Encyclopedia of
White Power

Dedication

To Buitre

Encyclopedia of
White Power

A Sourcebook on the
Radical Racist Right

Edited by Jeffrey Kaplan

A Division of
ROWMAN & LITTLEFIELD PUBLISHERS, INC.
Walnut Creek • *Lanham* • *New York* • *Oxford*

ALTAMIRA PRESS
A Division of ROWMAN & LITTLEFIELD PUBLISHERS, INC.

Published in the United States of America
by AltaMira Press
A Division of Rowman & Littlefield Publishers, Inc.
1630 North Main Street, #367
Walnut Creek, CA 94596
http://www.altamirapress.com

Rowman & Littlefield Publishers, Inc.
4720 Boston Way, Lanham, Maryland 20706

12 Hid's Copse Road
Cumnor Hill, Oxford OX2 9JJ, England

British Library Cataloguing in Publication Information Available

Library of Congress Cataloging-in-Publication Data

Kaplan, Jeffrey
    Encyclopedia of white power : a sourcebook on the radical racist right / edited by
Jeffrey Kaplan.
        p.   cm.
    Includes bibliographical references and index.
    ISBN 0-7425-0340-2 (cloth : alk. paper)
        1. White supremacy movements—Encyclopedias. 2. Right-wing extremists—
        Encyclopedias. I. Kaplan, Jeffrey, 1954–

HT1523 .E53 2000
305.8'003—dc21   99-059698

Printed in the United States of America

∞™ The paper used in this publication meets the minimum requirements of American National Standard for Information Sciences—Permanence of Paper for Printed Library Materials, ANSI/NISO Z39.48–1992.

Editorial Management by Erik Hanson
Project Management and Production Services by ImageInk, San Francisco
Cover Design by Raymond Cogan

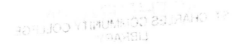

Table of Contents

Glossary

ADL	Anti-Defamation League
AGV	Aryan German Brotherhood
AJC	American Jewish Committee
ANP	American Nazi Party
ARA	Aryan Revolutionary Army
BIWF	British Israel World Federation
CDL	Christian Defense League
CNP	Canadian Nazi Party
COI	Church of Israel
COTC	Church of the Creator
CPDL	Christian Patriots Defense League
CPUSA	Communist Party USA
CSA	Covenant, Sword, and Arm of the Lord
ELF	European Liberation Front
FMI	People's Movement Against Immigration
HP	Hembygdspartiet (Native Place Party)
IHR	Institute for Historical Review
JOG	Jewish Occupation Government
KKK	Ku Klux Klan
NAACP	National Association for the Advancement of Colored People
NAAWP	National Association of the Advancement of White People
NS	National Socialist
NSDAP/AO	National Sozialistische Deutsch Arbeiter Partei/Auslands Organisation (National Socialist German Workers Party/Overseas Organization)
NSL	National Socialist League
NSLF	National Socialist Liberation Front
NSPA	National Socialist Party of America
NSV	National Socialist Vanguard

NSWPP	National Socialist White People's Party
NUNS 88	Norske unge nasjonalsosialister 88 (Norwegian Young National Socialists 88)
NYA	National Youth Alliance
NYO	National Youth Organization
ONA	Order of the Nine Angles
SD	Swedendemocrats
SFA	Scriptures for America
SPLC	Southern Poverty Law Center
UKA	United Klans of America
VAM	Vitt Ariskt Motsånd (White Aryan Resistance)
WAR	White Aryan Resistance
WUFENS	International Secretary of the World Union of Free Enterprise National Socialists
WUNS	World Union of National Socialists
YAF	Young Americans for Freedom
ZOG	Zionist Occupation Government

The book passes no judgments, and expresses no preferences. It merely tries to explain; and the explanations—all of them theories—are in the nature of suggestions and arguments even when they are stated in what seems a categorical tone. I can do no better than to quote Montaigne: "All I have to say is by way of discourse and nothing by way of advice. I should not speak so boldly if it were my due to be believed."

Eric Hoffer, *The True Believer*
(New York: HarperPerennial, 1951), p. xiii

Seekers of this world are like dogs,
wandering from door to door in wonder.

Their attention is riveted on a bone,
their lives wasted in bickering.

Short on intelligence and unable to understand,
they set out in search of water.

Apart from recollection of the Lord, Bahu,
all else is idle chatter.

Sultan Bahu [d. 1691. Sultan Bahu,
Death Before Dying, trans. by Jamal J. Ellias,
Berkeley, CA: University of California Press, 1998]

Among those who know them well, *the Gerhardt boys* are referred to as the "dingaling brothers." Without meaning to do so, they carry on a continuous Bud Abbott and Lou Costello routine, continually bumping into each other and falling over each other's feet and doing all that they can (quite unintentionally) to convince any chance observer that United States Nationalists must all be insane.

"Deguello Report on the American Right Wing" (1976)

Preface

During both the research and the writing phases, this project was enriched by the participation of numerous scholars, observers, and activists. Many of these submitted signed entries. To each of these contributors, I offer my thanks and gratitude. Many others, both in the United States and in Europe, were of great help as well in reading, critiquing, and offering insights on individual entries. To each of these individuals, too, I offer my appreciation. In this regard, I would like to thank especially Rick Cooper for allowing me to reprint his "Brief History of White Nationalism" in the "Resources" section of this volume; to Michael Moynihan of Blood Axis for his material on the Norwegian Black Metal scene; to James Mason and Tommy Rydén for their assistance and participation at a very early stage of this project, as well as for sharing their insights and experience; and to Harold Covington for his much-appreciated barbed humor. Special thanks, too, must be extended to scholarly participants on both sides of the Atlantic, including Heléne Lööw, Katrine Fangen, Fred Simonelli, Mattias Gardell, and Edvard Lind, to name but a few.

Thanks are also extended to the staff at the Wilcox Collection at the University of Kansas for their tolerance of my rather anarchic approach to research in the Special Collections section of the library. In this regard, I am most grateful to Ilisagvik College for its generosity in allowing me time to conduct this research, both in the United States and in Scandinavia, during my long sojourn in Barrow, Alaska, which I still think of in many ways as home.

To Laird Wilcox I owe thanks and more for his assistance and for his friendship, not only in this research, but throughout my academic career.

Most of all, however, I want to thank my wife, Eva Maria, for her extraordinary support and forbearance.

Introduction

When I was first approached with the idea of producing an encyclopedia dealing with the radical-right-wing, one of the first questions I had to deal with was, "what else is out there?" It was a good question, to which I soon added, "what would make the volume you now hold in your hands different from anything that has come before?" This introduction will seek to acquaint you with what is to follow by endeavoring to answer both of these questions.

The first is answered easily enough. There is only one volume in English that covers the radical right in encyclopedic form. This is the excellent, but sadly out of print, Phillip Rees, *Biographical Dictionary of the Extreme Right Since 1890* (New York: Simon & Schuster, 1990). A more narrowly focused encyclopedia, Michael Newton and Judy Newton, *Ku Klux Klan: An Encyclopedia*, Garland Reference Library of the Social Sciences, vol. 499 (New York: Garland, 1991), concentrates on the Ku Klux Klan. It too, however, is out of print and extremely difficult to find. Laird Wilcox publishes annually the *Guide to the American Right* (Editorial Research Service, P.O. Box 2047, Olathe, KS 66061), but this is simply a directory consisting of addresses of extant groups throughout the United States. Gordon Melton, in his series of encyclopedias of American religion, covers a few of the more overtly religious groups and leaders emanating from the far-right-wing. For example, Gordon Melton, *The Encyclopedia of American Religions*, 3 vols. (Tarrytown, NY: Triumph Books, 1991), provides some coverage of both the Christian Identity Church of Jesus Christ Christian (Aryan Nations) and Dan Gayman's Church of Israel, an entity that Pastor Gayman insists is no longer part of the Christian Identity community. However, the radical right is lightly represented in Melton's work.

There are, of course, a number of academic, trade, and journalistic works that treat some facet of the radical-right-wing. Of these, however, only one, John George and Laird Wilcox, *Nazis, Communists, Klansmen, and Others on the Fringe* (Buffalo, NY: Prometheus Books, 1992), and its nearly identical follow-up, John George and Laird Wilcox, *American Extremists, Supremacists, Klansmen, Communists and Others* (Buffalo, NY: Prometheus Books, 1996), seek to present a panoramic view of the far right in the manner of an encyclopedic work. Other attempts at such grand surveys have fared less well. Virtually all—like the prototype of the genre,

Seymour Martin Lipset and Earl Raab, *The Politics of Unreason*, 2d ed. (Chicago: University of Chicago Press, 1970)—either seek to make the case for a grand sociological or political theory, or fall into what may be termed "watchdog" literature that tries to warn the public of the dangers posed by the radical right. The latter includes the World War II–vintage efforts of the pseudonymous John Roy Carlson, *Under Cover* (New York: Dutton, 1943) and *The Plotters* (New York: Dutton, 1946); the most important of the 1950s-era texts, Ralph Lord Roy, *Apostles of Discord* (Boston: Beacon Press, 1953); and a more recent manifestation of the watchdog syndrome that had widespread impact, Ken Stern, *A Force Upon the Plain: The American Militia Movement and the Politics of Hate* (New York: Simon & Schuster, 1996). Such watchdog literature, however, was not designed to further a historical understanding of the phenomenon of far-right-wing activism. Rather, its objective is to warn the public about the perceived dangers emanating from the radical right, to mobilize support, and (especially) to raise funds to oppose radical-right-wing activism.

On specific aspects of the far-right-wing, there are a number of good academic studies and journalistic efforts to choose from. In the academic realm, Michael Barkun, *Religion and the Racist Right: The Origins of the Christian Identity Movement* (Chapel Hill: University of North Carolina Press, 1994), provides a fine history of Identity Christianity. James Aho, *The Politics of Righteousness: Idaho Christian Patriotism* (Seattle: University of Washington Press, 1990), is another good study of the milieu of the far right in the state of Idaho, while Aho's "greatest hits" volume, *This Thing of Darkness: A Sociology of the Enemy* (Seattle: University of Washington Press, 1994), seeks to gather his work into a focused, sociological perspective. My own *Radical Religion in America: Millenarian Movements from the Far Right to the Children of Noah* (Syracuse, NY: Syracuse University Press, 1997), brings a number of movements into focus via the lens of Colin Campbell's 1970s-era cultic milieu theory.

A number of academic anthologies are available treating various aspects of the far right. Tore Bjørgo and Rob Witte, eds., *Racist Violence in Europe* (New York: St. Martin's Press, 1993); Peter H. Merkl and Leonard Weinberg, eds., *Encounters with the Contemporary Radical Right* (Boulder, CO: Westview, 1993); Tore Bjørgo, ed., *Terror from the Extreme Right* (London: Frank Cass, 1995); Michael Barkun, ed., *Millennialism and Violence* (London: Frank Cass, 1996); and Jeffrey Kaplan and Tore Bjørgo, eds., *Nation and Race: The Developing Euro-American Racist Subculture* (Boston:

Northeastern University Press, 1998), to name but a few—all contain articles that recommend them.

Finally, a few high-quality journalistic studies of specific cases in the radical right have appeared in recent years. Of these, two in particular come to mind. The most recent, Jess Walter, *Every Knee Shall Bow: The Truth and Tragedy of Ruby Ridge and The Weaver Family* (New York: ReganBooks, 1995), is a sensitively crafted and well-balanced study of the Randy Weaver tragedy, which was instrumental in the formation of the American militia movement. Of earlier vintage, Kevin Flynn and Gary Gerhardt, *The Silent Brotherhood* (New York: Signet, 1990), is an equally good study of the American revolutionary movement called the Silent Brotherhood (the Order).

As this brief review of the literature suggests, there is a demonstrable need for an encyclopedia treating the radical-right-wing. The only comparable volume on the market, Rees's *Biographical Dictionary of the Extreme Right Since 1890,* is no longer in print. Moreover, that volume was oriented more toward European fascism than the American radical right. It thus had few entries on Americans, and in truth only a small percentage of the entries could be thought of as in any sense contemporary. Given the time of its publication, this European focus is understandable. However, in recent years, there appears to have been a sea change in the world of the radical-right-wing. Heretofore, ideas and leadership had flowed from east to west, from the fascist movements of Europe to a small but enthusiastic audience of American aficionados who were drawn into the dream by shared political beliefs or by ties of ethnicity to their nations of origin.

More recently, however, American ideological and theological exports such as the Ku Klux Klan, Christian Identity, and the Church of the Creator have made strong inroads into the European radical right. Moreover, even such distinctly European ideologies as National Socialism are, with due reverence paid to the shade of Adolf Hitler, being reexported to Europe not only in the form of agit-prop materials, but also through the leadership of such American adherents as the late George Lincoln Rockwell, Gerhard Lauck, and William Pierce.

Clearly, something new was stirring in the milieu of the transatlantic radical right. This shift is considered in some depth in Jeffrey Kaplan and Leonard Weinberg, *The Emergence of a Euro-American Radical Right* (Rutgers, NJ: Rutgers University Press, 1998). For the present, however, the increasing influence of the American movements and leaders in the world of the transatlantic radical-right-wing testifies to the need for a volume that would complement Rees's work through a focus on the American scene, albeit with a considerable European component as well.

The concentration on the contemporary United States, however, is not the only thing that makes this volume unique. When preliminary discussions began on the possibility of creating this encyclopedia, I suggested that, in my view, the study of the radical right in fact suffered from an overabundance of ethnographic works of wildly varying qualities, enough watchdog materials to stock a library, and a small but growing body of useful scholarly literature. Then there is, as if in a parallel universe, the esoteric world of the primary source data consisting of a relative handful of books; a mountain of pamphlets, fliers, and letters; cassette and videotape recordings; and, of late, Internet postings so voluminous as to be almost beyond reckoning. This plethora of material is described best by Ross Upton, head of the Jonathan Swift Society, who wrote in 1992:

> ...there is more to learn...mountains of paperwork, hundreds of audio cassettes, many video cassettes, books beyond counting all circulating within the patriotic underground. Either we will restore our constitutional form of government or we will be the best educated slaves in the history of mankind.

And then there are the adherents themselves, often written about, though seldom allowed to speak in their own voices. Given the widely held belief—fostered by the symbiotic interactions of the mass media and the watchdog groups—that the denizens of the radical right are dangerous, irrational, and violently unstable individuals, this is hardly a surprising state of affairs. But what, I wondered, would they say if given the opportunity to speak directly to a sophisticated mainstream readership? What light could (or would) they shed on their own world that no outsider, regardless of how knowledgeable he or she might be, could hope to provide?

Having interviewed a number of individuals over the years representing a wide variety of nonmainstream perspectives—from the radical right to the worlds of explicit Satanism, from the deeply committed Christianity of the pro-force end of the pro-life rescue movement to the gentle believers in a variety of Wiccan and neopagan belief systems, and indeed, among the numerous watchdog groups—I knew that each of these true believers has much of value to say, if only one were prepared to listen. In this book I wanted to give them a chance to speak.

This volume thus features not only my own writing, and that of scholars on both sides of the Atlantic, but also the words of activists in the United States and in Europe as well. Thus, in these pages you will read, for example, several entries by veteran American National Socialist James Mason, whose pedigree in the movement dates back more than three decades and whose current mission is to introduce Charles Manson as the natural leader of the global National Socialist movement through the vehicle of the Universal Order. Other activists, men such as the long-time American National Socialist Rick Cooper and the former head of the Swedish Church of the Creator, Tommy Rydén, speak candidly of the history of their respective movements with an insight born of often-bitter experience. And for the cutting-edge subject of the Internet as a recruiting tool by radical-right-wing groups, Milton Kleim, Jr., one of the primary theorists of the effort before leaving the racialist movement, explains how the ideas were formulated and candidly discusses their prospects for success. Moreover, many of the entries in this volume offer quotations from the writings of numerous groups and individual leaders so as to better provide the reader with a glimpse of the world as seen through the eyes of the adherents themselves. It is this kaleidoscope of perspectives that makes this volume truly unique.

The suggestion that the subjects of the volume might be allowed to be, in a very real sense, its creators may come as something of a surprise. To accomplish this ideal of allowing the subject to speak to the reader in the first person obviously raises important ethical questions and comes freighted with certain responsibilities. Having asked academic contributors from Europe and the United States to submit, to the greatest extent possible, detached and value-free analyses of their individual topics, no less could be required of the activists themselves. But would such a detached perspective really be possible for people who, after all, had dedicated their lives to a belief system that had marked them as pariahs in the eyes of the mainstream culture? And, should they succeed in providing a reasonably detached analysis of their lives and works, would a mainstream audience be prepared to put aside its own preconceptions and listen to what the activists themselves have to say? In truth, I suspected that this was doable, but I could not really be sure. To my knowledge it had not been attempted before.

So, borrowing the motto of the American Academy of Religion's Fundamentalism Project, in which I had participated at the University of Chicago in the early 1990s, I offered all potential contributors, activists, and academics alike a paraphrase of the philosopher George Santayana's (1863–1952) dictum that we are here "neither to laugh nor to cry, but to understand." Each contributor was thus asked to write an entry that would "neither demonize nor proselytize, but would leave an accurate and unbiased historical record." Remarkably, virtually every contributor took the opportunity seriously, and sought to provide the reader with a window of understanding into movements and belief systems that are banished to the furthest reaches of the American and European political fringes. To better alert the reader to the identity of a guest author, each such entry will be signed by the writer, and a very brief identification will be provided. Further information on guest authors will be provided in a separate list of contributors as well.

Having settled the question of *who* will be contributing to this encyclopedia, we must turn to the more difficult question of *what* will be included under the heading of "radical right." Put another way, how far out on the axis of right-wing ideology must we go before we enter the territory of the "radical right," as the term is understood in the context of this volume? Is the Christian Coalition, for example, sufficiently right wing as to be considered radical? The John Birch Society? Or the current media caricature of the irrational gun-toting right winger, the American militia movement? Or, as Russ Bellant argues in *Old Nazis, the New Right and the Republican Party* (Boston: Southend Press, 1991), a faction of the Republican Party itself?

Clearly, no definitive answer to this question will satisfy all readers. The criteria for inclusion in this volume must therefore be somewhat subjective, but criteria there are nonetheless. First, the movements and individuals you will find in these pages are strongly racialist. They see themselves, and they identify friend and foe, primarily on the basis of race and an assumption—often erroneous, as it happens—of a shared history and common culture. For many of these figures, nationalism and the kind of ultrapatriotism that was typical of the right wing in the postwar era has given way to a resigned acceptance that their countries of origin have become irredeemably lost—utterly hostile to their ideas and values and, moreover, under the control of a triumphal Jewish conspiracy that has been reified into the redolent epithet of ZOG, the Zionist Occupation Government.

The primacy of race is the chief litmus test for inclusion in this volume. It is this issue that separates the subjects of this volume from such candidates as the Christian Coalition, which at this writing is attempting to build bridges to the Black community in the hope of creating a larger, multiracial coalition to work toward a restoration of what its members understand to be traditional values in the United States. Put to the test of a primary emphasis on racialism, the militia movement too was eliminated from discussion in these pages. While the militias contain more than their fair share of racists, and some militia leaders do have demonstrable ties to racialist organizations ranging from the Aryan Nations to the Ku Klux Klan, these individuals in fact represent a distinct minority of a movement that has so far spurned the attentions of the racial right, concentrating instead on such issues as Second Amendment protections to keep and bear arms, fear of foreign subversion, and the grand-conspiracy scenario of the New World Order discourse. Readers desiring coverage of the militia movement might be directed to Neil A. Hamilton's contribution to the ABC-CLIO Contemporary World Issues series, *Militias in America* (Santa Barbara, CA: ABC-CLIO, 1996), or the more recent (and more useful) D. J. Milloy, ed., *Homegrown Revolutionaries: An American Militia Reader* (Arthur Miller Center: University of East Anglia, Norwich, 1999).

Racialism, therefore, is a necessary but not a sufficient test for inclusion in these pages. While those who would define themselves as racist activists form a tiny percentage of the population in either Europe or the United States, they are nonetheless too numerous to hope to cover adequately in a single encyclopedic work. As a result, secondary criteria were needed. The most important of these attitudinal variables are the closely intertwined elements of a revolutionary rather than a conservative outlook, together with a strong streak of religiosity. The key question in this context is this: How is it that the true believer in a racialist worldview can see himself as part of a tiny, powerless, and much persecuted "righteous remnant" in a nation that he has long since despaired of reclaiming to the truth as the believer understands it? And how is it, moreover, that such a tiny group—or, more commonly, a loose network of isolated individuals—can dare to dream of a revolutionary change whose outcome would see the believers actually triumph against all odds?

To answer this question, it is important to understand the religious zeal that lies so much at the heart of even the most avowedly secularist of racialist-right-wing ideologies. The dream is thus frankly apocalyptic, and the outcome of the timeless struggle between good and evil that the faithful see as the true reality underlying the dross of everyday events is invariably interpreted in a way strikingly similar to the Christian apocalyptic scenario of the

Bible's Book of Revelation. In this vision, God will rescue His faithful remnant at precisely the time when sin is at its apogee and the world is so oppressed under the weight of accumulated evil that a just and righteous God will bear no more. Thus, the best of times is always the worst of times, and, for the true believer, the most unpromising of strategic situations is ironically the situation that is most fervently desired.

All of this is not to say, however, that the groups and individuals you will meet in these pages are irrational. Quite the opposite. They are, for the most part, canny judges of the prevailing balance of forces and are thus loath to act on their revolutionary impulses until the signs of the End are unmistakable. Thus, while a few of the individuals and organizations covered in this encyclopedia have turned to violence, most are content to watch and wait. Accordingly, it is not necessarily the violent act that qualifies one for inclusion herein, but the revolutionary dream—a dream that in the context of the contemporary world is in and of itself an ultimately revolutionary statement.

Having established this set of criteria for inclusion, the most vexing aspect of the creation of an encyclopedic work must be dealt with next: whom of this now drastically reduced universe of activists and organizations to include, and, more to the point, whom to exclude? While there is inevitably an element of subjectivity in making these choices, more winnowing clearly must be done. The most important of these choices was for the contemporary over the historical. However, while the preponderance of entries here are contemporary—that is, from the 1980s to date—some historical figures are of such overwhelming import that it would have been unthinkable to exclude them. Such vital historical figures as Adolf Hitler, Gerald L. K. Smith, Gerald Winrod, or Savitri Devi, for example, are discussed both within the context of their own times and in terms of the influence they exert and the various interpretations to which their lives and works are subjected by activists of the present day.

The selection of contemporary figures, organizations, and belief systems presented a number of dilemmas. The task was simplified by the rather arbitrary division of the radical right into eight major categories: Christian Identity; National Socialism; Ku Klux Klan; Reconstructed Traditions (a catchall category for attempts to reconstruct movements based on a "Golden Age" fantasy such as the neopagan Odinism, the Phineas Priesthood, and the like); Demagogues and Right-Wing Populists; Single-Issue Constituencies and

Tightly Focused Racialist or Anti-Semitic Appeals; Violent Revolutionaries and Terrorists; and the Youth Scene (skinheads, White noise bands, and the virtual race warriors of the Internet). Within these categories, leading figures and organizations from North America and Europe were selected. So too were some lesser-known groups and individuals whose lives and activities were felt to be illustrative of important trends within the radical right.

It is hoped that the kaleidoscope of viewpoints represented in this volume will allow the reader to come to a greater understanding of the Euro-American White Power subculture. To facilitate this understanding, some rather unorthodox strategies are attempted in this volume. The most important of these is, of course, opening the book to a number of guest entries written by activists themselves. But there is more. The reader need only leaf through these pages to realize that some of the entries are far lengthier than one would expect in an encyclopedic work. For these entries, a good deal of interview material, primary source writings, and in-depth discussion of pertinent issues are included so as to provide the reader with a more global perspective than a brief encyclopedic notation would have made possible. "Black Metal," for example, is included as a way of introducing the reader to an entire subculture in a form that individual entries on figures unfamiliar to most readers outside of Norway could not hope to convey. The Black Metal underground was the breeding ground for church burning, several murders, and—of central importance to the subject of this encyclopedia—a racialist message that would adapt National Socialism and Odinism into a syncretic ideology attractive to a youth-culture following far beyond the borders of its Norwegian birthplace. Several of the longer essays in this volume adopt this strategy as a method of acquainting the reader in some depth with unfamiliar topics and rather obscure figures from the world of racialist occultism.

Along the same lines, a comprehensive "Resources" section is provided in this volume. This section includes two internal movement histories: the anonymous "Deguello Report" and veteran American National Socialist Rick Cooper's "Brief History of White Nationalism." The Deguello Report was circulated in the mid-1970s and is offered to provide the reader with the rather jaundiced view the American radical right have of themselves—with accusations of rival leaders as being "secret" Jews, "secret" communists, or "secret" homosexuals (or, more often, varying combinations of the three) being the essence of much internal movement discourse.

"A Brief History of White Nationalism" was first published a decade later in Cooper's publication, the *National Socialist Vanguard*, and since then has circulated to a somewhat wider audience via the Internet. For this encyclopedia, Cooper himself made slight revisions and allowed it to be published in this forum in the hope that its internal view of the American radical right would, in Cooper's words, be of value to "scholars, researchers, book authors, historians and sociologists" as a counterweight to the received wisdom of "the establishment educational system and any combination of government agencies such as the Justice Department, the Federal Bureau of Investigation (FBI) and various law enforcement agencies, most of which get their information directly or indirectly from the Anti-Defamation League (ADL) of the B'nai B'rith and other anti-White groups." It is offered, from the perspective of this volume, as a forum through which the reader might gain some insight into how the radical-right-wing faithful see themselves.

Also appended is something of a catchall repository for movement documents, intended as a supplement to the main body of entries. Here can be found key movement documents such as "The White Party Report," which appeared in 1968 and was addressed to American National Socialists; the foundational documents for the Aryan Nations; and many more. These documents are referenced in the main entries and appear in the order in which they appear in the entry section of the encyclopedia.

The insider/outsider approach of this volume invariably raises a question in the minds of readers: just how great a threat does the radical right present? This question is particularly apropos in the wake of the Oklahoma City bombing in 1995, and even more so following the senseless attack on children in a Los Angeles Jewish Community Center in August 1999. Yet it is a question that is difficult to assess with any accuracy. To the watchdog movement, and to a lesser extent in government reports, the radical-right-wing is an arena of undifferentiated evil—a world powered by the emotions of hate, anger, and resentment. It is a milieu, moreover, inherently given to violence. The picture thus painted is tautological and, like all tautologies, contains an element of truth. A tautology, after all, is defined as "an empty or vacuous statement composed of simpler statements in a fashion that makes it logically true whether the simpler statements are factually true or false."

Acts of violence *have* emanated from the radical right in recent years. Of those listed in this encyclopedia, for example, the Order embarked on a course of revolutionary violence that culminated in at least one murder (though probably more). National Socialist Joseph Franklin became the model of the lone-wolf assassin lionized in William Pierce's novel *Hunter*. Franklin is thought to have committed roughly 20 racially motivated murders. Racist skinhead groups have a well-deserved reputation for random and occasionally deadly violence. And Timothy McVeigh, whose lack of a racialist emphasis precluded his inclusion in these pages, was responsible for the single most destructive terrorist incident in American history in the bombing of the Federal Building in Oklahoma City.

Yet it is also true that, as demonstrated by the Randy Weaver incident at Ruby Ridge, Idaho; the Waco conflagration (which, while unconnected to the radical right in itself, was subsequently adopted as a symbol of government persecution of dissident views by the radical right); and a long series of increasingly deadly confrontations between the radical-right-wing and the state, the racialists whom you will meet in these pages may as often be the victims of violence as they may be perpetrators. In the self-view of the movement, much of the violence that has engulfed the radical right in recent years is reactive and defensive. Readers are left to judge this issue for themselves.

The next issue that must be addressed is the problem of tonality. If there is one unifying thread that runs through the numerous books, articles, and reports dealing with the radical right, it is this: virtually all take on a tone remarkable for dour humorlessness. Much of this is more than echoed in the publications and public pronouncements of the radical right-wingers themselves. Yet in their offstage behavior, the outside observer is often struck by the self-deprecating humor with which many of the activists view themselves and the even more caustic eye that they turn upon their erstwhile comrades. With this in mind, and while fully realizing the gravity of the issues raised by the racialist right, the reader will find an insider/outsider approach in this volume that provides an opportunity for some decidedly tongue-in-cheek observations in several of the entries. Once again, no better example might be cited than the entry on Harold Covington.

A final issue that may be of importance to readers of this encyclopedia is perhaps the most elemental: where do I stand in relation to this material? In academic conferences and public lectures, the author-versus-content question is, in one form or another, the most often-raised question I am asked. Certainly, it has been the most difficult for me to answer. It was to these questions, and to the very difficult issues that these questions raise, that I focused a formal address, given at the University of Helsinki on November 3, 1998. The relevant portions of this address, "Racism, Anti-racism, and the Americans: Reflections on the European Year Against Racism," should help to clarify these questions:

Racism, Anti-racism, and the Americans:
Reflections on the European Year Against Racism

I would like to do something this afternoon that I have never had the opportunity to do before. In my field of study—contemporary apocalyptic religious movements, modern millennialism and religious violence—it is imperative to separate intellect and emotions. The head and the heart. In doing fieldwork among racist and anti-Semitic groups in particular, this dichotomy of head and heart is as necessary for success as a working tape recorder, a pen and paper, and a sympathetic but not overly curious dean. This afternoon however, I would like to step out of the role of detached observer and try, if only for a moment, to speak to you from the heart about my work.

The title and the topic of today's address, "Racism, Anti-racism, and the Americans: Reflections on the European Year Against Racism," were born of a remarkable conference held in Stockholm last year to mark the European Year Against Racism. The adjective "remarkable" is here not taken lightly, for the conference *was* remarkable on a number of levels. The conference itself was structured in such a way as to bring together academic specialists from around the world with a cross-section of young European anti-racist activists. After the formal opening however, the two conference constituencies were, much to the relief of the academics and the consternation of the activists, rather rigorously separated.

But this was not really the remarkable feature of the conference. Rather, in the academic section of the European Year Against Racism conference, it soon became clear that the largest national contingent came not from any European nation, but from the United States! Indeed, such epicenters of European racial strife as Germany, England or Sweden, were represented only by a single scholar, while the United States was represented by no less than three academic researchers. This is all the more remarkable in light of the fact that, of the more than one hundred anti-racist activists invited to Stockholm, not a single representative of the well funded and highly active American groups was present. This was an important statement on the part of the organizers of the conference that the problem of European racism could not be addressed without recognizing the important role played by the American movement.

As you can imagine, the Americans present were somewhat bemused by our sudden prominence in the European Year Against Racism. Certainly, Americans do have a certain expertise in the area of racism, and perhaps some of our unhappy experiences could be of benefit to Europeans as they enter into a period of increasing multiculturalism. Yet the American participants could think of few precedents for such European solicitude for American input into European social problems.

...[As the conference sessions] wore on, the collected activists vented their frustrations, not so much with the racist groups who were hardly mentioned, as with the Swedish state. The complaints were many, but the consistent theme was the failure of European nations to readily adapt to multiculturalism which, in the vision of the participants, should be fashioned on the American model and implemented immediately by government decree. Toward the close of the increasingly impassioned workshop, the Swedish discussion facilitator noted as an aside that Swedes too have a culture, and that the assembled activists might take this insight into consideration in presenting their case to the government and to the wider Swedish public. At that moment, the many issues dividing the participants from each other dissolved as if by magic, and the [facilitator] was roundly denounced....

The altogether unremarkable observation that anti-racist activists *can* be, and usually *are,* as intolerant of dissenting views as are racist activists, brings us back to our topic of "Racism, Anti-Racism and the Americans." When I took up this research almost a decade ago, this observation from the American perspective was anything but obvious. This is not to say that the idea was in any way new. In 1951, Eric Hoffer made precisely this point in *The True Believer: Thoughts on the Nature of Mass Movements*. But even then, only a half dozen years since the defeat of Nazi Germany, and at the dawn of the first phase of the Cold War and the McCarthy period of anti-Communist hysteria in the United States, Hoffer was careful to avoid mentioning specific movements. And what's more, Hoffer anticipated the reception his carefully balanced descriptions of the extremist personality would evoke in academia, when he introduced his book with a quote from Montaigne:

> All I can say is by way of discourse, and nothing by way of advice. I should not speak so boldly if it were my due to be believed.

In this, Hoffer was prescient, for when I began my own research almost four decades later, a considerable—but utterly predictable—evolution had taken place. In the wake of the revelations of the horrors of the Holocaust, the success of the Civil Rights Movement, the fall of Joseph McCarthy and the subsequent discrediting of the anti-Communist right, and the massive social transformations of the 1960s, the American radical right had been banished to the most distant fringes of American culture.

This is where I found them when I began my own research. There, in angry isolation from the dominant culture, they existed in a seemingly separate universe of newsletters and booklets, of cassette tapes and small rural enclaves, which kept contact with each other—and with other oppositional belief systems as well. But for all we in the dominant culture knew of this world, it might as well have been, in Martin Marty's imagery, the terra incognita which medieval maps depicted as inhabited by the monsters of our deepest fears.

Prof. Marty's conception is important here, for what I expected to find when I set out on my own voyage of discovery were precisely these kind of monsters—angry and violent men, so consumed by hatred that they could scarcely have resembled human beings at all. And I was not alone in this conception, for it was a vision widely shared among my graduate student peers, and among each and every one of my professors.

That we all shared this vision is hardly remarkable, as for a number of years the information filtering back to the dominant culture about these distant figures, was supplied by a network of watchdog groups whose mission it was to keep tabs on the doings of the far right. Some of these watchdogs came from religious communities such as the American Jewish Congress and the Anti-Defamation League of the B'nai B'rith. Others came from smaller, private groups with a more left wing political orientation. But in either case, the reports which these groups issued were largely in agreement, and it was these, as filtered through the news media, that provided the stuff of dreams of which the monsters of terra incognita were constructed.

For my part, I did not question the validity of the construction of the radical right wing "other", to borrow from James Aho's work on reification, or the construction of cultural enemies. But I was determined in any event to carry out the research, for there was at that time a gap in the academic literature which I hoped that my work would fill. While there were a number of political and sociological studies of the American radical right, there was virtually nothing dealing with their millennialist religiosity. And even the briefest glance at the movement's literature would suggest that, for many in this sub-culture, a powerful apocalypticism was very, very close to the surface, and in fact seemed to be a primary force driving the movement.

Here I must confess that I was in those days very much under the spell of Norman Cohn's work on medieval millenarian revolutionary movements, and I felt that the American radical right would make a perfect case study of contemporary millenarian revolutionary activism. That religiosity is a key characteristic of American radical activism is hardly a fresh insight. Eric Hoffer had made the same observation in *The True Believer*. To again quote Hoffer:

> It is necessary for most of us these days to have some insight into the motives and responses of the true believer. For though ours is a godless age, it is the very opposite of irreligious. The true believer is everywhere on the march, and both by converting and antagonizing he is shaping the world in his own image. And whether we are to line up with him or against him, it is well that we should know all we can concerning his nature and potentialities.

If a single quotation could be said to encapsulate both the motivation and the methodology of my work, it is this one. So armed with my trusty tape recorder, a pen and paper, a sympathetic but not overly curious dissertation committee, and a singularly forbearing spouse, I set off for the particular portion of terra incognita occupied by the anti-Semitic and racist Christian Identity faith.

I spent some considerable time in this nether region. I spoke to leaders and simple true believers in the Identity creed, read a mountain of Identity materials and received enough tape recorded sermons to keep a radio station in programming for a month. Fortunately, this was still in the pre-Internet stone age of academic research, which made it possible to work with a finite number of published sources rather than an endless backlog of messages on a computer screen.

Ultimately, I did find as expected a millenarian sub-culture with at least the potential, fortunately only rarely actualized, of millenarian violence on the Norman Cohn model. These findings were duly published in my first academic article in the *Journal of Terrorism and Political Violence*. This was, I believe, the first academic article on the topic of right wing millennialism to appear in the academic literature.

But I found something else as well, and it took a considerable amount of time before I was able to fully understand it's import.

What I found most puzzling was that the monsters of terra incognita, upon closer examination, were not really monsters at all. They held political views which were repugnant, and religious views based on fantastically eccentric interpretations of sacred text. But whatever their belief structure, these were not monsters. They were not the violent and hate filled people I had expected to find.

More than anything else, they struck me as dispirited and confused. They were genuinely unable to understand the social changes that had in their life times reshaped America, and indeed the world. So they fell back for support on the starkly dualistic battle of good and evil which they had been taught since childhood from the "Book of Revelations," and upon the apocalyptic sermons which since the time of the Puritans have been a staple of American Christianity. This is the stuff upon which they had drawn to construct their enemies-—the Jews, racial minorities, communists, ad infinitum. They saw themselves in biblical terms, as a tiny and powerless "righteous remnant" whose faith and perseverance would be rewarded with terrestrial peace, power and plenty when Jesus returned to put the world to right.

Far from monsters, these strange and isolated people seemed, if anything, to feel too much and understand too little. In their words and deeds they harmed mainly themselves and their families.

But in these early days of my research, I was not at all sure what to make of this dissonance between what I had expected to find, and what I actually experienced in the field. Perhaps I had simply stumbled on the *wrong* millenarians and the monsters lay still further into the depths of terra incognita. Yet as the years went by, and I followed one idea to the next, one movement to another, and went ever deeper into the oppositional subculture of America, what I found was not remarkably different from the Identity sect, save that Identity believers tend to be much older and many of the groups with which I came into contact in America, and later in Europe, could be better characterized as youth sub-cultures.

If this finding could be given a name, it would be this: the shock of shared humanity. And in truth, this bothered me greatly. How could such people be so much like us? And why would this seem so obvious to me, and so opaque to the wider culture and the academic world alike? Surely I felt, the problem must lie with me. It was at this point that I seriously thought of finding some other avenue of research.

It was at this nadir that a colleague and good friend, Doug Milford of Wheaton College in Illinois, made an off-hand observation that would in a significant way change the course of my work.

Wheaton is a Christian college and Doug himself is a devout evangelical Christian. Thus, when he observed in the context of suggesting that perhaps aspects of my research—specifically, those dealing with Satanism and the occult, would be better left untouched—that the real problem was that I had been given a gift of discernment which allowed me to find, at the deepest level, the spark of goodness, of humanity, in even the most lost of souls, it caused me to reflect deeply on the implications of the idea.

In the evangelical worldview, evil is a literal, ever-present reality in the world. And discernment is understood as one of the gifts of the spirit which God grants to allow the faithful to discern between truth and deception. Thus the force of the idea. This after all is at the core of all of the great religious traditions. In Judaism, it is conceived as the Sacred Spark and in Christianity it is the human soul. In Buddhism, it is the Buddha nature. But by any name, and in any tradition, it is the power of discernment, the search for the core of humanity and the spark of the divine, that unites us all in the human family. And it is this universal truth of the oneness of all human creation which we so often forget in dealing with those with whom most violently disagree. It is this recognition of shared humanity which is so lacking in the popular constructions of the radical right, and it is precisely the lack of this recognition of shared humanity that allows for the creation of the imaginary monsters of terra incognita. There are real world implications of all this.

Before considering these real world consequences however, it is important to note at this point that none of this is said to condone racism as "just another idea" or, more subtlety, to rationalize evil. Rather, this is to suggest that all human beings can be approached on a human level. That contact can be made. This human contact will in turn invariably neutralize the caricatures which skew scholarly analysis and distort the historical record.

Eric Hoffer's warning, issued some forty-eight years ago, still rings true today:

> The true believer is everywhere on the march, and both by converting and antagonizing he is shaping the world in his own image. And whether we are to line up with him or against him, it is well that we should know all we can concerning his nature and potentialities.

The demonization of the radical right ill serves us when now, more than ever before, it is vitally important to know all we can about this esoteric milieu's nature and potentialities.

Moreover, at the end of this quest, I did find something even more remarkable than the fact that "we" and "they" are both human beings and have important commonalties. This discovery was more unsettling still, for just as Doug Milford had warned, I found that there IS genuine evil in the world. It is rare. It is subtle. But it *is* real.

By so demonizing the many, we cloak the few, and, however unwittingly, ourselves facilitate the existence of evil in the world.

We do this in two ways. First, by failing to recognize the humanity which binds us together, we lose the opportunity to do what anti-racism *should* be about: to try to bring the angry and the outcast back into our midst.

More subtlety, by condoning the use of stereotypes and caricature, we virtually invite a new generation of seekers to reject our own wisdom, our own way of seeing the world, when they discover for themselves that those whom we had portrayed as the embodiment of all modern evil are simply people like ourselves. People whose own journey into the terra incognita of racism often began with the dissonance produced by questioning received wisdom which, on closer examination, proved to them to be either exaggerated or simply false.

It is through such disillusionment that those few whose hatred is truly dangerous find followers, and new generations of the disappointed fill the ranks of the hate movement.

I have over the years seen what I believe to be genuine evil of this sort only twice. Both times, it was a considerable shock, and both times it was a frightening experience. But in both cases, it would have been impossible to discern what I believe is a genuine threat to society, if I had accepted the stereotypical view that ALL of the denizens of this milieu are equally bad.

As promised, there is a practical application to all this. Over the course of the last decade, I have in the US and in Europe done a number of formal interviews, and had innumerable conversations, with people from these oppositional subcultures. In virtually all of the interviews with core members of these groups, and in a number of more casual conversations as well, not one person who had reached adulthood did not report that, at some time or other, he or she had not harbored the dream of living a normal life in mainstream society. Peripheral adherents come and go all the time. But core members of these groups, people who are known to the police and the watchdogs and the general public, seldom have this option.

Yet on a few occasions several of these core members with whom I had dealt did leave the movement. Indeed, one of the primary subjects of my early Christian Identity research—a man who had been one of the two or three primary theorists of the American Identity creed, and who had, moreover, been in the milieu of the radical right for more than forty years, quietly left the movement. Even more remarkable, his Church newsletter which by the 1970s had become one of the most strident sources of religiously based anti-Semitic rhetoric in the nation, began in the 1990s to suggest that perhaps Jews were not really the servants of Satan on earth after all, but a people from whose survival and current prosperity we could learn much.

Well, if a loss to my research is a gain for society, I can hardly complain. But I *can* note that what I referred to as the shock of shared humanity is not a one way street. Rather, the discovery can be, for the denizens of the racist and anti-Semitic terra incognita, a shattering experience.

Which at last brings us back to the Stockholm conference and its American participants. Each of us, representing three very different generations of American academia, and coming from very different political and religious perspectives, *did* believe that Europeans *could* find some value in the American experience. From the theoretical perspectives brought by my American colleagues, and through my own experiences of fieldwork, we each in our own way stressed two overriding points.

First and foremost, America has over the years dealt with oppositional subcultures in three ways. The most successful strategy is, in the present era, no longer much of an option. That is, we had plenty of land and few laws, so virtually any oppositional group, so long as they were reasonably circumspect, could go west and establish their own enclaves. America today has far less available land, and far more laws, and so this is hardly more an option for us than it is for Europeans.

Second, as a long line of moral crusades of which the McCarthy era is only the most recent demonstrates, the option of suppression has been remarkably unsuccessful. By driving a movement underground, we have found that we have increased its virulence without markedly lessening its appeal. In fact, it is the aura of the forbidden which most attracts young people to oppositional movements in the first place! Indeed, my findings and those of a number of colleagues working on the skinhead and the Satanist subcultures in particular, indicate that it is the simple availability of an oppositional milieu, rather than an attraction to any particular ideology, which first brings young people into a radical group.

What then did we suggest? To us, the protections of speech and action as embodied in the First Amendment to the American Constitution seemed to be a far more promising avenue than outlawing speech or non-violent action. This appeared to us to be a necessary precondition to the kind of engagement that, recognizing the Sacred Spark that exists in us all, may allow even the most seemingly lost of souls to return to mainstream society.

The second suggestion follows naturally from the first. Anti-racism as embodied in government programs and private initiatives is extremely important. Such programs can help to break down the barriers of misunderstanding and mistrust which have prevented the successful integration of immigrant and refugee populations into the life of the nations of Western Europe. Indeed, the universities *must* play a central role in the design and the implementation of these programs. But the American experience of multiculturalism has taught again and again that the success of government and private initiatives depends on the cooperation and good will of all concerned—public and private institutions, citizens and newcomers, activists and the general public. The success of the multicultural project can not be achieved overnight, and to attempt to produce significant changes in public attitudes by official *dictát* can be counter-productive, and may in fact swell the ranks of the racist movements."

Finally, this encyclopedia will have succeeded in its intent if, to some degree, it brings to life for the reader not only the beliefs but also the personalities of the individuals who comprise the transatlantic radical right. In writing these words, I have had ample occasion to reflect on the words of Montaigne: "All I have to say is by way of discourse and nothing by way of advice. I should not speak so boldly if it were my due to be believed."

I hope that, in reading this volume, the reader too will bear in mind Santayana's cautionary dictum: that we are here neither to laugh, nor to cry, but to understand.

Jeffrey Kaplan
Helsinki, Finland
1999

American National Party   *See* Burros, Dan.

AMERICAN NAZI PARTY   The American Nazi Party (ANP) was founded in 1959 by George Lincoln Rockwell as the first explicitly postwar American National Socialist group. It was built on the corpse of the National Committee to Free America from Jewish Domination, which Rockwell had run under the patronage of Harold Noel Arrowsmith. Early adherents of the uniformed ANP cadre represented a cross-section of the American radical right, infiltrators from both government and private watchdog groups, defectors from the New York–based National Renaissance Party, and other idiosyncratic extremists. The American Nazi Party soon moved into a house in Arlington, Virginia, which came to be dubbed alternately "Hate House" or "Hatemonger Hill." They would remain at this address until 1965, when the chronically underfunded organization would lose possession of the property to the Internal Revenue Service in lieu of back taxes.

The party was never large. Estimates of actual ANP membership (as opposed to names on the mailing list) range from 100 to 150 at its height. The core of the party resided with Rockwell in Virginia, although a strong if highly divisive group was centered in California, and other dues-paying adherents were scattered throughout the country.

Beyond the problem of numbers, Rockwell was bedeviled by the wildly uneven quality of the American Nazi Party's "Stormtroopers," as he dubbed them. For every William Pierce—a Ph.D. mathematician—there were a number of followers who would aptly fit Rockwell's description in his autobiography, *This Time the World:* "90 percent [are] cowards, dopes, nuts, one-track minds, blabbermouths, boobs, incurable tight-wads and—worst of all—hobbyists...." Indeed, even the rising stars of the movement

1

would often prove to have feet of clay. One such case, that of Dan Burros, was particularly tragic. Lt. Burros, who rose to become the ANP's Political Education Officer and the author of the basic training document for recruits, the *Official Stormtrooper's Manual,* committed suicide on learning that the *New York Times* was about to write an exposé revealing him to be Jewish.

Be this as it may, the hallmark of the American Nazi Party was from the beginning high-profile activism. Headline-grabbing publicity stunts, street brawls, and histrionically racialist and anti-Semitic rhetoric were the ANP's tactics of choice. The aim was to garner as much publicity as possible. Rockwell shrewdly grasped the fact that America in the early 1960s had entered a new media age and that any publicity, however negative, was both a useful weapon and an invaluable recruiting tool. The ebullient Rockwell confidently predicted that the ANP would rise to power in the 1972 elections, following which a bloody reckoning would be had with the American Jewish community, and with racial minorities as well.

While much of the ANP's public energy was given to street theater, the group had a more lasting impact on the global radical right wing through the publication of its party newspaper and supporting newsletters. *The Stormtrooper,* the *Rockwell Report,* and other American Nazi Party publications would have a considerable impact throughout the milieu of the international radical right.

However, the American Jewish community quickly took action to silence Rockwell and his ANP to the greatest degree possible. Adapting a policy that had proved effective in dealing with Depression-era demagogues such as Gerald L. K. Smith, the American Jewish Committee's expert on anti-Semitism, Rabbi Solomon Andhil Fineberg, championed a policy he called "Dynamic Silence." This was aimed both at lobbying newspaper editors and broadcast stations to sway them to avoid reporting on Rockwell and the ANP and at persuading such activist Jewish groups as the Jewish War Veterans of America to cease confronting the ANP at their rallies and media events. It was these confrontations that drew the media to the scene in the first place. Rabbi Fineberg's policy was a success, and the American Nazi Party gradually disappeared from the headlines.

Ironically, 1966 would mark both the high point of American Nazi Party activism and the dissolution of the organization. In that year, Rockwell would at last break out of the media quarantine to express his views in a wide-ranging interview in *Playboy* magazine. The interviewer, Alex Haley, would go on to write the best-seller *Roots* about his search for his African family tree. As an organization, the ANP succeeded, in the face of intense opposition, in conducting a uniformed march in Chicago. The highly publicized march capped the career of George Lincoln Rockwell as the head of the American Nazi Party.

Little known to the outside world, a deepening split had occurred in party ranks. Rockwell sought a more "ecumenical" racialist platform than was possible under the swastika banner in America. True believers, led by Matt Koehl, held fast to National Socialist purism. Most ANP members, however, followed Rockwell's lead, and Koehl remained loyal. As a result, in 1966 the American Nazi Party was renamed the National Socialist White People's Party (NSWPP) in conscious imitation of the Black civil rights group named the National Association for the Advancement of Colored People (NAACP). This brought an end to the American Nazi Party.

The NSWPP soon turned in on itself, and most of the remaining American Nazi Party veterans quickly resigned or were expelled by Koehl. Rockwell himself was assassinated by disgruntled ANP veteran John Patler on August 25, 1967. The American Nazi Party name has been taken up by a number of tiny—usually one-man—organizations such as James Burford's Chicago-based American Nazi Party and the short-lived, Iowa-based American Nazi Party of John Bishop's.

See also: Burros, Dan; Koehl, Matt; National Renaissance Party; National Socialist White People's Party; Pierce, William; Rockwell, George Lincoln; Smith, Gerald L. K.

Further reading: John George and Laird Wilcox, *American Extremists, Supremacists, Klansmen, Communists and Others* (Buffalo, NY: Prometheus Books, 1996); William L. Pierce, *Lincoln Rockwell: A National Socialist Life* (Arlington, VA: NS Publications, 1969); George Lincoln Rockwell, *This Time the World!* (Arlington, VA: Parliament House, 1963); George Lincoln Rockwell, *White Power* (n.p., 1967, 1977); A. M. Rosenthal and Arthur Gelb, *One More Victim: The Life and Death of a Jewish Nazi* (New York: New American Library, 1967); Frederick J. Simonelli, *American Fuehrer: George Lincoln Rockwell and the American Nazi Party* (Champaign: University of Illinois Press, 1999).

Harold Noel Arrowsmith　*See* American Nazi Party; Rockwell, George Lincoln.

ARYA KRIYA   A system of Aryan meditation, Arya Kriya was formulated by Jost, the former head of the National Socialist Kindred
in northern California. Arya Kriya itself barely had time to get off
the ground before Jost's untimely death in 1996. In essence, Arya
Kriya was a holistic discipline, the practice of which, in Jost's view,
was "slowly & quietly bringing about a major change in the evolution of this world." Arya Kriya, a program whose roots (according to
Jost) may be traced back to time immemorial, begins with a course
of internal purification, including a vegetarian diet and the use of
meditation and mantra techniques. The benefits of this regime may
seem somewhat ironic, given the circumstances of Jost's death. In
his own words:

> Our Arya Kriya training course covers natural diet, which is of
> course vegetarian. I have been a vegetarian since 1970 and am in
> the best of health. Our children have never eaten dead animals, and
> they are really very radical about it. We always refuse any food
> which has meat.

The training program itself was distributed in segments via the
"Arya Kriya Initiate's Letter." The benefits of the training, in Jost's
view, constituted a weapon of supreme power in the arsenal of the
race movement. Arya Kriya is in essence an adaptation of the
Hindu Vedanta, whose efficacy is demonstrated in a series of examples that culminate in the tantalizing possibility of the White race
activists finding within themselves the power to overcome their
infinitesimally tiny numbers and current sense of vulnerability to
the overwhelming power of the state. As Jost explains:

> Our first subject was a German-American activist who, during a
> trip to Germany to see his family, had been jailed and charged with
> the usual hate crime nonsense. He was an older man who was prob-
> ably not up to the rigors of a German prison, and his chances
> against the German legal establishment looked pretty hopeless. We
> began transmitting a Ganesha Mantra to him each day. It was some
> time before we got word about his situation, and we were astounded
> to learn that when he got to court, the judge, against all precedence
> and very strong objections from the prosecution, granted him bail
> on his own recognizance! Naturally the activist hightailed it for the
> USA and out of reach of the German puppet regime. Although we
> had no idea at the time, we began our transmissions about two
> weeks before his court appearance. The activist noted that about
> two weeks before his court appearance he began to have the feeling
> that he was going to get out of prison (he had been in prison for

many months). We knew that this could be just a simple coincidence, and so we began a second experiment.

Our second subject was a German-Canadian who was faced with being charged under the new Canadian hate crimes law. He had been prosecuted earlier and convicted, but on appeal the law was ruled unconstitutional and his conviction reversed. This time, however, the prosecutors had made sure that the law would stand up under appeal, and under the pressure of powerful Jewish interests, prepared to charge him again. We began our daily transmissions with the same Ganesha Mantra. After some time, we learned that the prosecution had suddenly, completely unexpectedly, and in the face of hysterical remonstrations by the Jewish pressure groups, decided to drop all charges against him for lack of evidence. The activist, amazed at the turn of events, called it divine intervention. Now, this too could have been merely a coincidence, but, since our earlier experiments were beyond any probability of coincidence, it seems reasonable to believe that our efforts had some effect. And this brings us to the possibility of using the ancient Aryan science as a defensive weapon, as did our Aryan forefathers thousands of years ago.

If myself and two small children can have results of this sort, what would be possible for ten, twenty, fifty or a hundred individuals trained in Mantras? Could we not protect our activists from legal harassment from such creatures as Morris Dees or Janet Reno? Could we insure the success of honest political ventures? This is why I decided to introduce the science of Mantras to Arya Kriya initiates, in hope that some of you would like to join us in our experiments, and begin focusing our energy as a group to benefit some of our activists.

It is too soon to judge the post-Jost fate of Arya Kriya. Tommy Rydén continues the work of translating Arya Kriya materials into Swedish for distribution throughout Scandinavia under the imprimatur of his DeVries Institute, although he does not plan to carry the work forward himself. It is likely that Arya Kriya will remain a dream unrealized.

See also: Jost; National Socialist Kindred; Rydén, Tommy.

Further reading: Jeffrey Kaplan and Leonard Weinberg, *The Emergence of a Euro-American Radical Right* (Rutgers, NJ: Rutgers University Press, 1998).

ARYAN NATIONS   The Aryan Nations is both a national Christian Identity movement organization and a communal settlement
centered in Hayden Lake, Idaho, which came into being with Pastor
Richard Butler's 1973 move from multiracial southern California to
the primarily White region of northern Idaho near Cour d'Alene.
The founding premise of the Aryan Nations movement is a simple
statement of Identity theology:

> ...We believe in the preservation of our race, individually and collec-
> tively, as a people as demanded and directed by Yahweh. We believe
> our Racial Nation has a right and is under obligation to preserve
> itself and its members. We believe that Adam, man of genesis, is the
> placing of the White Race (sic) upon this earth. Not all races descend
> from Adam. Adam is the father of the White Race only.... We believe
> that the true, literal children of the Bible are the twelve tribes of
> Israel, now scattered throughout the world and now known as the
> Anglo-Saxon, Germanic, Teutonic, Scandinavian, Celtic peoples of
> the earth.... We believe that there are literal children of Satan in the
> world today.... We believe that the Cananite Jew is the natural
> enemy of our Aryan (white) Race. We believe that there is a battle
> being fought this day between the children of darkness (today known
> as Jews) and the children of light...the Aryan race, the true Israel of
> the Bible.... We believe that there is a day of reckoning. The usurper
> will be thrown out by the terrible might of Yahweh's people, as they
> return to their roots and special destiny....

The Aryan Nations would attract a disparate group of disaffected young White men, particularly recently released prison
inmates, as a result of its prison outreach ministry spearheaded by
the Aryan Nations prison journal *The Way*. Other Aryan Nations
publications over the years have include the periodicals *Calling
Our Nation* and *Aryan Nations*. The Aryan Nations outreach features the effective use of Pastor Richard Butler's sermons on cassette tape as well.

Relations with the citizens of Cour d'Alene have been rocky at
best, reaching their nadir in 1986–1987 with a series of bombings of
the homes of local human rights activists. Following the bombings,
an unspoken truce of sorts emerged, with both sides choosing to
leave each other well alone. This unwritten mutual tolerance pact
was broken in 1998 when the Aryan Nations, over fierce local opposition, applied for a permit to hold a march in downtown Cour d'Alene.
Tiring of the uproar, the Aryan Nations were given their permit, but
a public holiday was declared on the same day, ensuring that the

march would take place in a ghost town of shuttered shops and empty streets. Relations nonetheless continued to worsen, and in June 1998 a minor confrontation between police and Aryan Nations members on church property escalated to the point that the aged Butler was sprayed with pepper gas and four church members were arrested. By 1999, with an influx of undisciplined young skin-heads and the further deterioration of Pastor Butler's leadership because of age and infirmity, a series of violent incidents in the streets of Cour d'Alene have served to strain to the breaking point the tolerance of townsfolk for their Aryan Nations neighbors.

The most complete program of the Aryan Nations is found in the eponymous premier edition of the organization's newsletter. This foundational creed provides a remarkable insight into the mind-set of the separatist aspirations of the movement in the mid-1970s through the 1980s. Opening with a detailed explanation of the symbolism of the swastika-like Aryan Nations emblem, which is redolent with the arcane beliefs of the Identity creed, the document then segues into a detailed political manifesto that begins, fittingly enough, with the question of "population and race." Here, Identity's emphasis on the descent of Caucasian man from Adam is blended with the "science" of eugenics as exemplified by the nineteenth century figure of Sir Francis Galton and the contemporary lightning rods of the field, William Shockley and E. O. Wilson. In particular, miscegenation (marriage between a White person and a member of another race) is expressly forbidden.

Next, the Aryan Nations turn to the problem of private property. Here, what is demanded is a utopian socialism in which the nation's productive capacity in the forms of agriculture and industry will be placed under communal control, to be administered "in the national and racial interest." This is followed by a brief section on industry and finance in which the "financial system of International Jewish Capitalism" is to be abolished, all adults are expected to be productive contributors to society, and loaning money at interest is forbidden.

The subject of Aryan youth follows and is given more attention. Here the model is platonic by way of National Socialist Germany. Youth movements for both boys and girls are mandated. The ideal for the young Aryan male is held to be "physical and athletic fitness, reliability and determination of character, proficiency in chosen livelihood-occupation, and general usefulness to the community." For girls, the accent is "primarily on fitness for mother-hood and home-making, but also on athletics and arts."

For the rest, the Aryan warrior ideal is touted, as is a call for discipline, race consciousness, and obedience to the laws of God. The role of women is of particular concern to the Aryan Nations. Here, an Aryan woman's primary duty is clear: "Every child that an Aryan mother brings into the world is a battle waged for the existence of her people. The program of the National Aryan Women's Movement has a truly a single point—the child."

Then, among idealized calls for feminine purity and paeans to the complementary nature of the separate roles for the Aryan male and female, the manifesto cannot resist the passing observation that it is far better to be "the mother of healthy Aryan children than to be a clever woman lawyer."

When the document turns to more global questions, much of the specificity found in discussions of social relations vanishes. In a formulation that would appall the narrowly legalistic militia movement of the 1990s, Aryan law is described as something that is to be followed more in spirit than in the letter, and Aryan judges are given wide latitude to apply the law in both the racial and the national interest. Much the same applies to the formation of the Aryan armed forces. Here, the central concept is this motto: "At the beginning of our struggle there stood a people; at the end of our struggle there will once more stand a people." The underlying concept here is that the battle is for *race* and not territory. The Aryan army is to defend "Aryan freedom" and the "whole of the Aryan state."

But what constitutes the Aryan state? What are its borders? The section that follows, "Constitution and World Outlook," seeks to elaborate. First, the primacy of the leadership principle is affirmed. The putative Aryan state will be explicitly National Socialist in structure. Thus, the constitution will reflect the divinely ordained interests of the Aryan people, and will brook no dissent, for "Intolerance of opposing ideas is necessary to strength." But in 1979, the movement's vision had yet to disengage from the central paradigm of the nation-state. World leadership in the Cold War world was vested in the United States, and thus leadership of the world to come would rest with the *Aryan* United States. But the seeds of something greater are nonetheless present.

The sections that follow, on culture and education respectively, are both of a piece. On the one hand, they contemptuously reject "intellectualism" in favor of spirit. On the other hand, culture (which remains largely undefined) is seen as the genetic possession of the Aryan people. No other racial group, the creed posits, is capable of possessing this priceless gift from God to the Aryan folk. The education system is therefore geared primarily toward inculcating the young with this amorphous, divinely mandated Aryan culture.

Surprisingly, the only section dealing explicitly with religion is one of the document's briefest. The entire exposition is neatly summed up in the opening sentences, for which little follow-up is (or need be) attempted: "Christianity for the Aryan is Race; and Race is Christianity. Race is Soul seen from without; and Christianity is Soul seen from within." With this genetic vision of religion, all that need be added is the rather self-contradictory assertion that to be truly Aryan, Christianity "must be purged of all remnants of Jewish thought."

What is perhaps most important in the Aryan Nations' foundational document is its generic nature. There is little in it that is so specifically of a Christian Identity character that other sectors of the race movement would be put off from becoming associated with the organization. If anything, National Socialism rather than Identity Christianity provides the document's primary thrust.

The appeal thus attracted many of the disaffected. Most were content to attend the annual Aryan Nations Congress, although a few of the most committed donned Pastor Butler's snappy imitation Nazi uniforms and became full-time residents of the compound. It was here that men such as Robert Mathews, Gary Yarbrough, and Frank Silva talked late into the night of their hopes and dreams, and thus gave birth to the Order (also called the Silent Brotherhood). But the Order's emergence and brief but violent revolutionary career owed much to the frustration of Aryan Nations residents with the steady diet of dreamy promises of impending apocalypse and White renaissance that contrasted so sharply with Richard Butler's cautious disinclination to go beyond words to the propaganda of the deed.

Other contradictions ate away at the Aryan Nations' base of support among its resident faithful, making all but hopeless the outlook for the movements following Butler's demise. There has, for example, been in recent years a fruitless search for a successor to Butler that has, not coincidentally, coincided with the defection of several senior followers. The most interesting of these defections is arguably that of Floyd Cochrane, to whom the implications of the Aryan Nations' fixation with race eugenics was graphically driven home in bunkhouse conversation when a fellow race warrior casually noted that Cochrane's own son, born with a cleft palate, would probably have to be eliminated under the New Order! This seems to have brought home the practical implications of the ideology for the first time, whereupon Cochrane not only left the movement but renounced his racialist beliefs as well. Carl Franklin, a man who was widely expected to succeed Butler, also departed, forming the New Church of Jesus Christ Christian of Montana.

Throughout the 1980s, not only did the Aryan Nations' residential population decline, but the attendance at the Annual Congress dropped precipitously as well. Part of the problem was that in the wake of the successful efforts of the Anti-Defamation League (ADL) to outlaw paramilitary training at such gatherings, they simply weren't as much fun anymore. Moreover, acutely aware of the presence of federal agents and private spies working for groups like the ADL, the ever-cautious Butler had allowed little of the kind of fiery rhetoric that had once typified the Congress.

Thus it was probably something of a pleasant surprise in the late 1980s when Butler, searching for new ways to make his organization relevant, hit on the then-novel approach of inviting skinheads and, more precisely, skinhead rock bands, to perform at the Congress. The Aryan Nations regulars were, however, less than thrilled by the musical efforts of the White noise bands and were appalled by the skins' penchant for beer-drinking and hell-raising. The ploy did, however, bring a much-welcomed jolt of new life to the movement.

Therefore, it must have seemed like old times in 1986 when a young skinhead named Gregory Withrow, founder of the White Students' Union, mounted the podium to make a brief, four-minute speech calling for the "total extermination of all subhuman, non-Aryan peoples from the face of the North American continent: men, women, and children, without exception or appeal." The skinhead youth culture, however, has done little to halt the Aryan Nations' slide into oblivion. In recognition of their incompatibility with the older Aryan Nations regulars (in the best of times, composed of true racialist believers, federal agents and informants, and Jewish agents and informants), by the early 1990s skinheads had established Hitler's birthday, April 20, as the occasion for a skinheads-only birthday bash for the Führer. Tellingly, Withrow had by then left the movement and was literally crucified on a wooden board by his former comrades for his apostasy.

Efforts by such movement luminaries as Louis Beam, Tom Metzger (who was primarily responsible for bringing in the skinhead contingent), and Don Black (whose Stormfront web site has helped to create an Aryan Nations web site) have not succeeded in reviving the fortunes of the Aryan Nations.

Although the Aryan Nations appears to be in permanent eclipse, it is nonetheless of considerable importance. It provided a relatively stable communal experiment that outlived more radical contemporaries such as the Covenant, Sword, and Arm of the Lord. Pastor Butler established important connections with European movement activists, especially in Germany, that will continue to flourish long after the Hayden Lake compound is but a memory. Perhaps of greatest importance, the Aryan Nations spawned the Order, whose martyred leader, Bob Mathews, is lionized in the United States and Europe in song and story and whose imprisoned members—men such as Gary Yarbrough and David Lane—have become icons of the international race movement.

See also: Butler, Richard; Covenant, Sword, and Arm of the Lord; Lane, David; Mathews, Robert; Order.

Further reading: James A. Aho, *The Politics of Righteousness: Idaho Christian Patriotism* (Seattle: University of Washington Press, 1990); James A. Aho, *This Thing of Darkness: A Sociology of the Enemy* (Seattle: University of Washington Press, 1994); Michael Barkun, *Religion and the Racist Right: The Origins of the Christian Identity Movement* (Chapel Hill: University of North Carolina Press, 1994); Raphael Ezekial, *The Racist Mind* (New York: Viking, 1995); Kevin Flynn and Gary Gerhardt, *The Silent Brotherhood* (New York: Signet, 1990); Jeffrey Kaplan and Leonard Weinberg, *The Emergence of a Euro-American Radical Right* (Rutgers, NJ: Rutgers University Press, 1998); James Ridgeway, *Blood in the Face* (New York: Thunder's Mouth Press, 1990).

B

DAVE BARLEY A moderate Christian Identity pastor, Dave Barley inherited the Heirs of the Promise, the ministry of famed Identity minister Sheldon Emry. Emry, a Phoenix-based Identity preacher, was a prolific author and propagandist for the Identity faith in the crucial decades of the 1960s and 1970s as the doctrines of anti-Semitism and racism were becoming the dominant features of the Identity world. Emry's writings, such as the seminal booklet "Billions for Bankers," remain important texts in Identity circles to this day. With Emry's death in 1985, Barley eventually took over the Lord's Covenant Church in Phoenix, the *America's Promise* newsletter, and the all-important mailing list. Barley moved the ministry to Sand Point, Idaho, in 1991. There, he weathered considerable local opposition, based on fears that his ministry would prove as troublesome as the Aryan Nations had turned out to be for Cour d'Alene, Idaho. When these problems did not eventuate, Barley and his ministry were left in relative peace and caused no problems to the local citizenry.

Barley's primary distinction in the Identity world comes from his strong rejection of the violent currents flowing in the Identity world in the last decade as well as from his pioneering use of modern technology, particularly satellite television, to propagate the Identity creed. He continues the *America's Promise* newsletter and runs a thriving cassette tape ministry.

See also: Aryan Nations; Butler, Richard; Christian Identity.

Further reading: Jeffrey Kaplan, *Radical Religion in America* (Syracuse, NY: Syracuse University Press, 1997).

BATHORY The Swedish group Bathory, along with Venom, are torchbearers in the evolution of modern Black Metal. Bathory takes its name from the "Blood Countess" Erzebet Bathory, a Hungarian noblewoman in the 1700s who was put on trial for the murder of hundreds of young girls, in whose blood she allegedly bathed to maintain her youthful beauty. It is highly probable that an early Venom number, "Countess Bathory" on the *Black Metal* album, may have provided the direct inspiration for the name, as Bathory owes much of its initial sound and look to the English founders of Black Metal. The driving force behind the group is Pugh Rogefeldt, who uses the more exciting stage name of "Quorthon" (though, in fact, Bathory has never in their career played a live concert before the public).

Bathory's first three albums follow a similar mode of expression as Venom, though the music is made even more vicious by a potent arsenal of noisy effects and distortion. The hyperkinetic rhythm section blurs into a whirling maelstrom of frequencies— a perfect backdrop for the barked vocals of an indecipherable nature. Much of the explanation for this sound was simply the circumstances of recording an entire album in two and a half days on only a few hundred dollars. The end result was more extreme than anything else being done in 1984 (save maybe for some of the more violent English Industrial "power electronics" bands like Whitehouse, Ramleh, and Sutcliffe Jugend) and made a huge impact on the underground Metal scene. In retrospect Quorthon says of Bathory's first self-titled album, "If you listen to it today, it doesn't make you tickled or frightened, but in those days it must have made a hell of an impression. Thinking back on how it was recorded, it's amazing how big things can be made with small measures sometimes." The lyrics were centered on black magic and Satanism à la Venom, though funneled through a bit of Scandinavian innocence and teenage melodrama, which made them come off as even more extreme in the end. Quorthon is very honest in his assessment of the Satanism on the early records:

> Well, at the time it was very serious, because today, ten years later, I don't think I know anything more about it than I did then. I'm not one inch deeper into it than I was at that time, but your mind was younger and more innocent and you tend to put more reality towards horror stories than there is really. Of course there was a huge interest and fascination, just because you are at the same time trying to rebel against the adult world, you want to show everybody that I'd rather turn to Satan than to Christ, by wearing all these crosses upside down and so forth. Initially the lyrics were not trying to put some message across or anything, they were just like horror stories and very innocent. But nevertheless at the time you thought that you were very serious, and of course you were not.

As Bathory matured over the course of its subsequent records, *The Return...* (1985) and *Under the Sign of the Black Mark* (1987), the music slowed down noticeably, songs became more elaborate, and the subject matter began to convey a degree of subtlety and ambiguity that was a far cry from the earliest singles. At this point came a marked shift of focus that, like its early primitivity, would also become influential on the Black Metal scene of the future. *Blood Fire Death,* Bathory's fourth LP, hit record shops in 1988 and was eagerly grabbed by extreme Metal fans around the world. Instead of the B-grade horror cover art of the previous album, an entirely different image greeted them: a swarming, airborne army of enraged Valkyries on black horses, spurred on by the Nordic god Thor, hammer held aloft in righteous defiance as a wolf skin–cloaked warrior drags a naked girl up from the scorched earth below. This remarkable romantic painting by Norwegian artist Peter Nicolai Arbo, depicting the infamous "Wild Hunt" or Oskorei of Scandinavian and Teutonic folklore, was the ideal entryway into Bathory's new sound, which lay on the vinyl inside it. More accessible than the band's previous noise fests, the new album was, nevertheless, just as brutal. *Blood Fire Death* employed the same amount of raw aggression, but channeled it through orchestrated songs and understandable vocals, which were helped along by more realistic and thoughtful lyrics. The first track was an evocative instrumental, "Oden's Ride Over Nordland," which re-creates the soundtrack of sorts to the cover art, with the father of the Norse heathen gods, Odin (also called Oden, Wotan, and other names, depending on the Germanic language), riding his eight-legged horse, Sleipnir, across the heavens.

With *Blood Fire Death* Bathory had forsaken the childish and foreign Satanism of its original inspiration but uncovered something just as compelling and fertile—the heathen mythological legacy of its own forefathers. The tapping of ancestral archetypes would become a matter of primary importance for the generation of Black Metal to follow, and an essential component of the genre.

The same inspiration resurfaced intensely on the next release, 1990's *Hammerheart,* with the songs written from a more personal point of view. On *Hammerheart,* Bathory's music undergoes an epic restructuring. Most of the songs clock in at ten minutes apiece; the vocals are clearly sung and even surrounded by chanted choral backdrops. Richard Wagner is thanked in the credits. The cover art, another romantic oil painting titled "A Viking's Last Journey," depicts a Viking ship burial of a nobleman, where the corpse is pushed to sea in a longship, set alight by torches.

The final release in Bathory's "Ásatrú trilogy" came with 1991's *Twilight of the Gods,* which further emphasized the musical elements of European classical composition. Lyrical themes were drawn from Nietzsche's dire warnings about the spiritual malady afflicting contemporary mankind. Beside this came veiled references to the SS divisions of World War II Germany in the song "Under the Runes," which Quorthon admits was a deliberate provocation. This was not the first time Bathory trod questionable ground with symbolism. *Hammerheart* featured a sunwheel cross emblazoned on its back cover, an oft-used icon of radical-right-wing organizations. Quorthon professes some naiveté in the matter, but it's hard to believe he wasn't aware of the full potency of such visual elements.

Although not conscious of its influence, Bathory managed to create the blueprint for Scandinavian Black Metal in all its myriad facets: from frenzied cacophony to orchestrated, melodic bombast; reveling in excesses of medieval Devil worship to thoughtful explorations of ancient Viking heathenism; drawing inspiration from European traditions to deliberately flirting with the iconography of fascism and National Socialism. Bathory's first six albums encapsulated the themes that would stir unprecedented eruptions from the youth of Scandinavia and beyond.

Bathory's bizarre bloodline of demonic inheritance—and that of Black Metal itself—can be traced straight back through Venom, Mercyful Fate, and other darker-themed Metal bands of the early '80s, to the Heavy doom-ridden sounds of Black Sabbath and the mystical Hard Rock of Led Zeppelin, to their bluesy antecedents the Rolling Stones, and all the way to Robert Johnson, a poor Black guitarist from the American South who may have sold his soul to Satan in a lone act of desperation. An unlikely Black Metal pedigree, but there it stands, helped along the way by countless others who poured their own creative juices into an evolving witches' brew.

—Michael Moynihan, Blood Axis

See also: Black Metal; Odinism.

Further reading: Michael Moynihan and Didrik Søderlind, *Lords of Chaos* (Venice, CA: Feral House, 1998); Janne Stark, *The Encyclopedia of Swedish Heavy Metal 1970–1996* (Stockholm: Premium Publishers, 1996).

LOUIS BEAM   Unique in the world of the contemporary Ku Klux Klan, Louis Beam is a capable and talented ideologue who, despite being identified with the most radical factions of the racist right, has managed to avoid serious jail time through a combination of luck, audacity, and intelligence. These qualities, however, cannot obscure the essential futility of Beam's quest: to modernize the Klan and bring it kicking and screaming into the modern world as a serious racialist organization capable of posing a significant challenge to the American status quo.

For Louis Beam, the world is a starkly divided battleground in which the forces of good and evil, light and dark, wage a timeless battle for dominance:

> Throughout the millenniums of warfare between the Aryan and the Jew, neither we nor they have ever "won." The victories each has in turn known, when spread over the centuries, equal stalemate. However, Aryan technology has shrunk the whole earth to the size of one battlefield. The eternal war, which can most properly be called a Conflict Of The Ages, has taken a final turn. The age-long conflict approaches, the last battle—Ragnarök, Armageddon—is about to be fought, and there will be only one survivor of this struggle.

Louis Beam, the author of this manichaean and apocalyptic analysis of contemporary history, has lived the life that many Klansmen and would-be Klansmen fantasize over. A Vietnam veteran, Beam preaches the dream of revolutionary violence and has himself not been loath to take up the dangerous existence of the underground fugitive. The most celebrated of Beam's exploits may well be the shoot-out in which Mexican federal officers attempted to take Beam and his wife into custody. In the ensuing confrontation, Beam's wife managed to pin down the arresting officers, allowing her husband to make good his escape. Beam's charmed life did not end with his return to the United States. Here, he and his fellow defendants were acquitted of all charges in an ill-starred 1989 sedition trial held at Fort Smith, Arkansas. He remains free today.

Beam's personal successes should not, however, obscure the failure of his quest to modernize the Ku Klux Klan by unifying its many disparate factions and forging the organization into an effective vanguard revolutionary force. The theory, put together with the help of the late Robert Miles and others, was called the "Fifth Era Klan"—a Klan capable of a clear-eyed analysis of the incompetence and treason that has been the history of the Klan since the original movement was disbanded in 1869, as well as capable of an honest appraisal of the remarkably poor quality of recruits that the present-day Klan organizations have managed to attract.

Only when these difficulties are addressed and rectified will Beam's ecumenical call be more than a distant dream—a call, that is, to take up arms, overthrow the current socio-political order, and ruthlessly take vengeance on (in his words) "lying politicians, criminal bureaucrats, racial traitors, communists, assorted degenerates, culture distorters, and those who resist the implementation of lawful constitutional government." In the meantime, Beam's ecumenism is aptly demonstrated in his extra-Klan contacts, ranging from his close association with Richard Butler's Christian Identity Aryan Nations compound in Idaho to the sort of generic Odinism alluded to in his equating of the Christian apocalypse with the Norse apocalyptic scenario of Ragnarök in the quotation above.

Beam's career in the world of the organized radical right began conventionally enough. Returning in 1968 from Vietnam where he served as a helicopter pilot, Beam took up residence in his native Texas where, in the early 1970s, he acted on a long-standing racial animus by joining the United Klans of America. From that organization he joined David Duke's Knights of the Ku Klux Klan where he led the Knights' Texas branch. The match with the mediagenic Duke appeared viable for a time, with Duke providing the smooth public face of the group and the less flamboyant Beam taking charge of paramilitary training. It did not take long for Duke to begin to eye greater horizons than would be possible for a Klansman. Beam, for his part, remained a Klansman to the end, and the two would soon go their separate ways.

Beam emerged as a public figure in 1981 as a result of violent protests against Vietnamese shrimp fishermen who were in competition with native Texans in Galveston Bay. Violence flared, a Vietnamese boat was burned, and the resulting national publicity made Beam a well-known figure in right-wing circles. This was hardly a development that would endear him to David Duke, and it was at this point that the split occurred. Beam simply formed his own Klan faction and began his long-term association with Richard Butler and the Aryan Nations.

In 1987, Beam met and married Sheila Toohey, a Sunday school teacher from Sante Fe, Texas. The match was fateful, for it was not long after the wedding that news of Operation Clean Sweep began to make the rounds of the radical right. Operation Clean Sweep was a federal government operation, undertaken following the defeat of Robert Mathews and the Order, that intended to utilize the conspiracy laws to incarcerate the leadership of the American racialist right wing. Federal agents fanned out across the country arresting or serving with subpoenas everyone targeted by Operation Clean Sweep, including Louis Beam, along with such movement elders as Robert Miles and Richard Butler and surviving members of the Order.

For his part, Beam knew that while a conspiracy to overthrow the government is a thing much to be desired, in the context of the divisive and thoroughly infiltrated world of the radical right, it was at best a fantasy and at worst evidence of a government conspiracy against dissident citizens. Either way, Beam didn't care to ride the legal railroad into the prison system, and so he and Sheila fled to Mexico. It was here that the shoot-out with the federales occurred, resulting in Sheila's capture and incarceration under extremely harsh conditions in that country. Following the shooting, Beam was quickly captured by a combined force of Mexican federales and FBI agents. The story of what followed is an interesting one and it is taken up by J. B. Campbell in an essay found on Beam's web site titled "Louis & Sheila."

Sheila was ultimately freed and sent back to the United States, and whatever the circumstances of her release, Beam's future looked decidedly unfavorable as the Fort Smith sedition trial got under way. In the event, however, the government case at Fort Smith turned out to be a fiasco. Not only were all defendants acquitted of all charges, but in a suitably crowning irony one of the jurors ended up marrying David McGuire, one of the defendants. In a second irony, in the wake of the unsuccessful prosecution, the FBI agent who had arrested Beam lamented to him after his acquittal "My marriage broke up over this case," to which Beam replied, "I guess I did your wife a favor." Ironically, Beam's first serious brush with the law had been a bitter 1981 divorce and custody battle in which he fled with his infant daughter, rather than the Galveston Bay protests.

With Fort Smith out of the way, Beam made his most important contributions to the movement. Although very much a man of action, it is for his writings that he will be best remembered. His early prose is showcased in the collection *Essays of a Klansman,* which, as the title suggests, contains meditations on race and on the Klan as a vehicle for addressing the decline of Western civilization. *The Seditionist,* Beam's quarterly journal, appeared in winter 1988. In its pages over the next three years of its life would appear many of the most important essays to emerge from the radical right wing. In this lies the central contradiction of Beam's life: on the one hand his thinking is years ahead of that of many of the radical-right faithful, yet on the other his loyalty to the Klan concept is such that he has never been able to widen his influence, as did, for example, Richard Butler from the world of Christian Identity or the late Robert Miles, a Klansman whose eclecticism provided a big tent under which any racialist could comfortably shelter. Be this as it may, two of Beam's cutting-edge ideas are what most concern us here: the use of computers as a weapon in the racial struggle, and the concept of leaderless resistance that defines the movement's approach to revolutionary violence today.

By the time the *alarum* was sounded by the Anti-Defamation League in 1985, the movement had begun with limited success to take up the possibilities offered by the computer and modem through the construction of two national computer BBS (bulletin board) sites. Of these, the most influential BBS was sponsored by the Aryan Nations under the tutelage of Louis Beam. According to the ADL, it was Beam who was a guiding force in bringing the American movement from the age of the Xerox to the computer age.

Beam for his part is more modest than the ADL, noting that the existence of movement BBS sites dates back to 1964. The reference, however, is to telephone-based rather than computer-based technology. Indeed, when Beam began to publicize the Aryan Nations' leap into the world of high tech in the early 1980s, he was constrained not only to explain what a computer is, but also to urge on his fellow Patriots, assuring them that the technology is so simple that, of the approximately 40 then-active BBS sites throughout the United States: "One of the forty is run by a thirteen-year-old child!" It was indicative of the movement's adaptability to the new technology, however, that nearly a decade later, Beam would still feel the need to explain again the basics of the computer—in even simpler terms than before. Rather than wait for the movement to adapt to the new technology, the Aryan Net BBS was forced to operate a telephone-based message system that allowed the noncomputer literate to listen to menus of recorded messages, albeit at the price of an expensive long distance phone call. By 1995, however, Don Black, a former Klansman and associate of Louis Beam, used these ideas to create his Stormfront web site, which launched the movement into the innovative use of computers.

Government and private watchdogs alike consider Beam's leaderless resistance concept to be far more ominous than any uses to which he could put the computer. Beam's original "Leaderless

Resistance" essay was first publicized in Pastor Pete Peters's report on a meeting of Identity Christians that was convened to discuss the Randy Weaver drama. Suddenly, leaderless resistance, which had been an idea floated among the far right ever since 1962, was no longer an isolated theory. Following the Weaver killings and the Waco, Texas, holocaust, it was seen as a matter of survival in the face of a government now determined to eradicate once and for all the righteous remnant of the Patriot community. Beam was quick to comprehend the dire strategic situation of the far right at the end of the 1980s and he was eager to seek some way to keep burning the flame of violent opposition.

Louis Beam's writings show a serious interest in history and evince an academic's care to identify his sources. Thus, Beam takes no credit for coining either the concept or the term "leaderless resistance." Rather, he traces its origin to one Col. Ulius Louis Amoss, the founder of the Baltimore, Maryland–based International Service of Information Incorporated, who published an essay titled "Leaderless Resistance" in April 1962. Col. Amoss was suggesting guerrilla tactics in case of a communist invasion and conquest of America, but the scenario did not eventuate and so the essay was forgotten. Such might have been the fate of Beam's essay as well, had it not been written a mere few months before the events of Ruby Ridge, Idaho. As noted above, Beam's essay was included in Pete Peters's report on the Weaver tragedy, and suddenly the term "leaderless resistance" was on everyone's lips. The movement, seeing in Ruby Ridge and far more so in Waco evidence of a long-feared government plot to eliminate the Patriot community, and understanding full well the weakness and isolation of the movement, began to think of leaderless resistance as the only hope of striking a last, despairing blow before inevitable defeat.

In this supercharged atmosphere, Beam's essay seems somewhat discordant, given its despairing tone and limited expectations for success. The essay, however, perfectly reflected the mood of the late 1980s and the pre-Waco 1990s. The tone throughout the essay is hardly of a man confident in ultimate victory—Beam is too canny a judge of the prevailing balance of forces for such unwarranted optimism—but the essay is most notable for its exhortations to simply persevere. The essay is reproduced in part below:

> In the hope that, somehow, America can still produce the brave sons
> and daughters necessary to fight off ever increasing persecution and
> oppression, this essay is offered. Frankly, it is too close to call at this
> point. Those who love liberty, and believe in freedom enough to fight

for it are rare today, but within the bosom of every once great nation, there remains secreted, the pearls of former greatness. They are there. I have looked into their sparking eyes; sharing a brief moment in time with them as I passed through this life. Relished their friendship, endured their pain, and they mine. We are a band of brothers, native to the soil gaining strength one from another as we have rushed head long into a battle that all the weaker, timid men, say we can not win. Perhaps...but then again, perhaps we can. It's not over till the last freedom fighter is buried or imprisoned.

The concept of Leaderless Resistance is nothing less than a fundamental departure in theories of organization. The orthodox scheme of organization is diagrammatically represented by the pyramid, with the mass at the bottom and the leader at the top. The Constitution of the United States, in the wisdom of the Founders, tried to sublimate the essential dictatorial nature of pyramidal organization by dividing authority into three: executive, legislative and judicial. But the pyramid remains essentially untouched.

This scheme of organization, the pyramid, is however, not only useless, but extremely dangerous for the participants when it is utilized in a resistance movement against state tyranny. Especially is this so in technologically advanced societies where electronic surveillance can often penetrate the structure revealing its chain of command. Experience has revealed over and over again that anti-state, political organizations utilizing this method of command and control are easy prey for government infiltration, entrapment, and destruction of the personnel involved. This has been seen repeatedly in the United States where pro-government infiltrators or agent provocateurs weasel their way into patriotic groups and destroy them from within.

An alternative to the pyramid type of organization is the cell system. In the past, many political groups (both right and left) have used the cell system to further their objectives.

The efficient and effective operation of a cell system after the Communist model, is of course, dependent upon central direction, which means impressive organization, funding from the top, and outside support, all of which the Communists had. Obviously, American patriots have none of these things.

Since the entire purpose of Leaderless Resistance is to defeat state tyranny (at least insofar as this essay is concerned), all members of phantom cells or individuals will tend to react to objective events in the same way through usual tactics of resistance. Organs of information distribution such as newspapers, leaflets, computers, etc., which are widely available to all, keep each person informed of events, allowing for a planned response that will take many variations. No one need issue an order to anyone. Those idealists truly committed to the cause of freedom will act when they feel the time is ripe, or will take their cue from others who precede them....

With this formulation, the theory of leaderless resistance was presented in its most complete form. It would amplify other calls for lone-wolf tactics in the movement, with William Pierce's novel, *Hunter,* based on the original National Socialist leaderless resistor Joseph Franklin's 1970s era actions, as the best example.

Beam remains today one of the most important strategists and thinkers in the American race movement.

See also: Aryan Nations; Black, Don; Butler, Richard; Christian Identity; Duke, David; Franklin, Joseph; Mathews, Robert; Miles, Robert; Order; Peters, Pete; Pierce, William; Weaver, Randy.

Further reading: Louis Beam, "On Revolutionary Majorities," *Inter-Klan Newsletter and Survival Alert* 4 (1984); Louis Beam, "Computers and Patriots," *The Seditionist* 10 (summer 1991); Louis Beam, "Leaderless Resistance," in Pete Peters, n.d., "Special Report on the Meeting of Christian Men Held in Estes Park, Colorado, October 23, 24, 25, 1992, Concerning the Killing of Vicki and Samuel Weaver by the United States Government," Laporte, CO: Scriptures for America (n.d.); Louis Beam, *Essays of a Klansman* (Hayden Lake, ID: AKIA Publications, 1983); John C. Calhoun and Louis R. Beam, "The Perfected Order of the Klan," *Inter-Klan Newsletter and Survival Alert* 5 (1984); Jeffrey Kaplan, *Radical Religion in America: Millenarian Movements from the Far Right to the Children of Noah* (Syracuse, NY: Syracuse University Press, 1997); Jeffrey Kaplan and Leonard Weinberg, *The Emergence of a Euro-American Radical Right* (Rutgers, NJ: Rutgers University Press, 1998); Bill Stanton, *Klanwatch: Bringing the Ku Klux Klan to Justice* (New York: Grove Weidenfeld, 1991).

DON BLACK   Before 1995 Don Black's primary claim to fame was his role as David Duke's right-hand man in the Knights of the Ku Klux Klan—a group that he inherited in 1980 when Duke left the Klan for better things as a semirespectable politician. Black proved to be a capable enough Klan leader, though in the America of the 1980s that in itself was hardly a claim to fame. The Klan today has hit hard times and shows no signs of recovery any time soon. In any case, Black's reign ended ingloriously within a year.

In 1981, Black was arrested along with a group of Klansmen and National Socialists—the most notable of whom was Wolfgang Droege of the Canadian Western Guard. As befits so singular a group of defendants, the charges were suitably strange. It was alleged that, acting apparently as mercenaries, the would-be Rambos intended to invade the Caribbean island of Dominica, to overthrow the government there, and presumably to eventually turn the island into a racialist redoubt cum vacation paradise. Black was convicted for his role in the fiasco and was incarcerated for three years in late 1982.

On his release in 1985, Black drifted into various racialist activities, the high point of which was an abortive run for the U.S. senate under the Populist Party banner in his native Alabama. Failing this, he returned to the Duke orbit and cast about for a way to make his mark on the American racialist scene.

In 1995, Black came on an idea whose time had come. Seizing the promise of the Internet, Black set up Stormfront, the first and still the premier racialist World Wide Web site. Stormfront offers files from a number of racialist groups, hypertext links to a number of others, and several e-mail discussion and news lists that allow the White nationalist community to discuss issues of interest. Don Black moderates the site to prevent the risk of threats of violence that could result in action being taken by its Internet service provider, by the government, or by various watchdog groups, all of whom monitor the discussion.

Stormfront put Don Black in the spotlight, both for racialists throughout the world and for a number of watchdog groups— most notably the Simon Wiesenthal Center and the Anti-Defamation League. The efforts of these opponents have thus far proved ineffectual, and Stormfront remains at this writing the cyberspace flagship of the racist right.

See also: Duke, David; Internet Recruiting.

Further reading: Jeffrey Kaplan and Leonard Weinberg, *The Emergence of a Euro-American Radical Right* (Rutgers, NJ: Rutgers University Press, 1998).

BLACK METAL   A genre of music rather than a group, Black Metal traces its roots back to Death Metal and Heavy Metal, and its lyrical themes reflect on Satanism (frequently of a very primitive variety), neo-pagan Odinism, and, in certain examples, National Socialism. Some trademarks of typical Black Metal include shrieking, high-pitched songs played at breakneck speed, with band members generally wearing "corpse paint" makeup and spiked armor and brandishing weapons in promotional photos. It is today the basis of a musical subculture that is global in scope, but is most readily identified with Scandinavia—particularly Norway. From the ranks of the first generation of Black Metal came the young people involved in burning a number of Norway's churches, which included one medieval "stave" church—a national historical treasure. Many of the first generation of Black Metal musicians have left the Norwegian scene, because of suicide, incarceration, or, in the case of one of the founders of the genre, Øystein Aarseth (stage name "Euronymous"), through murder. His killer, Varg Vikernes, whose influential one-man band Burzum was on Aarseth's record label, proved to be the guiding force behind the church burnings. Nonetheless, the influence of Norwegian Black Metal is now global, and what follows is a detailed history of the genre.

It is difficult to offer an explanation of how Norway, a country on the outskirts of Europe with fewer than 4.5 million people, should become the epicenter of Black Metal, at least in the musical sense. The theories range from prosaic to spectacularly speculative. For example, one of the reasons suggested for why so many churches burned in Norway is that, compared to other Scandinavian countries, a much higher percentage of Norwegian churches are constructed of wood. It is much easier to set fire to a wooden church than one of stone—but even then it is not an entirely simple affair, as many failed arson attempts have proven.

The cultural legacy of Norwegian folktales presents a grotesque world of trolls, witches, and foreboding forests. These have had a profound influence on many younger Black Metal groups. Some bands, like Ulver, have altogether dropped traditional Black Metal imagery and symbolism for "Trollish" atmospheres. Today there even exists a band called Troll.

Modern folklore has had a more difficult time in Norway, and horror culture has never been allowed a place there. While America has figures like Edgar Allan Poe as a part of the literary heritage, and slasher movies are screened on national TV, Norway's otherwise highly prolific movie industry has produced only one horror film in its 70-year history. Horror films from abroad are routinely heavily censored, if not banned outright. This taboo against violence and horror permeates every part of Norwegian media. In one case, Norwegian National Broadcasting stopped a transmission of the popular children's TV series *Colargol the Singing Bear* on the grounds that the particular episode featured a gun.

The resulting void from cultural censorship of violence and the macabre may have made a significant contribution to Black Metal's overweening appetite for such imagery. When denied something, one tends to gorge on it when access is finally gained. Black Metal adherents tend to be those in their late teens to early twenties who have recently gained a relative degree of freedom and independence from their parents and other moral authorities. They are finally in a position to indulge their own interests without the interference of those who might frown on such behavior.

The cultural distance from Europe could be part of the explanation why Black Metal was carried to its logical, or illogical, conclusion in Norway. Early Black Metal bands like Venom might not have been very serious about their image, but many young Norwegians may have been unable to realize this. So when Venom was tongue-in-cheek, Norwegian kids took them dead seriously. Similar cases have happened before. The Sex Pistols, for example, were the product of a smart manager who knew how to make a buck off Rock music; it spawned a generation of bands who took Punk Rock, and the anarcho-politics that had been convenient slogans for the Pistols, very earnestly indeed. One weird aspect of the Black Metal mentality of the earlier days was the insistence on suffering. Unlike other belief systems, where damnation is usually reserved for one's enemies, the Black Metalers thought that they, too, deserved eternal torment. They were also eager to begin this suffering long before meeting their master in hell.

This gave rise to popular jokes like "Why don't Satanists drive cars? Because walking is really hellish." Funny enough, to be sure, but reality was more bizarre. In an interview in the February 1993 edition of the now-defunct Norwegian magazine *Rock Furore,* Varg Vikernes told the story about his arrest for suspected church burning. When asked if this world wasn't already hellish enough, and therefore no grounds existed for romanticizing a metaphysical Hell, Vikernes lashed out against the prison system:

> It's much too nice here. It's not hell at all. In this country prisoners get a bed, toilet, and shower. It's completely ridiculous. I asked the police to throw me in a real dungeon, and also encouraged them to use violence.

Because of its excesses, Black Metal has become synonymous with Scandinavia, and Norway in particular. Somehow, through a combination of subtle and not-so-subtle factors, it coagulated and took shape. The drive toward violence could have just as easily been dissipated in less cathartic ways if the same people had become involved in an already established genre like Hardcore Punk instead. But this was not to be. With an icy but fertile garden in place, all it took was the effort of a few visionaries to sow the seeds of barbarity.

Beyond doubt, the scene owes itself to Euronymous more than anyone. As he is no longer here to speak, we shall never know how deeply or seriously aware Øystein Aarseth was of the monster he was bringing to life. But animate it he did, and therefore his activities and associations deserve a closer scrutiny, to reveal the path of the sparks igniting the blaze in the northern sky.

In the realm of Black Metal, so thoroughly impregnated with the iconography of the occult by its perpetrators, names and pseudonyms appear to achieve a magical significance, becoming indelibly welded to the personalities of their bearers. This can be a blessing or curse, depending on the elements involved. In the case of Øystein Aarseth and his band Mayhem, the connection between such elements and outcomes is startling.

Mayhem began in 1984, inspired by the likes of Black Metal pioneers Venom, and later Bathory and Hellhammer. Judging from an early issue of *Slayer* magazine, Aarseth initially adopted "Destructor" for his stage name as guitarist. The other members of the earliest incarnation of the band were bassist "Necro Butcher," "Manheim" on drums, and lead vocalist "Messiah." Not long after this, Aarseth took on "Euronymous" as his own personal mantle—presumably it sounded less comical and more exotic than his previous pseudonym. His new name was allegedly Greek for "the prince of death."

In early interviews, members of Mayhem always refer to themselves as "Total" Death Metal, though in the fashion of many other Norwegian groups Aarseth would later claim the band exclusively played Black Metal from the beginning. Mayhem had no religious angle, beyond members sprinkling their signatures with upside-down crosses. Their image mainly emphasized an obsession with death, violence, and having "a fuckin' good time."

Mayhem played its first show in 1985. Its debut demo tape, *Pure Fucking Armageddon,* appeared a year later in a limited edition of numbered copies. By 1987 someone called "Maniac" replaced the previous singer, whom Aarseth henceforth referred to as a "former session vocalist," despite his appearance on the demo as well as the first proper release, that year's *Deathcrush* mini-LP. Released in an edition of ten on its own label, Posercorpse Music, the vinyl sold out fairly soon, demonstrating Mayhem's small but increasing position of importance in the underground. Aarseth commanded a powerful role among disenchanted younger music fans in Norway, as Mayhem was considered the most extreme band existing in an otherwise quiet, conservative land.

After the release of *Deathcrush*, vocal duties were exchanged once again and Dead, the distinctive singer for the Stockholm cult act Morbid, joined Mayhem and moved to Oslo. A new drummer was found in Jan Axel "Hellhammer" Blomberg, one of the most talented musicians in the underground. Even with the mini-LP selling briskly, and Mayhem's bestial reputation increasing, the band and its members remained dirt poor.

By early 1990 the modern face of Black Metal had now reared its grimly "corpse painted" face. It was a far cry from the vintage days of Venom concerts with their banks of flashing strobe lights, pyrotechnics, and cheesy outfits fashioned of studs and spandex. Norwegian Black Metal had found its soul and was happy to just settle for a few decapitated heads, self-mutilation, and an opposition to everything considered "good" or life-affirming.

Fanciful stories have circulated about Euronymous setting up a laboratory of sorts in the basement of the house he shared with Hellhammer and Dead. Supposedly he would descend into the cellar for hours, concocting recipes with volatile chemicals, attired in a white lab coat. Some of Euronymous's experiments were rumored to have caused dangerous combustions, creating fiery results. The same could be said of his Helvete record shop, though the consequences would reach far beyond the black walls that enclosed it. The combinations of impetuous personalities and impatient enthusiasms would play off each other in an escalating drama that quickly made national headlines.

Smaller "actions" escalated, until someone in the scene decided to torch the ancient Fantoft Stave Church in Bergen. Aarseth proudly alluded to church break-ins done to provide interior decorating props for the record shop, and a few such minor crimes were probably committed from mid-1991 onward.

In late 1991 an Oslo concert by the popular Satanic Death Metal band Morbid Angel was a meeting point for fans who would become integral to the inner core of the Black Metal scene. It was also linked to a rash of cemetery grave desecrations. The media would later paint a picture of the profanations occurring as a result of the excitement generated by the concert, but Vikernes clarified, "It wasn't *after* the concert, really it was the day before. I was accused of it, but they didn't have any witnesses. The witness withdrew his testimony, so I was actually freed of the charge."

Other small, fledgling crimes included a threatening attack against Stian "Occultus," a temporary member of Mayhem whom Euronymous later disowned entirely. In an old German fanzine interview from 1991, Vikernes boasted, "Under a full moon of June a cross was burnt in Occultus' garden. His window shattered under the raging storm clouds by the hands of evil beings tossing an iron crucifix. The false will be given a sign before they DIE! One night!" When recently asked about the nature of the incident, Vikernes explains there was "some idiot who said, 'I'll kill you.' We just took a cross which said 'My girl' on it, put it in his garden with gasoline all over it and lit it, and threw rocks through his bedroom window. Nothing came of it."

News of the destruction of Fantoft church, one of Norway's cultural landmarks, made national headlines. It would not be long before other churches began to ignite in nighttime blazes. On August 1st of the same year the Revheim Church in southern Norway was torched; 20 days later the Holmenkollen Chapel in Oslo also erupted in flames. On September 1st the Orm Øya Church caught fire, and on the 13th of that month Skjold Church likewise. In October the Hauketo Church burned with the others. After a short pause of a few months' time, Åsane Church in Bergen was consumed in flame, and the Sarpsborg Church was destroyed only two days later. In battling the blaze at Sarpsborg a member of the fire department was killed.

Beginning with a small, ineffectual fire at Storetveit Church in the month preceding the Fantoft blaze, there have since been a total of at least 45 to 60 church fires, near-fires, and attempted arson attacks in Norway. Roughly a third have a documented connection to the Black Metal scene, according to Sjur Helseth, Director of the Technical Department of the Directorate for Cultural Heritage. The authorities are reluctant to discuss the details of many of these incidents, fearing that undue attention may literally spark other firebugs or copycats to join the assault that Vikernes and his associates began in 1992.

The city of Oslo took Varg Vikernes to court to reclaim damages for the burning of Holmenkollen Chapel. The insurance company Gjensidige did the same for Skjold church and Åsane Church. The original charge was that Vikernes should compensate the entire cost of rebuilding the churches, which amounted to nearly 40 million kroner ($5 million). Later, however, the sum was reduced so that Vikernes would not have to pay for the actual consecrations of the rebuilt churches. Still, around 37 million kroner remained to be paid, and Vikernes, unsurprisingly, did not accept the charges. He would have to go through the court system again.

In the courtroom, Vikernes once more played the role of Public Enemy Number One, wearing green fatigues and leering, just as he had in his criminal trial. A certain tone was also set by the fact that those admitted to the courtroom were searched with metal detectors (not a common practice in Norway). During the trial, Vikernes's defense attorney claimed that he had been wrongly convicted of the church burnings, the charges were outdated, and furthermore, his client had no money to pay the damages. He pressed for acquittal on all counts.

Vikernes's protestations of innocence were not accepted by the court, and in December 1997 he was ordered to pay 8 million kroner ($1 million) in damages. Vikernes would also have to endure a 12 percent interest rate on the money owed, calculated from the summer of 1996. By the time of the trial the interest alone had already amounted to nearly 1 million kroner.

Churches were not the only things being disturbed by the middle of 1992. On July 26th, an 18-year-old girl, Suuvi Mariotta Puurunen, nicknamed "Maria," crept up to a quiet house belonging to Christopher Jonsson in Upplands Väsby, near Stockholm, Sweden. She attempted to set the domicile on fire and left a note tacked to the door with a knife, reading, "The Count was here and he will come back." Someone inside the house awakened at the smell of smoke and the fire was quickly put out before any serious harm was done. Jonsson is the front man of the Death Metal band Therion. He had been involved in an argument with Vikernes. Shortly after the attempted arson on his house, Jonsson received a letter from Norway:

> Hello victim! This is Count Grishnackh of Burzum. I have just come home from a journey to Sweden (northwest of Stockholm) and I think I lost a match and a signed Burzum LP, ha ha! Perhaps I will make a return trip soon and maybe this time you won't wake up in the middle of the night. I will give you a lesson in fear. We are really mentally deranged, our methods are death and torture, our victims will die slowly, they must die slowly.

The actual perpetrator of the attack, Maria, would later be arrested and her diary discovered by the Swedish authorities. In speaking of her actions, she wrote, "I did it on a mission for our leader, The Count. I love The Count. His fantasies are the best. I want a knife, a fine knife, sharp and cruel...he-he." She would later be sentenced to one year's observation in a mental hospital for her activities in connection with the Black Circle. Vikernes for his part would dismiss her with a contemptuous "Dirty gypsy, she wasn't even white," and would deny any relationship with her whatsoever.

It was only a matter of time before church burnings and threats of murder led inevitably to real killing. Several murders were attributed to the Black Circle of the Norwegian Black Metal scene, but the most famous was that for which Varg Vikernes was tried and convicted.

On August 10, 1993, Øystein Aarseth was found slaughtered in the stairwell of his apartment building. The death of "Euronymous" shook the Black Metal scene to its core. Until that point, many felt they could continue to escape the repercussions of their deeds unscathed—deeds that by now had become a veritable shopping list of church arson, murder, burglary, death threats, grave desecration, and vandalism.

It didn't take long, however, for the police to piece together what had actually transpired. After only four days of investigative work, the police had enough evidence and testimony to confidently make their move against the slayer of Øystein Aarseth. In August 1993 they arrested Varg Vikernes in Bergen. As the case unfolded, they would eventually be able to bring charges against him for far more than just the killing. Vikernes claimed self-defense, arguing that he'd simply made a preemptive strike against Aarseth, who was already planning to kill him, but the story was unconvincing and Vikernes was convicted both of murder and of several of the church burnings. He was sentenced to 21 years—an extremely heavy punishment in the lenient Norwegian court system. Arrests of those close to Vikernes proceeded apace, and thus ended the first wave of the Norwegian Black Metal scene.

—Michael Moynihan, Blood Axis

See also: Odinism; Vikernes, Varg.

Further reading: Martin Alvsvåg, *Rock og satanisme—destruktive elementer itungrocken* (Oslo: Credo, 1995); Michael Moynihan and Didrik Søderlind, *Lords of Chaos* (Venice, CA: Feral House, 1998).

British Movement   *See* Jordan, Colin.

George Burdi   *See* Hawthorne, George Eric; White Power Music.

JAMES BURFORD   Another of the American National Socialist leaders, James Burford has a following no more substantial than a limited mailing list composed primarily of the curious, the watch-dogs, and a handful of National Socialists. What distinguishes Burford somewhat from the pack is that he was audacious enough to adopt the name American Nazi Party. The original American Nazi Party was the name of George Lincoln Rockwell's prototype American NS group of the late 1950s and 1960s.

Burford, like most National Socialists of his generation, began his active career under the banner of Matt Koehl's National Social-ist White People's Party (NSWPP). Burford joined the NSWPP in 1974. And like most ranking members of the National Socialist White People's Party, Burford's break with Koehl was acrimonious. In his May 1981 letter of resignation, Burford states:

> As for me, I would rather shoulder axe (sic) & musket & march off into the savage wilderness to face unknown terrors, than to remain a part of an organization that is solely run by your personal whim and fancy. You say you are a leader, but you cannot make decisive decisions. You print that Matt Koehl is National Socialism, but refuse to reunify the entire movement, the reason is that you are the man who splintered it to start with. Your paranoic (sic) refusal to delegate authority has insured the Party's future to be that of a 3rd rate mail business, which is constantly on the brink of disaster. I CHARGE YOU WITH TREASON TO THE MOVEMENT.

A National Socialist true believer, Burford refused to let his unfortunate experiences with Koehl's National Socialist White Peo-ple's Party destroy his faith, and so joined the National Socialist Party of America, then headed by Frank Collin. Michael Allen and Harold Covington were ranking officers in the group. This associa-tion, too, proved short-lived. Frank Collin, who had been identified by the NSWPP as the son of a Jewish Holocaust survivor, was ousted from the leadership and incarcerated for homosexual pedophilia. Photographic evidence for the latter charge was sup-plied to the police by his NSPA comrades, most notably Covington. Burford then moved into a leadership position when Allen was exposed as an informant for the Bureau of Alcohol, Tobacco, and

Firearms in 1982. This glory was fleeting, however, as the group folded shortly thereafter.

Burford's American Nazi Party is based in Chicago, where he at times cooperates with, and at other times competes with, Arthur Jones's equally minuscule—but no less audaciously named—New America First Committee, which is itself a fanciful revival of the Depression-era populist movement of the same name formed around aviator Charles Lindbergh.

Burford's American Nazi Party's annual Christmas Party is a major event on the Chicago NS calendar.

Burford publishes the *ANP Newsletter*.

See also: American Nazi Party; Collin, Frank; Covington, Harold; Koehl, Matt; National Socialist Party of America; National Socialist White People's Party; Rockwell, George Lincoln.

Further reading: ANP Newsletter; John George and Laird Wilcox, *Nazis, Communists, Klansmen, and Others on the Fringe* (Buffalo, NY: Prometheus Books, 1992).

DAN BURROS   A core member of George Lincoln Rockwell's original American Nazi Party (ANP), Lt. Dan Burros was a violently anti-Semitic soap box orator, the author of the American Nazi Party's *Official Stormtrooper Manual,* which served as the basic training document for all ANP recruits, and a dabbler in such racist belief systems of the early 1960s as the Ku Klux Klan, the National Renaissance Party, and Odinism. His story may have been one of the most tragic yet instructive cautionary tales to arise out of American National Socialism. For on a night in October 1965 a distraught Burros, in the course of a visit to fellow Klansman (and, unbeknownst to Burros, government informant) Roy Frankhouser, put a pistol to his own head and bid a messy farewell to the world of the living. The source of Burros's despair was an upcoming *New York Times* exposé that contained definitive evidence that Dan Burros was, like a surprising number of American National Socialists, Jewish.

Shortly after his suicide, in the pages of the October–November issue of *The Rockwell Report,* George Lincoln Rockwell reminisced about the career of his one-time follower and later bitter enemy Daniel Burros. In his recollection, Burros made contact with the American Nazi Party in 1960 after a correspondence with ANP member James Warner. Fascinated by the uniforms as much as the ideology, Burros filled out the standard membership form, swearing his family roots were "German," and moved into the chaotic and impoverished barracks in Arlington, Virginia. It was during this residence that Burros's fellow Stormtroopers were to become intimately acquainted with the new recruit's eccentricities.

To his new comrades, Burros confided that while in the Navy he had undergone psychiatric treatment for what Rockwell described as "sadistic tendencies and Nazi leanings." Specifically, Burros had strangled an eagle, which was the mascot of the 101st Airborne Division. He later earned the enmity of many in the ANP headquarters when he attempted to do the same to the Party's pet dog, affectionately named "Gas Chamber." His free time would be spent regaling his disgusted comrades with his fantasies for designing new and ingenious tortures for Jews (with his pièce de résistance a kind of piano in which wires would be attached to sensitive parts of the victim's body and Burros, acting as the maestro, could then "play the organ and make the victims scream in various keys") and collecting pornography. It speaks volumes for the condition of the American Nazi Party that, despite abnormalities that were striking even by American Nazi standards, Burros rose to become National Party Secretary before his break with Rockwell in 1962.

Following his defection from the American Nazi Party, Burros returned to New York, formed the American National Party, and published *Kill!*, a viciously racist and anti-Semitic journal. In its second issue, published in September 1962, Burros writes of his former mentor:

> Without the swastika, Rockwell would be nothing. He uses a symbol for which millions of men died. Men from whom Rockwell now steals glory. Rockwell could never make it on his own, as we are. Also, I managed to expose Mr. Rockwell in the newspapers as a nigger loving liberal—a fact which his followers will soon discover for themselves!

Before long, however, rumors surrounding his Orthodox Jewish background began to surface. Many believe, and Rockwell fully concurs, that the information about Burros originated in one of the Jewish watchdog agencies that stumbled on Burros while investigating the Ku Klux Klan in the early stages of the civil rights movement. Whatever their source, Rockwell could only express amazement that "a man as brilliant as Burros [could] not to have foreseen the day when he would read about his Bar Mitzvah and his synagogue days all spread in the nation's press." Moreover,

Rockwell is surely correct when, in the midst of an anti-Semitic diatribe, he notes that:

> Burros hated himself and his Jewishness, and went a step further, planning to MURDER them all.
> It killed him.

In 1967, *New York Times* columnist A. M. Rosenthal and Arthur Gelb wrote a book on the tragedy of Dan Burros titled *One More Victim: The Life and Death of a Jewish Nazi*.

See also: American Nazi Party; National Renaissance Party; Odinism; Rockwell, George Lincoln; Warner, James.

Further reading: John George and Laird Wilcox, *Nazis, Communists, Klansmen and Others on the Fringe* (Buffalo, NY: Prometheus Books, 1992); A. M. Rosenthal and Arthur Gelb, *One More Victim: The Life and Death of a Jewish Nazi* (New York: New American Library, 1967).

RICHARD GIRNT BUTLER   Founder of the Church of Jesus Christ Christian and of the Aryan Nations (the prototype Christian Identity compound in Hayden Lake, Idaho), Richard Butler became in the 1980s the ubiquitous example of what the Anti-Defamation League (ADL) dubbed the "Theology of Hate." Butler's influence, however, has waned considerably in the 1990s as age, infirmity, the death of his wife, and his own innate caution in a milieu that was becoming increasingly radical, all took their toll.

As his full biography as published by the Aryan Nations may be found in the "Resources" section, this entry will note only the brief highlights of Butler's eventful life. In the late 1960s, Richard Butler was a settled family man with a promising engineering career with Lockheed Corporation. Then, in 1968, he suddenly resigned his job and determined to follow a new course in his life. Behind this dramatic change was an association with Dr. Wesley A. Swift, the patriarch of racialist Christian Identity, which in Butler's recollection began in 1961. It was the course of study of religion, current events, and, most of all, the perceived menace of "Jewish communism" that lay behind Butler's determination to dedicate his life to the Identity cause.

As Pastor Butler's official biography takes pains to note, it is the student/teacher relationship with Wesley Swift that forms the basis of Butler's claims to the mantle of that preeminent Identity figure. This is no small claim, for Christian Identity in the post-Swift era has no center of authority, no hierarchy, and indeed few dogmas on which all Identity pastors would agree. That Butler would for a decade be the most visible face of Christian Identity was no small accomplishment. While other Identity figures would reject Butler's claims to have succeeded to Swift's role as the central figure in the Christian Identity movement, there is no question that Butler was mesmerized by Swift and that their association constituted a life-changing event for Butler.

Butler's first public appearance as an Identity figure was in the 1960s-era Christian Defense League (CDL). The CDL was one of many organizational vehicles associated with Wesley Swift, though William Potter Gale (who for many years would vie with Butler for the claim to be Swift's successor), S. J. Capt, and Bertrand Comperet were instrumental in the organization as well. Each of these has offered differing accounts of the genesis of the group, but what is not in dispute is the fact that Richard Butler was the CDL's first president. The goals of the CDL included Christian (read: Identity Christian) unity in the face of perceived Jewish hostility and proselytizing for the Identity creed. When Butler departed California for Idaho in 1973, the CDL was taken over by James Warner, a younger Swift protégé.

Butler's move to Hayden Lake outside Cour d'Alene, Idaho, was undertaken for a number of reasons. Identity being an apocalyptic millenarian belief system, northern Idaho was deemed a safer place to be than southern California when the expected Soviet nuclear attack took place. Moreover, the demographics of the area—nearly all White in the towns with small but significant pockets of Native American tribes at a safe remove in the hinterlands—was considered more amenable to the growth of the movement than multiracial Los Angeles. Finally, land in the northern Idaho area in the 1970s was remarkably inexpensive. Thus, upon these rocks Pastor Butler built his church, the Church of Jesus Christ Christian, which was so named to distinguish it from the dread hybrid of "Judeo-Christianity" that Identity theology sees as the dominant religion in America today. In this way was the Aryan Nations born.

Relations with the citizens of Cour d'Alene were less cordial than Pastor Butler had hoped. Despite leafleting, proselytizing, and by 1986–1987 a series of bombings of the homes of local human rights activists, the people of Cour d'Alene not only proved unreceptive to Butler's message, but over time became downright hostile to their Aryan neighbors. Following the bombings, however—events that Butler neither authorized nor condoned—an unspoken truce of sorts emerged, with both sides choosing to leave each other alone.

Richard Butler and his Aryan Nations compound quickly evolved into a communal society with marked National Socialist elements. Barracks were constructed and young men were outfitted in snappy brown quasi–Third Reich uniforms. Church services were recorded, and a booming tape ministry resulted. Of greatest import for the future of Aryan Nations, a mail-order prison ministry was established. The premier issue of Butler's prison outreach newsletter, *The Way,* appeared in June 1987, proudly featuring a long letter from imprisoned Order veteran David Tate. The Aryan Nations' prison ministry was forced to compete with other racialist appeals—most notably that of Robert Miles' Mountain Church—but it was influential on two levels. First, it brought the Aryan Nations a steady stream of alienated young recruits who had been recently released from prison. Second, the ministry may have been of some importance in the formation of a national White prison gang, the Aryan Brotherhood, which was formed by White prisoners as a counterweight to other ethnic prison gangs.

While the prison ministry was the flagship project of the Aryan Nations' outreach ministry, the group also published newsletters, including *Calling Our Nation* and *Aryan Nations*. Pastor Butler, however, was slow to realize the potential of the Internet, and for a long time had only the most basic web site, through the auspices of Don Black's Stormfront site.

The signature activity of Richard Butler and his Aryan Nations is the annual Aryan Nations Congress, which brings together Identity Christians, National Socialists, Ku Klux Klansmen, and other denizens of the disparate tribes of American racialist thought with a few foreign colleagues, a legion of federal agents and informants, and, reportedly, enough agents of the Anti-Defamation League and other Jewish watchdog groups to form an Aryan Nations' Jewish caucus. Highlights of these gatherings in the late 1970s and early 1980s were weapons and survivalist workshops and an evening cross-burning performed by Robert Miles and other well-known Klan figures, to which all were cordially invited.

However, the adoption by many state legislatures of the Anti-Defamation League's "Model Paramilitary Legislation" precluded the pleasures of weekend warrior training, making such events less attractive. So too did the suspicion that friendships formed at the Congress could as easily be with federal or ADL agents or informants as with fellow racialists—a point that was driven home by the Randy Weaver tragedy when a "friend" from the Congress entrapped Weaver into selling him illegal sawed-off shotguns in an unsuccessful effort to "turn" Weaver into a government informant, leading directly to the bloody confrontation at Ruby Ridge, Idaho. For all these reasons and more, the Aryan Nations Congress became steadily less attractive until, in recent years, the event was fortunate to draw as many as 100 people.

To inject new life into the Congress, Richard Butler made the decision in 1988 to invite National Socialist skinheads to the event. The youthful skins did inject some needed excitement, but their predilection for guzzling large quantities of beer appalled the puritanical Identity faction, and their ear-splitting White Noise music proved less than popular fare with the Aryan Nations regulars. So negative was the reaction that a young skinhead named John W. Bangerter was constrained to write a heartfelt two-page article entitled "Skinheads—Why?" (*Aryan Nations* #56, 1988), which attempted to bring about some understanding on the part of older racialists of the trials and tribulations of urban White youth in multiracial American cities. Understanding, however, did not make the mix more comfortable, and as a result in the 1990s Butler elected to hold a separate but equal get-together for the skins every April 20th in honor of Adolf Hitler's birthday. Bangerter himself would later enjoy a moment of national celebrity for his bizarre standoff against a nonexistent government siege of his home, which caught the fancy of the national media in 1998.

Despite the avalanche of publicity that Richard Butler courted and received, by the mid-1980s a number of events contributed to the decline of both the Aryan Nations and Butler's standing in the movement. The most important of these was the formation of the Order, a violent revolutionary movement led by Robert Mathews. At the core of the Order were residents of Aryan Nations who had grown increasingly frustrated with the dissonance between Butler's incendiary rhetoric and his ultracautious actions. The Order's revolutionary career was brief but spectacular, and with the discovery that the group not only emerged from the Aryan Nations compound but had been using the Aryan Nations' printing press in an attempt to produce counterfeit currency, Butler, who knew nothing of any of this, found himself with a lot to answer for.

The answers came in the course of the 1989 sedition trial at Fort Smith, Arkansas, in which an aged Richard Butler was a star defendant. The prosecutors were unable to convince the jury to convict Butler and his codefendants. However, Butler received the message loud and clear, and in the 1990s Aryan Nations gatherings were notable for their comparatively tame rhetoric; the movement's publications reflected this caution as well. The trial was a close call—Butler surely believed that he would be found guilty, and with the verdict's reprieve, he was not about to press his luck further. Moreover, when the Order's fanciful successors, the Order Strike Force II, emerged from the Aryan Nations' ranks, Butler lost no time in disassociating himself from their actions.

By the 1990s, the decline of both the organization and its aging pastor was irrevocable. A series of high-profile defections hit the movement hard. Security chief Floyd Cochrane left the movement and publicly renounced his racist views, and heir apparent Carl Franklin too departed, forming the New Church of Jesus Christ Christian of Montana. Ku Klux Klan figure Louis Beam tried to shore up the group as the Aryan Nations' Ambassador at Large, but seemed to have little interest in replacing Butler. Indeed, so low had Richard Butler's fortunes sunk that at the 1993 Aryan Nations Congress, fewer than 100 people made the trek to Hayden Lake. There appear to be few realistic prospects for the movement to long survive Butler's demise.

See also: Aryan Nations; Beam, Louis; Black, Don; Christian Defense League; Christian Identity; Church of Jesus Christ Christian; Gale, William Potter; Hitler, Adolf; Mathews, Robert; Miles, Robert; Order; Swift, Wesley; Warner, James; Weaver, Randy.

Further reading: James A. Aho, *The Politics of Righteousness: Idaho Christian Patriotism* (Seattle: University of Washington Press, 1990); James A. Aho, *This Thing of Darkness: A Sociology of the Enemy* (Seattle: University of Washington Press, 1994); Michael Barkun, *Religion and the Racist Right: The Origins of the Christian Identity Movement* (Chapel Hill: University of North Carolina Press, 1994); Raphael Ezekial, *The Racist Mind* (New York: Viking, 1995); Kevin Flynn and Gary Gerhardt, *The Silent Brotherhood* (New York: Signet, 1990); James Ridgeway, *Blood in the Face* (New York: Thunder's Mouth Press, 1990).

C

CALIFORNIA RANGERS The California Rangers was founded in the early 1960s by William Potter Gale and several associates. In Gale's version of events, the Rangers were a civil defense group formed to protect the California shores from possible communist invasion. In his memory, the group was duly registered with the California secretary of state as a civil defense organization. and it was only the malign machinations of the Anti-Defamation League that created the entirely misleading public perception that the Rangers were a paramilitary tax resistance group.

According to a report published in 1965 by Thomas Lynch, California's Attorney General, however, the Rangers were portrayed as a potentially violent "secret guerrilla force" that constituted a "threat to the peace and security of the state." Both sides agree that one Ranger, George King, Jr., was convicted of selling illegal weapons to government undercover agents, but the Rangers had no other serious legal entanglements.

Whatever the truth of the situation, the California Rangers simply became too notorious to be useful, and faded away. They were, however, an important group that mirrored on the state level much of the activity and ideology of the more ambitious national paramilitary group of the day, the Minutemen, led by Robert DePugh. Because of its localist orientation and the status of William Potter Gale in the American racialist movement, the Rangers spawned a number of imitators in the tax protest movement of the 1980s and provided an important organizational model for the contemporary Patriot or militia movement.

See also: Gale, William Potter.

Further reading: Cheri Seymour, *Committee of the States: Inside the Radical Right* (Mariposa, CA: Camden Place Communications, 1991).

WILLIS CARTO   For more than forty years, Willis Carto has had a remarkable career as a publisher of anti-Semitic and racist literature, financier to racialist appeals, the founder of the Holocaust revisionist Institute for Historical Review, and head of the populist Liberty Lobby, which publishes the right-wing weekly *Spotlight.* Moreover, Carto has been remarkably consistent. None of his innumerable associations over the years has ended amicably. Rather, bitter splits and even more bitterly contested lawsuits have long been the lot of the irascible Carto.

Carto's first foray into anti-Semitic publishing was with the 1955 appearance of *Right,* a periodical that reprinted articles from a variety of sources. *Right* had little impact on the American right, but not so Carto's next project. In 1960, Francis Parker Yockey was arrested on a technical charge of passport violation. Yockey, under the name Ulick Varange, had written the massive *Imperium*—a book that in movement circles is considered either a brilliant analysis of the malaise of Western civilization (that is, the Jews are the root of all evil) or the impenetrable ramblings of a madman. Willis Carto was decidedly in the former camp.

The first edition of the sprawling work was issued in two volumes under the imprimatur of something called Westropa Press. It attracted a small but fanatical following, the most important of whom would be the fledgling American publisher Willis Carto. Carto picked up the rights to *Imperium* and published a comprehensive edition in 1948. When Carto created his Noontide Press over a decade later, *Imperium* was one of its featured offerings, with the first Noontide edition appearing in 1962. By then, however, Yockey had committed suicide by ingesting a cyanide pill in his San Francisco jail cell in 1960. Willis Carto was the last man to see the imprisoned Yockey alive, and there has been a persistent but probably untrue rumor in movement circles to the effect that Carto had somehow assisted Yockey in obtaining the poison pill. In any case, Carto to this day remains enamored of Yockey and his magnum opus.

The Liberty Lobby remains Willis Carto's most important flag of convenience. It was founded in 1957 as an umbrella for Carto's diverse publishing and organizational interests. The Liberty Lobby published a monthly newsletter, the *Liberty Letter,* and soon diversified with such publications as the *Liberty Lowdown* (an in-house organ for Liberty Lobby contributors), *Western Destiny,* and the *Washington Observer.* In 1966 Carto acquired the crown jewel of his publishing empire, the venerable *American Mercury,* which was the most important right-wing publication of its day.

Like many racialists of the day, Carto joined the George Wallace presidential campaign in 1968. There, the 42-year-old Carto ran a student group called Youth for George Wallace. Carto must have enjoyed the company of young people, for with the defeat of the Wallace candidacy Carto converted the Youth for George Wallace organization into the National Youth Alliance (NYA). The National Youth Alliance is of some importance, for as a national chairman Carto recruited none other than William Pierce, author of the *Turner Diaries* and one of the most important National Socialist figures in the country.

Pierce, a key figure in George Lincoln Rockwell's American Nazi Party, had by 1968 run afoul of Rockwell's successor, Matt Koehl. The American Nazi Party had by then become the National Socialist White People's Party and was busily engaged in the round of Koehl-inspired purges and forced resignations that would cripple the organization in the post-Rockwell era. Pierce was looking for a port of call, and in turn Carto was looking for a dynamic young leader for the National Youth Alliance. The match appeared perfect.

Under the imprimatur of the National Youth Alliance, Pierce published *Attack!,* the first issue of which appeared in the fall of 1969. At its inception *Attack!* was not explicitly National Socialist. Instead, it featured articles by writers like Revillo P. Oliver, graphic Israeli atrocity pictures, and critical articles about hippies.

The National Youth Alliance never amounted to much, but unlike so many later far-right-wing "organizations," it did have an organizational existence. The NYA elected officers and had several congresses—funded, of course, by Willis Carto. In reality, however, the National Youth Alliance foundered under the smothering attentions of the meddlesome Carto. William Pierce's bitter split with Willis Carto took place in 1970 or 1971, but not before he had written the *Turner Diaries* and published it in installments in *Attack!*

Despite all, the Liberty Lobby carried on, publishing an array of literature and holding occasional conventions. 1975 was a particularly important year for Carto and the Liberty Lobby. In that year, the Liberty Lobby ceased publication of the long-running *Liberty Letter* and premiered the *National Spotlight*. The *National Spotlight,* later renamed simply *Spotlight,* became the most important right-wing newspaper in the country, and even today it remains on sale in vending machines at major airports throughout the nation—a remarkable degree of market acceptance for a racialist publication. Moreover, much of the *Spotlight*'s material is currently available in ZIP-compressed packages on a year-by-year basis over the Internet.

Throughout the mid-1970s, the Liberty Lobby increased its influence, culminating in a syndicated radio program, *This Is Liberty Lobby*. That was too much for the Anti-Defamation League, which in 1974 began a concerted campaign to curtail Carto's activities. The ADL's campaign succeeded in getting *This Is Liberty Lobby* off the air in most markets, much to Carto's disgust. Carto's subsequent lawsuit failed to reverse the stations' decision to cancel the radio show, and *This Is Liberty Lobby* faded away.

Carto, however, was not about to be beaten so easily, and in 1979 he struck a telling blow in his personal war against the Jews. In that year, Carto organized and funded the Institute for Historical Review (IHR), an organization that soon became a global clearing house for Holocaust revisionist studies. The Institute for Historical Review was organized as a mirror-image of an academic think tank, with a board of directors, a central institute in Los Angeles, and, most important, a serious-looking, pseudo-academic journal, *The Journal of Historical Review*.

The Institute for Historical Review would have a checkered history, but by the 1980s the IHR began to take itself seriously as a research organization until Willis Carto and his outspoken anti-Semitism became an embarrassment to it. Harsh words and lawsuits fell like rain until *The Journal of Historical Review* in its November/December 1993 issue at last published an official repudiation of their founder:

WILLIS CARTO AND THE IHR

Willis Carto is perhaps best known as the founder and director of Liberty Lobby, an organization based in Washington, DC that publishes a weekly tabloid paper, *The Spotlight*. Carto has also been affiliated with the Institute for Historical Review since its founding in 1978. As those who have attended recent IHR conferences know, the IHR staff acknowledges the many hours of volunteer help that he and his wife Elisabeth have contributed over the years.

Neither, however, contributed financially to the IHR. Neither was involved in the IHR's day to day operations, nor was either ever a paid employee. Willis Carto did, however, occasionally act as an "agent" for the Institute and its non-profit corporate parent, the "Legion for the Survival of Freedom, Inc."

During the past several months, facts have come to light to persuade the IHR senior staff that Carto's relationship with the IHR had become a liability. After much careful deliberation, and on

advice of legal counsel, the Institute resolved to terminate this rela-
tionship. Accordingly, the corporate Board of Directors, meeting on
September 25, voted unanimously to end its relationship with the
Cartos. This decision has the full support of the IHR staff, including
Director Tom Marcellus and editors Mark Weber, Theodore O'Keefe
and Greg Raven.

This nasty public divorce is simply par for the course for most of
Willis Carto's associations.

As Willis Carto's relationship with the Institute for Historical
Review was souring, he was already involved with a new endeavor.
In the early 1980s, Carto was the leading force in putting together
the Populist Party to contest the 1984 presidential election. As a
candidate, Carto sought a figure untainted by a public image of
anti-Semitism or racism. In Bob Richards, a former Olympic
pole-vaulting champion, he seemed to have found the ideal candidate. The relationship was short even by Carto's standards, though.
Failing to make a discernible dent in the popular vote, Carto and
Richards ended up in court in a lawsuit following accusations of
campaign funding irregularities emanating from the Federal Election Commission.

Never one to be daunted by a fiasco, Carto carried on with
the Populist Party. Its 1988 presidential candidate was Nazi cum
Klansman cum politico David Duke. Polling a pathetic 47,047 votes,
Duke and the Populist Party came to a parting of the ways. And,
unsurprisingly, the Populist Party broke with Willis Carto as well.
Out of the welter of charges and countercharges stemming from
Carto's latest failed organizational romance came a March 1991
issue of the *Populist Observer* that devoted five pages to anti-Carto
invective. John George and Laird Wilcox in their book *American
Extremists, Supremacists, Klansmen, Communists and Others*
reprint a key section of one such article, "Carto's Endless Feuds."
The article reads like a virtual Who's Who of the American right:

> Although probably not more than one in a hundred *Spotlight* read-
> ers is even aware of who he is, the shadowy Carto has clashed with
> an impressive list of conservatives, nationalists, populists,
> racialists, and religious conservatives. Although the following list is
> not complete, it gives a good idea of some individuals and organiza-
> tions Carto has clashed with or attacked over the years.
>
> Eustace Mullins, Harold Covington, Tom Metzger, George Dietz,
> Dr. Revilo Oliver, Dr. Edward Fields, Ben Klassen, David McCalden,
> Michael Hoffman, Robert DePugh, Dr. William Pierce, the John
> Birch Society, John Reese, William F. Buckley, Robert Bork, Reed

Irvin, *Human Events,* Richard Vigurie, Rep. Vin Weber, Rep. Robert K. Dornana, Rep. Newt Gingrich, Jerry Falwell, Moral Majority, Pat Robertson, Jim Yarbrough, Bob Richards, Don Kimball, Don Wassall, Pat Buchannan, and David Duke.

One suspects the erstwhile authors of this impressive but far from complete name check of Willis Carto's legion of enemies may have run out of energy long before they ran out of names. Be this as it may, Willis Carto, now in his 70s, shows no signs of fatigue in his often lonely battles against the Jews, racial minorities, and his erstwhile allies of the racialist right wing.

See also: American Nazi Party; Covington, Harold; Duke, David; Klassen, Ben; Koehl, Matt; Metzger, Tom; National Socialist White People's Party; Pierce, William; Rockwell, George Lincoln; Yockey, Francis Parker.

Further reading: Kevin Flynn and Gary Gerhardt, *The Silent Brotherhood* (New York: Signet, 1990); John George and Laird Wilcox, *Nazis, Communists, Klansmen, and Others on the Fringe* (Buffalo, NY: Prometheus Books, 1992); Deborah Lipstadt, *Denying the Holocaust* (New York: The Free Press, 1993); Nizkor, *Holocaust FAQ: Willis Carto & The Institute for Historical Review* (e-text available from Nizkor web site).

ELSE CHRISTENSEN   In late 1970 or early 1971 Else Christensen founded the Odinist Fellowship in Crystal River, Florida, as the first organizational expression of racialist Odinism in the United States. Her discovery of Odinism was somewhat accidental. In the course of reading such right-wing staples as Francis Parker Yockey's *Imperium* and Oswald Spengler's *Decline of the West,* Else Christensen and her late husband Alex discovered a copy of Alexander Rud Mills's book: *The Odinist Religion: Overcoming Jewish Christianity.* Mills, an eccentric Australian admirer of Hitler's rising National Socialist party in the 1920s-era Weimar Republic, wrote *The Odinist Religion* as a religious alternative to what he saw as the root of the malaise of Western society: the Jews and Christianity, which emerged from Judaic roots. Mrs. Christensen recalls:

> When confronted with Rud Mills' ideas and the political atmosphere of the time, I suppose that I finally realized that the problems were more of a spiritual nature than political. We chose the Scandinavian mythology as, at the time, the animosity between Anglo Saxons and Teutons (aftermath of WWII) was still lingering; Scandinavian was neutral; a rational choice, not because I'm Danish.

Mrs. Christensen is said to remain so enamored with Mills's work that she has obtained a complete collection of A. Rud Mills's writings and effects.

It was this strain of right-wing thought that inspired the widowed Else Christensen to form the Odinist Fellowship. The publication in 1971 of the first issue of the Fellowship's journal, *The Odinist,* coincided with the discovery of the Norse pantheon by other seekers, most notably Steve McNallen, who would at virtually the same time found the Ásatrú Free Assembly. The Odinist Fellowship, however, from its inception would focus to a far greater degree on politics than any Ásatrú organization.

The premier issue of the Odinist Fellowship's journal, *The Odinist,* appeared in August 1971 with the banner headline "New Values from the Past." The essay set the tone for the next 20 years of *The Odinist.* The central themes focus on the decline of Western civilization, the erosion of the values and ideals that had existed in the Golden Age past of the Viking era, the relationship between the gods and humankind, and a powerful invocation of a religion of nature. Over the next two decades of publication, *The Odinist* would concentrate rather more on politics and philosophy than on theological speculation.

From its inception, the Odinist Fellowship was seen primarily as a mail-order church with a national outreach. Nonetheless, a few believers did visit Else Christensen in Crystal River, and on occasion she traveled throughout the United States and Canada. Here she played an important role in the lives of many contemporary Odinists and Ásatrúers. For example, the current head of the Ásatrú Alliance, Michael Murray, was an early director of the Odinist Fellowship, but as his spirituality deepened, he went on to join Steve McNallen in the Ásatrú Free Assembly. It was Murray who would be the driving force behind reconstituting the Ásatrú Free Assembly as the Ásatrú Alliance—an organization that flourishes to this day.

More ominously, Else Christensen focused a good deal of the Odinist Fellowship's outreach on prisons. Here, she sees her role as entirely positive, attempting to channel the anger of White prisoners into more constructive avenues than violence. Mrs. Christensen asserts that her constant counsel is for patience:

> When letters come in full of anger about obvious discrimination (and there is a lot!) (funny enough, the Blacks say the same!), I act as a conductor. I do not deny the problems, that would be stupid, but in some prisons I have suggested that our men get together with the

Muslims to keep order on the compound and/or to negotiate with the administration; a few times it has worked.

I try to get them to use logic and understand that working together is a lot more productive than fighting....

It is important to note, however, that Odinism for Mrs. Christensen is a warrior religion, and she thus holds in contempt the Christian concept of turning the other cheek. Nonetheless, extreme anti-Semitism or derogatory language "alienates those who might otherwise work with us, and...will put even more people into the jails and prisons."

It was ultimately the prison outreach that brought an end to the long-running saga that was the Odinist Fellowship. In 1993 the octogenarian Else Christensen was arrested and sent to prison after being caught in a car filled with marijuana. The car belonged to one of her less successfully rehabilitated alumni of the prison system. In the end, her refusal to testify was the cause of her incarceration, and by 1997 deportation proceedings were reportedly under way as well. Soon after her imprisonment, she gave the Odinist Fellowship's mailing list to Steve McNallen as the basis for his present organization, the Ásatrú Folk Assembly.

See also: Hitler, Adolf; Odinism; Religion of Nature.

Further reading: Jeffrey Kaplan, *Radical Religion in America: Millenarian Movements from the Far Right to the Children of Noah* (Syracuse, NY: Syracuse University Press, 1997); A. Rud Mills, *The Odinist Religion: Overcoming Jewish Christianity* (Melbourne, Australia: self-published, c. 1930); *The Odinist.*

CHRISTIAN DEFENSE LEAGUE   The Christian Defense League (CDL) was created in 1964 as one of many organizational initiatives credited to the Christian Identity patriarch Wesley Swift. While the idea for the CDL probably originated with a Swift associate, San Jacinto Capt, it was Swift who soon took the initiative in bringing together the core figures to make the dream a reality. Swift selected a young California engineer, the then-unknown Richard G. Butler, who would go on to fame if not fortune as the head of the Aryan Nations, as its National Director. From 1964 to 1973, the CDL was very much a Christian Identity vehicle, led by Butler with a core group consisting of such Identity stalwarts as William Potter Gale and Bertrand Comperet.

Under Butler, the Christian Defense League was envisioned as an activist organization. Its early public activities included opposing integration, fighting any initiatives emanating from the organized Jewish community, or simply trying to awaken White Americans to the perceived Jewish control of the nation, which by the early 1960s had become a Christian Identity dogma. An informational CDL pamphlet titled "Why What Who Where When?" stated this focus clearly:

> If you join the **Christian Defense League,** you must be prepared to do something. You may be asked to distribute pamphlets in the streets, to picket, to speak to a group, to manage a meeting, to talk to your neighbors about the **CDL.** You surely will be asked to sacrifice financially.

According to such sources as the Anti-Defamation League and the author of *Power on the Right,* William Turner, the Christian Defense League in these years also had a paramilitary function. While many of the exploits attributed to the CDL by these sources—dark tales of stolen explosives and a plot to assassinate Martin Luther King, Jr.—sound more than a bit fanciful and in any case are impossible to confirm, it is not unlikely that, given the presence of William Potter Gale on the scene, some CDL involvement in one of Gale's various paramilitary endeavors did take place.

With Butler's 1973 departure for Idaho, the Christian Defense League passed to James K. Warner. Warner, a native of Wilkes-Barre, Pennsylvania, was a longtime National Socialist figure and a veteran of George Lincoln Rockwell's American Nazi Party. Having broken with Rockwell's successor, Matt Koehl of the National Socialist White People's Party, Warner began an ideological drift that saw him take up Christian Identity and later Odinism. Warner, however, was a less charismatic figure than Butler and a figure viewed with considerable suspicion among many in the racialist right.

Under Warner, the Christian Defense League was moved to his new home base in Baton Rouge (and later Metterie), Louisiana, where it was ultimately merged with his New Christian Crusade Church and mail-order book business. Warner continued to publish the *CDL Report,* which over time came to be virtually indistinguishable from his own *Christian Vanguard,* organ of the New Christian Crusade Church. In practice, the Christian Defense League became simply another of the radical right's many mail-order organizations.

A sharp controversy erupted in 1979 between the Christian Defense League and John Harrell and Jack Mohr, two more-moderate Identity figures who had founded an organization that they dubbed the Christian Patriot's Defense League. In a sharp series of letters, Harrell responded to accusations of stealing the CDL's name with unconvincing denials of ever having heard of the Christian Defense League. Pointing to invitations to the Christian Patriot's Defense League's annual Flora, Illinois, gathering, which both Warner and Butler accepted, Harrell noted that neither raised the issue in person.

In the end, both sides agreed to disagree, and both confusingly named organizations were forced to live in uneasy proximity. By the 1990s, neither group appeared to be more than a mail-order franchise for their aging leaders.

See also: American Nazi Party; Aryan Nations; Butler, Richard; Christian Identity; Gale, William Potter; Koehl, Matt; Mohr, Jack; National Socialist White People's Party; Odinism; Rockwell, George Lincoln; Swift, Wesley; Warner, James.

Further reading: Michael Barkun, *Religion and the Racist Right* (Chapel Hill: University of North Carolina Press, 1994); Kevin Flynn and Gary Gerhardt, *The Silent Brotherhood* (New York: Signet, 1990); Cheri Seymour, *Committee of the States: Inside the Radical Right* (Mariposa, CA: Camden Place Communications, 1991); William W. Turner, *Power on the Right* (Berkeley, CA: Ramparts Press, 1971).

CHRISTIAN IDENTITY   A   contemporary   religious   movement, Christian Identity is centered in North America but has scattered adherents in Europe, southern Africa, and Oceania. It was named for its identification of the Anglo-Saxon, Germanic, Scandinavian, and other European peoples with the ten tribes of Israel who did not return to the Holy Land from the Assyrian Captivity of 740–721 B.C.

Modern Christian Identity evolved from the nineteenth century doctrine of British Israelism. The ideological transformations that would arise from this heretofore philo-Semitic (that is, favorable to the Jews) theology into the racist and anti-Semitic doctrines of Christian Identity took place in the interwar years of the twentieth century, primarily in the western United States and Canada, when many Americans were alarmed by profound changes in American social mores, perceived international entanglements, economic disruption, and a massive wave of immigration, particularly of eastern European Jews.

While it is impossible to locate the precise moment at which modern Identity Christianity was born, several key events are particularly notable. A 1930 Bible conference brought together a number of leading American British Israelites, including Howard Rand, the head of the Anglo-Saxon Federation of America, and William J. Cameron, the spokesman for Henry Ford, Sr., and the driving force behind the publication of the *Dearborn Independent* newspaper's anti-Semitic series of articles (1923–1925), which is today available as the four-volume set of books collectively known as *The International Jew*. The *Independent*'s series Americanized the motifs of the most prominent anti-Semitic tract of the day, the spurious European forgery called the *Protocols of the Learned Elders of Zion*. The *Protocols* and the *International Jew* series won widespread support in American British–Israel circles, convincing Rand and his more moderate followers of the truth of a Jewish conspiracy theory of history. This conspiritorialism mixed easily with more militant British Israelites such as Reuben H. Sawyer, who in the 1920s was the first to combine leadership in the Ku Klux Klan with the newly emergent doctrines of Christian Identity.

This mixture of British–Israel theology, anti-Semitism, and racism was further systematized at a series of prophesy conferences involving adherents from the United States and Canada that began in 1937 and was attended by such notable figures as Rand and Sawyer. By the end of World War II, however, the development of Christian Identity doctrine shifted to California, with the coterie surrounding Gerald L. K. Smith as the key figures.

No systematic dogma is universally accepted among contemporary Identity Christians, though there are some constants. The most important of these is the "two-seeds doctrine," which is the cornerstone of Identity theology. Identity has evolved several versions of a "two-seeds doctrine" in its approach to the centrality of the Jews. The two seeds refer to the belief that the Jews are the product of a literally satanic line of descent whose origins are posited as springing from the unholy sexual union of Satan (in the form of the serpent) with Eve in the Garden of Eden. Cain, the demonic issue of this mating, is thus believed to be the progenitor of the Jews.

In this view, the Bible is held to be the history of only one people, the descendants of the race of Adam, the true Israelites who are in reality the White race. The Jews, in this view, are not truly Israelites; rather, they are the Synagogue of Satan (Rev. 2:9 and 3:9), who are believed to have dispossessed the true Israelites from their identity as God's covenant people. Other races are identified with the "beasts of the field" (Gen. 2:19–2:20), who took human form as a result of illicit matings with the Jews. In a later elaboration of the two-seeds theory, some Jews are held to be the descendants of the conversion of the barbaric Khazar tribe to Judaism, a scenario drawn from Arthur Koestler's book *The Thirteenth Tribe*.

Overlaying the scripturalism of modern Christian Identity are other identifiable strands of belief. From British Israelism comes a marked strain of occultism, including pyramidology and homeopathy. Also found in modern Christian Identity are elements of Mormonism and fundamentalist Protestantism, shorn of its optimistic doctrine of rapture in which, during the worst times of the apocalypse, the faithful would be lifted into the air to wait at Jesus' side the moment of His return and judgment. The loss of faith in rapture explains the marked affinity of Identity Christians for storing private arsenals of weapons and stocks of food for use in the years of universal, apocalyptic chaos.

In the decades of the 1940s and 1950s, several key Identity figures gathered around the movement of the xenophobic orator Gerald L. K. Smith, learning in the process the techniques of organizing and managing a mass movement of national scope. These individuals, including Wesley Swift, William Potter Gale, and Kenneth Goff, emerged from Smith's movement with a confirmed sense of militancy. They would act as teachers for a new generation of Identity ministers, ordaining men such as Dan Gayman, Richard Butler, and Thom Robb. This generation of leaders would serve to illustrate the compatibility of Identity theology with other belief systems, including the Ku Klux Klan (Swift and Robb), National Socialism (Butler), the antitax Posse Comitatus (Gale), and a number of other right-wing movements. Today, Identity has a presence in these and other right-wing ideologies such as National Socialism and the skinhead movement, to name but a few.

The Christian Identity movement of the 1960s and 1970s is based on a post–Gerald L. K. Smith model. Ministries often locate their churches in isolated rural locations and form small congregations. These churches tend to be concentrated in the Pacific and mountain west and, increasingly, in the northeastern United States. From these local bases, leading Identity ministers rely on mailing lists to disseminate their teachings via publications, cassette recordings, and, increasingly, on the Internet. Radio time has been difficult to obtain, but Pete Peters in Colorado, among others, has managed to buy radio time, while Dave Barley from Idaho pioneered the use of satellite television. Shortwave radio is becoming an increasingly attractive medium for Identity ministries as well.

Christian Identity today is a deeply divided movement with no center of orthodoxy and a number of competitive ministries riven by disputes over doctrine and interpretation as well as by their susceptibility to violent discourse. Like those in earlier oppositional or millennial religious movements, Identity Christians are currently faced with two choices: either withdraw from society (primarily through individual survivalism or retreat into isolated rural compounds) or engage selectively with the dominant culture. While the vast majority of the faithful have opted for the latter, a further choice must be made. That is, either heed the counsel of the radical fringe of the movement and adopt a theology of violence, or submit to government authority and maintain their chosen way of life with as much autonomy as is feasible for an unpopular minority religion in the United States. This dichotomy of active/revolutionary vs. withdrawal/submission to authority constitutes the primary cleavage among Identity Christians today. However, the actions of most Identity Christians have changed little from the peaceful missionary imperative formulated by the late Howard Rand, who sought to awaken the Anglo-Saxon and kindred peoples to their true identity as Israelites and thus as heirs to the covenant. Success in this endeavor would, in the Identity view, constitute nothing less than universal redemption—a peaceful revolution that would change every aspect of the life of this world.

See also: Aryan Nations; Barley, Dave; Butler, Richard; Church of Israel; Covenant, Sword, and Arm of the Lord; Gale, William Potter; Gayman, Dan; Goff, Kenneth; Peters, Pete; Robb, Thom; Smith, Gerald L. K.; Swift, Wesley.

Further reading: James Aho, *The Politics of Righteousness: Idaho Christian Patriotism* (Seattle: University of Washington Press, 1990); Michael Barkun, *Religion and the Racist Right: The Origins of the Christian Identity Movement* (Chapel Hill: University of North Carolina Press, 1994); Howard Rand, "The Servant People: A Brochure on Anglo-Saxon Identity and Responsibility," undated pamphlet distributed by Destiny Publishers.

Christian Patriots Defense League *See* Christian Defense League; Ellison, James; Mohr, Jack.

CHURCH OF THE CREATOR   The Church of the Creator (COTC) is a church with roots in the early 1970s, though by its own official history it was founded in North Carolina in March 1982 by its self-proclaimed Pontifex Maximus, the late Ben Klassen. The Church of the Creator propounded an extreme antitheology that combined a violent abhorrence of Jews and non-White races with a complete rejection of Christianity as being a conscious Jewish plot to subjugate the White race. In place of Christianity, Klassen offered a religion that replaced worship of God with the veneration of the White race itself. The essence of Creativity as propounded in its creedal statement, the Sixteen Commandments of Creativity, is a blend of secularized Christianity, health faddism, conspiritorialism,and histrionic racism. (The Sixteen Commandments are reproduced in the "Resources" section of this volume.) Klassen was a prolific writer, producing lengthy albeit repetitive texts that were disseminated—often free of charge—to the small band of the faithful.

Klassen's dream for his church is encapsulated in the title of one of these tomes, *RaHoWa, The Planet Is Ours*, which is an acronym for Racial Holy War and spells out the Pontifex Maximus vision of, in COTC terms, "a whiter, brighter world." Following a period of instability in which an aging Klassen cast about for a successor, the Church was shattered following Klassen's 1993 suicide and for a time existed as a scattered group of would-be leaders lacking a significant following. In 1995, the church began to reunite under the leadership of Matt Hale in Wisconsin, and today as the World Church of the Creator it is showing signs of vibrancy that were sorely lacking in Klassen's final years.

The COTC's organizational problems were obvious from the movement's inception. While Klassen was willing to dedicate a good deal of his personal fortune to building a global organization, he realized that no one person could hope to both underwrite and organize a religion (or antireligion) on the scale at which he intended to operate. Therefore, much of his energy was diverted from the COTC's earliest days to searching for both "a financial angel" to help bear the costs of running the organization and printing its voluminous literary output and a young man capable of handling the administrative details of the organization while possessing the patience to work closely with the irascible Klassen.

Both efforts were ill-starred. Only one potential "financial angel" was identified—a middle-aged gentleman from New Orleans for whom the COTC sought desperately to obtain a Swedish wife.

No willing women were found, and the recruiting effort foundered as the individual in question soon fell out with Klassen, who dedicated a chapter in his final autobiographical work, *Trials, Tribulations and Triumphs,* to castigating the "perfidy" of the lonely bachelor from the South.

The search for office help fared no better. A succession of eager—and often dissolute—young men tried, with varying degrees of success, to impose order on the chaotic Church of the Creator. All would fail in the end, and in the process manage to antagonize both Klassen and the widely scattered COTC "reverends." These internal problems prevented the COTC from taking on more than a rudimentary organizational structure.

This diffuse organizational structure, combined with COTC's histrionic racialist appeal, brought the COTC a scattered group of adherents worldwide, which at its height (according to Gordon Melton) probably numbered no more than 3,000, of whom about 100 were "ordained ministers." Throughout the COTC's more than 20 years of tumultuous existence, Creators have been implicated in a number of acts of racially motivated violence. This violence is at once encouraged by the tone of COTC literature and overtly discouraged by the cautious Klassen's practice of framing the most violently racialist prose with disavowals of any intent to foment violent behavior among his church's "ministers."

Theologically, the COTC accepts the nearly universal perception that Christianity is built on the foundation of Judaism, and that Jesus himself was a Jew. Thus, Christianity itself is Jewish and therefore anathema—as is the society that would embrace such a Jewish religion (styled JOG, or Jewish Occupation Government). Following this line of reasoning, the Pontifex Maximus deduced that as Christianity is built on a lie, so then must all religions be false. Moreover, as the Jews are the font of all the lies of this world, it therefore stands to reason that all religions are Jewish creations constructed to enslave the world.

Having rejected the existence of God or any other supernatural being, the COTC has erected in His place a program that is primarily negative. Thus, COTC publications attack every belief system from Mormonism to Odinism, but it is Christianity that comes in for particular vilification:

> Where did the idea of Christianity come from?...[from] the Jews, who were scattered throughout the Roman Empire, [who] have been **Master Mind-manipulators** of other peoples from the earliest beginnings of their history. They have **always been at war**

with the host peoples they have infested like a parasite…. They had tried military opposition and failed miserably, being no match for the superlative Romans. They looked for an **alternative— mind-manipulation through religion**—and they found the right creed in a relatively unimportant **religious sect called the Essenes….**

So let us proceed further…exposing the ridiculous Jewish story known as Christianity, which I prefer to call the "spooks in the sky" swindle, the greatest swindle in history.

With so much time devoted to attacking other religious faiths, little wonder that Creativity provides little by way of a creed of its own. What passes for a COTC creedal statement is contained in the Sixteen Commandments of Creativity and a number of "credos" that do little more than recycle the aphorisms abounding in Klassen's writings.

Ben Klassen's suicide in 1993 capped a chaotic period in the existence of Creativity. Formed as either the fruition of a burst of religious illumination or a tax dodge, the Church of the Creator by then had come to appeal to an audience increasingly composed of skinheads and prisoners. The COTC had by the late 1980s enjoyed considerable growth while in the process gathering more than its share of enemies in the competing camps of the radical right. By 1992, however, the COTC had begun to falter. Klassen's advanced age and failing health—and at the end perhaps the death of his wife of many years—necessitated a search for a new Pontifex Maximus. In rapid succession, Klassen named as his successors Rudy Stanko, Charles Altvatar, Mark Wilson, and Dr. Rick McCarthy. Attacks on Klassen mounted, usually in the stereotypical form of far-right invective: with accusations that Klassen was a homosexual and a Jew. Finally, on August 6, 1993, Klassen took a number of boxes of documents to a local recycling center, returned to his home, and ingested the contents of four bottles of sleeping pills. He reportedly left behind a suicide note that referred to a passage in *The White Man's Bible* that asserted suicide was an honorable way to end a life no longer worth living.

Creators were officially notified of Klassen's demise through a letter dated August 12, 1993, from the COTC's successor of the moment, Dr. Rick McCarthy. That letter said, in brief:

In the early hours of Sunday, August the 8th our beloved founder and friend Mr. Ben Klassen passed away. I learned of this from Klassen's daughter Monday morning. She told me his last thoughts were about you. How important and significant each one of you are in the survival of our race and religion. The faith he has in each of you to continue with the courage you have always shown. To make a stand and not to back down. To take up the banner of the COTC and to carry it to victory...

In his last book, *Trials, Tribulations and Triumphs,* Klassen wrote: "At 75, this is undoubtedly the last book I will write. I have dedicated the last twenty years of my life and all my worldly resources to try and awaken the White Race to its impending peril, and I have done all I can. Now the younger generation must pick up the torch and fight the battle."

See also: Hawthorne, George Eric; Klassen, Ben; Kreativistens Kyrka; Stanko, Rudy.

Further reading: Jeffrey Kaplan, *Radical Religion in America* (Syracuse, NY: Syracuse University Press, 1997); Jeffrey Kaplan and Leonard Weinberg, *The Emergence of a Euro-American Radical Right* (Rutgers, NJ: Rutgers University Press, 1998); Ben Klassen, *The White Man's Bible* (Otto, NC: COTC, 1981); Ben Klassen, *RaHoWa! The Planet Is Ours* (Otto, NC: COTC, 1989); Ben Klassen, *Trials, Tribulations and Triumphs* (East Peoria, IL: COTC, 1993).

CHURCH OF ISRAEL The Church of Israel (COI) is the ecclesiastical organization presided over by Dan Gayman in Schell City, Missouri. The COI was for many years a primary source of Christian Identity theology in America. Since the mid-1990s, however, the Church has shunned the Identity label, believing it to be tainted by the violent activities of some Identity adherents and the antigovernment rhetoric of many Identity pastors.

The Church of Israel emerged from the Gayman family church, which was affiliated with the Church of Christ (Temple Lot), a dissident Mormon sect. The impact of Dan Gayman's increasing interest in racialist Identity theology and his crusading zeal had by 1972 split the Church, creating a divisive lawsuit pitting Dan Gayman and his faction against a faction championed by his brother Duane. The resulting court case cost Dan Gayman all but 20 acres of the Church's property.

From its inception, the COI's distinctive brand of Identity theology centered on an apocalyptic analysis of American society—a view that defines the Church of Israel to this day. This view is clear from the March 5, 1972, resolution through which Dan Gayman sought to effect the takeover of the Church. This resolution vowed to:

1. prepare a people for the return of Jesus Christ to earth;
2. establish [the Church] as a place of retreat for God's people;
3. establish a storehouse of the Lord as the economic order of God in these latter days; and
4. bring...Adam's race under the influence of the Gospel of the Kingdom of Jesus Christ...under the administration of...the Gospel as contained in the Articles of Faith and Practice.

The Church of Israel has been divided into 12 dioceses, each named for one of the tribes of Israel. Pastor Gayman heads the Diocese of Manasseh, named for the son of Joseph and covering the United States. How many of these dioceses are operational is unclear, though there is evidence of COI activity in Great Britain and South Africa. The congregation of the Church of Israel is at present about 100 individuals residing in the vicinity of Schell City, with an international mailing list of subscribers to the *Watchman* and a large cassette tape ministry that the church opened in 1977. The COI operated a Christian Day School in the late 1970s, but recent movement literature has stressed home schooling (as well as home birthing) and the operation of home churches presided over by the family patriarch where an Israelite congregation is unavailable.

By 1987, in the wake of the order's violent activities and with indictments in the Fort Smith, Arkansas, sedition trial on the horizon, Dan Gayman began to seriously reconsider the militant direction of the Church of Israel's stridently racialist and anti-Semitic stance. The Church of Israel passed a resolution on January 15 of that year:

> The CHURCH OF ISRAEL, realizing that the religious and political right in America is charged with many diverse ideologies, feels an urgent need to point those who desire to be Christians toward a Christ-centered walk in this evil world.
>
> In order that all may clearly understand the position of the CHURCH OF ISRAEL in the midst of this unsettled time in history, be it hereby known that the CHURCH OF ISRAEL has no mission apart from the above stated commitment, and the Board of Trustees, the Pastor, and the congregation of the same in America and throughout the world do not offer this Church as a sanctuary, cover, or "safe house" for any person or persons, organizations or groups, that teach civil disobedience, violence, militant armed might, gun-running, paramilitary training, hatred of blacks, reprisals against the Jews, posse

comitatus, dualist, odinist, Ku Klux Klan, Neo-Nazi, national socialism, Hitler cult, stealing, welfare fraud, murder, war against the government of the United States, polygamy, driving unlicensed vehicles,
hunting game without proper licenses, etc.

The capture of the Order and the resultant 1989 Fort Smith
sedition trial had a devastating impact on Dan Gayman and the
Church of Israel. Forced by the FBI to return some $10,000, which
had apparently been given to him by the Order, and to testify as a
prosecution witness at Fort Smith, Gayman suffered irreparable
harm to his reputation in the radical right and among the increasingly militant Identity faithful. These events served to expedite the
already ongoing process of alienation that by the 1990s saw
Gayman and the Church of Israel publicly disassociate themselves
from the Christian Identity world.

Today, the COI's theology is most noted for its withdrawal, to
the greatest extent possible, from a society and culture that they
see as facing Divine chastisement, urging self-sufficiency, and, in
accordance with the Bible's Romans 13, obedience to duly constituted secular authority. In recent years as well, COI literature has
avoided any overtly racialist or anti-Semitic material.

See also: Christian Identity; Gayman, Dan; Hitler, Adolf; Order.

Further reading: Kevin Flynn and Gary Gerhardt, *The Silent Brotherhood*
(New York: Signet, 1990); Dan Gayman, "The Bible and Civil Disobedience"
(Schell City, MO: COI, 1989); Dan Gayman, "Apocalyptic Millenarianism"
(Schell City, MO: COI, 1991); Jeffrey Kaplan, "The Context of American
Millenarian Revolutionary Theology: The Case of the 'Identity Christian'
Church of Israel," *Journal of Terrorism and Political Violence* 5:1 (spring
1993); Jeffrey Kaplan, *Radical Religion in America: Millenarian Movements
from the Far Right to the Children of Noah* (Syracuse, NY: Syracuse Univer-
sity Press, 1997); J. Gordon Melton, *American Religious Creeds*, vol. II (New
York: Triumph Books, 1991); *Zions Watchman.*

CHURCH OF JESUS CHRIST CHRISTIAN   The Church of Jesus
Christ Christian was founded by Wesley Swift as a Christian Identity ministry in Lancaster, California, in 1948 under its original
name, the Anglo-Saxon Christian Congregation. The 1940s was a
period in which Identity Christianity was becoming distinct from
its origins in British Israelism, primarily over the issues of racism
and anti-Semitism rather than of theology. Wesley Swift was the
seminal figure in this transformation.

The Church soon attracted a small but loyal following, among whom were the core leaders of the next generation of Identity Christianity. These men included Bertrand Comperet, William Potter Gale, and, of greatest importance, Richard Butler. When Swift died in 1970, the first of a number of struggles took place over his mantle of preeminence in the Identity world, pitting Butler against Gale. Despite the opposition of Swift's widow and the original board of directors of the Church, Butler gained the upper hand, finding himself in control of two of Swift's projects, the Christian Defense League and the Church of Jesus Christ Christian. Butler left California for Kootenai County, Idaho, in 1973.

Today, the Church of Jesus Christ Christian remains the official title of Richard Butler's ministry, though it is better known as the Aryan Nations. The official postal address for the group therefore reads "Church of Jesus Christ Christian, Aryan Nations."

See also: Aryan Nations; Butler, Richard; Christian Defense League; Christian Identity; Gale, William Potter; Swift, Wesley.

Further reading: James A. Aho, *The Politics of Righteousness: Idaho Christian Patriotism* (Seattle: University of Washington Press, 1990); Michael Barkun, *Religion and the Racist Right: The Origins of the Christian Identity Movement* (Chapel Hill: University of North Carolina Press, 1994).

Floyd Cochrane   *See* Aryan Nations.

FRANK COLLIN   One of the stranger, and sadder, life stories of the American National Socialist movement is that of Frank Collin. In the late 1960s, Collin was a promising member of the National Socialist White People's Party (NSWPP). He rose to become midwest coordinator and had responsibility for the key headquarters, in Chicago. As with so many promising adherents, it wasn't long before he ran afoul of NSWPP leader Matt Koehl, who arranged for his dismissal in 1970. With that, a lifelong enmity was born, and Collin moved on to found the National Socialist Party of America (NSPA), whose chief appeal was to other disillusioned former NSWPP members.

The National Socialist Party of America was an immediate success—inasmuch as success is a relative concept in the National Socialist world. It quickly attracted a capable core leadership in

Michael Allen and Gary Lauck, and soon Harold Covington brought his considerable writing talents and his not inconsiderable inheritance to the leadership as well. With Covington's funds, the group purchased a building in Chicago, which they dubbed Rockwell Hall, after the late Commander, George Lincoln Rockwell. They set to refurbishing Rockwell Hall, to serve as both headquarters and barracks for the group. In the end, it became a fatal source of embarrassment as well.

Collin ran for the powerful post of city alderman in Chicago in 1975 and actually garnered 16 percent of the vote, though how many of the voters knew that Collin was a Nazi is hard to gauge. The high point of the National Socialist Party of America's activism, however, came when Collin announced a uniformed march through the streets of the heavily Jewish Chicago suburb of Skokie, Illinois, in 1977. This brought an avalanche of publicity to the tiny party and to its leader, as the city fathers of Skokie attempted to prevent the march. To Collin's delight, civil libertarians jumped to his defense, and with backing from the American Civil Liberties Union, a Jewish lawyer named David Goldberger took the case on the NSPA's behalf.

Collin, always one to hedge his bets, had in the meantime announced a rally in Chicago itself. The event would have been nearly a decade after George Lincoln Rockwell's march through the Chicago suburb of Riverside in protest against Martin Luther King, Jr.'s civil rights activities and another Rockwell event that ended up in a riot in Chicago's Marquette Park. The Chicago Park District was in no mood to risk a replay of these events, and it was only after Collin was refused permission to march in Chicago that he took up the Skokie case seriously. In the event, Collin and the National Socialist Party of America won their case, and the march through Skokie was held on July 9, 1978. Collin and 25 uniformed followers marched through a gauntlet of thousands of jeering spectators and into National Socialist legend.

In the zero-sum world of American National Socialism, no good turn goes unpunished. In that same year of 1978, Matt Koehl and the National Socialist White People's Party opened a full-scale attack on Collin in the pages of their newspaper, *White Power*. There had been in the movement long-standing rumors that Collin was in fact of Jewish blood. The charge had some credibility despite the stereotypical use of the term "Jew" to smear opponents in internal movement discourse. Indeed, the movement well remembered the scandal when another former American Nazi Party stalwart,

Dan Burros, was shown to be a Jew. Koehl went one better, however, offering a $10,000 reward to anyone who could *disprove* the charge about Collin. Proving a negative being impossible by definition, no one claimed the reward, but the charge was not found terribly credible either, until *White Power* published what it claimed were the naturalization records of Frank Collin's father, Max. Max Cohen, that is. The photostats certainly looked real enough, despite the cries from Collin, Covington, and Allen of forgery and fraud. Collin and the National Socialist Party of America were left reeling by the onslaught from Koehl and company in the National Socialist White People's Party's redoubt in Arlington, Virginia. But worse was yet to come.

Through a combination of circumstances that are still far from clear, the NSPA leadership discovered in Collin's living quarters an archive of photographs of nude and seminude young boys, sometimes posed in uniforms or with weapons, which commemorated Frank Collin's frequent forays into the world of homosexual pedophilia. It seems the half-Jewish leader of the National Socialist Party of America had for several years been luring young boys into party headquarters for these photographic sessions, and, as it turned out, for sexual activities as well. It was too much for one and all, and a plot code-named "Operation Bobby Brown" was hatched to get rid of Collin. The police were duly summoned, and Collin was ultimately convicted and sentenced to a seven-year prison term.

Harold Covington, from the remove of two decades, is still dubious of the charge that Collin is a Jew:

> As odd as it may seem despite what it eventually turned out that he WAS, there was never any documented proof that Frank Collin was a Jew. [Chicago newspaper columnist] Mike Royko never actually produced any proof and simply repeated the allegation parrotwise from time to time; there were in fact some serious discrepancies in Royko's accounts over the years regarding when Max Collin came to this country, whether or not he was a so-called "concentration camp survivor", etc. The "immigration papers" alleged to be those of Collin's father published by the Arlington group were a clumsy forgery, and were created by a man named John Logan who was later expelled by Cedric Syrdahl when he was revealed to be a homosexual himself. (No, that is not me being "obsessed" with homos in the Movement, it is simply the truth. One reason I am "obsessed", if you want to call it that, is because we have attracted so many goddamned fruits in the past.)

I am one of the few people in the Movement who actually had occasion to meet Max Collin, and he did not strike me as particularly Jewish. I am well aware that this "Collin was a Jew" thing has assumed the status of a holy and sacred doctrine among the Movement and the Antifa [anti-fascist] industry alike, and like all religious doctrines it is based on faith and [it's] pointless for me to dispute it, but like so much you people believe about us, it seems to be one of your own hoaxes which has been enshrined as fact through constant monotonous repetition and assumed a life of its own. Collin was unfortunate in his physiognomy—he actually did NOT have the classically Jewish features, he was just a damned ugly little cuss with a big nose. All of the preceding is moot, of course, in view of his habit of buggering little boys.

The National Socialist Party of America did not long survive the leadership change, however. Harold Covington took over and moved the party to North Carolina, but without Lauck and Allen, both of whom had leadership aspirations of their own. Under Covington's command, the NSPA soon dissolved.

See also: American Nazi Party; Burros, Dan; Covington, Harold; Gale, William Potter; Koehl, Matt; Lauck, Gary; National Socialist White People's Party; Rockwell, George Lincoln.

Further reading: Laird Wilcox, *Nazis, Communists, Klansmen, and Others on the Fringe* (Buffalo, NY: Prometheus Books, 1992).

Combat 18   *See* Covington, Harold; Hawthorne, George Eric; and White Power Music.

COMMITTEE OF THE STATES   The Committee of the States was founded in California in 1984 by William Potter Gale and a lesser-known group of associates. The Committee was one of the most audacious (or foolhardy, depending on one's point of view) radical-right-wing initiatives of the 1980s. Harking back to a preconstitutional document called the Articles of Confederation, the Committee of the States announced its purpose as unseating the U.S. Congress and assuming power in its stead. Toward this end, letters were duly dispatched to every American congressperson and senator, as well as several federal judges, advising them to resign or face indictment by popular grand juries and risk a possible death sentence for treason. The recipients of the letters were not amused, interpreting (correctly) the letters as terrorist threats and triggering a wide-ranging crackdown code-named Operation Clean Sweep. Operation Clean Sweep targeted not only the Committee of the States, but the radical right as a whole. The operation was spearheaded by the Internal Revenue Service with the help of the Federal Bureau of Investigation and the Bureau of Alcohol, Tobacco, and Firearms. The leadership of the Committee of the States was indicted, tried in Las Vegas, and convicted on a variety of charges, including making terrorist threats against the lives of IRS agents and a judge, as well as violation of the tax laws. William Potter Gale's death in 1988 spared him the prison sentences meted out to his associates.

Ideologically, the Committee of the States brought together a number of the strands of the 1980s vintage far-right-wing while providing a bridge to the activism of the 1990s. From another Gale vehicle, the Posse Comitatus, the Committee adopted a radical localism that saw the county sheriff as being the highest legitimate government authority, as well as a view of states' rights that would virtually eliminate the need for the federal government to carry out any functions beyond national defense. From the tax protest movement's most extreme reaches in such organized armed guerrilla forces as the California Rangers (yet another Gale initiative), there came an aggressive rejection of the legitimacy of the IRS, the Federal Reserve Bank, and indeed the U.S. monetary system as a whole. In all of this, as well as in its veneration of the instruments of governance such as the U.S. Constitution and the aforementioned Articles of Confederation, the Committee of the States may be seen as a precursor to the most extreme sectors of the contemporary Patriot or militia movement.

See also: California Rangers; Gale, William Potter.

Further reading: Cheri Seymour, *Committee of the States: Inside the Radical Right* (Mariposa, CA: Camden Place Communications, 1991).

RICK COOPER A career National Socialist, Rick Cooper's NS activities date back to 1970 when he set up a White Power telephone message service in Fresno, California. He joined the National Socialist White People's Party when the NSWPP leader, Matt Koehl, personally offered him membership in 1975 in Tracy,

California. Cooper remained with the party's fractious West Coast branch until 1978, when he became the National Socialist White People's Party's business manager at its national headquarters in Arlington, Virginia.

Like virtually all NSWPP officers, he eventually ran afoul of Koehl and was transferred to Chicago in 1980. The immediate issue between Koehl and Cooper involved the former's sale of "victory certificates"—essentially National Socialist savings bonds, which would be redeemed following the institution of a National Socialist government in the United States. As relations with Koehl worsened, Cooper filed a lawsuit to recover his investment, and the National Socialist White People's Party responded by suspending Cooper's membership. In a letter in June 1980 from Dominic Lewitzke, NSWPP membership secretary, Cooper was advised that he faced three categories of charges:

a) Coprolagnia—i.e., you have an unhealthy interest in vile and disgusting things, bordering on obsession;

b) Personal habits and public actions which embarrass the Movement and bring it into disrepute—e.g., your rummaging through trash bins across the street in broad daylight, and talking to Party comrades and business associates about your obsessions mentioned above;

c) Lack of proper understanding and appreciation of the National Socialist world view and the objectives of our movement.

Within 24 hours, Cooper responded to this letter with an 11-page, single-spaced missive that furiously refuted each charge—and, pointing out the dictionary definition of "coprolagnia," he replied to this particular charge with an incredulous: "YOU'VE GOT TO BE KIDDING ME!!!" The letter went on to recount Cooper's decade of service to the cause. Lewitzke's reaction to Cooper's letter is hard to gauge as, in Cooper's recollection: "within 24 hours after Lewitzke read my letter, he became so demoralized and depressed that he shot himself in the head with the duty officer's 0.45 caliber hand gun. Even Matt Koehl admitted to his close associates that Lewitzke was mentally ill."

With such an introduction to the ways of American National Socialism, Cooper's next moves were eminently logical. Along with disgruntled fellow National Socialist White People's Party veterans Dan Stewart and Fred Surber, Cooper formed the National Socialist Vanguard effective New Year's Day 1983 in Salinas, California, and began publication of the long-running *NSV Report,* a breezy commentary on the White Nationalist Movement in America. Simultaneously, Cooper, Stewart, and Surber founded ST Enterprises, a business venture that aimed to finance the National Socialist Vanguard (NSV) and to provide jobs for activists. The NSV took seriously the sad lessons of the National Socialist White People's Party and from the outset announced that it neither sought nor would accept members. Moreover, the ultimate goal of the NSV was unabashedly separatist. Several businesses were in various ways associated with the three activists, though only some were under the aegis of ST Enterprises directly. These included Nordic Carpet and Upholstery Cleaning, Hessian Janitorial Service, Quartermaster Laundry, and the Galactic Storm Troop Amusement Center, all in Salinas, California. The National Socialist Vanguard ultimately hoped to create a separatist enclave for White refugees from what was perceived as an increasingly crime ridden multicultural America, to be named Wolf Stadt. While Wolf Stadt would never materialize, it did anticipate the turn to White separatism in the racialist movement in America.

In the bitter battle with Matt Koehl, Cooper would have the last word, however. In his 1990s vintage "Brief History of the White Nationalist Movement," Cooper would publish and distribute via the Internet a devastating critique of Matt Koehl's character and leadership. (A slightly updated version of this history is presented, in its entirety, in the "Resources" section of this encyclopedia.)

Rick Cooper remains one of the most accessible, and generally amiable, National Socialist survivors in the United States, and his *NSV Report* continues publication 15 years on—a remarkable accomplishment in the world of American National Socialism.

See also: American Nazi Party; Koehl, Matt; National Socialist Vanguard; National Socialist White People's Party; Rockwell, George Lincoln.

Further reading: Rick Cooper, "Brief History of the White Nationalist Movement," *NSV Report* ("Resources" section); John George and Laird Wilcox, *Nazis, Communists, Klansmen and Others on the Fringe* (Buffalo, NY: Prometheus Books, 1992); Jeffrey Kaplan, *Radical Religion in America* (Syracuse, NY: Syracuse University Press, 1997).

Cosmotheism   *See* Pierce, William; Rydén, Tommy.

FATHER CHARLES COUGHLIN   Charles Coughlin was a Catholic priest who, from his Detroit church, the Shrine of the Little Flower, in the 1930s became the nation's most readily identifiable public source of anti-Semitic rhetoric through his highly popular nationally syndicated radio show. Ironically, Father Coughlin's activism began in 1926 in response to the wave of nativist sentiment that swept the country in the decade of the 1920s. Those years saw a surge of immigration, not only of Jews from Eastern Europe, but also of Catholics from Ireland and southern Europe. In reaction, the Ku Klux Klan was reborn and became highly influential in the political life of a number of northern states. At the crest of that nativist wave, in 1926 the Klan burned a cross in front of Father Coughlin's church.

The Church of the Little Flower was located in Royal Oak, Michigan, a working-class suburb of Detroit. Royal Oak in the 1920s was a hotbed of Ku Klux Klan activity, and, in reaction to the anti-Catholic bigotry of the 1920s-era Klan and the cross burning in front of his church, Father Coughlin in 1926 took to the airwaves on Detroit station WRJ with a message of tolerance and religious brotherhood. He proved to be an exceptionally effective speaker, and the number of stations carrying his presentations grew quickly.

As a social and political thinker, Coughlin had been influenced by papal encyclicals such as *Rerum Novarum* ("Of new things," 1891) and *Quadragesimo Anno* ("After forty years," 1931) that expressed concern for the sufferings of the poor in an industrial society. *Rerum Novarum* was an encyclical issued by Pope Leo XIII that was of considerable importance to the American Catholic faithful. Breaking with the church's withdrawal from the world of secularism and modernism, with which the United States in particular was seen to be deeply infected, *Rerum Novarum* upheld the right to private property and strongly condemned socialism, but at the same time confirmed the rights of workers to unionize and to live at a decent standard, with fair wages and under reasonable working conditions. *Quadragesimo Anno,* the Depression era follow-up to *Rerum Novarum,* upheld the principles of the 1891 encyclical, but strongly condemned both communist tyranny and capitalist greed. Significantly, no mention was made of European fascism in this document. Father Coughlin's early broadcasts were not marked by significant or controversial political commentary. Following the pattern of a number of American populist voices, however, the Depression changed this.

At first, Coughlin, like many an American populist, expressed strong support for Franklin D. Roosevelt and the New Deal. Indeed, he was initially welcomed by the Roosevelt White House, and Coughlin in return signed his letters to the new president with the declaration "I love you" and publicly blessed the New Deal as "Christ's Deal." However, like his close associates Gerald L. K. Smith and the apostle of the universal pension system Dr. Francis P. Townsend, Father Coughlin felt the need to explain the suffering of the Depression to his ever-growing audience. This explanation was not long in coming. By 1934, Coughlin had declared America a Christian nation, and he went on to endorse the *Protocols of the Elders of Zion*. This transformation from a moderate, left-wing populism to singling out Jews as the primary cause of the nation's suffering was heralded by his public assertion that the continuing Depression was the product of flaws in the monetary system and the machinations of "international bankers."

On the radio waves, however, Father Coughlin was still circumspect with regard to overt public expressions of anti-Semitism at this stage of his career. By the mid-1930s, however, he began to take a far more critical attitude toward Roosevelt, especially after the president rebuffed his attempts to gain a direct influence on public policy-making. Growing increasingly frustrated by developments in Washington—for example, adamantly opposing the administration's attempt to have the United States join the World Court—Coughlin created the National Union for Social Justice. At the time, 1935, he claimed no fewer than 8.5 million active supporters, though he later offered the more realistic figure of 1.6 million active members and 6 million "passive supporters." He hoped to mobilize this vast audience on behalf of issues and candidates he favored. Coughlin went on public speaking tours to raise support for his social justice agenda. In 1936 he also promoted the third-party presidential candidacy of Congressman William "Liberty Bell" Lemke. When Lemke, in the context of the Roosevelt landslide, failed to win a significant percentage of the vote, Father Coughlin informed his followers that he was retiring from public life.

But less than two months later he resumed his career by delivering Sunday sermons on the CBS radio network. By 1938 and increasingly thereafter, the tone of Coughlin's remarks became stridently anti-Semitic, linking Jews to the spread of communism and to the nefarious activities of international bankers. He began to see virtues in the Nazi and Fascist dictatorships that he had overlooked in the past. *Social Justice,* the Coughlinite periodical, serialized the *Protocols of the Elders of Zion,* and Coughlin himself attacked the role of Jews in the Roosevelt administration.

It is also at this stage of his career that Coughlin urged his followers to create paramilitary units under the name Christian Front, to combat a largely imaginary communist menace. Obviously modeled after European fascist groups, Christian Front organizations were established in New York, Boston, Hartford, and a few other East Coast cities. The Christian Front groups, composed largely of young toughs, carried out street-corner attacks on Jews and other passersby in these communities. One of these local groups, the Christian Mobilizers led by Joe McWilliams, achieved some prominence in New York City in the summer of 1939 when it held a rally and paramilitary display jointly with Fritz Kuhn's German American Bund.

With the outbreak of World War II in Europe, Coughlin urged American neutrality and blamed Jews for seeking to drag the country into the conflict. He also praised the kind of "New Order" that Hitler was seeking to impose on the Continent. A few months after Pearl Harbor, Coughlin's public career was brought to an end when, with the threat of church prosecution hanging over his head, the Detroit Archdiocese officially demanded his silence.

In this sudden withdrawal from public life, Coughlin narrowly avoided being dragged into the widening net of conspiracy and sedition charges that were being filed against a number of figures in the American radical right of the day. By 1940, 17 members of his Christian Front were not so fortunate. Father Coughlin was thus in an agonizing dilemma. On the one hand he had been ordered to remove himself from politics by his superiors, on the other he nonetheless felt torn by loyalty to the men of his Christian Front. Out of this came a strange and compelling document, "I Take My Stand," which Father Coughlin published in January 1940. In it, he balances the interests of his movement with the discipline of the Roman Catholic Church—noting in the process the considerable support he had always enjoyed from his ecclesiastical superiors:

> This address then, is designed by me not to wash my hands, Pontius Pilate-like, of the Christian Front and its members, be they in jail or out of jail. But it is designed to notify those responsible for Mr. Hoover's [director of the FBI] descent upon a group of Christian young men—among whom it is possible that there is at least one borer-from-within—that the real Christians of this nation will not beat a retreat.

And why will we not beat a retreat? Because the Christians of America are asking themselves this question: "Why did not Attorney General Murphy and Mr. Hoover swoop down months ago upon the Communist organizations whose leaders, publicly and admittedly, proposed to overthrow the government?"

When I encouraged and still encourage the formation of a Christian Front, I did not stand alone in doing so, for the Christian Front movement was endorsed by many thousands of decent citizens who were and are heartsick as a result of the unimpeded and cultured growth of Communism in this nation over a period of years.

I speak of these things to indicate the need for establishing a genuine Christian Front, modeled upon the principles of Christ and encouraged by the words of the Venerable Pontiff to whose writings I formerly referred—a Christian Front that is tolerant with saint and sinner, with Catholic, Protestant and Jew; but a Christian Front that is not tolerant with the propagation of ideologies of sedition and treachery aimed at the destruction either of our form of government or our Christian ideals.

At this point may I quote for public record what [Pope] Leo XIII said about tolerance. He advised us "to cut off familiar intercourse not only with the openly wicked, but with those who hide their *real character under the mask of universal tolerance*——of the mania for reconciling the maxims of the gospel with those of the revolution, Christ and Belial, and the Church of God and the state without God." (Pope Leo XIII's Letter to the Italian People, December 8, 1892.)

When tolerance is so misinterpreted as to imply that we must shake hands with Satan, extend to him our friendship, become his bedfellow, and sit back complacently while communism is countenanced in the highest and lowest circles of government, the courageous Christians of America will not be intimidated by name calling such as "anti-Semitic" or the threats of investigation by a prejudiced press. And by no means am I including all newspapers in that category.

Father Coughlin's defense of the Christian Front was unstinting but, in the end, unavailing. Ecclesiastical pressure on him to pull back became irresistible until in 1942, following the Japanese attack on Pearl Harbor, he was at last ordered by his bishop to cease and desist from all political activities. At the same time, the U.S. Postmaster-General moved to ban Father Coughlin's primary publication, *Social Justice,* from the mails. Thus, the loss of the radio show and the inability to disseminate his ideas via the written word silenced Coughlin's voice as effectively as did the orders of his ecclesiastical superiors.

Father Coughlin returned to the life of a parish priest, far from the limelight, in suburban Detroit. He died in obscurity in October 1979.

See also: Hitler, Adolf; Smith, Gerald L. K.

Further reading: David H. Bennett, *Demagogues in the Depression* (New Brunswick, NJ: Rutgers University Press, 1969); Alan Brinkley, *Voices of Protest* (New York: Alfred Knopf, 1982); Jeffrey Kaplan and Leonard Weinberg, *The Emergence of a Euro-American Radical Right* (Rutgers, NJ: Rutgers University Press, 1998); Seymour Lipset, "Three Decades of the Radical Right," in Daniel Bell, ed., *The Radical Right* (New York: Doubleday & Co., 1963); Martin E. Marty, *Modern American Religion Volume 2: The Noise and the Conflict 1919–1941* (Chicago: University of Chicago Press, 1991); Richard McBrien, ed., *Encyclopedia of Catholicism* (New York: HarperCollins, 1995); Phillip Rees, *Biographical Dictionary of the Extreme Right Since 1890* (New York: Simon & Schuster, 1990); Leo Ribuffo, *The Old Christian Right* (Philadelphia, PA: Temple University Press, 1983); Donald Warren, *Radio Priest* (New York: Free Press, 1996).

COVENANT, SWORD, AND ARM OF THE LORD   The Covenant, Sword, and Arm of the Lord (CSA) was founded in 1976 under the leadership of James Ellison in a rural redoubt that hugged the Missouri border with Arkansas and that the biblically minded founders dubbed Zarephath-Horeb. Interestingly, the communal group that evolved into the CSA originated as a charismatic Christian community with no overt racial or anti-Semitic overtones. Rather, membership was composed of disaffected refugees from the Children of God and followers of the controversial evangelist William Branham, as well as an ever-changing number of other religious seekers who drifted into and out of the Zarephath-Horeb orbit. It was not until James Ellison's fortuitous discovery of a cassette sermon by long-time Missouri Identity preacher Dan Gayman that the Covenant, Sword, and Arm of the Lord as an Identity End-Time enclave (that is, a refuge for the faithful at the apocalyptic End of Days as foretold in the Book of Revelation) came into being. With this conversion to Identity beliefs—a process that took more than six months of argument and prayer—CSA emerged as a kind of final refuge for the Christian Identity faithful in the times of the oncoming apocalypse. Until the onset of the darkest days of the

Tribulation (the seven-year period of suffering under the reign of the Antichrist), however, the CSA came to fill the role of elite armorer and training ground for the most militant members of the American radical right. This powerful sense of mission is made clear in a statement published in the *CSA Journal* in 1982:

> In the early days of 1981, we received a prophesy [sic] form [sic] the Lord saying that as He established our name locally, so He would establish our name across the United States, to be a Beacon of Light unto Him and His people, that others could see what a Christian is to be. Two weeks later, we were on the NBC Nightly News.

This would not be the last evening news appearance for the CSA, though that publicity would not be as felicitous as this NBC report.

Throughout the 1970s and early 1980s, James Ellison was a charismatic, if highly divisive, figure in the American radical-right-wing scene. He attended and addressed numerous movement gatherings, including the Aryan Nations' annual meeting in Idaho and the Christian Patriots Defense League Freedom Festivals in upstate Illinois. As a result of these appearances and of the CSA's publications, a small but steady stream of seekers made their way to the CSA property on the Missouri–Arkansas border, often living in trailers or sharing quarters until such time as permanent housing could be found. To the frustration of the founders who saw the CSA as the "city on a hill," which would serve as a beacon for the White remnant community during the "soon-coming" horrors of the Last Days, many of those attracted to the CSA's various seminars and training sessions, as well as to the community itself, were motivated more by the violent message preached in the CSA's publications than by the religious faith that fired the original residents of the Zarephath-Horeb community. In this sense, the violence that followed was as much a response to the demands of the faithful as it was a result of the will of the leadership.

By 1981, sufficient interest in the doings of the CSA had been expressed that the group felt constrained to publish a 15-point statement of beliefs. These, together with what would prove to be a deeply ironic "Declaration of Non-Surrender," were duly published in the same 1982 edition of the *CSA Journal*. Based on James Ellison's interpretation of the Bible, these included:

1. Statements of belief in the Bible as the "inspired (though not necessarily perfect) Word of God".
2. Belief in the oneness of God.

3. Faith that Jesus Christ is the Son of God.
4. Faith that "the white race is the Israel race of God and is the superior race on this earth."
5. Belief in the "Born Again" experience, including the Pentecostal gifts of healing and speaking in tongues.
6. Belief that God is actively saving a remnant of the (White) nations, or, in Identity parlance, the nations or tribes of biblical Israel.
7. Faith that God is about to visit a wrathful judgment on the earth in these, the Last Days.
8. Faith that "the commonly-called Jews of today are not God's chosen people, but are in fact an anti-Christ race, whose purpose is to destroy God's people and Christianity, through its Talmudic teachings, forced inter-racial mixings, and perversions."
9. Belief that miscegenation is a sin and (again) in the dominion of the White race.
10. Belief in the Declaration of Independence and the Constitution as divinely inspired documents that "have become a farce today because of evil forces in our government."
11. Belief in a dispensational reading of history in which all things would in the fullness of time be gathered unto Christ.
12. Belief in the reality of the devil and his demons as spiritual beings who are nonetheless under the dominion of God.
13. A belief that "the Scandinavian-Germanic-Teutonic-British-American people [are] the Lost Sheep of the House of Israel which Jesus was sent for."
14. Belief in the God-given right of self-defense against the enemies of God and a conviction that the time is almost come for the people of God to take possession of the earth.
15. Belief that [it] is "mandatory to come out of the confusion of Babylon and its political, religious, worldly, city, sinful systems, and not to touch these unclean things."

All of this is standard Identity fare. What distinguished the CSA from even so histrionically racialist and militant an Identity community as the Aryan Nations, however, was the lack of a cautious elder statesman such as Richard Butler to curb the enthusiasm of such as Ellison. Thus, the CSA's rhetoric became increasingly revolutionary in the early 1980s, and its side business of gun smithing for the movement's firebrands boomed. Such was the bravado of the times that the CSA would boldly state in its "Decla-ration of Non-Surrender" that its members would "refuse any treaty, pact or declaration of surrender" with the hated "Babylon" government of the United States.

The population at Zarephath-Horeb/CSA reached almost 200 at its peak. Yet by the time the community turned to serious revolu-tionary violence in the early 1980s, the resident population was only about a quarter of that number. Moreover, the 50 to 60 people who remained at CSA were almost all newcomers, interested in the violent racialist message rather than what the leadership felt was the vital biblical foundation of the group's beliefs. In 1982, a mass exodus occurred in which almost two-thirds of the community parted ways with the group over the question of polygamy. When, over the virtually unanimous objections of the church elders, James Ellison insisted on taking a second wife, the original Zarephath-Horeb community fragmented, opening the way for the violent radi-calism that was to follow.

Even before the polygamy controversy, though, all was not well at the CSA. Disaffected adherents began to filter out of Zarephath-Horeb with lurid stories of sexual improprieties and fraudulent dealings with members' property and finances. Ellison, in particular, was charged with interpreting scripture to suit his whims and with forming a cult of personality, and the group in gen-eral was charged with such un-Christian activities as shoplifting in local stores. The latter charge was particularly telling in that it indicated the dire state of the group's finances as well as the CSA's convenient code of morality. The charges were taken seriously by the Identity community, while Ellison's constant battles with rival leaders and his polygamous lifestyle had already clouded the CSA with an aura of considerable suspicion. Moreover, some among the CSA faithful took Ellison's violent rhetoric more seriously than did the leader himself. A few, most notably Richard Wayne Snell, would become notorious in their own right for crimes up to and including murder (a charge for which Snell would be executed on the very day of the Oklahoma City bombing of the federal building, April 19, 1995).

The CSA's course of revolutionary violence took place between 1982 and 1984. As with everything else at the Covenant, Sword, and Arm of the Lord, the violence was incremental, resulting from the group's increasing impatience with the Lord to fulfill the group's prophesies of imminent apocalypse. The ingredients for vio-lence were there from the beginning. The group, living in isolation and under the authority of a charismatic and highly eccentric leader who was convinced of his role as a prophet of God in the Last Days, had amassed a considerable stockpile of illegal automatic weapons. Further, the group was "blessed" by the presence of no fewer than two experts in armaments and explosives, and soon the group boasted of a remarkable stockpile of weaponry. The CSA emerged in the early 1980s as the elite training ground of the radical right, and its *CSA Survival Manual* remains the standard work on irregular warfare to emerge from the American radical right.

Thus armed, it was only a matter of time before petty shoplifting and various forms of fraud evolved into more serious crime. One such, an armed robbery of a pawnshop in Texarkana, Arkansas, resulted in the murder of its owner by Richard Wayne Snell, who felt the man "looked Jewish" and thus needed to die. Other actions included an attempted arson of a gay church in Springfield, Missouri, and the bombing of a Jewish community center in Bloomington, Indiana, both in 1983.

Fortunately, CSA's more grandiose schemes were not carried out. One such, the bombing of a gay church during services, was aborted when the putative bomber, Kerry Noble, sat in the church with the bomb and then decided, for both instrumental and emotional reasons, that he simply could not do it. A hit list of assassination victims was drawn up but not acted on. And the most ambitious plot of all—the blowing up of the Oklahoma City Federal Center—was ultimately deemed too dangerous, and it too was forgotten.

While all of this was going on, the drumbeat of criticism of Ellison and the CSA from movement circles had, if anything, increased in intensity. As Ellison and the CSA leadership struggled to defend themselves in movement circles from the swirl of charges and countercharges, more serious problems loomed on the horizon. By 1984, the federal government began a series of prosecutions of the CSA membership that would culminate in the seizure of the property itself. Ellsion, Noble, and the CSA hard core, in keeping with their own "Declaration of Non-Surrender," vowed to defend the compound to the death, if need be. Given the large cache of armaments and supplies at their disposal, the threat was not taken lightly by the government, and in April 1985 the compound was besieged with a force of some 300 FBI agents. After an initial show of bravado, Ellison meekly surrendered without a shot being fired. Some residents were allowed to remain on the property after the arrests of the leadership, but the faithful soon dwindled to fewer than 30. With the news that Ellison had betrayed the movement and would testify for the government at the Fort Smith, Arkansas, sedition trial, the embers of the once-powerful Covenant, Sword, and Arm of the Lord flickered and died. Today, Ellison resides at the Elohim City Identity enclave in Oklahoma, while Kerry Noble has left the movement and renounced his racist beliefs.

See also: Aryan Nations; Butler, Richard; Christian Identity; Church of Israel; Ellison, James; Gayman, Dan; Snell, Richard Wayne.

Further reading: Michael Barkun, *Religion and the Racist Right: The Origins of the Christian Identity Movement* (Chapel Hill: University of North Carolina Press, 1994); *CSA Journal*; *CSA Newsletter*; CSA, *C.S.A. Survival Manual* (n.p., n.d.); Jeffrey Kaplan, *Radical Religion in America* (Syracuse, NY: Syracuse University Press, 1997); Kerry Noble, *Tabernacle of Hate: Why They Bombed Oklahoma City* (Prescott, Ontario: Voyageur Publishing in Canada, 1998).

HAROLD COVINGTON Veteran National Socialist Harold Covington is perhaps the most talented writer and propagandist that American National Socialism has produced. Indeed, even the writings of the Commander himself, George Lincoln Rockwell, were but candles in the wind before the blast of Covington's purple prose. Had this talent not been put to such effective use in the ongoing internecine wars of the racial right wing, Covington may well have realized his life's ambition of taking up Rockwell's torch and uniting the many disparate American National Socialist groups under his leadership. This was not to be.

Covington's writings are voluminous, and his unusual capacity for self-analysis offers an unparalleled view of the psychology and outlook of an American National Socialist. For this reason, as well as for the fact that Covington has for some two decades been a weathervane of doings of the American National Socialist subculture, this entry will be of unusual length, and will feature Covington's own words and ideas in an effort to render a National Socialist world view in a form that would be comprehensible to the uninitiated.

Covington comes from comfortably middle class circumstances. His grandfather, A. B. Glass, founded the Dixie Bedding Company in Greensboro, North Carolina. This company manufactured Serta mattresses, and it was his inheritance from this company that was to play a prominent role in Covington's early NS career. In common with a number of baby-boomer converts to National Socialism,

Covington's racial consciousness was born of the clash of Black and White cultures in the newly integrated school systems of the 1960s. In an interview with the French zine *14 Mots* [*14 words*], Covington, who closely guards his age, described this awakening:

> I was born and raised in North Carolina. When I was 15 I got my first dose of racial reality when my family moved to the leftist university town of Chapel Hill and I was thrust into an integrated high school. I left high school with a personal vow that I would devote my life to making sure that someday no White boy or girl would have to go through what I witnessed during those three years. I had always had a very strong attraction to National Socialism and the Third Reich but it was kind of instinctive; I didn't fully understand that NS was the racial solution I was looking for. I joined the United States Army at age 17 and while I was in the military I did a lot of private reading and research into racial matters. One of these was a superficially anti-NS book by a German named Heinz Hohne about the SS called *The Order of the Death's Head*. Once I had finished that I realized that National Socialism was it. I was able to get in touch with the old Franklin Road NSWPP and I joined when I was 19 years old.

While at Chapel Hill High School, Covington won a place at the annual Governor's School for Gifted Boys. However, a 1980 *Raleigh News and Observer* article quotes an exasperated but prophetic Chapel Hill High School teacher to the effect that: "Harold is a bright, creative boy. But his intelligence should be channeled— before he does something destructive to society." That undirected destructive streak would mark not only Covington's relationship to society, but his many movement associations as well.

Covington's early association with Matt Koehl's National Socialist White People's Party was ill-fated, but that could be said for a considerable number of NSWPP alumni. What set Covington apart, though, was the intensity of his antipathy for the NSWPP leader, Matt Koehl—a hatred that has hardly mellowed with time. While with the NSWPP, Covington's first official posting was with the El Monte, California, unit led by Joseph Tommasi. Tommasi's break with the NSWPP was even more spectacular than Covington's, and would cost him his life. Before these events, however, Koehl had recognized Covington's considerable gifts as a propagandist and recalled him to the NSWPP's Arlington headquarters to edit the party paper, *White Power*. It was not long before Covington became one of Koehl's most bitter enemies and a tireless purveyor of the long-time movement belief that Koehl is a homosexual. Darker plots, too, were attributed to Koehl, including using the NSWPP as a personal piggy bank and, through the circulation of a 1968 letter attributed to the pseudonymous Max Amman (a Texas follower of George Lincoln Rockwell's American Nazi Party), the strong implication that Koehl was involved in Rockwell's 1967 murder.

Estranged from the NSWPP, Covington was associated with veteran National Socialist George Dietz before returning to North Carolina—a pattern of retreat to that state that would recur throughout Covington's career. This period in the late 1970s through the early 1980s saw Covington operating on the fringes of the political system. Still a committed National Socialist, Covington nonetheless ran for several state and local offices. The most successful of these electoral endeavors was a run in the Republican primary for the office of state attorney general. Covington garnered no less than 43 percent of the vote in a losing effort. Other elections were less kind, with Covington garnering an anemic 172 votes in the Raleigh mayoral race and 885 votes for a seat in the state legislature. Covington also authored two books, the movement manual and autobiography *The March Up Country* and the historical novel *Rose of Honor*.

This same period was spent in building the North Carolina branch of the National Socialist Party of America (NSPA). The association promised much, but turned out to be one of the greatest disasters of Covington's long career—and that is saying much, given Covington's unfortunate organizational history. The NSPA was founded and led by Frank Collin in Chicago, another disgruntled NSWPP veteran, with Michael Allen as second in command and the ultimate American Germanophile Gerhard (Gary) Lauck—replete with his mock German accent—on the scene and vying for the leadership post as well. Once again, Covington's talents were quickly recognized, and he became part of the leadership group. This rapid rise had unfortunate consequences for both the North Carolina unit and the national headquarters.

Covington's North Carolina NSPA group held a bizarre collection of activists, even by the standards of American National Socialism. Best known of the group was Glenn Miller, whose primary claim to fame (before he became a government informant and entered the witness protection program) was to help update the Ku Klux Klan by outfitting his Klan group in camouflage fatigues and engaging in armed paramilitary maneuvers. Less famous, but no less colorful, was the head of the Raleigh headquarters before his expulsion from the party on the grounds of gross mental instability,

Stephen Daryl "Steph" Sumrall. Recruited from Philadelphia, Sumrall moved into the North Carolina headquarters with his invalid mother, a small menagerie of pets, and a not insignificant cache of firearms. The obese adjutant wore out his welcome, however, by flying into unpredictable rages, spreading hostile rumors, threatening other party members, and throwing tantrums that according to witnesses were like unto a "a bearded Gerber baby on a rampage."

Nor was this all. Prominent members of the North Carolina unit were Frank and Patsy Braswell. In Covington's recollection, Frank was "the quintessential wild eye," a lunatic whose dreams were of extravagant terrorist exploits of no particular operational value, but with the potential for collateral casualties of the magnitude of the Oklahoma City bombing. Patsy Braswell was beautiful in a Patsy Cline sort of way, and thus, in a movement as bereft of women as American National Socialism, had instant star quality. She supported Frank's grandiose schemes to the hilt. Covington seems to have tried to assert some control over this idiosyncratic crew, even issuing a three-page order in November 1980 noting that, as a result of alcohol and collective idiocy, there had been two accidental discharges of firearms in the headquarters in the previous two weeks—the last narrowly missing a woman—and that the situation was not improved by the slovenly condition of the building or the constant backbiting of its habitués. Steph Sumrall, the corpulent rampaging Gerber baby, was assigned the thankless task of restoring order on the premises. After the disaster that was inevitable with this company did eventually come to pass, Covington would opine in an essay entitled "Seigfried's Jabberwocky":

> Why did I tolerate Braswell if he was such a loon? The answer is simple and tragic. I *liked* him. I knew he was crazy, but he was crazy in an engaging sort of way. Both Frank and Pat have a personal charm which tends to mask their character defects, and this charm has allowed them to pull the wool over many a White patriot's eyes for some time. In this way they have had the operational assistance of a number of enthusiastic proponents, including me. I am as much responsible as anyone else for the Braswells' inflated reputations in the Movement. I covered their flamboyant gunfights in NS publications, neglecting to mention that the assailants were not Israeli commandos or gin mad niggers but the irate relatives of Braswell's first wife and his daughter's jilted boyfriend. Many people, like me, found the image of "feudin', fightin', fussin' Nazi mountain folk" titillating, and so we built up a completely

false image for these people as being the Hatfields in brown shirts when in fact they were dangerously unstable nut cases. A lot of people, not the least myself, were to pay dearly for that indulgence.

This passage is more revealing of Covington's modus operandi than he would probably care to admit. As a dedicated student of Joseph Goebbels and the art of propaganda, Covington too often sacrificed literal truth to the greater good of the cause. This tendency, coupled with his admittedly sometimes childish weakness for the snappy one-liner at the expense of others, has time and again come back to haunt him.

Covington's tribulations with his erstwhile North Carolina unit began in 1979 with the now infamous Greensboro, North Carolina, shoot-out between Ku Klux Klansmen and members of the Communist Workers' Party, which left five of the communists dead. Two of the "Greensboro 16" were NSPA members, and, worse, the violence appears to have been precipitated by a federal agent whom Covington was blamed for having introduced into the movement. Although Covington seems to have urged that no weapons be present at the site of the confrontation, weapons were brought—legally, under North Carolina law—in the trunks of the Klansmen's cars. While the "Greensboro 16" were ultimately acquitted of murder charges, stories of this time are legion, and the truth at this remove is hard to determine with absolute accuracy. But what is clear is that from this time forward the suspicion that Covington was an informer or agent of either the FBI or the ATF became widespread in the movement.

As if this were not enough, the North Carolina unit of the NSPA hatched a mad plan in 1980 that seems to have been intended to somehow divert attention from the Greensboro fiasco. Very much a Frank Braswell operation, the idea appears to have been to bomb a busy shopping center—at Christmas time, no less—with incendiary napalm bombs. The lunatic adventure seems to have been undertaken without the approval—and probably without the knowledge—of Covington, who expressed probably sincere horror at the prospect of the White women and children who would die in the conflagration. Fortunately, the NSPA was apparently so thoroughly penetrated by federal agents that the Brasswells' plan was circumvented by the arrests of the so-called "Ashville 6": Frank and Patsy Braswell, Joseph Gorell Pierce, Raeford Milano Caudle, James "Shorty" Talbot, and Roger Pierce. The case became a cause celebré in the radical right as Willis Carto's *Spotlight* newspaper took up the case on the side of the Braswells, who like the other plotters blamed Covington for the fiasco. By now the "Covington as agent" label, fairly or unfairly, became accepted movement dogma.

Covington's response was typical. On the one hand, he wrote to the Braswells, especially Patsy, whom he considered the more rational of the two. As in this March 1981 missive, the letters were alternately belligerent:

> You have finally succeeded in hurting both me and the Party. The public reaction to your arrest has been exactly the opposite of the reaction to the Greensboro killings. When we were greasing communists, everybody cheered for us. Now that we have been arrested for allegedly planning to blow up a crowded shopping center at rush hour, killing God knows how many innocent WHITE people, children, etc.; and other acts of absolutely imbecile terrorism, the public reaction is summed up by one phone call I got from a WHITE WORKING person: "Serves you bastards goddammed right!"

Or practical:

> The first thing we must do is get our act together and present a UNITED FRONT TO THE ENEMY. I am restoring the Party membership of Frank and yourself, for the duration at least. You were technically Party members while you were engaging in this shenanigan and we will not deny you, however much that tempting thought might occur. I learned a lot from the Greensboro 16 case and I believe I can put this to use in the "Carolina 6" campaign. That is your official designation, and you'd best get used to it. That is you, like it or not my lady, you and your husband and the four other good men you dragged in with you are the first martyrs of Carolina's independence.

Or conciliatory:

> I will forward you a check as soon as we can accumulate about fifty bucks or so.

But Covington would not be Covington if he could resist an opportunity for a gratuitously nasty gesture (one no less amusing for all that). Thus, the movement was entertained with an epic poem that Covington titled "The Braswell Rap." Again, the poem was classic Covington, for at the same time he and his North Carolina unit were promoting a fanciful plan to turn North Carolina and its White masses into a magnet for other White racialists who were urged to immigrate to the "Carolina Free

State," Covington publicly lampooned the Braswells, two of the few local followers he had managed to attract:

> Well, hello, y'all my name is Frank
> My feet are smelly and my breath is rank.
> My breath is rank and my feet are smelly,
> And my brain consists of petroleum jelly!
> I live in the mountains around Spruce Pine,
> And the folks up there think I'm outta my mind,
> And they're right, you know—I'm crazy as a cootie
> But now I'm in the hoosegow a-gin' up the booty!
> Had a really swingin' little gal named Tina,
> Who did things very bizarre and obscena,
> Then my cousin Jack, who was always high
> On chemicals nobody sane would try,
> Used to sit around shooting at leprechauns
> Who came out of the walls singing Gaelic songs.
> He plugged his old lady right between the eyes,
> And when she dropped dead, man was he surprised!
> Yea, shot his old lady right in the ass,
> And he took another slug of laughing gas!

While the North Carolina fiasco was unfolding, the national NSPA under Frank Collin was faring no better. Collin had recently been revealed in the pages of the NSWPP paper, *White Power,* to be the son of a Jew whose real name was Cohen and who was allowed into the country as a refugee, having survived the Dachau concentration camp. Complete with immigration records and Collin/Cohen's birth certificate, the evidence appeared to be indisputable. Worse, Covington and several confederates, in a search of Collin's quarters, discovered significant quantities of homemade pornography detailing homosexual pedophilia. It seems Commandant Collin had been entertaining young boys on the NSPA premises over the course of several years, and photographing these dalliances for posterity. Thus a coup, code named "Operation Bobby Brown," was engineered with Covington and Lauck among the leading figures. The operation was a success (it could hardly fail, after all), and Collin was turned over to the police and ultimately sentenced to seven years in prison. Covington assumed the leadership in 1980, but, according to Lauck, Covington had promised the coveted position to him. Whatever the truth of the claim, another coup was staged in December of that year and Covington was forced to submit his resignation—a particularly bitter blow, given the fact that he had invested his $90,000 inheritance in the NSPA's Chicago headquarters, which was dubbed Rockwell Hall in honor of the late Commander, George Lincoln Rockwell.

Today, Covington still refuses to accede to the received wisdom of the movement concerning the Collin fiasco:

> As odd as it may seem despite what it eventually turned out he WAS, there was never any documented proof that Frank Collin was a Jew. The "immigration papers" alleged to be those [of] Collin's father published by the [NSWPP] were a clumsy forgery.

In any case, after Ashville the heat was becoming too much for Covington, and whether as a result of death threats (as he claimed), or fear of prosecution in the North Carolina cases (as many thought), or because he was an agent protected by the witness protection program (as his legions of enemies believed), Covington fled the country in 1982. In Covington's own rendition, he left the country when "I received a credible threat against my life from FBI Special Agent Richard Goldberg and BATF Special Agent Bernard Butkovich, who hand delivered my U.S. passport to me in Charleston, South Carolina, in September of 1981 and ordered me to use it or be dragged into the forthcoming Greensboro Federal BS [bullshit] and subsequently destroyed."

He spent time in the United Kingdom (particularly Ireland and the Isle of Man), but he had already made his greatest mark in the mid-1970s in Rhodesia, then fighting a doomed war to preserve White control of the country. Covington served as a quartermaster in the Rhodesian Army Services Corps, "then as an ammunition and ordnance storeman and technician, then as a driver and convoy NCO, and finally in air supply during the beginning of the Angola war in 1976." In these years, he was one of the first American racialists to cast his lot with the battle against the African majorities in the countries of southern Africa. Even this epiphany was short-lived, however. Covington was expelled from Rhodesia when he was linked to a National Socialist group calling itself the Rhodesia White People's Party—a Bulawayo-based organization best known for issuing Nazi literature and threatening the local Jewish community. The group had in 1976 sent a missive to the Bulawayo Hebrew Congregation, assuring them of "an Eden-like future for all Rhodesians of the Jewish faith—free meals and accommodation at government expense in a healthy outdoor environment, bracing exercise and uplifting, character-building labour close to the soil: when National Socialism assumes power in Rhodesia, we'll make you an offer you can't refuse." The White government was not amused, Covington was declared a prohibited immigrant, and in 1976 he was on the road to North Carolina again.

The years that followed were lean times for Harold Covington. He certainly had his fans and followers, but organized NS groups were intensely wary of his cautious feelers. This is hardly surprising, for, as one of the recipients of these cautious missives, William Pierce of the National Alliances, pointed out, it was hard to envision Covington as a member after his multitudinous negative comments about the group and its professorial leader. Thus Covington turned with a passion toward intrigue and remarkably vicious battles against other movement leaders. Matt Koehl was of course a favorite target of Covington's lethal wit, but the most intense battle of Covington's long career was waged with the Church of the Creator (COTC) and its no less divisive leader, the Pontifex Maximus (or in Covingtonese, the Gluteus Maximus), Ben Klassen.

The battle with the COTC was intensified by the presence of Will Williams, then the second in command to Klassen with the title "hasta primus" (spear point). Williams, another native North Carolinian from equally affluent circumstances, was an old friend and neighbor of Covington and a partner in one of his earliest ventures, an effort to utilize local public access television to broadcast racist programs such as Tom Metzger's "Race and Reason." So vindictive did the Covington–COTC contest become that, following two viciously pejorative anti-Covington articles in the COTC paper *Racial Loyalty,* Covington filed a libel suit against the COTC, Klassen, and Williams. The suit was later dropped. However, as Covington would later ruefully admit, Klassen and the superior economic resources at his disposal got the better of the exchange, at least in the short term, tarring Covington not only with the label of "government agent" but with a number of other charges as well. Indeed, when belatedly convinced that the lawsuit was not simply a figment of Covington's ever-active imagination, Klassen and Williams struck back by having a few words with Covington's employer, resulting in the loss of his job. So intense was the overt and covert barrage coming out of the COTC that Covington was constrained to issue two circular letters in the summer of 1989, refuting Klassen's voluminous charges point by point. Covington was thus forced to deny that he was a government agent, a secret Jew, a closet Jewish rabbi, the perpetrator of the Greensboro fiasco, an Anti-Defamation League operative, a Mossad agent, and, best of all, a practitioner of black magic who ate his kitty cat in an occult ritual, among other assorted slanders. Covington's sole satisfaction from the exchange was to outlive Klassen, an elderly man who committed suicide in 1993. In a mocking eulogy, Covington could crow:

> Benny Klassen is dead, and it's a Whiter and Brighter world without him. The founder of the "Church of the Creator" sodomy cult, the man whose deviate sexual lifestyle was so notorious that American Skinheads nicknamed him "Old Benny Buttfuck", the self-proclaimed greatest Aryan genius who ever lived—most probably a rabbi's son from Vilna—came crawling back to his cult's ashram in Otto, North Carolina in the early weeks of July.
>
> For twenty years, Benny Klassen performed one gigantic act of psychological and political sodomy on us all. He never had any real religious or political message. It was all a gull, warmed-over classical anti-clericalism framed in the manner of Talmudic response, mixed with crude race baiting and pseudo-scholarship, garnished with soft core pornography and served up on a bed of crap....
>
> Yet the turgid gibberish in his interminable books was reverenced as inspired wisdom; the most arrant nonsense in his so-called theology was seriously debated; and flaming bird-brained idiots that we are, all but a few of us accepted the liver-lipped old baboon at his own estimation of himself. The reason is simple and shameful: money. Klassen was a millionaire, and with pitifully few exceptions Movement people and Movement leaders in particular genuflect in the presence of wealth. Our public spokesmen and most prominent personalities are largely self-seeking, venal frauds who are incapable of distinguishing between the cool riffle of a roll of hundred dollar bills and the Voice of God. I'd give anything if it weren't so. But it's true.

The intensity of the battle with Klassen overshadowed for a time the long-running feud with Covington's ultimate nemesis, Matt Koehl. Koehl, for his part, had no intention of so conveniently leaving the scene as had Klassen. Thus, beginning in the early 1980s, Covington—often in loose partnership with other angry NSWPP veterans such as Rick Cooper—made serious attempts to stir up a palace revolt against Koehl within NSWPP ranks. The most articulate such effort was a nine-page open letter in February 1982 that urged the NSWPP to depose Koehl, detailed his numerous failures, reviewed the various charges against him (especially his alleged homosexuality), and offered a number of possible scenarios by which Koehl could be induced to step down or be removed. Covington even recognized his own tenuous standing in the movement and promised to stay out of the newly resuscitated NSWPP. Covington, of course, was at the same time communicating with Koehl, offering condolences on the 1980 suicide of NSWPP officer

Dominic Lewitzke (whom Covington was concurrently suggesting Koehl had a hand in killing), and broaching various olive branches under the banner of National Socialist reunification. Koehl's replies ranged from a sincere thanks for the Lewitzke condolences to contemptuous refusals to discuss reunification in the light of Covington's decade of vilification of Matt Koehl and all his works.

By the end of the 1980s, Covington was a tired and bitter man, but he was no less a true believer in the National Socialist dream than he had been in his youth. Now long estranged from his family and on speaking terms with only a few members of the American NS community, Covington desperately needed a change. Thus, the 1990s saw yet a new initiative, plus a new identity to go with it. Caught up in the movement dream of establishing a White homeland in the Pacific Northwest, Covington moved to Seattle, adopted the name Winston Smith after the hero of George Orwell's novel *1984,* and published his newest and most successful newsletter, *Resistance.* Of course, the feuds were hardly a thing of the past. William Pierce and the National Alliance became Covington's latest bête noire, and a lawsuit may or may not have been filed against Covington from those quarters, depending on whose version of events one finds most credible. But the most noteworthy activity to take place in Seattle was the 1994 initiative of forming a new National Socialist White People's Party under the leadership of the erstwhile Winston Smith. Having for the better part of 20 years failed to wrest Rockwell's legacy from the tenacious grip of Matt Koehl, Covington/Smith decided to pretend that Koehl's organization had simply ceased to exist. Indeed, Covington argues in a 1997 letter that the original NSWPP *had* ceased to exist "on January 1st, 1983 when Koehl changed the name to 'New Order' and retired to Milwaukee, where he still issues periodic fund appeals out of force of habit. Koehl's literature mostly consists of bizarre stuff advocating the worship of the number '8'."

Thus in *Resistance* #46 (1995), Covington could boast:

> History must record that the Aryan racial resistance movement's break with lies and corruption and cowardice finally began on April 20th, 1994 and was cemented in 1995 with the creation of a true revolutionary Party. Future chroniclers of our people must someday write: "...just when all seemed lost and it appeared that no effective Aryan resistance to racial destruction would be attempted, in the mid-1990's the National Socialist White People's Party was resurrected virtually out of thin air by a small band of dedicated men and women who finally decided that it was time for the nonsense to stop.

However, as with so many of Covington's initiatives, the northwest migration too was short-lived and by 1997, Covington was back in North Carolina, using the Internet to spread the message via a private NSWPP mailing list. At the same time, Covington's opponents in the movement struck back. Hoisting Covington by his own satirical petard, a web site and the "Weird Harold" mailing list was inaugurated. The site was replete with files detailing all of the long-standing charges against the man they referred to as "Rabbi Covington" and news photos such as President Bill Clinton's swearing-in ceremony with the added caption, "I swear to pay Harold Covington on time and help him destroy the White Resistance."

Covington's long history in the American National Socialist movement may be thought of as something of a cautionary tale, and certainly he is far from the end of his colorful career. What will follow is anyone's guess—certainly Covington, least of all, could predict his next initiative. But if Covington's history is a cautionary tale, it is a deeply revealing one. In today's American National Socialist subculture, Harold Covington shares with his most bitter enemy of the moment, William Pierce, that rarest of combinations: long experience in the movement and incisive intelligence. Yet where the cautious Pierce carefully guards his private thoughts, Covington writes first and regrets later. Therefore, it is Covington who does the most to answer the question that has most puzzled even the most neutral of outside observers: how does an intelligent man persevere in a milieu so viciously divisive and, truth be told, so filled with madness and despair? In answering this question, Covington's internal and public expressions, for once, are in perfect accord. First and foremost, the activist must be ready to sacrifice everything to the cause. No greater example could be offered than the all-too-typical scenario of failed marriages and estrangement from family and friends. Covington has indeed suffered familial ostracism, but it is his two marriages that concern us here. Once again, no better source could be offered than Harold Covington's own mordant reflections on these tragicomic affairs:

> My first marriage was at age 19; she was 18. It was a teenaged mistake. We neither of us had any business getting married, and we damned sure had no business getting married to each other. My habit of dragging her halfway around the world to Rhodesia, South Africa, and other strange places certainly didn't help, neither did losing two children, one through miscarriage and the other through crib

death at four months. We were divorced in 1978 and I last saw her in 1980 when we spent the weekend together in Raleigh, and we parted more or less amicably along the "chalk it up to experience" line.

My second marriage in Ireland was a far more complex situation which I don't propose to get into, but it was one of those cases where the good times were really good, the bad times were hellish, and although the bad times were starting to outnumber the good we still might have made it were it not for certain outside forces interfering.

Louise was an Irish redhead of the crockery-throwing, picturesque brogue dialect-cursing Maureen O'Hara type. She was not a feminist bitch, she was just a bitch, the kind who used to be called a "scold" and for whom our ancestors used to have ducking stools and tongue clips. Her favorite benediction was "Begob, that square Protestant head of yours would look good on the end of a pike!" I never hit her except in self-defense, and no, that is not a joke. (She tried to kick me once while barefoot, missed me and hit a solid oak table and broke her big toe, which got her ROYALLY pissed off, I can tell you!) She once told me that as a child in Dublin she lived down the street from the young Bob Geldof [of the rock band the Boomtown Rats] and used to beat up on him and take his toys, on one occasion knocking him unconscious with a camogie stick, which I can well believe.

She filed for the divorce in the Isle of Man, ironically after voting AGAINST divorce in an earlier referendum in Ireland because she said she was afraid I might divorce HER against her will if it were legalized. ["...A foolish consistency is the hobgoblin of little minds."—Emerson] The divorce was pretty rancorous, but then everything Louise did was rancorous. She told a lot of lies about me in the petition but no more than is customary, and after a time I don't really hold it against her.

Where most activists become frustrated, lonely, or simply disgusted with the "movement" and, giving in to despair, quietly disengage from the scene, Harold Covington has steadfastly refused to try to find a way out. As he wrote in a letter to a financial supporter in 1980:

I for one, *can't* give up even if I wanted to. The Jews are the most cruel, vindictive, and viscous [sic] people on the face of the earth. They never forgive and never forget, and even if I tried to flee they would hound me and harass me and never rest until they had destroyed me. But what is more, I don't *want* to give up. I refuse to accept this incredibly evil world as it is. I refuse to accept the destruction of my race and my civilization. I refuse to lie down and die like a slave.

What then is left but the dream that is the one thing that serves to unite the fratricidal world of American National Socialism? It is the timeless dream that was given flesh by the Führer, and is a vision of hope and despair that the American movement shares only in its most private moments.

In the same 1980 letter, Covington asserts:

Does anybody really believe we can someday take over and put all the niggers on boats and send them back to Africa? Do YOU believe it? I don't. The niggers simply will not go—even if we could take power legally, we would have to kill them all. Do you have any idea how many men it would take to track down and wipe out thirty million jungle bunnies, fifteen or so million spics, plus all the Jews, Filipinos, Haitians, boat people, etc.? Is there any realistic chance that we are going to assemble that type of following in our lifetime?

Undoubtedly not, but what other vision could be so powerful as to sustain Harold Covington and the tiny community of the American National Socialist faithful in the distant dream of an apocalyptic New Dawn? How can they look beyond the madness and mediocrity that so defines the modern "movement"? In a 1998 message to the National Socialist White People's Party faithful, Covington tells of his own despair and determination in a form that may be thought of as universal to the battle-scarred veterans of the wars of the right-wing:

On December 1st, 1996, a Sunday morning, I stepped out of the door of my apartment in Carrboro, North Carolina, and almost stepped right into a mound of clearly human feces. I know to a moral certainty that this act was committed by the National Alliance, and since then I am told that a certain individual living in Raleigh, North Carolina, has boasted of committing this act, cackling with demented laughter as he did so; his demeanor as he told this jolly little anecdote caused a woman NA member to resign from the group, and she subsequently reported this incident to me. (By the by, the feces were on a piece of cardboard; no one actually dropped his drawers on my doorstep. The man responsible for this does not have the physical courage to remain that long in close proximity to me, as he has proven over the past nine years, and I personally disbelieve his claim to have personally delivered the "package". I think he probably incited someone else to do it while he waited in the car. But I digress.)

I have been accused of harping on this incident and being "obsessed" by it. Well, maybe there's something to that, although not in the sense that my critics mean. I happen to believe that as disgusting as it is, this is one of the most vitally significant experiences I ever underwent. It was, for me, a kind of epiphany.

I understood in a flash of comprehension who had placed the object there, and in one mind-expanding moment I understood what it all meant. There before me under my poised shoe was twenty-five years of my life. From 1971 until 1996 I served The Movement with my entire being, and there waiting for me to step forward was the cosmic commentary on my whole adult life. What I had been risking my life, my freedom and my future for was indeed the Movement—the Bowel Movement. I threw the filthy thing away, went and got my Sunday paper, washed and scrubbed my hands and arms to the elbows until they were almost scalded, sat down with a cup of coffee and marveled at my life.

I knew then—and I know now—that if I stay with this, it will always be the Bowel Movement. There will be no change. It is NOT going to get better. Twenty-five years later, in the year 2021, when I am 68 years old, I will one day step out of my door and find turds placed on my doorstep by deranged, dysfunctional morons who claim to speak for the Aryan race. Probably from that same walking cockroach over there in Raleigh, if he's still alive in 2021. It is written in the stars. I am quite mad, of course. Only a madman would stay with it. But I can't leave. Because the IDEA—the SPIRIT—the SOUL of National Socialism is a thing of such beauty, such intense power, such glory, that it is to me the very essence of life.

That's how crazy I am, people. I am willing to accept the turds on the doorstep in order to continue even the most tenuous, faintest contact with that wonderful, unspeakably beautiful and life-giving ideal of Adolf Hitler.

See also: American Nazi Party; Carto, Willis; Church of the Creator; Collin, Frank; Cooper, Rick; Hitler, Adolf; Klassen, Ben; Koehl, Matt; Lauck, Gerhard; Metzger, Tom; National Alliance; National Socialist Party of America; National Socialist White People's Party; Pierce, William; Rockwell, George Lincoln; Tommasi, Joseph.

Further reading: Harold Covington, *Rose of Honor* (Pittsburgh, PA: Dorrance & Co., 1980); Harold Covington, *The March Upcountry* (Reading, PA: Liberty Bell, 1987); Elizabeth Wheaton, *Codename Greenkill—The 1979 Greensboro Killings* (Atlanta: University of Georgia Press, 1987).

D

SAVITRI DEVI   Born Maximiani Portas, Savitri Devi was one of the most compelling figures to emerge from the wreckage of postwar National Socialism. More than any single figure, it was Devi who would carry the torch of occult National Socialism through the grim period following World War II. Through her writings and her personal example, she would inspire a new generation of National Socialists to explore the occult byways of racial mysticism that were once blazed by such nineteenth-century German figures as Guido von List and such Third Reich figures as Heinrich Himmler.

Originally a French citizen, Devi was born in 1905 of Greek and British parents. Educated in France and Greece, Devi earned master's degrees in philosophy and science in France in the 1920s and received a Ph.D. in chemistry on the basis of her dissertation, *La Simplicité Mathématique,* in 1931. Mathematics and science, however, held less allure for Devi than did contemporary politics, religious speculation, and (of greatest import) the Aryan philosophical and religious traditions of ancient India. India, in fact, would be her home for much of her life.

Before embarking on her spiritual quest, however, Devi took an active interest in politics. Even as a young girl, she was much attracted to Germany and to the German philosophical and intellectual traditions. Appalled by the betrayal of Germany at Versailles following World War I, as well as by the treatment of Greek refugees in the same period, Devi determined to learn more of what she instinctively felt were the deeper realities that determined the seemingly chaotic course of world events. It was during this youthful quest for knowledge both hidden and suppressed that Devi acquired her lifelong aversion to Judaism.

Devi's anti-Semitism was fed by several currents. First, there was the Bible, and in particular the Old Testament, which she felt was rife with examples of Jewish perfidy. This feeling would be considerably reinforced by reports of Zionist actions in Palestine in the 1920s. In 1929—the year of Arab riots and the killing of a number of Jews in Hebron—she visited Palestine and confirmed for herself the truth of these reports. Her studies brought her into contact with the intellectual anti-Semitism that was the common coin of the realm in the French academy, and this too seems to have been a factor. In this, the work of the intellectual anti-Semite Ernst Renan would be an important influence both in confirming her dim view of the Jews as racial and cultural outsiders and in fixing India and the Aryan myth of origins as the central interest of her life. Of considerable importance, too, was what she perceived to be the malign role Jews played in the defeat of Germany in World War I. This latter stream would come to dominate Devi's view of the Jews, as her admiration for Hitler and the Third Reich grew in the 1930s through World War II. Here, Devi seems to have been one of the select few to actually read Alfred Rosenberg's verbose and turgid 1930 opus *The Myth of the Twentieth Century*. Even the Führer would confide that, though he displayed this book prominently on his bedside table, he found it unreadable; Devi, however, was enchanted by it.

In the 1930s Devi moved to India and undertook what would prove to be a lifelong study of the classic Indian texts, the Vedas and the Upanishads. From these sources, and from their contemporary manifestations in the caste system, Devi felt that she had found the true sources of the once-and-future greatness of the Aryan race.

In 1940, Devi married a pro-Nazi Indian nationalist named A. K. Mukherji. This gave her a British passport and the possibility of deepening her work for the Third Reich. In Calcutta, the Mukherji home became something of a salon for Allied diplomats and military officers, and whatever intelligence could be gathered found its way quickly to the German consulate. Devi felt her greatest service to the cause, however, would be in her ongoing research and the book she was writing, which would set out a blueprint for the new Aryan religion that she believed would be instituted in Germany after the inevitable Nazi victory.

In the event, of course, Germany was defeated. Devi's dream of a global Aryan racial paradise would now never be realized, but through considerable adversity, she held fast to her ideals until her death in 1982. She returned to Europe in 1945, settling in England where her book on the religious heritage of ancient Egypt, *A Son of God,* was published and well received in British intellectual and occult circles.

It was the work that followed, however, titled *Impeachment of Man* (finished in London and published in 1946), that stands as a classic in the current world of National Socialism. Radical environmentalism, amounting indeed to a religion of nature, has always been strong in National Socialist thought and, with the wartime defeat, has become as much a trademark of the movement as anti-Semitism and racialist thought. *Impeachment of Man* remains the strongest statement of the National Socialist nature religion that may be found today. Opening with epigraphs from Alfred Rosenberg ("Thou shalt love God in all things, animals and plants") and Josef Goebbels (who in a diary entry quotes the Führer's resolve to create a postwar society that would eschew the eating of meat), the book is a passionate treatise on the rights of animals and of plants, as contrasted with humans' egocentric consumption and destruction of the natural world. The argument is couched in religious terms, and the proof texts are drawn from the Aryan Golden Age. The book, long out of print, underwent a revival when Willis Carto released a new Noontide Press edition in 1991.

In 1946, Savitri Devi moved from England to Iceland. There, the ancient Norse pantheon joined the ancient Indian heritage as a source for her Aryan religiosity. Here, too, Devi anticipated by decades Odinism's popularization of the Norse/Germanic pantheon as a fitting Aryan racial religion in the postwar movement.

Two years later, Devi undertook a more open pro-Nazi course of activism, traveling to occupied Germany and distributing propaganda leaflets. This resulted in her incarceration in 1949. While in jail, Devi expanded one of her leaflets into the book that she considered her magnum opus, *Gold in the Furnace*. In it, at once an autobiography and a dreamy meditation on what could have been, she states explicitly that which until 1948 she had never dared to publicly utter:

> I love this land, Germany, as the hallowed cradle of National Socialism; the country that staked its all so that the whole of the Aryan race might stand together in its regained ancestral pride; Hitler's country.
>
> Because for the last twenty years I have loved and admired Hitler and the German people, I was happy—oh so happy!—thus to express my faith in the superman whom the world has misunderstood and hated and rejected. I was not sorry to lose my freedom for the pleasure of bearing witness to his glory, now, in 1948.

Devi was released from prison after six months, and then entered her most productive literary period. The autobiographical *Defiance* appeared in 1950. Devi's example served as an inspiration to a new generation of National Socialists when a portion of the book was published in the winter 1968 edition of the American Nazi Party's intellectual journal, the *National Socialist World,* edited by the American Nazi Party's only intellectual, William Pierce.

Gold in the Furnace came out in 1952, followed by another memoir, *Pilgrimage,* in 1958 (though some sources give the publication date as early as 1953).

Her most important work, *The Lightning and the Sun,* appeared in 1956, and a condensed version was published in the premier edition (spring 1966) of the *National Socialist World. The Lightning and the Sun* is a remarkable exposition of occult National Socialism that explicitly deifies Hitler as the savior of the Aryan people. The first words of the book read:

> To the godlike individual of our times; the *Man against time*; the greatest European of all times; both Sun and Lightning: ADOLF HITLER.

The Lightning and the Sun ranges through the ages, suggesting a religious and political history in which the Third Reich is both the apex and the natural culmination of Aryan development. The book ends with at once a cry of despair and an affirmation of hope:

> Kalki will lead them through the flames of the great end, and into the sunshine of the new Golden Age.
>
> We like to hope that the memory of the one-before-the-last and most heroic of all our men *against time*—Adolf Hitler—will survive at least in songs and symbols. We like to hope that the lords of the age, men of his own blood and faith, will render him divine honors, through rites full of meaning and full of potency, in the cool shade of the endless regrown forests, on the beaches, or upon inviolate mountain peaks, facing the rising sun.

As if to belie the heroic tones of her National Socialist dream, Devi found the 1950s an empty time. While she could escape into the world of her literary dreams, and while she traveled intensively in these years, a terrible void remained in her life. The "man against time" and his iron heroes were gone—many were dead, others living in hiding, still others captured and brought to the bar of Allied justice. It was not until the 1960s that Devi could allow her hopes of a National Socialist revival to live again.

Through the jungle telegraph linking European Nazis, Devi soon got wind of a rising young star on the American scene, George Lincoln Rockwell. Rockwell, who founded the American Nazi Party in 1959, began to correspond with Devi in 1960. It was Devi who introduced Rockwell to the man who would quietly become a mentor, the unreconstructed German National Socialist Bruno Ludtke. Together with Britain's Colin Jordan, the three became the core of the World Union of National Socialists—an organization that sought, with little success, to link the far-flung National Socialist tribes from throughout the world. The high point of their effort was a 1962 meeting at Cotswold, England, that resulted in the Cotswold Agreement, the World Union of National Socialists' founding document that served as a theoretical blueprint for the revival of a global neo-Nazi movement. Cotswold, in which Savitri Devi served as the representative of France, was the first and last time that Devi and Rockwell would have the opportunity to meet.

By all reports, Rockwell was mesmerized by Devi. Here was a living link to the original font of National Socialism—Nazi Germany—and here too was a visionary whose religious vision of National Socialist revival immeasurably deepened and enriched Rockwell's more narrowly political conception of the movement. Moreover, the fact that Devi was the only woman in the upper echelons of National Socialism at that time was no small matter either.

In the end, it mattered little. The World Union of National Socialists never rose above the level of squabbling "leaders" more engaged in internecine plotting than in serious pursuit of revolutionary change and the institution of a neo-Nazi New Order. Worse, only five short years after Cotswold, Rockwell was dead, felled by bullets from the gun of a disgruntled former follower. The World Union of National Socialists soldiered on for decades, but as a mere shell of the organization envisioned by Rockwell, Ludtke, Devi, and Jordan.

Devi's remaining years were bleak. Much of her time was spent back in mother India with her husband, writing, corresponding, and marking time. She was an early convert to the field of Holocaust denial, and it was under her influence that such well-known Holocaust revisionists of the present day as Ernst Zundel were introduced to the faith. Indeed, Devi's chief contribution to the movement to which she had dedicated her life in the 1970s was her tireless correspondence with true believers throughout the world. Her personal circumstances did not fare so well, however, and at her death in 1982 she was reportedly penniless.

In the course of her life, Savitri Devi's achievements were meager, if measured on the scale of her dreams of re-creating a National Socialist revival. At her death, the world of explicit National Socialism was, if anything, more fragmented and powerless than ever before. But her writings, together with the powerful dream of a religio-mystical Aryan Golden Age that they so eloquently convey, are having a powerful impact on the movement, and indeed reaching beyond the narrow confines of the radical right and into the realms of radical ecology and New Age thought.

See also: American Nazi Party; Carto, Willis; Hitler, Adolf; Jordan, Colin; Ludtke, Bruno; Odinism; Pierce, William; Religion of Nature; Rockwell, George Lincoln; World Union of National Socialists.

Further reading: Savitri Devi, "The Lightning and the Sun (A New Edition)," *National Socialist World* 1 (spring 1966); Savitri Devi, "Gold in the Furnace," *National Socialist World* 3 (spring 1967); Savitri Devi, "Defiance," *National Socialist World* 6 (winter 1968); Savitri Devi, *Impeachment of Man* (Costa Mesa, CA: Noontide Press, 1991); Nicholas Goodrick-Clark, *Hitler's Priestess: Savitri Devi, the Hindu-Aryan Myth, and Occult Neo-Nazism* (New York: New York University Press, 1998); Fritz Nova, *Alfred Rosenberg: Nazi Theorist of the Holocaust* (New York: Hippocrene Books, 1986); Phillip Rees, *Biographical Dictionary of the Extreme Right Since 1890* (New York: Simon & Schuster, 1990); Frederick J. Simonelli, *American Fuehrer: George Lincoln Rockwell and the American Nazi Party* (Champaign: University of Illinois Press, 1999).

ELIZABETH DILLING   In her later years, Elizabeth Dilling played the role of the grandmotherly, blue-haired old lady who could always be counted on to respond to a mail solicitation with a few dollars for a variety of anti-Semitic causes. Older members of the American racist movement knew better, however. Dilling was the author of several of the most scurrilous attacks on Franklin Roosevelt and his administration to appear in the interwar years. Moreover, she apparently drew blood from the thin-skinned president, according to the official reaction to her "revelations." Her career spans two generations of the American radical right, and her influence is still felt somewhat today.

Elizabeth Dilling graduated from the University of Chicago, and after a visit to the Soviet Union in 1931 her life changed. The experience made of her a passionate anticommunist. She soon became convinced that Jews were responsible for the communist movement, and a fanatical anti-Semite was born. Dilling, a strikingly beautiful redhead in her youth, was married twice. Both her husbands would figure prominently, albeit indirectly, in her political activities. Albert Dilling, her first husband, was an attorney by whom she had a daughter; she would refer to him in public as "Mr. Dilling" even before their divorce. Albert left her in good financial condition, and when she was indicted in the Sedition Trial of 1942, he served as her lawyer. Her second husband, Jeremiah Stokes, shared her politics if not her activism and on his death left Dilling with a comfortable nest egg that allowed her to carry on her work virtually until her own death in Lincoln, Nebraska, in 1966.

Dilling's primary claim to historical fame stems from two books that she authored in the early years of the Roosevelt administration. To Dilling, Franklin Roosevelt was in all likelihood a Jew and his administration a Trojan horse for international communism. To publicize these views, she authored and published at her own expense two of the more vituperative books of the era. *The Red Network: A "Who's Who" and Handbook of Radicalism for Patriots* was published in 1934. *Red Network* opened with a primer on the horrors of socialism (seen as synonymous with communism), proceeded to an encyclopedic listing of organizations Dilling believed to be communist fronts, and then culminated with a list of no fewer than 1,300 prominent Americans connected in some way to the Roosevelt administration whom she felt to be active communists or "fellow travelers."

Never a woman given to subtlety, Dilling followed this tome with *The Roosevelt Red Record and Its Background* in 1936. *The Roosevelt Red Record* carried the attack to FDR himself and members of his inner circle, accusing them of being active communists. These literary efforts, together with a brief prewar visit to Nazi Germany, brought Dilling the distinction of being the only woman to be charged in the 1942 sedition trial.

Unlike many of her aging and insolvent codefendants, Dilling had the financial wherewithal to move to a small apartment in Washington, D.C., where she remained with her daughter and a typewriter throughout the long years of the trial. Her running commentary on the proceedings, carried in her Chicago-based *Patriotic Research Bureau* newsletter and promulgated in her private correspondence to a number of supporters around the country, remains the best defendant's-eye record of the proceedings available today.

After the war, Dilling remained active. She moved from Chicago to Kansas to Nebraska, increasing her output of anti-Semitic propaganda at each stop. Her anti-Semitism, in fact, became too extreme for many in the American race movement. She declined, for example, to become involved in the Korean War era movement to draft General Douglas MacArthur as a Republican candidate for president because of her suspicions that the general too may have harbored some Jewish blood.

Elizabeth Dilling is best remembered in the movement today for one of her last works, *The Plot Against Christianity,* published in 1964. The book may best be seen as an updated and Americanized *Protocols of the Elders of Zion.* It juxtaposes anti-Semitic texts with selectively chosen passages from the Babylonian Talmud to further the thesis that Jews are engaged in an age-old plot to destroy the

Christian religion, to murder Christians, and thus to inherit the earth. Renamed *The Jewish Religion: Its Influence Today,* the book is currently available from Willis Carto's anti-Semitic Noontide Press.

See also: Carto, Willis.

Further reading: Elizabeth Dilling, *The Red Network: A "Who's Who" and Handbook of Radicalism for Patriots* (Elizabeth Dilling, 1934); Elizabeth Dilling, *The Roosevelt Red Record and Its Background* (Elizabeth Dilling, 1936); Elizabeth Dilling, *The Jewish Religion: Its Influence Today* (Torrance, CA: Noontide Press, 1983); John George and Laird Wilcox, *Nazis, Communists, Klansmen, and Others on the Fringe* (Buffalo, NY: Prometheus Books, 1992); Leo Ribuffo, *The Old Christian Right* (Philadelphia: Temple University Press, 1983).

DAVID DUKE   It is hard to escape the suspicion that David Duke, if he had it to do over again, would have become a conservative populist politician rather than a Nazi or a Klansman. Who knows how far the mediagenic Duke might have gone? As it is, Duke is today reduced to making high-profile but doomed crusades for statewide office in Louisiana, tending to his web site, making speeches to the faithful across the nation, and in his spare time taking knowing part in the wry chuckles his name evokes by appearing on such television programs as the satirical *Daily Show* on the basic cable channel, Comedy Central, where he half-seriously answers a correspondent's query about how best to remove stubborn stains from white sheets. Given a different set of choices as a young man, Duke might well have achieved something better.

David Duke's first taste of media magic haunts him to this day. In a 1970 photo picked up by the wire services, Duke as a baby-faced teenager is depicted in full Nazi regalia in a one-man demonstration holding a sign saying, "Gas the Chicago 7"—a reference to the high-profile trial of a group of left-wing radicals in Chicago. Duke was then a student at Louisiana State University and a mail-order member of Joseph Tommasi's National Socialist Liberation Front (NSLF). The NSLF would later break with its parent group, the National Socialist White People's Party (NSWPP), and turn to revolutionary violence. But in 1970, it was still very much the youth arm of the NSWPP, and its primary appeal was aimed at earnest White college students such as David Duke. Duke, however, was one of the very few to answer the NSLF's call for support in a doomed effort to stem the tide of antiwar radicalism that was then sweeping the campuses of America.

Duke in these years drew considerable local attention handing out National Socialist Liberation Front and National Socialist White People's Party propaganda on the LSU campus and enlightening the student newspaper, the *Reveille,* with the finer points of NSLF doctrine. A portion of this dated discourse is offered by Michael Zatarian in his book *David Duke: Evolution of a Klansman:*

> The NSLF has different views from the run of the mill groups on campus, whether they support the right or the left. Their approach to the problems confronting our civilization is completely mechanical, economic and materialistic. National Socialism, on the other hand, is unique! Instead of stressing materialistic economic dogma as democratic-liberalism has in its Eastern version or Western version, we believe that the quality and spirit are by far the most important issues of our time.
>
> What are the goals of the NSLF? Our first goal is to break through the communications barrier in this country and to let the people know exactly what we stand for instead of what certain people say we stand for. Once people hear both sides, we are confident that they will choose ours; then we can proceed to build the leadership we need to liberate our people so that they can determine their own destiny.

Even at this young age, Duke was perfecting his ability to speak to different audiences in strikingly different ways. The identity of the malign cabal from which it would be necessary "to liberate our people so that they can determine their own destiny" is left unremarked, and indeed in an earlier paragraph in the same letter to the editor, Duke explicitly denies that the National Socialist Liberation Front intends to "Exterminate all Jews, and with more efficient methods than Hitler used! Ship all the Negroes back to Africa in cattle boats! Exterminate all people who politically disagree." Yet anyone familiar with Joseph Tommasi and his extraordinarily radical writings find plenty of support for scenarios quite similar to these. Tommasi and the National Socialist Liberation Front frightened the conservative majority of American National Socialists with their violent rhetoric, yet, for public consumption, Duke manages to render them only a shade to the right of the Young Americans for Freedom. This is vintage David Duke.

Never one to ride a dead horse for long, Duke realized that the National Socialist Liberation Front was going nowhere. In this he was prescient, for the NSLF by 1974 had broken with the National Socialist White People's Party, and by August 1975, its charismatic leader, Joseph Tommasi, was dead. Thus began a period of drift for

Duke, in both the physical and spiritual senses. In the latter, Duke decided to leave the United States for a time, and thus he embarked on a brief world tour. Of this period, he was most impressed with India, and his essay on the wonders of that mysterious civilization and its caste system, titled "My Indian Odyssey—A Ghost from India Haunts Me Still," can be found today on Don Black's Stormfront web site and on Duke's own home page.

Duke formed and later dumped an organization called the White Youth Alliance, and another called the National Party. Then, around 1972, Duke discovered the Knights of the Ku Klux Klan. Duke looked nothing like the popular conception of a Klansman, and that was the whole point. Young, telegenic, charismatic—Duke shattered the mold of the "good ol' boy" southern Klansman, and he was an immediate sensation in Klan circles. He soon gathered an influential group of supporters, including Klansmen such as Don Black and other long-time racists who had marched under many banners such as James Warner, a veteran of George Lincoln Rockwell's American Nazi Party, a short-lived Odinist ministry, and most recently the Christian Identity New Christian Crusade Church. Constantly at Duke's side in these years was his young wife, Chloe, also a White Power true believer. Taking the name National Director of the Klan rather than the traditional Grand Wizard, Duke set out across the South to spread the word.

The next few years were spent organizing, marching, going to jail, getting out of jail, and, most of all, building the Knights of the Ku Klux Klan's organization. Almost single-handedly, David Duke for a moment in history seemed to make the Klan almost relevant again. For Duke, it was an exciting time, and a frightening one. Duke's first experience of jail in the early 1970s had been, to say the least, unsettling. The then-unknown Duke found himself isolated behind bars, a baby-faced young White boy in a population of mostly Black inmates—few of whom were making their first visit to the facility. The situation did not improve as Duke's notoriety grew.

Duke and Chloe barnstormed through the South, and later expanded the campaign to a national level. They worked where they could in these years—the mailing list was hardly sufficient to support them as yet. Unsurprisingly, the smooth-talking Duke found an ideal job as a salesman for Kirby vacuum cleaners, and by his own testimony he was quite good at it.

The numbers Duke could draw to Klan rallies were impressive, occasionally gathering more than a thousand—an unheard-of number in the 1970s. As he traveled, Duke perfected the talent he had developed in his National Socialist Liberation Front days at Louisiana State University for tailoring his rhetoric to his audience and professing to see no contradiction between the violently racialist rhetoric spoken at a Klan meeting and the smoothly delivered ruminations on race and history he would offer to the press and the general public.

Duke's media profile soared in the 1970s. In this, Duke benefited from a change that was then in its nascent stages in the media's treatment of the radical right. In the immediate postwar period, such Jewish watchdog groups as the American Jewish Committee (under the leadership of Rabbi Solomon Fineberg) formulated a policy that came to be known successively as Quarantine and later Dynamic Silence; it sought, with considerable success, to isolate the voices of the radical right by convincing the mainstream media to simply ignore their activities. This worked remarkably well, and it was this policy that was most responsible for the marginalization of the once-powerful voice of the Depression-era demagogue Gerald L. K. Smith and of the angry rhetoric of George Lincoln Rockwell in the early 1960s.

By Duke's day, however, the advent of popular talk shows opened a door for the walking wounded of American society to publicly air their private demons. The medium was perfect for David Duke, and his appearances on such late-night fare as a 1974 edition of Tom Snyder's *Tomorrow Show* on NBC allowed Duke the priceless opportunity to present his new face of the Klan to a national audience, a few of whom were inspired enough to become involved in the race movement in general and Duke's Knights of the KKK in particular.

Occasionally, the wide disparity between Duke's movement rhetoric and his public professions would come back to haunt him. For example, the transcript of a Louisiana trial for incitement to riot in 1976 contrasted statements he made at a rally with those he made on the *Tomorrow Show*. More ominously, Duke's rise was hardly appreciated by rival Klan leaders and by less successful competitors throughout the radical right. Thus, while he was on trial for the 1976 incitement charges (he and James Warner were ultimately convicted and sentenced to six months and three months, respectively), Duke was obliged to respond to charges that internal opponents circulated in a letter-writing campaign. In an undated flier issued by the Knights of the Ku Klux Klan titled "A Legal Lynching: A Personal Account by David Duke," Duke complains:

> At a time when I face jail because of my work for the White race a
> couple of individuals calling themselves "Klansmen" have sent out

a vile smear letter against me and our Movement. The letter is "unsigned" with the letterhead of the Invisible Empire [Bill Wilkinson's Invisible Empire of the KKK].

What motivates such people. Is it petty jealousy? Do they think if I am "out of the way" in jail then Klansmen will look to them as true leaders of our Movement? Or are the same government and Jewish organizations that are trying to repress our movement and put me in jail behind their efforts? I don't know what the motivation is, but I do know that whoever indulges in such rumor-mongering is playing right into the Jews' hands. Indeed if they are in our own camp they are worse than Jews because at least Jews defend their own and stick together while these people if they are on "our side" have betrayed their own race, their own flesh and blood....

If indeed you receive any attacks on me or on our organization it very likely came from the mailing list that Jerry Dutton [a reporter who infiltrated the Klan and wrote a book based on his experience] stole from our organization when he worked for us last October. (Dutton had similarly stolen a copy of Edward Fields *"Thunderbolt"* mailing list some time ago). A list that I had worked hard building up for seven years.

While fighting battles in the courts and within the race movement, Duke would not infrequently find his carefully tailored internal and external messages thrown back at him in public forums and in the media. A classic example from March 28, 1991, found an unsuspecting Duke as a guest on the *David Brudnoy Show,* on Boston's WBZ Radio. (The full transcript of this show is found in the "Resources" section of this encyclopedia.)

The tension between the "Movement Duke" and the "Public Duke" became unbearable, and in 1980 it finally came to a head. Duke needed to get out of the Klan. Its constant internecine battles, its perpetual negative public image, and the lamentable quality of its recruits were, for a bright and ambitious young politico like David Duke, simply more baggage than he was willing to carry.

But how to get out and start anew? Incredibly, he turned to one of his oldest enemies, Bill Wilkinson, whose Invisible Empire of the KKK was responsible for the internal poison-pen campaign against Duke noted above. Duke offered to sell Wilkinson the highly prized mailing list that he "had worked hard building up for seven years" for the princely (by movement standards) sum of $35,000. Wilkinson, whose own career would be cut short in a few years when it was revealed that he had long been an FBI informant, readily agreed, and a meeting was set up to effect the transaction.

Of course, Wilkinson did not have $35,000, but the mailing list was not the point of the meeting. Rather, it was a marvelous chance for Wilkinson to do-in his more successful rival, and Duke walked smiling into the trap. Wilkinson secretly videotaped the meeting, and soon the duplicitous Duke's treason to his organization and his supporters, as well as his less than charitable view of his followers, was immortalized and gleefully repeated throughout the American radical right.

In the end, Duke got his wish. He was out of the Klan, but his reputation in the movement was indelibly tarnished. Few in the world of the American racialist right would ever trust David Duke again.

Duke's new vehicle was the semirespectable-sounding National Association of the Advancement of White People (NAAWP). An obvious takeoff on the National Association of the Advancement of Colored People (NAACP), the group served as both a symbol of Duke's new approach—a civil rights organization for beleaguered Whites rather than a racist group—and a much-needed fund-raising center. Indeed, the early issues of the *NAAWP News* were little more than a combination of fund-raising appeals and advertising fliers, though each managed to include color photographs of David Duke.

The early 1980s were a dry time for Duke. He continued to function with one foot in the movement and the other in the fringes of mainstream politics. In 1988, however, he took the plunge into the latter and announced his candidacy for the Democratic Party's nomination for president. Duke's campaign hardly caused either of the mainstream candidates to lose any sleep, but it did give Duke a taste for the electoral process that would have amazed the 17-year-old member of the National Socialist Liberation Front nearly two decades earlier. So much so, in fact, that in that same year Duke accepted the nomination of Willis Carto's pet project of the moment, the Populist Party, for president.

The Populist run was a natural for Duke, whose primary support, even as a Democratic candidate, was from the denizens of the radical right. The campaign went nowhere, of course, but Duke learned invaluable lessons about the nuts and bolts of running a political campaign. It was this new-found wisdom, combined with his innate talent for public speaking and his affinity for the media, that would serve Duke well in the 1990s as he sought to put away the skeletons of the radical right in a bid for mainstream acceptance.

Duke returned to Louisiana a confirmed electoral junkie, and he wasted no time gearing up his next campaign. If the nation was not yet ready for a President Duke, why not start at the grassroots and work up? Laboring quietly and taking full advantage of the fact that no one really took him seriously, Duke put together a run for the state House of Representatives and, to the shock of all, was elected in 1989 on the Republican ticket. Duke now had what he had always craved: a legitimate platform from which to proclaim a suitably muted right-wing message. Today, Duke claims as his legislative legacy authorship of House Bill 1013, which sought to curb affirmative action in the state; the bill passed easily in 1990.

Duke served a single term in the legislature, but the experience helped to make him a legitimate candidate in the eyes of many Louisiana voters. In a state that has produced such colorful characters as Huey Long, Edwin Edwards, and Moon Landrau, what, after all, is so unusual with electing a David Duke? And, for his part, Duke increasingly consigned his past to the euphemistic description of "youthful indiscretions" (though those indiscretions had an inconvenient habit of jumping into Duke's media events, to his great embarrassment).

In any case, Duke made a run for the U.S. Senate in 1990, garnering a more than respectable 44 percent of the vote against incumbent Democrat J. Bennet Johnson. More to the point, Duke received 57 percent of the White vote in an election in which the powers that be were paying keen attention to the race and in which Duke's past did emerge as a major campaign issue. Duke was now running on a straight populist appeal, opposing affirmative action, high taxes, and social welfare programs that many White voters believed unfairly benefited minority groups.

Undaunted by his loss, Duke jumped into the 1990 race for governor against corruption-tinged incumbent Edwin Edwards. By now, the anti-Duke forces had gathered and mounted a withering press attack on him. Indeed, a bumper sticker that appeared in the campaign may have summed up the sentiment of many: "Vote for the Crook! It's important." Most held their noses and took the advice, and Edwards was elected for another circus-like term as governor. Duke, however, garnered an astonishing 55 percent of the White vote.

Losses or no, the transformation of David Duke was now complete. Starting out as a Nazi, Duke became a Klansman in the 1970s, metamorphosed into a national gadfly in the 1980s, and by the 1990s had become a full-time professional candidate. The office seems to matter less to Duke than the pure zeal he has for campaigning and staying always one step in front of the next television camera. That Duke's vote totals seem to decline with each unsuccessful run seems to mean less than the fact that he can still count on sufficiently respectable numbers to keep him in the limelight. Indeed, one can almost envision him in the early decades of the next millennium as Louisiana's answer to Harold Stassen!

Media notoriety, however, does allow him to tour the nation in a whirlwind of speaking engagements and press interviews as he gears up for the next campaign. In his spare time, he continues to upgrade his state-of-the-art web site from which he hawks tapes and videos of his appearances, offers "greatest hits" sound bites for download to the curious, and pushes his latest publication, the *David Duke Report*. What this all means in the great scheme of American political life is probably very little. Duke's favorite topics—race, politics, and David Duke—hold endless fascination for him, however, and so there is little chance that he will fade quietly from the scene.

Duke is a man of considerable talent, charisma, and energy. Observers may only wonder what may have been if he had not run across a flier for the National Socialist Liberation Front in the waning days of the 1960s.

See also: American Nazi Party; Black, Don; Carto, Willis; Christian Identity; National Socialist Liberation Front; National Socialist White People's Party; Odinism; Order; Rockwell, George Lincoln; Smith, Gerald L. K.; Tommasi, Joseph; Warner, James.

Further reading: Tyler Bridges, *The Rise of David Duke* (Jackson: University of Mississippi Press, 1994); Betty A. Dobratz and Stephanie L. Shanks-Meile, *White Power, White Pride!* (New York: Twayne, 1997); John C. Kuzenski, ed., *David Duke and the Politics of Race in the South* (Nashville, TN: Vanderbilt University Press, 1995); Douglas D. Rose, ed., *The Emergence of David Duke and the Politics of Race* (Chapel Hill: University of North Carolina Press, 1992); Patsy Sims, *The Klan* (New York: Stein and Day, 1978); Michael Zatarian, *David Duke: Evolution of a Klansman* (New York: Pelican, 1990).

JAMES ELLISON   One of the more idiosyncratic characters to emerge from the violent end of the Christian Identity world in the 1970s and early 1980s was James Ellison. At the height of his influence in the mid-1970s, Ellison and another Identity firebrand, Kerry Noble, led the communal Identity group with the ungainly title of the Covenant, Sword, and Arm of the Lord (CSA) in a rural redoubt that hugged the Missouri border with Arkansas and that the founders called Zarephath-Horeb.

James Ellison today is a much reviled figure both in the Identity world and, beyond it, in the world of the American radical right. This was not always so, but it is true that Ellison's path from the beginning was somewhat singular. A believer, like many Identity adherents, in the sacrality of the "White seed," Ellison went beyond mere rhetoric and actually formed a polygamous marriage with two women, having children by each. A true believer in imminent apocalypse, Ellison lived in the belief that the End was near and that it would not be pretty. Indeed, he expected the full horrors of the apocalypse, with famine, pestilence, and, in particular, racial warfare, to be the hallmark of the Last Days.

The Covenant, Sword, and Arm of the Lord compound was thus seen as a fortress to preserve the "righteous remnant" of the White race in those terrible times and as a bastion for the training of the elite of the radical right wing in weapons and irregular tactics in preparation for the apocalypse. Weapons held an enduring fascination for Ellison, and soon the CSA compound became the armorer and preferred source of training for the most extreme elements of the American radical right.

With such a perspective, and with a fiery rhetoric to match his beliefs, Ellison did not have to wait long for trouble. Headstrong and unwilling to listen to the counsel or criticisms of others, he soon was embroiled in disputes with other Identity figures. This, however, is par for the course in the fractious Identity world. More serious were the complaints of defectors from the compound of the Covenant, Sword, and Arm of the Lord.

Ellison, who seems to have become somewhat unhinged as a result of his outsized ego and the effects of both the CSA's physical isolation and his now unchallenged leadership, came to style himself "King James of the Ozarks." While this was amusing to some, charges of sexual immorality, common criminality, fraud, and the abuse of his followers were not so lightly dismissed. The charges and countercharges ricocheted through the Identity world in the early 1980s and were most widely disseminated by John Harrell, head of the Christian Patriots Defense League in Flora, Illinois. Harrell, in fact, published the charges, his own correspondence with Ellison and Kerry Noble, and the CSA's response to the charges. By 1984, when the federal government began the process of charging and eventually incarcerating the CSA's faithful, Ellison had developed something of the reputation of a right-wing Jim Jones in the Identity community.

Ellison's star went into permanent decline in the wake of the inevitable confrontation with the federal government. As late as the winter of 1984–1985, he was vowing in the *CSA Newsletter* to "fight, and die if necessary," rather than give in to government efforts to seize the property of the Covenant, Sword, and Arm of the Lord. The threat was taken seriously, with good reason, given the CSA's considerable store of armaments, its daily military training regimen, and years of fiery rhetoric. Thus, it was something of a shock when, in April 1985, Ellison and company surrendered without a shot being fired when surrounded by some 200 FBI agents. Much of the credit for this peaceful denouement belongs to the level-headed negotiating prowess of Kerry Noble, who had become quietly disillusioned with Ellison, the radical course of the CSA, and the right-wing in general.

Still greater surprises were in store. In the 1987 sedition trial in Fort Smith, Arkansas, involving the members of the Order and the most visible leaders of the American racialist right, the star witness for the prosecution was none other than James Ellison! He testified in return for promises of immunity, but his testimony proved of little avail to the government, and the defendants were all acquitted. Ellison was imprisoned from the time of the surrender of the CSA compound until after the trial, and the experience devastated him. His testimony at Fort Smith had made him an outcast in the world of the far right, while endearing him not a whit to anyone else. Both Ellison's wives divorced him in this period.

Ellison today lives at Elohim City, Oklahoma, a more stable, far-right, communitarian property, whose patriarch, Robert Millar, is the grandfather of Ellison's current wife.

See also: Christian Identity; Covenant, Sword, and Arm of the Lord; Order.

Further reading: CSA Journal; *CSA Newsletter*; CSA, *C.S.A. Survival Manual* (n.p., n.d.); Jeffrey Kaplan, *Radical Religion in America* (Syracuse, NY: Syracuse University Press, 1997).

Sheldon Emry   *See* Barley, Dave.

European Liberation Front   *See* Yockey, Francis Parker.

F

RALPH FORBES An Arkansas-based Identity minister and frequent unsuccessful candidate for local office, Ralph Forbes possesses impeccable National Socialist credentials. In the 1960s, Forbes had risen to the leadership of the fractious California contingent of George Lincoln Rockwell's original American Nazi Party (ANP). From the beginning, however, Forbes's strongly religious bent contrasted with the more secular orientation of his compatriots. The result was constant friction, which turned into open rebellion after Rockwell's assassination on August 25, 1967.

According to Rockwell's biographer, Frederick Simonelli, Rockwell early on recognized the possibilities inherent in Forbes's attraction to religion. The ANP's inability to reach out to the White masses was a problem that plagued Rockwell's last years and, following an extended transatlantic correspondence with one of his mentors in the World Union of National Socialists (WUNS), Bruno Ludtke of Germany, he at last came to the realization that America was a deeply religious nation, and if National Socialism were to become a mass movement, it must be presented in religious terms.

The vehicle for this religious appeal would be Christian Identity, a theology to which Rockwell had been introduced by Wesley Swift. The mission of packaging National Socialism in Identity garb was secretly entrusted to Ralph Forbes in 1965. The choice was logical—for no one else in the American National Socialist community of the 1960s possessed as marked an affinity for the mystical as did Forbes. However, the increasing religiosity of the California commander served to further alienate the rank and file.

When the legitimacy conferred on Forbes as the ANP's California leader was withdrawn following Rockwell's demise, the group fell into disarray. The California party was split by a rebellion led by James Warner (who, ironically, would himself drift from National Socialism to Christian Identity to neopagan Odinism in later years) and Allen Vincent. Matt Koehl, Rockwell's successor in the ANP's successor organization, the National Socialist White People's Party (NSWPP), was called to California to mediate the dispute. When Koehl opted for Forbes, the California branch of the party shattered and a number of micro-NS groups were the result.

If Forbes's original conversion to Christian Identity was a clever ruse concocted by Commander Rockwell, it did not stay that way for long. Ousted from the California National Socialist leadership despite Koehl's best efforts, Forbes began an ideological and geographic drift that brought him to tiny London, Arkansas, as a true-believing Identity minister. His long-running Sword of Christ Good News Ministries boasts a national mailing list, if only a modest catalog of original materials.

In truth, Ralph Forbes will not be remembered for his intellectual gifts nor for his Identity writings, which read as turgid and derivative. His appetite for politics, however, remains undiminished. He has run for local office under a number of banners, most notably the New America First Party, which boasted impressive stationery bearing the signatures of such deceased stalwarts of the original Depression-era America First Party as Charles Lindbergh. He has also been active in other national campaigns under the banner of the Populist Party.

See also: American Nazi Party; Christian Identity; Koehl, Matt; Ludtke, Bruno; National Socialist White People's Party; Odinism; Rockwell, George Lincoln; Swift, Wesley; Warner, James; World Union of National Socialists.

Further reading: Frederick J. Simonelli, "Preaching Hate with the Voice of God: American Neo-Nazis and Christian Identity," *Patterns of Prejudice* 30 (April 1996); Frederick J. Simonelli, *American Fuehrer: George Lincoln Rockwell and the American Nazi Party* (Champaign: University of Illinois Press, 1999).

Henry Ford   *See* Coughlin, Father Charles; Smith, Gerald L. K.

JOSEPH FRANKLIN   Long before the contemporary radical right (recognizing its relative weakness and the hopeless nature of any attempt to strike a decisive blow against the state or its perceived Jewish masters) adopted the tactic of "leaderless resistance," there was Joseph Paul Franklin. Franklin, aka James Vaughn, joined the National Socialist White People's Party (NSWPP) in the late 1960s and was the archetype on which the movement's vision of the lone-wolf assassin was modeled. Eschewing the comforts of home and the love of his wife, Franklin threw himself wholeheartedly into the work of the party.

Yet he never really fit in and was wildly unpopular among party regulars. Why? For one thing, he made no effort to adopt the mock Third Reich spit-and-polish look favored by American National Socialists. Rather, he was scruffy and unkempt, reflecting the look of the "enemy" of the day, the New Left. Moreover, his predilection for direct action and revolution *now* would have no place in the conservative NSWPP. It was not until the dramatic break of Joseph Tommasi's National Socialist Liberation Front with the National Socialist White People's Party that there would be an organizational vehicle for revolutionary violence in the world of explicit National Socialism in America. By then, Franklin had despaired of the movement and struck out on his own.

The National Socialist White People's Party exploit for which Franklin was best remembered concerned the 1969 New Mobilization demonstrations in Washington, D.C., in opposition to the Vietnam War. In an effort to oppose the "New Mobe"—and incidentally to prove to the media and to themselves that they remained relevant in the left-wing atmosphere of the 1960s youth culture—the party members decided to attack the enemy's headquarters.

At first glance the operation seems unlikely. The Nazis were vastly outnumbered, and in any case their distinctively military look was unlikely to get them within shouting distance of their long-haired opponents. Thus the leader of the operation, James Mason, turned to Franklin. There was one catch, however. Not one of the NSWPP members chosen for the "glorious mission" would deign to take part in any operation that included Franklin. After much cajoling, Mason at last was able to gather a group to provide a diversion. Franklin, though, became part of movement mythology by singlehandedly storming the New Mobe Bastille and setting off tear-gas grenades, which forced the evacuation of the enemy headquarters.

This epiphany, however, marked the beginning of the end of Franklin's National Socialist White People's Party career. He soon disappeared, and several years later reports of mysterious killings of African Americans began to be issued across the country. Black cab drivers were found shot dead by a .22 caliber pistol in Buffalo. A Jewish synagogue in Chattanooga was bombed. Black civil rights leader Vernon Jordan was shot and wounded. So was the publisher of the pornographic magazine *Hustler*, Larry Flynt. And a mixed-race couple in Utah was shot and killed. Suspicion eventually fell on Franklin, and in 1980 he was convicted of numerous charges ranging from civil rights violations to murder.

Franklin, never a popular movement figure, was quickly and conveniently forgotten by his erstwhile comrades. Although his movement career spanned both the National Socialist and Ku Klux Klan groups in America, only James Mason and the National Socialist Liberation Front saw fit to acknowledge him. For everyone else, Franklin became an Orwellian "nonperson," written out of their history.

Prison life proved particularly difficult for Franklin. In the maximum security facility at Marion, Illinois, where he had been incarcerated since 1982, Franklin had been attacked by African-American inmates and stabbed no fewer than 15 times. Apparently determined to get out one way or another, Franklin began to confess to crimes of which he had long been suspected, but which the government could not prove in court. The Jordan and Flynt shootings were only two of the crimes to which Franklin has confessed (Flynt was targeted for publishing photographs depicting interracial sex). More deadly actions—including the murder of interracial couples in Utah and bank robberies across the country to finance his operations, as well as several as-yet-unsubstantiated confessions to other unsolved murders—were recounted in Franklin's statements.

As a result of these revelations and a promise he made to Indiana jurors that he would do it again given the opportunity, Joseph Franklin was granted his wish and sentenced to death. In a newspaper article recounting the case, Franklin is quoted as describing his motivation in these terms: "I was the executioner, the judge and the jury. I was on a holy war against evildoers."

On June 16, 1998, the Missouri Supreme Court upheld another death sentence for Franklin. In this case, he was convicted of killing one man and injuring two others as they left a synagogue after a bar mitzvah on October 7, 1977. In the 1997 trial, Franklin stated that he had taken a position outside the building with the intention of killing as many Jews as he could with the five bullets he had for his newly purchased rifle.

See also: Mason, James; National Socialist Liberation Front; National Socialist White People's Party; Tommasi, Joseph.

Further reading: Jeffrey Kaplan, "Real Paranoids Have Real Enemies: The Genesis of the ZOG Discourse in the American National Socialist Subculture," in Catherine Wessinger, ed., *Millennialism, Persecution and Violence* (Syracuse, NY: Syracuse University Press, forthcoming); James Mason, *Siege* (Denver: Storm Books, 1992).

G

WILLIAM POTTER GALE   In the recollection of senior Christian Identity figures such as Dan Gayman, it was William Potter Gale who, more than any other individual, played the key role in bringing an element of revolutionary violence into the Identity community. A career military man who rose to the rank of colonel and served as an aide to General Douglas MacArthur in World War II, Gale was no armchair warrior. His endeavors in this regard remain controversial, however, and he managed to avoid serious legal entanglements until his final years.

On returning to California after the war, Gale threw himself into far-right politics with the same passion he had given the army during his long military career. He met and became friendly with such national figures as Henry Ford, Sr., and Gerald L. K. Smith. It was not long before he came in contact with the coterie of Identity figures associated with the Smith movement, including Wesley Swift, Bertrand Comperet, and San Jacinto Capt.

Gale studied the Identity creed in California under Wesley Swift. Despite his later bitter split with Swift, Gale would contest with another Swift protégé, Richard Butler, for Swift's mantle of leadership in the divisive world of Christian Identity. In 1964, Capt, Comperet, Gale, and Butler formed the Christian Defense League under Swift's tutelage. Tellingly, it was Butler rather than Gale who was selected as the CDL's president. Butler would in fact inherit much of Swift's legacy and would eventually take the ministry to Idaho to form the Aryan Nations.

With Butler's departure, Gale turned to a number of outlets for his unabashedly revolutionary racialist and anti-Semitic message. The first, and perhaps one of the most influential, of these efforts was the California Rangers, founded roughly contemporaneously with the Christian Defense League.

The Rangers in many ways mirrored on a state level the organization of Robert DePugh's Minutemen. That is, it was a secretive, armed group that benefited considerably more from Gale's knowledge of irregular warfare than the Minutemen did from DePugh's inspired but amateurish training regimen. The Rangers remain controversial. In the view of California's attorney general, who issued a report on the group in 1965, it was a terrorist organization. Gale recalled it years later as a civil defense unit duly registered with California's secretary of state. By either name, the California Rangers would provide an organizational model for the tax protest movements of the 1980s and the militia movement of the 1990s.

More influential still was Gale's next venture, the Posse Comitatus. With the Posse, Gale achieved the dream—and the nightmare—of every far-right revolutionary: he managed to frighten not only the press and the public, but the federal government itself. The Posse was actually formed in 1969 by Gale and Henry Beach, but it was not until almost a decade later that, under the leadership of James Wickstrom, it would make much impact on public consciousness. The Posse combined a radical localism (no authority higher than the county sheriff was to be recognized as legitimate), a tax protest, and a deep sense of rural grievance fostered by the farm crisis of the early 1980s into a powerful ideological cocktail whose punch is still felt today.

The organization exploded into prominence with the 1983 shoot-out with police that left North Dakota farmer Gordon Kahl dead. The government mobilized, with the Internal Revenue Service taking the lead, and a severe crackdown on the far-right, code-named Operation Clean Sweep, followed in the mid-1980s. Unsurprisingly, it was Wickstrom rather than the more-sophisticated Gale who would suffer the legal ramifications of the crackdown.

Gale's final organizational effort was the Committee of the States in 1984. The Committee's brief was either audacious or ridiculous, depending on one's point of view. Based on the Articles of Confederation, which preceded the U.S. Constitution, the Committee sought members in each state who would act as a body to form the "legitimate" Congress of the United States.

Given the Committee's pronounced radical localism à la the Posse Comitatus, the first function of the Committee of the States would logically have been to dissolve itself. Instead, letters were sent to each U.S. senator and congressperson informing them that they had been indicted and faced trial by a popular Grand Jury of the people. This would be common fare in the most extreme sectors of the common-law wing of the 1990s Patriot Movement, but in the mid-1980s it was considered nothing less than a terrorist threat, so the government reacted accordingly. Gale and the rest of the Committee's leadership were indicted on a variety of charges, including making terrorist threats against the lives of IRS agents and a judge, plus violation of the tax laws. Gale and his codefendants were ultimately convicted in a Las Vegas trial. Once again, however, Gale avoided prison. He died in April 1988 and was buried with full military honors.

See also: Aryan Nations; Butler, Richard; California Rangers; Christian Defense League; Committee of the States; Gayman, Dan; Smith, Gerald L. K.; Swift, Wesley.

Further reading: Michael Barkun, *Religion and the Racist Right: The Origins of the Christian Identity Movement* (Chapel Hill: University of North Carolina Press, 1994); James Coates, *Armed and Dangerous: The Rise of the Survivalist Right* (New York: Hill and Wang, 1987); John George and Laird Wilcox, *Nazis, Communists, Klansmen and Others on the Fringe* (Buffalo, NY: Prometheus Books, 1992); Jeffrey Kaplan, *Radical Religion in America: Millenarian Movements from the Far Right to the Children of Noah* (Syracuse, NY: Syracuse University Press, 1997); Cheri Seymour, *Committee of the States: Inside the Radical Right* (Mariposa, CA: Camden Place Communications, 1991).

DAN GAYMAN   The pastor of the Church of Israel (COI) in Schell City, Missouri, Dan Gayman was from the 1960s to the 1980s considered one of the leading Christian Identity theologians in the United States. Gayman was born in Denver in 1937 to a family associated with the Church of Christ (Temple Lot), a dissident Mormon sect with centers in Denver and three other cities. He was raised by his mother. An honors graduate of Southwest Missouri State University in 1964 with a major in history, and residing since 1967 in Schell City, Gayman undertook a career in public education, eventually becoming the teacher-principal of Walker High School, before opting in 1976 for a full-time career in the ministry.

His interest in British Israelism, the genteel forerunner of Christian Identity, dates from the early 1950s by way of Herbert W. Armstrong's *Plain Truth Magazine* and Howard Rand's Destiny publications. Gayman later sent for British Israel World Federation (BIWF) material and soon veered away from the mild doctrines of British Israelism, opting instead for the racialist and anti-Semitic wing of the movement. In this, he was much influenced by the *Dearborn* (Michigan) *Independent*'s "International Jew" series.

In his more than 30 years of involvement with the Identity movement, Dan Gayman has come to know and be associated with nearly every major figure in the White supremacist constellation in the post–Gerald L. K. Smith era. Gayman was in fact the National Youth Chairman for Smith's movement. The names of his associates, or even mere contacts, in these years read as a veritable Who's Who of the White supremacist subculture and include such major figures as William Potter Gale, Buddy Tucker, Thom Robb, Richard Butler, Sheldon Emry, James Warner, and many more.

Dan Gayman received his primary training in Identity theology under the Denver-based Identity minister Kenneth Goff, a teacher to many current figures in the movement, at Goff's Soldiers of the Cross Training Institute in Denver in 1964–1965. Immediately prior to this education, however, Gayman took his first substantive step toward racialist activism, unsuccessfully attempting to turn the family's Schell City church youth camp into something of a Christian Identity adult seminary, which would provide, besides theological education, training in weapons and survivalism.

Armed with Goff's teachings and a much-strengthened sense of mission, Gayman returned to Schell City to win election as the Church of Israel's pastor and the editor of its newspaper, *Zion's Restorer,* which henceforth would become a stridently racialist organ.

The transition of the Schell City congregation into an Identity ministry was far from smooth, however. In 1972, a lawsuit pitted Dan Gayman against his brother Duane for control of the church and the land on which it was built. As a result of the suit, Dan lost control of the original church and all but 20 acres of the adjacent land. The family feud culminated in June 1976, with Dan Gayman, Buddy Tucker, and others entering the church, which had been lost as a result of the court case, sporting a banner of the organization to which both Tucker and Gayman belonged, "The National Emancipation of our White Seed." In the ensuing confrontation, a large number of policemen and state highway patrolmen entered the building, arresting both Gayman and Tucker, among others.

What is clear in retrospect is that in the wake of this arrest, Gayman had begun to rethink his position. The demonstration had accomplished nothing save to incur further legal fees. Indeed, the fanciful uniform adopted by Gayman and Tucker for the action, described by the local paper in Nevada, Missouri, the *Nevada Herald,* as "a white uniform, with knee length storm trooper boots, and an empty pistol holder and belt slung over one shoulder," could not have brought about a desirable public effect. And from Pastor

Gayman's recollections, there appears to have occurred in the course of this imbroglio an attempt by the Rev. Tucker to "steal" Gayman's congregation by preaching ever-greater militancy. Gayman would eventually break with Tucker over these strident calls for violence.

The key events in turning Dan Gayman and the Church of Israel away from confrontation with secular authorities and toward quietism appear to have been the violent activities of the Order, the revolutionary organization headed by Robert Mathews, in the early 1980s, plus the 1989 Fort Smith, Arkansas, sedition trial, which followed in its wake. Dan Gayman was called as a prosecution witness at Fort Smith, ostensibly to testify about the $10,000 allegedly passed to him by the Order. This event would lead to Gayman's ultimate break with both Christian Identity and the radical right.

Until Fort Smith, Gayman was a figure of considerable respect throughout the American radical right. Through his Church of Israel outreach ministry, which consisted of cassette tapes and the COI newsletter, *Zions Watchman* (later shortened to the *Watchman*), he attracted a number of followers in Europe and southern Africa as well. However, he became alienated by Christian Identity's drift toward increasingly violent antigovernment rhetoric in the 1980s and the appearance of the Order, and even before the Fort Smith fiasco, he had been leading his flock into a more passive, withdrawn mode in accordance with the teachings of Rom. 13 to obey state authority.

By the mid-1990s, this withdrawal was complete. Gayman today asserts that he is no longer a part of the Identity movement, and current Church of Israel publications eschew expressions of racism or anti-Semitism, concentrating instead on home birthing, home schooling, and other such apolitical pursuits.

See also: Butler, Richard; Christian Identity; Church of Israel; Gale, William Potter; Goff, Kenneth; Order; Robb, Thom; Smith, Gerald L. K.; Warner, James.

Further reading: Dan Gayman, "The Bible and Civil Disobedience" (Schell City, MO: COI, 1989); Dan Gayman, "Apocalyptic Millenarianism" (Schell City, MO: COI, 1991); Jeffrey Kaplan, "The Context of American Millenarian Revolutionary Theology: The Case of the 'Identity Christian' Church of Israel," *Journal of Terrorism and Political Violence* 5:1 (spring 1993); Jeffrey Kaplan, *Radical Religion in America: Millenarian Movements from the Far Right to the Children of Noah* (Syracuse, NY: Syracuse University Press, 1997); *Zions Watchman*.

German American Bund   *See* Hitler, Adolf.

KENNETH GOFF   One of the most colorful personalities to emerge from the world of Christian Identity in the 1950s and 1960s was Kenneth Goff. The 1944 national chairman of Gerald L. K. Smith's Christian Youth for America group, and a self-proclaimed reformed communist, Goff emerges from the literature and the reminiscences of those who knew him as a decidedly equivocal man, described alternately as a brilliant preacher, a mentally unstable individual, a great patriot, and a shady character, often all in the same breath. Separating historical fact from Goff's epic self-mythologizing is no easy task. Indeed, this difficulty is compounded by Goff's rigorous separation of his identity as an Identity minister and his better-known public persona as an anticommunist crusader. The latter role is far better documented.

In a short biographical extract provided to the media and as an advertisement for his numerous speaking engagements, Kenneth Goff dates his early membership in the Communist Party from May 2, 1936, to October 9, 1939. This gift for precision was brought into play in 1939 when he testified before the congressional Dies Committee investigating the threat of communist subversion in America. Goff told Congress tales of derring-do he performed on behalf of the Communist Party USA (CPUSA), including infiltrating youth organizations, activities he conducted on behalf of communist front groups, his involvement with the "special branch which laid the groundwork for Communist revolution in the United States," and close contacts he had with communist leaders both in the United States and the Soviet Union. Turning to anticommunism with the same missionary zeal that seems to have marked his years in the party, Goff claims with precision that his testimony "aided in removing 169 Communists from the federal payrolls." However, he said that, like all former communists, he was "a marked man, and has received many bodily injuries."

The latter claim appears unlikely, given Goff's peripatetic speaking tours (he appeared in every state of the union over the course of his long career). Goff was a productive writer as well, claiming to have authored 28 books, innumerable tracts, a periodical called *The Pilgrim Torch* from 1962 to 1967, a newsletter named *Christian Battle Cry* from 1966 through 1971, and finally a series of bizarre newsletters pitched to a particular theme (for instance, hippies are a communist plot) that were distributed as fund-raisers.

Goff's books make for some of the more eccentric prose to emerge from the radical right of his day. In his 1954 tome, *Hitler and the Twentieth Century Hoax,* for example, he asserted both that Hitler was a communist agent (hinting all the while that he was of Jewish ancestry and may not have been a real anti-Semite after all) and that he may not really be dead, but would make a dramatic reappearance when the time was right, to advance communist plans. In *Red Shadows,* Goff unveils the World War II–vintage conspiratorial history of the communist plan for world domination. And in *Reds Promote Racial War,* he makes a biblically based plea for segregation and claims, unsurprisingly, that integration is a communist plot.

Goff's more enduring contributions to the racial right wing stem more from his religious affiliations, however, than from his anti-communism. In 1943, he became the chairman of the newly formed National Youth Organization (NYO). The group grew out of a loose coalition of conservative Protestant churches. The NYO had three primary aims, in his words:

1. All out effort to win the war.
2. We hold that the regenerating power of the Lord Jesus Christ is the cure for Juvenile Delinquency.
3. To combat communistic plots among our Youth.

However, also in Goff's words:

By 1950, those who launched the organization were no longer youth, and therefore a new group called "Soldiers of the Cross" was formed with Christian Youth for America as their youth auxiliary.

It is the Soldiers of the Cross Training Institute for which Kenneth Goff is best remembered in Identity circles today. While it appears that the Soldiers of the Cross may have had some connection to Robert DePugh's Minutemen, its primary claim to fame was as a training school for aspiring Christian Identity ministers, among them such high-profile leaders as Dan Gayman of the Church of Israel.

The Institute was located in Evergreen, Colorado, and boasted many of the accoutrements of any unaccredited Bible college. Students were offered a range of study opportunities, from a full curriculum on the semester system to short courses and night school. Unlike Bible colleges, however, the school offered such courses as "The Bible's Answer to Communism," "The Christian History and Concept of the U.S. Constitution," "Communism and Socialism," "American History," "The United Nations and the World Revolutionary Movement," "Psychopolitics—the Conquest of the Mind," "Applied

Christianity," "Speech," "Debate," "Music," "Christian Resistance," "Survival Judo and Karate," and a survivalist class called "Storehouse and Christian Survival."

See also: Christian Identity; Church of Israel; Gayman, Dan; Hitler, Adolf; Smith, Gerald L. K.

Further reading: Michael Barkun, *Religion and the Racist Right: The Origins of the Christian Identity Movement* (Chapel Hill: University of North Carolina Press, 1994); John George and Laird Wilcox, *Nazis, Communists, Klansmen and Others on the Fringe* (Buffalo, NY: Prometheus Books, 1992); Glen Jeansonne, *Gerald L. K. Smith: Minister of Hate* (New Haven: Yale University Press, 1988); Jeffrey Kaplan, *Radical Religion in America: Millenarian Movements from the Far Right to the Children of Noah* (Syracuse, NY: Syracuse University Press, 1997); Ralph Lord Roy, *Apostles of Discord* (Boston: Beacon Press, 1953).

Karl Hand   *See* Mason, James; National Socialist Liberation Front; Pierce, William; Tommasi, Joseph.

John Harrell   *See* Christian Defense League; Ellison, James; Mohr, Jack.

GEORGE ERIC HAWTHORNE   Had he not quietly left the movement following his release from jail in 1998, George Burdi (aka George Eric Hawthorne) may have become the kind of seminal radical-right-wing figure of the decade of the 1990s that George Lincoln Rockwell was of the 1960s, that Joseph Tommasi (had he lived) could have been in the 1970s, and that Robert Mathews proved to be of the 1980s. This is all the more remarkable, given the fact that Hawthorne's rise to prominence has been in the skinhead milieu—hardly a source of great inspiration for the racialist subculture.

Hawthorne's roots in the movement were decidedly unpromising. His first appearance on the racialist scene was in his native Canada as part of the latter-day Church of the Creator (COTC). Creativity then as now attracted a tiny handful of capable and idealistic adherents whose actions were lost in the violence, negativity, and outright criminality that was more typical of COTC recruits. After Ben Klassen's 1993 suicide and the defection of his successor, Dr. Rick McCarthy (who took the COTC treasury with him), the Church of the Creator devolved into small, warring fiefdoms, and most of the first generation of COTC alumni reluctantly left the sinking ship. Two such alums, George Eric Hawthorne and Marc Wilson (a former Klassen-designated heir apparent), became the nucleus of Resistance Records.

Precisely where the start-up funds for Resistance were obtained is one of the more interesting lines of speculation in the contemporary racialist movement. Although it's unprovable, many believe that the Swedish skinhead movement provided its seed money. The Swedish movement, well ahead of its North American counterpart, had taken the lessons of Robert Mathews and the Order to heart, and so embarked in the late 1980s on a course of bank robberies as a means to fund racialist activities. In the early days, the money was squandered on vacations that saw groups of Swedish skins peacefully descending on various resorts throughout Europe where they soaked up sun and sea and vast quantities of cheap beer like many another Scandinavian tourist. The pointlessness of this soon stimulated some changes in direction, however, and what emerged was a surprisingly sophisticated investment strategy. Of greatest import, money was invested in the music business.

In 1994 Resistance Records, headquartered in Detroit, marked its appearance with the debut of a glossy eponymous magazine, while the Swedish Nordland label issued its premier magazine in January 1995. Save that one is in English and the other in Swedish, the layout of both magazines is virtually identical, and each magazine speaks warmly of its transatlantic counterpart. Moreover, product was exchanged between the companies more on the basis of a handshake and an e-mail message than by standard contracts—a fact that would come back to haunt both Hawthorne and Resistance Records. Nonetheless, Resistance proved to be a remarkable success on this side of the Atlantic, while Nordland succeeded beyond all expectations in Sweden, capturing a significant share of the domestic music market.

In the second issue of *Resistance,* George Eric Hawthorne reflected on his company's surprising success:

> I am proud to announce that instead of being a dying people with out-dated opinions, we are actually being revitalized by hope and promise, and finally working together for the type of future we all deserve. It may sound like an idealistic pipe dream, and heaven knows I have been a dreamer since I was a boy, but I can tell you with the right combination of ideas and promotion, the White youth of the world are capable of lifting themselves out of the quagmire of defeat and degeneracy. There is a bold new force on the horizon— and you guessed right—it is Resistance Records. We have proved ourselves capable of inspiring a dying cause in what I will venture to say was a dying movement desperately in need of a new beginning.
>
> The most important emotion you can feel is not hatred, nor love. It is empowerment. Empowerment is that feeling that results from

the positive influences, be they actions or ideas. The revolution—any revolution—begins in the hearts and minds of the most heroic elements of the population: the revolution begins with you. Your ability to allow feelings of empowerment to enter your life will ultimately determine your relative worth to the cause. I have said it time and again to those of you who know me: there is no jewish [sic] problem, there is no black problem, there is no government problem. In many ways, these factors only hold as much power over you as you allow them to. The problem lies within White people and our inability to recognize our uniqueness and to protect it.

So where do we stand here in 1994? It is important for you to realize that you are not living in the present, but that you are a product of the past and represent a hope for the future. You are a link in the long, golden chain of your people, and act as a torchbearer for all those who came before you. I urge you not to fight your White Racial Comrades, but to fight with them. Instead, swear an oath on the blood of your ancestors, the blood that flows within your veins and gives you life. Be your own god, your own master, your own leader and your own follower. In your veins lives an army of the undead that will give you hope and strength if you listen to your Racial soul.

To racialist ears, the words are undoubtedly stirring. The ideas are drawn from a variety of sources ranging from explicit National Socialism to the Church of the Creator, and even the famous Hawthorne ego is pledged to the glory that in this vision lies the racial past and, perhaps, the glorious future of the White race.

This remarkably positive message would be a consistent feature of all of George Eric Hawthorne's endeavors with Resistance Records. For Hawthorne, the kind of aimless and senseless violence associated with the skinhead movement is more than a negative feature of the subculture—it is an action that is in keeping with the self-destructive instincts he sees as inherent in the White race of these times, and as a service to the enemies of the race (that is, to the Jews and to their most successful creation, ZOG, or the Zionist Occupation Government). Thus, Hawthorne's counsel is for patience, as in the spring 1995 issue of *Resistance:*

These sort of attacks accomplish absolutely NOTHING, and have cost us hundreds of our best men who are currently rotting away in ZOG's dungeons because they lacked the foresight and direction necessary to act as revolutionaries instead of reactionaries. Beating some worthless mud [that is, a non-White person] to death is not an act of revolution, it is an act of poor judgment. The *Protocols of the Learned Elders of Zion,* which is the doctrine outlining ZOG's plan for global domination, says that our enemy can **count on the White man to sacrifice long term victory for short term satisfaction**. We must stop acting in accordance with their plans and start acting in accordance with our own *LONG RANGE PLAN FOR WHITE REVOLUTION*. This means staying out of jail whenever it is avoidable. Remember, this is a war and you are living behind enemy lines. Act accordingly.

From 1995 through 1997, Hawthorne's activities were frenetic. Resistance expanded its format to include a remarkably advanced web site at which Resistance bands could be sampled online and Resistance product ordered (Visa and MasterCard cheerfully accepted). *Resistance* magazine went from republishing widely circulated articles in the racialist right and lightweight interviews with lightweight bands to an expanded format that featured cutting-edge articles and interviews with such important figures as the imprisoned Order veteran David Lane and key movement debates such as the attempt by James Mason and the Universal Order to advance Charles Manson as the natural leader of the racialist movement. Moreover, a fortnightly *Resistance* e-mail publication discussed issues and news of note, as well as advertising upcoming Resistance releases.

As a record label, Resistance continued to expand apace. By 1997, Resistance had gathered an impressive roster of bands, including Berserker, Bound for Glory, Max Resist, Nordic Thunder, and No Remorse, to name a few. Moreover, Resistance was handling product not only from the Swedish Nordland label, which featured bands such as Svastika, Division S, and the premier Swedish White Power band Dirlewanger, but also from other labels throughout the world. This was important in that it allowed Resistance customers to purchase at domestic prices Ian Stewart Donaldson's seminal Skrewdriver catalog. Moreover, as Resistance diversified, key CDs from beyond the "White-noise" world became available. Thus, nonracialist but important works such as Blood Axis's *Gospel of Inhumanity* and Varg Vikernes's one-man band effort, *Burzum*, were introduced to an American White-noise audience.

But the single most important recorded work to emerge from Resistance Records was, fittingly enough, George Eric Hawthorne's band, Rahowa. The name *Rahowa* was chosen in homage to the Church of the Creator's book cum slogan, Racial Holy War (*RaHoWa! The Planet Is Ours!*). With the same perfectionism that Hawthorne uses to approach any task, Rahowa's *Cult of the Holy*

War CD offers beautifully crafted songs, flawless instrumental passages, and an innovative approach that saw a mixture of such genres as white noise and black metal to create a work that easily transcended the world of White Power music. Hawthorne himself noted that he was taking singing lessons to perfect his craft.

The *Cult of the Holy War* was an epiphany for Hawthorne. He was now a media presence, being interviewed in mainstream publications from the local newspaper to the august *New York Times*. But in 1997, the wheels came off the Hawthorne bandwagon. Hawthorne was becoming a star, which brought a typically adverse reaction from the racialist right. This went beyond the usual sniping and backbiting in 1996 when Resistance sided with Nordland in a fierce conflict over control of the lucrative music scene against Combat 18 (C18), the British heirs to Ian Stewart's Blood and Honour legacy. Several killings later, and after a rash of letter bombs were apparently mailed by C18 to Sweden (including one to a cabinet minister), the Nordland/ Resistance axis emerged victorious when C18's leadership were incarcerated on murder charges.

But of greater import, Hawthorne and Resistance were becoming much too successful for comfort in official quarters. Hawthorne himself had always been cognizant of the risks he was running, and sought to cushion himself and his label to the extent that he could.

Part of this effort was the decision early on to operate out of the United States rather than his native Canada. The attraction of Canada's southern neighbor is the First Amendment to the U.S. Constitution, which allows considerably greater freedom of action to racialist movements than is available under the more restrictive hate-speech codes in Canada or Europe. It is this relative license that explains the irony of the racialist Resistance Records label's operating from heavily Black Detroit rather than predominantly White Ontario. Thus, when asked why he centers his operations in the United States, Hawthorne candidly states:

> The main reason is that we are a U.S.-based group and therefore the U.S. Constitution protects us and lets us say what we want. We can write our version of truth in the United States. This has enabled racial ideologies in the States to be a lot more radical than in Canada. You would see a lot more radical ideologies coming out of Canada if it weren't for the hate laws that prevent it.

There are, however, limits to even the American tolerance of a racialist movement such as Resistance that is deemed to be overly successful. In April 1997 Michigan state authorities descended on the offices of Resistance Records and confiscated a considerable quantity of CDs, computer files, and the like. Simultaneously, Canadian authorities conducted similar raids on the more limited Resistance Canadian operations. The raids, which were immediately lauded by the Anti-Defamation League on both sides of the border, were officially based on tax charges and failure to pay Social Security taxes for Resistance employees—a credible enough charge given the loosely structured communal approach with which the movement tends to business. Hawthorne himself, meanwhile, was serving a year in jail in Ottawa on charges of assault.

The charges and the trial that led to Hawthorne's incarceration were controversial. The Resistance collective had this to say in the February 28, 1997, issue of the *Resistance Records Electronic Newsletter:*

Greetings Friends & Supporters,

The staff at Resistance Records would like to inform you of the results of George Hawthorne's appeal. Most of you know the details of the case. For those of you that don't, allow me to give them to you. In case you're really new to all of this, George Hawthorne is the founder of Resistance Records, the editor of RESISTANCE Magazine, the founder and lead singer of the band RAHOWA, and he puts together our email newsletter, the RREN [*Resistance Records Electronic Newsletter*].

George was arrested and charged a few years ago with "assault causing bodily harm" for an attack that occurred on an anti-racist in Canada's notorious "Ottawa Riots" following an aborted RAHOWA concert. He was found guilty of not actually committing the assault, but in "abetting". Yes, you got it right. They basically placed the blame of the entire riot on George's shoulders. He was sentenced to ONE YEAR in jail. Funny how that worked out. It was his first offense and there was no real "proof" of anything, just hearsay.

Some guys were caught on film in the act of assaulting people with chains and they only got 45 or 90 days. An anti-racist attacked a police officer with a steel pipe and got no time. All he had to do was write a 500 word essay on how kids should become "active" in promoting anti-racism. Just like him. Oh, he also had to give an "apology" to the cop. Is there any justice left in this world? You tell me.

George served 3 weeks and got out on appeal bail. He waited almost 2 years for the appeal. The appellant court upheld both the conviction and the sentence. So he has begun serving his 1 year sentence. He "should" be released on parole in 4 months (1/3 of the sentence) and at most in 8 months (2/3 of the sentence). Please note my "cynicism". We'll keep you posted.

Regardless, we at Resistance HQ are now handling George's email. We will be issuing a formal letter from George on his situation with our next mailing of Resistance Magazine (due out in a few weeks) and our next catalog mailing to non-subscribers. Subscribers to RREN should also be getting something. Please note that there hasn't been an RREN in quite some time. With George away, its release will be sporadic at best. We appreciate your understanding in this matter.

We would like to ASSURE YOU that BUSINESS WILL GO ON AS USUAL!!! Our WEB site will still be up and running. You will still be able to order music from it. Orders will still be processed FAST and efficiently. The service you expect from us will continue to be delivered. Also, RESISTANCE MAGAZINE WILL STILL BE PUBLISHED! It may come out a little later, but rest assured, if you paid for a subscription for 4 issues or for 8 issues, YOU WILL GET THEM, EVEN IF IT TAKES LONGER THAN NORMAL!

Resistance did attempt to soldier on in Hawthorne's absence, but the effort was, as stated, sporadic at best. With the tax raids, Resistance was put largely out of action. For two years, *Resistance* magazine failed to publish another issue, and subscribers were eventually "compensated" with complimentary subscriptions to Willis Carto's excruciatingly turgid *Spotlight* newspaper. Apparently the Swedish movement sent help, but Resistance continued to flounder. Then, in 1998, Hawthorne was released from prison and since then seems to have dropped out of the movement altogether. Finally, in 1999, a new glossy issue of *Resistance* magazine appeared. The new *Resistance,* however, is under new management, appearing courtesy of veteran American National Socialist William Pierce's National Alliance.

See also: Black Metal; Carto, Willis; Church of the Creator; Klassen, Ben; Lane, David; Manson, Charles; Mason, James; Mathews, Robert; National Alliance; Order; Pierce, William; Rockwell, George Lincoln; Skinheads (Origins and Music); Tommasi, Joseph; Universal Order; Vikernes, Varg; White Power Music; Zionist Occupation Government.

Further reading: Stanley R. Barrett, *Is God a Racist?* (Toronto: University of Toronto Press, 1987); Jeffrey Kaplan and Leonard Weinberg, *The Emergence of a Euro-American Radical Right* (Rutgers, NJ: Rutgers University Press, 1998); Warren Kinsella, *Web of Hate: Inside Canada's Far Right Network* (Toronto: HarperCollins, 1994); Heléne Lööw, "White Power

Rock 'n' Roll—A Growing Industry," in Jeffrey Kaplan and Tore Bjørgo, *Nation and Race: The Developing Euro-American Racist Subculture* (Boston: Northeastern University Press, 1998); Joe Pearce, *Skrewdriver: The First Ten Years* (London: Skrewdriver Services, 1987).

HEMBYGDSPARTIET [Native Place Party]   The   Hembygdspartiet (HP) was founded in April 1995 in Stockholm by Leif Ericsson, Leif Larsson, and other former members of the Swedendemocrats (SD). Tommy Rydén became the official party leader in 1996. The party has not yet published an official program, but its internal newsletters and magazine advocates an end to non-White immigration and the deportation of those non-Whites who are already in Sweden, opposes membership in the European Union, and wants free medical care for Swedes. The HP wants to distance itself from the Nazi subculture groups and seeks an image similar to the Deutsche Volks-Union in Germany. The Hembygdspartiet in 1996 has between 200 and 300 members. Its chief publication is called *Grindvakten* [Guarding the gate].

—Tommy Rydén, Swedish race activist

See also: Rydén, Tommy; Vitt Ariskt Motsånd.

Further reading: Grindvakten 1 (1995); and *Grindvakten* 2 (1996).

ADOLF HITLER   The figure of Adolf Hitler, born on April 20, 1889, is today the colossus whose legacy for good or ill must be confronted sooner or later by every adherent of the racialist right wing. So great is the burden of the history of World War II and the enormity of the Holocaust that one's attitude toward Hitler and Nazism serves at once as a litmus test of the faith of the far right and as a so-far-unbreachable barrier between the racialist right and mainstream acceptance. What concerns us here, therefore, is not so much Hitler the historical figure as the many shades of interpretation of the figure of Adolf Hitler and the Third Reich common to the radical right of the present day.

In the immediate postwar years, the image of "Hitler the monster" became fixed in the public mind. Ghastly images of the stacked bodies of concentration camp victims and the haunting images of the gaunt and emaciated human skeletons of the liberated survivors were disseminated around the world in newsreel films, newspapers, and magazines. The Nuremberg Trials that followed dissected the Third Reich in clinical detail, revealing to the world the cool gray bureaucrats who carried out the National Socialist policies, becoming forever (in the words of Hanna Arendt) the living embodiment of the "banality of evil."

In the United States, the largely German and Italian immigrant-based movements whose members had been most notably sympathetic—or subservient—to the wartime fascist regimes had long since vanished from the political stage. Before the war, however, these pro-German groups were a cause for significant official concern. A mere decade before the 1930s, though, what had been perceived as threatening was marginal to the point of being humorous. In *The Emergence of a Euro-American Radical Right,* Leonard Weinberg of the University of Nevada–Reno reflects on this history:

> The Teutonia Association was organized in 1924, shortly after the failure of Hitler's Beer Hall Putsch in Munich. Teutonia, centered in Chicago, was led by Fritz Gissibl, a German national, who extended membership both to Germans living in the United States and Americans of German descent. In both instances there were few takers. Teutonia had no more than 100 members by the time it dissolved in 1932.
>
> As the Nazi Party's electoral fortunes in Germany rose in 1932, the Party's ambitious Foreign Section established an American branch. It sent a party member, Heinz Spanknoebel, to the United States to achieve this aim. Spanknoebel formed a group headquartered in Detroit, but with locals in New York, Cincinnati, Chicago, Los Angeles and San Francisco. Its objective was to Nazify the German Americans (racial Germans) throughout the country. Spanknoebel had some success in promoting National Socialist ideas and his recruitment effort surpassed that of the old Teutonia Association. By 1933, there were 1500 members of this Nazi movement. However, its open anti-Semitic activities, including physical attacks on Jews in a few cities and use of Nazi agents from Germany brought it to the attention of the US State Department which proceeded to lodge a complaint with its German counterpart. Accordingly, in April 1933 the Nazi Party in Germany issued an instruction calling for Spanknoebel's return to the Fatherland and the dissolution of the organization he had created.
>
> In its place Rudolph Hess, Robert Ley and other Nazi officials in Berlin created another American organization, the Friends of the New Germany. As short-lived as its predecessor, Friends of the

New Germany embarked on an even more flamboyant campaign to promote National Socialist ideas in German American communities throughout the United States, but particularly in the Yorkville section of New York City. Membership, estimated at approximately 10,000 in 1935 (60% of whom were German citizens), was of course substantially higher than the earlier Nazi groupings. Correlatively, the Friends' newspaper and other publications achieved a wider circulation and its public demonstrations, often involved street-corner brawling which gave them a considerably higher visibility than the earlier promotional efforts. Further, the Friends of the New Germany was able to establish some links to emerging native fascist organizations as William Dudley Pelley's Silver Shirts.

But with Hitler firmly in power in Germany, the nature of National Socialism was becoming increasingly clear to American observers. Jewish groups, such as the American Jewish Committee, along with labor unions, acting under the auspices of the American Federation of Labor, staged their own protests, including a mock trial of Hitler in Madison Square Garden. Further, at the urging of Congressman Martin Dickstein, the Speaker of the House of Representatives appointed a committee, under the chairmanship of Rep. John McCormick, to investigate the Friends' substantial ties to Nazi Germany. This development along with practically unceasing internal rivalries among the Friends' leaders led Rudolph Hess to issue a directive in December 1935 requiring all Reich citizens living in the United States to withdraw their membership in the Friends organization, thereby bringing about its disintegration.

Over the next few months, National Socialist activity in the United States went through a period of disorientation with various fragments of the Friends seeking to find a new format. Fritz Kuhn, a naturalized American citizen who had fought for Germany during World War I and had then joined the Nazi party afterward, succeeded in establishing a new Nazi organization for the American context. At a meeting in Buffalo, New York, in March 1936, Kuhn and representatives of various splinter groups created the German American Bund. By contrast to its predecessors, the Bund would appeal to Americans and emphasize its American character. Kuhn indicated his goal was to promote German-American friendship and understanding. Symbolically, Bund rallies would include pictures of George Washington along with those of the Führer and American flags were conspicuously on display. For Kuhn and his followers the Bund was an attempt to Americanize National Socialism.

Kuhn's effort to divorce, or at least partially separate, the Bund from its roots in Nazi Germany produced ambiguous results, to say the least. Although its members were largely American citizens, many of whom were of German origins (according to the Justice Department Bund membership achieved its highest level of 8500 in 1937-38), the Bundists' organization mimicked that of the Nazis. Accordingly, the Bund divided the United States into three Gau or districts (comparable to the Nazis' format in Germany), for the East, Midwest and West. Each Gau had its own Gauleiter and staff to direct the Bund's operations in his region. In addition, Kuhn promoted the formation of a uniformed paramilitary unit, the Order Service, clearly modeled after the Nazi Brown Shirt organization; and the Bund's Youth Division, from its public display of the Swastika to the Hitler salute to the singing of the "Horst Wessel Song," represented a barely Americanized reproduction of the Hitler Youth. Even Kuhn's highly theatrical style of public speaking seemed patterned after that of the German dictator. And the fact that Kuhn and other uniformed Bund leaders were publicly photographed shaking hands with Hitler during a 1938 visit to Germany did little to promote the organization's reputation as an American entity.

The highlight of the German American Bund's history was its 1939 Washington's Birthday rally (Washington's warning against America entangling itself in European affairs provided the theme) at Madison Square Garden in New York City. Although Kuhn was able to fill the arena with 22,000 cheering supporters to hear him speak about the virtues of Christian Americanism, the gathering produced a massive backlash. Public officials and spokesmen for such groups as the American Legion denounced the Bund's alien ideas and ties to Nazi Germany.

Within several months of his Madison Square Garden triumph, Kuhn was indicted on charges of embezzlement for stealing funds from the Bund treasury and using them for various private purposes, including support for a female companion. With Kuhn's conviction and subsequent flight to Mexico to avoid incarceration, the Bund's fortunes declined rapidly; its activities were brought to an end with the American entry into World War II. Its effort to spread National Socialist ideas in the United States had been stymied by its transparent links to a foreign power. Nevertheless, it did achieve a few symbolic victories in this area, most conspicuously a joint rally with the Ku Klux Klan (at one of the Bund's New Jersey training camps) in 1940 and encounters with other American radical right groups, including such leaders as William Dudley Pelley and the Rev. Gerald Winrod.

What was clear from the brief heyday of the Bund was that, even in the 1930s, Adolf Hitler held little appeal to most Americans. Alternately seen as a madman or a clown, Hitler was always looked on with unease by Americans, whose isolationism (when considered in the light of the Depression era's absorption with more immediate concerns than European instability) precluded a close examination of the German political situation. Soon, the collective weight of negative reports from American journalists reinforced the popular view of Hitler first as a ruthless demagogue and then, after Crystalnacht, as a fanatic who headed a barbarous regime of thugs and killers.

The war put an end to the activities of the explicitly National Socialist right in America. With the indictment of a number of radical-right-wing figures (including Pelley, Winrod, and Elizabeth Dilling) on charges of sedition in 1942, Hitler's American sympathizers were suitably cowed. Although the trial would meander on for years before all charges were at last dismissed, the war had by then swept lingering pro-Hitler sympathies beyond the furthest margins of American political life.

Given this history, it is hardly surprising that when the pseudonymous John Roy Carlson wrote his undercover exposés of the American radical right, *Under Cover* (1943) and *The Plotters* (1946), the native fascists on display were a sad and pathetic lot who were collectively hardly worth the effort to keep tabs on. Indeed, in *Apostles of Discord,* the next major watchdog text to appear, in 1953, Ralph Lord Roy's diatribe against the religious elements of the American radical right contained nary a reference to serious pro-Hitler sentiment in postwar America.

This is not to say that Hitler lacked admirers on both sides of the Atlantic in the immediate postwar years. Far from it—there remained on both continents a core of ex-Nazis and Nazi sympathizers whose adoration for the Führer grew in direct proportion to the magnitude of the German defeat. Thus, for one such as Savitri Devi, Hitler had by the late 1940s already taken on a godlike stature. In her remarkable hagiography *The Lightning and the Sun,* the Third Reich emerges as the apex and the natural culmination of Aryan development, while Adolf Hitler is presented as the greatest Aryan in history:

> We like to hope that the memory of the one-before-the-last and most heroic of all our men *against time*—Adolf Hitler—will survive at least in songs and symbols. We like to hope that the lords of the age, men of his own blood and faith, will render him divine honors,

through rites full of meaning and full of potency, in the cool shade of the endless regrown forests, on the beaches, or upon inviolate mountain peaks, facing the rising sun.

Devi was not alone in these florid sentiments. Although they were both numerically and organizationally insignificant, a few true believers in the late 1940s and early 1950s began—cautiously—to reemerge. James Hartung Madole in the United States, Bruno Ludtke in Germany, Göran Assar Oredsson in Sweden, and Colin Jordan in England were a few of the most important of these early leaders. It was, however, not until the 1959 formation of George Lincoln Rockwell's American Nazi Party that uniformed National Socialists owing explicit fealty to Adolf Hitler exploded back onto the public consciousness.

The reasons for the key importance of the relative latecomer Rockwell on the present-day centrality of the figure of Adolf Hitler for the radical right are many and complex, but of greatest import is the relatively open nature of the American political system. Where most European National Socialists had to carefully tailor their message to the anti-Nazi legislation found throughout postwar Europe, the American First Amendment allowed Rockwell and company to publish explicitly National Socialist literature, parade around in authentic re-creations of Third Reich uniforms, and disseminate paeans to the memory of the Führer. This relative freedom was misinterpreted as political significance by the Europeans, whereupon the image was born of Rockwell and his American Nazi Party as being at the forefront of a global National Socialist revival. Moreover, it was on this rock that the World Union of National Socialists, with Rockwell at its head, was built.

It would be misleading to suggest that Rockwell and the American Nazi Party "rehabilitated" the dead Hitler so as to be acceptable to both the mainstream political culture and, for that matter, the radical right of the day. What Rockwell did accomplish was to throw down the gauntlet to the racialist right in a way that forced all to recognize that Hitler's legacy could not be ignored. Although both sides would be loath to admit it, the interests of Rockwell and the American Jewish community converged on this point. The Nazi regime and the Holocaust demonstrated, in a way that no amount of outreach by the Anti-Defamation League or the American Jewish Committee could, that anti-Semitism can lead to profound and deadly consequences. Indeed, after World War II, anti-Semitism in the United States came to be banished to the furthest reaches of the

American political scene, until today, as Leonard Dinnerstein notes in *Antisemitism in America:*

> Today antisemitism in the United States is neither virulent nor growing. It is not a powerful social or political force. Moreover, prejudicial comments are now beyond the bounds of respectable discourse and existing societal restraints prevent any overt antisemitic conduct except among small groups of disturbed adolescents, extremists, and powerless African-Americans (p. 243).

George Lincoln Rockwell was among the first in the American race movement to recognize the problem, and his near-deification of Adolf Hitler was one answer. Hitler, for Rockwell and for the majority of American National Socialists who followed, became a kind of religio-political savior whose life and death became a tale of selfless sacrifice with strong parallels to the life of Jesus. Few in the radical right were prepared to go so far, but all came to recognize the centrality of Hitler and the Holocaust as an obstacle to connecting with mainstream society.

From this recognition came the widespread acceptance of Holocaust revisionism and ultimately Holocaust denial throughout the Euro-American radical right from the 1970s to the present day. Holocaust denial had a number of advantages for the racialist right. Over time, it was hoped, the seeds of doubt that could be planted about the historicity of the Holocaust would grow into popular indignation at the Jews, in whose interests the "Holocaust myth" (as the far right has come to term it) was thought to be perpetrated. Internally, Holocaust denial serves an even more immediate purpose—to provide a psychological bridge that allows true believers to convince themselves that the Holocaust is a vast, conspiratorial hoax. Every member of the radical-right-wing subculture today was raised on the same popular images of Nazi brutality that we all have internalized. In the process of questioning all forms of received wisdom, which is so characteristic of the far right, the Holocaust became one more "deception" aimed at keeping the people in the dark and, in the same sense, one more psychological barrier that must be breached if the seeker hopes to grasp the radical right's esoteric "truths."

Having accepted the message of Holocaust denial and reevaluated the figure of Adolf Hitler along with the history of the Third Reich, not every seeker, it must be stressed, will accept Hitler in the same lofty terms as have the National Socialists. Hitler cultism, with its uniforms, Nazi regalia, pictures of the Führer, and its grandiose April 20th celebrations of the Führer's birth, remains very much a minority camp within the radical right, and is today the almost exclusive province of National Socialists (especially of the American variety), neo-Nazi skinheads (again, not a majority of the skinhead subculture), and a handful of other true believers on the fringes of such other belief systems as Christian Identity.

On the other hand, the popularity of Hitler—suitably reinterpreted—is on the rise throughout the radical right. In a number of guises, the figure of Hitler may be found in the literature of virtually every radical-right-wing belief system today. Much of this discussion (or idealization, depending on one's point of view) has strongly millennial overtones, with Hitler emerging as an End Time savior. This in itself is significant, for the intensity of millennial hopes attached to Hitler provides a valuable insight into the radical right's current sense of despair at ever being able, of its own volition, to right the course of a world that they see as utterly hostile to their values and beliefs. In such a situation of hopeless longing, it is not uncommon to dream of a messiah who will, at the moment when all hope seems lost, appear and miraculously lead the tiny, righteous remnant of the faithful to victory.

Thus, for example, Hitler becomes one of a line of warrior heroes to racialist Odinists, a kind of doomed prophet of the Aryan race for Identity Christians, the "greatest White man in history" for the Church of the Creator, and to Satanists a man who more than any human being in the modern world knew the secrets of the art of power (though Satanists may simply be nihilists who find Satanism a flag of convenience). This process of interpretation and reinterpretation continues unabated to this day, as Adolf Hitler and National Socialism become increasingly central to the race movement on both sides of the Atlantic, despite the paltry numbers attracted to explicit National Socialism.

Thus, in the songs and iconography of the White Power music scene and in the web sites and zines of the racist right, no less than in the pages of National Socialist publications, the visage of Adolf Hitler is literally everywhere. With so profound a change in the status of Hitler the man—from a pariah in the immediate postwar movement to his central role as a godlike figure today—it should come as no surprise that in the most radical reaches of the race movement the cult of Adolf Hitler has evolved into a religion. Thus, in a *Reuters* article of February 19, 1998, titled "Neo-Nazis Whose World Began With Hitler Detained," we read:

> Nine suspected members of a neo-Nazi network who believed the
> world began when Hitler was born have been detained in France

and Britain over death threats against Jewish personalities, police said Tuesday.

They said the international network was living in year 109, as it had made up its own calendar starting with Hitler's birth date in 1889.

Eight people were being held in France. Another, named as Herve Guttuso and belonging the group "Charlemagne Hammer Skins,'" was being held in Britain and expected to be handed over to France.

They were being investigated on suspicion of making death threats against France's Simone Veil, a former cabinet minister and ex-president of the European Parliament, and Anne Sinclair, a popular journalist married to Finance Minister Dominique Strauss-Kahn.

They were also being probed for inciting racial hatred and denying Nazi crimes against humanity, and on suspicion that they started a fire in a Jewish-owned shop in Rouen.

See also: American Nazi Party; Christian Identity; Church of the Creator; Devi, Savitri; Dilling, Elizabeth; Jordan, Colin; Ludtke, Bruno; Madole, James; Odinism; Pierce, William; Rockwell, George Lincoln; Winrod, Gerald; World Union of National Socialists.

Further reading: Hanna Arendt, *The Origins of Totalitarianism* (New York: Harvest, 1951); Leland Bell, *In Hitler's Shadow* (Port Washington, NY: Kennikat Press, 1973); Alan Bullock, *Hitler: A Study in Tyranny* (New York: Harper and Row, 1962); John Roy Carlson, *Under Cover* (New York: Dutton, 1943); John Roy Carlson, *The Plotters* (New York: Dutton, 1946); Lawrence Dennis and Maximillian St. George, *A Trial on Trial: The Great Sedition Trial of 1944* (Torrance, CA: Institute for Historical Review, 1945, 1984); Leonard Dinnerstein, *Antisemitism in America* (New York: Oxford University Press, 1994); Robert Ellwood, "Nazism as a Millennialist Movement," in Catherine Wessinger, ed., *Millennialism, Persecution and Violence* (Syracuse, NY: Syracuse University Press, forthcoming); Charles Higgham, *American Swastika* (Garden City, NY: Doubleday, 1985); Adolf Hitler, *Mein Kampf*, trans. by Ralph Manheim (Boston: Houghton Mifflin, 1971); Jeffrey Kaplan, *Radical Religion in America* (Syracuse, NY: Syracuse University Press, 1997); Jeffrey Kaplan and Leonard Weinberg, *The Emergence of a Euro-American Radical Right* (Rutgers, NJ: Rutgers University Press, 1998); Deborah Lipstadt, *Denying the Holocaust* (New York: The Free Press, 1993); Heléne Lööw, "The Swedish Racist Counterculture," in Tore Bjørgo and Rob Witte, *Racist Violence in Europe* (New York: St. Martin's Press, 1993); Heléne Lööw, "'Wir Sind Wieder Da'—From National Socialism to Militant Racial Ideology—The Swedish Racist Underground in an Historical Context," in *Strommar i tiden*, Mohamed Chaib, ed. (Göteborg, Sweden: Diadalos Forlag, 1995); Phillip Reese, *Biographical Dictionary of the*

Extreme Right (New York: Simon & Schuster, 1990); James M. Rhodes, *The Hitler Movement: A Modern Millenarian Revolution* (Stanford: Hoover Institution Press, 1980); Ralph Lord Roy, *Apostles of Discord* (Boston: Beacon Press, 1953); Gaetano Salvemini, *Italian Fascist Activities in the United States* (New York: Center for Migration Studies, 1977); Morris Schonbach, *Native American Fascism During the 1930s and 1940s* (New York: Garland Publishing, 1985); Fredrick J. Simonelli, "The World Union of National Socialists and the Post-War Transatlantic Nazi Revival," in Jeffrey Kaplan and Tore Bjørgo, *Nation and Race* (Boston: Northeastern University Press, 1998); Frederick J. Simonelli, *American Fuehrer: George Lincoln Rockwell and the American Nazi Party* (Champaign: University of Illinois Press, 1999); Gerald B. Winrod, *Hitler in Prophecy* (Wichita, KS: Defender Publishers, 1933).

Richard Kelly Hoskins   *See* Phineas Priesthood.

Institute for Historical Review   *See* Carto, Willis.

INTERNET RECRUITING   The advent of cheap, easy access to the international computer network known as the Internet has accorded previously voiceless individuals and groups a powerful medium to express their rigid opinions to a worldwide audience. Adherents of the White Power movement were among the first to maximize the potential of Internet access for recruiting and propaganda.

The Internet is composed of several elements, the most important of which is the World Wide Web. The Web allows anyone with a "webpage" to express their thoughts to anyone anywhere who wishes to view such a page, more cheaply, more quickly, and often with greater impact than other forms of advertising. Composed of tens of thousands of sites, the Web is rapidly changing the method and character of individual and business communication.

Reuben Logsdon's Texas-based "CyberHate" (later the "Aryan Crusader's Library") and Don Black's Florida-based "Stormfront White Nationalist Resource" page appeared first, in early 1995. The latter continues to be the most influential of White Power pages. By the end of 1995, the National Alliance, White Aryan Resistance, Aryan Nations, and other groups recognized the potential of the Web, and created their own sites. Of particular note is the rapid proliferation of skinhead-oriented and White Power music sites, the most important of which is the Detroit-based Resistance Records site. Resistance and its imitators peddle hate- and violence-themed music and wares worldwide on their webpages, largely to youth.

Today, there are dozens of individuals and groups who have published webpages, of varying degrees and composition of racial philosophy, technical sophistication, and graphical artistry, but all share the same racist bent. Most work together for their common benefit, usually "linking" to others; that is, each site offers the addresses of its colleagues' pages.

On the Internet, everyone can have an equal voice. Besides the Web, this can be seen most clearly on the Usenet network. Usenet comprises thousands of newsgroups, each in essence an electronic memo board about a specific topic, where people may freely discuss, argue, or often exchange insults about a myriad of topics, from food, to politics, to music, to, of course, computers. Most newsgroups are "unmoderated" (unregulated), their proper functioning dependent on the self-discipline of participants.

Dan Gannon, a Holocaust "revisionist" and neo-Nazi sympathizer who started to be noticed in 1991, is known for his early work in spreading anti-Semitic propaganda far and wide. Gannon was often engaged in "spamming"—excessive cross-posting of material to inappropriate newsgroups. Eventually, Gannon resigned himself to operating his Oregon-based BBS, which archives much of his material, but his efforts caused much discussion regarding the right to air highly controversial views without restraint, and led to the beginnings of organized anti-Nazi activism on the Internet, most notably the creation of Ken McVay's British Columbia–based "Holocaust and Fascism Archives" (now the "Nizkor Project" web site).

Gannon was a beginning, with even greater White Power efforts to come. In 1993, organized racist activism arrived with Arthur LeBouthillier, Milton John Kleim, Jr., and Jason Smith.

Kleim took the lead in developing Usenet into one of the White Power movement's most profitable propaganda media, outlining his plans in a now infamous essay, "On Tactics and Strategy for Usenet." Kleim and his associates became seemingly omnipresent in 1995 and early 1996. In late 1995, in response to the O. J. Simpson verdict, Kleim, White Aryan Resistance's Wyatt Kaldenberg, George Burdi (aka George Eric Hawthorne) of Resistance Records, and others undertook an intensive but makeshift recruiting campaign on the alt.fan.oj-simpson newsgroup, appealing to the resentment of many toward the not-guilty verdict by arguing that the decision was based on racial grounds.

In January 1996, Kleim single-handedly created a massive Internet freedom of speech controversy by proposing the creation of rec.music.white-power. The proposal, admitted by the author to be a publicity stunt, was utterly defeated: nearly 600 "yes" votes vs. over 33,000 "no" votes. However, severe damage was done to the "good-will" basis of Usenet newsgroup creation. Ironically, soon after the results were announced, Kleim denounced the movement, and eventually renounced neo-Nazism in mid-1996. In his wake, other individuals, such as the National Alliance's Kevin Alfred Strom, and the crude-penned Matt Giwer, have not let racist Usenet activism fall by the wayside.

Electronic mail is one of the most accessible of Internet conveniences, and for White Power activists, it is indispensable. Several electronic mail lists, such as the semipublic Stormfront mailing list, and private lists, such as Harold Covington's "NSNet" and Ernst Zundel and Ingrid Rimland's "Zgram" e-mail list, are used for information and news distribution, and, in the case of Stormfront, discussion of movement issues. Unique among White Power mailing lists is the "Aryan News Agency" list, founded by Kleim in 1993, and now run by a pseudonymous editor in conjunction with the Stormfront web site. Until pressure on its Internet provider forced the list off the net, ANA distributed daily news bulletins compiled from many sources.

In the past, File Transfer Protocol (FTP) sites were instrumental for recruiting for a short time, but have been replaced by the Web. The National Alliance and the Colorado-based Scriptures for America were the first groups to use an FTP site.

Internet Relay Chat (IRC) is used by many White Power activists, but it is not a particularly effective vehicle for recruitment. IRC "channels" mainly serve as virtual arenas for social gathering.

Undoubtedly, the Internet has enabled White Power adherents to appeal directly to prospective recruits and sympathizers, as never before. The youthful nature of most Net users, a large percentage of them college students, makes the Net fertile ground for White Power recruiters. Because of this, antiracist groups have taken special notice of the pervasive character of White Power activities on the Net.

Rabbi Abraham Cooper of the Los Angeles-based Simon Wiesenthal Center has been most outspoken against White Power expression on the Net, calling for Internet service providers to refuse access via their systems to racists. His campaign has received a mixed reception. While some members of the public stridently agreed, many others, and most members of the Internet community, vehemently opposed such efforts, and suggested that complete freedom of expression for racists does more damage to their cause than censorship.

Regardless of the effectiveness of White Power recruitment via the Internet, the presence of racist and anti-Semitic views in the new medium will continue to offer challenges to both the Net community and society at large, calling into question race and ethnic relations as well as issues of freedom of speech and expression. The

Internet has changed the face of telecommunications and, with it, every element of society that depends on effectively communicating with others. As long as the Net has few restrictions on freedom of expression, White Power supporters will be found using it.

—Milton John Kleim, Jr.,
former Internet recruiter for the National Alliance

See also: Aryan Nations; Beam, Louis; Black, Don; Covington, Harold; Hawthorne, George Eric; National Alliance; Peters, Pete; Scriptures for America; White Aryan Resistance.

Further reading: Anti-Defamation League, *The Web of Hate: Extremists Exploit the Internet* (New York: ADL, 1996); Les Back, Michael Keith, and John Solomos, "Racism on the Internet: Mapping Neo-Fascist Subcultures in Cyberspace," in Jeffrey Kaplan and Tore Bjørgo, eds., *Nation and Race: The Developing Euro-American Racist Subculture* (Boston, MA: Northeastern University Press, 1998); Milton John Kleim, Jr., "On Strategy and Tactics for the Usenet," full e-text version archived at http://www.io.com/~wlp/aryan-page/tac.html and short version available from Nizkor archives at http://www.nizkor.org/.

J

COLIN JORDAN   Today Colin Jordan operates on the most distant fringes of the British National Socialist scene. This is a remarkable state of affairs for a man whose National Socialist pedigree dates to the years of World War II and before. The story of Jordan's descent from the center of British fascist politics and the inner circles of the World Union of National Socialists (WUNS) is a remarkable tale of bad decisions, inexplicable actions, and the divisiveness common to the far right subculture on both sides of the Atlantic.

Colin Jordan's National Socialist roots run deep. His pedigree may be traced back to Oswald Moseley's prewar British Union of Fascists and National Socialists and, in particular, Arnold Leese's more rabidly anti-Semitic Imperial Fascist League. Leese, who set up the League in 1928, was one of the most extreme anti-Semites of the era. His writings, which cover any number of charges against the Jews—most notably the revival of charges of Jewish ritual murder—were of such influence on Jordan that today Jordan's newsletter, *Gothic Ripples,* borrows the name of Leese's own mimeographed vehicle. Leese's writings are still available and serve as an important source for the racialist right wing in both Europe and the United States.

Although Jordan is best known for his own National Socialist Movement, which he founded in 1962, it would be no exaggeration to say that every explicitly National Socialist organization and most of the more generically racialist right-wing groups in Britain from the early 1960s to date owe their existence, directly or indirectly, to Colin Jordan. Thus, from the National Front to the British Movement, the ideological children of Jordan are ubiquitous on the British scene. That Jordan would break with each movement, and that he today is held in general contempt by the milieu he did so much to found, speaks volumes both to the volatility of the radical right and to Jordan's own unsuitability for a position of leadership.

Jordan's moment in the sun in the international movement came with the founding of the World Union of National Socialists, which resulted from the Cotswold Conference in 1962. Jordan was at this point the key player, and the choice of Great Britain for the conference reflected this importance. It was Jordan who, putting aside his initial distaste for America and Americans, spotted a rising young star of the movement in George Lincoln Rockwell, whose American Nazi Party was established only in 1959. It was Jordan who introduced Rockwell to Savitri Devi and to Germany's Bruno Ludtke, who together with Jordan formed the backbone of the World Union of National Socialists. And it was Jordan who was selected as the first chairman of the World Union.

Jordan, however, proved to be a better subordinate than a leader in his own rite, and he was forced to cede the leadership to Rockwell after a series of jail sentences made his running the organization impractical. Soon, Jordan's relationship to the dynamic Rockwell was one of sycophantic follower to charismatic leader. When Rockwell was assassinated in 1967, Jordan was the natural choice to reclaim the leadership of WUNS, because Ludtke was constrained by the anti-Nazification laws of his native Germany and Devi, as a woman, could not aspire to leadership in the National Socialist world of the 1960s. This was not to be, however, and Rockwell's American successor, Matt Koehl of the renamed National Socialist White People's Party, claimed Rockwell's mantle of leadership. Koehl proved to be no more capable of leading a world movement than he was of commanding an American one, and throughout the 1970s, the World Union of National Socialists faded into impotence.

Despite the ultimate failure of the World Union, the reports of the Cotswold meeting caught the attention of a wealthy and aristocratic Frenchwoman, the Comtesse R. H. de Caumont La Force—Françoise Dior. The couple were duly wed in October 1963 in a flashy National Socialist ceremony that, among numerous toasts and Nazi salutes, featured a revival of an ancient Germanic blood ceremony, which was described in a 1963 issue of Rockwell's *Stormtrooper:*

> The couple took their places behind a table draped with a Swastika and on which stood two red lighted candles.
>
>   Each in turn made to the other a declaration of Aryan descent and racial fitness, and a pledge of loyalty as man and wife.
>
>   Each then made a small incision on the upper part of the ring finger and the two fingers were held together for a moment to symbolize the union of blood. A drop of the blood so mixed was then allowed to fall on the blank fore page of a copy of "Mein Kampf" belonging to the couple.

Then each in turn placed a ring engraved with a Swastika on the finger of the other.

The couple joined hands and the marriage was declared as enacted.

The gathering gave the National Socialist salute, and the Horst Wessel anthem was played.

The wedded couple were toasted in mead, the ancient drink of the Nordic peoples.

The marriage brought Colin Jordan not only a companion and life partner, but financial security. In the event, even this did not save Jordan from the minor scandal that, in National Socialist circles, undid him.

Politics did not go well for Jordan in the decades of the 1960s and 1970s. He was imprisoned intermittently in the early 1960s for his political activities, forcing him to rely increasingly on his subordinates to keep going both the British National Socialist Movement and the British activities of the World Union of National Socialists. This brought to the fore such future stars of the British radical right (and, ironically, implacable opponents of Colin Jordan) as John Tyndall, Denis Pirie, and Peter Ling. Tyndall and Martin Webster split from the National Socialist Movement in 1967 to form the more effective National Front.

Jordan reorganized the National Socialist Movement itself in 1968 as the British Movement, but by 1974 he had been forced to step down in favor of Michael McLaughlin. The split was far less than amicable. It was Jordan, however, who provided McLaughlin with the sword with which to do in the movement's founder, and Jordan further obliged his enemies by taking a running start and skewering himself in a manner guaranteed to bring maximum public humiliation. It seems that, for reasons best known only to him, Jordan was arrested on charges of simple shoplifting. Worse, Jordan's booty was comprised of lingerie—to wit, pairs of women's panties. Why the financially secure Jordan would resort to this method of shopping was a mystery to the British movement, but soon the internal correspondence of many of the faithful had brought to Jordan the nickname of "Knickers Stealer," and the McLaughlin faction of the British Movement had a field day with the news. The label stuck, dogging Jordan's ill-fated campaigns in the 1970s to seize back control of the British Movement and, indeed, to reenter the British National Socialist scene that had, in truth, long since left him behind.

The last two decades have not been notably kinder to Colin Jordan. His voluminous National Socialist writings span almost the last half century, and even today, in his twilight years, Jordan remains productive. Each year, on Hitler's birthday, Jordan updates and reprints his "National Socialism: Then and Now: A Philosophical Appraisal." His *Gothic Ripples* newsletter still appears regularly, increasingly with an Odinist flavor and in a form not unlike James Hartung Madole's long-running "New Atlantis" series in his 1970s era *National Renaissance Bulletin*. And in 1997 Jordan had completed a new book, *Merrie England 2000*. The book is currently available only on the World Wide Web, because, according to its author's mocking "Dedication":

> This book is dedicated to Gerald Kaufman, Jewish Member of Parliament for the U.K., ancestrally from Poland, who not only in his policies typifies trends towards an England in the year 2,000 [sic] as depicted in it, but has taken a lead in trying to prevent its publication by penal action against its author for his writings.
>
> In June 1991, acting merely on a complaint by Kaufman, police invaded and ransacked the author's home, and seized a copy of the first draft of this book. Thereafter, with the necessary scrutiny and consent of the Attorney General, a prosecution was started against him for some other literature seized. This was at the outset suspended by a High Court injunction which the author obtained, pending a Judicial Review by that Court of the legality of the warrant used for the raid, leave for which Review he had previously applied for and had been granted. When that Judicial Review was about to take place in November 1992, the police finally at the last moment, to avoid a High Court decision of censure, admitted that the warrant was invalid, and the search and seizure consequently unlawful; and abandoned the prosecution, agreeing to return all of the property seized and since then retained.
>
> The Attorney General—the highest law officer in the land appointed by the government of the day—thus stands condemned for having sanctioned under Jewish pressure a prosecution of a political opponent for expressing freedom of thought, an attempt at suppression based moreover on what he must have known was an illegal raid. Such was the threat to freedom in 1992.
>
> What will it be like in the year 2,000 ? [sic]

There is little doubt that Colin Jordan will still be with us to see for himself what the new millennium brings.

See also: American Nazi Party; Devi, Savitri; Koehl, Matt; Ludtke, Bruno; Madole, James; National Socialist White People's Party; Odinism; Rockwell, George Lincoln; World Union of National Socialists.

Further reading: Colin Jordan, *Merrie England 2000* (self-published, 1997); Ciarán Maoláin, *The Radical Right: A World Directory* (Santa Barbara, CA: ABC-CLIO, 1987); Fredrick J. Simonelli, "The World Union of National Socialists and the Post-War Transatlantic Nazi Revival," in Jeffrey Kaplan and Tore Bjørgo, *Nation and Race* (Boston: Northeastern University Press, 1998); Frederick J. Simonelli, *American Fuehrer: George Lincoln Rockwell and the American Nazi Party* (Champaign: University of Illinois Press, 1999).

JOST   In the 1980s and early 1990s, Jost led the National Socialist Kindred, a movement that sought to meld National Socialism and racialist Odinism into an ideology that would attract similarly disaffected individuals dedicated to the creation of a separatist community in the mountains of Northern California. The idea of a National Socialist haven was hardly new. Donald Clerkin of the Euro-American Alliance had dreamed of such a National Socialist enclave even before the formation of the Aryan Nations. The dream has been shared by such high-profile figures as Rick Cooper of the National Socialist Vanguard, whose vision of a community known as Wolfstadt is the stated reason for the group's existence. And most recently, we have seen the efforts in Britain involving the Reichsfolk, the Order of the Nine Angles, and the Order of Balder to form communal separatist groups that would adhere to National Socialist ideals. Jost tried to bring these dreams into reality.

It was not to be. Jost died of a heart attack in late 1996, while still in his early 50s, and, out of deference to his family's wishes, this entry will not use his birth name. By 1996, he had already abandoned the National Socialist Kindred and the communal dream in favor of a remarkable theology that brought New Age ideas into the already heady mix of Odinism and National Socialism to form Arya Kriya, a holistic belief system that combined health faddism, meditation techniques, and racialist ideology into a kind of correspondence course. At the time of his death, Arya Kriya had subscribers throughout the United States and was being translated into Swedish by Tommy Rydén for distribution in Scandinavia.

The best source for Jost's biography is Jost himself. Jost's "Aryan Destiny: Back to the Land," which is presented in full in the "Resources" section, describes in vivid detail the author's alienation after his return to America from two tours in Vietnam, his sense of culture shock when confronted with the counterculture of the early 1970s, and the withdrawal of Jost and his family from the multiracial city they lived in to the mountains of northern California. There, in rural isolation, Jost describes the idyllic life of the day—a time in which alienated right wingers and equally alienated hippies coexisted in harmony, united by their shared disdain for the American establishment. This harmony would be shattered by the rise of marijuana cultivators whose wars with each other—and with the federal government—would shatter forever the live-and-let-live atmosphere that Jost prized so highly. It was then that the National Socialist Kindred was born, and that the dream of the longed-for folk community of Volksberg was offered to the National Socialist faithful.

As Jost and his family patiently laid the foundation for the Volksberg community, he published a large number of tracts under the imprimatur of the National Socialist Kindred. The NS Kindred too republished the work of such foreign neo-Nazis as the Aryan Nations' regular Manfred Roeder, as well as pieces by imprisoned veterans of the Order such as David Lane.

Jost's writings can be divided roughly into three categories; those dealing with National Socialism, and particularly with the person of Adolf Hitler, who in Jost's formulation is raised to the level of the gods themselves; religious tracts on racialist Odinism; and, increasingly through the 1990s, earnest exhortations toward self-improvement that would point the way towards Arya Kriya. One point should be noted, however. Jost's Odinism was deeply felt and quite sincere. But the NS Kindred was very much apart from the organized Ásatrú community. This isolation may have contributed in large measure to Jost's drift out of Odinism into Arya Kriya.

With the failure of the National Socialist Kindred to attract the quality of adherents to the Volksberg community that would have made the experiment viable, Jost in his final years turned inward. His concentration was increasingly on Arya Kriya, a kind of Aryan yoga system that concentrated on diet, meditation techniques, and spiritual self-discovery. Even this experiment did not go far, however, before Jost suffered a fatal heart attack and died in 1996. What will survive of his work remains, at this writing, an open question.

See also: Arya Kriya; Aryan Nations; Cooper, Rick; Hitler, Adolf; Lane, David; National Socialist Kindred; National Socialist Vanguard; Odinism; Order; Order of Nine Angles; Reichsfolk; Rydén, Tommy.

Further reading: Jost, "Aryan Destiny: Back To The Land," (undated e-text distributed by the National Socialist Kindred); Jost, *The Essentials of Mein Kampf* (Volksberg, CA: NS Kindred, 1988); Jost, "Love: An Eternal law of Nature and first Tenet of National Socialism" (undated flyer from the National Socialist Kindred); Jost, "ARYAN DESTINY: Why Hitler had to be Overcome" (pamphlet from the National Socialist Kindred, 1989); Jost, "Arya Kriya: Vetenskapen om påskyndad evolution" (undated poster issued by the DeVries Institute, 1989); Jeffrey Kaplan and Leonard Weinberg, *The Emergence of a Euro-American Radical Right* (Rutgers, NJ: Rutgers University Press, 1998).

KEEP SWEDEN SWEDISH   The group named Keep Sweden Swedish (Bavara Sverige Svenskt or BSS) was a small anti-immigrant organization that was the beginning of the Swedish parliamentary parties formed in the late 1970s to oppose (non-White) immigration. The BSS was in essence an interest group formed to push for a national referendum on immigration. It never coalesced into a political party and never grew very large, with an estimated 300 members by 1984. Nonetheless, passing through BSS ranks were a number of Swedish racialists such as Tommy Rydén who were destined for careers in both the parliamentary and the extra-parliamentary far right.

See also: Rydén, Tommy.

Further reading: Jeffrey Kaplan and Leonard Weinberg, *The Emergence of a Euro-American Radical Right* (Rutgers, NJ: Rutgers University Press, 1998); Heléne Lööw, "'Wir Sind Wieder Da'—From National Socialism to Militant Racial Ideology—The Swedish Racist Underground In An Historical Context," in *Strommar i tiden*, Mohamed Chaib, ed. (Göteborg, Sweden: Diadalos Forlag, 1995).

MATTHIAS "MATT" KOEHL   If gold watches were awarded to Nazis for longevity of service, Matt Koehl would be among the first of the generation that came into the movement under George Lincoln Rockwell to receive such a golden handshake. While a few others in the first generation of American postwar National Socialists are still active in leadership positions, only Koehl and William Pierce may lay claim to an uninterrupted fealty to National Socialism to the exclusion of all other ideologies on offer to the radical-right faithful.

By his own reckoning, Koehl's National Socialist consciousness dates back to 1948 when, as a 13-year-old in the Milwaukee public schools, he loudly took the unpopular position that Hitler was the good guy in the war. In that same capsule biography, which ran as an installment of a regular feature titled "Know Your Party Officers" in the American Nazi Party's *Stormtrooper* magazine (December–January 1965), Koehl recounted his years as a student in Milwaukee and Chicago, as well as his brief and unsatisfactory experience in the insurance industry and in the Marine Corps Reserve.

Koehl's early interest in Hitler had by adulthood blossomed into a fanatical adherence to National Socialism in its classic 1930s German form, a reverence for Adolf Hitler that assumed cultic proportions, and a powerful anti-Semitism. Armed with these beliefs, Koehl while still a teenager began his search for a comfortable niche in an American racist right that still retained its wartime distaste for Nazism.

Upon his graduation from high school, Koehl was at last free to travel. Like the next two generations of American National Socialists, Koehl looked to the East Coast for some organization that would give him the chance to see real action in the company of fellow true believers. His first such experience was with James Madole's National Renaissance Party in New York. There he became a uniformed guard for the diminutive Madole, whose anti-Semitic street corner invective had a sure knack of inciting fights in which the orator invariably came out the worst for the experience. Koehl remained for about a year with the NRP before returning to Chicago around 1953. There, he attended college, found work, and continued his anti-Semitic activities in a number of largely mail-order movements, most notably Ed Fields's States' Rights Party.

In 1960, Commander Rockwell made his first recruiting trip to Chicago on behalf of the then barely one-year-old American Nazi Party. The young Koehl was one of the first to meet with him there, and Koehl's life would be forever changed. He quickly joined the ANP, donned the Stormtrooper uniform, and was named head of the key Chicago unit, where he distinguished himself for his loyalty and steadfastness in the face of universal public hostility.

Meanwhile, the situation in Rockwell's Arlington, Virginia, headquarters was going from bad to very bad to very much worse, as poverty, infighting, and defections increasingly commanded the Commander's attention. When National Party Secretary Daniel Burros defected and began to publish anti-Rockwell broadsides in his journal, *Kill!,* in 1962, Captain Koehl was recalled from Chicago to assume the key post of party secretary. He was then promoted to major, which would be his rank upon the formal dissolution of the American Nazi Party in 1966. By then, Deputy

Commander Alan Welch had resigned and Koehl had become Rockwell's second in command.

1966 was a key year in the history of American National Socialism. In that year, a highly publicized march in Chicago turned violent and brought the party much needed visibility, and in that year too Rockwell gave his famous interview in *Playboy* magazine. But by then, the Commander had come to recognize the futility of attempting to turn Nazism into a mass movement in America. Thus, over Koehl's opposition, Rockwell forced through a fractious party congress the dissolution of the American Nazi Party in favor of the National Socialist White People's Party (NSWPP)—a name chosen in conscious imitation of the highly successful civil rights organization, the National Association for the Advancement of Colored People. Within a year, however, Rockwell was dead, assassinated by a disaffected Nazi named John Patler. Koehl found himself in command of the NSWPP. It was Koehl who gave the eulogy for the fallen Commander, and thus it was Koehl who found himself in the position of unchallenged leadership. This rare moment of unity would not last.

Ironically, Koehl's tenure saw both the high-water mark and the functional end of the National Socialist movement in America. Always minuscule, the ranks of the "organized" American National Socialist community attracted, in the immediate post-Rockwell period, a small but steady stream of the committed and the curious. Koehl thus appeared to outside observers to work on two concurrent tracks: a highly successful effort to anger and alienate the old guard while simultaneously leaving the new recruits with such a bad taste in their mouths that many left the movement, and others became lifelong enemies of the new Commander. It was by all accounts a singular performance.

The roster of those harried from the National Socialist White People's Party reads like a virtual "Who's Who" of American National Socialism. William Pierce, James Warner, Ricky Cooper, Harold Covington, Joseph Tommasi, James Mason—the list of victims of Koehl-era purges and angry resignations could go on for pages. Part of the problem was Koehl's unbending adherence to the leadership principle as propounded in classic fascist doctrine. Koehl had after all remained loyal to Rockwell during his tenure, and he expected his own subordinates to do the same. To the rank and file, however, to paraphrase a mordant commentary on Vice President Dan Quayle's fixation on John Kennedy: the veterans knew George Lincoln Rockwell, and Matt Koehl was decidedly no

Rockwell. Thus, for example, in December 1968 the California branch of the party pooled their meager resources to fly Koehl out to solve the divisive conflict that pitted the California leader, Ralph Forbes, against Alan Vincent and core American Nazi Party member James Warner. It was Koehl's stubborn insistence on the primacy of the leadership principle, rather than the clear evidence of Forbes's inability to lead the group, that moved Koehl to support Forbes, a decision that split the West Coast branch of the party. This atomization is replicated on a national scale in the world of National Socialism to the present day. Similarly, at party headquarters in Virginia, a succession of party officers came and went with monotonous regularity, each blasting Koehl as he stomped out the door (save for one, Dominic Lewitzke, who went quietly, feet first, having committed suicide in party headquarters).

Koehl fared no better with Rockwell's dearest project, the World Union of National Socialists, which sought to unite National Socialists throughout the world under his leadership. As with the National Socialist White People's Party, Koehl attempted in vain to assume the Commander's mantle of leadership over the far-flung leaders of the World Union of National Socialists. And, not unlike the NSWPP, the World Union would carry on in a zombie-like fashion long after the breath of life had departed the corpse.

It was during this period too that Koehl was forced to battle long-standing rumors of his homosexuality. The rumors have never been proven, but they have been repeated so often in both conversation and in print over the last two decades that they have come to be virtual articles of faith in the American National Socialist community, despite the fact that Koehl has lived with a woman, Barbara von Goetz, for many years.

The 1980s were hardly kind to Koehl and the National Socialist White People's Party. In 1982, the Internal Revenue Service foreclosed on the American Nazi Party's Arlington, Virginia, headquarters. Koehl responded with a crash fund-raising drive and a move to a piece of rural property in his native Wisconsin, which was pitched as a new and more secure party headquarters, but which from the beginning seems to have been intended as more of a Matt Koehl retirement home.

The 1980s would see constant mass-mailing appeals for funds under this and a variety of other guises as the National Socialist White People's Party increasing took on the look of a second-rate televangelism ministry that was always falling just short of the funds needed to stay on the air. Koehl sold literature, dreams, and promises, but it was his bizarre "Victory Bonds" scam that may be seen as classic Koehl.

Koehl, who unlike most American National Socialists could remember the wartime success of government bond drives, applied these lessons to the National Socialist White People's Party and offered worthless bonds for sale, bonds that would be redeemed at a handsome profit after the party's assumption of power! While it speaks volumes for how tenuous was the grasp on reality of those who made the investment, Koehl once again proved the prescience of P. T. Barnum's mordant estimation of the American consumer, and money was raised. One such unlucky investor, former National Secretary Ricky Cooper, sued to recover some $888. The suit was unsuccessful, but it did have the effect of bringing the operation to the attention of the Securities and Exchange Commission, which promptly put a stop to it.

Koehl responded by changing the name of the National Socialist White People's Party to the New Order and withdrawing deeper into his semiretirement in Wisconsin. Unlike the controversy surrounding Rockwell's transformation of the American Nazi Party into the National Socialist White People's Party, the emergence of the New Order went largely unremarked. No one, it seems, really cared any more.

Today, the New Order puts out the *NS Bulletin,* issues occasional fund-raising appeals, and keeps Koehl's 1960s-era writings in circulation. These include a number of rather lightweight theoretical pieces such as his "Some Guidelines for the Development of the National Socialist Movement" and his 1967 eulogy for the Commander. Koehl's primary legacy, however, lies less in his contributions to American National Socialism than in his example of survival in the vortex of a movement famous for its tendency to devour its own.

See also: American Nazi Party; Burros, Daniel; Cooper, Rick; Covington, Harold; Forbes, Ralph; Hitler, Adolf; Madole, James; Mason, James; National Socialist White People's Party; Pierce, William; Rockwell, George Lincoln; Tommasi, Joseph; Warner, James; World Union of National Socialists.

Further reading: John George and Laird Wilcox, *American Extremists, Supremacists, Klansmen, Communists and Others* (Buffalo, NY: Prometheus Books, 1996); George Lincoln Rockwell, *This Time the World!* (Arlington, VA: Parliament House, 1963); George Lincoln Rockwell, *White Power* (n.p., 1967, 1977); Frederick J. Simonelli, "The World Union of National Socialists and Post-War Transatlantic Nazi Revival," in Jeffrey

Kaplan and Tore Bjørgo, eds., *Nation and Race: The Developing Euro-American Racist Subculture* (Boston: Northeastern University Press, 1998); Frederick J. Simonelli, *American Fuehrer: George Lincoln Rockwell and the American Nazi Party* (Champaign: University of Illinois Press, 1999).

KREATIVISTENS KYRKA   The Kreativistens Kyrka was founded in 1988 by Tommy R. Rydén as the Swedish chapter of the Church of the Creator (COTC). Rydén was sentenced to four months in jail in 1991 for distributing the COTC's English language material to the public. The Kreativistens Kyrka later changed its name to the Ben Klassen Academy and the Reorganized Kreativistens Kyrka, because of conflicts with the COTC leadership after Klassen's 1990 retirement. The Kreativistens Kyrka in all its forms always remained loyal to Klassen, who they said "came as a light in the darkness." Ben Klassen in turn praised Rydén in his last book, *Trials, Tribulations and Triumphs*. The Kreativistens Kyrka was dissolved in 1995 due to a lack of members and problems related to the mother church in the United States, but some of its material is still sold through a project called the DeVries Institute, which is named after the author of the COTC book *Salubrious Living*.

—Tommy Rydén, Swedish race activist

See also: Church of the Creator; Klassen, Ben; Rydén, Tommy.

Further reading: Ben Klassen, *Trials, Tribulations and Triumphs* (East Peoria, IL: COTC, 1993); Heléne Lööw, "Racist Violence and Criminal Behavior in Sweden: Myths and Reality," in Tore Bjørgo, ed., *Terror from the Extreme Right* (London: Frank Cass & Co., 1995); Tommy Rydén, "Kreativistens Kyrka, en kort introduktion" [The Church of the Creator, a short introduction] (booklet, no date); "De utvaldas skara" [The chosen ones] (flier from the Reorganized Church).

OLE KROGSTAD   A leading Norwegian rightist activist, Ole Krogstad in 1983 became the secretary of Nasjonalungdommmen, the youth organization of Nasjonalt folkeparti [National People's Party]. In 1985, Krogstad was charged with taking part in the planning of a bomb attack on a Muslim mosque. He was remanded into custody for four months, but was set free since there was no clear evidence against him, and he was never sentenced for the bombing.

However, he was sentenced to four months for illegal possession of weapons, handing over weapons to persons under the age of 18, having fired dynamite outside the Immigrant office in Oslo, and having smeared slogans on Jewish tombstones.

In 1987, he started Bootboys, a "comrade club for skinheads," and he was the editor of the skinhead fanzine *Bootboys*. Krogstad has been the main leading figure of the skinhead part of the rightist underground. However, he has never been the sole leader of the underground. The reason for this is that the underground is led collectively by several figures who coordinate their efforts. Krogstad's task has been to organize trips to Oi-rock concerts in Sweden, as well as being a front figure during confrontations with militant antifascists.

Krogstad believes that the world is ruled by ZOG (the Zionist Occupation Government). In the early 1990s, he labeled himself a radical nationalist, whereas he currently refers to himself as a National Socialist, albeit somewhat less militantly than previously.

Krogstad was a personal friend, and a loyal follower, of former Skrewdriver vocalist Ian Stewart Donaldson. In 1995, he started his own White Power band called Vidkuns Venner [the friends of Vidkun]. He had wanted to call it Rinnans Band, after Henry Oliver Rinnan, a Norwegian who had worked as an executioner for the German Nazis during their occupation of Norway. As a result of Rinnan's family threatening to sue Krogstad for using this name, Krogstad chose the name Vidkuns Venner instead, after Vidkun Quisling, the head of Nasjonal samling [National Unification], the Norwegian National Socialist Party during the 1930s and 1940s.

Today Krogstad's main task is to distribute White Power CDs, patches, posters, and other ideological material through his company, Bootboys Records.

—Katrine Fangen, University of Oslo

See also: Skinheads (Origins and Music); Zionist Occupation Government.

Further reading: Attakk No. 1 (February 1983); *Bootboys* No. 9 (1990); Katrine Fangen, "Living out our Ethnic Instincts: Ideological Beliefs Among Right-Wing Activists in Norway," in Jeffrey Kaplan and Tore Bjørgo, *Brotherhoods of Nation and Race: The Emergence of a Euro-American Racist Subculture* (Boston: Northeastern University Press, 1998); Katrine Fangen, "Skinheads I rødt, hvitt og blått En sosiologisk studie fra innsiden" [Skinheads in red, white, and blue: A sociological study from inside] (1994).

Fritz Kuhn   *See* Hitler, Adolf.

VÄINÖ KUISMA   The Patriotic Right, a far-right-wing religio-political movement centered in Lahti, Finland, is led by Väinö Kuisma. Despite the presence of a White Power music label named *Pro Patria* and an active skinhead subculture centered in Turku, there is comparatively little radical-right-wing activity in Finland. Kuisma's movement is therefore extremely small. But like the National Renaissance Party of James Hartung Madole in the United States in the 1960s and 1970s, the remarkable religious and occult explorations of Kuisma and the core membership in the Patriotic Right are worthy of consideration in these pages. More-over, unlike the colorless Madole, Kuisma does have a physical presence, which he uses to advantage in gaining public attention for his tiny movement, together with an ideology with deeper roots in Finnish culture than Madole's forays into modern Satanism did with U.S. culture.

It is somewhat surprising for the founder of a folkish movement to have had his moment of conversion in, of all places, Los Angeles. But it was during a stay in that epicenter of plastic Americana in the 1970s that Väinö Kuisma's awakening to the richness of his own Finnish heritage took place. Armed with this new vision, Kuisma returned to his native Lahti and underwent an intense course of study that focused first and foremost on the Finnish national epic, *The Kelevala*. *The Kelevala* is an epic poem (some 650 pages of text in a recent English translation) that was first published in its entirety in 1849 by Elias Lönnrot as the crowning achievement of the Finnish romantic revival. Based on the oral traditions of the Kerelian region of Finland, *The Kelevala* is an epic myth that recounts the cultural history of Finland from the creation of the world through the Golden Age of Finnish culture as seen through the eyes of a quasidivine character, Väinämöinen.

Kuisma became deeply enamored of the poem, finding esoteric and exoteric (hidden and open) meanings in the text that, he believed, only a native Finn could fully comprehend. Through his study of *Kelevala,* Kuisma created a theology and an evolving set of rituals based not only on the poem's text, but also on the paintings that accompanied the original Finnish editions of the poem, and eventually on such other aspects of Finnish culture as the use of Sibelius's musical suite *Finlandia* as a meditative tool.

Kuisma's studies took him in other directions as well, and his early political endeavors took on some occult aspects of German National Socialism, as recounted in the eccentric literature that has grown from this aspect of the Third Reich. From this convergence of Finnish folk mysticism and occult National Socialism was born Kuisma's Aryan German Brotherhood (AGV). The AGV was nothing if not colorful. Black shirts with the AVG logo, posters, stickers, and literature in the black-and-white, German National Socialist–derived symbolism did capture a good deal of attention in a country that has had little far-right activity in the postwar era. Internally, Kuisma and his core adherents continued to explore the occult path through ever-more-elaborate rituals, and the native shamanism of Kuisma's native Kerelia made its appearance in the core leadership as well.

Soon, television cameras appeared, and a brief documentary segment of the AGV's activities was broadcast to the nation. This much-needed publicity was a mixed blessing at best, however. While Kuisma stood out with a body builder's physique and an ascetic lifestyle that would be the envy of radical-right leaders in countries more amenable to far-right politics than Finland, his band of followers left a more comic impression. Indeed, two more mismatched partners would be hard to imagine.

One of these erstwhile adherents was rotund, coarse, and possessed of a prominent, bright-red nose that was the result of decades of chronic alcoholism. Playing Bud Abbot to this character's Lou Costello was an equally bizarre figure—as sepulchrally thin as his comrade was corpulent—who wore a flowing cape throughout the production and looked nothing so much as the hyperactive manager of an American professional wrestler as he hopped from foot to foot, gesticulated wildly, and seemed oblivious to the open-mouthed stares he elicited from the public as he sought to hand out the group's literature. To many Finns, the Aryan German Brotherhood became an instant cause for mirth.

This impression was unfortunate, in that Kuisma's deepening mysticism and marked personal charisma was in stark contrast to the impression made by the Finnish television documentary. Indeed, many who have privately met with Väinö Kuisma attest to an almost hypnotic quality to his discourse and demeanor, an observation that has been made about other hereditary practitioners of Kerelian shamanism. Indeed, so great was the disparity between the AGV's public image and private reality that it became clear that, if Kuisma's ideas were to gain a wider audience, the

Aryan German Brotherhood and its more dysfunctional adherents would have to go. Thus in 1993 the Patriotic Front was born.

The Patriotic Front was conceived as a more broadly based movement than the Aryan German Brotherhood. On the political level, the Patriotic Front would stand for parliamentary elections, and thus the Third Reich symbolism was jettisoned. The Patriotic Front was to be a purely Finnish folkish party. At the same time, Kuisma sought to unite the small Finnish radical-right community under his leadership.

The latter bid for primacy in the small world of the Finnish far right had some initial success. Kuisma's Patriotic Right was for a time able to cooperate with the established Patriotic National Alliance, but, of greater interest, Kuisma was able to make significant inroads into the skinhead scene in Turku and elsewhere. The founder of Pro Patria and the most influential figure in the Finnish skinhead world, Remi Leskonnen, was for a time attracted to Kuisma and became a member of Kuisma's inner circle.

Neither the alliance with the Patriotic National Alliance nor the connection with Leskonnen and Pro Patria would last for long. In the highly divisive world of the far right, Kuisma's Patriotic Right was in competition for a very small pool of potential voters, and an even more rarefied group of potential contributors. Ideological considerations aside, this fact mitigates against the creation of stable coalitions.

Kuisma's connection with Leskonnen was even more star crossed. From the beginning, the differences between Kuisma and the skinhead subculture were profound. Kuisma is ascetic, disciplined, and abstentious. He notes that his only real indulgence in life is enjoying a good cigar. Beyond this, he eschews alcohol and even the company of women—in fact, he avoids anything that would distract him from his studies and his preparations to assume power. Kuisma's taste in music runs to the classical, with Sibelius's deeply Finnish compositions first and foremost. It need hardly be said that the skinhead scene is not of the same temper. Thus, after an initial flirtation, Leskonnen departed, and Kuisma's support among Finnish skinheads has diminished considerably as well.

Despite these political setbacks, Kuisma's ideological and religious quest continues unabated. For Kuisma, the essence of "Finnishness" has assumed such centrality that all else has been excluded. Thus the National Socialist imagery has largely disappeared from the movement, replaced primarily by concepts of what is termed in this encyclopedia as "a religion of nature," in which *The*

Kelevala is elevated to the level of sacred and inerrant text. From this source springs Kuisma's sense of mission, together with his conception of the Finns as a spiritual elite. As quoted by Dr. Kyösti Pekonen of Helsinki University:

> Our own people is the most important in the world. We will fight with this people and for it. Leadership of every People should well forth from the People's holy roots and books, its holy spirit. Only the people who has found its roots and spirit is able to fulfill its mission in the world.

And it is *The Kelevala* that serves as the source for this timeless mission. It is, moreover, a mission exclusive to the Finnish people. Thus, Kuisma's appeal transcends the borders of Finland, with a Patriotic Right "overseas office" to spread the message of *Kelevala* culture to ethnic Finns throughout the world:

> We can honestly say that the principles of the Patriotic Right gushes out of *The Kelevala*. The dynamics, energy and will power of our organization are feasible only for the reason that we have elevated our national epic to a worthy position as the Finnish People's own sacred book. As our own bible. THE KELEVALA REFORMATION IS GOING ON.

See also: Madole, James Hartung; Religion of Nature; White Power Music.

Further reading: Mari Kalliala, "Pekka Siitoin: Mixing the Extremes and Surviving," in Jeffrey Kaplan and Heléne Lööw, *Sekter, sektmotståndare och sekteristiska miljöer, en förnyad granskning* (Stockholm: Swedish National Council of Crime Prevention, forthcoming); Kyösti Pekonen, ed., *The New Radical Right in Finland in the Nineties* (Helsinki: University of Helsinki Press, 1999).

KU KLUX KLAN   In the contemporary demonology of American culture, no organization elicits a more negative reaction than does the Ku Klux Klan (the KKK). Fear of the Klan, and perhaps a shared collective shame for the power that the movement accrued both in the Reconstruction Era American South (c. 1865–1876) and in a number of northern states in the 1920s, is deeply rooted in the collective American consciousness. It is a fear that at once attracts and bedevils Klan recruits, who often find their initial attraction to the Klan's mystique of secrecy and popular fear waning with the realization that virtually any public activity undertaken by the Klan is certain to be met by a far greater crowd of counterdemonstrators. Worse, covert

Klan operations appear to be undertaken at the sufferance (if not the outright invitation) of government authorities, given the success of federal agencies at infiltrating Klan ranks and inducing Klan leaders to cooperate in federal investigations. Thus, for a Klan group to undertake or even seriously contemplate violent action is tanta-mount to organizational suicide. On the one hand, members face not only indictment for whatever criminal acts may occur, but also face lengthy incarceration as a result of the imaginative utilization of standing conspiracy statutes and the newly adopted hate-crime sen-tence enhancement provisions available in many states. Moreover, the successful use of civil litigation initiated by such watchdog orga-nizations as the Klanwatch Project of the Southern Poverty Law Center on behalf of victims of Klan violence has the intended effect of putting out of business those Klan organizations whose members do perpetrate acts of violence.

Given these powerful disincentives to violence, it is not surpris-ing that the already fragmented Klans in North America would enter into a bitter battle of polemics over the tactics of nonviolence versus the Klan's tradition of violent activism. Emerging from this internecine debate are two very different approaches: the call to violence championed by such firebrands as Louis Beam of Texas and Dennis Mahon of Oklahoma, as opposed to the mediagenic call to nonviolence, best embodied by Arkansas-based Thomas Robb.

Louis Beam is a rarity among Klansmen. Undeniably intelligent, articulate, and widely read, Beam is the author of the "Leaderless Resistance" essay that remains the single vital theoretical model for radical-right-wing violence extant today. Beam, however, has not succeeded in his primary objective—unifying the Klan's many dispa-rate factions and forging the organization into an effective vanguard revolutionary force along the lines of what the late Robert Miles called the "Fifth Era Klan."

Dennis Mahon is no Louis Beam, but he too has come to represent a revolutionary voice in Klan circles—so much so, in fact, that, having come to much the same analysis of the Klan's current status as Louis Beam, he amicably left the Klan in 1992 for Tom Metzger's White Aryan Resistance (WAR). Prior to his defection to WAR, Mahon was best known for his association with Terry Boyce's Confederate Knights of America Klan chapter and for his calls to arms in the Knights' journal, the *White Beret,* as well as for his occasional forays to Europe and Canada on behalf of the Klan. Mahon's drift from the KKK to WAR was announced with an unusually frank analysis of the Klan. Interspersed between intemperate attacks on Thom Robb ("the

Grand Lizard") and Robb's attempts to remake the image of the Klan from a revolutionary force to, in effect, a civil rights group, comes Mahon's telling appraisal of the current state of the Klan:

> ...after 12 years of proudly wearing the robe of the Invisible Order, I feel that Tom Metzger's leadership and personal strategies fit my personality and mind set better at this time of my life. Also, I just got tired of seeing so many mistakes in tactics and ideology of the leaders of the other 25 or so Klan groups in Zoglandia. So many of these mini-fuhrers of these other Klans have embarrassed me with these displays of weakness and idiotic statements of "Niggers are the cause of all our problems—we got to kill the niggers—nigger this, nigger that." It's like a broken record.
>
> The Jewsmedia always link the Klan with "lynching niggers." The average "Joe Six-pack" out there, whenever he thinks of a Klansman, pictures an uneducated hick half drunk, in bib overalls, with tobacco juice dripping down his chin, burning a cross on some poor Blacks [sic] lawn, and the Klansman stating how he "put the nigger in his place." Unfortunately, many Klansmen knowingly fit the media stereotype.

Mahon continues his analysis throughout the premier issue of his post-Klan vehicle, *The Oklahoma Excalibur*. The effortless penetration of Klan leadership ranks by government agents as well as by informants reporting for private watchdog groups is decried, as are the tactics of nonviolence and staged events in which Klan groups are seen as demonstrating peacefully until they are attacked by anti-Klan demonstrators, the forte of Thom Robb. For Mahon, the contradictions of the modern Klan became intolerable, and thus the switch to WAR.

During an interview with this writer in Chicago in 1991, Identity minister and Klan leader Thom Robb made the surprising declaration that, virtually alone among members of the radical right in America, he was pleased with media coverage of his Knights of the Ku Klux Klan. Indeed, inasmuch as the Ku Klux Klan could get positive media coverage, Robb's message of love for the White race while eschewing any (public) negative comments on any other race has dovetailed nicely with a certain trend in American society toward the reinforcement of ethnic as opposed to national identity. Robb's kinder, gentler Klan is unlikely to do much to erase the intensely negative associations that the organization engenders in Americans, and, as Dennis Mahon's writing amply demonstrates, it has done much to further divide an already disintegrating movement.

How low the Ku Klux Klan's fortunes have ebbed in recent years is clearly documented by the watchdog community. According to Anti-Defamation League figures, total Klan membership had by 1988 hit a record low of between 4,500 and 5,000 members. These figures represent the lowest Klan membership total in 15 years, according to the ADL, and Klanwatch's 1990 estimate of 5,000 too shows little hope of upward growth. So dire are the Klan's current fortunes that in its 1991 report on the KKK ("The KKK Today: A 1991 Status Report," *ADL Special Report*), the ADL was moved to write:

> Although the Klan's decade-long decline has stopped, and it may begin to grow again—especially if the current recession becomes lengthy and severe—there is little prospect of the hooded order once again becoming a significant force in the land.... As long as it continues to exist, it poses a danger to the communities in which it operates. The danger consists specifically of violence and terrorism. The Klan's very presence in a community constitutes a source of anxiety to members of minority groups and a standing threat to peaceful and friendly relations among the citizens.... Nevertheless, considered from the standpoint of the nation as a whole, the KKK has only limited present and potential significance.

Since 1991, ADL material dealing with the Klan has reiterated these findings, and, according to watchdog and academic sources alike, the Klan remains a marginal force in the world of the radical right, as well as an insignificant factor in the mainstream culture.

See also: Aryan Nations; Beam, Louis; Butler, Richard; Metzger, Tom; Miles, Robert; Odinism; Robb, Thom; White Aryan Resistance.

Further reading: Louis Beam, "On Revolutionary Majorities," *Inter-Klan Newsletter and Survival Alert* 4 (1984); David Chalmers, *Hooded Americanism* (Chicago: Quadrangle Books, 1965); John George and Laird Wilcox, *Nazis, Communists, Klansmen, and Others on the Fringe* (Buffalo, NY: Prometheus Books, 1992); Kenneth T. Jackson, *The Ku Klux Klan in the City, 1915–1930* (Chicago: Oxford University Press, 1967); Michael Newton and Judy Newton, *Ku Klux Klan: An Encyclopedia*, Garland Reference Library of the Social Sciences, vol. 499 (New York: Garland, 1991); Patsy Sims, *The Klan* (New York: Stein and Day, 1978); Bill Stanton, *Klanwatch: Bringing the Klan to Justice* (New York: Grove Weidenfeld, 1991).

L

DAVID LANE   An imprisoned member of the Order and leading proponent of Odinism, David Lane is presently serving a 190-year-term in a maximum security prison beneath the ground in Florence, Colorado. Born 1938 in Woden, Iowa, Lane was adopted by a rigid Lutheran family, thus developing his distaste for Christianity. Opposed to racial integration, which he came to see as part of a Zionist conspiracy aimed at exterminating the Aryan race so as to facilitate a global takeover, Lane grew increasingly radical. Passing through the John Birch Society, the Ku Klux Klan, and the Christian Identity movement, Lane adopted a pagan philosophy based on his understanding of Nature's Law, one that would be greatly developed after his incarceration.

Already an experienced activist operating out of Denver, Lane met Robert Mathews at the 1983 Aryan World Congress at Aryan Nations and subsequently joined the Order.

Captured in March 1985 after Ken Loff, an Order member turned FBI informant, gave him up to the agents in exchange for a five-year sentence reduction, Lane was convicted for racketeering, conspiracy, and violating the civil rights of the Denver-based radio personality Alan Berg. Berg was murdered, allegedly by members of the Order, in the garage of his apartment house in June 1984.

In prison, Lane turned to the study of history, philosophy, mystery religions, and Odinism, gradually developing an Aryan creed based on the pre-Christian Norse religion. Lane cast himself as being called by the Gods of the Blood to "stop the Zionist murder of the White race" and "bring down the present Zionist World Order."

Convinced that Aryan man is at the brink of extermination, Lane coined the "14 Words" as a rallying point for a pan-Aryan militant uprising: "We must secure the existence of our people and a future for White children." He married Katja in October 1994 and together the Lanes established the *14 Word Press* and a monthly news sheet called *Focus Fourteen* to channel the message of racial revival. Lane's "88 Precepts," like the 14 Words, enjoy a considerable vogue in the world of the racialist right. (The "88 Precepts" essay may be found in its entirety in the "Resources" section.) Together with artist Ron McVan, the troika established Wotansvolk as a vehicle for an Ariosophist, Odinist revolution. "You cannot share Gods with other races," Lane says, urging a return to the ancestral faith as a remedy for the spell of universalist religion. He goes on to describe Christianity as diametrically opposed to the natural order, singling it out as the principal cause of Aryan degeneration. Otherworldly oriented, Christianity is said to glorify weakness and defeat. In teaching the White man to love his enemies it undermines the instinct of self-preservation. "God is not love," Lane emphasizes. "God the Creator made lions to eat lambs, he made hawks to eat sparrows. Compassion between species is against the law of nature. Life is struggle and the absence of struggle is death." Reconnecting with the ancestral faith rekindles the warrior spirit in the slumbering Aryan Folk Soul, Lane argues, thereby instilling the heroic qualities deemed necessary for racial survival and prosperity.

Increasingly gaining notoriety around the White racialist world, David Lane has been built up as a White "prisoner of war," sometimes ironically called the "[Nelson] Mandela of the White revolution." Strategically, Lane embraces the leaderless resistance concept suggested by Louis Beam, arguing for the necessity of a tactical separation between an overt propaganda arm and an underground action arm. Ideally, the latter operates as small autonomous cells to avoid infiltration and to help activists understand what needs to be done by listening to those in the propaganda arm. Lane is not concerned that this could lead to misguided acts of terror. "In the coming revolution there will be no innocents," he states uncompromisingly. "There are only those who are for our cause and those who are our enemies. The masses are selfish, greedy asses. They have always been and they always will be. They will either follow us or follow them. They are now following their terrorism. When the time comes that our terrorism is superior to theirs, they will follow us. They will worship and adore whoever is the greater tyrant. That's the nature of the masses."

In the postrevolutionary era, Lane envisions an all-Aryan nation of Odin based on a tribal structure and ruled by the Philosopher-Elect. By necessity, Lane believes, it will become reality only through a transitory phase of strong dictatorship where individual rights must be sacrificed to secure racial regeneration and advancement. Considering the corrupting nature of absolute power, Lane suggests himself as "the leader of this particular phase in the history of our people."

—*Mattias Gardell, Stockholm University, Sweden*

See also: Beam, Louis; Christian Identity; Lane, Katja; Leaderless Resistance; Mathews, Robert; McVan, Ron; Odinism; Order; Religion of Nature; Wotansvolk [Wotan's Folk]; Zionist Occupation Government.

Further reading: Kevin Flynn and Gary Gerhardt, *The Silent Brotherhood* (New York: Signet, 1990); *Focus Fourteen* [newsletter]; Mattias Gardell, *Rasrisk* (Stockholm & Uppsala: Federativs & Swedish Science Press, 1998); Jeffrey Kaplan, *Radical Religion in America: Millenarian Movements from the Far Right to the Children of Noah* (Syracuse, NY: Syracuse University Press, 1997); David Lane, *The Auto-Biography of David Lane* (St. Maries, ID: 14 Word Press, 1994); David Lane, *The Mystery Religions & The Seven Seals* (St. Maries, ID: 14 Word Press, 1994); David Lane, *Revolution by Number 14* (St. Maries, ID: 14 Word Press, 1994); David Lane, *White Genocide Manifesto* (St. Maries, ID: 14 Word Press, undated); Ron McVan, *Creed of Iron: Wotansvolk Wisdom* (St. Maries, ID: 14 Word Press, 1997); Stephen Singlar, *Talked to Death* (New York: William Morrow, 1987).

KATJA LANE   Wife of David Lane, mother of his five children, and a leading proponent of racially based Odinism, Katja Lane was born in 1951. She was the daughter of an intelligence officer for the Air Force and was given a conservative upbringing, traveling extensively outside the United States. In 1967, her father was shot down in Vietnam and has been missing ever since, an event that propelled Katja into antiwar activism in an organization called Vietnam Veterans Against the War.

Cross-culturally competent through her travels and later university studies, Katja Lane gradually came to the conclusion that international capitalism not only was threatening indigenous cultures abroad but also was destroying the Aryan civilization. Adopting an increasingly more radical position racially and politically, she moved through Christian Identity into Odinism in the late 1980s.

In October 1994, Katja married David Lane, who was serving a 190-year-prison term for his involvement in the Order, and with him cofounded *14 Word Press* and the monthly *Focus Fourteen* newsletter as a vehicle for disseminating his political writings dedicated to the "14 Words": "We must secure the existence of our people and a future for White children."

In 1995, Ron McVan had moved to St. Maries, Idaho, and together the troika established the group Wotansvolk [Wotan's Folk] as "a vehicle to unite the Aryan race and give us a sense of identity as well as destiny." Although emphasizing the virtues of motherhood and traditional gender roles, Katja Lane's part in spreading the call of Ariosophic Odinism and revolutionary racialism should not be underestimated. Beside home-schooling her children, Katja Lane is the channel of communication between David Lane and the outside world, thus serving a key function in the build-up of his reputation as a prisoner-of-war ideologue.

Skilled in computer technology and graphic lay-out, Katja Lane is responsible for editing the writings of her husband David and of Ron McVan and the Wotansvolk Internet home page.

—*Mattias Gardell, Stockholm University, Sweden*

See also: Christian Identity; Lane, David; McVan, Ron; Odinism; Order; Wotansvolk [Wotan's Folk].

Further reading: Focus Fourteen [newsletter]; Mattias Gardell, *Rasrisk* (Stockholm & Uppsala: Federativs & Swedish Science Press, 1998); David Lane, *The Auto-Biography of David Lane* (St. Maries, ID: 14 Word Press, 1994).

GARY "GERHARD" LAUCK   Gary Lauck is an anomaly in the contemporary National Socialist movement. His fancifully named NSDAP/AO (National Sozialistische Deutsch Arbeiter Partei/ Auslands Organisation, or National Socialist German Workers Party/Overseas Organization) borrows the name of Hitler's original German National Socialist Party. Lauck's idolatry of all things German hardly stops with the name of his tiny Nazi party. Lauck is one of the select few American neo-Nazis to have learned German, and, going even this talented cadre one better, he has for many years affected a mock-German accent, signed himself Gerhard rather than Gary, grown a pencil mustache in imitation of his Führer, and from his home in Lincoln, Nebraska, he has aimed his activities primarily at a European (read: German) audience. Perhaps most remarkable of all, where many young European National Socialists profess both amusement and contempt for their American counterparts as "Hollywood Nazis" caught in a 1930s time warp and more drawn to the leather and black of Nazi uniforms than to the depth of National Socialist philosophy, Lauck alone has managed to gain a respectful following in Europe. Why that should be is an interesting tale.

Lauck is a long-time National Socialist whose roots are conventional enough. Passing through the ranks of the National Socialist White People's Party (NSWPP), he became part of the core leadership of the National Socialist Party of America (NSPA) under Frank

Collin in Chicago in the early 1970s. There, he joined Mike Allen and Harold Covington in a National Socialist party that briefly appeared to have the potential to supplant Matt Koehl and the NSWPP as the premier National Socialist Party in the country. The NSPA's moment in the sun was the highly publicized march through the heavily Jewish Chicago suburb of Skokie, Illinois, in 1978.

Following this epiphany, however, the National Socialist White People's Party responded with a campaign that offered strong evidence that Frank Collin was in fact the son of Max Cohen, a Jewish concentration camp survivor. This shock was followed by the discovery by Lauck, Allen, and Covington of photographic evidence that Collin was a homosexual child molester. In an internal plot, code-named "Operation Bobby Brown," to rid the National Socialist Party of America of its embarrassing Führer, Collin was removed from the leadership and turned over to the police. Collin was ultimately convicted and incarcerated, but the NSPA did not long survive the coup.

Lauck, convinced that he had been promised the leadership, found the title usurped by Harold Covington (whose funds had bought the NSPA's headquarters, Rockwell Hall, and kept the group afloat as well). Covington moved the group to North Carolina, and Lauck retreated to Nebraska to devote all his time to his NSDAP/AO, a vehicle he had actually founded in 1974 as a riposte to the German government, which had the temerity to expel him for making pro-Nazi speeches.

With the NSDAP/AO, Lauck found a vital niche in the international National Socialist movement. European governments take a dim view of National Socialist propaganda and the German government in particular has gone to great lengths to outlaw such material. For almost two decades in the United States, however, Lauck, protected by the First Amendment, produced tremendous quantities of such propaganda, translated it into German (and later, with help from a global network of National Socialist collaborators, into a variety of other languages as well), and smuggled it into Germany with apparent ease. Indeed, the German National Socialist leader Ingo Hasselbach went so far as to claim that the German neo-Nazi network would collapse without Lauck. While this is a considerable overstatement, Lauck's contributions to the German movement are enormous.

Throughout the 1980s and early 1990s, Lauck skipped back and forth from Europe to America frequently, meeting with German National Socialists in third countries, most notably Denmark.

Lauck's flagship publications, *New Order* in English and *NS Kampfruf* in German, did remarkably well and were translated into a variety of languages for wider dissemination throughout the world. The NSDAP/AO also ran a highly successful mail-order line of National Socialist–oriented books, tapes, and films, as well as flags and other Third Reich memorabilia. However, the item Lauck most enjoyed, a computer game in several languages that gives the young player entrepreneurial experience as a "virtual" concentration camp commandant, was never made available on the U.S. market through the mail-order house. Yet so successful was the venture that the Germans adapted an updated version to allow the electronic concentration camp to hold Turkish immigrants, rather than Jews, as prisoners. As usual, the German movement is less fixated on the 1930s model of National Socialism than are the Americans.

Lauck's luck ran out in 1995 when, at last, the Danish government acted on the German warrant and arrested him. In a crowning irony, Lauck, who for years deified all things German and vilified all things American, fought extradition to Germany with every legal means at his disposal. He even requested—and was denied—political asylum in Denmark. Both in Denmark and in his subsequent trial in Germany, Lauck complained that he had broken no American laws and that his right to publish and export his propaganda material was guaranteed by the First Amendment to the U.S. Constitution. The Germans were unmoved, and in August 1996 Lauck was sentenced to a maximum of four years in prison.

The NSDAP/AO sans Gary Lauck tries to soldier on. Two of Lauck's rare American followers are currently trying manfully to keep up with orders for *New Order,* but admit to falling further behind by the day. Moreover, contrary to the dire predictions of imminent ruin for a Lauckless German movement, young Germans— particularly in the East—are drawn to the movement in greater numbers than ever. But perhaps of greatest importance is that even as Lauck was at last brought into the embrace of his beloved German Fatherland, his operation had already become passé. Since 1995, the explosion of Internet technology has revolutionized the German movement and made obtaining National Socialist propaganda, bomb-making recipes, and secure communications as easy as logging on to a computer.

See also: Collin, Frank; Covington, Harold; Hitler, Adolf; Internet Recruiting; Koehl, Matt; National Socialist Party of America; National Socialist White People's Party.

Further reading: Anon., "Free Gerhard!," *New Order* 116 (May/June 1995); Anon., "Free Gerhard!: Gerhard's Case Goes to the Danish Supreme Court," *New Order* 117 (July/August 1995); Anon:, "Gerhard Jailed!," *New Order* 118 (September/October 1995); Anon., "Fifteen Years for Free Speech!," *New Order* 123 (July/August 1996); John George and Laird Wilcox, *Nazis, Communists, Klansmen, and Others on the Fringe* (Buffalo, NY: Prometheus Books, 1992); Ingo Hasselbach with Tom Reiss, *Führer-Ex* (New York: Random House, 1996); Jeffrey Kaplan and Leonard Weinberg, *The Emergence of a Euro-American Radical Right* (Rutgers, NJ: Rutgers University Press, 1998).

LEADERLESS RESISTANCE   More a mark of despair than a revolutionary strategy, leaderless resistance as it was formulated and disseminated to the far-right faithful sought to make a virtue of weakness and political isolation. Leaderless resistance may be defined as a kind of lone-wolf operation in which an individual, or a very small, highly cohesive group, engage in acts of antistate violence independent of any movement, leader, or network of support. This violence may take the form of attacks on state institutions or operatives, or it may take the form of random targets of opportunity selected on the basis of their perceived vulnerability and their symbolic importance. Thus acts of leaderless resistance may be aimed at targets as diverse as interracial couples, gay book stores or clubs, or, indeed, at government agents or buildings.

The leaderless resistance concept was popularized in the late 1980s as a last gasp of defiance by the American radical right, which was then at the nadir of its already bleak fortunes. This entry will examine the historical context that gave birth to leaderless resistance, follow it through its National Socialist, Christian Identity, and neopagan Odinist formulations, and close with a speculative consideration of Timothy McVeigh as a possible case study of the strategy of leaderless resistance.

The internal debates that produced the leaderless resistance strategy did not begin in the 1980s. Rather, they are of considerable vintage and reflect a long-standing division in the far right. On the one hand, a conservative majority of the movement has always seen—correctly, as it happens—that to engage prematurely in revolutionary violence against a vastly more powerful state would be foolhardy at best, suicidal at worst. The political strategy of choice was thus to utilize propaganda and legal demonstrations so as to build a "revolutionary majority." This theory is best articulated by the author of the most influential tract on leaderless resistance, Louis R. Beam, Jr., whose original essay appears in the "Resources" section. This approach in National Socialist circles came to be known as the theory of mass action.

All but the most idealistic adherents of National Socialist mass action theory realized full well that the American masses were hardly likely to flock to the swastika banner, short of some catastrophic turn of events. Thus, throughout the 1960s and 1970s, the literature of American National Socialism blended prognostications of the impact of integration and school busing to achieve racial balance, lurid crime stories with a racial slant that would have done the supermarket tabloids proud, and hopeful speculations of impending cataclysm, economic collapse, and urban mayhem. In one of the great ironies of American National Socialism, George Lincoln Rockwell, the sole charismatic figure produced by the postwar movement, was himself one of the architects of the mass-action strategy.

Following the assassination of Rockwell in 1967, the party began to fragment. Matt Koehl succeeded the commander, soon renamed the American Nazi Party the National Socialist White People's Party (NSWPP), and initiated an endless round of purges that would soon cost the party its bare handful of capable adherents. Two of the victims of these purges and angry resignations, William Pierce and Joseph Tommasi, figure prominently in the development of the leaderless resistance concept.

Of Pierce much more will be said later. Joseph Tommasi concerns us first. Tommasi ironically was a Koehl loyalist almost to the day he was unceremoniously purged from the NSWPP and subsequently assassinated by an NSWPP member in 1975. Tommasi, like Pierce, was acutely aware of the bold actions undertaken by the Weathermen and the Symbionese Liberation Army, to name but two of the left-wing combatant organizations of the day. They were determined to create a campus-based revolutionary movement of the right on the same model. Thus was born the National Socialist Liberation Front (NSLF).

In 1973 or 1974, Tommasi published his now famous poster, "THE FUTURE BELONGS TO THE FEW OF US WILLING TO GET OUR HANDS DIRTY. POLITICAL TERROR: It's the only thing they understand." And he printed a seminal pamphlet, *Building the Revolutionary Party,* to announce the formation of the NSLF. The NSLF's revolutionary ideology was based on the rejection of the conservative theory of mass action that Tommasi correctly believed was paralyzing the NS movement. For Tommasi, the mass-action doctrine meant in reality that no serious antistate actions were possible, given the patent absurdity of creating a mass-based National Socialist party in the United States.

Tommasi gathered more than 40 adherents to the foundational meeting of the NSLF in El Monte, California, in March 1974. But this number is somewhat deceiving. Few of these young National Socialists were sufficiently suicidal to act on Tommasi's rhetoric. In the end, only four NSLF "members" undertook revolutionary action: Tommasi himself, Karl Hand, David Rust, and James Mason.

The NSLF soldiered on at least in name for another decade. In that time, however, Tommasi was murdered, Hand and Rust were incarcerated for acts of racially motivated violence and firearms charges, and James Mason found a new avatar in Charles Manson. But the NSLF's contribution to the leaderless resistance concept is incalculable. The NSLF was the first to act on the theory that, regardless of the dearth of public support, a blow could be struck against the hated state, provided that the determined revolutionary was prepared to act resolutely and alone. Tommasi was among the first to fully grasp the truth of the strategic situation—in the milieu of the radical right, no one is to be trusted, anyone could be (and probably is) an informer for the government or for one of the many watchdog organizations monitoring radical-right-wing activity, and, short of divine intervention, public support would not be forthcoming no matter what tactical approach the movement was to adopt. Yet, in this state of weakness, there is ultimate strength. With nothing left to lose, a man is totally free to act as he will. For while the state had proven over and over again that it could effortlessly penetrate any right-wing organization, it had yet to develop the capability to thwart the will of one man acting alone!

This revelation would do the NSLF little good. The group actually died with Tommasi. The actions of Hand and Rust were, in reality, pathetic outbursts of pointless violence that succeeded only in bringing them into the care of the prison system. But the example, once proffered, could not be erased. Although it had yet to be given a name, radical-right-wing leaderless resistance was born.

At the same time, it is important to remember that the conservative majority of the far right did *not* approve of the unauthorized actions of leaderless resistors. Their well-grounded fear was of precisely the sort of pointless and undisciplined actions that landed the tiny NSLF combatant cadre in prison. Rather, between mass action's impotent dreams and leaderless resistance's antinomian reality, there was a third path that would become a model for the more extreme fringes of the present-day militia movement. Borrowed from Leninist theory, the cell structure under a centralized command was the mark of the 1960s era Minutemen under the leadership of Robert Bolivar DePugh.

The decade that followed Tommasi's death and the fall of the NSLF were, from the perspective of the far right, both eventful and deeply disheartening. Most notable, a true revolutionary movement, the Silent Brotherhood, more popularly known as the Order, under the leadership of Robert Mathews, arose and, after a brief but incandescent revolutionary career, was smashed by the state. It was not until the Order was nearing its inglorious end that many in the radical right were able to accept that the group could be anything other than a diabolically clever federal entrapment scheme.

The death of Robert Mathews in a shoot-out with the FBI was thus traumatic to the movement, but far worse was to come. The 1989 Fort Smith, Arkansas, sedition trial brought into the dock a virtual "who's who" of the radical right. Louis Beam, the author of the original "Leaderless Resistance," tract was there. So were surviving members of the Order. And so too were such venerable movement patriarchs as Richard Butler of the Aryan Nations and the ever-jovial Robert Miles. The defendants were in the end found not guilty of all charges, but not before a parade of their erstwhile allies, men such as the head of the Covenant, Sword, and Arm of the Lord Identity compound James Ellison and the Church of Israel's Dan Gayman, betrayed the movement by appearing as witnesses for the prosecution. Little wonder in such a bleak situation that the power of the federal government, and of what was seen as its Jewish puppeteers (personified as the Anti-Defamation League of B'nai B'rith), were reified into ZOG, the all-powerful Zionist Occupation Government, now seen as the masters of the nation and, indeed, of the world.

The ZOG discourse offered a form of comfort and an ironic sense of security for the faithful. Against so all-pervading a foe, what could be done but to withdraw and wait and seek to persevere? Movement discourse, thus, in the late 1980s became increasingly chiliastic. The mass action theories of the previous generation were discarded as hopeless dreams. And so things may have stayed had two searing events not galvanized the movement. In 1992, a heretofore obscure Identity adherent, Randy Weaver, became an unlikely movement icon when, in the wake of a botched federal government sting operation, Weaver's wife, young son, and family dog were killed in a siege in Ruby Ridge, Idaho, that took the life of a federal agent as well. Then the next year—in the midst of the Weaver trial as it happened— there was the massacre at Waco, Texas. Suddenly, previously isolated voices calling for individual acts of violent resistance to state tyranny began to be heard, and to a limited degree heeded, by a few in the milieu of the far-right wing.

No better symbol of this newfound credibility can be posited than the inclusion of Louis R. Beam's original "Leaderless Resistance" essay in Pastor Pete Peters's published report on a meeting of Identity Christians that was convened to discuss the Randy Weaver drama. Suddenly, leaderless resistance was no longer an isolated theory. It was seen as a matter of survival in the face of a government now determined to eradicate the radical right once and for all. With this brief historical context, it is time to examine the texts that gave form and substance to the Leaderless Resistance strategy. These texts were, in chronological order, William Pierce's *Hunter,* a sad sequel to the *Turner Diaries;* Richard Kelly Hoskins's foray into imagined history, *Vigilantes of Christendom;* Louis Beam's seminal essay, "Leaderless Resistance"; and David Lane's reprise of the theory in Viking garb, "Wotan is Coming."

William Pierce, a confidant of George Lincoln Rockwell, was the spiritual father of the NSLF and the ghost in the machine whenever serious acts of radical-right-wing violence are contemplated or undertaken. His *Turner Diaries* was said to be a major source of inspiration for both the Order and Timothy McVeigh, the convicted Oklahoma City bomber. Yet Pierce himself has kept cautiously in the background, carefully building his National Alliance organization cum book distributorship and living the life of a gentleman farmer on his West Virginia estate.

For all the attention given to the *Turner Diaries,* however, his long-awaited follow-up, *Hunter,* is a dispirited affair that has garnered little public attention. Yet *Hunter,* like its more famous predecessor, well reflects the ethos of the time in which it was written. *Hunter* is the story of one Oscar Yeagar, a character closely modeled on the real-life prototype of the lone-wolf killer, James Vaughn, aka Joseph Franklin, to whom the book is dedicated. *Hunter*'s hero, stoically accepting the hopeless situation of the right in the wake of the fall of the Order, the Fort Smith fiasco, and the perceived ever-present reality of Jewish control of both the nation and the world, sheds his attachments to family and friends, to career and creature comforts, and provides a fictional model of the lone-wolf assassin, stalking the enemies of the White race. The ultimate goal is to demonstrate the weakness of the system, and eventually to ignite a race war. But unlike the exuberant *Turner Diaries,* in which the protagonist, Earl Turner, helps to unleash a revolution that changes the very face of the planet, *Hunter* ends not with a bang but with a resigned sigh:

> He sighed. Well, he would be very busy during the next few days discharging responsibilities he had already incurred. But after that it would be time to do some more hunting.

Where *Hunter* offered a plausible if rather unpromising model for action, Richard Kelly Hoskins offered the Christian Identity faithful something better: a safe but deeply satisfying dream. Hoskins's 1990 magnum opus, *The Vigilantes of Christendom,* offered the dispirited faithful the age-old dream of supernatural succor as personified by a timeless band of selfless avengers, the Phineas Priesthood (Num. 23:6–13; Ps. 106:29–31). The Phineas Priests in the pages of *Vigilantes of Christendom* are presented as an order of assassins whose sacred role is to cull from the pure flock of Christ those wayward sheep who, through race mixing or other transgressions, would do the work of Satan and his earthly servants, the Jews. The Phineas Priesthood came with a catchy motto:

> As the Kamikaze is to the Japanese
> As the Shiite is to Islam
> As the Zionist is to the Jew
> So the Phineas Priest is to Christendom

And who are the Phineas Priests? A long list of claimants to the title is presented. Robin Hood, St. George, Beowulf, King Arthur, John Wilkes Booth, Jesse James, Gordon Kahl, Robert Mathews, and Doug Sheets (accused of murdering homosexuals) are but a few of the worthies in Hoskins's elaborate fantasy.

The Phineas Priesthood was, in the context of the times, a fantasy so alluring that it was only a matter of time before a few brave or deranged individuals would take up for themselves the title and set out in search of God's enemies. Given the fanciful nature of the Phineas Priesthood, such a quest must unambiguously qualify as an act of leaderless resistance.

Clearly the most important text to emerge concerning leaderless resistance is Louis R. Beam's essay on the subject. Beam, a Klansman with close ties to Richard Butler's Christian Identity Aryan Nations compound, has for many years been at the cutting edge of movement theory. Beam was quick to comprehend the dire strategic situation of the far right at the end of the 1980s and was eager to seek some way to keep the flame of violent opposition alive.

Louis Beam's writings take a serious interest in history and evince an academic's care to identify his sources. Thus, Beam takes no credit for coining either the concept or the term "leaderless resistance." Rather, he traces its origin to one Colonel Ulius Louis Amoss, the founder of the Baltimore-based International Service of Information Incorporated, who published an essay titled "Leaderless Resistance" in April 1962. Colonel Amoss was suggesting guerrilla tactics in case of the communist invasion and conquest of America, but, in the event, the scenario did not eventuate and the essay was forgotten. Such might have been the fate of Beam's essay as well, had it not been written a mere few months before the events of Ruby Ridge, Idaho. As noted above, Beam's essay was included in Pete Peters's report on the Weaver tragedy, and suddenly the term "leaderless resistance" was on everyone's lips. The movement, seeing in Ruby Ridge and far more so in Waco, evidence of a long-feared government plot to eliminate the Patriot community, and understanding full well the weakness and isolation of the movement, began to see leaderless resistance as the only hope of striking a last, despairing blow before inevitable defeat. The watchdog community, too, seized on the concept as evidence of a resurgence of radical-right-wing violence. And the government appears, in the aftermath of Waco, to have undergone some paralysis as it sought to understand what had gone wrong and, with the sudden rise of the militias across America in response to Waco, where such widespread antistate anger could have come from so suddenly.

In this supercharged atmosphere, Beam's essay seems somewhat discordant, given its despairing tone and limited expectations for success. The essay, however, reflected perfectly the mood of the late 1980s and the pre-Waco 1990s. Beam begins:

> In the hope that, somehow, America can still produce the brave sons and daughters necessary to fight off ever increasing persecution and oppression, this essay is offered. Frankly, it is too close to call at this point. Those who love liberty, and believe in freedom enough to fight for it are rare today, but within the bosom of every once great nation, there remains secreted, the pearls of former greatness. They are there. I have looked into their sparking eyes; sharing a brief moment in time with them as I passed through this life. Relished their friendship, endured their pain, and they mine. We are a band of brothers, native to the soil gaining strength one from another as we have rushed head long into a battle that all the weaker, timid men, say we can not win. Perhaps...but then again, perhaps we can. It's not over till the last freedom fighter is buried or imprisoned.

Hardly the words of a man confident of victory. But, following a discourse on other seemingly doomed causes that somehow turned out well in the end, Beam offers his tactical suggestions:

> The concept of Leaderless Resistance is nothing less than a fundamental departure in theories of organization. The orthodox scheme of organization is diagrammatically represented by the pyramid, with the mass at the bottom and the leader at the top. The Constitution of the United States, in the wisdom of the Founders, tried to sublimate the essential dictatorial nature of pyramidal organization by dividing authority into three: executive, legislative and judicial. But the pyramid remains essentially untouched.
>
> This scheme of organization, the pyramid, is however, not only useless, but extremely dangerous for the participants when it is utilized in a resistance movement against state tyranny. Especially is this so in technologically advanced societies where electronic surveillance can often penetrate the structure revealing its chain of command. Experience has revealed over and over again that anti-state, political organizations utilizing this method of command and control are easy prey for government infiltration, entrapment, and destruction of the personnel involved. This has been seen repeatedly in the United States where pro-government infiltrators or agent provocateurs weasel their way into patriotic groups and destroy them from within.
>
> An alternative to the pyramid type of organization is the cell system. In the past, many political groups (both right and left) have used the cell system to further their objectives.
>
> The efficient and effective operation of a cell system after the Communist model, is of course, dependent upon central direction, which means impressive organization, funding from the top, and outside support, all of which the Communists had. Obviously, American patriots have none of these things.
>
> Since the entire purpose of Leaderless Resistance is to defeat state tyranny (at least insofar as this essay is concerned), all members of phantom cells or individuals will tend to react to objective events in the same way through usual tactics of resistance. Organs of information distribution such as newspapers, leaflets, computers, etc., which are widely available to all, keep each person informed of events, allowing for a planned response that will take many variations. No one need issue an order to anyone. Those idealists truly committed to the cause of freedom will act when they feel the time is ripe, or will take their cue from others who precede them....

With Beam's formulation, the theory of leaderless resistance was essentially complete. All that remained was to adapt and disseminate it to ever-wider constituencies of the far-right wing. One of the more interesting of these endeavors was that of imprisoned Order veteran David Lane. Lane, an Odinist and an icon in the racialist wing of that movement, juxtaposed the leaderless resistance strategy with the Phineas Priests concept and arrived at the dread Wotan, a man alone—a true beserker—who will carry on the battle against impossible odds until the day of Ragnarök:

> So, let's go on to strategy. Resistance to tyranny within an occupied country necessarily forms into certain structures. Most basic is the division between the political or legal arm, and the armed party which I prefer to call Wotan as it is an excellent anagram [sic] for the will of the Aryan nation. The political arm is distinctly and rigidly separated from Wotan. The political arm will always be subjected to surveillance, scrutiny, harassment, and attempted infiltration by the system. Therefore the political arm must remain scrupulously legal within the parameters allowed by the occupying power. The function of the political arm is above all else to disseminate propaganda. The nature of effective propaganda is magnificently detailed in *Mein Kampf,* and condensed in Lane's *88 Precepts*. The political arm is a network and loose confederation of like minded individuals sharing a common goal.
>
> Wotan draws recruits from those educated by the political arm. When a Wotan "goes active" he severs all apparent or provable ties with the political arm. If he has been so foolish as to obtain "membership" in such an organization, all records of such association must be destroyed or resignation submitted.
>
> The goal of Wotan is clear. He must hasten the demise of the system before it totally destroys our gene pool. Some of his weapons are fire, bombs, guns, terror, disruption, and destruction. Weak points in the infrastructure of an industrialized society are primary targets. Individuals who perform valuable service for the system are primary targets. Special attention and merciless terror is visited upon those white men who commit race treason. Wotan has a totally revolutionary mentality. He has no loyalty to anyone or anything except his cause. Those who do not share his cause are expendable and those who oppose his cause are targets. Wotan is mature, capable, ruthless, self-motivated, silent, deadly, and able to blend into the masses. Wotan receives no recognition for his labors for if the folk knows his identity then soon the enemy will also. Wotan are small autonomous cells, one man cells if possible. No one, not wife, brother, parent or friend, knows the identity or actions of Wotan.

By its very nature, leaderless resistance is an act undertaken through individual initiative. How then to determine with certainty whether a crime was committed as an act of leaderless resistance, or as an impulsive act of opportunity? Certainly Joseph Franklin, Karl Hand, and David Rust would appear to have been engaged in leaderless resistance, though it is most unlikely that they either read Colonel Amoss's 1962 essay or believed that their actions would have much of an effect on the government or on the course of the nation.

The Oklahoma City bombing is a case in point. Certainly, by any objective analysis, Timothy McVeigh would appear to be the veritable paradigm of the leaderless resistance concept. Estranged from any right-wing group, rejected by the militia movement for whom his angry words appeared to be either the ravings of a madman or, more likely, a federal plot, McVeigh with the help of one or two close friends planned and executed the most destructive act of domestic terror in American history. Moreover, McVeigh was very much a denizen of the cultic milieu of the radical right, giving him access to a vast array of conspiratorial and hate literature. It is not at all unlikely that McVeigh was familiar with Beam's essay. Indeed, given his widely reported fondness for the *Turner Diaries,* it is almost inconceivable that he would be unfamiliar with *Hunter.* But, as is usual in the world of the American radical right, things are not so simple, and McVeigh is not inclined to discuss the subject.

When McVeigh was arrested, he was carrying Patriot literature in his car. Subsequent publicity brought forward McVeigh friends and associates who offered further literature distributed by McVeigh, as well as his personal letters. This entry will close with a brief consideration of some of these documents and letters in the context of McVeigh's possible intention to act on the leaderless resistance concept.

First, it must be emphasized that nothing found in McVeigh's possession in any way indicated an interest in, or a knowledge of, any of the texts dealing with leaderless resistance theory. In McVeigh's car at the time of his arrest, an envelope was found containing fragments of what appear to be several articles culled from various unnamed Patriot publications. These documents deal with the question of when a citizen has the right and duty to resist a tyrannical government. Most notable among these documents are a series of quotations from such luminaries as Thomas Jefferson, Alexander Solzhenitsyn, and John Locke on the subject. The latter is of particular note, in that McVeigh writes this on the papers in his own hand, and the same quote recurs several times in McVeigh's effects:

> "I have no reason to suppose that he who would take away my liberty would not when he had me in his power, take away everything else; and therefore, it is lawful for me to treat him as one who has put himself into a 'state of war' against me; and kill him if I can, for to that hazard does he justly expose himself, whoever introduces a state of war and is aggressor in it." —John Locke, Second Treatise of government

Leaderless resistance envisions an individual battle against hopeless odds in which the long-range strategic objective appears to be little more hopeful than perseverance. There is scant hope that the American masses will rise against a state that the fighter sees as the embodiment of evil. The Patriot literature found with and distributed by McVeigh, however, suggests no such suicidal course of action. Rather, exhortations to awaken, to organize, and to resist are formulated here in terms of the creation of a mass movement that will call America back to the ideals of the Founding Fathers. Thus, one article, "The American Response to Tyranny," juxtaposes Waco with the American Revolution and urges the faithful: "Don't Get Discouraged."

Other articles, "U.S. Government Initiates Open Warfare Against American People" and "Waco Shootout Evokes Memory of Warsaw '43," decries government actions, but stops well short of urging violent reprisals. Rounding out McVeigh's traveling collection is that staple of every Patriot home and automobile, a copy of the Declaration of Independence and the Bill of Rights.

Through the years, McVeigh sent a number of documents to his sister, Jennifer. These appear to be little different from those found in his car on the day of his arrest save for one typewritten sheet titled "Constitutional Defenders." Apparently written by McVeigh himself, the last line of the undated text has been widely quoted—sans context—in the news media. The brief text bears directly on our concern with the leaderless resistance concept, and so should be quoted in full.

Constitutional Defenders

We members of the citizen's militias do not bear our arms to overthrow the Constitution, but to overthrow those who PERVERT the Constitution; if and when they once again, draw first blood (many believe the Waco incident was "first blood").

Many of our members are veterans who still hold true to their sworn oath to defend the Constitution against ALL enemies, foreign AND DOMESTIC. As John Locke once wrote "I have no reason to suppose that he who would take away my liberty, would not, when he had me in his power, take away everything else; and therefore, it is lawful for me to treat him as one who has put himself into a 'state of war' against me, and kill him if I can, for to that hazard does he justly expose himself, whoever introduces a state of war, and is aggressor in it." The (B)ATF are one such fascist federal group who are infamous for depriving Americans of their liberties, as well as other Constitutionally-guaranteed and INALIENABLE rights, such as one's right to self defense and one's very LIFE. One need only look at such incidences as Randy Weaver, Gordon Kahl, Waco, Donald Scott, (et ILL [sic]), to see that not only are the ATF a bunch of fascist tyrants, but their counterparts at the USMS [sic], FBI, and DEA (to name a few), are, as well.

Citizen's militias will hopefully ensure that violations of the Constitution by these power-hungry stormtroopers of the federal government will not succeed again. After all, who else would come to the rescue of those innocent women and children at Waco?!? Surely not the local sheriff or the state police! Nor the Army—whom are used overseas to "restore democracy", while at home, are used to DESTROY it (in full violation of the Posse Comitatus Act), at places like Waco.

One last question that every American should ask themselves: Did not the British also keep track of the locations of munitions stored by the colonists; just as the ATF has admitted to doing? Why???... Does anyone even STUDY history anymore???

ATF,

All you tyrannical motherfuckers will swing in the wind one day, for your treasonous actions against the Constitution and the United States. Remember the Nuremburg War Trials "But...but...but...I was only following orders!"...

Die, you spineless, cowardice [sic] bastards!

Finally, McVeigh corresponded with a Michigan woman, who made the material available to the FBI after the bombing. There is in this material a considerable quantity of Patriot articles expressing rage at government actions at Waco, Texas:

The people of this nation should have flocked to Waco with their guns and opened fire on the bastards! The streets of Waco should have run red with the blood of the tyrants, oppressors and traitors that have slaughtered our people. Every person responsible for this massacre deserves nothing less than to die. If we want to live in peace, then sometimes we must go to war.

If this is too extreme for you, then bow down, lick the hand of your master like a willing, complacent whore and shut your mouth. Take whatever is dealt to you and your children and do not dare to complain to me about your fate. I do not have the patience to listen to the whining of cowards.

There will be future massacres because we allow them to occur.

Angry words, to be sure. But, once again, the thrust of this and all of the other articles sent to the Michigan woman by McVeigh is for a mass uprising, not lone-wolf actions. Yet in a letter to her dated April 30, 1995, other thoughts emerge. Writing from an isolated desert encampment, McVeigh expresses themes of loneliness, isolation, fear of aging, frustrated sexual desire, and, most of all, a newfound sense of personal mission. Noting that passing out literature is proving to be a futile gesture of defiance against the power of the state, and taking as a model the example of those revolutionaries of a previous day who risked all to sign the Declaration of Independence, McVeigh notes that while he is today at the peak of his mental and physical prowess, it will not be long before time dulls his lethal edge. Thus:

Hell, you only live once, and I *know*. You know it's better to burn out, then [sic] rot away in some nursing home. My philosophy is the same—in only a short 1–2 years my body will slowly start giving away—first maybe knee pains, or back pains, or whatever. But I will not be "peaked" anymore. Might as well do some good while I can be 100% effective!

In short, if a popular revolution is not on the horizon, what is left but the despairing bravado of the lone-wolf assassin?

See also: American Nazi Party; Aryan Nations; Beam, Louis; Butler, Richard; California Rangers; Christian Identity; Church of Israel; Covenant, Sword, and Arm of the Lord; DePugh, Robert; Ellison, James; Franklin, Joseph; Gayman, Dan; Koehl, Matt; Lane, David; Mathews, Robert; Miles, Robert; National Socialist Liberation Front; National Socialist White People's Party; Odinism; Order; Peters, Pete; Phineas Priesthood; Pierce, William; Rockwell, George Lincoln; Tommasi, Joseph; Waco; Weaver, Randy; Zionist Occupation Government.

Further reading: Louis R. Beam, "Leaderless Resistance," *The Seditionist* 12 (February 1992); Richard Kelly Hoskins, *Vigilantes of Christendom* (Lynchburg, VA: Virginia Publishing Co., 1990); Jeffrey Kaplan, "Leaderless Resistance," *Journal of Terrorism and Political Violence* 9:3 (Fall 1997); Andrew Macdonald [William Pierce], *Hunter* (Arlington, VA: National Vanguard Books, 1989).

Arnold Leese   *See* Jordan, Colin.

Liberty Lobby   *See* Carto, Willis.

BRUNO ARMIN LUDTKE   Bruno Ludtke played a pivotal role in the political education of George Lincoln Rockwell, the moving force in the postwar Nazi revival in the United States. With Rockwell and Britain's Colin Jordan, Ludtke organized the World Union of National Socialists (WUNS) in 1961–1962 and attended the WUNS founding conference in July 1962 in the Cotswold hills of Gloucestershire, England.

As Rockwell's mentor, Bruno Ludtke helped shape Rockwell's crude anti-Semitism and unfocused anticommunism into a more integrated political philosophy. Ludtke's guidance enabled Rockwell to place his racism and virulent anti-Semitism within the context of an international Nazi revival.

Through voluminous correspondence that lasted from 1960 until Rockwell's assassination in 1967, Bruno Ludtke helped Rockwell develop the philosophical and tactical foundations of his political program: defining "White" simply as not being a Jew or of African or Asian descent, rather than the far more restrictive criteria of possessing Nordic or Aryan ancestry; the exploitation of "White Power" as an organizing principle; the creation of an international network of national Nazi and neo-Nazi parties to coordinate disparate elements into a worldwide movement; the infiltration of "Holocaust denial" propaganda into the media and worldwide educational systems; and the exploitation of religious imagery to legitimize the anti-Semitism that remained at the core of Rockwell's belief system.

Bruno Armin Ludtke was born in Harburg on the Elbe, Germany, on November 15, 1926. Ludtke's parents belonged to the Christian Church of God, a fundamentalist sect that attracted a small core of adherents in primarily Lutheran Greater Hamburg in the years following World War I. Ludtke's father, a stern, autocratic disciplinarian, was a vehement anti-Nazi. From an early age, young Ludtke idolized Adolf Hitler, precipitating frequent clashes with his father. In 1940, at age 14, Bruno Ludtke joined the Hitler-Jugend [Hitler Youth] over his father's objections, leading to an irreparable break between father and son.

When he attempted to enlist in the S.S. in 1943, Ludtke was rejected because of poor health. In 1944, due largely to the decimation of the German army and the lowering of physical standards in a desperate attempt to replenish the Wehrmacht, Ludtke succeeded in joining the German army. Ludtke served in the German occupation forces in Denmark until the end of the war.

In the postwar years, Ludtke studied engineering in Cologne. A brief three-month marriage in 1953 produced an infant son. Ludtke remarried in 1956. That union produced four daughters. Ludtke worked as an engineer in Cologne from the early 1950s until he lost his job in 1960, when he moved to Frankfurt and found a job as an Olivetti office machines salesman. In Frankfurt, Ludtke's fragile health deteriorated, and he was diagnosed with multiple sclerosis. Frequently unemployed, Ludtke barely supported his family through part-time sales work and freelance writing.

Although physically debilitated, Ludtke never lost his passion for Germany's Nazi past. He assiduously tracked the locations of former minor Nazi party functionaries and Nazi expatriates worldwide, building a network of Nazi sympathizers for what he hoped would be a political revival leading to a Nazi restoration to power.

As his health deteriorated, Ludtke worked obsessively to gather the remnants of the Reich's true believers. His work finally seemed to have a purpose when he read of George Lincoln Rockwell's new American Nazi Party in 1960. Ludtke's files became the basis for World Union of National Socialists recruitment worldwide in the early 1960s. Rockwell, the tall, charismatic former American Navy pilot, seemed to Ludtke the perfect leader for his anticipated worldwide Nazi revival, and he committed his passion and energies to his new Führer and to the fulfillment of his old dream.

—Frederick J. Simonelli, Mount St. Mary's College

See also: American Nazi Party; Jordan, Colin; Rockwell, George Lincoln; World Union of National Socialists.

Further reading: Frederick J. Simonelli, "The American Nazi Party, 1958–1967," *The Historian* 57 (spring 1995): 553–66; Frederick J. Simonelli, "Preaching Hate with the Voice of God: American Neo-Nazis and Christian Identity," *Patterns of Prejudice* 30 (no. 2, 1996): 43–54; Frederick J. Simonelli, "The World Union of National Socialists and Post-War Transatlantic Nazi Revival," in Jeffrey Kaplan and Tore Bjørgo, eds., *Nation and Race: The Developing Euro-American Racist Subculture* (Boston: Northeastern University Press, 1998); Frederick J. Simonelli, *American Fuehrer; George Lincoln Rockwell and the American Nazi Party* (Champaign: University of Illinois Press, 1999).

Dennis Mahon *See* Ku Klux Klan; Robb, Thom; White Aryan Resistance.

CHARLES MANSON At first glance, the inclusion of one of the most highly publicized murderers in recent American history would seem incongruous in this *Encyclopedia of White Power*. Yet, for a number of reasons, Charles Manson is an important influence on many of the younger adherents of American National Socialism—many of whom had not been born when the "Manson Family" was active in Southern California. Indeed, so great has this unspoken influence become that long-time National Socialist activist James Mason has formed an organization specifically centered on the leadership of Charles Manson, called the Universal Order, and has taken the case for Manson's leadership to the National Socialist faithful, as well as to the young aficionados of White Power music. The example of Manson and his original Family is of such interest that both a discussion of the historical Manson and an interpretation of the Manson legend as it stands today are warranted in these pages.

It is fitting for so ambiguous a figure as Charles Manson that, beyond the murders for which he was convicted and sentenced to death, the activities of the so-called Manson Family remain shrouded in myth some 30 years on. Certainly, the killings for which he and his codefendants Leslie Van Houten, Patricia Krenwinkle, and Susan Atkins were convicted are clear enough. The murder spree, which took place in the Los Angeles area in 1969, began more by chance than design, with the killing of UCLA student and Zen devotee Gary Hinman in the course of a bungled robbery attempt. Hinman had in the past provided temporary lodging to Manson and a few of his female core followers. Whatever the motivation of the Hinman murder, the killing was the precipitating event of the August 1969 murder of Sharon Tate, Jay Sebring,

Abigail Folger, Voytec Frykowski, and Steve Parent. The Tate killings were quickly followed by the slayings of Leno and Rosemarie LaBianca.

The motivations for these killings have been hotly debated. To Vincent Bugliosi, the prosecuting attorney and the author of *Helter Skelter,* the most widely read book on the case, Manson was motivated by an apocalyptic belief in the imminent end of the world through a race war in which the White population was doomed to defeat. The victorious Black population would in time realize that the White man is genetically more fit to govern, and would seek in vain for White survivors of the racial Holocaust to assume the reins of power. The Manson Family, having survived the apocalypse by hiding in a timeless cave at the center of the world, would then emerge to take power.

To the surviving female Family members, the motivation was more prosaic—to commit a string of copycat murders and thus to free Bobby Beausoleil, the Family member then being held for Hinman's murder. To still others in the world of religious fundamentalism, the murders were part of a wider satanic conspiracy spearheaded by the now-defunct Process Church of the Final Judgment. To still other Family members—and it is likely that the notoriously opaque Manson (who has never actually admitted guilt for any of the killings) would hint his agreement—radical environmentalism through an ideology called ATWA (Air, Trees, Water, Animals) was the Family's raison d'être.

Whatever the motive—or, more likely, combination of motives—that brought about the murders, all of the above suggestions are vital strands of the contemporary radical right wing, especially in its National Socialist form. Apocalyptic scenarios have long been a dominant motif in National Socialist writings. These range from the kind of depression/social collapse/race war scenarios that the American National Socialist movement understand all too well form their only hope of mobilizing a significant number of Americans to their banner. Indeed, one such elaborate apocalyptic fantasy, William Pierce's now famous *Turner Diaries,* has emerged from the wilderness of the radical right to become widely known. Moreover, the *Turner Diaries* centers on the imminence of race war, which has been the American movement's "apocalypse of choice" for many years, easily out-polling such biblical staples as floods, pestilence, and earthquakes. It is indeed rivaled only by the specter of economic collapse as a way to recruit the masses. Charles Manson's actions, if they were intended to foment a race war (as attorney

Vincent Bugliosi contends), provided an early model that a few other National Socialists such as Joseph Franklin (himself the model for Pierce's second book, *Hunter*) and Perry "Red" Warthan (who claimed a direct connection to Manson) would seek to emulate.

While American movement annals contain no records of "copycat" terrorism to free imprisoned movement members, there have been cases of terrorist actions and hostage taking in the European movement, acts intended to force the authorities to free imprisoned cadres. Italy in particular comes to mind in this regard.

Explicit Satanism would seem odd in the present-day National Socialist movement, and indeed it is the province of a small number of adherents. But the occult is a long-standing feature of National Socialist thought. Heinrich Himmler was devoted to occult explorations in the original Third Reich, Savitri Devi became in the immediate postwar years the high priestess of occult National Socialism, and such early American radical right wingers as William Dudley Pelley in the Depression years and James Hartung Madole in the postwar years kept the flame alive. Madole and his long-running National Renaissance Party established contacts with Anton LeVey's Church of Satan, and the Detroit-based Order of the Black Ram was led by a former follower of Madole's. Today, an occult underground still thrives in the National Socialist world, featuring such groups as the British-based Order of the Nine Angles and one called Reichsfolk, as well as the Swedish version of the Black Order. In these circles, the appeal of Manson is very strong.

Where Manson most connects with the "mainstream" of the modern National Socialist movement, however, is in his emphasis on ATWA (Air, Trees, Water, Animals). From its inception, National Socialism has been to a considerable degree a "religion of nature." In every country with an active National Socialist movement today, one of the key—and most dearly held—planks of the groups' programs gives ecological concerns an equal billing with questions of race and religion. The reasons for this are complex, centering on the National Socialist quest for purity in all its forms, be they racial or environmental. Thus the emphasis on ATWA by Manson's faithful today, as they seek to make the case for the leadership offered by their imprisoned leader.

According to Nuel Emmons's *Manson In His Own Words,* Manson himself ties these themes neatly together:

> Look around you, the worm's turning on the white man. Him and his pigs have put the dollar in front of everything. Even his own kids. Blackie's tired of being the doormat for the rich man's pad. So

while the white man is locked into his dollars, blackie's balling the blond, blue eyed daughters and making mixed babies. It's all leading to bad shit. Real madness is going to explode soon—everything is going to be Helter Skelter. But that won't effect us 'cause we'll be in a beautiful land that only we know how to survive in.

Over the years, this racialism would become more pronounced. In the CD *Manson Speaks,* still available today, racial stereotypes are frequent. Add to this Manson's denunciation of Jews in the Hollywood recording industry, whom Manson partially blames for his lack of success in the 1960s-era music business, and the affinity of Manson's thought with National Socialist ideology becomes clear. Yet another point of contact between Manson and the modern National Socialist movement is his unreconstructed patriarchy. This is hardly surprising, given the fact that Charles Manson's following was primarily female; in a movement that manages to attract very few women, this is no small matter.

With so many historical and ideological points of reference, it was only a matter of time before the American National Socialist movement discovered Charles Manson. In 1980, James Mason established contact with two imprisoned female members of the Manson Family, Sandra Good and Lynette Fromme, both being held in Alderson, West Virginia. Through them, he contacted Charles Manson at Vacaville, California. (James Mason recounts these events in his "Universal Order" entry in this encyclopedia.)

Certainly, the Universal Order's insistence on this recognition of the role and leadership of Charles Manson has not met with much success among the conservative majority of National Socialists. It has, however, attracted a following. Conversely, the Universal Order has encountered significant criticism among the young fighters of the skinhead movement. The reaction to James Mason's proposal that Charles Manson be recognized as the natural leader of the National Socialist movement by the young readers of *Resistance* magazine was so overwhelming that the editor, George Eric Hawthorne, presented in the next issue a full-fledged debate on the proposition from two of his magazine's readers. His introduction to this debate provides a fair representation of the "resistance" the Universal Order has faced in its quest to promote the thought and example of Charlie Manson:

> In the last issue of RESISTANCE Magazine, James Mason, author of *Siege,* took a fairly unpopular platform and proceeded upon a difficult thesis: although few people in the pro-White movement realize it, Charles Manson is actually ideally suited to be "the" leader of

our generation, and for us to win, we must recognize it. We were literally flooded with letters and phone calls from irate readers who firmly disagree with this concept, stating that any connection to Manson is pointless and dangerous to our credibility. One distributor even clipped out the Manson article from the issue before distributing it.

But on the other side of the subject, there is a growing body of Manson supporters that see the public view of Manson as a late 20th Century icon who carries weight and influence with his name, so much so that it may be the tool we need to sway the youth of our generation.

How great a success the Universal Order will have in promoting Charles Manson as the movement's last best hope for victory is questionable. What is certain is that the Manson legend resonates powerfully in the world of National Socialism on a number of levels, and that he will continue to cast a long shadow on the American National Socialist movement for years to come.

See also: Devi, Savitri; Hawthorne, George Eric; Madole, James; Mason, James; Order of the Nine Angles; Pierce, William; Reichsfolk; Religion of Nature; Universal Order.

Further reading: Vincent Bugliosi with Curt Gentry, *Helter Skelter* (New York: Bantam reissue, 1995); Nuel Emmons, *Manson In His Own Words* (New York: Grove Press, 1986); Nicholas Goodrick-Clark, *Hitler's Priestess: Savitri Devi, the Hindu-Aryan Myth, and Occult Neo-Nazism* (New York: New York University Press, 1998); Jeffrey Kaplan, "The Postwar Paths of Occult National Socialism: From Rockwell and Madole to Manson," paper delivered at the conference: Rejected and Suppressed Knowledge: The Racist Right and the Cultic Milieu, Stockholm, February 1997; Ron Kenner, *The Garbage People* (Los Angeles: Amok, 1995); James Mason, *Siege* (Denver: Storm Books, 1992); W. L. Reese, *Dictionary of Philosophy and Religion* (Atlantic Highlands, NJ: Humanities Press, 1980); Ed Sanders, *The Family: The Story of Charles Manson's Dune Buggy Attack Battalion* (New York: E. P. Dutton & Co., 1971).

JAMES MASON The life story of James Mason is typical of the National Socialist faithful of his generation. Born in 1952 in Chillicothe, Ohio, Mason awakened to the world of radical political activism with the onset of puberty. This radicalization was, however, primarily oppositional rather than racial. Mason grew to despise the status quo, and in the days of his youth the primary opponents of the values of the American middle class were Black. The Civil Rights movement of the mid-1960s was in full swing, and Mason recalls being, on the whole, rather admiring of his Black classmates. A common thread running through the biographies of many current National Socialist activists is a feeling of always being oppositional, always different. In this, it is the availability of an oppositional milieu rather than the persuasiveness of a particular ideology that will often first draw the activist to the movement. Mason is no exception:

> My interests always diverged from the mainstream. I rather don't like competition, preferring to have a field more or less to myself. If necessary, I'll always invent one of my own. I've seen it that what I pick out early often has a way of catching on. Not surprising that when that happens I usually move on. When just beginning in this [National Socialism] about 1966 or 1967, I felt absolutely confident I'd make some mark, if only through sheer default.

His epiphany came from seeing a news report broadcast about an American Nazi Party (ANP) march in Chicago. Here was a movement that was *both* oppositional *and* universally despised by Americans. Better yet, it was led by a charismatic and fearless fighter of his own race, George Lincoln Rockwell. Here was a movement to which Mason could belong, and here too was a form of political activism that, under the swastika banner, could strike fear into the hearts of its opponents in a way that robes of the Ku Klux Klan no longer could. At the age of 14, a lifelong National Socialist was born.

Determined to be a Nazi, what could a poor boy from backwater Ohio do to contact these distant urban heroes? Showing the same remarkable ingenuity that many another fledgling race activist would demonstrate in establishing his first tenuous link to the movement, Mason made contact with a classmate who had a reputation of being something of a "Hitler Youth," and thus was given a book, *Extremism U.S.A.* The book contained a picture of American Nazi Party West Coast activist Allen Vincent standing in front of a truck emblazoned with the address of the Berkeley, California, party headquarters. A letter to Vincent quickly produced the address of George Lincoln Rockwell's American Nazi Party in Arlington, Virginia. James Mason became a dues-paying member, perhaps one of its youngest, again at the age of 14.

Soon finding himself in trouble for chronic truancy, Mason saw the opportunity to leave Chillicothe behind for the more exciting world of American Nazi Party headquarters in Virginia. A call to ANP central resulted in a conversation with Mason's hero, William

Pierce, who told him (perhaps unwisely, given his age) to hop on a bus and "come on down." Mason was then still a minor at 16. Pierce for his part was indeed concerned about Mason's age, thus nothing was at first kept in writing, and Pierce paid Mason's expenses out of his own pocket.

Mason loved the life of the party activist. Indeed, his enthusiasm for doing whatever needed to be done was less than universally popular with older and less daring adherents. It would be the first, but hardly the last, conflict Mason would have with the movement's conservative majority. Nonetheless, when he reached 18, he was sworn in as a full-fledged member of the National Socialist White People's Party, by none other than Matt Koehl, the successor to the assassinated Rockwell. But Koehl's leadership fragmented the movement; an event that ironically swung a small portion of the National Socialist movement in a revolutionary direction with the creation of the National Socialist Liberation Front, under the command of Joseph Tommasi in El Monte, California.

As with so many individuals caught up in the Koehl-era NSWPP, the years rolled by uneventfully. Eventually, James Mason became a close friend of Tommasi and a collaborator with him and the group, though he never officially joined the National Socialist Liberation Front. Within a year, however, Tommasi was dead, and it was not long thereafter that Tommasi's successors, Karl Hand and David Rust, were imprisoned for their acts of racial violence. The NSLF underground died with Tommasi.

Mason continued for some time to publish the National Socialist Liberation Front journal, *Siege!*, and to head his own one-man band, the short-lived National Socialist Movement, which by Mason's own admission soon was foundering. Then came Mason's discovery of the teachings of Charles Manson. This association ended Mason's connection with his old comrades. Manson urged Mason to jettison the National Socialist Liberation Front in favor of a new grouping, the Universal Order, and as a result Mason and Karl Hand amicably agreed to part ways, with Mason holding *Siege!* as the organ of the Universal Order and Hand keeping its sister publication, *Defiance,* as official journal of the National Socialist Liberation Front.

Mason's adulation of the Manson Family and his tireless efforts through his current vehicle, the Universal Order, to present Manson to the international movement as an avatar on the level of a Rockwell or a Tommasi, and perhaps even of Hitler himself, of the coming National Socialist revolution—these efforts have isolated Mason in the world of contemporary National Socialism. From 1982 until the journal's demise, *Siege!* became the primary vehicle for the glorification of Charles Manson.

Mason himself was no stranger to the occult aspects of National Socialism, and like so many of the movement's '60s generation, he was drawn for a time to the teachings of Anton LaVey and the Church of Satan. Mason notes that in 1969, he purchased a copy of Anton LaVey's LP *The Satanic Mass* from a fellow National Socialist White People's Party trooper, and has "cherished it ever since." But while Satanism, particularly in its Church of Satan guise, was no stranger to the world of National Socialism, the figure of Charles Manson was quite something else. The selection of Manson and his largely female following as National Socialist heroes seems as unlikely, at first glance, as the elevation of Horst Wessel from dissolute street fighter to the selfless martyr of the original NSDAP (National Sozialistische Deutsch Arbeiter Partei, or National Socialist German Workers Party).

Certainly, the Universal Order's insistence on this recognition of the role and leadership of Charles Manson has not met with much support from the conservative majority of National Socialists. It has also encountered significant criticism from the young fighters of the skinhead movement—men (and they were virtually all men) who for the most part were not born until after 1969—the year of the sensational capture and trial of the Manson Family. Yet, to James Mason, the Manson allure as the prototypical NS Führer runs deep. In the pages of *Siege!,* as the journal after 1982 became, in effect, the organ of the Universal Order, the case for Manson as a movement archetype is put forth in depth. This appeal goes beyond the Manson Family's chiliastic dreams of race war—a fantasy that has never lost its allure to the American movement. On a deeper level, Mason points out the painful fact that Charles Manson's following was primarily female. In a movement that manages to attract very few women, this is a major attraction. James Mason's view is simple and to the point:

> ...good as it now poses is limp prick at best and people who are still alive sense this. Hence, the fascination with "evil" which at least has some life to it. Hitler being the best example. Manson being another. Women flocked to them both.

More, Manson and his women were no mere armchair revolutionaries. Like Joseph Tommasi, they seized the moment and acted. The Manson murders are thus of little consequence to Mason, given the apocalyptic intent of the crimes. Manson in this conception emerges as the ultimate realist: a leader who, like Hitler and

Rockwell, had torn aside the veils of illusory sentiment and the blinders of "system lies" to reach true freedom in that Nietzchean plateau that transcends mundane considerations of good and evil. It is a detachment to which Mason himself aspires, but even such *apologias* as his dismissal of the murder of Sharon Tate's unborn baby with the contemptuous words "With regard to the eight-month-old fetus Tate was carrying, it was, after all, a Jew" falls far short of Charles Manson's amoral example.

Thus when Mason took his case for the consecration of Charles Manson as movement leader to the aficionados of White noise music in the pages of *Resistance* magazine, in the 1990s, it was a kinder, gentler Führer that was on offer. Manson was presented as the logical successor to Rockwell's mantle of leadership, accompanied by a photograph of him smiling and bespectacled, looking uncannily like a grandfatherly version of Alan Berg, the Jewish radio talk show host who was murdered by the Order in Denver. After all, not only did Manson carve the swastika into his own flesh, announcing to the world his irrevocable allegiance to the National Socialist dream, but the motto of the Family, ATWA (Air, Trees, Water, and Animals) was presented, dovetailing well with the current National Socialist movement's emphasis on ecology as a natural outgrowth of its obsession with purity in every form. Mason concludes his magazine piece with the exhortation:

> White man, now is the time to use your secret weapon, your *brain,* and see and embrace your leader. Charles Manson. Then and only then can you effectively use your renowned weapon, fury and skill in battle, without being undone by the scheming Jew and his filthy, ZOG system.

The plea for Manson's accession to Rockwell's role as leader is, however, unlikely to be widely heeded. The Universal Order remains a tiny band of dreamers, though the group's minuscule size is not atypical of the explicitly National Socialist groups in both Europe and the United States. Each is numerically insignificant, but a few have had an impact far beyond their numbers. Mason and the Universal Order have had such an impact as well, and their ideas (if not their prescription for the universal acceptance of Manson's leadership) have filtered out beyond the world of explicit National Socialism.

It is an interesting fact, however, that many who cross paths with Manson and his faithful followers quite often come to grief. Whether by chance, design, or simply bad karma, the Manson Family seems to cast a black cloud over the lives of most with whom they come into contact. So it was with James Mason. Mason, whose association with the most violent aspects of American National Socialism would seem a sure prescription for extended sojourns as a ward of the prison system, had actually remained relatively above the fray and out of serious trouble with the law until his connection to the Manson Family. Then his life became remarkably turbulent. While in Ohio in the early 1990s, he became romantically involved with a 14-year-old girl. Despite the fact that the girl was an emancipated minor who had been previously married, Ohio authorities took a dim view of the liaison. That Mason took a number of nude photographs of the girl didn't help. Nor did the quantities of National Socialist material and the collection of firearms on the premises. And the large guard dogs in the yard, whose presence complicated the task of police surveillance, did nothing to endear Mason to the local constabulary. It was, in sum, a volatile brew that finally exploded in Mason's face when, following a nasty breakup, the girl went to the police. Apprised of the existence of the photographs, the police had probable cause to intervene, and this they did.

Seeing his legal situation worsening in Ohio, Mason moved to Colorado, all the while carrying on an unseemly dispute with the girl in the pages of movement publications. The girl's age, Mason's photographic propensities, and the less than benign specter of Charles Manson in the minds of many of the National Socialist faithful did little for Mason's reputation in movement circles. This was especially true with the conservative majority of American National Socialists, whose attitudes about women tend toward idealization in an archaic sort of way, and whose interactions with women are, to say the least, limited.

In any case, Mason clung to his principles and his photographs, and soon wound up in the custody of the state of Colorado. Released briefly in 1997, within weeks Mason found himself back in maximum security over alleged parole violations centering on three specific charges: possession of a deadly weapon (actually, several bullets to a gun he had thrown away), associating with Nazis (after a lifetime in the movement, he has few other associates), and, once again, possession of pornography.

In a hearing in February 1998, an attorney for Mason, who had been hired as a result of a pass-the-hat fund-raising effort, succeeded in having Mason's parole revocation set aside and the state of Colorado being reprimanded for its handling of Mason's case. Mason was duly released in March 1998, albeit with such parole restrictions as being forced to wear a leg monitor through mid-August 1998. Upon his release, he remained in Colorado, working on his follow-up to *Siege,* a book with the working title *Out of the Dust.* With the help of what he describes as "an antique but serviceable computer system," he was able to carry on correspondence, write, and tend to his web site. In 1999, however, he was returned to prison, although by the turn of the millennium, he was free and preparing to publish several books on prophetic and apocalyptic themes.

See also: American Nazi Party; Hawthorne, George Eric; Hitler, Adolf; Koehl, Matt; Manson, Charles; National Socialist Liberation Front; National Socialist White People's Party; Order; Pierce, William; Rockwell, George Lincoln; Tommasi, Joseph; Universal Order; Zionist Occupation Government.

Further reading: John Carpenter, *Extremism U.S.A.* (Phoenix: Extremism USA, 1964); Jeffrey Kaplan and Leonard Weinberg, *The Emergence of a Euro-American Radical Right* (Rutgers, NJ: Rutgers University Press, 1998); James Mason, *Siege* (Denver: Storm Books, 1992); James Mason, "Charles Manson: Illusion vs. Reality," *Resistance* 4 (spring 1995).

ROBERT J. MATHEWS   A legendary leader of the Aryan guerrilla group the Order, Robert J. Mathews is hailed as a martyr in White racialist circles. Born in Texas in 1953, Mathews was raised in a lower-middle-class family and grew up in Phoenix. Early in life Mathews developed an interest in conservative politics, joining the John Birch Society at age 11. He was attracted to Mormonism because of its discipline and conservative morals, and later adopted a more radical and militant position. In his late teens, Mathews cofounded the Sons of Liberty, a paramilitary underground of constitutionalist fundamentalists composed of far-right Mormons and survivalists, dedicated to counter what they perceived as the corruption of true Americanism.

A publicity stunt brought them to the attention of the FBI, which began a surveillance, but it was Mathews' refusal to pay income tax that got him into his first trouble with the law, earning him a sentence of six months on probation. Disappointed on a personal level with the Sons of Liberty, in 1974 he decided to move up to Metaline Falls, Washington, to start anew. He built a homestead there, married a woman named Debbie, and convinced his family to join him up north, but none of these events could long prevent Mathews from gravitating again toward radical politics.

Joining the National Alliance and getting acquainted with the circle around Pastor Richard G. Butler's Church of Jesus Christ Christian/Aryan Nations at nearby Hayden Lake, Idaho, Mathews grew increasingly frustrated with the impotence of the Aryan revolutionary organizations. Delivering "A Call to Arms," a much-publicized speech, at the 1983 National Alliance convention, Mathews graduated from words to deeds. Deciding that the time had come for revolutionary action, in that year he formed his second underground, named Brüder Schweigen [Silent Brotherhood], popularly known as the Order.

Mathews, who by that time had moved away from Christianity into Norse paganism, attracted a following of unruly men from Christian Identity circles and beyond, casting their task as a holy war "to deliver our people from the Jew and bring total victory for the Aryan race." The short but intense activities of the armed underground would transform Mathews into a legendary Aryan warrior. Keeping his band together through his personal charisma and diplomatic skills, Mathews embarked on an accelerating path of violent activities that would crown his career with martyrdom. Blaming him for a series of successful armored car robberies, a money-counterfeiting operation, and the murder of talk show host Alan Berg, the FBI was set on tracking him down as the leader of the armed Order. Developing informants allowed FBI agents to surround Mathews' safe house at Whidbey Island, Washington, in December 1984. Refusing to surrender, Mathews died in the flames that resulted, his gun in hand, on December 8. That date is described in David Lane's newsletter, *Focus Fourteen,* as a "holy day for Aryans," in commemoration of the day when "the Feds ruthlessly exterminated Bob Mathews," in the "massacre on Whidbey Island."

One man can hardly be exterminated, much less massacred. The wording indicates that Mathews has grown larger than life after his death, assuming the role of a legendary Aryan warrior martyr. In poems, artwork, and the lyrics of White Power music, Mathews is hailed throughout much of the Aryan revolutionary world, extending his name recognition as an exemplary Aryan man far beyond the United States. In a poem by Order member David Lane, Mathews is depicted as the slain warrior issuing a call to those yet living: "Arise, you Aryan Warrior/I've shown you how to fight!/You owe it to my children/To battle for the right."

The cult of Robert Mathews continues to grow, aided by two widely circulated documents. One, the Order's "Declaration of War," may be found in several journalistic sources, most notably

Kevin Flynn and Gary Gerhardt's *The Silent Brotherhood*. Less readily available in the mainstream media is a letter attributed to Mathews that was written to a local newspaper even as the FBI was closing in on him. Both may be found in their entirety in the "Resources" section of this volume.

—Mattias Gardell, Stockholm University, Sweden

See also: Aryan Nations; Butler, Richard; Christian Identity; Church of Jesus Christ Christian; Lane, David; Odinism; Order; Pierce, William; Wotansvolk.

Further reading: James A. Aho, *The Politics of Righteousness: Idaho Christian Patriotism* (Seattle: University of Washington Press, 1990); Michael Barkun, *Religion and the Racist Right: The Origins of the Christian Identity Movement* (Chapel Hill: University of North Carolina Press, 1994); Kevin Flynn and Gary Gerhardt, *The Silent Brotherhood* (New York: Signet, 1990); Mattias Gardell, *Rasrisk* (Stockholm & Uppsala: Federativs & Swedish Science Press, 1998); Richard Kelly Hoskins, *Vigilantes of Christendom* (Lynchburg, VA: Virginia Publishing Co., 1990); Jeffrey Kaplan, *Radical Religion in America* (Syracuse, NY: Syracuse University Press, 1997); David Lane [Wodensson], "ODINISM" (St. Maries, ID: 14 Word Press, n.d.); Andrew Macdonald [William Pierce], *The Turner Diaries* (Arlington, VA: National Vanguard Books, 1978); Thomas Martinez with John Gunther, *Brotherhood of Murder* (New York: Pocket Books, 1990); Stephan Singlar, *Talked to Death: The Life and Murder of Alan Berg* (New York: Beech Tree Books, 1987).

Mayhem   *See* Black Metal.

RON MCVAN   Author and cofounder of Wotansvolk [Wotan's Folk], Ron McVan is also a racialist artist. Born in 1950 in Philadelphia, McVan moved to Washington state and got involved in rock music and art. For 15 years, McVan toured the United States taking his surrealist and fine arts paintings to different cities. During these years, McVan developed an increasingly radical antigovernment and pro-White political position. In the late 1970s, he became involved in the militant racist Church of the Creator (COTC), contributing to the Church with his artwork, including various COTC logos. Moving to its Otto, North Carolina, headquarters in 1990, McVan became editor of the COTC paper *Racial Loyalty* and commander of the White Berets, the Church's paramilitary wing.

Although in agreement with Ben Klassen's iconoclastic anti-Christian fervor, McVan in time found Creativity spiritually shallow. Looking for a religious alternative, McVan began searching for his ancestral roots and developed an interest in Ásatrú, the pre-Christian Norse religion, cofounding the northern Oregon/southern Washington group Wotan's Kindred in 1992. Two years later McVan moved to St. Maries, Idaho, to work with the 14 Word Press of David and Katja Lane. Together, they established Wotansvolk as a vehicle for disseminating Aryan revolutionary Odinism, which they defined as "an ancestral faith that puts race first."

To McVan, Whites must "again learn to think with their blood," while Ariosophic Odinism is perceived as a spiritual path of "restoring" the "lost Folk consciousness" of Aryan man, deemed necessary for racial survival and expansion. McVan authored *Creed of Iron: Wotansvolk Wisdom,* an Odinist manifesto and ritual handbook, and also furthered Wotansvolk through his artwork. Besides illustrating each Wotansvolk publication with his artistic skills, McVan continuously expands the line of Odinist artifacts sold, such as rune-staffs, Thor's hammers, Odin's amulets, and ceremonial drinking horns. His artistry adds a special aura to the Wotansvolk headquarters and its surroundings. Magnificent wood sculptured wolves, dragons, and ravens can be found in the mountainous woodlands in which also a wooden Hof (temple) with elaborate carvings is situated. The interior of the main building is filled with shields, swords, sculptures, Viking art, runes, and paintings. Basing his work on historical, mainly pre-Christian Norse prototypes, McVan's artistry adds an important cultural dimension to the Wotansvolk efforts to re-create a perceived separate Aryan identity and revive its ancestral faith.

—*Mattias Gardell, Stockholm University, Sweden*

See also: Church of the Creator; Klassen, Ben; Lane, David; Lane, Katja; Odinism; Wotansvolk.

Further reading: Focus Fourteen [newsletter] (St. Maries, ID: 14 Word Press); Mattias Gardell, *Rasrisk* (Stockholm & Uppsala: Federativs & Swedish Science Press, 1998); Ron McVan, *Creed of Iron: Wotansvolk Wisdom* (St. Maries, ID: 14 Word Press, 1997).

TOM METZGER   **203**

TOM METZGER For many years, Tom Metzger has positioned himself as the lowest common denominator of American racism. This was a conscious choice that for a time brought Metzger to the front ranks of the American racialist movement and attracted a strong following overseas as well. At the same time, it has made Metzger a lightning rod for the attentions of the government and of various private watchdog agencies. While Metzger has managed to avoid the worst of state prosecutions, he was not so fortunate with a civil suit by the Southern Poverty Law Center under Morris Dees. It was the surprising aftermath of that suit that badly tarnished Metzger's reputation in movement circles. The shock waves from these developments have yet to abate.

Tom Metzger's entrée into the movement was conventional enough. In the early 1960s, he was one of many California right wingers who joined the John Birch Society. As his views hardened into anti-Semitic, racialist, and anti-immigration positions, he left the Birch Society's conservatism behind—especially after the 1963 book *The Neutralizers* in which Birch Society founder Robert Welch explicitly disavowed racism and anti-Semitism as divisive distractions from the greater anticommunist crusade. In the early 1970s Metzger began a drift through ideas, leaders, and organizations that is typical of those in the race movement.

Being a Californian, an obvious first stop was Christian Identity, where under the tutelage of American Nazi Party veteran James Warner (who himself was only passing through Identity on his way to Odinism before returning to Identity in the 1980s) he established a short-lived Identity ministry of his own. Metzger, however, was not truly of a religious bent, finding the Knights of the Ku Klux Klan under the mediagenic David Duke to be a more comfortable belief system.

Metzger did well as a Klan leader, forming a relatively stable following and undertaking a course of activism that brought him to the attention of the local media. However, as so often happens, the media spotlight was not big enough to share, and Metzger soon split with Duke in a particularly nasty public breach that, by the 1980s, would lead Metzger in the pages of his *WAR* newspaper to fantasize about the killing of "[Willis] Carto, Duke, [Edward] Fields, various National Socialists and Klan leaders. It had to be done, and oh it felt so good" (*WAR* 7:5). Metzger then formed his own Klan group, the California Knights of the Ku Klux Klan in 1980, but soon found more interesting diversions than Klan leadership.

In 1980, Metzger announced his candidacy for United States Congress, running on the Democratic ticket in California. Where David Duke sought to play down his past as a Nazi and a Klan leader, Metzger remained a Klansman and addressed questions relating to this involvement squarely. And while Duke's political campaigns won attention from the national press, Metzger ran a quietly effective campaign and won the Democratic primary, garnering some 33,000 votes. It was a remarkable performance, and even though he was wiped out in the general election, he got 35,000 votes (14 percent of the total votes cast in his district). Metzger was now on the map.

The Klan, however, proved a limited vehicle for Metzger's vision, and in 1983 the White Aryan Resistance (WAR) was born. From the beginning, WAR was something of a family business. WAR's headquarters, as well as Metzger's television repair business, were in his home in Fallbrook, California. Metzger's son, John, became active as well, both in WAR and in his own vehicle, the White Students' Union. Indeed, John's activities were sufficiently attractive that Church of the Creator (COTC) founder Ben Klassen tried unsuccessfully to recruit the younger Metzger as his successor in the COTC.

From the beginning, WAR was one of the rare racialist organizations in the United States to set out a coherent ideology in its recruiting efforts. This platform contrasts so sharply with Metzger's thuggish public image—an image that he has carefully cultivated both in his propaganda and in his home-made videos—that the WAR ideological appeal is worth a more careful examination. The key aspect of Metzger's ideology is its Strasserite focus, which Metzger dubs the "Third Force position." In the German National Socialist movement of the 1920s, a leftist wing of the party developed under the leadership of the Strasser brothers, Otto and Gregor. The Strasser brothers advocated a form of National Socialism that would take more seriously the "socialist" elements of the platform than Hitler was prepared to accept. Gregor actually rose to become head of the Party Propaganda office in 1926—a post he held until 1930—but with the National Socialist assumption of power, both Strasser brothers were effectively isolated. Otto fled the country, while Gregor stayed and was shot by the Gestapo in 1934. Metzger's championing of the Strasserite line put him in a position to appeal to a White working class constituency whose family roots lay in trade unionism, but for whom changes in America's social and political atmosphere since the 1960s have been anathema. At the same time, however, the Strasserite line alienated Metzger from many American National Socialists, whose veneration of Hitler and all things Third Reich has long been a kind of religious cult.

WAR's platform may be found in its entirety in the "Resources" section of this volume. In the document "What We Believe As White Racists," which is available from WAR's web site, Metzger sets out WAR's ideology at length. The primary theme running through the document centers on White separatism—the belief that America had by the 1980s become irredeemably hostile to racialist beliefs and that all that is left for the beleaguered White majority is withdrawal into a separatist enclave. Many of the ideas contained in the document were nothing less than visionary, in the context of racialist thought in the 1980s (when the document was written).

Metzger's leadership style, combined with the bonus of a thought-out political program, brought WAR a number of followers throughout the 1980s. Converts ranged from such movement veterans as Klansman Dennis Mahon to a number of skinheads throughout the nation. Metzger's outreach efforts were consistently innovative. His WAR telephone line offered callers a taped "hate-o-gram" of the day with an inimitably crude, race-baiting message recorded each morning. More influential still was his cable access television show, *Race and Reason,* which gave movement figures a moment in the media sun in the period before afternoon talk shows, in search of ever more exotic acts with which to draw viewership, discovered the radical right as a dependable substitute for the usual parade of America's walking wounded. Indeed, when the talk shows came a-knocking, Tom and John Metzger were always available to do some talking. They were thus present when a melee erupted on the episode of Geraldo Rivera's execrable talk fest in which the sleazy host had his nose broken by a chair-wielding skinhead.

Not to be outdone, that inveterate Geraldo wannabe, Jerry Springer, invited the Metzgers for an afternoon of chat and bloodshed, an episode that was filmed in Chicago and televised on May 11, 1993. The scene was remarkable. The panel was composed of such radical-right stalwarts as Tom and John Metzger and such self promoting nonentities as the Nazi-uniformed Art Jones, National Chairman of the America First Committee, who was accompanied by the entire membership of that organization (all two of them), similarly garbed and prominently displayed in the front row of the audience. On the other side stood Black nationalists Michael McGee and Doris Green. There was less to the confrontation than met the eye, however. Jones, a last-minute addition to the spectacle, was assured a place on the panel only by his willingness to follow the suggestions of the producers and "say something outrageous." When Jones protested that to do so could start a fight, he was assured that there was nothing to worry about on that score, since the show would have plenty of security guards. Still dubious, Jones was not sufficiently incendiary on a first run through, causing the host to call a halt to filming and start again!

Jones responded with a recitation of FBI crime statistics, which Commander of the Black Panther Militia McGee took to imply that Black women and prostitution were synonymous—and the tussle was on. This epiphany was short lived. Jones immediately apologized for the misunderstanding and shook hands with McGee. Worse, as the discussion wore tediously on, it became clear that the panel had more areas of agreement than disagreement, and indeed, the Metzgers were ultimately invited to address McGee's group—a meeting that went well, according to all concerned. The duplicitous host was left to end the show with a platitudinous soliloquy to the effect that none of the guests were nice people, even as the mailing addresses of each participating group were flashed on the screen.

The Metzgers' invitation to address McGee's supporters was not the first time that Tom Metzger had found himself on friendly terms with Black nationalist leaders. No less a personage than the Nation of Islam's leader, Louis Farrakhan, had held talks with Metzger and, according to Metzger, was poised to go into a business venture with the WAR leader before political circumstances changed sufficiently to sink the deal.

Metzger followed up on his high-media profile with the World Wide Web, where his WAR page, with its racist cartoons, sets new standards for primitively racist recruiting propaganda. In fact, by the early 1990s it was almost as if there were *two* Tom Metzgers. Privately, Metzger could be reflective, thoughtful, and, as always, iconoclastic. But at the same time, Metzger could play the thug, and do it well. So well in fact that, when most established racialist leaders tried to steer well clear of the skinhead movement, Metzger saw in the youthful skinheads the vanguard of racial revolution in America. Much of his outreach in the late 1980s was thus geared to the decidedly nonintellectual skinhead groups around the country. It was this flirtation that would derail Metzger's bid for primacy in the American race movement.

The putative alliance became costly in the wake of a civil suit won by the Southern Poverty Law Center (SPLC), holding Metzger responsible for the murder of a black Ethiopian immigrant in

Portland, Oregon. The plaintiffs asked for an award of $10 million (they ultimately received $12.5 million) in an action to, quoting SPLC founder Morris Dees, "Build a fence $10 million high" to keep the Metzgers out of Oregon. Tom Metzger and his son acted in their own defense, contending that "skins can't be organized." They in fact did more to lose the case than the plaintiffs did to win it.

The trial graphically demonstrated the interconnections between skinheads and racialist leaders when Dees played a videotape of Metzger in Tequila, Oklahoma, talking to a group of skins and suggesting that they "kick a little ass." Dees then played a tape of Metzger's telephone bulletin board that justified the killings after the fact, claiming that these "beautiful Blacks" (the victims) were "high on crack" and that the killers were doing "a civic duty." Another tape claimed that "One young fighter, Ken Mieske, received life" and that the victims should "get their Ethiopian ass [sic] out of this country." Losing the civil action temporarily closed down Metzger's operation, as well as making him technically homeless and garnishing 40 percent of any future moneys he may manage to earn.

The real effectiveness of the suit is best illustrated by the nearly hysterical warnings emanating from such a movement figure as Harold Covington to potential WAR recruits that, as a result of the suit, Morris Dees has gained control of the organization's post office box. This, according to Covington, not only makes Klanwatch and thus the FBI privy to every communication sent to Metzger, but also it allows Klanwatch to seize a significant percentage of the funds sent to WAR's burgeoning mail-order trade.

In fact, Covington seems once again to have been prescient in warning of yet another danger to the movement. In November 1995, another set of *alarums* reverberated throughout the movement. From Dr. Edward Fields's virulently racist newspaper *The Truth at Last* to the e-mail service associated with the former National Socialist figure Milton John Kleim, Jr., the Aryan News Service, the word belatedly spread. Dr. Fields offers the observation that "(if) they want their letters to reach Metzger faster, they should write directly to Tom Metzger c/o Morris Dees" (at the Southern Poverty Law Center's Alabama address). Harold Covington is typically more outspoken. In an open letter to Ed Fields, he writes:

Dear Dr. Fields,

Regarding your article about Morris Dees of the Poverty Law Center receiving Tom Metzger's mail, it should be emphasized that this has been going on for over three years now. Metzger's treachery has given the radical left the most important "observation post" into the activities of the patriotic movement that they have ever enjoyed.... I am especially concerned about the number of young people who have written to Metzger and had their correspondence turned over to Dees. At least one young man, Mark Lane of Birmingham, Ala., has been sentenced to prison in part due to "evidence" provided to the federal government by Morris Dees, in the form of Lane's private correspondence sent to Tom Metzger's WAR post office box. The truth is that Morris Dees is now the de facto publisher of the WAR newspaper.... Dees allowed Metzger to remain in business in return for allowing Dees' legally appointed agent, San Diego attorney James McElroy, the authority to open all the mail going to Metzger's Fallbrook P.O. Box, forwarding copies of all letters to the Southern Poverty Law Center and depositing all the money in a Dees controlled bank account. At the end of each month. McElroy writes Metzger a check for 50% of the "take" so he can keep publishing and keep his increasingly bizarre and hysterical telephone recordings on the air.

In the same letter, Covington perceptively describes the utility of the most virulent examples of racist propaganda to the watchdog groups' fundraising appeals:

A year ago, Metzger published a crude cartoon showing beheaded Mexicans lying in a field. Then Dees ran this cartoon in a fund raising letter to show how awful these "evil racists are". Thus Dees is actually financing an operation which spies on the right-wing and also provides ammunition for his money-begging racket at the same time.

This two-pronged attack took Metzger very much by surprise. He reacted with outrage and with counterattacks against his critics, but he was never able to fully deny the charges. National Socialist figure Rick Cooper tried to mediate by launching his own investigation. Cooper found that while it was true that Metzger's mailbox is (or was: Cooper is not certain of the current situation) probably under the control of Morris Dees through the San Diego attorney, the young skinhead whose arrest Covington attributes to a letter to WAR that was intercepted by Klanwatch was incarcerated as the result of the incriminating letter having been sent to another organization—also named WAR—under the leadership of Bill Riccio, who is widely thought to be a government informant (and in any case is in jail at the moment as well).

The explosion caused by the post office box controversy has deeper roots than appear on the surface. Every racialist suddenly was faced with the question: If a figure of the stature of Tom Metzger can be brought down and forced to cooperate with the movement's most implacable foes, who then is safe? And who in the movement can be trusted?

See also: American Nazi Party; Carto, Willis; Christian Identity; Church of the Creator; Cooper, Rick; Covington, Harold; Duke, David; Hitler, Adolf; Klassen, Ben; Odinism; Warner, James; White Aryan Resistance.

Further reading: Jeff Coplon, "The Skinhead Reich," *Utne Reader* (May/June 1989); Morris Dees and Steve Fiffer, *Hate on Trial* (New York: Villard Books, 1993); Mattias Gardell, "Black and White Unite In Fight?: On the Inter-Action Between Black and White Radical Racialists," paper presented at the conference: Rejected and Suppressed Knowledge: The Racist Right and the Cultic Milieu, Stockholm, February 13–17, 1997; John George and Laird Wilcox, *Nazis, Communists, Klansmen, and Others on the Fringe* (Buffalo, NY: Prometheus Books, 1992); Mark S. Hamm, *American Skinheads: The Criminology and Control of Hate Crime* (Westport, CT: Praeger, 1993); Jeffrey Kaplan, *Radical Religion in America* (Syracuse, NY: Syracuse University Press, 1997).

ROBERT MILES   In the viciously divisive world of the American radical right, one would be hard pressed to find a harsh word spoken against the late Pastor Bob Miles. Had he done nothing else in his three decades of activism, this alone would be achievement enough to warrant his presence in these pages. But Miles was much more than the genial face of a decidedly uncongenial movement. He was a Klan leader in an era when the declining Ku Klux Klan was becoming increasingly irrelevant, and yet Miles never allowed robed nostalgia to blur his analysis of the contemporary world. He created a rich religious stew that he called Dualism, in honor of his idealized vision of the medieval French heretical sect the Cathars. He created a prison outreach that both competed with, and yet complemented, Richard Butler's angry Aryan Nations prison ministry. And most remarkably, when the increasingly marginal voices of the American racialist right began in the 1980s to withdraw into angry isolation, Miles maintained friendships outside of the movement, never letting his strident anti-Semitism get in the way of a good conversation (or, when push came to shove, of finding good legal representation—a lesson learned too late by such other movement leaders as Tom Metzger!). Bob Miles was a racist for all seasons.

Miles was born of working class parents in 1925 in Bridgeport, Connecticut. His parents were ardent anticommunists, but even so it must have come as a surprise to them that the young Miles, upon his graduation from high school, would enlist in the Free French Forces fighting the Nazi occupation of France. Years later, Miles would recall the choice as motivated by his family's bitter disappointment at the short-lived Nazi–Soviet pact. A fluent French speaker, Miles served with the Free French until the United States entered the war.

Like a generation of young American artists in the interwar years who lived the life of the impoverished intellectual and would only in retrospect wax nostalgic about the romance of the experience, Miles found that his future course was much affected by his life in France. But for him, the romance was with a distant and much idealized past: that of the Cathars, a medieval dualist sect whose appeal to popular resentment of the power and corruption of both church and state swept through southern France and for a time, under the leadership of the minor nobility, managed to unseat the powers that be and live the dream of sinless perfection on earth.

In the thirteenth century, the Cathars were crushed by a papal crusade, but for Bob Miles they provided both a revolutionary model and a rich source of theological inspiration. From this stuff of dreams, Miles constructed his fanciful faith, Dualism. The primary text for his dualist Mountain Church was contained in a reprinting of a scholarly article by Eric Wyants, "The Church's Attack on the Cathars," which appeared in the fall/winter 1986 issue of *Critique*. The Wyants article was accompanied by Miles's running commentary in the guise of his favorite alter ego, Fafnir (the mythological Norse dragon slain by Sigurd). For those ill equipped to make much sense of Wyants's academic prose, Miles helpfully published a small pamphlet, "The Identity of Dualism and The Duality of Identity," which in simple terms contrasted his religious appeal with the better-known Christian Identity creed.

Robert Miles's Dualism was at root an imaginative act of selective retrieval in which the primary focus is on the Cathars, but with secondary elements drawn from Genesis, the *Book of Jubilees,* and various other intertestimental texts, as well as selected aspects of Christian Identity doctrine, which are brought together to present the White race as a race of giants, a superhuman elite who have but to realize their inherent greatness to be freed of the travail of this earth, and to return whence they came—to the stars, to the Light:

> We came to this earth. We are not akin to those who were made of
> it nor were created on it. The Sixth Day (soulless non-white male

and female based on Gen. 1:26–27) and the Eighth Day creations (Adam and Eve) are in our blood line of the flesh, but they are not of our soul lineage. The soul, your true self, rides in the flesh as a driver rides in a vehicle. Yet they are not one and the same. You enter the Old Testament briefly, and are noted in Genesis 6:1–4. You came to earth and took daughters of men! You were mighty and men of renown! You were GIANTS in the beginning! You still carry the ASTRAL SEED within your flesh. That seed is pure and untouched by all the matings with earth creatures. You can regain the powers and can be again the Giants of this earth! Prisoners of the flesh, prisoners of chains, you shall be free if you so will it and follow the light!

Dualism provided Miles, as well, with a remarkably creative formulation of the timeless theft of culture myth that provided Dualism with its core anti-Semitism:

First of all, Jesus was not a Jew. He was a Galilean. Jesus came out of the North! Not out of the desert lands. Understand that the population of Galilee, during the time of Jesus, was composed of relocated northern Folk tribes. Our folk!... Historians of a subsequent age attempted to give Jesus lineage socially acceptable to the masses, to fulfill prophecy.... This attempt to make history support a certain status, rewriting history as it were, is not new. It has been going on since man began.

Dualism, however, was still well in Miles's future in the 1960s when his horror of the demographic changes in Detroit and throughout Michigan, combined with the impact of the 1967 Detroit race riots, brought him to his personal Rubicon: the decision to leave the Republican Party, which he had served as state finance chairman, to work full time for George Wallace's presidential campaign in 1968. A number of the prominent figures in the racist right got their start in the Wallace campaign, and so it was for Miles. Thus began his sojourn in the wilderness of the American racist right, and he never looked back.

Following the Wallace campaign, Miles joined Robert Shelton's United Klans of America (UKA), where he quickly rose to the position of Grand Dragon, in charge of UKA activity in Michigan. It was in these years that Miles had his first serious brush with the law. In response to court-ordered desegregation, Miles was convicted in 1973 of bombing empty school buses and of tarring and feathering a Willow Run, Michigan, school principal. He drew a nine-year prison sentence, which he served while noting that a number of Klansmen should be grateful that he alone took the rap for the crimes. His prison time convinced him that reform was impossible in the United States. His demand now was for separation from the entity dubbed ZOG, the Zionist Occupation Government.

Following his release from prison, Miles retired to his Cohactah farm, the setting that gave a name to his newsletter, *From the Mountain*. He had long since broken his ties to the dominant culture, or, more precisely, had his ties broken for him. He had lost his job in 1970 as an insurance broker as a result of his Klan involvement. Now he would exist as did so many other leaders of the racist right—on donations brought in by his mailing list and whatever other money-making schemes he could dream up. Miles's prison experience also brought home to him the tremendous recruiting potential offered by the pool of alienated young White men in the prison system. For them, Miles created a newsletter, *Beyond the Bars...The Stars!*, which made its debut in June 1983. Although it was often confused with Richard Butler's prison newsletter on behalf of the Aryan Nations, *The Way*, *Beyond the Bars...The Stars!* was considerably different, promulgating Miles's Dualist religion and offering glimpses of the ironic sense of humor for which he was noted. In his introductory statements, Miles introduced the new religion to his captive audience:

> To those of the Astral Seed, welcome to your newsletter! We bring to you the theological news of your Folk. We bring to you articles written by ones also in chains. We write to you that are in chains to bring to you the good news that chains only bind the flesh. Your true self, the prisoner within the flesh who has struggled to be free since birth, can never be chained if you so will.
>
> The name of our newsletter comes from some anonymous soul in the past. The full statement was, "TWO PRISONERS GAZED OUT OF THE WINDOWS AND THROUGH THE BARS OF THEIR CELL. ONE SAW ONLY THE BARS. THE OTHER SAW ONLY THE STARS. BE EVER LIKE THE LATTER AND BE FREE."
>
> You who are called out of the earth worshippers of this age, and are called to the Old Religion, the Faith of your Fathers, will have questions and will have comments. Each individual letter will be answered and each question will be responded to as promptly as possible. This is your Church in Correspondence as you are our congregation behind the wire. The word "parish" is defined as "the ecclesiastical unit of area committed to one pastor." Having served as a prisoner of the anti-Christ, the staff now serves you!

From his Mountain Church, Miles in the early 1980s played host to a remarkable cross-section of the White Power world. Cross lightings alternated with Odinist festivities, while Klansmen and uniformed neo-Nazis rubbed elbows with skinheads and Christian Identity family folk. Over the years, it seemed that virtually everyone in the White supremacist world, as well as journalists, documentary film makers, and academic researchers made their way to Michigan, where the Miles family made all feel equally welcome. However, Miles's withdrawal to his Cohactah farm did not last long, and by 1987 the old man of the mountain was hailed into court once again.

This time, the charges were at once serious and, in Miles's sardonic view, deeply comical. The early 1980s were the heyday of the revolutionary Order under the charismatic leadership of Robert Mathews. Of course, Miles knew of the Order, and he knew its members well. Indeed, he wrote a thinly disguised, fictional account of their exploits, *The Secret Army Or WENN ALLE BRUDER SCHWEIGEN* in 1985. *The Secret Army* reprinted the 1814 poem by Max von Schenkendorf (in German and English) from which Mathews selected the name Brüder Schweigen, Silent Brotherhood, for his organization. Thus, when the government instituted its Operation Clean Sweep to roll up the leadership of the racist right following the defeat of the Order, Miles was a prime target.

Miles recorded the complaint in what became known as the Fort Smith, Arkansas, Sedition Trial in a pamphlet titled "White Separatist or Aryan Seditionist?," which was published after the acquittal of all defendants:

> FROM ON OR ABOUT JULY 1983, AND CONTINUOUSLY THEREAFTER, UP TO AND INCLUDING APRIL 1985, IN THE WESTERN DISTRICT OF ARKANSAS, AND ELSEWHERE, A GROUP OF PERSONS WILLFULLY AND KNOWINGLY COMBINED, CONSPIRED, CONFEDERATED AND AGREED TOGETHER WITH EACH OTHER TO OVERTHROW, PUT DOWN AND TO DESTROY BY FORCE THE GOVERNMENT OF THE UNITED STATES AND FORM A NEW ARYAN NATION.

Miles was further charged with having supplied a member of the Order with a drum of cyanide with which to poison the water supply of an unnamed northwestern city. The cyanide drum did in fact exist, though it was James Ellison, of the Covenant, Sword, and Arm of the Lord, who received the poison. From there the story becomes hearsay at best. Kerry Noble, Ellison's second in command at CSA, today notes that he is convinced that Miles intended for Ellison to use the cyanide in the water supply of a city, but he notes as well that he had no evidence to support the theory. Ellison for his part wanted to use the cyanide to coat bullets, but the group never did this either. In the end, the drum went unused for anything, and the unintended irony of an anti-Semite—particularly an anti-Semite with a marked fixation for medieval history—being charged with "poisoning wells" is so striking that no scholar of religion could fail to remark it. In any case, the Fort Smith conspiracy charges were at best fanciful, and the weakness of the government's case was well illustrated in Miles's often hilarious running commentary in his newsletter, *From the Mountain*. The most apt comment, however, came in retrospect. In the "White Separatist or Aryan Seditionist?" pamphlet, Miles asks:

> Why bother with an army, navy or airforce if two old men [Miles and Richard Butler], plus some not so old...form such a threat to the mighty power of this goliath called the USA? Do you really think that there is an underground army, sort of a Geriatric League on Wheelchairs, that is threatening the power of La Cesspool Grande, DC?

But if the trial failed to secure convictions, it did have the effect of forcing Miles to use scarce funds for legal fees and living expenses in Fort Smith. His wife, already in poor health, worsened, and finally lost her battle with cancer early in 1993. During her convalescence, *From the Mountain* began to recycle earlier stories, publishing in particular a number of photographs of comrades who had long since succumbed to age and infirmity. Like so many racialists of his generation, Robert Miles did not long survive the death of his spouse. Dualism, *From the Mountain,* and *Beyond the Bars...The Stars!* all went to the grave with him.

Robert Miles was the one figure in the American radical right whose innate sense of the absurd and all too rare ability to laugh at himself allowed him to consistently eschew bitterness, even as he recognized the futility of realizing his racialist quest within his lifetime. In a very real sense, he was the Abby Hoffman of the racialist right, and no figure has emerged in his wake with his ability to bring together the American radical right's warring tribes.

See also: Aryan Nations; Butler, Richard; Christian Identity; Covenant, Sword, and Arm of the Lord; Ellison, James; Mathews, Robert; Metzger, Tom; Order; Zionist Occupation Government.

Further reading: James Ridgeway, *Blood in the Face* (New York: Thundermouth Press, 1990).

———————————

JACK MOHR   Lt. Colonel Gordon "Jack" Mohr is a long-time Christian Identity figure from Bay St. Louis, Mississippi. Although in his voluminous movement writings he styles himself as "Brig. General," the impressive military title reflects his role in the Christian Patriots Defense League (CDPL), which he cofounded with John Harrell. Nonetheless, Mohr has a long and distinguished military record that includes service in World War II and the Korean conflict. It was during the latter that Mohr adopted a strident anticommunism that he would later combine with anti-Semitism and racism as staples of his long-running Christian Identity ministry. Mohr's frank memoirs of this evolution were published in his undated booklet, *Communist Terror in Peaceful Heaven.*

Like many of his generation of Identity ministers, Mohr's roots are in fundamentalist Protestantism, and his fundamentalist and Identity ministries overlapped for a time. This pattern of drift from fundamentalism to Identity also marked the careers of such key Identity figures as Gerald Winrod, Kenneth Goff, and John Harrell, among others. In each case, the break with their churches came over the issue of anti-Semitism. Given a literalist reading of such biblical passages as John 8:44 and Revelation 2:9 and 3:9, which posit the Jews in strongly negative terms (for example, Rev 3:9: "I will make those who are of the synagogue of Satan, who claim to be Jews though they are not, but are liars—I will make them come and fall down at your feet and acknowledge that I have loved you"), why, they wondered, were Jews and the state of Israel seen in such positive terms in the fundamentalist world? Lacking an acceptable answer, each began a religious quest that ended in Christian Identity. In every case, the result was the publication of polemical attacks on their former fundamentalist colleagues. For Kenneth Goff, the result was a 60-page treatise published in 1946 entitled *Traitors in the Pulpit and Treason Toward God.* Mohr, a more modest intellect, would offer a shorter but no less heartfelt contribution to this literature with a long, undated pamphlet, *Woe Unto Ye Fundamentalists!*

Over the years, Mohr has authored a vast number of Christian Identity materials, though these tend to be rather derivative of other Identity ministries. This tendency to recycle at length the work of others is best seen in his quarterly newsletter, the *Christian Patriot Crusader,* which he began in 1984.

Despite Mohr's involvement with the Christian Patriots Defense League and his military background, Jack Mohr is no William Potter

Gale. Mohr has outspokenly opposed the increasing inroads of National Socialism and violent rhetoric into the Identity world.

Old and enfeebled, Jack Mohr reportedly lives out his remaining years in Bay St. Louis in difficult economic circumstances, but holds true to the Identity faith that has sustained him for more than three decades of tireless activism.

See also: Christian Identity; Gale, William Potter; Goff, Kenneth; Winrod, Gerald.

Further reading: Kenneth Goff, *Traitors in the Pulpit and Treason Toward God* (Englewood, CO: Kenneth Goff, 1946); Jack Mohr, *Communist Terror in Peaceful Heaven* (no publication data); Jack Mohr, *Jesus—The Rock That Will Not Roll! (An Expose of Satan's Minstrels of Music* (no publication data); Jack Mohr, *The Satanic Counterfeit* (no publication data); Jack Mohr, *Woe Unto Ye Fundamentalists!* (no publication data).

DAVID WULSTAN MYATT   A fixture on the British National Socialist scene since the early 1970s, David Myatt is a prolific writer who headed the National Socialist organization, Reichsfolk. Myatt is most commonly identified with the occult wing of the National Socialist movement, and for him National Socialism is unambiguously a religion while the figure of Adolf Hitler is treated unabashedly as the savior of mankind. His story tells much of the nature of the spiritual quest that brought many young men into the National Socialist movement.

Myatt's biography is typical of the National Socialists of the generation of the 1960s. A true seeker, Myatt sampled many belief systems in his search for *the* answer to the riddle of the illusive pattern underlying the seemingly random jumble of world events, until he found National Socialism—especially as propounded by such mystics as Savitri Devi—at the age of 16. Even before this propitious discovery, however, Myatt's history was decidedly unconventional.

David Myatt was raised as a child in East Africa and the Far East, and notes that his earliest memories are of Tanganyika. However, he soon undertook his quest for the truth in a global odyssey that included extended stays in the Middle East and East Asia, accompanied by studies of religions ranging from Christianity to Islam in the Western tradition and Taoism to Buddhism in the Eastern path. In the course of this Siddartha-like search for the truth, Myatt sampled the life of the monastery in both its Christian and Buddhist forms.

Myatt's National Socialist career has been somewhat checkered, and has included prison time for his political activities and an extended battle with the British watchdog publication *Searchlight,* which prefaces every story about his doings with the title "cat strangler," in reference to his alleged occult experiments. Myatt for his part strongly objects to these charges, stating: "I have denied and do deny the malicious stories about cat-strangling and harming animals and challenged to a duel anyone who spread such allegations—for I find these particular allegations, involving cruelty to animals, quite detestable, being, like Savitri Devi and Adolf Hitler, a person who loves and respects animals."

Myatt's writings have been widely disseminated throughout the National Socialist world. His own journals, *The National Socialist, Das Reich,* and *Future Reich,* are far from the only vehicles for these writings. His essays have in fact been widely republished, and have most recently been made available via the Internet. He cooperated closely with the National Socialist–oriented Satanist organization, the Order of the Nine Angles (ONA), as well as with a number of other small occult or magical racialist groups throughout the world. The subject of his involvement with the Order of the Nine Angles is something of a sensitive point, given the widespread belief both within the National Socialist world and among the watchdog community that the Order of the Nine Angles is in fact a Myatt vehicle operated under the pseudonym Christos Beest. While this is unlikely to be the case, Myatt emphasizes that "I have denied and do deny such involvement/cooperation."

Then, in 1999, Myatt abandoned the movement. Following a front-page exposé on Reichsfolk and the ONA that appeared in *Searchlight,* which declared Myatt to be "the most dangerous Nazi in Britain," both David Myatt and Christos Beest announced that they were going underground.

Shortly thereafter, rumors began to surface in the movement to the effect that Myatt had converted to Islam. This may seem anomalous, but in the milieu of the radical right, it is not surprising, really. Myatt, as noted, is a true religious seeker who has sampled Buddhist and Christian monastic paths. Moreover, whenever the personality types that are drawn to the radical right wing decide to take their leave and try to return to mainstream society, they often require a text, a dogma, and a more or less absolutist set of truth claims to replace the beliefs that had bound them to the movement. In the United States, born-again Christianity has been one faith community that welcomes such seekers while absolving them of their past and offering the benefits of a supportive community of fellow-seekers. Conversely, in Europe, where highly formalistic state churches are the norm, a communitarian religion such as Islam can reasonably be expected to serve much the same role as the born-again faith. And thus, as with the amalgamation of Satanism and National Socialism, David Myatt may be once again just a bit ahead of his time.

See also: Devi, Savitri; Hitler, Adolf; Order of the Nine Angles; Reichsfolk.

Further reading: Jeffrey Kaplan, "Religiosity and the Radical Right: Toward the Creation of a New Ethnic Identity," in Jeffrey Kaplan and Tore Bjørgo, eds., *Nation and Race: The Developing Euro-American Racist Subculture* (Boston: Northeastern University Press, 1998); David Myatt, "Arts of Civilization," "The Galactic Empire and the Triumph of National Socialism," "Reichsfolk—Toward a New Elite," "Why I Am a National Socialist" (all available as e-text).

N

NATIONAL ALLIANCE   The National Alliance is William Pierce's National Socialist organization, which grew out of the ashes of the National Youth Alliance that Pierce had fronted for Willis Carto. After Pierce's split with Carto in 1970 or 1971, the National Alliance came into being in 1974. Its headquarters in those days was Arlington, Virginia. Pierce took with him the National Youth Alliance's journal, *Attack!,* which was renamed the *National Vanguard* in April 1978. The *National Vanguard* remains the flagship organ of the National Alliance today, though this is supplemented by a number of other publications, including the *National Alliance Bulletin* and, in 1999, the white noise music journal *Resistance.*

Closely related to the National Alliance is Pierce's designer religion, Cosmotheism, which appeared on the scene in the late 1970s. Cosmotheism's tax-exempt status was revoked by the Internal Revenue Service in 1978 following protests from the Anti-Defamation League and other watchdog organizations.

Pierce moved his operation from Arlington to rural West Virginia in 1985 where he formed the Cosmostheist community composed of himself and his immediate National Alliance followers.

The National Alliance today is the center for a successful book distributorship, a short-wave radio program named *American Dissident Voices,* a web site, and a thriving e-mail outreach. It remains, however, very much a personal vehicle for William Pierce.

See also: Carto, Willis; Pierce, William.

Further reading: John George and Laird Wilcox, *American Extremists, Supremacists, Klansmen, Communists and Others* (Buffalo, NY: Prometheus Books, 1996); National Alliance, *The Best of Attack!: Revolutionary Voice of the National Alliance* (Hillsboro, WV: National Vanguard Books, 1984, 1992); Frederick J. Simonelli, *American Fuehrer: George Lincoln Rockwell and the American Nazi Party* (Champaign: University of Illinois Press, 1999); Brad Whitsel, "Aryan Visions for the Future in the West Virginia Mountains," *Terrorism and Political Violence* 7:4 (winter 1995).

National Front   *See* Jordan, Colin.

NATIONAL SOCIALIST KINDRED   The National Socialist Kindred was a California-based organization whose existence was based on a communal dream: a separatist enclave for mystically oriented National Socialists who could withdraw into a self-sufficient, racialist utopia. The National Socialist Kindred was the brainchild of Jost, a Vietnam veteran who, in the 1970s, despaired of the racial pluralism, crime, and chaos of the cities and with his wife and sons moved deep into the wilderness of the northern California mountains. In the early days, they lived in a variety of shelters, from teepees to a rough wooden cabin, learning as they went the arts of survival and self-sufficiency.

The National Socialist Kindred, however, aimed to create a separatist enclave where Jost and his family could enjoy the support of a like-minded community. The dream was called Volksberg, and the National Socialist Kindred's large output of literature, which centered on the themes of National Socialism, explicit Hitler worship, and racialist Odinism, was originally designed to propagate this communal vision. For Jost and the National Socialist Kindred, however, the communal dream was not to be, and the National Socialist Kindred was officially dissolved, to be replaced by a system of Aryan meditation called Arya Kriya.

In a letter to a friend, Tommy Rydén in Sweden, Jost candidly explains what had gone wrong:

> We stopped using the name NS Kindred for three reasons: first, our scope is so much different now that the name is misleading; second, legally, the NS Kindred is considered a business name, and this requires bi-annual fees and bureaucratic paperwork which we no longer wanted to deal with; third, Arya Kriya training and our whole program is unique and it requires a much more personal relationship than any organization could afford. So, we decided to drop NS Kindred and publish and correspond simply under Jost, which eliminates the bureaucratic BS, is more personal, and has no connotation which might be misleading.
>
> Yes, we has some problems with Nazis. They destroyed years of hard work. We found the Folk-community concept was very alluring, but few people were willing to forsake job, home, friends, family, etc., to move here. We found that more often than not, those who were willing to pull up stakes and move here were willing to do so

because [they] had no job, no home, no family, no friends, nor anything else. They were looking for somebody to take care of them! Most were psychopaths and dangerous.

We learned (the hard way) that a Folk-community must be organic, that is, it must spring from those who are already established in the area. So, now that we are working with our neighbors, who we know and who are already established, to build an organic Folk-community here, and this is working much better. However, for fear of attracting psychopaths (the racial movement is full of them) we decided not to publicize it anymore. We publish the ideas so that others can form Folk-communities in their own areas, but are quiet about our work here.

We had hesitated for many years about introducing Arya Kriya. We didn't want to "cast pearls before swine" (pardon my paraphrasing of the dead Jew.) But realizing its awesome potential, we finally decided to give it a try. To our surprise, there has been lots of interest, even though we have not really advertised it. Also, since it requires some Aryan discipline, it doesn't attract the psychos. We have a number of prisoners taking the course, but they are of higher intelligence than most, and the Kriya seems to be really helping them. Meanwhile, our Folk-community here is becoming a Kriya community as well. Interest is growing in all quarters.

With the National Socialist Kindred's communal dream in tatters, Jost turned increasingly inward. The result was Arya Kriya, but even this did not get far before Jost's untimely death in 1996.

See also: Arya Kriya; Hitler, Adolf; Jost; Odinism; Rydén, Tommy.

Further reading: Jeffrey Kaplan and Leonard Weinberg, *The Emergence of a Euro-American Radical Right* (Rutgers, NJ: Rutgers University Press, 1998).

NATIONAL SOCIALIST LIBERATION FRONT   The National Socialist Liberation Front (NSLF) was a political front conceived in early 1969 by Dr. William Pierce and intended to compete against the leftist movements on U.S. college campuses. The NSLF was a deliberate takeoff on the National Liberation Front of the Vietnamese, whose struggle was then dominating the news. In this instance, national liberation meant an end to Jewish control of government in a land where Whites are a majority.

The NSLF was an experimental offshoot from the parent organization, the National Socialist White People's Party (NSWPP), formerly known as the American Nazi Party. For its first few years of existence under this new name, it issued a quarterly publication, *The Liberator,* and activities were carried out mainly by regular party personnel. During this time, memberships were issued and control was headquartered at Arlington, Virginia.

In 1974, the NSLF was reborn when former NSWPP Captain Joseph Tommasi of El Monte, California, took over the name to serve as the political front for his new, revolutionary brand of National Socialism. A deep schism had developed within the party between the conservative, orthodox faction and the younger, more radical members. It was Tommasi's philosophy to abandon the long-standing strategy of attempting to raise a mass movement in order to effect change legalistically and instead to begin conducting guerrilla warfare against the government.

In line with the new approach, Tommasi and his hard-core followers retired their traditional Nazi uniforms and military haircuts—which Tommasi claimed only gave the impression of an invasion from Mars—in favor of army fatigues and longer hair and beards. Emphasis was moved from political protocol to physical strikes against the enemy. Toward this end, Tommasi led a four-man underground dedicated to carrying out what would be referred to as terrorist activities.

In a dispute with National Socialist White People's Party members in August 1975, Tommasi was shot and killed in El Monte, California. Lieutenant David Rust took over the leadership of the NSLF until he was arrested not long afterward on firearms violations.

To prevent the NSLF from disbanding, other former NSWPP members in Cincinnati, Ohio, adopted the name, issued literature, and carried on with organizational matters from 1977. In this they were joined by units in Louisville, Kentucky; Wilmington, Delaware; and elsewhere. The object was now to influence all other far-right-wing groups in favor of Tommasi's own revolutionary way of thinking.

During the summer of 1980, Tommasi's publication, *Siege,* was resurrected as a monthly newsletter of the NSLF by James Mason, also of Ohio and a former party member. The title had been borrowed by Tommasi from the Weather Underground. Simultaneously, *Defiance* was issued by John Duffy as another NSLF publication.

By 1982, Karl Hand had assumed NSLF leadership in Louisiana as well as the publication of *Defiance*. It is ironic that, under

Hand's direction, the NSLF resumed the more traditional type of uniformed political demonstration and refrained from overt illegality. Despite this, Hand was arrested on a weapons charge and imprisoned for a number of years. This signaled the end to the National Socialist Liberation Front. It is also ironic that at about the same time, the National Socialist White People's Party itself closed its doors in Arlington.

Developments in the United States, which had initially prompted the formation of both the American Nazi Party in the late 1950s and the NSLF through its various incarnations throughout the 1960s, '70s, and '80s, continued to intensify. The influence projected by these early forerunners now has Adolf Hitler, along with a reliance on violence, generally accepted among the present-day radical right.

James Mason, Universal Order

See also: American Nazi Party; Hitler, Adolf; Mason, James; National Socialist White People's Party; Pierce, William; Tommasi, Joseph.

Further reading: Jeffrey Kaplan, "Leaderless Resistance," *Journal of Terrorism and Political Violence* 9:3 (fall 1997); Jeffrey Kaplan, "Religiosity and the Radical Right: Toward the Creation of a New Ethnic Identity," in Jeffrey Kaplan and Tore Bjørgo, eds., *Nation and Race: The Developing Euro-American Racist Subculture* (Boston: Northeastern University Press, 1998); James Mason, *Siege* (Denver: Storm, 1992).

National Socialist Movement *See* Jordan, Colin.

NATIONAL SOCIALIST VANGUARD The National Socialist Vanguard (NSV) and its associated business venture ST Enterprises were founded in January 1983 in Salinas, California, and then moved to Goldendale, Washington, in the fall of 1985. ST Enterprises folded in 1986. The National Socialist Vanguard, an unincorporated association that operates under the First Amendment to the U.S. Constitution guaranteeing freedom of association, remains in existence to this day. The address is P.O. Box 328, The Dalles, Oregon 97058.

The NSV advocates a survival program. It recommends that all Americans arm themselves with legal firearms and plenty of ammunition, store food, ensure a drinkable water supply, and stock survival items. The NSV also recommends that White people move to rural areas and network with other White survivalists for mutual defense and support in preparation for that day when death and chaos engulf the world in Armageddon (essentially a race war). Other than the survival program, the NSV recommends that White people engage in legal, organizational, and political activities that are to their liking.

The National Socialist Vanguard publishes the *NSV Report,* which primarily serves as a quarterly progress report of what the organization is doing, its trials and tribulations. Rather than publish propaganda for the masses, the reports are geared to movement activists, leaders, and others who understand the basic problems and who can identify with our experiences. Secondarily, the reports serve as an educator regarding the present state of the movement overall, the situation in the Northwest, and some philosophy.

National Socialist Vanguard activities are financed basically by the activists themselves. The National Socialist Vanguard is not a membership organization, so there are no dues or membership cards. There is no literature or book list. The *NSV Report* is self-financed except for that portion that is offset by freewill donations from various supporters and sympathizers, most of whom are not movement activists.

Rick Cooper, National Socialist Vanguard

See also: Cooper, Rick.

Further reading: Rick Cooper, "Brief History of the White Nationalist Movement," *NSV Report* (see the "Resources" section of this volume); John George and Laird Wilcox, *Nazis, Communists, Klansmen and Others on the Fringe* (Buffalo, NY: Prometheus Books, 1992); Jeffrey Kaplan, *Radical Religion in America* (Syracuse, NY: Syracuse University Press, 1997).

NATIONAL SOCIALIST WHITE PEOPLE'S PARTY Paraphrasing Hegel, Karl Marx once remarked that history repeats itself, first as tragedy, second as farce. No better proof of the truth of this axiom may be offered than the story of the National Socialist White People's Party (NSWPP). In this conception, the tragedy phase of American National Socialist history was the attempt by Matthias Koehl as the leader of the American Nazi Party's successor organization, the NSWPP, to fill the shoes of the ANP's founder, George Lincoln

Rockwell. The current efforts to function under the purloined NSWPP banner by the bombastic Harold Covington must qualify as the stage of historical farce.

The National Socialist White People's Party was born in 1966 out of the growing realization on the part of Rockwell and a few of his senior followers that not only was the American public immune to the blandishments of Nazi ideology and repelled by the uniforms, swastikas, and other accoutrements of 1930s Germany, but most members of the American radical right wing were unable to put aside their distaste for Hitler and all things Nazi sufficiently to cooperate with Rockwell on the many issues on which they were in agreement. Thus, the Nazis marched alone against the civil rights movement, against Martin Luther King, Jr., and against a host of other 1960s-era developments that the far right deemed inimical to all that was good and true.

Whether the National Socialist White People's Party could have become the answer to Rockwell's public relations problems will never be known. In August 1967 Rockwell was assassinated by a dissident Nazi, John Patler, whereupon his second in command, Matthias "Matt" Koehl, took control of the party. In short order, Koehl's inept leadership alienated the old guard and would soon drive them out of the organization. William Pierce, James Warner, Ricky Cooper, Harold Covington, Joseph Tommasi, James Mason, and many, many more either resigned or were expelled from the party under Koehl's direction. At the same time, a steady stream of younger adherents drifted into NSWPP ranks, served for a time, and then departed with the same bitterness as had their predecessors. Within a year of Koehl's assumption of power, the National Socialist White People's Party began a process of disintegration that would mark the rest of its organizational existence.

Shortly after assuming power, Koehl issued a pamphlet titled "An Introduction to the National Socialist White People's Party," which presented a short history of the organization and offered potential recruits a 12-point program that, in effect, summed up much of the thinking of the American radical right in the late 1960s.

First, the National Socialist White People's Party demanded the creation of a White republic for all Aryans, a move that presaged the separatist currents of the 1980s. Next, assuming the creation of such a separate state, the National Socialist White People's Party appeared to demand an end to non-White and Jewish immigration to the United States, and the separate republic in turn would restrict citizenship to only "those White people who prove themselves worthy of it." The third point in the program demanded the provision of a social safety net, as well as social justice for Whites. Next came a demand for the defense of the family farm, followed by a call for the strengthening of the family unit, including a paean to motherhood, which should be "universally recognized as the noblest profession to which any White woman can aspire." Along the same lines, the party called for a new education system that would place equal emphasis on character building, physical training, and "mental abilities."

Point seven tackled the economic sphere, demanding public (that is, state) control of banking and credit. The next point centered on the often overlooked environmental concerns of the far right, demanding "the phasing out of all forms of energy which befoul the environment, such as petroleum and nuclear fuels." These would be replaced through intensive research for alternative sources of energy. This specificity disappears in the ninth point, a demand for "Aryan cultural endeavor" and an end to other forms of popular culture. What exactly constitutes an Aryan cultural form is left to the imagination. Foreign policy was next, and its program plank offered little more of substance than a predictable call for a strong military. Point eleven demanded a eugenics program for "the propagation of the highest racial elements" within the putative White republic. Finally, a sweeping call was issued for the new Aryan state to take the lead in the spiritual life of the people so as to combat the modern ills of "materialism, cynicism, and egoism" in favor of "a rebirth of Traditional Aryan spiritual values." Once again, however, what constituted Aryan spiritual values was left unspecified.

Beyond the twelve-point program, little agreement was forthcoming from the ranks of the National Socialist White People's Party in the Koehl era, as the organization from the late 1960s through the 1970s continued to fragment. So well known was the organization—and so few were the alternatives for American National Socialists seeking an organizational home—that even though many left the group, others continued to fill out the membership forms and pay dues. Some of this scattered following were actually able to form local units—usually tiny aggregations of no more than a half dozen in any given place. A few, particularly in the Midwest, did for a time function with relative effectiveness, sending in their monthly action reports, engaging in leafleting, or managing to make an appearance in the local media. Koehl would frequently call the most effective (or, more precisely, the most literate) of the local leaders to headquarters in Arlington to fill the gaps left by the constant stream of angry resignations from party positions.

Several factors seem to have been at the root of this constant turnover. On an ideological level, Koehl's reverence for the 1930s model of German National Socialism had made it virtually impossible for him to adapt his own organization to the realities of 1970s America. In particular, his insistence on the Leadership Principle, which, in his interpretation, demands absolute obedience from subordinates, had the practical effect of alienating virtually every capable adherent the NSWPP managed to attract. This disinclination to tolerate any potential challenges to his leadership, together with the remarkably poor quality of the recruits drawn to American National Socialism, compounded the centrifugal tendencies inherent in the volatile mix of borderline personalities that are attracted to explicit National Socialism in the first place, making "organizational stability" in this milieu an oxymoron.

Thus, virtually every National Socialist who became active in the decades of the 1970s and early 1980s has the NSWPP on his (or, more rarely, her) résumé, but virtually none stayed with the group for long. Moreover, of the myriad of tiny National Socialist splinter organizations that exist in America today, most have roots in the NSWPP. Some of these achieved a degree of notoriety. Examples include William Pierce's National Alliance today, or such defunct aggregations as Joseph Tommasi's National Socialist Liberation Front in El Monte, California, and the National Socialist Party of America in Chicago, which was led by such well-known American Nazis as Frank Collin, Gary Lauck, and Harold Covington. Most, however, more closely followed the pattern of James Burford's revamped American Nazi Party, also in Chicago, and functioned as one-man units.

In 1982, the Internal Revenue Service foreclosed on the Arlington headquarters of the National Socialist White People's Party. Koehl responded with a crash fund-raising drive and moved to a piece of rural property in his native Wisconsin, which he pitched as a new and more secure party headquarters. The 1980s would thus see constant mass-mailed appeals for funds under this and a variety of other guises as the NSWPP struggled to keep afloat. Koehl sold literature, dreams, and promises, but it was his sale of "Victory Bonds" that may have been the final nail in the National Socialist White People's Party's coffin. Koehl sold these worthless bonds to the National Socialist faithful against the promise that they could be redeemed at a handsome profit after the party's assumption of power. Former National Secretary Ricky Cooper sued to recover the money he had invested in the scheme, and though the suit was unsuccessful, it had the effect of bringing the operation to the attention of the Securities and Exchange Commission, which promptly put a stop to it. Koehl responded by changing the name of the National Socialist White People's Party to the New Order and withdrawing deeper into his semiretirement in Wisconsin. Thus, by 1984 the National Socialist White People's Party was dead.

Today, the New Order puts out the *NS Bulletin,* issues occasional fund-raising appeals, and keeps Koehl's 1960s-era writings in circulation.

In 1995, Harold Covington laid claim to the name National Socialist White People's Party, and the group took wing as a virtual National Socialist group. It exists today in Covington's fertile imagination as well as in his private e-mail list. In 1998, Covington found himself named in a copyright infringement suit filed by an entity called the George Lincoln Rockwell Foundation, chaired by veteran activist Steve Kendall. The action capped an intensely divisive battle over Covington's unauthorized attempt to revive the NSWPP under his own leadership, and will probably mark the culmination of the NSWPP's evolution from the stuff of tragedy to its final appearance in the guise of high farce.

See also: American Nazi Party; Burford, James; Collin, Frank; Cooper, Rick; Covington, Harold; Koehl, Matthias; Lauck, Gary; Mason, James; National Alliance; National Socialist Liberation Front; National Socialist Party of America; Pierce, William; Rockwell, George Lincoln; Tommasi, Joseph; Warner, James.

Further reading: John George and Laird Wilcox, *American Extremists, Supremacists, Klansmen, Communists and Others* (Buffalo, NY: Prometheus Books, 1996); George Lincoln Rockwell, *This Time the World!* (Arlington, VA: Parliament House, 1963); George Lincoln Rockwell, *White Power* (n.p., 1967, 1977); Frederick J. Simonelli, *American Fuehrer: George Lincoln Rockwell and the American Nazi Party* (Champaign: University of Illinois Press, 1999).

National Youth Alliance   *See* Carto, Willis; National Alliance; Pierce, William.

Kerry Noble   *See* Covenant, Sword, and Arm of the Lord; Ellison, James.

O

ODINISM   A reconstruction of the Viking-era Norse pantheon, Odinism plays a vital role in the world of the radical right. Odinism today is becoming increasingly distinct from Ásatrú. Devotees of the same Norse/Germanic pantheon, Ásatrúers tend to eschew overtly racist constructions of their tradition, concentrating instead on the ritual and magical elements central to all Wiccan/neopagan religions.

As with other neopagan belief systems, Odinists practice an imaginative blend of ritual magic, ceremonial forms of fraternal fellowship, and an ideological flexibility that allows for a remarkable degree of syncretism with other White supremacist appeals—National Socialism in particular. Ironically, Odinists tend to subscribe to a number of beliefs that are explicitly Christian. Anti-Semitism, for example, would have puzzled the pagan-era Norse, as would the various conspiratorial fantasies that are ubiquitous among the radical right.

Although Odinism's precise origins are far from clear, its intellectual roots lie in the world of such nineteenth- and early twentieth-century German occultists as Guido von List, Georg Lomer, and Rudolf von Sebottendorff, as well as in such occult groups as the Edda Society. Of more direct organizational impact on the modern Odinist movement, however, was the profound social and political crises that engulfed Germany in the chaotic period of the Weimar Republic. In this time of intermingled chaos and decadence, wandering groups of displaced or simply disillusioned German youth (known collectively as the German Youth Movement) began—perhaps as a lark, perhaps with more serious intent—to make sacrifices to Wotan. Many of these young people would in the Nazi era give up their wanderings for the excitement of helping to build the Third Reich. Indeed, the old gods were hardly alien to the architects of the Third Reich. A fascinating, if eccentric, literature has grown up around the mystical endeavors of leading figures in the Nazi party, of which the revival of Germanic paganism was but one manifestation.

As Hitler was rising to power in Germany, the occult implications of German National Socialism were gaining the attention of
mystics outside of Germany. One such, an eccentric Australian
named Alexander Rud Mills, was an unabashed Nazi sympathizer
and a believer in a form of racial mysticism that posited
pre-Christian Anglo-Saxon society as the Golden Age of the British
people. Mills in the 1930s began to turn his dreams toward the
reconstruction of that perfect time in this degenerate age. Mills's
diagnosis held that the contemporary malady of civilization was the
result of the malign influence of the Jews, and, because Christianity was built on the foundation of Judaic thought, it had to be sev-
ered from the soul of the descendants of the Anglo-Saxon race as
surely as one would excise a cancer.

Out of this process of reasoning came Mills's first and most
influential book, *The Odinist Religion: Overcoming Jewish Christianity*. It was the first of a number of writings—mostly in tract
form—that Mills would churn out, but it is the most revealing of the
gradual process through which he attempted to disengage his
thought from the deeply ingrained paradigms of the dominant
Christian culture.

Mills would win few converts to his Anglecyn Church of Odin,
but his writings would be kept alive in the world of the right-wing
publishing houses. It was in this milieu that Mills would be discovered by Else Christensen and her late husband Alex in the early
1960s during the course of reading such right-wing staples as
Yockey's *Imperium* and Spengler's *Decline of the West*. But it was
Mills who would inspire the widowed Else Christensen to form the
Odinist Fellowship. The publication in 1971 of the first issue of the
Fellowship's journal *The Odinist* coincided with the discovery of the
Norse pantheon by other seekers, most notably Steve McNallen,
who would at virtually the same time found the Ásatrú Free
Assembly.

The heady combination of National Socialism, the occult, the
Viking mystique, and the quest for community proved irresistible
to others as well. Of these, perhaps most revealing of the processes
by which these racialist adherents seek to exploit the Norse/Ger-
manic revival are the activities of George Dietz. A German immigrant and long-time figure in American neo-Nazi circles whose
primary income appears to be derived from the sale of anti-Semitic
and racist literature through his Liberty Bell Publications, Dietz
took note of the revival of Odinist groups around the United States.
Through one of his younger associates, Ron Hand, Dietz created the

Odinist Study Group as a front operation for his own National Socialist movement. Hand, operating under his own name in Odinist affairs and the name Reinhold Dunkel in NS circles, enjoyed complete autonomy as leader of the group.

By the late 1970s or early 1980s, Dietz had come to realize that Germany was probably dead to a possible National Socialist revival and imagined that the last hope for a Nazi resurgence was the United States. Odinism, he reasoned, might be the engine for a future National Socialist America. The extent of George Dietz's knowledge of the Odinist revival is in some doubt. He clearly knew of Else Christensen, but whether he knew much more is questionable. The original plan appears to have been to gather a list of local Odinist groups and to infiltrate them, turning them gradually toward National Socialism. This plan could not be carried out, as Dietz had decided to sell his mailing list, of which the Odinist Study Group was a part, to other groups. This had the ironic effect of bringing the Odinist Study Group to life. That life consisted of a mail-order "kindred" (local group) in which the inclusion of the Odinist Study Group's address in certain right-wing lists—especially those of Joseph Dilys in Chicago—and by word of mouth, brought in a number of seekers from across the country, many of them in prison. Losing interest in Odinism, Hand eventually began to direct letters to the Odinist Study Group to Mike Murray of the Ásatrú Alliance.

In the late 1980s, with the discovery that the leader of the Order, Robert Mathews, was an Odinist, as was core Order member David Lane, the question of violence is one that must be addressed in relation to contemporary Odinism. Given that Odinism is a religion of battle, that Odin and Thor in their warrior aspects are seen as the models for emulation, and that much of the literature of youthful Odinists is given to the glorification of the berserker ideal, it is remarkable how little actual violence is associated with American Odinists. Else Christensen, the founder of the first organized racialist Odinist organization in the United States, saw her mission as one of diffusing this potential violence, particularly among her prison constituency. Violence emanating from the Odinist community has thus been largely rhetorical. The calls for violence—invariably posited as either vengeance for the "machinations of the predatory Jew" or as berserker rage—are ubiquitous in the Odinist world. Threats emanating from racialist Odinists have on occasion been directed at Ásatrúers as well. Few if any of these threats have been carried out, however.

This relatively nonviolent state of affairs is somewhat surprising given the fact that a key recruiting ground for racialist Odinism is the prisons of America. Throughout the 1980s, Odinist centers have conducted—invariably at the request of the inmates themselves—an important outreach ministry in the prisons. There, Odinism competes with Christian Identity for the allegiance of White racialist prisoners. Skinheads too have increasingly turned to Odinism, and Odinist lyrics and artistic motifs had by the 1990s become prominent features of White Power music.

Within the Odinist community itself, the justification for the resort to force in defense of the race has been encapsulated by David Lane's ubiquitous "14 words": "We must secure the existence of our people and a future for White children." With this formulation, the recourse to violence is both justified and encouraged. Yet again with the sole exception of the Order, such violence has to date been episodic—the province of Odinist skinheads indulging in street violence with little or no planning and less justification. This sort of random skinhead violence is the province of a minority of the movement, however, and would seem far more the product of skinhead than Odinist teachings. Most Odinist skinhead leaders call instead for perseverance, noting the futility of impulsive street violence to effect real change and asserting as well that the government would like nothing better than to warehouse racialist fighters in the prisons of America.

The incarcerated Order activist David Lane, by contrast, dreams of a revolution imbued with the violence needed to cleanse the earth of the corruption he sees as inherent in modern multiracial society. Lane's Odinist writings provide the most clearly articulated Odinist theology of violence available. Moreover, based on his Order pedigree, Lane's writings are becoming ubiquitous throughout the milieu of the radical right. This gives his pronouncements an authority that extends far beyond the narrow confines of the Odinist community.

Lane's discourse employs the image of the White warrior and the revolutionary as a "Wotan"—a god on earth. This imagery fits well with the "leaderless resistance" concept of lone-wolf actions as being directed against symbols of the status quo. And for those who decide to take the lonely course of the Wotan, David Lane's advice is succinct:

Death to Traitors
    In particular, if you are a white male who commits race treason, the day is coming when you will be visited by Wotan. Your demise will be unpleasant.

Judges, lawyers, bankers, real estate agents, judeo-christian preachers, federal agents, and other assorted treasonous swine take note, Wotan is coming. Your wealth, your homes, your women, and your lives are at risk when you commit treason. Pray that you die quickly. One day Wotan will feed your repulsive carcasses to the vultures and bury your bones under outhouses that our folk may forever pay fitting tribute to your memory. That day is called "Ragnarok."

See also: American Nazi Party; Beam, Louis; Christian Identity; Church of the Creator; Klassen, Ben; Koehl, Matt; Lane, David; Mathews, Robert; National Socialist White People's Party; Order; Phineas Priesthood; Pierce, William; Religion of Nature; Skinheads; Wotanism (Jungian); "Resources" section, "88 Precepts."

Further reading: Stephen E. Flowers, "Revival of Germanic Religion in Contemporary Anglo-American Culture," *Mankind Quarterly* XXI:3 (spring 1981); Kevin Flynn and Gary Gerhardt, *The Silent Brotherhood* (New York: Signet, 1990); Mattias Gardell, *Rasrisk* (Stockholm & Uppsala: Federativs & Swedish Science Press, 1998); Carl Jung, *C. G. Jung, The Collected Works,* vol. 10, Bollingen Series XX (New York: Pantheon, 1964); Jeffrey Kaplan, *Radical Religion in America: Millenarian Movements from the Far Right to the Children of Noah* (Syracuse, NY: Syracuse University Press, 1997); David Lane, *The Auto-Biography of David Lane* (St. Maries, ID: 14 Word Press, 1994); David Lane, *The Mystery Religions & The Seven Seals* (St. Maries, ID: 14 Word Press, 1994); David Lane, *Revolution by Number 14* (St. Maries, ID: 14 Word Press, 1994); David Lane, *White Genocide Manifesto* (St. Maries, ID: 14 Word Press, undated); Thomas Martinez with John Gunther, *Brotherhood of Murder* (New York: Pocket Books, 1990); A. Rud Mills, *The Odinist Religion: Overcoming Jewish Christianity* (Melbourne, Australia: self-published, c. 1930).

THE ORDER The Order, or the Brüder Schweigen [Silent Brotherhood], was an armed underground of Aryan revolutionaries operating in the early 1980s. Frustrated with the White radical racialists' lack of action, Order founder Robert J. Mathews (1953–1984) in September 1983 gathered a small group of militant young men for a solemn initiation ritual at his Metaline Falls, Washington, homestead. Swearing an oath upon the children in the wombs of their wives, the group cast themselves as a Holy Order of Aryan warriors determined to fulfill their "sacred duty to do whatever is necessary to deliver our people from the Jew and bring total victory to the Aryan race."

Involved in right-wing circles since his high school days in Phoenix, National Alliance member and Odinist Bob Mathews propelled a disparately composed group of Identity Christians, Odinists, long-time activists, and inexperienced men along the path of stepped-up action. The much-repeated claim that William Pierce's novel the *Turner Diaries* provided the blueprint for the Order must be taken with some caution. Members differed widely in their perception of what they were doing, ranging from modest hopes of contributing financially to racialist organizations to optimistic expectations of inspiring a chain reaction, thus fomenting an armed Aryan revolution. By trial and error, making new plans as they went along, members of the Order graduated into successful armored-car robbers and counterfeiters.

In this manner, the Order assembled a multimillion-dollar war chest that both enabled them to acquire arms, vehicles, and technical equipment and contributed to escalating the chain of events. Rather than consolidate its gains, however, the Order rapidly ventured into new areas of activity, involving more and more people. Following the armored-car robberies and the June 1984 assassination of Denver racist-baiting talk-radio host Alan Berg, the FBI began closing in on the group. Engaging its Aryan Nations informants and recruiting collaborators from within the Order, the FBI soon gained a fairly good picture of what was going on.

Assisted by trusted Order members whom they turned into FBI informants, the agents eventually surrounded Mathews in his hideout on Whidbey Island on the Washington coast. Refusing to surrender, Mathews died as his house caught fire and he perished still fighting as the flames consumed him. The date, December 8, 1984, still is hailed as the Day of Martyrs in Aryan revolutionary circles.

Hunting down the remaining inner circle with the help of less than silent members of the Brotherhood, the FBI had the whole Order behind bars by spring 1986. Receiving a total of more than 900 years, Order activists Frank Silva, Randy Evans, Richard Scutari, Richard Kemp, Gary Yarbrough, David Tate, Randy Duey, David Lane, and Bruce Pierce are hailed as heroic Aryan "Prisoners of War" in numerous poems and White Power music lyrics.

Achieving larger-than-life legendary status in racialist lore, the Order has grown in significance over the years. "The killing of Alan Berg was about as meaningless as assassinating the White House gardener," wrote George Hawthorne, vocalist in RaHoWa [Racial Holy War] and editor of the White Power magazine *Resistance*. "But in the wider context, it was of unfathomable significance. It marked the radicalization of the right-wing."

A growing segment of the American right wing has abandoned as unrealistic the means of conventional politics in favor of a revolutionary stand, at least theoretically, against the perceived powers that be. Although some Order members voice disappointment that their call to arms went practically unheard, isolated instances of new groups formed on the model given have surfaced in Europe and the United States. In 1997, for example, a group called the Aryan Revolutionary Army (ARA) was convicted for 22 bank and armored-car robberies in the Midwest. Ironically, not only did the ARA model itself closely on the Order, but their saga ended in a similar way as proud declarations of racial solidarity did not prevent activists from becoming FBI informants.

Mattias Gardell, Stockholm University, Sweden

See also: Christian Identity; Hawthorne, George Eric; Lane, David; Mathews, Robert J.; National Alliance; Odinism; Pierce, William.

Further reading: James A. Aho, *The Politics of Righteousness: Idaho Christian Patriotism* (Seattle: University of Washington Press, 1990); Michael Barkun, *Religion and the Racist Right: The Origins of the Christian Identity Movement* (Chapel Hill: University of North Carolina Press, 1994); Kevin Flynn and Gary Gerhardt, *The Silent Brotherhood* (New York: Signet, 1990); Mattias Gardell, *Rasrisk* (Stockholm & Uppsala: Federativs & Swedish Science Press, 1998); Richard Kelly Hoskins, *Vigilantes of Christendom* (Lynchburg, VA: Virginia Publishing Co., 1990); Jeffrey Kaplan, *Radical Religion in America* (Syracuse, NY: Syracuse University Press, 1997); Andrew Macdonald, *The Turner Diaries* (Arlington, VA: National Vanguard Books, 1978); Thomas Martinez with John Gunther, *Brotherhood of Murder* (New York: Pocket Books, 1990); Stephan Singlar, *Talked to Death: The Life and Murder of Alan Berg* (New York: Beech Tree Books, 1987).

Order of the Black Ram   *See* Madole, James; Manson, Charles.

ORDER OF NINE ANGLES   A British-based Satanist organization, the Order of Nine Angles (ONA) is an important source of Satanic ideology/theology for the welter of organizations that exist in what might be called the occultist fringe of National Socialism—a broad category including the Black Order and a number of other vehicles created by New Zealander Kerry Bolten, the Swedish Black Order, and other groups ad infinitum. This has put the Order of Nine

Angles in opposition to the more-well-known Satanic mail-order religions such as the Church of Satan and the Temple of Set.

In its internal history, the roots of the ONA are said to date back "aeons," predating the rise of Christianity. The so-called "sinister tradition," which is the basis of ONA theology, is said by Christos Beest "to be a continuation of the solar cults of Albion (some 7,000 years ago) with its esoteric origins in the region now known as Shropshire, on the Welsh borders." In the Christian era, the "sinister tradition" was carried on by a number of small temples in the Welsh marshes bearing such names as "Camlad," "Temple of the Sun," and the "Noctuliams." Each of these formations was led by a Grand Master/Mistress. In the early 1960s, a Grand Mistress decided to open the Tradition to a select group of outside adherents. This is the immediate origin of the Order of Nine Angles. Anton Long, the current Order of Nine Angles Grand Master, was initiated at that time. In subsequent years, the massive corpus of ONA material was written, most of it by Long, but some of the manuscripts were said to be written by the Mistress who initiated Long. Today, the ONA's most accessible public figure is Christos Beest.

The source of the ONA's influence is not its size—it is admittedly tiny—but its voluminous materials. Today, the ONA has authored literally thousands of pages of philosophical speculation, ritual instructions and guides, historical documents, letters, gothic fiction, and much, much more. In addition, the ONA has adapted every medium to its purposes. Thus, music (both written and recorded), an esoteric three-dimensional board game called "Star Game," gothic fiction, and a beautifully hand-painted deck of tarot cards known as the "Sinister Tarot" have been produced by the organization. Although the ONA is a secret (and secretive) organization, many of these materials have been broadly disseminated via the published word; through the Order of Nine Angles' connection with other Satanist, occult, and National Socialist organizations; and most recently over the Internet. Together, they have brought the organization considerable influence, if not adherents.

This small size is not surprising, given the rigorous requirements for membership. At the earliest levels, the Order of Nine Angles requires its fledgling recruits to be in superior physical condition, and a training regimen is suggested. The culmination of this physical preparation is a night when the would-be adherent is required to find a lonely spot and to lie without moving or sleeping for an entire night. The next major step on the "sinister path" requires a shamanic journey in which the neophyte must withdraw from civilization for a period of weeks or months. This rigorous selection process is reflective of the ONA's conception of itself as a vanguard organization composed of a tiny coterie of Nietzschean elites.

The most controversial aspects of the ONA are its insistence on the primacy of the traditional Black Mass (albeit with pronounced National Socialist elements), the use of crime as a "sacrament," and "culling" (that is, human sacrifice).

The ONA's adherence to occult National Socialism is best illustrated by a passage from one of its rites, the "Mass of Heresy":

Adolf Hitler was sent by our gods
To guide us to greatness.
We believe in the inequality of races
And in the right of the Aryan to live
According to the laws of the folk.
We acknowledge that the story of the Jewish "holocaust"
Is a lie to keep our race in chains
And express our desire to see the truth revealed.
We believe in justice for our oppressed comrades
And seek an end to the world-wide
Persecution of National-Socialists.

Crime represents a vast array of sinister behaviors that, in Order of Nine Angles literature, seem to have different connotations for male and female adherents. One male novice recalls choosing burglary as his crime of choice. The victim was "allowed" to select himself as someone particularly deserving of being robbed. The difficulty of the crime, too, was an important consideration, as the greater the difficulty, the more efficacious the act in terms of Satanic and "magickal" development. The sinister "crimes" of a female adept are posited in more frankly sexual terms.

With the success of a criminal act or acts, the final step is the sacrifice of a human being. The victim must be allowed to "self-select"—that is, he or she is tested by the adept and through his or her own character failings is deemed to have demonstrated a need to die. This element of self-selection explains the ONA's insistence that children are never to be involved in sacrifice. Whether this death is accomplished through "magickal" or physical means, the adept is said to gain considerable power from the body and the spirit of the victim, thus entering a new level of sinister consciousness. The primary Order of Nine Angles texts dealing with this form of "culling" are "A Gift for the Prince—A Guide to Human

Sacrifice"; "Culling—A Guide to Sacrifice II"; "Victims—A Sinister Exposé"; and "Guidelines for the Testing of Opfers."

The ONA's journal, *Fenrir,* after a period of dormancy, began to appear again in 1996.

See also: Myatt, David.

Further reading: Fenrir; Jeffrey Kaplan, "The Role of Oppositional Religious Movements in the Creation of a New Ethnic Identity," in Jeffrey Kaplan and Tore Bjørgo, eds., *Nation and Race: The Developing of a Euro-American Racist Subculture* (Boston: Northeastern University Press, 1998); Elizabeth Selwyn, "The Right Wing Left Hand Path," *Black Flame* (winter XXIV A.S. [Anno Satanis]).

Göran Assar Oredsson *See* Rockwell, George Lincoln; World Union of National Socialists.

P

John Patler   *See* American Nazi Party; Koehl, Matthias; National Socialist White People's Party; Rockwell, George Lincoln; "The White Party Report," "Resources" section.

PETE PETERS   Self-styled "cowboy preacher" Pete Peters presides over the LaPorte (Colorado) Church of Christ (LCC) and its outreach arm, Scriptures for America (SFA). Peters today is arguably one of the preeminent figures in the Christian Identity world. His prominence may be traced to a number of factors: his relative youth in an Identity world otherwise noted for its geriatric leadership; his audacity; his innovative use of technology to spread the SFA gospel; his unabashed militancy; and his willingness, for better or worse, to confront the state at all levels when he believes himself to be in the right.

Pete Peters offers his own capsule biography:

Who Is Pastor Peters?

He comes from a ranch background in Western Nebraska, is a husband and father. He is a graduate of the University of Nebraska, School of Agriculture. He obtained his Bachelor of Science degree from Colorado State University in Ag-Business and Economics and has had a successful career with the United States Department of Agriculture.

Pastor Peters received his Bible education at the Church of Christ Bible Training School in Gering, Nebraska, where after three years of study he received a Bachelor of Sacred Literature degree in Bible and Bible related studies. He is a writer, columnist, radio speaker, television teacher, editor of *Scriptures for America* newsletter and has a sizable national audio tape ministry. He has authored several books such as *Whores Galore, Baal Worship, The Greatest Love Story Never Told,* and *America the Conquered* as well as several tracts such as *Death Penalty for Homosexuals is Prescribed in the Bible, Saving the Environment New World Order Style* and *Strength of a Hero.*

239

Pete Peters first came to public attention through his peripheral association with the Order, when it was learned that, in 1984, several Order members (including its charismatic leader, Robert Mathews, and David Lane, who would emerge as a primary Odinist figure with an international following) attended services in Peters's LaPorte, Colorado, church. When Denver radio "shock jock" Alan Berg was murdered by members of the Order, the LaPorte Church of Christ, which opened its doors in 1977, began to receive some very unwelcome publicity. From that time forward, Peters has steadfastly refused to speak to any member of the press.

Despite his shunning the mainstream media, Peters engaged in a number of projects throughout the 1980s and 1990s that were designed to keep his name in the front ranks of the competitive Christian Identity world. He was among the first Identity figures to realize the potential offered by the Internet for disseminating the Identity creed as well as a forum for his own ideas. Even before Don Black's pioneering Stormfront web page, Peters set up an FTP (File Transfer Protocol) archive under the Scriptures for America banner to distribute copies of the *Scriptures for America* newsletter, Peters's essays on a wide variety of topics, and selected "classics" such as the late Identity patriarch Sheldon Emry's "Billions for Bankers" tract. FTP is a comparatively primitive affair, allowing for the downloading of large files, but lacking an on-line reading function, leaving the visitor with only a vague idea of what he or she is getting. But in spite of these technical limitations, the idea was a good one, and complemented Scriptures for America's more traditional use of written materials, cassette tapes, shortwave radio, and eventually satellite television.

Peters's intensive activism was bound to have repercussions, and indeed the SFA ministry has had a rough road to follow. Perhaps the most damaging controversy to engulf him resulted from his outspoken call for the imposition of the death penalty for homosexuality in his eponymous 1993 tract. Invoking such biblical injunctions as:

"If a man also lie with mankind, as he lieth with a woman, both of them have committed an abomination: they shall surely be put to death; their blood shall be upon them." Leviticus 20:13 KJV

"Thou shalt not lie with mankind, as with womankind: it is an abomination." Leviticus 18:22 KJV

"Or do you not know that the unrighteous shall not inherit the kingdom of God? Do not be deceived; neither fornicators, nor idolaters, nor adulterers, nor effeminate, nor homosexuals, nor thieves, nor the covetous, nor drunkards, nor revilers, nor swindlers, shall inherit the kingdom of God." I Corinthians 6:9,10 NASV

Peters called for the immediate imposition of the death penalty on all homosexuals in America as a precondition for forestalling God's judgment on an unrighteous nation. It was Peters's intransigence on this point that created a break between the Identity world and the quixotic 1992 Bo Gritz Populist Party presidential campaign (with Gritz telling a group of Identity pastors that Peters's proposal "sounded a little harsh"). Worse, the LaPorte Church of Christ's involvement in the controversy in Colorado over the passage of a constitutional amendment designed to deny special protection to homosexuals was found to constitute a minor violation of Colorado election laws. By refusing all efforts toward compromise, Peters soon amassed a fine of over $10,000 plus interest, resulting in February 1993 in the seizure of the church by state officials.

Undaunted, Peters tried step into the vacuum of Identity leadership brought on by the decline of Richard Butler's influence and the further splintering of the movement in the wake of the 1989 Fort Smith, Arkansas, sedition trial—efforts that have been less than successful. An opportunity to assert this claim to influence presented itself in 1992. This occasion followed the events that took place in Ruby Ridge, Idaho, on August 21–22, 1992. There, in an event that would eerily resemble a small-scale version of the federal action at the Branch Davidian compound in Waco, Texas, an 18-month stakeout of the cabin of Identity adherent Randy Weaver culminated in the deaths of a federal marshal, Weaver's 14-year-old son, and his wife—who was shot in the head while holding her infant daughter in her arms. The battle electrified the world of Christian Identity. By chance, this drama was played out during the August 22–28 Scriptures for America Bible Camp that Peters was conducting in Colorado.

Following the camp, Peters attempted with limited success to channel the outrage felt throughout the far-right wing into an organized movement that would seek to prevent such an event from happening again. Thus, at a men-only meeting convened under Peters's leadership in the mountain resort of Estes Park, Colorado, on October 23–25, 1992, a decision was taken to fight back against what was seen as an attempt by the federal government to eliminate right-wing opposition once and for all. The means of resistance were seen as either legal political action or, if no other recourse were possible, by fighting back rather than allowing the federal government to eliminate the faithful one by one. This meeting has been posited by some as a central factor in the sudden appearance of the militia movement in America after the Waco tragedy.

So fractious is the world of Christian Identity that it almost goes without saying that Pete Peters has had little success in his quest to unite the small, far-flung kingdoms that are the Identity ministries in North America. For this reason, Identity appears to have played a minimal role in the formation of the militia movement.

Today, Pete Peters continues to head one of the most stridently racialist and anti-Semitic Identity ministries in the country. The Scriptures for America web page is among the most sophisticated in the Identity world.

See also: Black, Don; Butler, Richard; Christian Identity; Internet Recruiting; Lane, David; Mathews, Robert; Odinism; Order; Scriptures for America; Waco; Weaver, Randy.

Further reading: Michael Barkun, *Religion and the Racist Right: The Origins of the Christian Identity Movement* (Chapel Hill: University of North Carolina Press, 1994); Kevin Flynn and Gary Gerhardt, *The Silent Brotherhood* (New York: Signet, 1990); Jeffrey Kaplan, *Radical Religion in America: Millenarian Movements from the Far Right to the Children of Noah* (Syracuse, NY: Syracuse University Press, 1997); Pete Peters, *Death Penalty for Homosexuals* (LaPorte, CO: Scriptures for America, 1993); Stephen Singlar, *Talked to Death* (New York: Beech Tree, 1987).

―――――――――

PHINEAS PRIESTHOOD   The Phineas Priesthood, a literary invention of Identity figure Richard Kelly Hoskins, consists of a timeless order of avengers who are selflessly dedicated to tracking down the worst of God's enemies and slaying them without mercy. The Phineas Priesthood proffers an attractive dream in that its members can safely yearn for the appearance of a Phineas priest with all the ardor that other true believers invest in the dream of being rescued from this sea of troubles by UFOs.

Richard Kelly Hoskins offered the Phineas Priesthood to the Christian Identity faithful as such a safe but deeply satisfying dream. Following the arrest of the Order's members and the spectacle of the Fort Smith, Arkansas, sedition trial in which the radical-right-wing elite were hailed before a court and forced to testify against each other in an ultimately unsuccessful prosecution in 1989, Hoskins's 1990 magnum opus, *The Vigilantes of Christendom,* sought to provide the dispirited faithful with the age-old dream of supernatural succor as personified by a timeless band of selfless avengers, the Phineas Priesthood (Num. 25:6–13; Ps. 106:29–31). Numbers 25:6–13, the key Bible text, reads:

> Then an Israelite man brought to his family a Midianite woman right before the eyes of Moses and the whole assembly of Israel while they were weeping at the entrance to the Tent of Meeting. When Phineas son of Eleazar, the son of Aaron, the priest, saw this, he left the assembly, took a spear in his hand and followed the Israelite into the tent. He drove the spear through both of them— through the Israelite and into the woman's body. Then the plague against the Israelites was stopped; but those who died in the plague numbered 24,000.
>
> The LORD said to Moses, "Phineas son of Eleazar, the son of Aaron, the priest, has turned my anger away from the Israelites; for he was as zealous as I am for my honor among them, so that in my zeal I did not put an end to them. Therefore tell him I am making my covenant of peace with him. He and his descendants will have a covenant of a lasting priesthood, because he was zealous for the honor of his God and made atonement for the Israelites."

The Phineas Priests in the pages of *Vigilantes of Christendom* are presented as a Templar-like order of assassins whose sacred role is to cull from the pure flock of Christ those wayward sheep who, through race mixing or other transgressions, would do the work of Satan and his earthly servants, the Jews. The Phineas Priesthood came with a catchy motto:

> As the Kamikaze is to the Japanese
> As the Shiite is to Islam
> As the Zionist is to the Jew
> So the Phineas Priest is to Christendom

And who are the Phineas Priests? A long list of claimants to the title are on offer. Robin Hood, St. George, Beowulf, King Arthur, John Wilkes Booth, Jesse James, Gordon Kahl, Robert Mathews, and Doug Sheets (accused of murdering homosexuals) are but a few of the worthies in Hoskins's elaborate fantasy.

The Phineas Priesthood was, in the context of the times, a fantasy so alluring that it was only a matter of time before a few brave or deranged individuals would take up for themselves the title and set out in search of God's enemies. Given the fanciful nature of the Priesthood, such a quest must unambiguously qualify as an act of leaderless resistance. And indeed, a few did style themselves Phineas Priests, not only among the radical right, but in the most radical fringes of the pro-life (antiabortion) rescue movement as well.

WILLIAM PIERCE

Today, the Phineas Priest concept is little used, having been displaced by the Army of God, another state of mind terrorist organization that began life in the decidedly antiracist world of the pro-life rescue movement.

See also: Christian Identity; Leaderless Resistance; Mathews, Robert; Order.

Further reading: Louis R. Beam, "Leaderless Resistance," *The Seditionist* 12 (February 1992); Richard Kelly Hoskins, *Vigilantes of Christendom* (Lynchburg, VA: Virginia Publishing Co., 1990); Jeffrey Kaplan, "Leaderless Resistance," *Journal of Terrorism and Political Violence* 9:3 (fall 1997); Jeffrey Kaplan, *Radical Religion in America: Millenarian Movements from the Far Right to the Children of Noah* (Syracuse, NY: Syracuse University Press, 1997).

WILLIAM PIERCE In the contemporary world of National Socialism, William Pierce; his organization, the National Alliance; and its would-be tax shelter cum religion, the Cosmotheist Church, stand alone. Pierce is today arguably the most important, and best known, figure in American National Socialism. His fictional works, the *Turner Diaries* and *Hunter,* served as inspirations for some of the most spectacular acts of violence to emerge from the radical right wing in North America and in Europe. The National Alliance is the center for a successful book distributorship, a shortwave radio program named *American Dissident Voices,* a World Wide Web site, and a thriving e-mail outreach. Most impressive of all, perhaps, is the fact that Pierce, in stark contrast to most other veteran National Socialists, has had scarcely any serious brushes with the law. This despite the fact that for more than 30 years he has been the "ghost in the machine" whenever serious acts of violence are contemplated or undertaken by American National Socialists. From the beginning of his long National Socialist career, William Pierce was altogether a different kind of Nazi.

When William Pierce, a Ph.D. physicist, joined George Lincoln Rockwell's American Nazi Party in 1966, no one could have been more surprised than the Commander himself. Since it was founded in 1959, the American Nazi Party (ANP) had struggled in vain to attract more than a bare handful of capable recruits. That a man like Pierce would give up a comfortable life and a promising career to join the foundering, impoverished, and deeply divided American Nazi Party must have been a much needed boost to Rockwell. No doubt about it, the party had uses for such a man.

Where most of the American Nazi Party faithful were distinguished as street fighters, Pierce was clearly meant for other tasks. The year Pierce joined the party a new publication, the *National Socialist World,* was produced alongside the ongoing party vehicles, the *Stormtrooper* and the *Rockwell Report.* But where *Stormtrooper* and the *Rockwell Report* were intended as propaganda and news-and-views organs, the *National Socialist World* was an intellectual journal—replete with footnotes—that was intended as a forum for extended theoretical pieces and for articles of historical importance to the National Socialist movement.

The premier issue of the *National Socialist World* was published in the spring of 1966. It was a remarkable document on a number of levels. It allowed Rockwell to proudly introduce Pierce to the National Socialist movement in the United States and abroad and, in a separate (footnoted) article, to ruminate on the vagaries of "Ph.D. right wingers"—a subject to which, it is safe to assume, he had given little thought before making the acquaintance of William Pierce, Ph.D. Moreover, it allowed Pierce to address the same audience in his own voice in the prefaced "Editorial." William Pierce, however, modestly declined to sign his own name to the "Editorial," styling himself instead simply "The Editor." This becoming modesty, or excessive caution as the case may be, would be a constant throughout Pierce's long National Socialist career. Even his key contributions, the fictional *Turner Diaries* and *Hunter,* would be published under a pseudonym, Andrew Macdonald. Here, then, is Rockwell's brief introduction of William Pierce:

> Dr. William L. Pierce, the editor of the *National Socialist World,* is a newcomer to the National Socialist movement. A physicist by profession, Dr. Pierce spent three years on the faculty of Oregon State University after completing his doctoral work at the University of Colorado. Prior to that, he studied at Rice University and the California Institute of Technology. His only previous literary experience consists in the publication of research results in several physics journals, so the publication of *National Socialist World* represents an entirely new undertaking for him, in which we pledge him our full and wholehearted support.
>
> —George Lincoln Rockwell

The remainder of that first issue of *National Socialist World* offered a key reprint, an abridged version of Savitri Devi's long-unavailable Golden Age fantasy and ode to Adolf Hitler "The Lightning and the Sun," as well as lighter fare such as British

National Socialist Colin Jordan's comparatively brief "National Socialism: A Philosophical Appraisal." There are even book reviews of a text about William Joyce (!) and a ten-page, heavily footnoted, critical review of Alan Bullock's *Hitler: A Study in Tyranny*. In sum, the *National Socialist World* was a unique effort. There has been nothing like it since in the world of American National Socialism. Reproductions of that first issue are still sold today by right-wing booksellers.

Pierce quickly became a close confidant of Rockwell, though the association would of necessity be short lived. The American Nazi Party became the National Socialist White People's Party (NSWPP) in late 1966, and Rockwell was assassinated on August 25, 1967. Pierce's homage to Rockwell came fittingly enough in the fifth issue (winter 1967) of the *National Socialist World*. His "George Lincoln Rockwell: A National Socialist Life" is still widely available in the National Socialist subculture. Of greater import, Pierce's account of the Commander's deeply religious experience surrounding the "religion" of National Socialism and the person of Adolf Hitler would later serve as a central motif in the *Turner Diaries,* whose main character, Earl Turner, undergoes precisely the kind of life-changing experience after reading "the organization's holy book" that Rockwell experienced upon reading *Mein Kampf.*

There would be little time in the wake of the Commander's death to mourn his passing. Matt Koehl assumed the leadership of the National Socialist White People's Party, with Pierce and Robert Lloyd as his key aides. Koehl, however, is not a man who will long tolerate rivals (or, truth be told, even equals), and within two years, both Pierce and Lloyd were gone—victims of the unending purges that would mark the entire history of the National Socialist White People's Party under Koehl.

Beyond the personality quirks of the new National Socialist White People's Party leader, however, there was in the increasingly conservative NSWPP little room for Pierce to delve into two related areas of interest: college recruitment and revolutionary violence. Of the former, the working-class composition of the American Nazi Party and its successor, the National Socialist White People's Party, in some ways resembled Hitler's original brown-shirted SA cadres in that it was largely composed of street toughs, ne'er-do-wells, and more than a few homosexuals who were ideal cannon fodder in the battle for the streets. The exigencies of power, however, required a better educated and more sophisticated following. Pierce may well have been looking toward this day, in view of his zeal to recruit college students to the cause. Moreover, the New Left activity on American campuses in the late 1960s and early 1970s appeared to offer an ideal climate for the creation of a counterforce of young National Socialists. Whatever the actual possibilities of realizing the vision may have been, such an endeavor would seem to have held little allure for Koehl and company.

Partly to achieve this vision of a campus-based cadre of highly educated and articulate National Socialists, and partly to explore (at a safe distance) the possibilities of revolutionary violence, Pierce cultivated within the National Socialist White People's Party a personal following of young firebrands who dreamed of taking up the gun against the hated American government. He brought young men into the Arlington headquarters, such as the 16-year-old James Mason from small-town Ohio. In Mason's case, Pierce paid his expenses until he reached the age of 18 and could legally join the party. He surely knew Joseph Franklin, whose campaign of lone-wolf revolutionary violence cost the lives of as many as 20 people, including several interracial couples in Utah. Franklin has admitted shooting and wounding civil rights leader Vernon Jordan and *Hustler* magazine publisher Larry Flynt (shot for publishing pictures of interracial sex in his magazine). Whatever the relationship between Pierce and Franklin in their National Socialist White People's Party days, Pierce's book *Hunter* is dedicated to him, while the protagonist, Oscar Yeagar, is closely modeled on Franklin's story.

Of greatest import, however, was the link between Pierce and a young West Coast adherent, Joseph Tommasi. Tommasi, a loyal member of the National Socialist White People's Party until he was unceremoniously purged from the party by Matt Koehl in 1973, came to Pierce's attention through his outspoken militancy and his demand for revolution *now*, regardless of how unpromising the strategic situation. Tommasi's speech to this effect at the Second Party Congress in 1970 confirmed Pierce's high estimation of him, and from this alliance the National Socialist Liberation Front (NSLF) was born as an explicitly revolutionary organization. The NSLF did not go far, however. Tommasi himself was gunned down by a young National Socialist White People's Party adherent in 1975 in El Monte, California. The only combatant members of the group, Karl Hand and David Rust, were soon jailed for acts of racial violence, leaving the corpse of the organization in the hands of James Mason. But what most interests us here is another of William Pierce's patterns: the use of younger and more reckless adherents to actuate hopeless campaigns of revolutionary violence while he himself remains at a safe remove. The success of the *Turner Diaries* would perfect Pierce's skills as a cheerleader from the sidelines.

William Pierce's first post-NSWPP vehicle, the National Youth Alliance, opened up shop in 1969 under Willis Carto's tutelage. Carto is the publisher of the flagship newspaper of the American far right, *Spotlight,* a veteran purveyor of racist literature, and the founder of the Holocaust denial organization, the Institute of Holocaust Research. Many in the American racist right have been associated with the irascible Carto, though virtually none of these associations long survive his smothering embrace. However, it was under the imprimatur of the National Youth Alliance that Pierce published *Attack!,* the first issue of which appeared in the fall of 1969. *Attack!* featured graphic pictures of atrocities and dead bodies, interspersed with as many female nudes as possible—in racially significant contexts, of course: to this day, a constant feature of Pierce's work. *Attack!* began the drift to more overt expressions of National Socialism in 1975 with a prepublication serialization of the *Turner Diaries*.

The National Youth Alliance (NYA) never amounted to much, but unlike so many later far-right-wing "organizations," it did have more of a presence than a name on a postal box and a line of literature. The NYA elected officers and had several congresses— funded, of course, by Willis Carto. In reality, however, the National Youth Alliance foundered, because many potential adherents for the kind of broad coalition of young right wingers that the NYA envisioned could as easily opt for more socially acceptable groups, such as the Young Americans for Freedom (YAF). The YAF at least found the attentions of its patron, William F. Buckley, far less stifling than those of the meddlesome Carto.

Pierce's split with Willis Carto took place in 1970 or 1971. From the ashes of the National Youth Alliance rose the National Alliance, Pierce's current vehicle, which opened its doors in 1974 in Arlington, Virginia. Pierce's primary journal, *Attack!,* mutated into the *National Vanguard* in April 1978. Two decades later the *National Vanguard* remains the flagship organ of the National Alliance, though it is supplemented by a number of other publications, including the *National Alliance Bulletin*.

Cosmotheism, Pierce's religious vehicle, appeared on the scene in the late 1970s. The Cosmotheist Church owes much of its "theology" to Ben Klassen's Church of the Creator (COTC). Like the COTC, it offers a heady mixture of Golden Age fantasy, dreams of a utopian future, and frank worship of the White race as both bearers of a superior culture and heirs to the promise of a magnificent destiny. Cosmotheism, however, is the product of a far more sophisticated mind than Klassen's, and thus the Church of the Creator's crude race-baiting and bizarre health faddism are absent from the Cosmotheist belief system.

At first, the Internal Revenue Service granted Pierce's church a tax exemption as a matter of course. Following sharp protests, notably from the Anti-Defamation League, this status was revoked in 1978—a point of considerable bitterness from Pierce's perspective. Undaunted, Pierce moved his operation from Arlington to rural West Virginia in 1985, forming a Cosmostheist community composed of himself and his immediate National Alliance followers. Indeed, what differentiates the Cosmotheist belief system from the secular National Alliance is not entirely clear, and this may well be a major impediment to realizing one of the chief dogmas of the Church: tax-exempt status.

Throughout the 1970s and into the 1980s, Pierce remained on good terms with the Church of the Creator's founder, Ben Klassen. This was no mean feat, for, like Willis Carto, Klassen had a remarkable talent for alienating friend and foe alike. Pierce's reward was the opportunity to buy Klassen's North Carolina property at the bargain price of $100,000. This, however, has brought Pierce only more trouble. After Pierce sold the property at a $100,000 profit, Morris Dees and the Southern Poverty Law Center filed a civil suit against him for the murder of a black man in North Carolina by a racist who had read the *Turner Diaries*. On May 20, 1996, a jury in Bryson City, North Carolina, found for the plaintiff. The case remains on appeal, and, win or lose, the legal fees alone will ultimately cost Pierce considerably more than his $100,000 windfall.

Despite these setbacks, William Pierce today lives something of the life of a country gentleman, presiding over his West Virginia estate, profiting from his book-selling operation, and disseminating his views via a shortwave radio program called *American Dissident Voices* and the Internet. He is poised to see the *Turner Diaries* pass into mainstream bookstores following the surge of notoriety the text and its author received following the Oklahoma City bombing. Convicted bomber Timothy McVeigh, it seems, was a serious fancier of the *Turner Diaries,* which he sold (or gave gratis) to one and all. This sudden burst of publicity brought Pierce and his new Hungarian bride considerable publicity in 1997 with a segment on the popular television news program *60 Minutes* and a feature on CNN. The latter was followed by the equivalent of a virtual autograph session, with Dr. Pierce answering viewers' questions through the CNN Internet site.

By 1999, Pierce had acquired Resistance Records, the premier White Power record label in the United States, which had been in limbo since the defection of George Burdi, its founder and the frontman of the label's best band, Rahowa. As a first step in reestablishing the enterprise, Pierce cut the prices of Resistance CDs, and he followed this by reintroducing the long-dormant, glossy *Resistance* magazine.

Life for William Pierce at the turn of the millennium is very, very good—an outcome he could hardly have foreseen more than three decades ago when, as a younger and more idealistic physics professor, he forsook all to follow George Lincoln Rockwell's National Socialist dream.

See also: American Nazi Party; Carto, Willis; Church of the Creator; Devi, Savitri; Franklin, Joseph; Hitler, Adolf; Jordan, Colin; Klassen, Ben; Koehl, Matt; Mason, James; National Alliance; National Socialist Liberation Front; National Socialist White People's Party; Rockwell, George Lincoln; Tommasi, Joseph.

Further reading: John George and Laird Wilcox, *American Extremists, Supremacists, Klansmen, Communists and Others* (Buffalo, NY: Prometheus Books, 1996); Charles Higham, *American Swastika* (Garden City, NY: Doubleday, 1985); National Alliance, *The Best of Attack!: Revolutionary Voice of the National Alliance* (Hillsboro, WV: National Vanguard Books, 1984, 1992); William Pierce, *Lincoln Rockwell: A National Socialist Life* (Arlington, VA: NS Publications, 1969); George Lincoln Rockwell, *This Time the World!* (Arlington, VA: Parliament House, 1963); George Lincoln Rockwell, *White Power* (n.p., 1967, 1977); Frederick J. Simonelli, "The World Union of National Socialists and Post-War Transatlantic Nazi Revival," in Jeffrey Kaplan and Tore Bjørgo, eds., *Nation and Race: The Developing Euro-American Racist Subculture* (Boston: Northeastern University Press, 1998); Frederick J. Simonelli, *American Fuehrer: George Lincoln Rockwell and the American Nazi Party* (Champaign: University of Illinois Press, 1999); Brad Whitsel, "Aryan Visions for the Future in the West Virginia Mountains," *Terrorism and Political Violence* 7:4 (winter 1995).

Populist Party   *See* Carto, Willis.

Posse Comitatus   *See* Committee of the States; Gale, William Potter.

R

REICHSFOLK   A vehicle for the dissemination of the teachings of David Myatt (a British National Socialist who cooperated closely with the Satanist organization the Order of the Nine Angles), the Reichsfolk shares elements common to all of Myatt's organizational endeavors. Reichsfolk thus combines elements of National Socialism, a near-deification of Adolf Hitler, the occult, and a pronounced form of escapism that Myatt calls the "galactic empire," that is, the dream of escape from the earth to some cosmic paradise of racial purity and mutual cooperation.

The fundamental aims of Reichsfolk, according to its literature, are: "(1) to create a new type of individual—a new Aryan elite; (2) to prepare the way for the creation of a new Golden Age by championing the enlightened and higher religion of National-Socialism, and (3) to fight the Holy War that is necessary to destroy the present profane, tyrannical anti-Aryan System and the sub-human values of the old order on which this System is based."

This new elite, according to the Reichsfolk, will be called The Legion of Adolf Hitler, a National Socialist elite who:

> ...will create the next National-Socialist Reich, the Golden Age itself.... It is this new elite which will stand fast against the rising tide of sub-humans and the rising tide of decadence which is engulfing our societies, as it is the loyal and honourable National-Socialists of this elite who will uphold and champion the noble Aryan ideals of honour, loyalty and duty in a world where these values are little understood and seldom practiced. It is this elite which will represent all that is best about the Aryan, as the members of this elite will not only be pure Aryans in race, they will also be pure Aryans in spirit—understanding as they will their glorious Aryan heritage and their glorious Aryan culture. It is this Legion of Adolf Hitler who will think and act and if necessary die like noble Aryans in a world increasingly anti-Aryan and increasingly controlled by the dark, sub-human, uncivilized forces of Zionism.

Myatt's Reichsfolk materials are considerable, but the key documents are "Reichsfolk—Toward a New Elite," on which much of this entry is based; "Arts of Civilization," which details the Aryan Code of Honour; and "The Galactic Empire and the Triumph of National Socialism." Reichsfolk sees itself as a vehicle through which its adherents can train and guide this new elite.

In the words of David Myatt:

> Reichsfolk is thus not just another religious or even National-Socialist organization—it is the future of the Aryan race and thus of civilization itself, just as Adolf Hitler is our future. Reichsfolk is fighting in the name of Adolf Hitler himself and for the holiest cause of all—that of the Cosmic Being itself, manifest to us in Nature, the evolution of Nature that is race and the evolution of race that is individual excellence, civilization and enlightenment. Reichsfolk is thus striving to bring the divine light of the Cosmic Being back into an increasingly dark, uncivilized and sub-human world.

In 1999, Reichsfolk activities were suspended when Myatt went underground in the wake of the defection of the Indiana-based head of the organization's American activities to the world of fundamentalist Christianity, plus the appearance of an exposé in the British watchdog publication *Searchlight* that dubbed Myatt "the most dangerous Nazi in Britain." During this period of introspection, Myatt—an inveterate religious seeker— discovered Islam and renounced his life-long racist views. Reichsfolk thus appears to be, at least for the moment, defunct.

Reichsfolk had few members, but through David Myatt's voluminous writings, his contacts throughout the occult and National Socialist worlds, and the power of the Internet, it will continue to be influential.

See also: Hitler, Adolf; Myatt, David; Order of the Nine Angles; Religion of Nature.

Further reading: Jeffrey Kaplan, "Religiosity and the Radical Right: Toward the Creation of a New Ethnic Identity," in Jeffrey Kaplan and Tore Bjørgo, eds., *Nation and Race: The Developing Euro-American Racist Subculture* (Boston: Northeastern University Press, 1998); David Myatt, "Arts of Civilization," "The Galactic Empire and the Triumph of National Socialism," and "Reichsfolk—Toward a New Elite" (available as e-text).

RELIGION OF NATURE   The "laws of nature" are proclaimed by several of the modern racial religions. Nature is believed to consist of a number of laws, the strongest and foremost of them being the law of survival. Nature's only objective is the "survival of the fittest." The strong will always defeat the weak, and nature is the best example of this; there exists no mercy or compassion in the natural world. Nature is only interested in the collective, the race, and its expansion and survival. This worldview or "Religion of Nature" has a long history in racist thought, and one historian even claims it to be the ideology responsible for the Holocaust.

The roots of the Religion of Nature may be found in nineteenth-century German romanticism. In several aspects, German romanticism was a reaction against the French Enlightenment, which claimed the superiority of reason over emotion, intuition, and tradition. Romanticism asserted that some truths could be found outside the province of reason. One of these truths was the unique status of natural and cultural identity.

Romanticism lacked the religious belief in a God, replacing it with a pantheistic worship of nature. Romanticism also believed in a unity and interconnectedness between all existence, from the inanimate to mankind and up to God. Another idea that was about to be very influential was the belief in culture as an organism in which religion, art, and science were bound to political and social structure, thereby together expressing the spirit or *Geist* of the society. The German philosopher Johann Herder claimed that the organic growth of the folk spirit and folk character was the result of time and history, not of present intellect. Another German philosopher, Johann Fichte, stated that there was something in the German character that enabled its development to the highest form. This romantic *Naturphilosophie* (philosophy of nature) presented evolution and development in a way that would influence others later in the century. This form of cultural romanticism came to be closely tied to German nation building of the early nineteenth century.

The second half of the nineteenth century was an age that saw rapid development of the biological sciences. Thus, the concept of forming a moral system on a biological basis became very popular. In Great Britain, this concept became, through Herbert Spencer, an extension of laissez-faire politics. In Germany, by contrast, it took the shape of nature worship and racial mysticism.

In 1859 Darwin published his *Origin of Species*. Darwin's ideas had an enormous impact on the contemporary sciences. One who was very impressed by Darwin's writing was the German zoologist Ernst

Haeckel. For him, evolution became a cosmic power, a manifestation of nature's creative energy. Haeckel saw evolution as the unifying principle that would explain the cosmos as an all-embracing whole. It would also explain, and bridge, the split between matter/spirit and man/nature, which he believed was created by the anthropocentric (human centered) Judeo-Christian tradition.

In the 1890s Haeckel started to conceptualize an approach called monism, and in 1904 he formed a group called the German Monist League. Monism is the name of a group of views that stress the oneness and unity of reality. One of the foremost representatives for the monist view is Spinoza, of whom Haeckel was a great admirer. Haeckel called his approach monism, in contrast to previous doctrines and ideas that he contemptuously called dualism.

Haeckel believed in a world soul, which he conceptualized as a project in which all forms of life, from the inorganic to the organic, are evolving in an upward direction. All matter was considered to be alive and in possession of mental attributes that are normally only prescribed to the higher animals. By "lifting" the lower forms of life, he also "degraded" humanity. Pointing at evolution, he wanted to show how illusory the conception of mankind's unique status in nature was. For Haeckel, evolution and man's animal heritage proved how close man was to nature and to our animal forebears. As man was part of nature, Haeckel tirelessly pointed out that human beings also were subject to the laws of nature.

The struggle for survival was the foremost drive of human nature, just as for the rest of the animal kingdom. Nature did not have any conscience or "moral order." Nature's only interest was "the survival of the fittest." This struggle implied a race with specialization that diverged from other races, even those races that closely resembled each other. The greater the struggle, the higher the grade of perfection. It was, according to Haeckel, of the utmost importance that we adjust to these laws and apply them to society in general. There was no possibility for humans to escape their animal heritage into a world free from conflicts or aggression. Struggle is inherent in the nature of human beings. This pessimism and cynicism separated Haeckel and the monists from earlier "naturalists."

Even though Haeckel considered all of humanity to be close to nature, there was a great difference between a Goethe and "the wildest of savages." It was because of the fact of this difference that he regarded as a great fallacy all talk about humanity as being one great family. Instead, each race was considered as possessing a different nature, with different characteristics. Not only was one's skin color different, but so were a race's intelligence, morality, and the ability to create a higher culture.

Haeckel divided humanity into different species and races, of which the "woolly haired" were generally on a lower level of development. Haeckel regarded hair type as a most reliable indicator of race. The differences were biological, and thus it was impossible to reduce the differences by education. He believed that the inferior races would have to "...completely succumb in the struggle for existence to the superiority of the Mediterranean races."

Haeckel looked at the cultures of the "woolly-haired" and could find nothing of value. The woolly-haired people were considered unable to aspire to higher development. It was to the White race, and especially the Germanic race, that one had to turn to find human perfection. It was the White race that had created civilization and history. Those accomplishments were in the blood of the Aryan people. That way, Haeckel linked man's appearance to inner qualities.

Race determined the ability to think, create, and live in accordance to the laws of nature, not the personality. The personality is dependent on race. Race-mixing was, of course, regarded as a terrible crime against both nature and the German race. Haeckel repeatedly warned against it. Advocating a conscious form of racial politics, he lamented actions aimed at the preservation of sick and unhealthy children, and blamed needless wars for taking the lives of the strong and healthy male combatants, while the sick, weak, and cowardly remained home to breed.

Johann Haeckel's attacks on traditional religion had many facets. He reacted against the unscientific view that had a considerable influence on society as a whole, and he tried to prove that theological beliefs were incompatible with scientific data. By preaching "love thy enemy" and "turning the other cheek," Christianity had led the people away from the laws of nature. Haeckel pitted revelation against reason and claimed Monism to represent the latter. One of his most controversial attacks on Christianity was the rejection of immortality. Convinced that all fallacies stemmed from traditional religion and that truth could be found in the scientific view of monism, he declared that it was time to establish a new religion of nature, a "monistic religion."

This mystical and religious approach to science caused a breach with his scientific colleagues. Nevertheless, Haeckel's writings were widely distributed and had a great influence. Monism spread to the radical non-Christian, pagan, and proto-Nazi groups that also shared the desire of a new Germanic faith for the German people. Such important occultists as Guido von List and Jörg Lanz von Liebenfelds were influenced by the concept of biological struggle and the need to purify the race to avoid the deterioration of the German race (Lanz also contributed to a semiofficial Monist journal). Monism led to the revival of many symbols and practices of the ancient German pagan religion. A common practice within the Monist League, for example, was sun-worship.

By the twentieth century, Social Darwinism had become influential all over Europe. Imperialistic endeavors drew support from social Darwinism and from more frankly racist ideas. Haeckel died in 1914, but his monist philosophy was clearly a part of the ideological milieu that fed National Socialist ideology. Several substantial links can also be drawn between the principles of the German Monist League and those of National Socialism.

The historian Robert A. Pois believes that National Socialist ideology, at its core, should be understood as a "Religion of Nature." He also regards this religion as the ideology that led to the Holocaust.

To the Nazis, nature's inner principle was eternal struggle. The will to fight was identical with the will to live. Those who didn't fight would perish, and this was all in accordance with the laws of nature and thus something positive. By submitting to nature's inexorable laws, mankind was liberated from history's variability, and the limit between life and death was erased. The Nazis regarded it as their mission to restore and maintain the "natural order." This way, time would be revoked, a "new man" would be created, and the millenarian kingdom could be built.

This religion also sanctioned totalitarianism. All criticism was interpreted as attempts to reverse nature, since the German state was rooted in, and therefore acting in accordance with, the laws of nature. When an S.S. commander gave an order, it had to be right, since he was rooted in nature. Thus, only decisions that were in harmony with nature's laws were made—decisions that strove for the good of the Aryan race. The extermination of the "impure" and "unnatural" was considered necessary and was looked upon as an unsentimental duty.

The Nazi "Religion of Nature" philosophy shares several features with Ernst Haeckel's monistic "Religion of Nature," but still there are differences. Adherents of National Socialism, for example, completely rejected the conception that man descended from the apes or other animals. The world was, according to them, a struggle between the major races, of which the most fit would win. Anti-Semitism also got a more prominent place in National Socialism. Haeckel was an anti-Semite, but mostly because of the cosmopolitanism of the Jews and their inability to adapt to German culture and nationalism. National Socialism, on the other hand, "uplifted" the Jews to the position of the greatest enemy of the Aryan race. According to the Nazis, the Jews were well aware that race had to come first, and they had long since adapted their religion so as to ensure the survival of their race. The Jews were also using the colored people to weaken and finally destroy the Aryan race. This made the war an inevitability. To survive as a race surrounded by hostile races, of which one was a real threat, war was a necessity for survival and for an extension of *Lebensraum* (living space).

Hitler didn't intend to create a "Religion of Nature" when he wrote *Mein Kampf,* but the seeds are there. He speaks about the "aristocratic" and "undemocratic" laws of nature: "The earth continues to go round whether it's the man who kills the tiger or the tiger who kills the man. The stronger asserts his will, it's the law of nature. The world doesn't change; its laws are eternal."

To Robert Pois, National Socialism is a revolt against the Judeo-Christian tradition and the lines it has drawn between man and nature, life and death. National Socialism managed, as had the monists, to bridge these two dualisms.

The "Religion of Nature," or the theories on natural law, exist as a part of, or as a complement to, several modern racial religions, such as Odinism and Nazi-occultism, but the most apparent heir is the Church of the Creator [COTC]. This church was founded in 1973 by Ben Klassen, whose first book was called *Nature's Eternal Religion* (1973). Still, there are differences between the Church of the Creator and the previous nature religions. To begin with, the Church of the Creator regards the White race as holy and uniquely endowed by nature to be the world's ruling elite. This still does not mean that members of the White race are destined to be the rulers of the world—the struggle is ongoing and its outcome is not assured. The Church of the Creator also criticizes National Socialism for being national. The COTC members are National Socialists and internationalists who believe that the struggle concerns White people all over the world. This vision of a worldwide pan-Aryan community is something that goes through most modern "Naturalists." The Church of the Creator also put an emphasis on race, declaring that: "Our race is our religion." It also takes anti-Semitism a step further, claiming that all evil stems from the Jews. All other evils are manifestations, not causes, of the White race's miseries.

David Lane, an Odinist and former member of "the Order," has written much on the natural/life law. This writing has, now and then, been so close to the teachings of the Church of the Creator that he has had to publicly deny all connections.

The ideas of "the eternal struggle," evolutionary strife, a global pan-Aryan psyche, the inevitable race war, the natural law, and the criticism against the dualist, liberal, and Christian ideas (which, it is argued, have led the people astray)—these ideas are also common among the Nazi-occult Swedish Black Order as well as in William Pierce's Cosmotheism.

When regarding, as Pois does, National Socialism and the "Religion of Nature" as a revolt against Christianity, Richard Butler's Church of Jesus Christ Christian is an interesting case in point. Butler claims that National Socialism is true Christianity. This way he has managed the impossible: combining Christianity with National Socialism. In his own version of Christian Identity he says that "Christianity for the Aryan is Race and Race is Christianity." Even though he speaks of the Father, the Son, and the Holy Spirit, that is not where you will find redemption: "The only hope for the redemption of the Aryan racial household is the total return to the fundamental life law."

—Edvard Lind, Stockholm University, Sweden

See also: Butler, Richard; Christian Identity; Church of the Creator; Church of Jesus Christ Christian; Hitler, Adolf; Klassen, Ben; Lane, David; Odinism; Order; Pierce, William.

Further reading: Daniel Gasman, *The Scientific Roots of National Socialism* (New York: American Elsevier Inc., 1971); Mike Hawkins, *Social Darwinism in American and European Thought 1860–1945* (Cambridge: Cambridge University Press, 1997); Adolf Hitler, *Mein Kampf* (Boston: Houghton Mifflin, 1971); Ben Klassen, *Nature's Eternal Religion* (Otto, NC: Church of the Creator, 1973); Robert A. Pois, *National Socialism and the Religion of Nature* (London: Croom Helm, 1986).

———————

THOM ROBB   Few Klansmen are to be found in this encyclopedia, for good reason: few Klansmen in 1999 have anything either very interesting or very new to say about the state of the racialist movement. It is this state of affairs that makes the exceptions to the rule so exceptional. Louis Beam is one such, notable for his "ecumenical" calls for revolutionary violence. The late Robert Miles was another, notable for his unfailing humor and, again, for his big-tent approach, which sought to bring together a wide range of belief systems in the milieu of the American radical right wing. And Thom Robb is a third figure worthy of some consideration. Robb's contribution to the movement is the idea that a kinder, gentler Ku Klux Klan might borrow a page from Martin Luther King, Jr.'s book and repackage racism as a "civil rights movement for the oppressed white majority."

Robb is a native of Michigan who moved to Harrison, Arkansas, in search of a more secure environment to raise his family as far from large, Black population centers as possible. Harrison seemed perfect, and it was there that Robb set up his branch of the Knights of the Ku Klux Klan and his separate Christian Identity organization, the Kingdom Identity Ministries. Both endeavors were remarkably successful, given the minuscule numbers of adherents that the Klan and Identity Christianity can hope to attract. Soon Robb became a national figure on the radical-right-wing scene, taking the title "National Chaplain" of the Knights and traveling intensely throughout the country.

Almost from the beginning, Robb took care to keep his religious activities and his Klan activities as distinct as possible. In this, he was following long-standing precedent. As early as the 1920s, Ruben Sawyer was wearing two hats, functioning as a Klan leader on the one hand and as a minister of the British Israel faith on the other. (British Israelism was the forerunner of modern Identity Christianity.) Thus, from the 1970s to date, Robb's far-flung publication interests included the *White Patriot* for the Klan, the *Message of Old Monthly* (which later became *The Torch* for his Identity church), and *Robb's Editorial Report* for himself.

In all of these endeavors, however, several consistent patterns can be discerned. First, Thom Robb has the talent to say one thing in public and quite another in print without appearing disingenuous in either forum. Robb's message of love for the White race and professions of respect for all other races (so long as they do nothing to harm the White race), which he offers to the press and to the wider American public, are sharply at variance with his writings, which contain a profusion of racist and anti-Semitic expressions. Second, Robb is genuinely interested in reaching beyond the narrow world of Identity Christianity and the even narrower world of the Ku Klux Klan so as to build alliances with racialists of every stripe and hue. Thus, in 1984 following widespread press reports of Nation of Islam leader Louis Farrakhan's anti-Semitic statements,

Robb published an open letter to Minister Farrakhan in the August issue of *White Patriot*. It was one of the more public efforts to contact and build an alliance relationship with the Nation of Islam to come out of the racialist movement, though it would be Tom Metzger of the White Aryan Resistance who would carry the effort furthest. The letter, so redolent with the separatist aspirations of the racialist movement in the 1980s, is reprinted in full in the "Resources" section.

This kind of ecumenical outreach brought Robb a national following of younger, better-educated Klansmen. It also brought him a good deal of opposition from the bitterly factionalized world of the modern Ku Klux Klan. Thus, Dennis Mahon dismisses Robb as the "Grand Lizard," while other movement brickbats are both less colorful and less printable. Aside from Robb's high media profile—never a thing meant to endear in the intensely jealous world of the American radical right—it is Robb's approach to the Klan that is the reason for the intensity of anti-Robb sentiment in Klan circles.

A typical Klan rally under Robb's direction calls for the Klan to stage a legal, well-publicized rally, after (and only after) obtaining the required local permits and meeting with the local police to discuss plans for the rally. As the event takes place, the reason for this elaborate legality quickly becomes clear. The small contingent of Klansmen, plus those sympathetic to their message of love for the White race and conciliation with all of God's creatures, turns out to march amidst a phalanx of police and a comparative army of anti-Klan demonstrators. Invariably, the anti-Klan groups become violent and a melee quickly ensues. As the police and demonstrators do battle, the Klansmen are expected to smile beatifically and opine to the press about the fallen state of the nation and of the left's sad lack of civility and respect for free speech. It is a spectacle ready-made for television, where Robb hopes the similarity between these pictures and those of the Rev. King's civil rights demonstrators—besieged by the repressive forces of the state and forced to endure the taunts and acts of violence of the local citizenry—will become apparent to White viewers who will then flock to the Klan's banner.

While this awakening of racial consciousness among White Americans has yet to eventuate, the spectacle of robed Klansmen being forced to flee from a leftist mob under police protection drives more traditional Klansmen than Robb to impotent fury. Thus Robb's status as the media's favorite Klan leader has not brought the universal approbation of the beleaguered Klan faithful!

Undaunted, Robb continues to hold his rallies, publish his papers, distribute audio and video tapes under both his Klan and Identity imprimaturs, and invent newer and more outrageous gambits with which to entice the rubes of the national press. Of the latter, it is surely his reported plans for a Klan version of a Disneylandesque amusement park that got him a full page in *Time* magazine that must win the award for the most creative piece of media hucksterism to emerge from the White racialist movement in recent years.

See also: Beam, Louis; Christian Identity; Dilling, Elizabeth; Ku Klux Klan; Metzger, Tom; Miles, Robert; Religion of Nature; White Aryan Resistance; Zionist Occupation Government.

Further reading: Mattias Gardell, *In the Name of Elijah Mohammad: Louis Farrakhan and the Nation of Islam* (Durham, NC: Duke University Press, 1996); Mattias Gardell, *Rasrisk* (Stockholm & Uppsala: Federativs & Swedish Science Press, 1998); Jeffrey Kaplan, *Radical Religion in America* (Syracuse, NY: Syracuse University Press, 1997).

GEORGE LINCOLN ROCKWELL Before he was felled by an assassin's bullet on August 25, 1967, "the Commander" was the one preeminent figure produced by American National Socialism in the postwar era. American National Socialism, always a tiny and fractious subculture, would never recover the loss of the one man whose charisma alone held the movement together with some semblance of unity.

Rockwell was a most unlikely candidate for conversion to National Socialism. His father, George "Doc" Rockwell, was a famous vaudeville comedian who successfully made the transition to radio. Given the considerable advantages of financial security and a home environment in which the rich and famous—including such well-known Jewish entertainers as George Burns and Jack Benny—were frequent house guests, the radicalism of Rockwell's later years is all the more puzzling. This violent racialism and anti-Semitism was, however, nowhere in evidence in his formative years.

George Lincoln Rockwell graduated from Brown University, after which he joined the navy as a pilot. He was a carrier-based reconnaissance and transport pilot in World War II, though he never flew in combat. Honorably discharged from service, Rockwell was recalled to active duty in 1950 during the Korean War. He was then stationed in San Diego. This tour took him to Iceland as well, where he met and married Thora, his second wife. Both of Rockwell's marriages ended in divorce.

It was during the Korean War years that he began to develop the racial consciousness that would lead him to National Socialism. Rockwell recalled this awakening in almost mystical terms. In a scene that the Commander would confide to a bare handful of his most trusted confidants, Rockwell describes his own fortuitous discovery of the "savior," Adolf Hitler, and the religious significance of the National Socialist dream. This should come as little surprise. For Rockwell, National Socialism would become his religion in every sense of the term, and he reverenced the figure of Adolf Hitler as a racial martyr. In his autobiography, *This Time the World!,* and even more openly in the writings of two generations of movement hagiographers, Rockwell describes his own conversion to National Socialism in explicitly religious terms.

First, there was the motif of the spiritual quest. While he was based in San Diego in the early 1950s, he spent many hours in the public library in a frantic search for the truth underlying the dross of everyday events. Then there was the discovery of *Mein Kampf* on a back shelf in a musty bookshop. This was a truly life-changing experience, and early follower William Pierce's description of Rockwell's fascination with the book eerily presages the scene in his influential apocalyptic novel *The Turner Diaries* in which the protagonist, Earl Turner, is allowed to read the Organization's Holy Book, which, like Rockwell's reading of *Mein Kampf,* suddenly parted the veil of illusion that masked the numinous realities of the world. In Pierce's accounts, recorded in his *Lincoln Rockwell: A National Socialist Life,* neither Rockwell nor the fictional Turner would ever again see the world in the same way following this deeply mystical experience. Moreover, Rockwell confessed to having had a series of extraordinarily vivid and nearly identical prophetic dreams in which he was called aside from crowded, commonplace situations to a private room where standing before him was his newfound god, Adolf Hitler. It was not long before Rockwell was moved to build a literal alter to his deity, hanging a Nazi flag that covered an entire wall of his home, under which he placed a table containing a bust of Hitler, three candles, and candle holders, and in Pierce's account he:

> ...closed the blinds and lit the candles, and stood before my new altar. For the first time since I had lost my Christian religion, I experienced the soul thrilling upsurge of emotion which is denied to our modern, sterile, atheist "intellectuals" but which literally

moved the earth for countless centuries: "religious experience." I stood there in the flickering candlelight, not a sound in the house, not a soul aware of what I was doing—or caring....

William Pierce then attempts to describe this mystical experience:

It was a religious experience that was more than religious. As he stood there he felt an indescribably torrent of emotions surging through his being, reaching higher and higher in a crescendo with a peak of unbearable intensity. He felt the awe inspiring awareness for a few moments, or a few minutes, of being more than himself, of being in communion with that which is beyond description and beyond comprehension. Something with the cool vast feeling of eternity and of infinity—of long ages spanning the birth and death of suns, and of immense, starry vistas—filled his soul to the bursting point. One may call that Something by different names—the Great Spirit perhaps, or Destiny, or the Soul of the universe, or God—but once it has brushed the soul of a man, that man can never again be wholly what he was before. It changes him spiritually the same way a mighty earthquake or a cataclysmic eruption, the subsidence of a continent or the bursting forth of a new mountain range, changes forever the face of the earth.

Rockwell now had a direction, but he needed guidance and support to develop this vision. He found this through the patronage of a wealthy anti-Semitic publisher in Virginia named Harold Noel Arrowsmith. The partnership was not long lasting, but Arrowsmith's support allowed Rockwell to find his early voice in the production of incendiary racialist and anti-Semitic prose.

With the break from Arrowsmith in 1959, Rockwell was left with the skeleton of their jointly founded National Committee to Free America from Jewish Domination. He quickly converted this into the American Nazi Party (ANP), and the first unambiguously American National Socialist organization was born. The American Nazi Party was never large. Estimates of ANP membership (as opposed to names on the mailing list) range from 100 to 150 at its height. However, the American Nazi Party was influential far beyond its meager following. The ANP would attract, among those that Rockwell's autobiography would accurately describe as "90 percent of cowards, dopes, nuts, one-track minds, blabbermouths, boobs, incurable tight-wads and—worst of all—hobbyists...," such stalwarts of the later National Socialist scene as William Pierce and Matt Koehl, Identity figure Ralph Forbes, and Identity-cum-Odinist James Warner, to name but a few.

Koehl was drawn, along with several of this first postwar generation of American National Socialists, from James Hartung Madole's National Socialist–oriented National Renaissance Party, then based in New York. An important group of National Socialists affiliated with Rockwell emerged in California as well, though this group was never successfully integrated with Rockwell's immediate entourage.

The American Nazi Party founded its headquarters and barracks for Rockwell's Stormtroopers in Arlington, Virginia, in a residence that was alternately dubbed "Hate House" or "Hate Monger Hill." The group's activities involved high-profile street confrontations centered on Rockwell's speeches and publicity stunts designed to garner media attention, such as the 1961 picketing of the film *Exodus,* which earned Rockwell a short jail sentence.

By the early 1960s, Rockwell and his American Nazi Party had succeeded in their quest for publicity. The appearance of the swastika and a spokesman willing to say or do almost anything to attract attention brought the ANP and its leader an avalanche of publicity, far in excess of what its tiny following would appear to have warranted. The FBI penetrated the group early, reporting that the American Nazi Party aimed to take power in the 1972 elections, following which there would be "gas chambers, hangings, depriving citizens of their homes and heritage."

This rhetoric obviously attracted the attention of the organized Jewish community. The early Jewish response to Rockwell came in the form of street confrontations, both verbal and physical. The Jewish War Veterans of America were the primary source of this response. It soon became apparent, however, that this street theater was precisely what the publicity-craving Rockwell wanted, as it drew the press to witness and report on the events.

A more measured approach was thus called for. This came under the leadership of the American Jewish Committee's (AJC) Rabbi Solomon Andhil Fineberg. Rabbi Fineberg adapted the "Quarantine" policy, which had proved successful in depriving such Depression-era demagogues as Gerald L. K. Smith of a public forum from which to voice their anti-Semitism. Renaming his policy "Dynamic Silence," Rabbi Fineberg undertook a two-pronged strategy to deal with Rockwell. On the one hand, local AJC officials would lobby the media to refrain from covering a visit by Rockwell. On the other, Jewish organizations such as the Jewish War Veterans were urged to stay home rather than to confront the Nazis. This robbed the event of whatever newsworthiness it might have had. "Dynamic Silence" proved so successful that Rockwell, in his famous 1966 interview in *Playboy* magazine, lamented:

> So you see, the Jew blackout on us is as real as a hand over my mouth. They know we're too poor to buy air time or advertising space, so they ban our publications from all channels of distribution, and they refuse to report our activities in the daily press. I could run naked across the White House lawn and they wouldn't report it. I'm being facetious. But I'm dead serious when I say that the only kind of free speech left in this country is that speech that doesn't criticize the Jews.

Rockwell and his group soon faded from the headlines.

Frustrated at home by the media blackout, and ever more distracted by the need to mediate the never-ending squabbles of his fractious Stormtroopers, Rockwell increasingly turned his attention to "foreign policy." Rockwell for years had been in correspondence with a variety of European National Socialist figures. The most important of these contacts were the British Nazi Colin Jordan, the German Bruno Ludtke, and the French mystic Savitri Devi. Together, they would form the core of the World Union of National Socialists (WUNS). In 1962, a meeting was held in England in which a global assembly of National Socialists met to draft the Cotswold Agreements and to lay the groundwork for the World Union of National Socialists.

Rockwell would subsequently emerge as the undisputed leader of the movement. Even European National Socialists, such as Sweden's Göran Assar Oredsson, who could not accede to a movement led by an American—a natural reaction, given the American role in defeating Nazi Germany—would nonetheless prove uncharacteristically laudatory in their descriptions of George Lincoln Rockwell. The World Union of National Socialists would enjoy no more success on the world stage than the American Nazi Party did in America, but this transatlantic correspondence would nevertheless occupy much of Rockwell's time and attention in his later years.

The assassination of the Commander at the hands of a disgruntled National Socialist named John Patler brought to an end the hopes of a unified American National Socialist movement. By the time of his death, in 1967, Rockwell had renamed the American Nazi Party, calling it the National Socialist White People's Party (NSWPP) in conscious imitation of the black civil rights group the National Association for the Advancement of Colored People (NAACP).

Under Rockwell's successor, Matt Koehl, the NSWPP fragmented and eventually dissolved. WUNS would carry on through the early 1990s, but without Rockwell, this organization too was a shadow of its former self.

See also: American Nazi Party; Devi, Savitri; Hitler, Adolf; Jordan, Colin; Koehl, Matt; Ludtke, Bruno; Madole, James Hartung; Pierce, William; Smith, Gerald L. K.; Warner, James; World Union of National Socialists.

Further reading: John George and Laird Wilcox, *American Extremists, Supremacists, Klansmen, Communists and Others* (Buffalo, NY: Prometheus Books, 1996); William L. Pierce, *Lincoln Rockwell: A National Socialist Life* (Arlington, VA: NS Publications, 1969); Phillip Reese, *Biographical Dictionary of the Extreme Right Since 1890* (New York: Simon & Schuster, 1990); George Lincoln Rockwell, *This Time the World!* (Arlington, VA: Parliament House, 1963); George Lincoln Rockwell, *White Power* (n.p., 1967, 1977); Frederick J. Simonelli, "The World Union of National Socialists and Post-War Transatlantic Nazi Revival," in Jeffrey Kaplan and Tore Bjørgo, eds., *Nation and Race: The Developing Euro-American Racist Subculture* (Boston: Northeastern University Press, 1998); Frederick J. Simonelli, *American Fuehrer: George Lincoln Rockwell and the American Nazi Party* (Champaign: University of Illinois Press, 1999).

David Rust   *See* Mason, James; National Socialist Liberation Front; Pierce, William; Tommasi, Joseph.

TOMMY RAHOWA RYDÉN   For more than a decade, Tommy Rydén has been the key figure in linking the Swedish racialist movement with its American counterpart. Beginning with a youthful flirtation with the Ku Klux Klan, Rydén has maintained contacts with most of the major figures—and a good number of the bit players as well—in the American racialist scene. In the process, Rydén has sampled Christian Identity, has founded the Swedish branch of the Church of the Creator from whose teachings he legally adopted RAHOWA (Racial Holy War) as a middle name, and has been a leading proponent of National Socialism. In many ways, Tommy Rydén's life may be paradigmatic of the emerging transatlantic race movement, and for this reason, it seems valuable to consider his life in some detail in this entry.

Tommy Rydén was born in Linköping, Sweden, in January 1966. He has a younger brother and sister. His father was a salesman, a profession that Rydén has recently taken up as well. His family background was, by Swedish standards, strongly religious and quite oppositional. In a nation with a state-church tradition, the Rydén family were revivalist Baptists. Today he lives with his wife, Maud, and five children in the small town of Mullsjö in the Jönköping district of Sweden.

From his earliest memories, Rydén was a true seeker. He was fascinated by ideas, particularly religious ones, and he was an inveterate letter writer. He wanted to know about everything, and would send letters of inquiry far and wide to obtain information. At the age of 15, an incident occurred that would have a considerable impact on Tommy Rydén's life. Such events are not uncommon in the recollections of race activists, and serve a variety of functions. Most important, they serve in a sense as bridge-burning events. The activist, faced with the consequences of his or her actions, is forced to make a decision: either continue along the racialist path, or abandon the belief system and return to the safety and comfort of the status quo. This decision, of course, had always been implicit, but the young activist will often be shocked at the negative sanctions that result from acting upon what he or she had perceived to be widely held racist attitudes. The backlash is therefore often interpreted as evidence of the hypocrisy of the dominant culture. In this regard, the young racialist is little different from other seekers who find their way to a wide variety of oppositional belief systems in a quest for hidden truths underlying the seemingly chaotic rush of everyday events. The search is for absolutes, and any deviation or compromise will be contemptuously rejected. So it was with Tommy Rydén's bridge-burning event.

In 1981, Rydén and two of his friends attacked the home of a local Gypsy family with stones. They were acting out the hostility of the neighborhood to the arrival of the family—a hostility that was expressed in private conversations but never within earshot of the Gypsies. Rather than approbation, however, the community reacted with shock, and Rydén and his friends were soon caught. In the end, the Gypsy family moved out of the neighborhood (to the quiet satisfaction of their neighbors), Rydén's friends apologized for their actions, and an unrepentant Tommy Rydén was left with his first taste of local notoriety.

Determined to further explore racialist ideas, Rydén was in a quandary. There was little organized activity in the Swedish far right of the day. Thus it was of some interest when a local newspaper article detailed in highly negative terms the activities of the

American Klansman Bill Wilkinson. Wilkinson's Klan group, the Invisible Empire Knights of the Ku Klux Klan, came into being in reaction to David Duke's mediagenic approach to the Klan. Wilkinson's Klan was positioned as a traditionalist, action-oriented group, and until the 1980s it was moderately successful. Indeed, in Wilkinson's grandiose telling, the Invisible Empire was the only viable Klan organization in the country. Yet in the same time period, it was revealed that Imperial Wizard Wilkinson was an FBI informant, and had been for many years. Such disappointments become the common lot of those who persevere in the racialist milieu for any length of time. Be this as it may, the very fact that the Klan in the United States could publish a newspaper and dis- tribute cassette tapes—a package of which was duly dispatched to Rydén, in reply to a letter he sent to something approximating the Invisible Empire's address—gave the appearance of the move- ment's viability, from the distant vantage point of Scandinavia.

This early American connection may also have acted as a sort of solace for the isolation that Rydén suddenly experienced in his home town. Shunned by the community, the Americans appeared to offer a welcoming hand and a vital sense of community in a world infinitely more exciting than that of small-town Sweden. Unlike the Swedes, the Americans appeared to be active and effective, confer- ring by association a sense of power on the young Tommy Rydén.

Rydén's contacts with the United States in this period were wide ranging. On the one hand, he sought to contact as many radical- right-wing groups as possible. On the other, his interest in funda- mentalist Protestantism brought him into contact with such luminaries as the Rev. Jerry Falwell of the Moral Majority and radio commentator Cal Thomas. In all cases, Rydén showed great ingenuity in unearthing even the most obscure addresses. And none were more obscure than the American National Socialists, who began to occupy more of his curiosity. Here, fate intervened in the form of the ever-helpful United States Information Agency, which, according to Rydén, responded to his request for information by providing him with a list of contact addresses for American rac- ist and National Socialist groups.

The first Swedish movement that Tommy Rydén would become involved with was Keep Sweden Swedish (Bavara Sverige Svenskt, or BSS). BSS was a small anti-immigrant organization that was the beginning of the parliamentary parties formed in the late 1970s to oppose non-White immigration. The BSS was in essence an interest group formed to push for a national referendum on immigration. It never coalesced into a political party and was never very large, with an estimated 300 members by 1984. Nonetheless, passing through BSS ranks were a number of adherents destined for careers in both the parliamentary and the extraparliamentary far right. The BSS, however, offered little that would hold Tommy Rydén's interest for long. Rather, ironically enough, he had by then begun to think of emigrating himself. His vision was of a White redoubt where the dream of community could be realized in a more concrete fashion than could be achieved through the mails. In the 1980s, South Africa became the destination of choice for a number of young White racialists from Europe and the United States. Tommy Rydén arrived in South Africa in May 1988.

Rydén was to spend some four months in South Africa. There, he would have a number of experiences that in retrospect would be life changing, but none had as dramatic a symbolic impact as his observation of a beautiful White woman whom Rydén describes as the "Aryan ideal" on one side of the street, while on the other side was walking a "typical African Black woman" weighed down with packages. At once, Rydén knew with absolute certainty that the races were different and ordained to be forever separate, forever unequal.

For Tommy Rydén, the South African trip was as much of a religious pilgrimage as it was a political statement. Ever the searcher, at the time he departed for South Africa Rydén was immersed in two contradictory religious traditions: conservative Christianity and Christian Identity. Further, he had already begun to make the contacts that would lead him in yet another direction—toward the American-based Church of the Creator. When he left Sweden, Rydén was already in contact with several American Christian Identity churches, and this would play a large role in his activities in South Africa. In the light of what he saw and experienced in South Africa, Rydén's attachment to Christianity was first eroded and then abandoned entirely.

Tommy Rydén today is somewhat loath to accept that he was once a Christian Identity believer. This may be attributed in large part to the strongly negative view that the Church of the Creator takes of Christian Identity. As his South African days drew to a close, Rydén felt alienated from the Identity creed's Jewish roots, and yet more convinced than ever that the answer to what he believed to be the disastrous situation facing the White race is a racial religion. The obvious place to turn after a visit home to Sweden was to the United States and to the small but growing Church of the Creator (COTC) under the leadership of the self-styled "Pontifex Maximus," Ben Klassen.

The COTC seemed to Tommy Rydén to be, at long last, *the* answer. Here was a racial religion that, unlike Identity, did not seek to contest with the Jews for the prophetic mantle of Old Testament roots. Rather, the COTC heartily agreed with the "Judeo-Christian" mainstream that Christianity was indeed built on the foundation of Judaism. That being the case, Klassen derisively dismissed Christians as dupes in an age-old Jewish plot to subvert the White man's glory, yet he reserved even greater contempt for the Identity Christian community that would seek to wrest from the Jews the poisoned fruits of this religious legacy.

Before going to South Africa, Rydén had briefly corresponded with Klassen, but on his return this correspondence became more serious. Ben Klassen replied personally to this new round of questions:

Dear Mr. Ryden:

This will acknowledge receipt of your interesting letter of July 31. Evidently you have had a number of revealing and educational experiences since we last corresponded five years ago, and I detect that you have increased your learning considerably as far as our program of survival, expansion and advancement of the White Race. I am glad that among these is the realization about what a farce is the spooks in the sky swindle.

Regarding some of your questions starting with No. 1, if you will explain to me what a "spirit" is, I might be able to answer your question about "spiritualism". As far as following the program in Salubrious Living, it is not mandatory to do so to become a member of our church. It is a helpful guide to better health, and the individual can take the advice and benefit from it.

Do we ever have members in South Africa! One of the most flourishing church groups in our movement is under the leadership of Rev. Jan S. Smith,...

We would be happy to hear from you again soon and have you as a member. In the meantime, RAHOWA!

For a Whiter and Brighter World,

Creatively Yours,

B. Klassen, P. M.

Thus began Tommy Rydén's association with the Church of the Creator. The COTC would prove to be his longest-lasting organizational commitment; he did not officially resign from the COTC until 1995. The Swedish COTC period was eventful, exciting, but ultimately unsuccessful. The Church (Kreativistens Kyrka), despite the efforts of both Tommy Rydén and his wife, was never able to attract more than a handful of adherents.

The Kreativistens Kyrka period, however, meant a great deal to Tommy Rydén. Of greatest import, Tommy met his wife, Maud, during this period, and they joined the COTC together. It was in connection with the COTC that Rydén was arrested for distributing the COTC paper *Racial Loyalty* and was sentenced to four months in prison in 1991. And it was through his association with the COTC that Rydén would come into his most intensive contact with an American group. The results, in retrospect, were often less than edifying. While Rydén's respect for Ben Klassen remains very much intact, he nonetheless is candid in describing the man's shortcomings. Rydén is even more critical of the revolving "successors" to Klassen and the too-often lazy, incompetent, or simply criminal parade of "Hasta Primus" ("Spear Head"—the COTC term for the director of day-to-day affairs) title holders.

The situation would go from bad to worse in the American COTC in the waning years of Klassen's life. For some time, the Swedish COTC (or Kreativistens Kyrka) tried to soldier on, despite the increasingly chaotic situation in the American mother church. This meant, in effect, opting for a kind of quasi-independence and several name changes, including the Ben Klassen Institute. As the situation worsened in the American mother church, Rydén at last despaired of the COTC and tendered his resignation.

In the wake of the demise of the Swedish COTC, Tommy Rydén has moved on to a variety of interests. In 1996–1997, he adapted some of the old Ásatrú Free Assembly rituals created by Steve McNallen in the United States to perform an Ásatrú 'baptism'; in an abortive move, he attempted to form a Cosmotheist church (Cosmotistkyrkan) modeled on that of the American National Socialist figure William Pierce, translated Jost's Arya Kriya materials into Swedish for dissemination in Scandinavia, put aside his distaste for skinheads and their "revolution by compact disc" to become associated with the music magazine *Nordland,* and became part of a new political party that has had some localized success, the Hembygdspartiet (Native Place Party).

But at the same time, Rydén is a husband and father, and these responsibilities became acute in 1997. It would be an understatement to say that the Rydéns are no materialists, and they live on a modest amount of money. Yet even under Sweden's once-generous social welfare system, five small children and a wife who must remain in the home to care for them represents a considerable responsibility. For many years, Rydén was able to eke out an existence as a full-time activist, thanks to the Swedish social support, supplemented by occasional contributions from family members and other activists. When these sources proved insufficient for a growing family, Tommy Rydén began to search for a job in earnest.

This is no easy task for such a figure. His notoriety is such that there is a constant risk of antiracist activists finding his employer and seeking to get him fired—if, that is, an employer could be found willing to give him a chance to work. This isolation represents a primary impediment to those seeking to leave the movement—the bridges have been burned, making reintegration into society problematic at best. Rydén faced this frustration, but refused to give up and, in 1997, he found a job as a salesman. This opportunity to support his family like any other husband and father represented yet another life-changing event for Tommy Rydén. Rydén's pride in this achievement is evident, and there is no better note on which to conclude this entry. In a fax dated April 13, 1997, Rydén states:

> Let me first give you the good news that I now got employment as a salesman at a company! I found the job through my own hard work. Began to hunt for a job like never before, and booked job interviews (not bad at all, since most people do not even get that far!), but this job as a salesman was the one that I really wanted, and perhaps they could see that in my eyes!
>
> For years I have put the cause before my own wellbeing and our family's economy, but with this employment I have now decided to withdraw from the nationalist scene…no articles, no party leader, etc. No, I have not changed my views. But I must concentrate 100 percent on my family and see to it that my children get a decent future. No one else will do it for us.
>
> The projects I have been involved in will be taken over by other activists, or will disappear entirely.
>
> The big problem in Sweden is that the citizens have been so passivated by the state's Marxism—so they still sit there and expect "big brother" (the politicians) to save them. They do not support us who try to do something, no matter how you try to market it.
>
> And to this the sad fact that that I am the only one in this whole nationalist movement here who has the guts to stand for my views with name and picture (even on the Internet), while so many others hide behind made-up names and protected identities.
>
> So I will not waste the upcoming years on these lazy Swedes. It is more productive to invest time and money in family and

friends—the only things of value in the Ragnarök that awaits us around the corner.

As a poor man, I cannot fight the forces that we are up against, nor can I help others. So I am leaving the battle scene for a moment—everyone who has studied Sun-Tzu's writing on the art of war will understand me (the others will continue to listen to their compact disks and understand nothing).

Yet Tommy Rydén remains committed to his racialist and anti-Semitic *weltenschaung*. Virtually every long-time activist has dreamed of what it would be like to live a "normal" life, with wife and children and the respect of the community. In this, Tommy Rydén is no different. He too has toyed with such thoughts. But weighed against such dreams are the years of contacts with distant activists, the notoriety that accrues to even the infamous in the form of television talk shows and newspaper articles, and the attentions of academics from around the world. But perhaps of greatest import, there is the fact that after having lived so long as an outsider, as an object of curiosity and, indeed, of fear, it is no easy task, given the best of intentions, to be allowed to act the part of the normal husband and father. As Rydén writes:

> Yesterday I was at an information meeting for parents in the school our oldest child will attend in August. The school is nearby and the female teacher seems to be OK as a human being. There will be 14 in the class. 3 of them non-Whites, one is racemixed (Chinese/White, the mother is adopted from somewhere) and the two others from the Middle East with parents who can hardly speak Swedish at all. Their children will receive home language training (the only thing they never cut down on in our lovely country). We had preferred an all-Swedish class, but I guess the situation could have been worse. I could see that the Asiatic woman recognized me (tell me who does not!) and looked very uneasy. I would not be surprised at all if she demands that her kid is moved to another class! I am dangerous you know! Anyway, we teach our children to be proud in a positive way. To focus on positive things (11 against 3) and to become problem solvers. At the same time I realize, like Maud, that sooner or later we will have to stand up and fight for our children. Funny, at the parents meeting I was the only one who asked most of the questions—and will continue to do so.

See also: Christian Identity; Church of the Creator; Duke, David; Hembygdspartiet; Jost; Keep Sweden Swedish; Klassen, Ben; Kreativistens Kyrka; Ku Klux Klan; Odinism; Pierce, William; White Power Music.

Further reading: John George and Laird Wilcox, *American Extremists, Supremacists, Klansmen, Communists and Others* (Buffalo, NY: Prometheus Books, 1996); Jeffrey Kaplan and Leonard Weinberg, *The Emergence of a Euro-American Radical Right* (Rutgers, NJ: Rutgers University Press, 1998); Heléne Lööw, "Racist Violence and Criminal Behaviour in Sweden: Myths and Reality," *Terrorism and Political Violence* 7:1 (spring 1995); Heléne Lööw, "The Fight Against ZOG—Anti-Semitism Among the Modern Race Ideologists," *Historisk Tidskrift* 1 (1996); Heléne Lööw, "White Power Rock 'n' Roll–A Growing Industry," in Jeffrey Kaplan and Tore Bjørgo, eds., *Nation and Race: The Developing Euro-American Racist Subculture* (Boston: Northeastern University Press, 1998).

SCRIPTURES FOR AMERICA   The group called Scriptures for America (SFA) is the outreach ministry for Christian Identity minister Pete Peters and his LaPorte (Colorado) Church of Christ. Scriptures for America publishes Peters's periodical, the *Scriptures for America* newsletter, as well as a number of books, pamphlets, and tracts on a wide variety of subjects. SFA is also the umbrella under which operate an extensive cassette tape service, shortwave radio, videos, satellite television, and, most recently, an Internet webpage.

Some of the more important titles published by Pete Peters's Scriptures for America include: *Whores Galore, Baal Worship, The Greatest Love Story Never Told,* and *America the Conquered* as well as several tracts such as *Death Penalty for Homosexuals is Prescribed in the Bible, Saving the Environment, New World Order,* and *Style and Strength of a Hero.*

Perhaps the most important outreach tool employed by Scriptures for America today is the World Wide Web. Beginning with a primitive FTP (File Transfer Protocol) site, the new Scriptures for America web site is remarkably sophisticated.

See also: Peters, Pete.

Further reading: Jeffrey Kaplan, *Radical Religion in America: Millenarian Movements from the Far Right to the Children of Noah* (Syracuse, NY: Syracuse University Press, 1997); Pete Peters, *Death Penalty for Homosexuals* (LaPorte, CO: Scriptures for America, 1993); Pete Peters, *Baal Worship* (LaPorte, CO: Scriptures for America, 1995); Pete Peters, *Whores Galore* (LaPorte, CO: Scriptures for America, 1995).

Frank Silva   *See* Aryan Nations; Order.

SKINHEADS (ORIGINS AND MUSIC)   The skinhead movement is today a global phenomenon, one fraught with remarkable contradictions. Skinheads belong to a youth movement whose first generation is no longer youthful. The movement is saddled with a well-deserved reputation for random racial violence, yet some of the deadliest confrontations involving skinheads have been internal—the product of sudden explosions of anger, internecine battles with the large contingent of antiracist and apolitical skinheads over the soul of the movement, or, in recent years, deadly warfare over control of the lucrative White Power music scene in skirmishes that more resemble organized crime than a political race movement. But the most central contradiction of all is that the skinhead movement first emerged in the multiracial districts of London where White working-class youth acquired a taste for Jamaican ska music and where a multiracial club scene was born.

In the early 1970s, skinhead culture emerged both as a form of working-class opposition to the hippie movement, which even then was in decline, and as a refusal to join the long-standing tribes of the British youth scene: the mods and the rockers. It was at this time that the prototypical skinhead uniform evolved as short, closely cropped hair, Ben Sherman work shirts, and especially Doc Marten boots and braces (suspenders). As with most British youth culture phenomena, violence was very much part of the mix, though this violence was directed primarily at Whites deemed economically more advantaged.

From the mix of early skinhead culture and Jamaican Rastafarian-inspired music came the first bands, either composed of skinheads or catering to a mixed audience that included skinheads. One of the first skinheads to rise to music stardom was Jimmy Pursey, who fronted a "three chords and a cloud of dust" punk band called Sham 69. For a few years, Sham 69 were the kings of the scene and Pursey the first skinhead star. His reign was brief, however. Pursey was at heart a liberal, and when the skin scene turned to racialism, Pursey became a pariah.

Although boasting only a few skinheads, a scene called Two Tone also enjoyed a brief vogue among British skins. Two Tone was the name of a record label that soared to popularity behind such bands as the Specials, the Selector, and Madness, to name a few of the most popular groups. Two Tone's hook was to bring the interracial London club scene to the concert stage with bands made of up of both Black and White musicians playing music that was a hybrid of the Jamaican reggae and ska styles and British pop. The Two Tone message was decidedly integrationist and antiracist. Two Tone's run was meteoric, but brief. By the end of the 1970s racial polarization had grown in recession-choked England, and Two Tone concerts were so plagued by racial fights in the audience that its bands had to stop touring. In a bitter farewell, the Specials released their last single, "Ghost Town," which lamented: "bands don't play no more, too much fighting on the dance floor."

The extraordinary racial polarization that doomed the idealistic Two Tone venture and made an outcast of Jimmy Pursey was a marked feature of skinhead culture by the mid-1970s. Increasingly, skinhead violence was turned from preppy Whites to immigrants and non-White targets of convenience. But the skinhead subculture remained diffuse, lacking the focus that a leader, a band, or a coherent ideology could provide. Into this void stepped Ian Stewart Donaldson.

In 1975, Ian Stewart formed a Rolling Stones–inspired band called Tumbling Dice, which played covers of hits by the popular bands of the day in workingmen's clubs in the Blackpool area. Stewart soon grew tired of playing other bands' material, and as a vehicle to play his original songs he created Skrewdriver in 1977, just in time for England's summer of punk, which saw the emergence of such flamboyantly antiestablishment groups as the Sex Pistols and the Clash. A surprising number of today's racialist skins in England and throughout Europe trace their roots to this time, starting out as punks and for various reasons deserting the punk movement for the skinhead subculture. Ian Stewart and Skrewdriver would play an important role in this evolution.

Skrewdriver's early recordings show little sign of the racialist anthems that would come. Their first single, an antidrug-message song named "You're So Dumb," was released to little acclaim by Chiswick in 1977. A second single, "Anti-Social," followed. The record was notable mainly for its B-side, a Stones cover, with "19th Nervous Breakdown." Skrewdriver followed these singles with its first album, *All Skrewed Up,* which continued largely in the punkish vein of the singles. By then, however, Ian Stewart had joined the first wave of punks to shave their heads and adopt skinhead culture as a working-class protest against the "gentrification" and commercialization of punk.

Following its oppositional early days, punk had become simply another commercial commodity that became a mild fashion statement for bored, middle-class kids with money in their pockets and nothing in their heads. That fate was not likely to befall racialist skinhead culture. The skinhead ethos was defiantly working class, utterly opposed to the social status quo, but, until Ian Stewart Donaldson and Skrewdriver's conversion to racialist skinhead beliefs, it was largely directionless and painfully inarticulate. Just as Bob Dylan would give voice to a generation of White, middle-class teens in an America emerging from the deepest chill of the Cold War, Ian Stewart provided the sound track for alienated White, working-class youths for whom postindustrial Britain could find no productive role.

By 1978, however, disillusioned with the band's lack of success and the incessant bad press it drew, Stewart dissolved Skrewdriver and worked for a time in a car wash. It wasn't long, though, before he was back in London ready to try again. He was assisted in the effort by Suggsie, the lead singer for Madness, the antiracist Two Tone band, who had once been a Skrewdriver roadie. From the beginning, class consciousness and neighborhood ties would be more important than ideology in the creation of the skinhead sub-culture. In this new incarnation, Skrewdriver released several EPs that hinted at an increasingly racialist direction. This evolution would be completed by 1982's *White Power* EP.

The early 1980s were Skrewdriver's heyday. As with so many British youth styles, the skinhead movement had by then gone inter-national. European skins copied the attire, music, and manners of the British movement, blending the skinhead scene's racialism with their own socioeconomic marginalization. Immigration became a ral-lying cry throughout the continent, though in this era Britain and Germany were the movement's epicenters. Soon Scandinavia would experience a skinhead boom, and, to a lesser degree, the United States and other nations in Western Europe followed suit. Against this backdrop, Skrewdriver in 1984 released its seminal album, *Hail the New Dawn*. Each cut on *Hail the New Dawn* is an anthem in itself, redolent with the imagery of a collapsing Britain as juxtaposed to an increasingly explicit vision of a British renaissance under the banner of National Socialism.

By 1984, a small but intense cult followed Skrewdriver, and Ian Stewart became the focal point of the racialist skinhead subculture. It is important to note, however, that by then there were a number of other popular skinhead bands, such as the British bands Brutal Attack and Public Enemy, that joined Skrewdriver for a mocking answer to the mainstream Rock Against Racism festivals—Rock Against Communism.

Skrewdriver topped *Hail the New Dawn* in 1985 with *Blood and Honour*. In keeping with the internationalism of the movement, the CD was released by a racialist German label, Rock-O-Rama. This would later prove problematic, as the label was quickly proscribed by the German authorities and its product seized. This would for a time in the 1990s make Skrewdriver's records somewhat difficult to obtain.

Blood and Honour became an international phenomenon in the skinhead subculture, and Stewart and Skrewdriver began a period of intensive touring throughout Europe. Skrewdriver gigs became the model for racialist skinhead concerts, with the band and the audience rejecting the rock star concept of distance. The band played, the largely male audience did a drunken imitation of dancing (more a series of violent collisions than anything coherent enough to be called a dance), and band and audience would drink beer and chat between sets. The band traveled to gigs by van, staying with fellow skins along the way. Stewart and Skrewdriver brought together the first generation of racialist skins, and today Stewart is deified by those who can trace their movement lineage to him. Consider one such eulogy offered in 1995 by a founder of the racialist Nordland music label in Sweden:

> Ian Stewart was like our generation's version of Hitler, to put forth the dream of a harmonious future for White people. [Stewart] invented the concept of spreading our ideas through music.

Blood and Honour was adopted as the name of Stewart's organization as he attempted—with, at best, mixed success—to parlay Skrewdriver's popularity into an institutional presence. Stewart's growing international celebrity did not go unnoticed, and in the mid-1980s skinhead gigs throughout Europe came under heavy police pressure. Halls were increasingly hard to rent, and local skinhead groups became remarkably resourceful at putting up a false flag under which space could be found to hold concerts.

Racialist skinhead gigs had to become even more clandestine as antiracist activists began to try to prevent the performances from taking place, leading to large-scale fights. Eventually, quite a sophisticated word-of-mouth operation was adopted in which trusted fans would contact local skinhead leaders to be given a meeting point and a time, following which a bus or car convoy would take the eager group to a secret location for the evening's festivities.

Stewart himself was jailed in 1985 for a street fight in which a Pakistani man was beaten. Stewart responded that he had merely been defending himself, and that the Jewish judge in the case refused to listen to his defense. Whatever the circumstances, Stewart emerged from prison with his standing, if anything, higher than ever. Stewart was lionized on his travels, and he was the driving force behind *Blood and Honour,* this time a magazine centered on the doings of the skinhead musical subculture. He announced his engagement to a strikingly beautiful girl named Diane, and all seemed well with the world.

On September 24, 1993, Ian Stewart Donaldson was killed in an automobile accident on the way to a Skrewdriver gig. From that day forward, in tribute concerts and in CDs dedicated to his memory, Ian Stewart's legacy lives on in the racialist skinhead subculture. Eerily, one of Ian Stewart's last songs, "Suddenly," asks:

If suddenly, I am forced to take my leave,
Will you carry on with the things that we believe?
One day if suddenly they take my life away,
Will you be fighting to win a bright, new day?

See also: Skinheads (Norwegian); White Power Music.

Further reading: Katrine Fangen, *Skinheads in Red, White and Blue: A Report from the Inside*, *Youth Research Report* (April 1995); Mark S. Hamm, *American Skinheads: The Criminology and Control of Hate Crime* (Westport, CT: Praeger, 1993); Erik Jensen, "International Nazi Co-operation; A Terrorist-Oriented Network," in Tore Bjørgo and Rob Witte, *Racist Violence in Europe* (Basingstoke: Macmillan, 1993); Laszlo Kurti, "Rocking the State: Youth and Rock Music culture in Hungary, 1976–1990," *East European Politics and Societies* 5:3 (1991); Anna-Lena Lodenius, "Blood, and Honour and Blue and Yellow Rock," *Arbetaren* 17 (1994); Anna-Lena Lodenius and Per Wikström, "Nazism Behind a Viking Mask," *Kommunalarbetaren* 6 (1994); Heléne Lööw, "White Power—Dark History," *Uppväxtvillkor* 3 (1993); Heléne Lööw, "Racist Violence and Criminal Behaviour in Sweden: Myths and Reality," *Terrorism and Political Violence* 7:1 (spring 1995); Heléne Lööw, "The Fight Against ZOG—Anti-Semitism Among the Modern Race Ideologists," *Historisk Tidskrift* 1 (1996); Heléne Lööw, "White Power Rock 'n' Roll—A Growing Industry," in Jeffrey Kaplan and Tore Bjørgo, eds., *Nation and Race: The Developing Euro-American Racist Subculture* (Boston: Northeastern University Press, 1998); Joe Pearce, *Skrewdriver: The First Ten Years* (London: Skrewdriver Services, 1987); Eric Weisband and Craig Marks, *Spin Alternative Record Guide* (New York: Vintage Books, 1995).

SKINHEADS (NORWEGIAN)   The skinhead subculture emerged in Norway in the early 1980s. As in many other countries, the skinhead subculture split into a nationalist and an antiracist faction. The nationalist faction was initiated by Ole Krogstad, who established the Bootboys Club. According to Krogstad, he got the inspiration when visiting his fellow rightist activists in Sweden. The Bootboys Club was not, according to Krogstad, intended to be political. The aim of the group was for skinheads to be able to come together to "talk and have a few beers."

Relations between the Bootboys and more ideological organizations like Zorn 88 and INO have been tense. The latter group has publicly said that it will not have anything to do with these youngsters, whereas Zorn 88's line, according to Krogstad, has been, to speak up against the Bootboys in public "because they are so violent." Behind closed doors, though, they think "..it is good to have the skinheads around when the reds come."

The leftist part of the skinhead subculture grew out of the punk scene in Norway, especially after the oi-rock band Sham 69 held a concert here in 1983. Furthermore, some of the White Power skinheads had previously been punks, but later preferred the skinhead style. They wanted to rebel and shock, but found the punk style too untidy. In contrast, the skinhead lifestyle was elegant, at the same time as it was proletarian and appeared to be tough.

Some of the White Power skinheads became members of Nasjonalt Folkeparti (National People's Party), an extraparliamentary party with a National Socialist profile. Several White Power skinheads were excluded from the Blitz house (an anarchist cultural center) because their nationalist symbols and attitudes contrasted greatly with the house's antiracist profile. According to a leading figure within the White Power skinhead movement, skinheads are "a reaction against the hippie subculture, cultural decline and blending of races, whereas the SHARP skinheads [Skinheads Against Racial Prejudice] are a...bunch of confused anarchists who live for chaos, sex, violence, and hash."

At the present, there are two groups of SHARP in Norway. Some of these skinheads are active both within the Blitz house and within the so-called *Vålerenga klanen* (Vålerenga Klan). The latter is the supporter club of one of the capital's football teams. They are famous both for their songs and their loyal support of the team, whether at good and bad matches. From time to time they have also been criticized for being violent and making racist statements. The leader of the Klan has tried to stop the racist talk and cut down on violence. Thus, the nationalist members of the Klan still take part, but no longer show their support openly. For example, they no longer wear White Power T-shirts, as they had done previously.

A couple of the SHARP skinheads have been skinheads as long as some of the leading White Power skinheads have. The White Power skinheads say that the SHARP skinheads are "a plague which tries to split the skinhead movement. ...they say that the skinhead movement originally was in favor of multicultural society with some reggae (ska) in their music. But the truth is that the first skinheads hated everybody!" On the other hand, the SHARP skinheads claim that the White Power skinheads are not real skinheads. Rather, they are boneheads or Nazi skinheads, who deny the skinheads' original link to Black culture.

Being experienced with the various codes of the skinhead lifestyle and knowing a great deal about the subculture entitles skinheads to a certain status in every area of the skinhead subculture. The men who are known to be central figures within the subculture are seen as important, no matter which part of the movement they belong to. Many aspire to attend skinhead concerts abroad where skinheads with different political opinions stand side by side, without this leading to fights. Many of the leading skinheads among the nationalists look back upon the period before the factions became more clearly defined with nostalgia.

The SHARP skinheads emphasize the fact that skinheads originally were not racists or nationalists, and the goal of several SHARP skinheads is to fight the Nazi skinheads. A distinct group of skinheads is called the Oslo-skins. Some of the group's members define themselves as being SHARP; others do not want to define themselves as antiracists, but neither like the fact that people associate skinheads with Nazis. This group has its own oi-rock band, the Fuck-Ups.

There is also a group of skinheads who define themselves as being politically neutral. Some of them wear patches with the Norwegian flag, similar to those used by the nationalist skins. But they define themselves out of the ongoing conflict between militant antifascists and White Power skinheads. They are very upset about the way matters have developed, and one of them said "the whole thing is so pathetic that there is hardly any use in talking about it." A few of them have become friends with some of the leading White Power skinheads, and respect them because they are "real" skinheads. This criterion of being a "real skinhead" is heard in every area of the skinhead subculture. The most common traits associated with being a real skinhead are a complete commitment to the lifestyle and musical preferences of skinheads, as well as a strong identification with and knowledge of the history of the skinhead subculture. Most skinheads do not have either a political or an ideological view of what it means to be a skinhead, other than the fact that skinheads love football, beer, street-fights, and girls, and that skinheads are comrades and do not adhere to the leadership principle. In the White Power subculture, it is common to speak of "leaderless resistance."

During the 1980s, the different kinds of skinheads could visit the same pubs and talk, despite their political disagreements. After Arne Myrdal (the former leader of FMI, the People's Movement Against Immigration) held a political rally in Brumunddal in 1991, the factions have become clearer. Then White Power skinheads and local bikers joined Arne Myrdal and the FMI members. On the other hand, the SHARP skinheads joined the anarchist Blitz youths on the antiracist side. Following this event, there have been many violent clashes between SHARP skinheads and the White Power skinheads.

Despite these points, the groups still have some areas in common. This is not least due to the fact that people from both groups belong to *Vålerenga klanen*. Quite a few of the football supporters frequent the same pubs as the right-wing activists, and some of the football supporters even join the rightist activists' trips to Sweden to attend rock concerts and nationalist demonstrations. The skinheads who belong to the supporter club mostly keep a friendly tone. However, problems have arisen when the White Power skinheads of the club have taken their nationalist friends with them to parties where other Klan members have been present.

—Katrine Fangen, University of Oslo, Norway

See also: Krogstad, Ole; Leaderless Resistance; White Power Music.

Further reading: Bootboys 9 (1990), *Rock Furore, Nasjonalisten* nos. 5–6, vol. 47–48 (June 1982); Katrine Fangen, "Skinheads I rødt, hvitt og blått En sosiologisk studie fra innsiden" [Skinheads in red, white and blue: A sociological study from "inside"] (1994); Katrine Fangen, "Living Out Our Ethnic Instincts: Ideological Beliefs Among Right-Wing Activists in Norway," in Jeffrey Kaplan and Tore Bjørgo, eds., *Nation and Race: The Developing Euro-American Racist Subculture* (Boston: Northeastern University Press, 1998).

GERALD L. K. SMITH   Of all of the Depression era demagogues, Gerald L. K. Smith has had by far the most impact on the American racialist movement today. It was Smith's Committee of One Million and his Christian Crusade, which gathered under one large tent the most important of the leaders of the radical right, that would emerge in the 1960s and 1970s to offer a sense of common destiny to a diverse group that represented belief systems from conservative anticommunist to Identity Christianity. Smith's innovative mass-mailing techniques set the standard for movement fund-raising and provides a model for the present day in which a particular leader's mailing list becomes his most precious possession. More-over, Smith was for a time able to walk the thin line of acceptability that allowed him to offer an extraordinarily radical and anti-Semitic message to the faithful while steering clear of the legal entanglements that hamstrung most of the American radical right during World War II.

Smith's story is a fascinating tale of a meteoric rise to fame fol-lowed by a gradual fade into obscurity. Smith was born in Pardeeville, Wisconsin, in 1898 to a family who taught him early to take a literalist approach to the Bible and to never shy away from making his views known. This he did, blessed with a seemingly inexhaustible reservoir of energy, a golden voice, and, as he later recalled, a "superabundance of wind." If ever a man was destined for the ministry, Gerald L. K. Smith was that man. He graduated from Valparaiso University in only two years, began to work his way through a succession of ever larger and more important churches, and in 1922 married his wife, Elma. She would be at his side constantly in good times and in bad for the next 50 years, pub-lishing his autobiography, *Besieged Patriot,* as a final tribute upon his death in 1976.

Smith's early years showed much of the promise of what was to come. In churches throughout the Midwest, Smith honed his consid-erable oratorical skills. By 1929, he had moved to the King's High-way Christian Church in Shreveport, Louisiana. It was there that the stock market crash and subsequent Depression brought Smith into politics full time. Smith became an intimate of "the Kingfish," Louisiana Governor Huey Long, and controlled in his own right an organization with the hopeful title Share Our Wealth. The success of the Share Our Wealth clubs provided Smith with over 200,000 names for his initial mailing list. With Long's assassination in 1935, Smith was on his own.

The 1930s were a fertile, albeit erratic, period for Smith. He was becoming either increasingly anti-Semitic or increasingly outspoken about his anti-Semitism, and it was surely this prejudice that explains his prewar flirtation with such extreme anti-Semites as William Dudley Pelley and his Silver Shirts (which group, despite Smith's denials, he and his wife appear to have joined). Going further, Smith's biographer Glen Jeansonne uncovered a letter in Smith's FBI file that the writer intended for Adolf Hitler via the German embassy. Dated January 8, 1933, the letter is worth quoting in full:

> Dear Sir,
>
> I write to you concerning a very confidential matter based on the confidence that some of my friends have in you.
>
> I am anxious to get in touch with his Honor, Adolf Hitler, but, knowing that you are recently removed from Germany, before doing so I desire your opinion of conditions in that country. They look good to me. Can you give me a code for getting in touch with Herr Hitler or one of his representatives in America?
>
> The Semitic propaganda in America is growing more serious every day. I enclose herewith a bulletin that was put on the streets of our country as the result of an attempt on the part of a Jew to take hundreds of homes away from our people. I am convinced that the Jews are trying to rob American people just as they attempted to do in Germany and Germany and America will be closer together than any two nations in the world.
>
> You will be interested to know that my grandfather's name was Herr Schmidt, and that I was reared in the state of Wisconsin. You may feel free to write to me directly or through one of your friends in Shreveport. Surely there must be an organization now existing in America to overcome the terrible anti-German propaganda being promoted by the Jews. Please enlighten me.
>
> Guten tag,
>
> Gerald L. K. Schmidt

It was a strange letter, which Jeansonne finds generally creditable. But whatever the circumstances under which it was written, the letter does fit in well chronologically with Smith's increasingly outspoken anti-Semitism.

Anti-Semitism, however, was only one facet of Gerald L. K. Smith's activities in the Depression years of the 1930s. Smith was better known for his tireless activities in support of populist appeals that in many ways transcend the narrow right-wing/left-wing dichotomy of American politics. Thus, Smith's next association was with the eccentric campaign waged by Dr. Francis Townsend for a national pension plan. The organized vehicle for this was the Old Age Revolving Pension Plan Ltd., which at Smith's suggestion was later changed to the easier-on-the-ear Townsend Recovery Plan. The plan had undeniable popular appeal, and it was in the midst of this campaign that Smith became an ally of the most important anti-Semitic voice in the nation, Father Charles Coughlin. Smith barnstormed with Townsend for his pension plan, but it soon became obvious that the campaign was going nowhere. What was missing was a political machine capable of sufficiently breaking the two-party stranglehold on politics so that the pension plan—and indeed, other populist reforms—could be enacted into law.

With this in mind, Smith, Townsend, Coughlin, and a congressman from North Dakota named William Lemke formed the National Union for Social Justice in 1935 to contest the 1936 election against the popular incumbent, Franklin Roosevelt. The election was a disaster for the National Union for Social Justice. The ticket headed by William Lemke polled a paltry 2 percent of the vote, with 891,858 popular votes and no electoral votes. Worse, Smith and Coughlin were competing more with each other than with Roosevelt, ending the campaign scarcely on speaking terms. For his part, Lemke could count himself fortunate to have (barely) retained his congressional seat. And to add insult to injury, Roosevelt's New Deal adopted key elements of the populist appeals in his dramatic expansion of the role of the federal government.

Smith did not do badly from the debacle of the National Union for Social Justice. His mailing list burgeoned and he had become a well-known public speaker, able to draw crowds in tent-revival-style appearances throughout the country. With this backing and name recognition, Smith formed his most important vehicle, the Committee of One Million, in 1937. The Committee allowed Smith to give vent to his anti-Semitism, but, of greater interest, Smith's Committee was increasingly shedding its populist skin in favor of a right-wing agenda that was explicitly anti–New Deal, antilabor, anticommunist, and in favor of a vague "Americanism" that affirmed a kind of generic Christianity along with exuberant public expressions of patriotism.

Standing with Smith now were such pillars of the American establishment as conservative congressmen and senators, governors, and, of greatest import, industrialist Henry Ford. Ford's contributions to anti-Semitism in America are incalculable. It was Ford's press outlet, the *Dearborn Independent,* that published the "International Jew" series of articles. The articles were later reprinted in a four-volume set of books also titled *The International Jew*. The "International Jew" is the key link that brought the Old World anti-Semitism of the *Protocols of the Elders of Zion* into the context of contemporary American life. More than any single source, the "International Jew" brought together a generation of right-wing true believers, and material from this series of articles provided the ammunition for most of the anti-Semitic agitation of the of the last half century of American life.

In Gerald L. K. Smith's Committee of One Million, Henry Ford found a powerful voice for Americanism as he envisioned it, and he was prepared to be generous in helping the Committee along. Ford's support was much appreciated. In *Besieged Patriot,* Smith proudly asserts:

> ...I received a message from a mutual friend to the effect that Mr. Henry Ford had heard about my address and would like to see me. I was flattered and inspired because I knew that he and the late Huey P. Long were friends. This was the beginning of the development of a friendship.... It will be recalled that Mr. Ford was universally hated by the international Jews because he published a terrific book entitled "The International Jew." It was published in serial form in the official magazine of the Ford Motor Co. known as the "Dearborn Independent." He also gave much publicity to the document known as "The Protocols of the Learned Elders of Zion." Due to pressure from certain members of his family and junior officers in the company, he ceased publishing "The International Jew," but on a visit with him he revealed to me that he hoped to publish it again, and if he didn't publish it, he hoped I would. At this time, I was broadcasting over the largest radio station in Detroit and had a phenomenal radio audience. Two of my admirers and chief listeners were Mr. and Mrs. Henry Ford. In fact we have flattering letters from Mrs. Ford written by hand and signed "Clara."...
>
> Without boasting or going into detail, I can truthfully say in this dramatic career of mine, one of my staunchest admirers was the late Henry Ford. He at one time said to a group of his friends: "I wish Gerald L. K. Smith could be President of the United States."
>
> I have been smeared and abused. My character has been assassinated. My life has been threatened, and virtually millions of dollars have been spent to destroy me and curb my influence, but to be appreciated and admired by such men as the late Henry Ford, to me is the equivalent of, or even better than, a Congressional Medal.

Indeed, enough of Smith's powerful new allies were prepared to bankroll the Committee of One Million that in 1942 Smith formed the Inner Circle—a kind of special donor's club within the Committee that would receive the most "sensitive" of Smith's newsletters. Smith, for his part, was loath to let the failed populism of the Depression years come between him and his new-found backers. Thus, for example, the Committee of One Million was able to discern the hidden hand of "Jewish Communism" behind American labor unrest.

By 1942, Smith announced that the Committee of One Million had grown to over 3 million dues-paying members. The money was rolling in, and Smith lived well. As always, he was a frenetic activist, writing innumerable newsletters, crafting fund-raising appeals, and carrying on a voluminous correspondence while continuing with his first love—barnstorming speeches throughout the country. Although he was now given over wholly to politics, Gerald L. K. Smith was at heart what he had always been—a fire-and-brimstone revival preacher.

One important activity undertaken by the Committee of One Million would have considerable benefit later and is thus worthy of mention here. In 1942, Smith circulated a petition that gathered 420,000 signatures supporting the creation of the Dies Committee to investigate un-American activities. The support would not be forgotten. When the great Sedition Trial, which sought to incarcerate the leadership of the American far-right wing on fanciful conspiracy charges, opened in the same year, Gerald L. K. Smith's name was conspicuously absent. This is all the more remarkable in the light of Smith's fan letter to the Führer recounted above! And when at last the Dies Committee called Smith to testify about his activities in 1946, though Smith took the hearing as evidence of a high-level conspiracy against him by the Roosevelt administration and international Jewry, the transcripts demonstrate that Smith was treated with kid gloves. For his part, Smith used the hearing to promote his evenhandedness, condemning both fascism and communism as un-American and praising the work of the Committee in rooting these evils out of the fabric of American political life.

But if the Congress was prepared to give Gerald L. K. Smith the benefit of the doubt, not so the American Jewish community, and not so increasing numbers of other Americans. Smith's public appearances became the venue for violent confrontations between leftists and members of the Jewish community on the one side and Smith's followers on the other. At the same time, Smith's primary publication, *The Cross and the Flag,* which appeared in 1942 and continued uninterrupted until 1978, two years after his death, became ever more shrill in its denunciation of Jews. Soon, *The Cross and the Flag* and the many other publications Smith sent to his supporters began to carry dark tales of plots against his life and that of his wife, while offering a myriad of tantalizing hints of mysterious documents delivered to Smith by secret sympathizers in government and intelligence circles (which proved, Smith asserted, the truth of Jewish plots against the republic). These repeated *alarums* had considerable short-term fund-raising utility, but at the cost of making Smith's message ever more esoteric.

Despite this turn to extremism within his movement, Smith in the decade of the 1940s and 1950s continued to run unsuccessfully for office. The high point of the effort was his creation of the America First Party to contest the 1944 presidential election. The America First Party was succeeded in 1946 by the Christian Nationalist Party, though this amalgamation fared no better at the polls.

At the same time, the Committee of One Million, which had served as Smith's personal vehicle (and was kept rigidly separate from the political parties Smith founded), had run its course and was replaced in 1947 by the Christian Nationalist Crusade. The Christian Nationalist Crusade provided a platform for Smith's most extreme anti-Semitic rhetoric, and it was under the banner of the Crusade that Smith's barnstorming activities were carried out. Moreover, the Christian Nationalist Crusade provided a flag of convenience for a cross section of the American racist right. By the late 1940s and through the 1950s, Smith's movement had begun to attract a core group of adherents who would emerge in the next decades as the most prominent figures in the American radical right. Veteran racists such as Wesley Swift, Kenneth Goff, Bertrand Comperet, William Potter Gale, as well as younger men such as Dan Gayman and Thom Robb, all emerged from Smith's Crusade.

Against the backdrop of rising violence at Smith's events and increasingly bizarre claims put forth in his publications, the organized Jewish community at last resolved to act. The American Jewish Committee (AJC) first focused on the activities of Gerald L. K. Smith on a formal level in May 1947 when, alarmed at the apparent success of Smith and other right wingers at linking Jews to Soviet communism, the AJC executive committee met to form a plan of attack against the Smith Crusade. This and subsequent meetings failed to come to an agreement on a coherent strategy, due primarily to the delicate balance of the body politic in this, the first flush of the Cold War. Russian Jews were simply too deeply involved in the Soviet state, and in the international communist movement as well, to risk weighing in fully on any particular aspect of the communism controversy.

Making a virtue of indecision, the strategy that both the Anti-Defamation League (ADL) and AJC eventually arrived at was termed at the time "dynamic silence." Championed by Rabbi S. A. Fineberg of the AJC, the idea was to close off all access to the public media—and thus the larger culture—to "rabble rousers" such as Smith. This decision would mark the moment in time when the American radical right would gradually fade from direct access to the popular media, and thus the public consciousness.

It was not until the attempt by Smith and others to block the appointment of Anna M. Rosenberg as an assistant secretary of defense in 1950 that both the American Jewish Committee and the Anti-Defamation League opened a full-fledged attack on Gerald L. K. Smith, bringing charges of anti-Semitism against him before the U.S. Senate. For the rest of Smith's career, the pressure from the Anti-Defamation League and the American Jewish Committee would be unrelenting.

No better example of the lengths to which the Jewish watchdogs would go to isolate Smith may be offered than the 1969 effort by the Anti-Defamation League to prevent the building of a road at public expense that would link an aging Gerald L. K. Smith's biblical theme park and an annual passion play in Eureka Springs, Arkansas, with the main highway. Using tactics perfected in the 1950s, the Anti-Defamation League acted along two tracks: a somewhat covert press campaign that attempted to influence local and national newspapers to write in opposition to the road-building effort, and a high-profile campaign headed by ADL National Chairman Don Schary to appeal to prominent government officials to intervene. Included in this latter campaign were President Richard Nixon, Secretary of Commerce Maurice Stans, and Secretary of Transportation John Volpe. Smith's theme park did, in the end, get its road, but not before the ADL set out to punish any individual or company having any connection with the project.

The biblical theme park, which was to have been a life-sized re-creation of Jerusalem in the days of Jesus, with a giant "Jesus of the Ozarks" statue as its primary attraction, may symbolize the irrelevance of the latter-day Gerald L. K. Smith. By the 1960s, Smith was a man out of time. The ultimate Depression-era tent revival orator, Smith was a fish out of water in the age of television. While he could continue to make a living from his massive but graying mailing list, his appeals reflected a frank incomprehension of the changing times.

The 1960s, with its civil rights movement and the legislation that accompanied it, the hippie movement and its antiestablishment ethos, and, perhaps most of all, the increasing acceptance of Jews as fully a part of the American mainstream, baffled and outraged Smith. Thus, he was reduced to disseminating such bizarre tracts as "75 Prostitutes—United States Senators—In a Brothel—Run By Jews"; "Sex Politics Subversion Blackmail, The Washington Story"; "Jews Rule America, We Are In Bondage, Can We Escape?'; and the memorable "Sex 'Education' (?) Phoney Name for Academic Pornography Resulting in Corruption of Youth, Free Love, Popularization of Premarital Sex, Venereal Disease Epidemics, Libertinism, Repudiation of Moral Standards, Juvenile Perversion, Community Degeneration, Ridicule of the Church, Evaporation of Religious Standards."

Gerald L. K. Smith died in April 1976.

See also: Christian Identity; Coughlin, Father Charles; Gale, William Potter; Gayman, Dan; Goff, Kenneth; Hitler, Adolf; Robb, Thom; Swift, Wesley.

Further reading: Michael Barkun, *Religion and the Racist Right: The Origins of the Christian Identity Movement* (Chapel Hill: University of North Carolina Press, 1994); David H. Bennett, *Demagogues in the Depression* (New Brunswick, NJ: Rutgers University Press, 1969); Arnold Forster and Benjamin R. Epstein, *The New Anti-Semitism* (New York: McGraw-Hill, 1974); House Committee on Un-American Activities, *Investigation of Un-American Propaganda Activities in the United States (Gerald L. K. Smith)*, 79th Congress, 2d sess., 1946, H. Res. 5; Glen Jeansonne, "Combating Anti-Semitism: The Case of Gerald L. K. Smith," in David A Gerber, ed., *Anti-Semitism in American History* (Urbana: University of Illinois Press, 1986); Glen Jeansonne, *Gerald L. K. Smith: Minister of Hate* (New Haven: Yale University Press, 1988); Phillip Rees, *Biographical Dictionary of the Extreme Right Since 1890* (New York: Simon & Schuster, 1990); Gerald L. K. Smith, *Besieged Patriot*, Elma M. Smith and Charles F. Robinson, eds. (Eureka Springs, AR: Elma M. Smith Foundation, 1978).

RICHARD WAYNE SNELL   On April 19, 1995—the day of the Oklahoma City bombing—Richard Wayne Snell was executed in Texarkana, Texas, for the murder of a Black Arkansas state trooper during a routine traffic stop. Previous to this murder, Snell was involved in a series of terrorist acts, culminating in the murder of a pawnshop owner during a robbery in Texarkana, Arkansas. The victim, William Stumpp, was believed by Snell to be Jewish, and thus he "needed to die." Snell apparently acted out of a sense of frustration with the reluctance of the Covenant, Sword, and the Arm of the Lord, of which he was a member, to turn its violent rhetoric into revolutionary action. He may have been emulating the revolutionary violence of the Order as well.

Snell's murders were those of an individual, not as a member of the Covenant, Sword, and the Arm of the Lord. For the CSA, Snell was involved in a series of robberies, weapons violations, shoplifting from local (White owned) stores, and other "revolutionary" acts. James Ellison, leader of the CSA, together with the inner circle of the group, was considerably irritated with Snell's killings, feeling that murder would bring more heat down on the group than they were ready to handle. On the other hand, Snell's explanation of the pawnshop murder was accepted by the leadership, who thought that Jews did indeed need to die.

Snell's case offers some insight into the question of what can be said of the individual psychology of the adherent in the more violent reaches of the movement. Psychological explanations for extremism of any sort are a risky venture, one best left to the province of psychiatrists. On rare occasions, however, a source emerges through which the mind of the extremist may be held up to view, both through the external perspective of the psychiatrist and through the self-view of the adherent. Such a source may be found in Richard Snell's prison newsletter, *The Seekers*.

During his appeal process, Snell published—with some considerable embarrassment—a transcript in which his psychological state is discussed in most unflattering terms by a court-appointed forensic psychiatrist. The testimony of the expert, Dr. Brad Fisher, is printed by Snell because, he writes:

> Whether it's expedient or not, fairness demands we let you read what the enemy thinks of us, after all it was your tax dollars that paid the expert to dig out all this info. After reading, you will not only have what we wrote, what our friends have to say, or what dear old mother may have said, but a balance of opinion assisting you to arrive at your own conclusions. We believe we owe this to you who have stood by us in this ordeal and to all who may read our opinions in the future. Is this fair?

Dr. Fisher's conclusions are straightforward enough. He finds that from at least 1983, Richard Snell was suffering from a "paranoid delusional disorder," with a second axis diagnosis of a "paranoid personality disorder." The symptoms of this delusion are primarily a conspiratorial view of history, the view that the U.S. government has fallen to a shadowy group of conspirators known as ZOG (Zionist Occupation Group [sic]), that the minions of this cabal have participated in the persecution of Snell personally, that said persecution commenced years before his attraction to Christian Identity theology, and that it drove him out of his photography business in the 1960s. Worse: "He believes that Armageddon and race wars will happen within the next two years." So advanced was this paranoia that the suicide of his son, Ken, connected to despair over drug use, was posited by Snell as the fault of ZOG—the entity he believed was ultimately responsible for the proliferation of drugs in America.

And what does Snell have to say to all this? On the death of his son:

> Ken's suicide: abruptly my thoughts were plucked as by an eagle snatching his prey and lifted back in time to an event shrouded in the cloak of attempted forgetfulness. A chilling rain was falling on that cold December morning in '78, the weeping family, a circle of friends who could find no comfort, the preacher intoning "Ashes to ashes, dust to dust..." as an unopened casket was lowered into a dark hole in the sandy loam of South Arkansas. Unopenable because a twelve-gauge shotgun under the chin does a trick to one's head.

And was Snell insane?

> Deluded? God, let it be so! A prison cage will become a palace if suddenly evidence is presented that this nightmare was only paranoia, merely a bad dream without reality. Time will tell. I must—and can—rest in this.

Appeals were fruitless, and Snell was put to death only hours before the Oklahoma City bombing. His last words proved prophetic: "[Oklahoma] Governor [Buddy] Tucker, look over your shoulder. Justice is coming."

Richard Wayne Snell is buried at the Elohim City Christian Identity compound in Oklahoma.

As a postscript, Governor Tucker was convicted in 1998 of corruption charges arising out of the Whitewater investigation against President Bill Clinton and his wife, Hillary, and a skein of others.

See also: Christian Identity; Covenant, Sword, and Arm of the Lord; Order; Zionist Occupation Government.

Further reading: Michael Barkun, *Religion and the Racist Right: The Origins of the Christian Identity Movement* (Chapel Hill: University of North

Carolina Press, 1994); James Coates, *Armed and Dangerous: The Rise of the Survivalist Right* (New York: Hill and Wang, 1987); Kevin Flynn and Gary Gerhardt, *The Silent Brotherhood* (New York: Signet, 1990); Mark S. Hamm, *Apocalypse in Oklahoma* (Boston: Northeastern University Press, 1998); Jeffrey Kaplan, "The Millennial Dream," in James R. Lewis, ed., *From the Ashes: Making Sense of Waco* (Lanham, MD: Rowman & Littlefield, 1994); Jeffrey Kaplan, *Radical Religion in America* (Syracuse, NY: Syracuse University Press, 1997); Jeffrey Kaplan, "Leaderless Resistance," *Journal of Terrorism and Political Violence* 9:3 (fall 1997); *The Last Call*; Richard Wayne Snell, *The Shadow of Death! (Is There Life After Death?)* (self-published and privately distributed, c. 1986).

RUDY STANKO   First in a line of putative successors to Ben Klassen's title of "Pontifex Maximus" as head of the Church of the Creator was Rudy "Butch" Stanko. As with every other would-be successor in Klassen's lifetime, the relationship was too short-lived to result in an orderly succession before Klassen's 1993 suicide.

The brief Klassen–Stanko relationship began with Stanko's 1988 letter written from prison praising Klassen's writings. Never one to eschew praise, Klassen responded, and there soon flowered a warm correspondence. This liaison resulted in the Church of the Creator's paper, *Racial Loyalty,* taking up Stanko's cause, as well as in an eventual invitation to visit the COTC's headquarters in Otto, North Carolina, upon his release. In the meantime, Klassen endeavored to visit the incarcerated Stanko, who was moved to several penitentiaries, causing the frustrated Klassen to make long automobile trips to visit his admirer. In his final book, *Trials, Tribulations and Triumphs,* the punctilious Klassen helpfully informs his readers of the exact odometer mileage of each of these jaunts. The first meeting eventually took place on June 3, 1989, in a Texas prison.

Even before his brief Church of the Creator experience, Stanko was something of a notorious figure. An outspoken anti-Semite, the 23-year-old Stanko joined his father in opening a meat-packing business in Gordon, Nebraska, in 1970. The business soon flourished, and Butch Stanko went on to open other packing houses under his own name in Nebraska and Montana. It was not long, though, before Stanko's business ran into trouble with the law.

Accused of selling tainted meat products, Stanko was indicted in 1976 in the first of what would be a blizzard of legal difficulties. Stanko, for his part, placed the blame for his legal problems on what he termed the Jewish meat cartel, with which he tried to do as little business as possible. Things took a considerable turn for the worse in 1983 when an NBC newsmagazine television show titled *First Camera* made Stanko's business the subject of its premier episode. The fallout from this broadcast greatly worsened Stanko's legal standing, and he soon found himself in prison. There he wrote a remarkably long book with a title to match: *The Score: An Autobiography Exposing the Forces That Remain Studiously Concealed and Masked*. The book both offered the reader a view of Stanko's life and thought, and echoed much of the language of the *Protocols of Zion*. *The Score* further recommended Stanko to Klassen, who was himself no slouch at writing remarkably long and painfully repetitive autobiographical anti-Semitic screeds.

On his release from prison in December 1991, Stanko called Klassen and arranged to visit the Otto headquarters. This he did, staying only long enough to borrow $500 and promising to return three months hence. On his return, he informed Klassen that he did not intend to take up the reigns of the Church after all, but not to worry—they could sell the Church of the Creator properties. This Klassen refused to do, and Stanko departed for Arizona, though not before purloining the Church of the Creator mailing list.

Ironically, Butch Stanko in 1996 resurfaced with splashy, full-page advertisements in such racialist journals as the glossy *Resistance* music magazine offering *The Score* and Klassen's books at fire-sale prices.

See also: Church of the Creator; Klassen, Ben.

Further reading: Ben Klassen, *Trials, Tribulations and Triumphs* (East Peoria, IL: COTC, 1993); Rudy "Butch" Stanko, *The Score: An Autobiography Exposing the Forces That Remain Studiously Concealed and Masked* (Gering, NE: Institute for Christian Bankers, 1986).

Ian Stewart   *See* Skinheads (Origin and Music).

Stormfront   *See* Black, Don.

WESLEY SWIFT   Dr. Wesley Swift is considered the father of modern racialist Christian Identity. So great is his influence that a generation of Christian Identity ministers—men such as Richard Butler of the Aryan Nations, William Potter Gale of Posse Comitatus fame, and Dan Gayman of the Church of Israel—trace their lineage to him and measure their "orthodoxy" by fealty to his teachings. Even today, with Swift long since in his grave, the Jewish watchdog groups such as the Anti-Defamation League hold up Wesley Swift as the personification of Christian Identity, and every ADL publication touching on Identity does not fail to feature Wesley Swift prominently as "[t]he best known advocate of the 'Identity' doctrine in the United States...." Swift's story is an interesting one.

Swift's attraction to religion may reliably be attributed to his family background. The son of a Methodist minister, Swift was born in New Jersey in 1919. How he moved from a conservative but conventional Methodism to British-Israelism, the forerunner of Christian Identity, is not known, though each of Smith's disciples, and his widow as well, offer differing theories. In any case, by the mid-1940s, Swift had opened his own church in Lancaster, California, which would remain his base of operations for the rest of his life. The congregation took the name of the Anglo-Saxon Christian Congregation, indicating considerable influence from Howard Rand and his British-Israel Anglo-Saxon Federation. The name was soon changed, however, to the Church of Jesus Christ Christian, and Swift's conversion to racialist Identity would by then be complete and irrevocable.

Swift might have remained an eccentric but unknown preacher in small-town California had he not been attracted to the crusade of Gerald L. K. Smith in the later 1940s. Smith was then at the height of his powers as a traveling populist whose anti-Semitic oratory rivaled that of the leading anti-Semitic populist of the prewar era, Father Charles Coughlin. How this contact was made and the dynamics of the Swift–Smith relationship are controversial. According to his autobiography, *Besieged Patriot,* Smith recalls that at a particularly fractious rally, when it appeared that Smith himself was in danger from enraged spectators:

> I turned to the right, and there sat a young man about 30 years old. He turned to me and said, "Don't be afraid Mr. Smith. Anyone who comes toward you will be sorry." He lifted up his coat and there he held a black automatic pistol.

According to the 1950s-era watchdog Ralph Lord Roy:

Perhaps Gerald L. K. Smith's most influential supporter is Anglo-Israelite Wesley Swift, who operates a hate enterprise costing over $40,000 annually in the Los Angeles area. Swift has directed the activities of the Great Pyramid Club, the Anglo-Saxon Christian Congregation, and the Anglo-Saxon Bible Study Group; collectively they are said to constitute the strongest racist element on the West Coast.

At one time Swift was Smith's chauffeur, bodyguard, and research assistant. He has remained intensely loyal to his former boss, cooperating with his program and accompanying him on many of his trips. Smith considered him "one of the great Bible students of the nation, and one of the three or four most eloquent preachers to whom I have ever listened."

Michael Barkun discounts many of Roy's claims, but credits Smith with providing Swift with his first copy of the leading anti-Semitic book of the era, *The International Jew*. What Swift did for Smith, however, was of even greater import. In Smith's recollection, it was Swift who introduced him to Christian Identity doctrine, and in this same passage of *Besieged Patriot*, Smith seems to indicate that he embraced the new faith:

One day, [Wesley Swift] said to me: "Mr. Smith, I would like to bring my Bible up to your hotel room and talk to you." He did, and he made one of the greatest contributions to my life that any man ever made. He opened the Bible and demonstrated to me with proper texts that Christ's worst enemies were not God's chosen people. He identified the "true Israel" which gave us the Messiah, and demonstrated to me that we were heirs to the covenant that God made with Abraham, and we were indeed Israelites. He later pointed out the text which reads, concerning those who had accepted Jesus Christ who might not be able to trace their lineage to Abraham: "Ye have been circumcised by faith."

He demonstrated that the crucifiers of Christ were apostates, sons of Satan, and the seed of Cain. He proved by scriptures that Jesus Christ was not a Jew as we now know Jews, and that God is going to give His kingdom to those who have accepted Jesus Christ, and not to those who caused His crucifixion and still justify it. The modern apostates may say that if they had it to do over again, they would not nail Him to a cross; but they, in fact "crucify our Lord anew" every day.

Ralph Lord Roy was correct in one respect: Swift had no intention of restricting his activism to Christian Identity. As early as 1946, Swift was involved in organizing a Ku Klux Klan group in Los Angeles, and there were some cross burnings there at that time. Indeed, Swift's organizational flair was evident in a vast number of spin-off projects through the years, though the most important of these was clearly the Christian Defense League (CDL). The CDL was born in 1964 as one of many of Swift's organizational initiatives. Swift selected a young California engineer, the then-unknown Richard G. Butler, as its National Director. From 1964 to 1973, the Christian Defense League was very much a Christian Identity vehicle, consisting of a core group of leaders under Butler, such as Identity stalwarts William Potter Gale and Bertrand Comperet. It is no accident that Comperet, Butler, and Gale were students and associates of Swift at his Church of Jesus Christ Christian.

Swift died in 1970. As with so many of the longer-lived leaders of the racialist right, by then he had broken his relations with virtually all of his former mentors and students. Gerald L. K. Smith, Richard Butler, William Potter Gale, James Warner—all had become estranged, and some became bitter rivals. Be this as it may, Swift remains the seminal figure in the transformation of British Israelism into Christian Identity. It is Swift whom many Identity ministers credit for the radicalism of modern Identity theology. It was Swift, too, who did much to add ever more fantastic layers of doctrine to the Identity creed—UFOs, intergalactic wars at the dawn of time, and much more. But most of all, it was Swift's teaching, preserved today in cassette sermons and the transcripts of those sermons, that provide a core curriculum for aspiring Identity ministers.

In the wake of Smith's passing, a brief struggle for his legacy pitted Richard Butler against William Potter Gale, James Warner, and Swift's own widow. Butler got the better of the battle, taking the Church of Jesus Christ Christian label for his own Identity ministry, which he moved from California to Idaho in 1973. Warner and Gale seized the large archives of Swift's recorded sermons, and these they sold under their own imprimaturs. Swift's widow retained some of the tapes, the Lancaster church, and, of greatest import, Swift's name. She is today the keeper of the flame of Swift's ministry.

See also: Aryan Nations; Butler, Richard; Christian Defense League; Christian Identity; Church of Israel; Church of Jesus Christ Christian; Coughlin, Father Charles; Gale, William Potter; Gayman, Dan; Smith, Gerald L. K.; Warner, James.

Further reading: Michael Barkun, *Religion and the Racist Right: The Origins of the Christian Identity Movement* (Chapel Hill: University of North Carolina Press, 1994); David H. Bennett, *Demagogues in the Depression* (New Brunswick, NJ: Rutgers University Press, 1969); Jeffrey Kaplan, *Radical Religion in America* (Syracuse, NY: Syracuse University Press, 1997); Ralph Lord Roy, *Apostles of Discord* (Boston: Beacon Press, 1953); Gerald L. K. Smith, *Besieged Patriot*, Elma M. Smith and Charles F. Robinson, eds. (Eureka Springs, AR: Elma M. Smith Foundation, 1978); William W. Turner, *Power on the Right* (Berkeley: Ramparts Press, 1971).

Teutonia Association *See* Hitler, Adolf.

JOSEPH TOMMASI Were he alive today, Joseph Tommasi may well be recognized as one of the three most important American National Socialists of the postwar era, in the company of George Lincoln Rockwell and William Pierce. Tommasi was only 24 when he died at the hands of Jerry Jones, a young and very frightened follower of the National Socialist White People's Party, in front of NSWPP headquarters in El Monte, California, in August 1975. Had he lived, there is a chance—albeit a small one—that the history of the National Socialist movement in America would have been different.

Tommasi was a rarity in the milieu of American National Socialism: a young man with leadership quality, the ability to admire the 1930s German model without being captured by it and thus losing touch with the fact that 1970s America bore scant resemblance to Weimar Germany, and a keen recognition that the dominant Nazi strategy of the day—the creation of a "mass action" front of disgusted and discouraged Whites—was, short of an apocalyptic social collapse, simply not going to happen.

Joseph Tommasi emerged from the fractious California cadre of Rockwell's American Nazi Party that became the National Socialist White People's Party in 1966, the year before Rockwell's death. A deeply committed National Socialist, Tommasi held out for some years after the Commander's assassination before he too fell victim to successor Matt Koehl's ongoing purge of the party. But where so many others similarly disgusted with Koehl and company departed for other belief systems throughout the radical right, Tommasi was an NS true believer who, until his expulsion from the party, believed in Koehl to the end. His analysis of the sad state of affairs of the post-Rockwell movement marked the first attempt to adapt the stereotypical Nazi subculture of the 1950s to the youth culture of the late 1960s and early 1970s. The results were intended to be revolutionary, and they were.

Addressing the Second Party Congress in 1970, he denounced the conservative majority of the party in a speech that electrified some and appalled most with his call for revolution *now*. The speech impressed William Pierce—then in the throes of his own bitter dispute with Matt Koehl. Pierce, like Tommasi, was acutely aware of the bold actions undertaken by the Weather Underground and the Symbionese Liberation Army, to name but two of the left-wing combatant organizations of the day. They were determined to create a campus-based revolutionary movement of the right on the same model. Thus was born the National Socialist Liberation Front (NSLF).

Unknown to most of those present at the Second Party Congress, Tommasi already had, with William Pierce's (well) behind-the-scenes encouragement, founded the NSLF in 1969. It was headquartered at the National Socialist White People's Party headquarters in El Monte, California, where Tommasi was based. The original intent of the National Socialist Liberation Front was as a youth auxiliary of the National Socialist White People's Party that hoped to concentrate its recruiting efforts on college campuses.

This was a project particularly dear to the heart of William Pierce, a former college professor. Pierce realized all too well that, just as the rabble of the original brown-shirted S.A. cadres who were Hitler's earliest supporters gave way to a more sophisticated following after the ascent to power, a future National Socialist government in America would need a more capable cadre of functionaries than could be found among the street fighters who peopled the American Nazi Party–cum–National Socialist White People's Party. The National Socialist Liberation Front's campus recruiting efforts made few converts, but could not be counted a complete failure. By 1970, it had attracted a young student in Louisiana who would go on to a notable career in the radical right. That one-man unit was a teen-aged David Duke.

The NSLF concept did not really go anywhere until 1973, however, when Tommasi was unceremoniously booted out of the National Socialist White People's Party by Matt Koehl for his un–National Socialist behavior of smoking marijuana in party headquarters, entertaining young women within those hallowed precincts, leading unauthorized armed-paramilitary maneuvers, and, it was rumored, misusing the scant party funds.

In 1973 or 1974, Tommasi's slogan—which remains current to this day in National Socialist circles—became known to East Coast party members, and in that year too the NSLF held its foundational meeting. Tommasi's dictum, "THE FUTURE BELONGS TO THE FEW OF US WILLING TO GET OUR HANDS DIRTY. POLITICAL TERROR: It's the only thing they understand," appeared on a poster featuring a .38 caliber pistol and a swastika. It would not be the last time Tommasi would borrow slogans, style, and eventually even dress and physical appearance from the New Left of the 1960s. Even more striking in this vein was the slogan that opened Tommasi's *Building the Revolutionary Party* pamphlet, the Maoist truism: "POLITICAL POWER STEMS FROM THE BARREL OF A GUN." Indeed, even the group's name was inspired by the communist Vietnamese National Liberation Front, while the name of the group's journal, *Siege!*, was borrowed from the Weather Underground.

According to National Socialist Liberation Front propaganda, the group's foundational meeting held on March 2, 1974—a full five years after Tommasi created the group—hosted "forty-three National Socialist revolutionaries" in El Monte. It was at this meeting that the mass action strategy was officially put to rest in favor of "revolution now." The NSLF was conceived as an activist, and thus violent, revolutionary organization. It was structured with an above-ground membership that may have numbered perhaps 40 or more, plus a tiny underground contingent of lone-wolf revolutionaries. The underground core of the NSLF never numbered more than 4, including Karl Hand, David Rust, and James Mason (who ironically was not an official member of the group). Mason recalls of these days:

> Yes, the N.S.L.F. of Tommasi had four persons who carried out the illegal activities. The remainder, the majority, weren't that much different from the N.S.W.P.P. members except they were a lot more forward thinking.

The brief *Building the Revolutionary Party* pamphlet is of some importance in that it openly breaks with the mass action strategy and demands that sterner action be taken. Moreover, its all too accurate portrayal of the anemic state of the American National Socialist movement and its dim prospects for power is as true now as then. It is thus worthy of some attention. As a preamble to the NSLF's demand to "SEIZ[E] THE TIME!" Tommasi writes:

> Winning the hearts and minds of the people takes intense organizing activity and a willingness on the part of people to get involved and be organized. Both at this time do not exist.
>
> Since a mass movement cannot be "pulled off" in America because of the anti-mass movement nature of the American people

(which stems from their ever-growing apathy), the only recourse for National Socialist Revolutionaries is to go underground and build their own armed struggle to wage war against the State.

National Socialist activities have never produced one significant result in the U.S.A. Any mob resistance our people have been engaged in has always been a spontaneous eruption (like Boston) with the participation and agitation of no political party or National Socialist activist. They did it themselves without our help.

Tommasi, whose gift for flaming oratory would live on long after he himself had died a lonely death in the streets of El Monte, ends with a flourish that produced one of his most memorable slogans, "Pray for victory and not an end to slaughter":

> In times of revolution, just wars, and wars of national liberation, we must love the angels of destruction and disorder as opposed to the devils of conservatism and law and order. To hell with all those who block the Revolution with rhetoric—revolutionary rhetoric or counter-revolutionary rhetoric! We will not make our most eloquent statements in courtrooms and at press conferences, but in the streets of Jew-Capitalist America!
>
> The choice of weapons belong to him who moves; and NSLF moves into the streets and we have made our choice of weapons and tactics. The weapon of criticism will never equal the criticism of weapons. NSLF prefers a paralyzed enemy to a well criticized one.
>
> Those who can't stand the sight of blood, especially their own, should stay home and pray for those who come outside the master's rules to "move," to DO IT, and pray for victory and not an end to slaughter. Pray for us to succeed for if we do succeed, you will be safe. If we don't, then kiss the baby good-bye.

Building the Revolutionary Party was a powerful call to action couched in the New Left phraseology of the day. From the conscious parody of Jerry Rubin's book *DO IT,* to the Maoist cliché "POLITICAL POWER STEMS FROM THE BARREL OF A GUN," which opens the pamphlet, to the very name of the organization, Tommasi's organization was the very antithesis of the nostalgic Hitler cultism and organizational paralysis that was (and is) the norm in the world of American National Socialism. And therein lay the problem. Tommasi was ahead of his time, and only the barest handful of the faithful were prepared to follow him.

The National Socialist Liberation Front's brief, active life produced an important theoretical journal, *Siege!,* and a number of remarkable posters and pamphlets. Yet in the end, the NSLF could not escape the reality of its minuscule numbers. It was fine for Tommasi to borrow the communist belief in a cell structure, but the grim truth was that, had the NSLF's combatant core formed a fighting cell, it would have had to put all its eggs in one basket. On an ideological level, however, it was not difficult to find a rationale, and a hope, for ultimate victory in the face of overwhelming odds. For one, the National Socialist faith has always been at heart deeply religious. Ultimate victory was assured to the faithful simply by virtue of their faith and of their ultimate "rightness."

On a more immediate level, Tommasi believed with Rockwell and Evola and Hitler too that the masses were in essence female, waiting to be swept off their collective feet by a strong male leader whose daring and charisma would guide them into the timeless racialist dream. Thus the suicidal audacity of the National Socialist Liberation Front's "operations." Thus too the ease with which the organization was smashed and surviving members were jailed. David Rust, Tommasi's first successor, went down on firearms charges. Karl Hand, Tommasi's final successor, was imprisoned briefly in 1980 for firing a gun into the home of a Black neighbor, and then received a 15-year sentence for other weapons violations and attempted murder.

Tommasi was the first American National Socialist leader in the post-Rockwell era to openly break with the conservative National Socialist majority and not only to urge, but also to actuate, an organizational campaign of guerrilla warfare against the American state, regardless of the obvious disparity of forces available to the respective sides. (Joseph Franklin predated Tommasi, but his war against America was strictly a private affair.) By his example, he left a lasting mark on the movement as well as on those who knew him. Even those who opposed his radicalism in the El Monte days—one former National Socialist, for example, recalls how the group referred to him contemptuously as "Tomato Joe" as both a play on his name and as a comment on his less than Nordic features—cannot help but admire his daring in the face of hopeless odds.

Those who looked up to him, even if they were not willing to follow him into hopeless battle with the state, revere him to this day. Harold Covington, for example, reflects that he would never have managed to persevere throughout his long and checkered career as a National Socialist had it not been for the fact that his first Commander was Joseph Tommasi and his first posting was in the El Monte headquarters. James Mason, too remains, fiercely loyal to the memory of Joseph Tommasi, and it may well be that it was his search for an equally strong and charismatic leader for the National Socialist movement that brought him to discover Charles Manson and create the Universal Order. What is certain is that American National Socialism has not produced another leader of Tommasi's caliber. James Mason thus says today of Tommasi:

> Joseph Tommasi, as founder of the NSLF [National Socialist Liberation Front], was the first of a new breed. A hero and a martyr to the Cause. What he wanted most was to provide the movement with its much overdue HIT TEAM and not to set himself up as some sort of cheap, tin horn demi-god like the rest. Tommasi personified the kind of man we MUST have: those desiring to serve the movement—and do so with great facility—not pose around in gaudy uniforms as "Hollywood Nazis"...
>
> ...[it's as if] Tommasi never went away. He'd have admired Oklahoma City. "Pray for Victory and not an end to slaughter."

See also: American Nazi Party; Covington, Harold; Duke, David; Franklin, Joseph; Koehl, Matt; Manson, Charles; Mason, James; Pierce, William; National Socialist Liberation Front; National Socialist White People's Party; Rockwell, George Lincoln; Universal Order.

Further reading Jeffrey Kaplan, "The Postwar Paths of Occult National Socialism: From Rockwell and Madole to Manson," in Jeffrey Kaplan and Heléne Lööw, *Rejected and Suppressed Knowledge: The Racist Right and the Cultic Milieu* (Stockholm: Swedish National Council of Crime Prevention, forthcoming); James Mason, *Siege* (Denver: Storm Books, 1992).

U

UNIVERSAL ORDER   The Universal Order is the operational front adopted at the direct suggestion of Charles Manson by James Mason, the publisher and editor of *Siege,* which had been a newsletter of the National Socialist Liberation Front (NSLF) beginning in 1980.

Mason had been a member of first the National Socialist White People's Party and then the NSLF, but had been growing increasingly disillusioned with the conservative, legalistic stance of the hard-right-wing organizations and their apparent lack of relevance and impact upon national and world events. Having run the entire gamut of political extremism, Mason sensed that by 1980 there existed no conventional political solution to the dilemma of Whites in America, i.e., increasing non-White presence and Jewish domination of government and media.

In 1980, Mason was moved to contact Manson Family members Lynette Fromme and Sandra Good, confined at the Federal Women's Penitentiary at Alderson, West Virginia, and Charles Manson himself at the state prison at Vacaville, California. The heavy exchange of letters and telephone calls that resulted led to a visit to Alderson in March 1981 and, due to the input of Manson's ideas, the formal move away from the NSLF and to the Universal Order by mid-1982.

It was also Charles Manson's contention that there was no political solution to the world's problems, which, in his view, extended well beyond the parameters of government and race, encompassing such issues as the poisoning of the earth's environment and the deadly damage being done to the human psyche by the modern, materialistic society. In line with this greater reality, Manson suggested that the name National Socialist Liberation Front was no longer valid and put forth Universal Order instead to reflect the philosophy and program itself.

Along with the change of name, Manson proposed a new symbol for the effort. Rather than a Swastika positioned with an M-16 rifle, it would now be a Swastika superimposed over the scales of justice. In deference to Manson, Mason utilized a leftward-revolving

Swastika in the new symbol. At the same time, Manson reversed the direction of the Swastika in his forehead to now revolve to the right.

From 1982 until it ceased publication in 1986, *Siege* promoted Manson's philosophy as the logical extension of Hitler's philosophy as it applied to today's world. Despite much initial rejection on the part of traditional Movement stalwarts on the basis of imagery and the lack of orthodoxy, the sentiments, priorities, and strategies of Manson gradually came to pervade areas of the U.S. radical right over the following decade.

Although few would realize or admit it, the gradual move away from "White Supremacy" toward White Separatism, from any hopes of recovering the U.S. government, toward establishing new, independent regions, is precisely what animated the creation of the Manson enclaves in Death Valley during the 1960s. At issue is bare survival as a species as the world system begins to crumble and die.

—James Mason, Universal Order

See also: Manson, Charles; Mason, James; National Socialist Liberation Front.

Further reading: Vincent Bugliosi with Curt Gentry, *Helter Skelter* (New York: W. W. Norton, 1974); Nuel Emmons, *Manson in His Own Words* (New York: Grove Press, 1986); John Gilmore and Ron Kenner, *The Garbage People* (Los Angeles: Amok, 1995); Jeffrey Kaplan, "The Postwar Paths of Occult National Socialism: From Rockwell and Madole to Manson," in Jeffrey Kaplan and Heléne Lööw, *Rejected and Suppressed Knowledge: The Racist Right and the Cultic Milieu* (Stockholm: Swedish National Council of Crime Prevention, forthcoming); *Manson Speaks,* a CD from White Devil Records; James Mason, *Siege!* (Denver: Storm Books, 1992); Nikolas Schreck, *The Manson File* (Los Angeles: Amok, 1988).

VALKYRIA Valkyria is a group of militant women in the Norwegian right-wing underground. The group was created in January 1995. The women's wish to organize themselves was motivated by the fact that they felt stigmatized by the men (the men divided the women into either "straight" or "mattress" depending on their sexual availability), and because they were dissatisfied that the men often excluded them from trips to Sweden and other gatherings. The women felt that it was easier to expose their feelings when the men were not present, and also, they wanted to make something on their own, and thereby gain more respect from the males. "It feels safe to be within an all-female group, and not having boys around you all the time," one of the initiators explained.

Even though Valkyria is a separate organization, it shares a lot of activities with males from the paramilitary Viking group. These two groups share the same post box address, and Valkyria is defined as Viking's "sister" on Viking's home page on the Internet. In the Viking's fanzine, also called *Viking,* the Valkyria women have a page of their own, where they write short articles signed "Jeanne d'Arc." Leading members of both groups take part in the same meetings, where they plan future actions, camps, and training. Weapons training is organized jointly for the two groups.

There is no formal leader of the Valkyria group. Still, there are more-experienced women who tell less-experienced women what to do. Valkyria is organized into several local cells. The main part of the group is located in Oslo. The Oslo cell has about ten members, whereas another ten women are spread into four other cells all located at smaller places surrounding Oslo. The Oslo women may be considered the inner circle of Valkyria women. However, all the women meet once a month. The main purpose of this meeting is to come together and create a sense of being a group, but also they plan actions or discuss ideology. Sometimes the Valkyria women organize their own training camps where like-minded women from other countries also take part.

A separate cell of Valkyria is located in Drammen. It emerged in the summer of 1995 and was temporarily dissolved after March 1996 because its leader left the underground. Later on, its activity was started up again at the initiative of the other members. The women of the Drammen department think the Oslo Valkyria women are too much ruled by the male members of the Viking group. The Oslo women, on their side, argue that the Drammen women are more fond of pub life, whereas the Oslo women are more militant and demand that their members drink less. Another difference is that the Drammen women tend to be more ideologically extreme, as they have not distanced themselves from National Socialism as the Oslo women did.

The Valkyria women have created their own symbol, which is a mixture of the Celtic cross, the women's sign, and the circle: "The women's sign [♀] because we are women, the Celtic cross because we are nationalists, and the circle to symbolize the unity and solidarity between us." The Oslo women later dropped this sign because the Celtic cross often is associated with Nazism, and these women want to be considered nationalists rather than National Socialists. Therefore, they only use the Norwegian flag and the official national symbol of Norway, the lion, because these symbols are purely national and have no connotations to Nazism.

New Valkyria members are recruited through leaflet actions and by "snowball" methods (recruiting the friends of one's friends). Before the emergence of a separate women's group, the sole route into the movement for women had to do with their relationships with men. However, after the emergence of the Valkyria group, some women have made direct contact with the women's group, without having become involved with the underground's men beforehand. The prime reason for women to join the underground is excitement. Some of them also give political motives for entering, such as the frustration they feel after having been assaulted by foreign (typically Muslim) men.

After a test period, the newcomer is allowed to meet all the members of the local Valkyria cell. One woman from the local group is responsible for taking care of the newcomer and is bound to secrecy concerning any problems the newcomer wants to discuss. This mentor relationship is meant to last until the other members fully trust the newcomer, whereupon she is allowed full membership.

There are no initiation rituals that the newcomer has to pass. A trustworthy member of Valkyria should handle information with discretion, not drink much, practice kick-boxing and shooting, not give Nazi salutes, be a true nationalist, wear military clothes when needed, but in daily life dress in casual clothes, and, last but not least, live "straight." Some women are denied membership, usually because they drink too much. This is especially true of a few Satanist women who wanted to join Valkyria. However, according to a leading Valkyria woman, they were too fond of pub life and Nazi salutes. Valkyria members should act more seriously than that.

Another claim is that Valkyria women should be straight, that is, not change partners often. More formal requirements are that all members are bound to keep information secret and, most important of all, they are not allowed to give away the identity of other group members. They are also forbidden to discuss information or mention names on the telephone. Members are not allowed to discuss internal issues with outsiders. However, members are allowed to discuss the general guidelines of the group and give examples of their common activities. Some members function as spokespersons in contact with the media.

Even though the Valkyria group is a militant nationalist group, the newcomer does not have to prove ideological proficiency or excellence in shooting or fighting. Rather, the newly recruited member has to prove herself capable of following certain procedures in relation to appointment-making, alert behavior, and discretion.

Only women above the age of 15 are allowed to be members. The reason for this is that the members often enter into serious conflicts with teachers, parents, or even the Child Welfare Authorities after joining Valkyria. Many of the girls received high grades at school. Then one day they come home wearing army caps and boots. Their parents try to stop them going out with their new friends. But often they calm down after a while. In other words, participation in this group is in many ways being in opposition to parents. These women want to be valued as tough.

The Valkyria women collaborate with women from many different countries, some of whom have already organized their all-female groups, whereas others want to start up, and need advice from an existing organization. For example, a Danish women's group was organized the summer of 1995, after its founder had contacted the Valkyria women, asking for information. The Valkyria members also exchange letters and information with women in Germany. Also, there have emerged other nationalist females' groups in Norway during 1996, such as Embla (named for the first woman in the Norse creation myth) and Jenter for Norge (Girls for Norway).

The women of Valkyria wear fatigues and U.S. army caps every time there is a concert or a counterdemonstration. They look so ultramilitant that some of their Swedish acquaintances have labeled them "the Death Squadron." The women copy many elements from masculine uniforms. However, these elements are counteracted by their long hair, which they sometimes bleach.

The Valkyria women take part in strategic meetings with the males, undergo weapons training, and organize their own study meetings and underground actions. According to the militant Valkyria members, "mattresses" are unacceptable as activists, but, on the other hand, they do not reject these women as friends.

The Valkyria women's participation in weapons training is partly motivated by things beyond the specific militant elements: being together in the wood, making a fire, the excitement of hiding from the police, and the feeling of taking part in an complicated stage play. However, the training is also motivated by a feeling that they are in danger of being severely wounded after attacks by anti-fascists, so using weapons is the only possible way to fight back. The females say they would not hesitate to use weapons "if it should come that far." However, to date, there have only been a few incidents of street-fighting between women from the militant antifascist group. The women practice kick-boxing, train with dogs, learn camouflage and communication techniques. They say that when they achieve sufficient courage, they will join the men on the front lines during confrontations.

The women agree with the view held by the males that Norwegian politics are governed by the proimmigration left wing, and accordingly, the hate targets of these women include both the official authorities as well as militant groups on the left. First and foremost, the Valkyria members are against immigration. They say that they are scared by the way many immigrants (mostly Muslim men) view women. They argue that Islam will, over the course of years, become more dominant, and that this will mean the rise of a backlash against women's emancipated status in Norway. Some women are more openly "racist" in the narrow sense of the word, saying that they have to protect the White race and prohibit mixed marriages.

A small number of women are sympathetic to parts of Nazi ideology, but the women are more resistant to the persecution of Jews than some of the males. They say they want to defend the Norwegian character and protect the White race by stopping immigration.

Nazism becomes an important issue for the Oslo Valkyria members because outsiders tend to think of them as being Nazis, and also, these women adhere to an international subculture in which Nazi elements are highly prevalent. One of these women, together with her friends at school, tried to sort out what separated militant nationalism from neo-Nazism, and found out—after having interviewed researchers, journalists, politicians, and right-wing activists—that "nationalist" (in *their* sense of being a nationalist) and "neo-Nazi" are in practice more or less the same thing. Despite wanting to be considered nationalists themselves, they realize that since they participate side by side with neo-Nazis, they must accept being reckoned as Nazis as well. This insight seems to make them less anti-Nazi than they originally wanted to be. They are thus resigned to the label, and say they don't care if some activists are Nazis.

Even though the women are not openly anti-Nazi, they certainly are anticommunist. They tend to define as communist all groups and parties ranging from the social democratic Labor Party to the militant street-group from Blitz House.

The Valkyria group arranges study meetings, in order both to heighten members' "political, cultural, and historical consciousness" and to protect Norway and Norwegian culture. At the meetings, they discuss the Viking era, the history of the Norwegian National Socialist party during the 1930s and 1940s, "our historical roots" in more general terms, immigration policy, and nationalism. The most experienced women see their role as being to teach the other women, but also to have an impact on people who disagree openly with their views.

Despite the Valkyria members' outspoken stand against immigrants, they do not usually carry out leaflet actions, violence, or harassment against foreigners. According to a leading male activist, the reason for this is that these actions are "taken care of" by male activists, so that the women do not see the need to engage themselves in this way. Instead, they carry out their own actions on issues that do not engage the men as much. A lead issue is defined by the women as "to create a future for our children and for girls in the nationalist milieu."

The Valkyria members are concerned with several contemporary women's issues, such as their stance against the emergence of brothels, and against pornography and prostitution. In this regard, they resemble their female opponents from Blitz House more than their male counterparts from the rightist underground. Women from Blitz House have frequently organized demonstrations against brothels. According to the Valkyria women, a problem with these demonstrations is that they have not managed to cause the brothels to suffer economical losses. The Valkyria women have not yet organized their own antibrothel demonstrations, though they have organized actions to stop men from using prostitutes. The way they managed to do so was by walking the streets where prostitution occurs, to see for themselves how this happened. To prevent it, the Valkyria telephoned the men, saying that "We do not want this to happen again. Prostitution pollutes women's nature."

The Valkyria women are also against pornography, as are the left-wing women. This is further proof that female participation in the rightist underground must be viewed in a context other than the males' participation, especially since many of the men are high consumers of pornography. One other incidence of men's attitudes being unappetizing to these women is the politician Jack Kjuus's statement that all adopted children should be sterilized. This view, which is equivalent to the racial hygienic views that were widespread in the 1920s and 1930s, has no appeal to these women.

They also claim that so-called "red stockings"—that is, left-wing feminist women—only want higher wages, whereas the Valkyria think that women should receive full wages for working at home. Several of them want to remain home with their future children, rather than sending them to day care.

In this way, the Valkyria women tend to distance themselves from parts of feminist policy. They tend to think that emancipation in some regards has gone too far. Many of the females are interested in equal rights for men and women, and view Viking women as female ideals because they were strong and combative.

Even though the Valkyria women define themselves partly in opposition to left-wing feminism, they are curious about the policies and knowledge of women on the left. According to one Valkyria member, they would like to find out more about what various leftist groups stand for, and would like to do so by actually joining their courses. They once contacted women from Rød Ungdom (Red Youths) in the street and asked whether they could join their communication courses. According to this Valkyria member, the communist women refused to answer the question and seemed furious to have been asked. She asserts that "The Blitz girls are scared to death that we will say, 'Hi, we are tough girls who want to study together with you.' They are scared because we are tough girls like they are, but still stand for something other than what they do."

In addition to their activism against the suppression of females, the members of Valkyria take part in volunteer work for elderly people. This is in no way a common trend among young women in Norway. They also choose traditionally female occupations at a period when it is more the norm that women take longer education than men and women enter more and more of the traditionally male spheres of the economy. One of them works in a kindergarten, another one is a day-care center worker who dreams of being a midwife. Some females work in shops, while some of them go to school.

This combination of females supporting the males' militance and studying ideology, but at the same time practicing exceptionally traditional female roles (taking care of children and elders), is also prevalent in rightist undergrounds in other countries. However, the Valkyria girls also support several women's-rights issues.

The fact that there had been so few women within the underground previously seems to be a strong indicator that the role as passive audience was not sufficiently satisfying for the women. They wanted to do something on their own, and not merely serve as an audience for the males. Therefore, the motivating factor behind the all-female group was that they felt subordinated. The separate women's group has had the consequence that the women are given a responsible role of which they previously could only dream. The leading women of Valkyria are part of the inner circle, taking part in meetings where strategic underground activities are planned. However, it is still male activists who set the main premises of this underground, and even the leading Valkyria women ask central male activists for counsel before giving interviews.

By beginning their own organization, the women created their own loyalty to the movement. They organize their own actions, with emphasis on certain "women's issues" not shared by the males. Women make contact with the movement on their own initiative to a larger extent than before, not merely by becoming involved with one of the males. The establishment of the women's group has also led to more women becoming attracted to the movement. The activities of the Valkyria group have also led to an increase in politicization and in the support of militant activities. These women thus have become more equal to the men in the right-wing movement, and thus they have developed such stereotypical male roles as being tough, militant, and politically extreme.

—*Katrine Fangen, University of Oslo, Norway*

See also: Women (Norwegian).

Further reading: Katrine Fangen, "Separate or Equal? The Emergence of an All Female Group in the Norwegian Rightist Underground," *Terrorism and Political Violence* 9:3 (fall 1997); Katrine Fangen, "Skinheads I rødt, hvitt og blått En sosiologisk studie fra innsiden" [Skinheads in red, white, and blue:

A sociological study from "inside"] (1994); Katrine Fangen, "Living Out Our Ethnic Instincts: Ideological Beliefs Among Right-Wing Activists in Norway," in Jeffrey Kaplan and Tore Bjørgo, *Brotherhoods of Nation and Race: The Emergence of a Euro-American Racist Subculture* (Boston: Northeastern University Press, 1998);

RUSSELL VEH   It has long been one of the dirty little secrets of postwar American National Socialism that the movement has, from its inception under George Lincoln Rockwell and his American Nazi Party, attracted a significant contingent of homosexuals to its ranks. Why this should be—in a movement where homophobia is a central ideological dogma and whose "Golden Age" model, the German National Socialist state of the 1930s through the end of World War II, ultimately placed its own homosexual population in concentration camps—is best left for psychologists rather than historians. It is a fact nonetheless, and much internal discourse has centered almost obsessively on the subject. Typically, the problem is set out most clearly (and most obsessively) by Harold Covington:

> Right now this movement is plagued with little self-appointed SS groups who spend huge bucks in assembling SS paraphernalia and putting it on for secret photographic sessions that almost smack of queers coming out of the closet—indeed, in some cases, that is what it is. The fact is (and we had better start admitting some of these unpleasant facts) that this movement has a distinct tendency to attract faggots because of the leather-macho image that the System Jew media imparts to the SS uniform....

Given this anomalous state of affairs, it was only a matter of time before the appearance of an explicitly gay National Socialist group. The first such openly gay neo-Nazi group was organized in 1974 by Russell Veh in Los Angeles. Originally called the National Socialist League (NSL), with a publishing arm called the World Service, the NSL published an exceedingly strange journal originally named *NS Kampfruf* (no relation to Gary Lauck's newspaper of the same name that appeared a decade later). The journal was later renamed *Race and Nation* (definitely no relation to the similarly named anthology of the radical right edited by Jeffrey Kaplan and Tore Bjørgo, which appeared two decades later).

Russell Veh was a National Socialist from Toledo, Ohio. Before moving to California, Veh ran a variety of National Socialist "organizations" in which he comprised both the leadership and the entire

known membership. Several hard-to-find journals are all that sur-
vives of the period. By 1973, however, Veh had apparently tired of
the organizational equivalent of onanism and, spurred on by a
mail-fraud conviction, headed for the more cosmopolitan environs
of California.

In Los Angeles, Veh's following probably did not increase greatly
from his Ohio days, but *NS Kampfruf* came out of the closet with a
vengeance. The cover of the March 1974 premier issue appeared conventional enough, with a drawing of Richard Nixon nailed to a cross
in parody of the then-ongoing Watergate scandal. However, any illusion of conventionality was dispelled by an (unsigned) open letter
addressed to all National Socialists, intended as a National Socialist
League recruiting pitch, which strangely echoed Harold Covington's
mocking observations:

> ...We are now organizing a national membership to again replant
> the seeds of National Socialism.
>
> Here is where we separate the men from the boys.
>
> The N.S.L. believes that there are many who dig National Social-
> ist uniforms, medals, and the "sexual trip" that was prominent in
> Nazi Germany with the S.S. and the S.A.....

And to drive home the point, the journal ends with a drawing of two
obviously gay Nazis in a barracks with swastikas covering their
genitals and the logo "$6.00 Subscribe! This Year!"

Subsequent issues of *NS Kampfruf* would be less subtle. Photos
of homosexual orgies in (and out of) Nazi regalia vied with more
tasteful male nude statues from the heroic imagery of the original
Third Reich. Short articles and news briefs vied as well with letters
to the editor extolling the organization, which had dared to offer a
home for openly gay National Socialists. Ironically, through a series
of interviews in the mainstream and gay press, Veh seems to have
made his bizarre National Socialist "group" something of an object of
debate over the openness of the gay community to all gay men,
regardless of their political ideology, and an object of interest to the
mainstream press, whose respectful interviews called into question
how far newspapers would go to find ever-more-exotic filler for an
otherwise slow news day.

Veh appears to have taken this curiosity as approbation, and
soon *NS Kampfruf* began to run personal ads that probably would
not have met the fairly low standards of taste and decency of the
underground newspaper of the day, the *Berkeley Barb,* much less
the puritanical ethos of American National Socialism. Thus, the
American National Socialist community was treated to ads that ran

heavily into leather fetishism and S&M as a vital component of National Socialist belief. Needless to say, there was little positive response throughout the American National Socialist subculture. In fact, the graphic personals simply provided ammunition for the movement's internecine wars in which a charge of homosexuality was simply a convenient term of abuse, as in this *NS Kampfruf* personal ad, reprinted in the *Deguello Report* (which itself is reprinted in its entirety in the "Resources" section of this encyclopedia):

> Subservient young man, dedicated to National Socialism, desires to provide complete oral service for dynamic male holding leadership position within the American Nazi movement.

Finding no support for his efforts in Los Angeles, Veh inexplicably moved to the even-more-conservative environs of San Diego in 1982, changing the name of the National Socialist League to the World Service in the process. From there he faded from the National Socialist scene.

See also: American Nazi Party; Covington, Harold; Lauck, Gary; Rockwell, George Lincoln.

Further reading: John George and Laird Wilcox, *American Extremists, Supremacists, Klansmen, Communists and Others* (Buffalo, NY: Prometheus Books, 1996).

VARG VIKERNES   Kristian Quisling Lafranzson Vikernes, more popularly known as Varg Vikernes, is one of Norway's most notorious criminals. He is currently serving a 21-year-prison sentence for murdering Øystein Aarseth, a prominent figure both in Norwegian satanic circles and in that country's black metal music scene. The rock star status that Vikernes has acquired as the creative force behind the one-man band known as Burzum significantly boosted his notoriety in Norway. Although the Norwegian press labeled Vikernes a Satanist because of his involvement in the Black Circle (a group of youths who made use of Satanic symbols and who participated in church arson to drive Christianity out of Norway), he claims that above all he is a dedicated Odinist. Vikernes argues that the only way the "Satanist" label that has been imposed upon him can be justified is if it is taken according to its literal meaning. That is to say, Vikernes asserts that he is a Satanist only insofar as he is an enemy of the Judeo-Christian God.

Born in 1973, in Bergen, Norway, Vikernes first became involved with the extreme right as a National Socialist skinhead while he was an adolescent. In 1991, Vikernes began to associate with Øystein Aarseth, godfather of the black metal scene in Norway, guitarist in the band Mayhem, and owner of both a small record store (Helvete, or Hell) and record label (Deathlike Silence). Aarseth, who preferred to be called Euronymous (a name he borrowed from the Prince of Death in Greek mythology), was infatuated with the concept of "evil." He praised the devil, cursed Christians, and preached that it was time the powers of evil were spread. Also, he was noted both within the movement and later in the popular press for his misogyny and sexual sadism. In 1992, Aarseth and Vikernes (who initially adopted the alias "Count Grishnackh" before calling himself "Varg," which means "wolf" in Norwegian) headed a group of youths drawn from the black metal scene whom Aarseth had baptized "the Black Circle." The objectives of the Black Circle were to drive Christianity out of Norway and to reinstitute the worship of Old Norse gods, particularly Odin. Approximately 40 churches were destroyed by arson in Norway between 1992 and 1996. The Norwegian press attributed much of the damage to the Black Circle, who were dubbed by the media, and by Aarseth himself, as "Satanic terrorists."

As a result of what is variously described as a power struggle between rival leaders of the Satanic circle, a conflict over a girl's affection, or a dispute over a record contract, Vikernes murdered Aarseth on the night of August 9, 1993. For his part, Vikernes contends that Aarseth planned to kill him and that he was striking first in self-defense. Vikernes states, too, that the substantial amount of explosives recovered from his apartment after his arrest was intended to blow up Blitz House, the radical leftist and anarchist enclave in Oslo. Vikernes's plan to destroy "the Blitz" was reportedly on the verge of execution when his arrest for the murder of Aarseth prevented it from being carried out. Vikernes was convicted of Aarseth's homicide and several counts of church arson in 1994.

Vikernes has been busy promoting his Odinist and National Socialist philosophy from behind bars via the periodical *Filosofem*, the first issue of which he coedited with the French activist Vidarrh von Herske (*Filosofem* is also the name of his most successful CD). He continues to record music in prison, and he runs a record company that produces albums with nationalistic overtones from there as well. Vikernes is also the self-proclaimed leader of the Norsk Hedensk Front (Norwegian Heathen Front) and of an international heathen brotherhood he calls Cymophane.

He advocates racial paganism (that is, exclusive and culture-specific worship of deities or archetypes), "race hygiene" (that is, the maintenance of territorial divisions based on racial differences), and anti-Semitism. He is dedicated to the liberation of Scandinavia and Germany from ZOG (the so-called Zionist Occupation Government), and he has even stated on at least one occasion that he wishes he were dictator of Scandinavia. Vikernes claims that if he had known his prior reliance on Satanic symbols would have caused so much confusion with respect to his goals and allegiances, he never would have used them.

On April 4, 1997, Vikernes's mother, Lene Bore, and four National Socialists were arrested for allegedly conspiring against the state. The Norwegian police found a hit list featuring the names of prominent Norwegian politicians, clergy, and police officers in Bore's home. Reportedly, military equipment and survivalist gear also were seized from her house.

—*Xavier Cattarinich, University of Alberta, Canada*

See also: Black Metal; Odinism, Skinheads (Norwegian); Zionist Occupation Government.

Further reading: Jeffrey Kaplan, "The Role of Oppositional Religious Movements in the Creation of a New Ethnic Identity," *Nation and Race: The Developing Euro-American Racist Subculture* (Boston: Northeastern University Press, 1998); Michael Moynihan and Didrik Søderlind, *Lords of Chaos* (Venice, CA: Feral House, 1998).

VITT ARISKT MOTSÅND   The group name Vitt Ariskt Motsånd (VAM) translates to White Aryan Resistance (WAR), and these Swedish revolutionary National Socialists were the most important European group to borrow the WAR name from Tom Metzger's eponymous California organization, with which they maintained close contact. Vitt Ariskt Motsånd was active in Sweden from 1990 through 1992. In that time, however, they demonstrated more of an affinity for Robert Mathews's revolutionary Silent Brotherhood (the Order) than Metzger's mail-order racism.

In an early circular, Vitt Ariskt Motsånd stated its purpose succinctly:

> VAM is not a traditional organization, but an efficient network that
> helps regional groups, local cells and individuals to get started in

their fight for freedom…. VAM distributes race-revolutionary propaganda through magazines, posters, stickers, leaflets and literature.

Whether VAM was here being modest or disingenuous, or whether it simply had decided by 1992 to make a change of course, Vitt Ariskt Motsånd soon found that propaganda of the pen was ineffective and turned to propaganda of the deed. In this, its members found the model of the Order to be irresistible, and they soon set out on a course of revolutionary violence. Their first action was audacious: a successful raid at the Lidingö, Sweden, police station, where they stole a number of weapons. Now armed and dangerous, the core activists who formed Vitt Ariskt Motsånd set out to finance the movement. Where Robert Mathews had used armored car robberies for the purpose, VAM adapted the tactic to Swedish conditions and undertook a series of bank robberies beginning in 1991. This was both the high point of Vitt Ariskt Motsånd activism and the beginning of the end of the core cadre of the organization. Swedish police soon arrested those involved in the robberies—most notably through a series of comic-opera car chases. The driving skills so notable in the American movement were simply not transferable to the Swedes, whose flights from the police invariably ended up in a ditch or against a guard rail.

The arrests of the Vitt Ariskt Motsånd leadership throughout 1992 did not put an end to the organization, however. VAM was constructed as a loose network rather than as an organization, so as to preclude police infiltration. Many actions undertaken under the Vitt Ariskt Motsånd banner therefore rather more closely resembled the leaderless resistance concept than any organized group on the model of the Order. VAM could thus draw on the support of activists throughout the Swedish White Power subculture, and at its height was connected to such prominent movement figures as members of the White Power rock groups Vit Aggression (White Aggression) and Division S.

The crimes attributed to Vitt Ariskt Motsånd include the bombing of the main railway station in Stockholm, a number of armed robberies, and as many as three murders. In a sense, however, this may be deceiving. The informal structure of VAM did have some success in weeding out potential infiltrators, but at the cost of giving the core leadership little if any control on what was done in the organization's name. As one leading Vitt Ariskt Motsånd activist noted to Dr. Heléne Lööw of Stockholm University, the media notoriety that VAM had achieved by 1992 was "like advertising for psychopaths—and unfortunately, the response was overwhelming."

The last issue of Vitt Ariskt Motsånd's publication, *Storm*, appeared in 1993. With the leading activists in prison, the VAM network faded away at that time. By then, though, VAM had become something of a legend, and the name, materials, and symbols of the organization lived on for a time among imitators throughout Scandinavia.

See also: Leaderless Resistance; Mathews, Robert; Metzger, Tom; Order; White Aryan Resistance; White Power Music.

Further reading: Heléne Lööw, "The Swedish Racist Counterculture," in Tore Bjørgo and Rob Witte, *Racist Violence in Europe* (New York: St. Martin's Press, 1993).

WACO   On April 19, 1993, the federal siege of the Branch Davidian compound in Waco, Texas, reached its fiery denouement. Within the American cultural heartland, there were expressions of sadness for the tragic fate of the children, which only slightly softened the consensus that the cult had in some way "got what they deserved." Attorney General Janet Reno was lionized as the most popular personality of the then-floundering Clinton administration.

To the radical right, however, the perception of Waco was considerably different. For many adherents of the myriad ideologies of the radical right wing, here was proof positive that our government had declared open season on each and every one of them. Two years to the day later, a bomb destroyed the Federal Building in Oklahoma City, Oklahoma. The accused bomber's correspondence indicated that his primary motivation was his anger over the Waco tragedy. Why the reaction from the radical right was as strong as it was—indeed, Waco and its aftermath was the genesis of the sudden appearance of the militia movement in America—tells much about the fears and vulnerabilities of the denizens of the American racialist right. This reaction was particularly puzzling to federal authorities and academic observers alike, in light of the fact that the beliefs and lifestyle of David Koresh and his followers were utterly inimical to all that the right wing holds dear. The key to this seeming mystery rests in two factors: historical context and the conspiritorialism that is a central facet of radical-right-wing ideology.

In terms of timing, Waco came at the tail end of a long series of increasingly violent confrontations between members of the radical-right-wing subculture and federal authorities. From the perspective of the right wing, the federal government, now acting as agents of the conspiratorial entity known as ZOG, or the Zionist Occupation Government, had since the early 1980s been embarked on a violent campaign of suppression of dissent from the right. This view did, in fact, have some justification. As James Gibson points out in his outstanding study *Warrior Dreams,* the paramilitary culture typified by movies such as *Rambo* and magazines such as *Soldier of Fortune* were no

323

less attractive to government agents than to armchair adventurers in the post-Vietnam era.

Thus, as government agents sought to enforce the federal writ against individual survivalists, tax resistors, and the inhabitants of rural compounds, there was a remarkable upsurge of violence as federal authorities, clad in camouflage fatigues or, later, black uniforms and ski masks to obscure their faces, adopted increasingly muscular solutions to handle confrontations. Most of the time, the strategy was successful and, after a brief show of defiance, the targets surrendered without a shot being fired.

The Covenant, Sword, and Arm of the Lord in southern Missouri, for example, was, for almost a decade, the elite armorer of and center for paramilitary training for the far right before its ignominious surrender to federal authorities in 1985. Not a shot was fired in anger, and worse, its idiosyncratic leader, James Ellison, became the star witness for the prosecution in the 1987 Fort Smith sedition trial!

Sometimes, however, the strategy had tragic consequences, and a long line of movement martyrs was the result. Gordon Kahl in North Dakota, Arthur Kirk in Nebraska, David Moran in California—the list could go on. But, of greatest import, it was the killing of Vicki Weaver and her 14-year-old son, Samuel, near Naples, Idaho, on August 21–22, 1992, that was the key event in the interpretation of Waco as a declaration of war on the far right.

The attempt to arrest Randy Weaver—a fiasco from the beginning—is a dispiriting tale of government ineptitude. Indeed, the ham-fisted handling of the slow-motion siege at Weaver's rural cabin and the inept attempts to cover up the facts of the incident after the fact violated every procedure set down by the FBI for handling such situations, endangering not only the putative target of the raid but his young children as well. The imbroglio ultimately cost the government a hefty monetary settlement with Weaver, cost Larry Potts his position as number two man at the Bureau, and nearly cost the freedom of the FBI sharpshooter who fired the bullet that killed Vicki Weaver. From the viewpoint of the radical right, however, not only was the Weaver tragedy the logical culmination of the pattern of recent government actions, but it was also seen as evidence that the state would stop at nothing to liquidate its enemies. The vision of Vicki Weaver, shot in the head as she cradled her infant in her arms, hit too close to home to be ignored.

At the same time, there had been since the mid-1980s a palpable rise in temperature throughout the radical right. The Order, led by the charismatic figure of Robert Mathews, had in the early 1980s taken up arms and risen in hopeless rebellion against the power of the state. Individual right-wing figures such as Richard Wayne Snell (a former member of the Covenant, Sword, and Arm of the Lord) were increasingly turning to violence, and the ranks of law enforcement too began to suffer casualties. It was into this tinder-box that Waco threw the final match.

Ironically, the holocaust at Waco took place during the Weaver trial—a trial in which Weaver and codefendant Kevin Harris were found not guilty of all charges. Waco was thus seen by the far right as not only a logical culmination of a decade of federal actions against the right wing, but, in its full-scale military assault on the Branch Davidians, a terrible harbinger of things to come. But nothing that had occurred before prepared the right for the incineration of the women and children at Waco. It was a message that not a single member of the American far right could mistake: There but for the grace of God go I, and with me my entire family. Waco was thus the breaking point for the hopes that a compromise could be found with the hated state and its perceived Jewish masters. The ZOG discourse thus became embedded as movement dogma.

The reaction was not long in coming. Militia groups began to spring up throughout the country as a response to both the events at Waco and the interpretations given to those events by videotapes such as "America Under Siege," by Linda Thompson, and more recently, "Waco: Rules of Engagement." Soon, these graphic videos were joined by World Wide Web sites such as one that includes the morgue photographs of the dead children.

Expressions of shock and outrage reverberated throughout the milieu of the radical right. And for some, a decision was taken to exact vengeance. Thus did America come to learn the name of Timothy McVeigh and to witness the bombing at the Federal Building in Oklahoma City, Oklahoma, on April 19, 1995, the second anniversary of the Waco tragedy.

See also: Covenant, Sword, and Arm of the Lord; Ellison, James; Mathews, Robert; Order; Snell, Richard Wayne; Weaver, Randy; Zionist Occupation Government.

Further reading: Richard Abnes, *American Militias: Rebellion, Racism and Religion* (Downers Grove, IL: InterVarsity Press, 1996); Michael Barkun, "Reflections After Waco: Millennialists and the State," in James R. Lewis, ed., *From the Ashes: Making Sense of Waco* (Lanham, MD: Rowman & Littlefield, 1994); Michael Barkun, *Religion and the Racist Right: The Origins of the Christian Identity Movement* (Chapel Hill: University of North

Carolina Press, 1994); James Coates, *Armed and Dangerous: The Rise of the Survivalist Right* (New York: Hill and Wang, 1987); Kevin Flynn and Gary Gerhardt, *The Silent Brotherhood* (New York: Signet, 1990); Mark S. Hamm, *Apocalypse in Oklahoma* (Boston: Northeastern University Press, 1998); Jeffrey Kaplan, "The Millennial Dream," in James R. Lewis, ed., *From the Ashes: Making Sense of Waco* (Lanham, MD: Rowman & Littlefield, 1994); Jeffrey Kaplan, *Radical Religion in America* (Syracuse, NY: Syracuse University Press, 1997); Jeffrey Kaplan, "Leaderless Resistance," *Journal of Terrorism and Political Violence* 9:3 (fall 1997); Jim Keith, *OKBOMB!: Conspiracy and Cover-Up* (Lilburn, GA: Illuminet Press, 1996); Pete Peters, *Special Report on the Meeting of Christian Men Held in Estes Park, Colorado October 23, 24, 25, 1992 Concerning the Killing of Vicki and Samuel Weaver by the United States Government* (LaPorte, CO: Scriptures for America, n.d.); Kenneth S. Stern, *A Force Upon the Plain: The American Militia Movement and the Politics of Hate* (New York: Simon & Schuster, 1996); Brandon M. Stickney, *"All American Monster": The Unauthorized Biography of Tim McVeigh* (Amherst, NY: Prometheus Books, 1996); Jess Walter, *Every Knee Shall Bow: The Truth and Tragedy of Ruby Ridge and the Weaver Family* (New York: ReganBooks, 1995).

George Wallace   *See* Carto, Willis; Miles, Robert; Warner, James.

JAMES WARNER   One of the most isolated veterans of the incessant wars of the radical right in America is James Warner. From his Louisiana home, Warner subsists on the income from his mail-order book dealership and on his memories of better days. Indeed, his impeccable racialist pedigree makes his current near-pariah status in the movement all the more striking.

Warner was a core member of George Lincoln Rockwell's American Nazi Party in the early 1960s. The diminutive Warner was known as pugnacious—even by American Nazi Party (ANP) standards. This, however, was considered a positive quality by the street fighters who formed the backbone of the ANP. He was, on the other hand, irascible and unpredictable—again, in the context of the ANP this is no small distinction. Yet, though in the late 1960s and early 1970s Warner would base much of his claim for movement leadership on his American Nazi Party days, in fact Warner's association with the Commander was short and his parting far less than amicable.

By Warner's testimony, offered in a 1968 Open Letter to the National Socialist movement via California Nazi leader Allen Vincent (reproduced in the "Resources" section), the Commander owed much to Warner:

> When the Party was launched in 1959, I was one of the five original members, and have been credited by Commander Rockwell with being the one individual who gave the Commander the encouragement to go ahead with organizing the American Nazi Party. In the Commander's words:
>
> "Just about as I regained 'consciousness', James Warner, the young man who sent the Nazi flag, was discharged from the Airforce for his Nazi sympathies, and appeared at Louis' home ready to do what he could to advance Nazism.
>
> "The fact that this young kid was ready to devote his life to our cause and to *my leadership* was the shock I needed to snap out of depression." (p. 342, *This Time the World*)

While the quote from Rockwell's 1963 autobiography is accurate enough, what Warner fails to mention is that in 1962, before the ink on the *This Time the World* manuscript had dried, the Commander had already had enough of Warner. In the November 1962 issue of the *Rockwell Report,* the Commander lambasted Warner for his disloyalty and dishonesty. The breaking point came in the course of Rockwell's nasty battle with Dr. Edward Fields of the National States' Rights Party—a fight that eventually ended up in court in a defamation suit, which Fields prudently settled out of court. In an article titled "Emory Burke Quits NSRP!!," the Commander singles out Warner for particular vilification:

> Then an unprincipled scoundrel named James K. Warner slithered into the scene and tried to get me to let him use the ANP mailing list for his own personal profit! When I put a firm stop to this attempt to MAKE MONEY out of the tragic concern of right-wing patriots, Warner STOLE the mailing list, pretending he was leaving to visit his "dying" mother....
>
> But apparently the ANP mailing list was a great temptation, because soon after Warner left to visit his "dying mother," he (Warner) authored and published an unspeakable and unprovoked attack against me—and recommended that patriots join the NSRP (Giving the address and membership information).
>
> ...Ed Fields finally kicked the money-grabbing Warner out of the NSRP, and printed a notice to that effect in the "Thunderbolt".

But then, several months later, Fields suddenly announced that profiteering Warner was to become an EDITOR of the "Thunderbolt," and began to print worse and worse smears and lies against myself!

...it became obvious that Warner had some kind of evil hold over Ed Fields....

The "evil hold" didn't last long, and neither did Warner's tenure with the National States' Rights Party. The parting was less than amicable, and again, Warner was accused of stealing the NSRP's mailing list. According to the *Deguello Report* (also included in the "Resources" section):

It was only a few months later that Warner talked one of Field's secretaries into thinking that he planned to marry her. The two disappeared from the *NSRP* headquarters (along with a copy of Field's mailing list) and the next thing Fields heard about it was a phone call from his secretary saying that Warner had left her stranded and asking for bus fare home....

Warner [then] formed an organization called *"Sons of Liberty"* using the various mailing lists he had stolen from the *American Nazi Party*, the *National States Rights Party*, etc.... [Roger] Pearson claimed that *Warner* had stolen his mailing list also.

In the world of the American radical right, no more serious charge can be lodged than theft of a mailing list. The mailing list represents the sole source of income for many leaders of the racialist right, and leaders from George Lincoln Rockwell to David Duke all attest that building it up over time is among their most important achievements. The suspicion—now grown to the stature of movement dogma—that Warner habitually absconds with the precious mailing lists does much to explain his current isolation. Much, but not all.

Having worn out his welcome with both the American Nazi Party and the National States' Rights Party, Warner headed west. In California, his *Sons of Liberty* newsletter sought to pick up a subscription base from the purloined mailing lists, and to this he added an innovative telephone line offering callers a recorded hate message of the day. Of greater import, he quickly made contact with the fractious California contingent of the American Nazi Party, which, by 1968 when he made his bid for power, had mutated into the National Socialist White People's Party (NSWPP). The California leader in those days was Ralph Forbes, who had been personally selected for the job by Rockwell. But Rockwell was assassinated in 1967, to be replaced by Matt Koehl, and the always-divisive California Party was by 1968 in full revolt against Forbes's leadership.

The precise charges against Forbes are many and varied, but what it all boiled down to was the charge—correct, as it happened—that Forbes had become increasingly absorbed in Christian Identity and had by 1968 become so fanatical on questions of religion that many of the more secular National Socialists had become alienated from party activities. James Warner jumped into the fray on the side of the rebels, brandishing his tarnished but still serviceable reputation as an original member of the American Nazi Party. Pooling their resources, the California party members flew Matt Koehl to the state to adjudicate the dispute. Koehl, however, was a dedicated follower of the National Socialist Leadership Principle (especially now that he was the leader), and his predictable decision was to keep the status quo and to insist that the party close ranks behind Forbes.

Warner, now styling himself Dr. James K. Warner, threw in his lot with the dissident faction headed by Allen Vincent, who led an exodus from the National Socialist White People's Party. This was the first fissure of what became the fragmentation of the Koehl-era NSWPP. The California rebels set up a new version of the American Nazi Party, and in the 1968 letter quoted above, Warner made his bid for control. In view of his later career, "Dr." Warner's charges against Forbes and the line of reasoning he followed in making this bold claim for leadership are of considerable interest.

Warner began with an *apologia* for his past transgressions against the party and its leader, George Lincoln Rockwell. Then, following a (necessarily) brief review of his American Nazi Party accomplishments, Warner set out the bill of particulars against Ralph Forbes, emphasizing his "misuse of Party funds, inactivity, incompetence and lack of leadership...." But Warner's primary charges, that Forbes was obsessed with "off beat religious cults" and that pressure was put on party members to join "KKK rallies," are deeply ironic in that much of Warner's own career would be developed in the same Christian Identity world that he condemns Forbes for being involved with and, while in Louisiana, an aging Warner would try to hitch his fading star to that of the fast-rising young Klansman David Duke. Be this as it may, it is Forbes's religiosity that served as the pretext for the party split and for the invitation to Matt Koehl to fly to California and try to mediate the dispute. In the end, Koehl opted for Forbes, and the California NSWPP dissolved as a result.

It almost goes without saying that Warner's bid for leadership got little support in the National Socialist subculture. He therefore turned to the same Identity Christians whom he had condemned as "religious fanatics" and members of "off beat religious cults" in his battle with Ralph Forbes. In 1971, Warner unveiled his New Christian Crusade Church. Warner's ministry soon thrived, and such high-profile (and highly secular) movement leaders as Tom Metzger were duly ordained by the now Rev. Dr. Warner in the early 1970s.

The California Identity circle into which Warner gained a foothold was extraordinarily fertile, comprised as it was of the elite group of ministers around Wesley Swift, and included such notable movement figures as Richard Butler, Bertrand Comperet, and William Potter Gale. This brought Warner into the Christian Defense League (CDL) under Richard Butler. When Butler moved to Idaho in 1973, Warner inherited the organization, which was by then nearly moribund but which did have the advantage of a mailing list, of which Warner gratefully took possession.

Publishing rather than leadership was in any case Warner's forte. His first effort, the Sons of Liberty's *Action Magazine,* began in the mid-1960s. It was a literate effort that endorsed George Wallace for president, though *Action* was explicitly National Socialist. Another Sons of Liberty newsletter, creatively titled *Sons of Liberty,* from Hollywood, California, hit the stands in June 1969 as a forum from which to denounce *everything,* from the Young Americans for Freedom to all points on the political compass, as pawns of the Jewish conspiracy.

Warner's Christian Identity newspaper, the *Christian Vanguard,* premiered with the April–May 1971 issue. It mixes Identity with generic anti-Semitic and racialist articles. Nazism made infrequent appearances, but occasionally surfaced, as in the "Julius Streicher Memorial Edition," *Christian Vanguard* 50 (February 1976). This was preceded, however, by a special Identity issue, *Christian Vanguard* 49 (January 1976). By the late 1970s, the *Christian Vanguard* was offering a very wide range of books and other racist and anti-Semitic materials, heralding Warner's eventual move from activism into the mail-order book business. By the mid-1980s, Warner's production had slowed considerably, and the paper relied on guest writers and on transcriptions of Identity sermons, particularly from Wesley Swift. From issue 46 (October 1975), *Christian Vanguard* was issued from Metairie, Louisiana. Warner's separate *CDL Report* was first published from Metairie in 1979. It offered much the same fare.

The move to Louisiana occasioned Warner's last glimpse of public notoriety. By the mid-1970s, Warner had largely worn out his welcome in California, where dark rumors about Warner's sexuality and of his alleged seizure of the Wesley Swift mailing list were widely believed. These charges are presented in both the *Deguello Report* and the *History of White Nationalism,* which are offered in the "Resources" section of this encyclopedia. Starting again in Metairie, Warner came to know a local boy who appeared to be going somewhere fast in movement circles, David Duke. Duke headed the Knights of the Ku Klux Klan, though the Klan was not Warner's favorite flavor of the American race movement in 1968.

Never one to stand on principle however, Warner joined forces with Duke until a 1976 arrest when the two were detained on the way to a Klan rally. Warner was ultimately sentenced to three months—half of Duke's sentence. However, it marked the beginning of the end of the relationship. The media-wise Duke, it turned out, always got twice the publicity of the colorless Warner, and the older racist grew tired of standing in the hooded shadow of the dynamic young "National Director" of the Knights of the Ku Klux Klan.

Following the Klan fiasco, Warner became increasingly reclusive, doing what he did best, in any case: publishing and working his now-burgeoning mailing lists for his Christian Vanguard book-distribution business.

See also: American Nazi Party; Butler, Richard; Christian Defense League; Christian Identity; Duke; David; Forbes, Ralph; Gale, William Potter; Koehl, Matt; Metzger, Tom; National Socialist White People's Party; Rockwell, George Lincoln; Swift, Wesley.

Further reading: Michael Barkun, *Religion and the Racist Right: The Origins of the Christian Identity Movement* (Chapel Hill: University of North Carolina Press, 1994); Betty A. Dobratz and Stephanie L. Shanks-Meile, *White Power, White Pride!* (New York: Twayne, 1997); John George and Laird Wilcox, *American Extremists, Supremacists, Klansmen, Communists and Others* (Buffalo, NY: Prometheus Books, 1996); George Lincoln Rockwell, *This Time the World!* (Arlington, VA: Parliament House, 1963); Patsy Sims, *The Klan* (New York: Stein and Day, 1978); Michael Zatarian, *David Duke: Evolution of a Klansman* (New York: Pelican, 1990).

RANDY WEAVER   An accidental (and unlikely) hero if ever there was one, Randy Weaver inadvertently rose to national fame as a young Christian Identity believer loosely tied to Richard Butler's Aryan Nations. In August 1992, the Federal Bureau of Investigation's Hostage Rescue Team, mistakenly believing that two federal agents were pinned down by fire from Weaver's Naples, Idaho, cabin, descended in force. What followed was a tragedy for all concerned. The case of Randy Weaver became national news, and for once the White supremacist beliefs of the suspect were considered to be less important than either the force utilized by government agents in the effort to apprehend him or the fanciful explanations offered for government conduct at the ensuing trial.

Weaver's story is straightforward enough. A financially strapped Christian Identity believer of no particular distinction, Weaver was entrapped into selling undercover agents a sawed-off shotgun with a barrel slightly under the legal length. Offered an opportunity to avoid prosecution by becoming an informer, Weaver refused and a trial date was set. At this point the tale becomes murky. What appears to have happened is that Weaver was given the wrong trial date—not an unusual occurrence in the chaotic American court system—and when he failed to appear at the correct time, a bench warrant was issued for his arrest. Fearing that a ZOG (Zionist Occupation Government) plot was afoot, Weaver fled with his family to a cabin in the Idaho hills where federal agents soon materialized and placed the site under surveillance...for 20 months! Finally, in August 1992, the Weaver's dog rushed at one of the agents, who panicked and shot it. Weaver's 14-year-old son, Samuel, was shot in the back and killed at this point, as was Federal Marshall William Degan, who was killed by a shot fired by Weaver family friend Kevin Harris, and what had been a low-level surveillance was transformed into a siege. For 11 days the Weavers and Harris held out. Finally, a federal agent using a high-powered rifle fired a bullet that entered the skull of Vicki Weaver as she stood by an open door holding their 10-month old baby. She was killed instantly.

At last, Populist Party candidate Bo Gritz negotiated Weaver's surrender. Weaver and Harris were charged with murder in the killing of William Degan, and Weaver was further charged with the original weapons violation and unlawful flight to avoid prosecution. And there it should have ended, had precedent held true. This time, however, popular indignation spread beyond the insular world of the radical right. Part of this may be explained by the way in which Vicki Weaver died while cradling her baby in her arms, part of it with the killing of a 14-year-old boy whose primary sin seems to have been investigating the death of his dog and firing back when shot at by men concealed in dense underbrush and firing high-powered weapons. Part of it, too, had to do with timing.

Weaver's trial coincided with the Branch Davidian siege at Waco, Texas, and the similarity of the two events was lost on no one. In any case, Gary Spence, a flamboyant defense attorney from

Wyoming, took the Weaver case on a *pro bono* basis and proceeded to put the government on trial for its actions. In a classic defense that would be imitated with nearly as much success by the attorneys representing the Branch Davidians, the government's often-contradictory explanations for the events surrounding the Weaver case were held up to ridicule. More seriously, Spence's warnings that what the government did to Randy Weaver it could easily one day do to any other citizen were suddenly credible to a white, middle-class American jury that had the cataclysmic denouement of the Waco siege fresh in mind. Ultimately, to the surprise of one and all, the jury voted to acquit both Weaver and Harris of all charges against them.

In the aftermath of the violence, a civil suit ultimately cost the government a hefty monetary settlement with Weaver, Larry Potts forfeited his position as number two man at the FBI, and the sharp-shooter who fired the bullet that killed Vicki Weaver for a time faced trial for manslaughter.

In retrospect, Randy Weaver is neither a hero nor a martyr. Rather, he is a true believer, a religious fanatic who exasperated his family (save for Vicki and his children), alienated his friends, and managed to outrage even so distant a group of neighbors as those surrounding his isolated Ruby Ridge, Idaho, property. Apart from his religious zeal, however, Weaver emerges as a decidedly weak man who leaned on the iron will of his wife. After her death, he turned to his teenage daughter for guidance. Hardly the stuff of legend in the patriarchal world of the radical right!

Jess Walter, in his excellent book on the Weaver tragedy, *Every Knee Shall Bow,* finds a consistent thread running throughout the story of a government that, far from being the all-pervading and utterly malevolent entity of the radical right's nightmares, is in real life every bit as fallible as its right-wing opponents. The Weaver fiasco, in this view, was entirely avoidable—beginning with the clumsy attempt by a federal informant to entrap Weaver into selling illegally sawed-off shotguns as a step toward inducing him to become a government informer, continuing with a local magistrate whose incomprehension of the law caused Weaver to first miss his court date and then to flee, and culminating with a garbled message in which the U.S. Marshals Service, believing erroneously that its agents were pinned down by fire from Weaver's cabin, asked the FBI to respond with its hostage response team.

From a movement perspective, however, the shoot-out on what became known as Ruby Ridge, followed as it was by the holocaust at

Waco, served notice on all within the milieu of the radical right that the federal government had determined to eliminate them one by one. A meeting of Identity adherents called by Pete Peters in Colorado produced a consensus that the time had come to fight back—a show of bravado that would have meant little had the siege at Waco not taken place so soon after the Weaver killings. As it was, the American militia movement took wing and Randy Weaver found himself testifying tearfully to Congress, and receiving a remarkably sympathetic hearing. To the radical right, Weaver's stand was the stuff of legend, and Randy Weaver, who wished by then only to be left alone with the surviving members of his family, had become an icon.

See also: Aryan Nations; Butler, Richard; Christian Identity; Peters, Pete; Waco; Zionist Occupation Government.

Further reading: Richard Abnes, *American Militias: Rebellion, Racism and Religion* (Downers Grove, IL: InterVarsity Press, 1996); Michael Barkun, *Religion and the Racist Right: The Origins of the Christian Identity Movement* (Chapel Hill: University of North Carolina Press, 1994); James Coates, *Armed and Dangerous: The Rise of the Survivalist Right* (New York: Hill and Wang, 1987); Kevin Flynn and Gary Gerhardt, *The Silent Brotherhood* (New York: Signet, 1990); Mark S. Hamm, *Apocalypse in Oklahoma* (Boston: Northeastern University Press, 1998); Jeffrey Kaplan, *Radical Religion in America* (Syracuse, NY: Syracuse University Press, 1997); Jeffrey Kaplan, "April 19," *Journal of Terrorism and Political Violence* 9:2 (summer 1997); Jeffrey Kaplan, "Leaderless Resistance," *Journal of Terrorism and Political Violence* 9:3 (fall 1997); Jim Keith, *OKBOMB!: Conspiracy and Cover-Up* (Lilburn, GA: Illuminet Press, 1996); Pete Peters, *Special Report on the Meeting of Christian Men Held in Estes Park, Colorado October 23, 24, 25, 1992 Concerning the Killing of Vicki and Samuel Weaver by the United States Government* (LaPorte, CO: Scriptures for America, n.d.); Kenneth S. Stern, *A Force Upon the Plain: The American Militia Movement and the Politics of Hate* (New York: Simon & Schuster, 1996); Brandon M. Stickney, *"All American Monster": The Unauthorized Biography of Tim McVeigh* (Amherst, NY: Prometheus Books, 1996); Jess Walter, *Every Knee Shall Bow: The Truth and Tragedy of Ruby Ridge and The Weaver Family* (New York: ReganBooks, 1995).

WHITE ARYAN RESISTANCE   The White Aryan Resistance, better known by its acronym WAR, is the brainchild of Tom Metzger. Metzger, a former Klansman and a former Christian Identity minister, was in search of a vehicle by which he could popularize his Third Positionist message of racism and a labor-oriented National

Socialism that is the direct ideological descendant of the 1920s-era National Socialists Gregor and Otto Strasser. Because the Klan's intellectual horizons were not such that a Strasserite philosophy was a common form of discourse, Metzger created WAR in 1983.

WAR operated out of Metzger's Fallbrook, California, home where he was assisted by his son John, whose White Students Union was operated as a kind of youth branch of WAR and for a time made inroads among young people—especially skinheads. The WAR concept of left-wing National Socialism, in a belief system that eschewed the religiosity that is so marked in the world of the American radical right, soon began to win adherents in the United States. Such established American racialist figures as Klansman Dennis Mahon and many others flocked to the WAR banner. By the late 1980s WAR had also made a significant impact on the European scene with the formation of branches in Scandinavia and Great Britain. But the most important WAR constituency consisted of the most stridently racialist American skinheads, leading not only to the recruitment of individual skins, but to the formation of WAR skinhead chapters throughout the country. Metzger explains the appeal of the skinhead subculture in a magazine interview with journalist Jeff Coplon:

> I became friends with the British skins about three years ago. The more I worked with them, the more I saw their potential to drag the racialist movement out of the conservative right-wing mold and into a newer era. I figured the music of these people could do that. I am 50 years old, and I grew up with early rock 'n' roll—Elvis Presley, Jerry Lee Lewis, Fats Domino. I don't always catch all the words (in skinhead music), but I'm impressed with the power of it. I feel the anger coming from these white street kids—I get taken up in it.

The advantage Metzger and WAR had in its battle for the allegiance of the young racialists on both sides of the Atlantic was due in no small part to the innovative use of media for which WAR became best known. Starting with a simple answering machine that offered callers a taped hate message of the day, Metzger consciously sought to emphasize the primitive emotional appeals that are the racialist movement's lowest common denominator. The eponymous *WAR* newspaper carried on the tradition, interspersing occasional literate expositions with repellent racist cartoons and inarticulate anger. Metzger worked hard to position WAR as an organization for White men who were both angry and ready to fight rather than to talk, and in the end, he drew far too many to his camp who wanted to fight because they had little capacity to do anything else.

The crown jewel in WAR's media arsenal is the cable access television show *Race and Reason*. The program allows well-known racist figures and lesser-known skinheads to get their 15 minutes of
fame by speaking to an audience of true believers, antiracist watchdogs, and channel-surfing insomniacs around the nation. For the
many television markets not carrying the show, WAR marketed
videocassette recordings of the proceedings. The show did wonders
for Metzger's profile within the movement.

WAR moved quickly into the world of the World Wide Web as
well. The WAR web site is notable for its racist cartoons scanned
from the pages of the *WAR* newspaper, its racist jokes in the same
vein, and the cynicism of its appeal to the segment of the race movement who would hardly qualify as the best and the brightest.

WAR's success aroused the predictable ire of many another
racialist leader who was forced to compete for the limited number of
dollars that the faithful had to offer. By the late 1980s, in fact, WAR
appeared to be the primary racialist organization in the United
States, and Tom Metzger seemed poised to emerge as the most
important leader on the American scene. It was at about this point
that the wheels started to come off the WAR bandwagon.

Metzger's problems stemmed from his intensive outreach to the
skinhead movement. In 1987, Dave Mazzella, a young associate of
Metzger's, met with a group of Portland, Oregon, skinheads. The
meeting followed an intensive and fairly successful drive by WAR to
recruit skinheads from around the nation. What took place in this
meeting, and its immediate aftermath, is somewhat murky. What
is clear is that the skinheads, Ken Mieske, Kyle Brewster, and
Steve Strasser, later got into a street fight with an Ethiopian immigrant, Mulugetta Seraw, who was killed in the altercation. The
skinheads were arrested, tried, and convicted of murder.

Enter Morris Dees of the Southern Poverty Law Center (SPLC),
which filed a $7 million civil suit against Tom and John Metzger
and WAR for the wrongful death of Seraw. It was a novel and risky
legal strategy, raising a number of First Amendment questions.
Stupidly, and against the advice of many, Metzger decided that he
was on the side of the angels and would thus conduct his own
defense. Whatever the factual merits of the case, the SPLC's legal
team made the plodding Metzger appear foolish throughout the
trial, and in the end the jury upped the ante by awarding the plaintiffs $10 million rather than the mere $7 million that they had
requested. Metzger was a television repairman whose WAR operation, while successful by movement standards, obviously did not

generate anything like the kind of money he now owed the family of Mulugetta Seraw! Worse, Metzger lost his wife to cancer in this period. It was a bleak period for him.

Metzger belatedly acceded to the advice of others and solicited the services of a lawyer. Michael Null, a Jewish civil liberties attorney from Chicago, worked diligently on Metzger's appeal—so much so that Metzger would later privately confide that he and the movement would need to rethink "the Jewish thing, but this will take some time." In any case, the mess that Metzger's inept defense had made of the case has so far proved to be more than any attorney could rectify, and the Southern Poverty Law Center moved to seize any and all of WAR's assets. Here is where the tale turns from murky to Machiavellian.

In his published account of the case, *Hate on Trial* (1993), lawyer Morris Dees states:

> The real hero since the trial has been San Diego attorney Jim McElroy, who took responsibility for collecting the judgment. He has devoted over a thousand hours, free of charge, in California courts, trying to corner the assets of an increasingly secretive and devious Tom Metzger. After Jim obtained a court order allowing a receiver to open mail coming to WAR's post office box and remove checks, Tom directed that money be sent to a number of out of state addresses.... (pp. 276–77)

Dees's claim of access to WAR's post office box was repeated in one of the Southern Poverty Law Center's ubiquitous fund-raising appeals as well. Such is the attentiveness of the movement, however, that it wasn't until 1995 that Dr. Ed Fields in his racist newspaper, *The Truth at Last,* apprised the American racialist movement of the situation in an article titled "Metzger's Secret Deal with Morris Dees." Not to be outdone, in a letter to the editor, Harold Covington (using his pen name of the moment, Winston Smith, borrowed from *1984*), wrote an incendiary missive on the subject that Fields ran under the title "Morris Dees is the De Facto Publisher of Metzger's WAR." Unsatisfied, Covington then took the issue to the Internet, warning potential WAR recruits that, as a result of the suit, Morris Dees has gained control of the organization's post office box. This, according to Covington, not only makes the Southern Poverty Law Center and thus the FBI privy to every communication sent to Metzger, but it allows the SPLC to seize a significant percentage of the funds accrued by WAR's burgeoning mail-order trade.

National Socialist figure Rick Cooper launched his own investigation, finding that it was true that Metzger's mailbox is (or was—Cooper is not certain of the current situation) probably under the control of Morris Dees through Jim McElroy. However, Covington's estimation of the damage this has done to WAR's members was greatly exaggerated. Even this limited vindication was insufficient for Metzger, however, and he broke off his friendship with Cooper as a result (he later relented, however).

In the end, the damage done to WAR through the Southern Poverty Law Center civil suit and its aftermath has been significant. No longer is WAR at the forefront of the American movement, though it does remain a significant player.

See also: Cooper, Rick; Covington, Harold; Christian Identity; Hawthorne, George Eric; Metzger, Tom.

Further reading: Jeff Coplon, "The Skinhead Reich," *Utne Reader* (May/June 1989); Morris Dees and Steve Fiffer, *Hate on Trial* (New York: Villard Books, 1993); Mattias Gardell, "Black and White Unite In Fight?: On the Inter-Action Between Black and White Radical Racialists," paper presented at the Conference: Rejected and Suppressed Knowledge: The Racist Right and the Cultic Milieu, Stockholm, Sweden, February 13–17, 1997; John George and Laird Wilcox, *Nazis, Communists, Klansmen, and Others On the Fringe* (Buffalo, NY: Prometheus Books, 1992); Mark S. Hamm, *American Skinheads: The Criminology and Control of Hate Crime* (Westport, CT: Praeger, 1993); Jeffrey Kaplan, *Radical Religion in America* (Syracuse, NY: Syracuse University Press, 1997).

WHITE NATIONALISM Many racialists use the term *White nationalism* to denote their determination to separate from the surrounding culture. This separation, in the present circumstances, will be more psychological and spiritual than physical. However, in the future, White nationalists will likely dream of a separatist enclave that will allow its inhabitants to build their lives free from the interference of a government that they see as controlled by Jews, other "racial enemies," and non-Whites who White nationalists believe endanger their survival as a species through miscegenation and physical violence. Increasingly, an important school of thought within White nationalist circles holds for a transatlantic nationalist community based on race and a perceived shared history and culture. For one such White nationalist interpretation of the movement's internal history, see Rick Cooper, "A Brief History of White Nationalism," in the "Resources" section of this volume.

See also: Cooper, Rick; National Socialist Vanguard.

Further reading: Jeffrey Kaplan and Leonard Weinberg, *The Emergence of a Euro-American Radical Right* (Rutgers, NJ: Rutgers University Press, 1998).

White Party   *See* "Resources" section, "The White Party Report."

WHITE POWER MUSIC (AKA WHITE NOISE MUSIC)   White noise recordings, concerts, music magazines, and the like, are the key instruments of propaganda among the youth of the White Power world. They have enabled activists to reach out beyond their "normal" recruiting ground, to reach a larger number of young people. George Eric Hawthorne, lead singer of RAHOWA and editor of *Resistance* magazine, stated in an interview in *National Alliance* that the very fact that the music was outside the mainstream was an attraction in itself. He then added:

> If something has an underground flavor or the image of being forbidden, the youth are naturally attracted to it. Now, in the past this is something that harmed our youth because they were attracted to things which were forbidden or at least discouraged for very good reasons. Examples would be race mixing or the use of drugs. However, in 1995, the mainstream media have made everything OK except being proud of your race and culture, and this tendency of youth is now having a very undesired effect from the perspective of the mainstream media giants, because these young people are now interested in the new forbidden thing, and that is being proud to be white.

The Swedish music magazine and record label *Nordland* expands upon this difference between White Power musicians and mainstream rock stars:

> Our people are unknowingly committing a collective suicide, which is part of the trend that has been created by destructive masters with a global influence. A sickening trend, that they daily feed our youngsters with, by MTV and their networks. In order to resist this threat, White youngsters have spontaneously created the Pro-White music movement which is fighting MTV on the same arena with the same weapon.... Our musicians are not dapper or drugged

rock stars who perform for the sake of their personal profit. They are performing because their rock hard dedication drives them to it. They are the racialist forerunners, who preach pride, strength and unity, who teaches our youngsters to think for themselves—instead of letting MTV think for them.

Matti Sundquist, the singer of the Swedish group Swastika, adds: "The music is very important, both as entertainment, to keep the flame burning, and to recruit people. We have noticed that a lot of people become interested because of the music." And in an article in *Nordland,* Sundquist stated: "*Nordland* speaks the language of the young. They belong to the MTV generation. They listen to music and watch music videos. We are giving them an alternative to their dirty music. Our message is racial pride, strength and separation instead of race mixing and decadence."

A special branch of White noise music is the American KKK-inspired country & western music, which first appeared in the American south in the 1960s. Among the musicians who played this special kind of country & western were Cliff Trahan, Leroy LeBanc, and James Crow. One of the record companies that started to record KKK country & western, or separatist rock as it's also called, was Jay Millens's Rebel Records in Crowley, Louisiana, which recorded the "classic" record "For Segregationists Only" in 1960. Ian Stewart Donaldson, the father of skinhead White Power rock, produced a number of songs and records in this style under the name of The Klansmen. Another sub-branch of the music is Aryan folk music, featuring among others the American singer Eric Owens. Still other examples of Aryan folk are the German singer Frank Rennicke and the Swedish singer Odalmannen.

Until the beginning of the 1990s, the major recording companies for White noise music were Rebelles Européens in France and Rock-O-Rama in Germany. Today there are countless White noise record companies. White Terror Records (U.S.A.); Excalibur and MSR production (Germany); Toubo Records (Italy); Lion Records, Pit Records, and Bulldog Records (France); Hammer records (U.K.); and Viking Sounds (The Netherlands) are just a few of these companies. The estimated number of White noise bands around the world is probably between 200 and 250.

In 1993 Rebelles Européens started to have cooperation problems with, among others, Division S, and lost its role as one of the leading companies. In 1994, George Eric Hawthorne, lead singer of RAHOWA (which was formed in 1990 with other former Church of the Creator members who had left the organization after Rick

McCarthy took over the leadership), founded the magazine *Resistance* and the record company Resistance Records.

The company quickly signed up a number of White noise bands like No Remorse, Fortress, Berserker, and New Minority. In 1995 Resistance Records established itself on the Internet, and it also transmited an electronic newsletter. By 1996, Hawthorne and *Resistance* had largely assumed the role of Donaldson, at least on the American scene. In 1997, Hawthorne was sentenced to one year in prison for assault and battery. This, coupled with a series of raids by tax authorities in the United States and Canada, nearly led to the near dissolution of both the record label and *Resistance* magazine. In 1999, however, Dr. William Pierce and his National Socialist organization, the National Alliance, stepped in to revive both the label and the magazine.

Ian Stewart Donaldson was born in 1958 in Poulton-le-Fylde near Blackpool in Lancashire. In 1975 he formed a band called Tumbling Dice, named after one of the Rolling Stones's hits. The band mostly played cover versions of the Stones, The Who, and Free songs in local working-men's clubs in the Poulton-le-Fylde and Blackpool areas. In 1977 the band changed its name to Skrewdriver. Skrewdriver's first record release came the same year—the single "You're so Dumb," on Chiswick Records. "Anti-social" came out the same year. During that period, the group changed its punk image in favor of cropped hair, and Screwdriver became a skinhead band. According to Donaldson, the decision was motivated by a belief that punk music at the time was becoming too left-wing. In 1978, a riot started when Skrewdriver played the Vortex Club, as a result of which the group was banned from the clubs and were forced to split up.

In 1979, Donaldson formed a political action group called White Noise. The goal of this organization was to promote Skrewdriver's philosophy of survival and rebellion. The White Noise group soon forged an alliance with the neofascist British National Front. Between 1983 and 1985, a number of White supremacist bands adopted the heavy metal sound of Skrewdriver, playing in working-class clubs throughout England, East and West Germany, Holland, Belgium, Sweden, France, Canada, Brazil, and Australia.

In 1984 Skrewdriver signed a contract with the German record company Rock-O-Rama Records. *Blood and Honour* was the publication Donaldson and his associates began in 1985. In the late 1980s Donaldson found himself behind bars. In an interview in the Swedish White Power magazine *Streetfight,* he explained why: "I and three of my mates were attacked by eight niggers and when the police came they only arrested us whites. When we were in court the Jewish judge didn't pay any attention to our defense." Apart from his tours and records with Skrewdriver, Donaldson also recorded a number of solo albums with such names as the Klansmen, White Diamond, and Patriotic Ballads.

The lyrics of Ian Stewart Donaldson are almost religious. They dream of ancient powers returning at the end of time to save their people, that is, the White race. "Warlord" is a good example:

No one's ever going to take away his land
Not while he has the power in his hands
He appears when his nation is in danger
to all our enemies he is the slayer.

Skrewdriver is not the only band whose lyrics are quasi-religious. No Remorse, RAHOWA, and Division S, for instance, all have the same kind of motifs in their lyrics. Donaldson's idea was to exchange boring meetings and endless speeches with rock concerts featuring Hitler salutes and National Socialist banners. He created a political platform without membership cards, or an administration. In 1988 Donaldson wrote:

Our fight begins in Europe and will spread all over the White world. There are certain moments in our lives when we grasp the magnitude of our task. I have walked from Antwerp during the first hours of the night when the nationalists gather at the pubs. The marvelous architecture of the cities of Flanders embodies the soul of Europe—sunset in Rotterdam when the lights of the city glitter and we are made welcome by our friends—an afternoon in Stockholm, frost on the ground and thereafter a journey to Gothenburg where the Swedish and Nordic beauty is hypnotizing.

After the death of Ian Stewart Donaldson, a number of memorial concerts have been held and songs dedicated to his memory. In 1996, *Resistance* and *Nordland* issued a memorial album, *The Flame That Never Dies,* in memory of Ian Stewart. For movement people around the world, he is surrounded by a rich mythology.

The mythology of the White Power music network is perpetuated through the ritual celebration of the anniversary of Hitler's birthday on April 20th, and the Day of the Martyrs on December 8th. The 8th of December is the date of The Order's Robert Mathews's death; the date has since become an international memorial day for the White Power world. Its constituents commemorate not only the death of Mathews, but also those of "all White warriors who have fallen in battle." The day also observes the remembrance of imprisoned brothers and sisters around the world. Tributes to dead or imprisoned members of various organizations frequently appear in White Power magazines around the world.

In 1987, a number of White noise magazines and groups launched a campaign in favor of Kev Turner, lead singer of Skullhead, who had received a four-year prison sentence. The martyrs and heroes of the movement are naturally a central theme in the lyrics of the White noise groups. The following text is by Division S and dedicated to Robert J. Mathews, leader of the American revolutionary group the Order, and the Swedish volunteers in Waffen-SS division Nordland:

> A tribute to the men of Nordland, a tribute to Robert J, a tribute to the struggle, and a tribute to Brotherhood. You are now seated around the table of Valhalla, victims of a corrupt and evil world. To some you are just a memory, but in our hearts you live on.

The National Socialists of the prewar and the wartime period—particularly the soldiers in the Waffen SS—are important themes in the music, as in the song "Perssons Unit," by Swastika:

> Then I think about our future and the ones that will come after us
> Then I wish them to be strong, so they can handle the fight
> I wish they were free and not slaves like us
> I want to see hard men and women, yes that's what the north will
> be like
>
> A couple of hundred Swedish men stood up like one
> A couple of hundred Swedish men, their memory still lives on.
> They were the voice of Sweden, when cowardice was the rule
> around here
> They fought against the evil Zion, who feed on our people.

Together with two other songs—"Faith, Hope and Struggle," by Storm and "Banner of Blood," by Vit Aggression—"Perssons Unit" was dedicated to Gösta Hallberg-Cuula, an important hero in the mythology of the prewar Swedish National Socialists. In 1926, at the age of 16, Gösta Hallberg-Cuula joined Sweden's Fascist Struggle Organization. During the 1930s, he was a party functionary of the NSAP/SSS. In 1932 he was arrested for his political activities. He took part in a protest against the play *God's Green Fields,* in which God was presented as a man of color. Gösta Hallberg-Cuula was the first Swede to enlist as a volunteer in the Finnish Winter War and in the so-called "War of Continuation." During the Winter War he lost one eye. He was killed in action in Finland in May 1942. His death marked the beginning of one of the longest traditions in the history of the Swedish National Socialists: the ceremony on April 14th at his grave in Stockholm.

The memory of imprisoned or dead members of extreme nationalist/National Socialist/racist groups is honored in the music. Skullhead, a British band, was founded in 1984, to spread the truth about the death of Peter Mathewson, a good friend of the band members, who was killed when a group of Blacks attacked a group of skinheads in London. Another important figure from the cadres of White noise musicians (apart from Ian Stewart) is Joe Rowan, the singer of the American band Nordic Thunder, who was killed in October 1994. He was an innocent bystander in a convenience store robbery.

In the lyrics, the combination of the European and the American race ideological traditions becomes evident. As in Swastika's "In Hoc Signo Vinces" (In this sign we will be victorious), which was taken from the seminal essay of the same name by George Lincoln Rockwell of the American Nazi Party:

It as been our symbol since time immemorial
brought power and strength in the battle for the men from the north
lightning and thunder has followed its trace
happiness and light, a new dawn will break

In Hoc Signo Vinces,
In Hoc—In Hoc—In Hoc Signo Vinces

1889—our leader [Hitler] was born,
he held the banner high for freedom and breed
George Lincoln Rockwell continued our battle
a global holy racial war

1994—Svastika is our name
we lead an army in the fight for our land
we are the last ones of our kind—unbeatable because...
Tomorrow belongs to us.

In this song, we find the SS-man, the modern-day race warrior, and the Nordic Ásatrú (Odinist) mythology—all central elements in the racist discourse.

Mark Hamm, in his book *American Skinheads,* points to the importance of the music in the socialization process of the activists, and concludes: "This transformation process occurs at a metaphysical level through a sort of seat of the pants shamanism. That is, players in white power bands transform themselves from ordinary musicians to extraordinary ones through the expression of highly forbidden messages and symbols that are part of a larger and widely known consciousness. Listeners to this music, in turn, seek to transform themselves from their ordinary realities to something wider, something that enlarges them as people. They become skinheads."

The modern racist propagandist is not, as was his 1930s predecessor, a party strategist or skilled speaker. Rather, he is a combination of rock star, speaker, and street fighter. It's no longer a question of music *for* the National Socialists/racists, but rather a music that *is* National Socialism and racism in itself. A study of the choreography of the White noise concerts makes it evident that the singer walks stiffly like a speaker back and forth over the stage. He is the high priest of a ritual celebration, the leader who controls the public in the very same way the National Socialist speaker of the 1930s did.

White noise music and the racist/extreme nationalist counterculture has grown during the past ten years. Its members are predominantly born in the 1960s and 1970s. George Eric Hawthorne explains their outlook:

> It came out of their hearts. It came out of feeling neglected. White Youth today are abandoned before they are even born. So many millions of them are abandoned while they are still in the womb. By the time they are born judgment has been passed on them. They are guilty of the crimes of their ancestors. They've held the world back. They enslaved the planet. They are the evil people.

Today, White Power music is making considerable inroads into youth culture—particularly in Europe. In Sweden, for example, a recent school survey demonstrated that Swedish White Power music has found an incredible 30 percent share of the youth music market. With this success has come an unprecedented inflow of wealth, which is shared within national movements and, to a remarkable degree, through the international network of racialist groups.

In 1997, the lucrative music market occasioned a kind of civil war that resulted in several deaths, a bomb sent to a Swedish cabinet minister, and sundry other mayhem that occurred as the alliance of the Swedish label Nordland and the American Resistance Records were challenged by the British Combat 18, the heir to Ian Stewart's Blood and Honour organization. C18, as it was called, was attempting to force bands associated with the Nordland/Resistance axis to leave those labels and perform for C18's labels. In the end, C18 went down to defeat when its leaders were imprisoned for murder.

By 1998, the Swedish half of the Nordland/Resistance axis were investing their money in rural properties to pursue the dream of a separate communal existence. Resistance, after a period of uncertainty following George Eric Hawthorne's defection and the tax raids on Resistance properties in Canada and the United States, is in 1999 showing signs of renewed vigor under the auspices of the National Alliance.

—*Heléne Lööw, Stockholm University, Sweden*

See also: American Nazi Party; Church of the Creator; Hawthorne, George Eric; Hitler, Adolf; Mathews, Robert; National Alliance; Odinism; Order; Rockwell, George Lincoln.

Further reading: Katrine Fangen, *Skinheads in Red, White and Blue: A Report from the Inside, Youth Research Report* (April 1995); Mark S. Hamm, *American Skinheads: The Criminology and Control of Hate Crime* (Westport, CT: Praeger, 1993); Erik Jensen, "International Nazi Co-operation; A Terrorist-Oriented Network," in Tore Bjørgo and Rob Witte, *Racist Violence in Europe* (Basingstoke: Macmillan, 1993); Laszlo Kurti, "Rocking the State: Youth and Rock Music culture in Hungary, 1976–1990," *East European Politics and Societies* 5:3 (1991); Anna-Lena Lodenius, "Blood, and Honour and Blue and Yellow Rock," *Arbetaren* 17 (1994); Anna-Lena Lodenius and Per Wikström, "Nazism Behind a Viking Mask, *Kommunalarbetaren* 6 (1994); Heléne Lööw, "White Power—Dark History," *Uppväxtvillkor* 3 (1993); Heléne Lööw, "Racist Violence and Criminal Behaviour in Sweden: Myths and Reality," *Terrorism and Political Violence* 7:1 (spring 1995); Heléne Lööw, "The Fight Against ZOG—Anti-Semitism Among the Modern Race Ideologists," *Historisk Tidskrift* 1 (1996); Heléne Lööw, "White Power Rock 'n' Roll—A Growing Industry," in Jeffrey Kaplan and Tore Bjørgo, *Nation and Race: The Developing Euro-American Racist Subculture* (Boston: Northeastern University Press, 1998); Joe Pearce, *Skrewdriver: The First Ten Years* (London: Skrewdriver Services, 1987).

White Students' Union   *See* Aryan Nations; White Aryan Resistance.

GERALD WINROD   In the Depression years, the Rev. Gerald Winrod was one of the most stridently anti-Semitic voices in the nation. His antipathy toward Jews was based on the twin pillars of the Bible and the anti-Semitic forgery *Protocols of the Elders of Zion*. This unswerving view led him into an inadvisable embrace of Nazi Germany in the 1930s. It was then that the so-called "Jayhawk Nazi's" difficulties began.

Before his turn to political activism, Gerald Winrod was a fundamentalist preacher in Wichita, Kansas. His primary issues in those years were a staunch opposition to "modernism" in general and the theory of evolution in particular. Toward this end, in 1925 the Rev. Winrod assembled a meeting of like-minded individuals to form the Defenders of the Christian Faith in Salinas, Kansas. The next year the organization issued the premier issue of the *Defender,* a magazine that in various forms the Winrod family would publish for the next five decades. The *Defender*, together with Winrod's tireless travels, brought him to the attention of a national audience.

The Depression and Franklin Roosevelt's election to the presidency in 1932 heightened Winrod's political concerns. He condemned the New Deal as not only ineffective, but as a conspiracy designed to rob Americans of their freedom. It did not take Winrod long to identify the source of this conspiracy. He concluded, based on his reading of the *Protocols of the Elders of Zion,* that Jews were conspiring to control the United States by infecting it with liberalism. He placed this perceived Jewish threat squarely within the context of the standard conspiratorial scenarios of the far right, identifying the illuminati and the Jews (among a host of others) as direct instruments of Satan on earth. From the crucifixion of Christ to the torture of Russian Christians and the plowing under of Kansas wheat in a hungry nation, Winrod said that a "Jewish elite had played satanic roles in a divinely directed drama now drawing to a close." The presence of such Jewish figures as Bernard Baruch in the circle of Roosevelt's advisers led Winrod to this judgment. As a platform for his political views, Winrod founded the *Revealer,* a newspaper that was published from 1934 to 1937 and that reached more than 100,000 readers at the height of its popularity.

Although he was initially critical of Hitler, Winrod came away from a visit to Nazi Germany in 1934 with a favorable impression of the dictator and his new regime. Winrod was able to overlook the Nazi movement's manifest paganism because of what he perceived to be its violent opposition to the Antichrist, communist Russia, and the Satanic Jews whose hidden hand he detected behind Soviet communism. Although the *Revealer* series detailing Winrod's visit to Nazi Germany took pains to stress that the "Hitlerite dictatorship" (as he termed it) could not be transplanted to America due to Americans' inborn love of freedom and the guarantees of individual liberty enshrined in the U.S. Constitution, the Roosevelt administration indicted Winrod in the Sedition Trial of 1942. Charges were eventually dropped after the war when the long-running trial was halted by an exasperated federal judge.

Early on, Winrod came to champion Christian Identity—a faith he may have passed on to the most influential Identity pastor of the twentieth century, Wesley Swift. Winrod's Identity legacy was inherited by his sons, who attempted to carry on the remnants of the Winrod ministry.

Gerald Winrod died in 1957. His sons continued the ministry and the *Defender* magazine well into the 1980s, though the magazine gradually lost the militant racism and anti-Semitism that was the Winrod hallmark. Gordon Winrod was the most outspoken of the sons, publishing the *Winrod Letter,* an anti-Semitic, mimeographed newsletter of limited circulation.

Another son, David Winrod, had a brief moment of notoriety when he led a small contingent of transplanted Kansans to Ketchikan, Alaska, in 1991. The intrepid homesteaders found the climate chilly—both in political and meteorological terms—and soon returned to the more hospitable plains of Kansas.

When the Defenders of the Faith ministry at last closed its doors, the organization had become, quite literally, a retirement community in Wichita. The location, however, was in the middle of a once-White, working-class neighborhood that had fallen on exceedingly hard times. The property was sold, and the surviving Defenders of the Faith entered more conventional retirement homes.

See also: Christian Identity; Swift, Wesley.

Further reading: Anon., *Fire By Night and Cloud By Day: The Amazing History of the Defenders of the Christian Faith* (Wichita, KS: Mertmont Publishers, 1966); Michael Barkun, *Religion and the Racist Right* (Chapel Hill: University of North Carolina Press, 1994); John George and Laird Wilcox, *Nazis, Communists, Klansmen, and Others on the Fringe* (Buffalo, NY: Prometheus Books, 1992); Martin E. Marty, *Modern American Religion Volume 2: The Noise and the Conflict 1919–1941* (Chicago: University of Chicago Press, 1991), pp. 265–67; Martin E. Marty, ed., *Modern American Protestantism and its World, Vol. 10: Fundamentalism and Evangelicalism* (Munich: K.G. Sauer, 1993); J. Gordon Melton, *Religious Leaders of America* (Detroit: Gale Research Inc., 1991); Phillip Reese, *Biographical Dictionary of the Extreme Right Since 1890* (New York: Simon & Schuster, 1990); Leo Ribuffo, *The Old Christian Right* (Philadelphia: Temple University Press, 1983); Gerald B. Winrod, *Hitler in Prophecy* (Wichita, KS: Defender Publishers, 1933); Gerald B. Winrod, *Adam Weishaupt: A Human Devil* (no publication data, c. 1935).

WOMEN (NORWEGIAN)   There are about 80 women in the Norwegian rightist underground, if one includes the less active sympathizers. About 25 percent of these women may be reckoned as activists. The women constitute some 30 percent of the total number of activists in the rightist underground. The females are in general much younger than the leading male activists. In 1993–1994, there were several partnerships between women at the age of 16–18 and men at the age of 30–32. Most of the females are between 16 and 24 years old, whereas the males are between 16 and 34 years old. During 1995–1996, several young men have joined the underground, so the age difference between the sexes is somewhat normalized.

Women in the Norwegian rightist underground during the early 1990s played subordinate or passive roles in comparison with the men. For some females this was a result of their lack of self-confidence, as well as their passive acceptance of being secondary in relation to the men. For other women this was clearly not so. They were tough and extroverted, they disliked the men's raucous behavior, and they did not like the way the men treated them. The different gender role-patterns partly reflect the different degree to which the women viewed themselves as equal to the men. Some women talked about not feeling oppressed by the males, while others held that the men were dominant figures but that it was no worse there than in other gangs.

Even the more self-conscious women who disagreed with parts of the men's practices acted rather passively in comparison with the males. They often had their private talks in the background, or they sat together with the males and laughed at what they said or what they did. Very young and inexperienced males often played the same passive role as the women in their first phase as participants, but quickly felt comfortable and became more active after a while. In contrast, even women who had participated for years would continue to play passive roles. Most of them did not participate as frequently as the men at the underground's monthly pub meeting. Some women said openly that these gatherings were of little value to them. Thus, the underground gave a clear impression of being dominated and defined by the men.

Some of the women who felt disappointed by the way the men excluded them resigned. They stayed within the underground, but did not participate that often, or they accepted their less-visible position. Others left the militant underground, but continued to play more ideological roles by writing for the nationalist monthly *Fritt Forum*. Some females, being more convinced of National

Socialism than most of the other women, acted independent of all the underground's groups. These women have contacts with some of the leading rightist activists on a personal basis. They variously explain their adherence to an ideology that is radically different from the way National Socialist men belonging to the rightist underground expound their views. One woman says that for her, the most important factor is the National Socialist morality. She thus views National Socialism as a private affair, as it deals with family life; the upbringing of children; the prohibition of abortion, prostitution, and pornography; and the emphasis on an anti-materialistic lifestyle.

These more ideologically convinced women, who left the underground after a while because they found that the raucous skinheads dominated it too much, speak of the underground and its participants as "nonserious." In particular, they have a negative view of many of the youngest women of the underground. They consider these women "cheap" and immature, and too passively accepting of their underprivileged position in relation to the men. It seems like two alternative routes, for the ideologically convinced woman is either working together with the editor of *Fritt Forum* or is making contact with elder nationalists or National Socialists. A third route is to join that part of the Ásatrú society that Knut Westland, also the leader of Norway's Patriot Unionist party, controls.

Most of the women are active within the underground as long as their relationship with a particular male is working. A few women remain within the underground after the breakup of their relationships. In 1993 some women saw the need for women meeting without men being present so as to gain more self-confidence. In 1995, they initiated Valkyria, a separate group for women in the movement. One of their aims was to persuade women to remain within the underground, despite the breakup of their partnerships.

What separates the females' roles from the males' roles is that more men have positions of leadership, and no men participate only as partners, or define themselves as politically neutral, as some women do. After the emergence of a separate women's group, some women joined the underground directly, without having been affiliated with a male activist beforehand.

In 1996, some new visible gender role-patterns emerged among women. Young and inexperienced women still played more passive and subordinate roles. However, the new trend is that women take part in all actions. These female activists are militant nationalist women, mainly members of the Valkyria group. Their reason for joining is political, and they take part in all kinds of actions. For example, they join strategic meetings with the males, they undertake weapons training, and they organize their own study meetings and underground actions. Another role is that of the National Socialist skinhead women, some of whom are members of the group NUNS 88 (Norske unge nasjonalsosialister 88; Norwegian Young National Socialists 88). The militant nationalist women label these women "nonserious" because they drink a lot and give Nazi salutes. Both the militant nationalist women and the National Socialist skinhead women partake in major actions of the underground. In addition there are sympathizers, that is, women who do not participate directly in underground activities.

Women typically make their first contacts with the underground because of political ideas, such as being against immigration, because of their attraction to a male activist, and/or because of the excitement connected to this secretive and potentially dangerous movement.

The situation is very tense for both male and female activists as a result of attacks from the outside, police surveillance, and frustration within the movement. This pressure has had an impact on romantic relationships as well, with the effect that few couples last within the movement. Nevertheless, there are several couples who live together, and several have children. Some couples have broken up, though, resulting in there being a few single mothers within the movement. The fathers of their children are males within the underground, except for one female who became a mother long before she entered the rightist underground.

The female right-wing activists often experience more severe conflicts with parents because of their entrance into the militant underground than do male activists. Some of the women have broken the ties to their families, whereas others remain in contact (though often with considerable conflict). According to a leading right-wing woman, the parents usually calm down when the girls become 18, as then they have become of age, and can according to the law decide for themselves.

The women are afraid of being attacked by antifascist opponents. All of them carry mobile phones, so that they can call up males if necessary. They carry tear gas, or wear shoes with steel caps to protect themselves. If someone attacks them, they say they want to fight back.

Some women have a few reservations against the militant profile of the rightist underground. Nevertheless, they see the need for

protection and, if attacked, they want to know how to defend themselves. Most of the women do, however, support militant strategies.
This attitude from the women is new in the Norwegian rightist
underground. Instead of being hesitant to endorse the militant
actions of the men, they actively support such a policy.

—*Katrine Fangen, University of Oslo, Norway*

See also: Odinism; Valkyria.

Further reading: Katrine Fangen, "Separate or Equal? The Emergence of an
All Female Group in the Norwegian Rightist Underground," *Terrorism and
Political Violence* 9:3 (fall 1997); Katrine Fangen, "Living Out Our Ethnic
Instincts: Ideological Beliefs Among Right-Wing Activists in Norway," in
Jeffrey Kaplan and Tore Bjørgo, *Brotherhoods of Nation and Race: The
Emergence of a Euro-American Racist Subculture* (Boston: Northeastern
University Press, 1998); Katrine Fangen, "Skinheads I rødt, hvitt og blått
En sosiologisk studie fra innsiden [Skinheads in red, white, and blue: A
sociological study from "inside"] (1994).

WORLD UNION OF NATIONAL SOCIALISTS   In political terms,
the World Union of National Socialists (WUNS) never realized its
ambition to link the scattered National Socialist faithful into a centralized global network, but it was a dream that, for a moment in
the 1960s, appeared to have some potential as a vehicle for facilitat-
ing communications between the scattered tribes of National
Socialist parties from around the world. The story of how the World
Union of National Socialists came into being, and of its long, slow
demise, is an object lesson in the hopes and grim realities of the
postwar National Socialist movement.

In the immediate aftermath of World War II, the National
Socialist movement was shattered. The Third Reich lay in ruins,
and German Nazi leaders were dead, put to trial, or on the run.
Overtly National Socialist parties were banned throughout Europe,
and Germany itself underwent a stringent de-Nazification.

Only in the later 1940s did National Socialist–oriented groups
begin to reemerge, and these had to contend with the enormity of
the Holocaust in their efforts to gain political legitimacy and popular support. Under such unpromising conditions, it should come as
no surprise that National Socialism failed to attract the "best and
the brightest" to its ranks. In fact, despite the small handful of
capable leaders and the even smaller number of capable adherents,

the "movement" was composed primarily of egocentric mini-führers whose vision stretched no further than their own national borders and whose time was spent in constant and pointless bickering.

Against this backdrop, there arose a few who envisioned something greater, but, lacking a charismatic figure under whose leadership the distant dream of National Socialist unity could be achieved, these were little more than pipe dreams. It was only in 1960 that such a leader emerged in, of all places, the United States—George Lincoln Rockwell.

Rockwell was a newcomer to the scene. He formed the American Nazi Party only in 1959. Yet even from that unpromising beginning, Rockwell hoped for a movement that would be global in scope. The vehicle he suggested in 1959 was the clumsily named World Union of Free Enterprise National Socialists. The idea went nowhere, but Rockwell's efforts caught the eye of Britain's Colin Jordan, a National Socialist whose roots stretch to the prewar fascist movement of Arnold Leese, perhaps the most extreme anti-Semite of his day and the rival of the better-known British fascist leader Oswald Mosely. Jordan initiated a correspondence with Rockwell in 1960 or early 1961. Jordan then introduced the young American führer to such key European National Socialists as the French mystic Savitri Devi and the German true believer Bruno Ludtke. As the correspondence among them deepened, they decided to come together in a secret conclave to lay the groundwork for the creation of a unified international National Socialist movement.

The meeting was duly held in Great Britain in 1962, though it did not remain secret for long. Nonetheless, the decisions that were taken, known collectively as the Cotswold Agreement (so named for the location of the meeting), laid the basis for the creation of the World Union of National Socialists.

Rockwell soon emerged as the unchallenged leader of WUNS. Devi added encouragement and schooled Rockwell in the importance of religiosity in the creation of a new Reich. Jordan, the original choice as leader, soon found his natural place as a sycophantic follower of the younger and more dynamic Rockwell. He was rewarded with the title of European Commander. Ludtke, precluded from any aspirations for leadership by the strict anti-Nazi laws in Germany, as well as by his own frail constitution, emerged as something of a father figure for Rockwell. He offered sage advice, wrote long letters to keep up the American's spirits when all seemed lost (as it often did in the poverty, chaos, and madness of the American Nazi Party headquarters in Arlington, Virginia), and, perhaps of greatest import from Rockwell's point of view, provided a living link to the German National Socialism that Rockwell idealized.

Such were the World Union of National Socialists' beginnings, but the road was far from smooth. Two interrelated obstacles inhibited WUNS's growth: the unwillingness of many local leaders to cede any portion of their authority to a transnational National Socialist movement, and a deeply felt resistance to according an American a position of leadership in the world of National Socialism. Memories of World War II remained fresh, and for many, the role of the United States in bringing down the Third Reich simply could not be forgiven. Typical of these views was the ambivalence of the Swedish National Socialist leader Göran Assar Oredsson, who in 1956 founded the Nordiska Rikspartiet in Malmö, Sweden:

> I can never forgive the USA's war against Europe, even if the guilt is not to be put on the US National Socialists....
>
> But I want to stress that my friendship with Lincoln Rockwell was total, and so was our co-operation with him as a person and American NS-leader.

As to the local chapters of the World Union of National Socialists, Dr. Frederick J. Simonelli describes the situation well:

> On the American side of the Atlantic, WUNS activities divided into three segments: the United States, which was essentially Rockwell's ANP, Canada, and South America. WUNS efforts in South America bore most fruit in Chile and Argentina, where open and active WUNS chapters flourished. In Chile, Franz Pfeiffer, a former SS-Colonel and the last commander of Hitler's "Leibstandarte," drew on large numbers of Nazi exiles to create an active—and, to the Chilean government, an extremely dangerous—National Socialist party, the Partido Nacionalsocialista Chileno. Pfeiffer impressed Rockwell and he suggested to Colin Jordan that Pfeiffer might be a suitable WUNS continental commander for all of South America. Pfeiffer's performance in a potentially devastating crisis particularly stirred Rockwell. Three months after being named leader of WUNS-Chile, Chilean authorities arrested Pfeiffer's closest friend and long-time comrade, Werner Rauff, and extradited him to West Germany on war crimes charges. West Germany accused Rauff, a top aide to Adolf Eichmann during the war, with personally murdering 90,000 Jews. Pfeiffer did not abandon Rauff, which impressed Rockwell. Instead, he openly defended him and hired a Chilean lawyer to fight the extradition order. In a letter to Rockwell during the crisis, Pfeiffer

even hinted that he was considering employing physical force to free Rauff—a suggestion that certainly would only have elevated his stature in Rockwell's eyes. In a letter to Bruno Ludtke, Rockwell described Pfeiffer as "quite a leader" who "will make history some day." In late 1964, the Chilean government outlawed Pfeiffer's party and WUNS-Chile. Pfeiffer refused to moderate his statements or curtail his activities and was arrested and jailed in February of 1965.

As Chilean authorities shut down WUNS-Chile, Rockwell turned his South American focus to Argentina, where Horst Eichmann, Adolf Eichmann's son, headed the Argentine National Socialist Party. Eichmann had a substantial following within the German expatriate community in Argentina and a recognized name worldwide, making him very useful to Rockwell, but he was never as fully loyal to Rockwell as Franz Pfeiffer. Young Eichmann believed, with good cause, that he had greater visibility among South American Nazis than did Rockwell. In his view, a new Fuehrer would more likely emerge from the German enclaves of South America than from suburban Virginia. Rockwell tolerated Eichmann because his name had value, but he never really controlled him. After 1965, WUNS in South America did not reach the potential that Rockwell expected of it under Franz Pfeiffer.

WUNS-Canada was limited by aggressive anti-Nazi governmental action, including vigorous prosecution of WUNS operatives under laws designed to control racist and revolutionary political movements. Early Rockwell efforts in Canada, from 1961 to 1965, were in cooperation with Andre Bellfeuille's Canadian Nazi Party (CNP). Rockwell appointed Bellfeuille's deputy, Janos Pall, the first International Secretary of the World Union of Free Enterprise National Socialists (WUFENS), who then helped Rockwell with the initial organization of WUNS. Bellfeuille's CNP was the first WUNS-Canada chapter. Infighting among the Canadian racist right fragmented the small support base of the movement. By 1965, Rockwell faced the unpleasant task of choosing among diminished and rival racist groups to be the WUNS designate—Bellfeuille's CNP, Jacques Taylor's Canadian National Socialist Party, and Don Andrews's Western Guard Party. Instead, Rockwell took a chance on a dynamic newcomer to the racist right political wars, John Beattie. Selecting Beattie as leader of WUNS-Canada—though practical political concerns negated the actual designation of Beattie as such—proved a wise decision. Ludtke guided Rockwell to the right choice and wrote of the young Beattie, "That is the face of the Canadian Hitler."

By early 1966, Beattie had consolidated much of the racist right around his leadership and was one of the few bright spots in Rockwell's world order. Rockwell met regularly with his protégé and reported to Colin Jordan, "Our Canadian leader, John Beattie is doing absolutely fabulously—in fact, the most professional and thorough job now going on in any other country outside of your own" (the latter comment a concession to Jordan's fragile ego). "He is religiously studying and putting into action the course in legal, political and psychological warfare we have been publishing.... He suffers from the usual agony of lack of, or no funds, but manages to continue nevertheless." Rockwell was convinced that Beattie, his "magnificent young leader," would someday "make history in Canada."

Europe contained the largest concentration of WUNS chapters. Three chapters—Hungary, Italy, and Switzerland—appear to have been little more than chapters in name, with no active organization and limited, or nonexistent, public programs. WUNS found particularly fertile ground in Scandinavia, forging working bonds with active indigenous National Socialists in Sweden, Denmark, and Iceland. In Sweden, Göran Assar Oredsson's Nordic Reich Partywas already deeply involved in extended legal disputes with the Swedish government over the distribution of anti-Semitic literature when Rockwell contacted him about joining WUNS. Oredsson's emergence as a National Socialist advocate in Sweden predated Rockwell's own conversion to Nazism and the formation of both the ANP and WUNS. While Oredsson maintained the independence of his Nordic Reich Party, he cooperated fully with Rockwell and Jordan on all strategic matters concerning the National Socialist revival in Scandinavia.

In Denmark, Sven Salicath, leader of the Danish National Socialist Workers Party, was an enthusiastic organizer of WUNS-Denmark and a devoted Rockwell disciple. Bernhard Haarde led an active WUNS chapter in Iceland that claimed over 300 members. Sweden's Göran Oredsson helped introduce Rockwell and WUNS to the incipient National Socialist movement in Iceland.

Ireland and Spain had moderately active chapters, but failed to meet Rockwell's expectations primarily because of strong government opposition. The failure of the Irish National Union particularly disappointed Rockwell. The Irish Nazis had expressed tacit approval of the principles contained in the Cotswold Agreements, but refused to publicly endorse them. They pleaded with WUNS's European leader, Colin Jordan, to intercede with Rockwell and to explain to the Commander that they were too "young and weak" to carry the movement to the streets. Rockwell patiently replied, "I can thoroughly understand their position about being young and weak, but as all of us have found, the way to get old and strong is not to remain in hiding in cellars." It wasn't until Bernard E. Horgan took command of WUNS-Ireland in 1966 that political and propaganda activities became visible, though the Irish Nazis never met the lofty expectations Rockwell held for them.

A German expatriate and Third Reich veteran, Friedrich Kuhfuss, organized and led WUNS-Spain. While Kuhfuss remained the de facto leader of WUNS-Spain, he put forth his deputy, Antonio Madrano, a native Spaniard, as the nominal leader to avoid the appearance of foreign, especially German, intrusion into Spain's internal politics. Rockwell's and Jordan's WUNS efforts in Spain tried to build on an earlier Spanish National Socialist organization, Joven Europa España, which had been encouraged and nurtured by Sweden's Oredsson.

England, France, and Belgium boasted the largest, strongest, and most active WUNS chapters in Europe. Although this entry does not attempt to quantify the numerical strength of WUNS chapters, the description of any WUNS chapter as "large and active" must be understood in a relative light. As Frederick Simonelli accurately notes, at no time during the period under examination did a WUNS-affiliated political party establish electoral significance in *any* country. WUNS supporters outside the United States, as with the ANP within the United States, are more accurately numbered in the hundreds than in the thousands. Their significance, as with Rockwell and the ANP in the United States, lies more with the sustenance of a virulent and violent racist and anti-Semitic political impulse and antidemocratic political tradition than with any real potential to seize political power through legitimate means.

Whatever fleeting hopes the World Union of National Socialists may have had to unite the tiny world of explicitly National Socialist movements effectively died on August 25, 1967, when a disgruntled American Nazi named John Patler ambushed Rockwell as he emerged from a Maryland laundromat and killed him. The National Socialist world reacted with shocked disbelief. This sense of shock and grief is nowhere better expressed than by the words of Swedish leader Göran Assar Oredsson:

> I was on my way down south [when]...I stopped to pick up the evening papers. The headlines cried out to me:
>
> "He wanted to be America's Hitler" (*Afonbladet*);
>
> "[A] Sniper killed America's Hitler" (*Kvallsposten*);
>
> "He wanted to be a new Hitler.... His dream ended here" (*Expressed*).
>
> At that movement I wanted to believe—yes wish—that I was dreaming, that I had read wrong. BUT NO, It came clear to me that George Lincoln Rockwell, the USA's National Socialist leader, was no more among us. Again I had to face how a friend, an ideological companion and battle comrade had fallen in our united battlefield in the struggle against our united enemy.
>
> In movements like this...there are no barriers and distances between the different continents. The distance to a friend and battle companion is never more far away then the distance to your own hearth. It was sometime during 1957 that I first came into contact with Rockwell. It was from letters. Rockwell's letters were many and long. My English was surely not what it should be, but with a friend's help our correspondence was the best you could ask for. Rockwell's letters revealed a brain as sharp as a knife.... He gave in his letters almost philosophical explanations and had the most interesting explanations...regarding National Socialism and it's [sic] ideologists. Why he had the swastika as a symbol, why he called his party Nazi etc. etc.
>
> ...I first judged him as a deskfighter. Yes even as a fruitless theoretician. But I was soon to change my mind. It was when his papers, *The Rockwell Report, National Socialist Bulletin* and *Stormtrooper* arrived. From pictures and articles, his movement proved to be the most brave and hard fighting Stromtroopers as any one could ask for. And everywhere in these pictures of the struggle, the leader Rockwell was in the front, as the leader, the speaker, the organizer and the hero, when it comes to courage and fighting spirit.

Matt Keohl, Rockwell's successor in the American movement, sought to inherit Rockwell's mantle of World Union of National Socialists leadership, but in this he did no better than he had managed with the American Nazi Party's successor, the National Socialist White People's Party. Under Koehl, the NSWPP soon began to fragment, and the World Union of National Socialists on the global stage in truth fared no better.

That the World Union of National Socialists carried on, at least in name, through the 1990s is testament to the importance adherents gave to the idea of National Socialist unity in the face of an unremittingly hostile world. Moreover, as Rockwell found in his last years, the fantasy of a global Reich offered a healthy diversion from the mediocrity, madness, and failure that were the reality of the national movements. In the correspondence of distant comrades, one could dream of far-off lands, of orders given and secret information received in a network that, with a bit of imagination, almost seemed to be a kind of government in exile awaiting the day when economic collapse or racial animosity would bring the slumbering White masses to the Swastika banner.

However, the ironic effect of the propaganda churned out by the disparate local National Socialist groups was to convince foreign readers of the proposition that the grass was definitely greener "over there." That is, that all of the real action and the hope for a fighting National Socialist organization that would in time threaten the hated status quo were always in another country. It was precisely to this phenomenon that the Swedish National Socialist leader Göran Assar Oredsson alludes in his eulogy to Rockwell, and it was this sense of local impotence that further marginalized the national-level activities of the World Union of National Socialists.

Nevertheless, Rockwell and the WUNS in its 1960s heyday claimed the power to make and unmake National Socialist leaders from around the world, to solicit the support of the "old fighters" of the original German National Socialist state, and to carefully plan for the coming upheavals by creating grandiose blueprints for the assumption of power and by awarding positions of prestige to the faithful in the future National Socialist utopia.

The World Union of National Socialists was a dream whose time would never come. When in the mid-1990s the organization was allowed to lapse, it was a clear-enough sign to anyone who still cared enough to listen, that a dream had died unmourned.

See also: American Nazi Party; Devi, Savitri; Jordan, Colin; Koehl, Matt; Ludtke, Bruno; National Socialist White People's Party; Rockwell, George Lincoln.

Further reading: Jeffrey Kaplan, "The Postwar Paths of Occult National Socialism: From Rockwell and Madole to Manson," in Jeffrey Kaplan and Heléne Lööw, *Rejected and Suppressed Knowledge: The Racist Right and the Cultic Milieu* (Stockholm: Swedish National Council of Crime Prevention, 1999); Frederick J. Simonelli, "The World Union of National Socialists and the Post-War Transatlantic Nazi Revival," in Jeffrey Kaplan and Tore Bjørgo, *Nation and Race* (Boston: Northeastern University Press, 1998); Frederick J. Simonelli, *American Fuehrer: George Lincoln Rockwell and the American Nazi Party* (Champaign: University of Illinois Press, 1999).

WOTANISM (JUNGIAN)   The end of the 20th century has witnessed attempts by contemporary men and women to resurrect a wide array of pre-Christian religions. The instinctual or atavistic nature of heathen religion itself is nothing new, and many of these "revivalists" have experienced its magnetic allure. The gods of the North seem particularly prone to stirring feelings that may unexpectedly resurge among the descendants of those who once worshipped them.

According to Carl Jung, it is not always modern man who actively seeks to consciously revive a pre-Christian worldview, but rather he may become involuntarily possessed by the archetypes of the gods in question. In March 1936, Jung published a remarkable essay in the *Neue Schweizer Rundschau* that remains highly controversial to the present day. Originally written only a few years after the National Socialists came to power in Germany, it is entitled "Wotan."

Jung states in no uncertain terms his conviction that the Nazi movement is a result of "possession" by the god Wotan on a massive scale. He traces elements of the heathen revival back to various German writers, Nietzsche especially, who he feels were "seized" by Wotan and became transmitters for aspects of the god's archetypal nature. He states:

> It is curious, to say the least of it…that an old god of storm and frenzy, the long quiescent Wotan, should awake, like an extinct volcano, to a new activity, in a country that had long been supposed to have outgrown the Middle Ages.

Jung would some years later reveal his conviction that both Nietzsche and he himself had experienced personal visits in their dreams from the ghostly procession of the "Wild Hunt," the German equivalent of the *Oskorei*.

In the "Wotan" essay he goes on to describe *Jugendbewegung* (Youth Movement) sacrifices of sheep to Wotan on the solstice, and explains in detail his belief that Germany is being led away from Christianity via "possession" by the ancient deity. Jung concludes his explication with the prediction that while Germany in the 1930s may be under the specific sway of Wotan's more furious attributes, in the "course of the next few years or decades" other, more "ecstatic and mantic" sides of the god's archetype will also manifest themselves.

—Michael Moynihan, Blood Axis

See also: Odinism; Religion of Nature.

Further reading: Carl Jung, "Wotan," in *C. G. Jung, The Collected Works*, v. 10, Bollingen Series, XX (New York: Pantheon, 1964); Jeffrey Kaplan, *Radical Religion in America: Millenarian Movements from the Far Right to the Children of Noah* (Syracuse, NY: Syracuse University Press, 1997); Michael Moynihan and Didrik Søderlind, *Lords of Chaos* (Venice, CA: Feral House, 1998).

WOTANSVOLK Wotansvolk (Wotan's Folk) is a propaganda center for racial Odinism established at St. Maries, Idaho, in 1995 by a creative troika, David Lane, Katja Lane, and Ron McVan. Wotan is the ancient German name for Odin, a leading warrior God and Master of Mysteries in the pre-Christian Norse pantheon. To Wotansvolk, Wotan symbolizes "the essential soul and spirit of the Aryan folk made manifest." As an iron-willed warrior God, Wotan is said to instill in the White race the determination and qualities necessary to arise victoriously in the ongoing struggle for Aryan survival and prosperity. Thus the acronym Will of the Aryan Nation, WOTAN. Wotansvolk cast their work as a continuation of the efforts of turn-of-the century Ariosophists like Guido von List, philosophers like Friedrich Nietzsche, and psychoanalysts like Carl Gustaf Jung, to return Aryan man to his perceived true nature.

Wotansvolk teaches that each race is by nature unique and given distinct qualities truly their own. To survive and evolve along the desired path of racial greatness, a race must develop a high level of "folk consciousness." Each race is said to possess a spiritual heritage understood as a Jungian collective unconscious. Engraved in each racial member are powerful archetypes that could be reached through rituals and ceremonies developed by the ancestors in times immemorial. These archetypes are the Gods of the Blood, who will exist as long as there are living members of the race. When the aboriginal Aryan culture was suppressed by universal Christianity, a process of degeneration began and the folk consciousness gradually diminished. As the Gods of the Blood are transmitted genetically, they remained alive though mainly lay dormant through the centuries of Christian dominion. Forced underground, the ancient Aryan knowledge was cultivated by secret societies and esoteric sects until the *volkish* revival of the late 19th century Germany.

The resurgence of Paganism, Wotanism, Ariosophy, and Rune Magic shows, the Wotansvolk argues, that the racial Gods are powerful psychic forces that suddenly can burst forth. Following Jung, Wotansvolk likens Wotan to a long-quiescent volcano that at any moment may forcibly resume its activity. With overwhelming power, the suppressed Gods of the Blood might return with a vengeance, Wotansvolk say, pointing to the ascendancy of Hitler as a historical example: "Nowhere since Viking times has the direct, singular effect of Wotan consciousness been more evident than in the folkish unity of National Socialist Germany."

By reconnecting with the ancestral roots, Wotansvolk aims at nothing less then re-creating the lost Folk Consciousness that it deems necessary to regain in order to destroy the perceived enemies of the race and to restore Aryan independence and racial greatness. Wotansvolk devotes much time to historical research and disseminates much material on pre-Christian Norse religion, traditions, rituals, rune wisdom, and artifacts through pamphlets and the monthly *Focus Fourteen,* published by its own 14 Word Press.

Since its modest beginning, the Wotansvolk has rapidly expanded their reach. In addition to serving likeminded souls in or outside prisons throughout the United States, Wotansvolk has developed contacts with Aryan nationalist pagans and other kindred spirits all over Eastern and Western Europe, Australia, New Zealand, Canada, Argentina, Mexico, Brazil, and Chile.

—*Mattias Gardell, Stockholm University, Sweden*

See also: Lane, David; Lane, Katja; Odinism; Religion of Nature; Wotanism (Jungian).

Further reading: Focus Fourteen (newsletter); Mattias Gardell, *Rasrisk* (Stockholm & Uppsala: Federativs & Swedish Science Press, 1998); David Lane, *Creed of Iron: Wotansvolk Wisdom* (St. Maries, ID: 14 Word Press, 1997).

Gary Yarbrough   *See* Aryan Nations; Order.

FRANCIS PARKER YOCKEY   The key figure in one of the earliest stirrings of the postwar effort to reestablish links between the American and European racialist movements was one Francis Parker Yockey. He was a mysterious figure who was one of the few American supporters of Adolf Hitler and European fascism who was not cowed by the wartime crackdown on fascist sympathizers, which culminated in the great Sedition Trial of 1942.

Yockey's prewar history is remarkably conventional, somewhat belying his rather inflated reputation as a key figure in the Euro-American fascist underground. He was born in 1917 in Chicago, and he received his law degree from Notre Dame, graduating cum laude in 1938. Yockey opposed the American entry in the war, but he nonetheless joined the army, where he served until he received a medical discharge in 1942 on the grounds of gross mental instability, having been diagnosed as suffering from "dementia praecox, paranoid type."

With the end of the war, Yockey accepted a position on the legal staff of the Nuremberg War Crimes Tribunal in 1946. In Germany, he was assigned to the trial of the second-tier Nazi operatives, which took place at Wiesbaden. His pro-Nazi sentiments, however, made his continuing in the position impossible, and in less than a year Yockey resigned and returned to America. He stayed in the United States only briefly, however. Within months he was back in Europe.

Establishing a base in Ireland, Yockey began to write the tome for which he is best known today, *Imperium,* which he would publish under the name of Ulick Varange. This time also saw him involved with the remnants of the wartime fascist network in Britain and throughout Europe, and, according to persistent rumor, with Soviet intelligence as well. With Yockey, anything is possible.

He was apparently a key figure in the formation of the European Liberation Front (ELF)—a profascist organization of which little is known. The group announced its existence in 1949 with a document pretentiously titled *The Proclamation of London*. Little came of it, and by the time the American State Department refused to renew his passport in 1952, Yockey appears to have collected a remarkable number of travel documents, including German press credentials.

With or without Yockey, the European Liberation Front itself remained a shadowy if persistent entity. The name did turn up occasionally through the years, however. As recounted by William L. Pierce in his hagiographic treatment of George Lincoln Rockwell, *Lincoln Rockwell: A National Socialist Life,* the Commander received an angry letter in the late 1950s from an American European Liberation Front adherent decrying Rockwell's attacks on America.

A less-enlightening document emerged in the late 1970s purporting to be from the ELF as well. This, however, was a simple, rather incoherent, anti-Semitic screed, titled "About 'The European Liberation Front': A Bulwark Against 'The Outer Forces'." The document is notable only for its claims of direct descent from Yockey and the claim that the group is forced to live a semiclandestine life in London. Its words, however, would prove prophetic for much of the movement view of the 1990s:

> Europe is a tired old man—more like a tired old lady—and if Western culture is to be saved, it will be saved by the last Western barbarians, the American barbarians I love.... You and your egghead gang of dandies are in love with what is gone and insist on ignoring what is here. Rome is no more. You keep trying to resurrect it, but you can't, because there are no more noble Romans over there, at least not enough to make a real fight of it. Europe is like one big France—all empty shell, fine words, pretty songs, *and dead men*.

Yockey's magnum opus fared better than the European Liberation Front itself. The book hit the market in 1948. It offered interpretations of history that combined elements of such anti-Semitic classics as *The Protocols of the Elders of Zion* with the sweeping historical analysis of Spengler's *Decline of the West*. The first edition of the sprawling work was issued in two volumes under the imprimatur of something called the Westropa Press. It attracted a small but fanatical following, the most important of whom would be the American publisher Willis Carto. Carto picked up the rights to *Imperium* and published a comprehensive edition in 1948. When Carto created his Noontide Press over a decade later, *Imperium* was one of its featured offerings, with the first Noontide edition appearing in 1962.

Yockey, meanwhile, had returned to the United States where, through a combination of careless handling of his baggage and buzzard luck, he was arrested and charged with violating passport laws. Held under an unheard-of (for the time) $50,000 bail for the passport charges, Yockey apparently feared he would be forced to reveal sensitive information about the European Liberation Front and other of his European endeavors.

Francis Parker Yockey committed suicide by ingesting a cyanide pill in his San Francisco jail cell in 1960. Willis Carto was the last man to see the imprisoned Yockey alive. Through *Imperium,* however, Yockey's legacy lives on. Carto's Noontide Press edition is readily available, replete with his fawning introduction. Else Christensen, a founder of the racialist wing of the Odinist movement in America, was much influenced by *Imperium* as well, and she introduced Yockey's ideas to the international Odinist community through a series of articles in her publication, *The Odinist.*

See also: Carto, Willis; Christensen, Else; Hitler, Adolf; Odinism; Pierce, William; Rockwell, George Lincoln.

Further reading: Kevin Coogan, *Dreamer of the Day: Francis Parker Yockey and the Postwar Fascist International* (Brooklyn, NY: Autonomedia, 1999); John George and Laird Wilcox, *American Extremists, Supremacists, Klansmen, Communists and Others* (Buffalo, NY: Prometheus Books, 1996); Jeffrey Kaplan and Leonard Weinberg, *The Emergence of a Euro-American Radical Right* (Rutgers, NJ: Rutgers University Press, 1998); Ulick Varange [Francis Parker Yockey], *Imperium* (Costa Mesa, CA: Noontide Press, 1991).

ZIONIST OCCUPATION GOVERNMENT (ZOG)   The Zionist Occupation Government discourse is at once the most caricatured and the most characteristic facet of the American radical right wing today. Moreover, the ZOG conception has found a secure beachhead with the European—and particularly the Scandinavian—racialist subculture. Why this seemingly eccentric view of modern society has found such a remarkable resonance in the transatlantic radical right reveals much of how the far-right faithful see the world around them and, of greater import, how they see themselves.

The Zionist Occupation Government (ZOG) may be defined as a deeply Manichaean conceptualization of the federal government and of what is seen as its Jewish puppeteers, often personified as the Anti-Defamation League of B'nai B'rith. ZOG is today considered to be the all-powerful master of the nation and, indeed, of the world. That the timeless Jewish conspiracy personified by the epithet ZOG has come to rule the world like a colossus is now unquestioned dogma for the most radical reaches of the American race movement, and enjoys a wide vogue among the European movements as well. How this came to be is strongly centered on the success of the Jewish organizations in the United States that in the postwar years turned to the battle against anti-Semitism with a vigor that was much fueled by the enormity of the Holocaust.

In the late 1940s, the American Jewish Committee (AJC) held a position very much akin to that of the Anti-Defamation League today. That is, one of the functions of the AJC was to monitor the doings of anti-Semites who might present a threat to the American Jewish community. At the head of this effort was Rabbi Solomon Andhil Fineberg. At the time, Rabbi Fineberg was concerned with the high-profile activities of the surviving Depression-era demagogues, in particular Gerald L. K. Smith. In conjunction with other Jewish organizations, Rabbi Fineberg developed and championed what he called a "quarantine policy." Quarantine meant exactly what the word implied—an attempt to sever the lines of transmission through which the anti-Semites' message could be disseminated to the mainstream culture.

The policy succeeded to a degree in dealing with Gerald L. K. Smith, but its real efficacy was demonstrated in the effort to neutralize George Lincoln Rockwell and his American Nazi Party in the early 1960s. In dealing with Rockwell, "Quarantine" was renamed "Dynamic Silence," but the objective was the same. When a Rockwell media event was planned, local Jewish organizations would seek to limit the impact of the performance. This involved on the one hand securing the cooperation of local newspaper editors and broadcast journalists in ignoring the event. To facilitate this process, every effort was made to render the spectacle less newsworthy. This necessitated limiting the kind of angry confrontations that had been par for the course at Rockwell's public appearances, for it was precisely these theatrical clashes that drew the press in the first place. At the moment at which Rabbi Fineberg's policy was accepted and militant Jewish groups ceased opposing Rockwell at his marches and public rallies, Rockwell's real troubles began, as an increasingly frustrated Commander was left to try to devise ever-more-outrageous stunts to publicize his movement. If a point of conception for the ZOG discourse can be posited, it may well have been at this fateful juncture when the American Nazi Party faded from the headlines.

But if the suspicion that the nation was being controlled by a shadowy Jewish conspiracy operating behind the facade of federal government became increasingly credible in the Rockwell era, its roots are considerably older. Moreover, the perception that the conspirators had in fact triumphed and that the nation could no longer be wrested from their grasp would take another two decades to find widespread acceptance in the American radical right.

As to the ideological stuff upon which the ZOG discourse is built, it is necessary to look to the 1920s. It was then that Henry Ford's newspaper, the *Dearborn Independent,* began the publication of the "International Jew" series. Later published as a four-volume set of books under the title *The International Jew,* the series based itself on the most important anti-Semitic document of the modern era, *The Protocols of the Learned Elders of Zion. The Protocols* was, however, a document steeped in the atmosphere of the dying days of tsarist Russia. Moreover, *The Protocols,* in the English translation by Victor Marsden, may have been one of the dullest reads ever committed to paper. Granted, its melodramatic portrait of a cabal of Jewish rabbis meeting once a century in a desolate cemetery in the dead of night to exchange news of the age-old plan is a timeless reencapsulation of anti-Semitic themes from the Middle Ages. Yet these scenes were not easily translated into the context of modern American life. *The International Jew* provided the link between the Old World anti-Semitism of *The Protocols* and the urban world of modern America. *The International Jew* introduced a generation of radical right wingers to the notion of a Jewish conspiracy boring away from within at the values of White Christian America.

Nonetheless, the patriotism of World War II and the ideological mobilization of the Cold War's battle against communism left little room for the kind of disaffection from the state that the ZOG discourse implies. Granted, Elizabeth Dilling, Gerald Winrod, Gerald L. K. Smith, and a handful of other radicals could lead the charge in accusing Franklin Roosevelt and his administration of being either Jews themselves or in thrall to Jewish interests, but these charges were so out of touch with the times that they simply failed to resonate.

Much the same could be said of the Cold War decades of the 1950s and early 1960s. Gerald L. K. Smith and company could (and did) attempt to paint President Dwight Eisenhower as a "Swedish Jew" and his administration as a largely Jewish enterprise, but once again the battle against communism, the McCarthy crusade against internal subversion, and the threat of nuclear annihilation made the federal government, while surely corrupt and inimical to the interests of the righteous remnant of the far right, the only game in town. Indeed, even when the federal government after the 1954 Brown vs. the Topeka Board of Education decision began to put its armed weight behind the effort to desegregate the American South, the call was for reform and states' rights rather than separation.

No better example of this reformist mood can be offered than the contrast between an anonymous apocalyptic novel of the day, *The John Franklin Letters,* with the 1970s vintage *Turner Diaries*—a novel by William Pierce. Published in 1959 and attributed to John Birch Society sources, *The John Franklin Letters* is remarkable for the way it reflected the mood of the far right of the day. In the 1950s, the movement's vision was more reformist than revolutionary. In *The John Franklin Letters,* the apocalyptic confrontation between the forces of good and true Americanism and the "enemy within" of international communism results in a reconstituted American state in which constitutional government is restored. In this resurrected status quo ante, the constitutional line of succession to the presidency is followed with such meticulous care that the novel ends with the swearing in of a Black president! The *Turner Diaries* offers no such heartwarming prognostications. Rather, the planet is devastated by "chemical, biological and radiological" means in a war of extermination against Jews, non-Whites, and racial traitors, a war that is conducted on a global scale. The apocalyptic dream is of an elite band of survivors inhabiting truly "a new heaven and a new earth."

But it was not long after the publication of *The John Franklin Letters* that the mood darkened. The success of Rabbi Fineberg and the American Jewish Committee at marginalizing the Rockwell phenomenon—and indeed most overt expressions of anti-Semitism—was only part of the problem. Of far greater import were the social and political changes that occurred throughout the culture in the 1960s and 1970s. The message of the radical right was simply losing relevance to most Americans. As the racialist right were increasingly cast to the most distant margins of the culture, the search for the reasons for this isolation came to preoccupy the radical right. The conspiratorial suspicions and anti-Semitism inherent in the movement had by the late 1970s come to conceptualize these complex socioeconomic factors as "the hidden hand" of a global Jewish conspiracy.

With the increasing perception of the culture as irretrievably lost to the "righteous remnant" of the far right, there was a push for separatism that became most visible in the sudden appearance of individual survivalists and the growth of rural settlements or compounds throughout the American heartland. From this era came such high-profile outposts as the Aryan Nations compound in Idaho and the Covenant, Sword, and Arm of the Lord in rural Missouri. From this era, too, came a series of armed confrontations with the radical right that made clear to one and all the hostility of the federal government to manifestations of right-wing opposition. The "martyrology" of the radical right served as eloquent testimony to this chilling perception.

Gordon Kahl, Arthur Kirk, Robert Mathews, David Moran, Vicki and Samuel Weaver, all died at the hands of police or federal agents. With the exception of Kahl (about whom a television movie was made), these names and many more are largely unknown in the American cultural heartland, but are instantly familiar throughout the milieu of the radical right. From the sieges of the Covenant, Sword, and Arm of the Lord's compound, Randy Weaver's cabin, and ultimately, that at Waco, there has in recent years been an escalation in the use of force against dissidents in

America. The reasons for this increase in violence are complex, necessitating a study in itself, but what concerns us here is the effect that this resort to force may have on the movement's perception of a triumphal Jewish conspiracy now able to command at will the forces of the state to eliminate once and for all anyone who would object to the writ of Jewish power.

What is certain is that even in the more sophisticated reaches of the radical right wing, the view that the U.S. government has become the agent of a triumphant Jewish conspiracy has become accepted orthodoxy. The occasional armed skirmishes that began with the effort to suppress the tax resistance movement in the early 1980s and the compound dwellers after that have come to involve adherents of other appeals in the milieu of the radical right.

The key event in this regard may, in retrospect, prove to be the siege of Randy Weaver's cabin in 1992. There, in an event that would eerily resemble a small-scale version of the federal action at the Branch Davidian compound in Waco, Texas, an 18-month stakeout of the cabin of Identity adherent Randy Weaver culminated with the deaths of a federal marshal, Weaver's 14-year-old son, and his wife, who was shot in the head while holding her infant daughter in her arms. The battle electrified the world of Christian Identity and the wider world of the radical right. The anger of the radical right boiled over that year at the August 22–28 Scriptures for America Bible Camp conducted in Colorado by Pete Peters.

Following the camp, Peters convened a meeting of Christian Patriots who resolved to prevent such an event from happening again, either through legitimate political action or by joining in a collective defense. As if for good measure, Weaver's trial coincided with the Branch Davidian siege at Waco, and the similarity of the two events was lost on no one.

The horrific deaths of the children of Waco broke whatever tenuous hope the radical right may have had for the possibility of reform in America. Now, the Zionist Occupation Government discourse took on the aspect of unquestioned dogma in the American radical right. And remarkably, virtually untranslated, it leapt the Atlantic to become part of European movement discourse as well.

In the late 1980s and throughout the 1990s, the ZOG discourse has become a feature of European radical right—even in countries suffering from an inconvenient dearth of local Jews! This development was most advanced in Scandinavia—particularly in Sweden—where the slogan "Död Åt ZOG" (Death to ZOG) remarkably saw no need to translate "Zionist Occupation Government" from its native English. Thus, White Power bands picked up the term and further popularized it in song and story, culminating in the Swedish band Vit Aggression's (White Aggression) song and eponymous CD, *Död Åt ZOG*.

Today, the Zionist Occupation Government discourse, and the sense of helpless despair in connotes, is ubiquitous in the most extreme reaches of the Euro-American radical right.

See also: American Nazi Party; Aryan Nations; Covenant, Sword, and Arm of the Lord; Dilling, Elizabeth; Mathews, Robert; Peters, Pete; Pierce, William; Rockwell, George Lincoln; Scriptures for America; Smith, Gerald L. K.; Waco; Weaver, Randy; Winrod, Gerald.

Further reading: Anon., *The John Franklin Letters* (New York: Book Mailer Inc., 1959); Michael Barkun, "Reflections After Waco: Millennialists and the State," in James R. Lewis, ed., *From the Ashes: Making Sense of Waco* (Lanham, MD: Rowman & Littlefield, 1994); Michael Barkun, *Religion and the Racist Right: The Origins of the Christian Identity Movement* (Chapel Hill: University of North Carolina Press, 1994); Kevin Flynn and Gary Gerhardt, *The Silent Brotherhood* (New York: Signet, 1990); William Gibson, *Warrior Dreams* (New York: Hill and Wang, 1994); Jeffrey Kaplan, "Right-Wing Violence in North America," in Tore Bjørgo, ed., *Terror From the Far Right* (London: Frank Cass & Co., 1995); Jeffrey Kaplan, *Radical Religion in America* (Syracuse, NY: Syracuse University Press, 1997); Jeffrey Kaplan, "Real Paranoids Have Real Enemies: The Genesis of the ZOG Discourse," in Catherine Wessinger, ed., *Millennialism, Persecution and Violence* (Syracuse, NY: Syracuse University Press, forthcoming); Jeffrey Kaplan and Leonard Weinberg, *The Emergence of a Euro-American Radical Right* (Rutgers, NJ: Rutgers University Press, 1998); Andrew Macdonald, *The Turner Diaries* (Arlington, VA: National Vanguard Books, 1978); Pete Peters, *Special Report on the Meeting of Christian Men Held in Estes Park, Colorado October 23, 24, 25, 1992 Concerning the Killing of Vicki and Samuel Weaver by the United States Government* (LaPorte, CO: Scriptures for America, n.d.); Jess Walter, *Every Knee Shall Bow* (New York: ReganBooks, 1995).

Resources

Title	Author or Source	Date
Deguello Report on the American Right Wing	Anonymous	1976
A Brief History of White Nationalism	Rick Cooper	1998 revised
In Hoc Signo Vinces	George Lincoln Rockwell	1960
The White Party Report	"Max Amann"	1968
Aryan Nations Creed	Richard Butler	n.d.
Foundations Biography of Aryan Nations Richard G. Butler	Aryan Nations	n.d.
The Sixteen Commandments	Ben Klassen	n.d.
The Movement's Fatal Fascination	Harold Covington	1998
David Duke: The Messenger and His Message	Chip Berlet and Margaret Quigley	1991
Aryan Destiny: Back to the Land	Jost	n.d.
88 Precepts	David Lane	n.d.
Leaderless Resistance	Louis R. Beam	1992
Reichsfolk— Toward a New Elite	David Myatt	n.d.
Why I Am A National-Socialist	David Myatt	n.d.
Declaration of War	Robert J. Mathews	n.d.
Letter to the Editor	Robert J. Mathews	n.d.
Alert Update and Advisory	Gary Lee Yarbrough	1983
What We Believe As White Racists	Tom Metzger	n.d.
Open Letter to Minister Louis Farrakhan	Thom Robb	1984
Open Letter	James K. Warner	1968

Part I   Movement Reports

Deguello Report on the American Right Wing
Anonymous — 1976

There has been a great deal of movement speculation as to authorship of the "Deguello Report." We will not add to the guessing game here. What is important about the document is not the stereotypical charges of socialism, Judaism, and/or homosexuality that are leveled against the movement figures of the day. These are impossible to prove (and in any case are for the most part unlikely to be true). Rather, it is the jaundiced "insider" view of the movement, the rhetoric in which these views are presented, the movement's conspiratorial view of history, and the all too typically fratricidal nature of the movement that make the "Deguello Report" an invaluable historical document. Virtually all of the figures noted in the Report are very much alive and active today, though as the addresses for those included in the "Deguello Report" are badly outdated, these have been omitted. For current contact addresses, the reader is directed to Laird Wilcox, *Guide to the American Right 1997* (Editorial Research Service, P.O. Box 2047, Olathe, KS 66061). Finally, it should be noted that the "Deguello Report" was never published. It was mimeographed and circulated to a selected number of individuals, who then passed it on to others. It is impossible to know how many people actually saw the "Deguello Report," and of those, how many found credible the charges contained in the document.

The document reproduced in the "Resources" section is unchanged from the original version of the "Deguello Report," save for some minor formatting changes. Otherwise, the "Deguello Report," typos and all, is given as it first appeared in 1976.

———————————

You have been identified as a person whose integrity is highly regarded among patriotic Nationalists of the United States. For this reason we are sending you this material free of charge and without obligation on your part.

We do not make any requests or recommendations as to how you may use this material. This is something we leave to your good judgment and discretion. You may keep it to yourself or share it with others as you see fit.

DEGUELLO

This may be our only communication with you or we may see fit to communicate with you again in the future. In any case, we will identify ourselves only as Deguello.

We can describe ourselves to you only to this extent: all members of Deguello are either present or past employees of government intelligence Services from a number of different nations in the so-called free world. As such, we have access to the intelligence sources of several different Western governments.

Our group is composed of a comparative few members within these intelligence organizations each having in common an extraordinary deep appreciation for our own nation. Working together, and in strictest secrecy, we pool our efforts and resources in a purely personal effort to fight back against those forces that would destroy all free nations of the world, supplanting them with a one world government.

THE PURPOSE OF THIS COMMUNICATION

Freedom loving peoples throughout the entire world look to the United States in their hope for salvation. What a feeble hope that is!

Even with many great advantages of wealth and comparative freedom, the Nationalist movement of the United States is pathetically inadequate, ineffective and misinformed.

Even most of those individual nationalists who have studied the so-called communist conspiracy for decades, we find practically none that have a realistic conception of their enemy. Very few understand the nature of the anti-nationalist conspiracy or its organizational structure. There are practically no individual citizens within the United States whom we have been able to find that have a deep understanding as to the forces that motivate their enemies in their tireless and unceasing drive to destroy the freedom of all nations.

It may be said also that of all Nationalist movements to be found within the major nations of the Western world, the Nationalist movement within the United States is the most heavily infiltrated by those whom they seek to defend themselves against.

THE ANTI-NATIONALIST CONSPIRACY

We can say it this way: communism has three faces. These three faces are socialism, Judaism and homosexualism.

Each of these faces represents a Vast and semi-independent conspiratorial apparatus. So vast is each one of these three separate conspiracies that none of them is completely controlled at the top by any one person or small council of persons. Within each of these three separate conspiracies we find numerous leaders and groups of leaders existing throughout different parts of the world, having various aspects and different degrees of power, each engaged in both cooperation and friendly competition.

Although basically independent of each other, these three vast conspiracies are interlocked and intertwined in such a manner as to move their energies forward along roughly the same paths and toward approximately the same destination.

Among these many millions of individuals, most will belong to only one of these three conspiracies. Some will belong to two conspiracies simultaneously and a comparative few will belong to all three.

To be more definite, the fact that a person is a Jew does not necessarily make him either a socialist or a homosexual. On the other hand, he may be either or both. The fact that a person is a homosexual does not necessarily make him a socialist and obviously, it does not necessarily mean that he must be a Jew. There are many socialists that are neither Jews nor homosexuals although many socialists may be one or the other or they may be all three: a socialist, Jew and homosexual.

The exchange of information between members of these three conspiracies is not always planned or exact. The sense of obligation between members of one conspiracy and members of a different conspiracy may be great or small depending on the individuals involved. For the most part the exchange of both information and assistance occurs through those individuals that simultaneously participate in two or more of the various conspiracies.

The relative strength of these conspiracies is a matter of debate. In general, it may be said that the socialist conspiracy is the most direct, forceful and aggressive. The Jewish conspiracy is perhaps most persistent, clever and conniving. The homosexual conspiracy is most apt to have surprising, subtle and unexpected effects.

Taken together, the three faces of communism maintain a continuous and unrelenting attack on national states of the world and against the individual freedom of all peoples everywhere.

We must now investigate the nature of these three conspiracies separately and in turn.

THE SOCIALIST CONSPIRACY

The theories of Karl Marx were anticipated by twenty-five centuries in the writings of the philosopher Plato. Between the lives of these two men there were hundreds of other authors and contributors to the generalized theory of communism. This history is well documented and we presume, well-known to all who will read this communication.

The communist manifesto, written by Karl Marx in 1848, became the focal point at which theory was transformed into practice. The history of socialism since the manifesto is known equally well and fully documented. The anti-communist organizations of most Western nations are fully acquainted with this history and are guided accordingly. Within the United States however, we find that most Nationalists and Nationalist organizations have been strangely diverted from the facts. The thinking of many United States nationalists has been misdirected against persons and organizations of comparatively small importance and away from those facts and organizational activities that constitute the real and immediate threat to the freedom of the United States. For this reason we will briefly review the nature of the socialist conspiracy and point out some errors of fact and judgment commonly circulated among United States Nationalists.

Almost at once, after writing the communist manifesto, a division of opinion occurred, not as to the ultimate objectives, but regarding the best means to obtain those objectives. One group favored violent revolution whereas the other favored a gradual drive for control through infiltration and subversion.

Marx first attempted to implement his plan for world wide socialist revolution on September 24th, 1864 by organizing the International Working Mans Association which became known as the First Socialist International.

In 1868 a socialist party was formed in New York which met with some early success. In 1872 the headquarters of the first

Socialist International was moved from London to New York where it combined with the Socialist party there. Still the division between the two groups prevented any unity of action and the original Socialist party was dissolved at a meeting in Philadelphia on Feb. 15, 1876.

A second International was founded in Paris on July 14, 1889 but succumbed to the sane division of opinion.

After the death of Karl Marx, the two groups split apart entirely. Those favoring violent revolution organized in 1903 as the Russian Social Democratic Labor Party. Their first meeting was convened in Brussels but soon moved to London after conflict with Belgian authorities. This party included Nikolai Lenin and Leon Trotsky with fifteen faithful followers. From this central core developed the bolshevik segment of the Marxist party.

In November, 1917, the bolsheviks overthrew the Kerensky government and seized control of Russia. Lenin assumed power as dictator of Russia and leader of the Third Socialist International (also known as the Comintern).

The Third International has continued through the years under control of the Communist party of the Soviet Union as the primary instrument for obtaining a one world communist dictatorship by means of violent conquest and revolution.

When the Comintern nations (USSR, Red China and their respective satellites) use non-violent means of espionage and infiltration, they do so more in a military manner. Their respective spy systems are organized along military lines and all agents are under strict control and discipline.

After the death of Marx 1883, that group which favored infiltration as the sole means of conquest immediately organized the Fabian Society which shortly came under the leadership of George Bernard Shaw along with Sidney and Beatrice Webb. The Fabians did not differ with the bolsheviks in their ultimate objectives, a socialist one world dictatorship, but only in the means by which it could be best obtained. George Bernard Shaw did not disapprove of violent revolution on principle. He completely agreed with Marx that any tactic leading toward a total collective state were justified. He and the Webbs simply concluded that in the more advanced Western nations, the tactics of violence and revolution would be less effective than those of infiltration and political conversion.

Whereas the bolsheviks worked mostly among the working classes, the Fabians sought out young intellectuals whose egotism could be exploited in the building of a "planned society".

The Fabian Society rejected all suggestions to form an independent political party. Their members preferred to infiltrate the colleges, the news media, religious groups, labor unions, business organizations and other political parties. In England they were immediately successful. By 1888 they had two of their members on the London school board and by 1892 two Fabian Socialists had been elected to Parliament. A magazine called Fabian Essays began publication in 1889 and soon afterwards, the Fabians founded the London School of Economics which became world renowned as an open vehicle for the teaching of socialism and socialist economic theories.

The importance of the United States was quickly recognized by the Fabian Socialists and in 1888, Sidney Webb made an extensive lecture tour through the United States. His book "Socialism in England" was soon circulated through leading American Universities as the Fabians made an extensive recruiting effort among liberal minded American educators. The Rand School of Social Science was formed in 1905 in New York City as the Fabian's equivalent to the London School of Economics. In 1907 the United States Fabians organized the Intercollegiate Socialist Society with chapters in many of the leading Universities of that country. Among the early converts to Fabian socialism in the United States were Felix Frankfurter who became a Justice of the Supreme Court, Walter Lippman whose career as a political columnist spanned four decades, as well as persons like John Dewey, the father of "progressive education" at Columbia University.

When Franklin D. Roosevelt was elected president, he opened the doors of government to socialist planners of all shades. During the following forty-five years, the Fabians achieved immense power and influence throughout almost every segment of the social structure of the United States. Always they have maintained a position of both secret cooperation and friendly competition with bolshevik agents as well as with the Jewish and homosexualist elements of the anti-nationalist conspiracy.

A big majority of the bolsheviks that came to power in Russia were Jews. The Fabian socialist movement included several prominent Jews among their early members. Thus the interlock between the Jewish conspiracy and the socialist conspiracy was early established and is continued to this day.

In the United States the Fabians have dominated the universities and the teacher's unions. In the news media, control has been jointly held by the Fabians and Jews. Here the Fabians have dominated the editorial and journalistic aspects while the Jews concentrated on extending the business and financial power of their respective newspaper chains, magazine publishing firms, radio and television networks. This symbiotic cooperation between the Jewish and Fabian conspiracies within the news media has resulted in almost total control over the source of information upon which citizens of the United States must base their judgments and reach their political conclusions. This control is in part responsible for the confusion that exists within the thinking of United States Nationalist organizations but infiltration by Fabian, Jewish, and especially homosexual agents has been a more important cause for this confusion as will be demonstrated in a later section of this communication.

This confusion, of which we speak, includes a failure to understand the three faces of communism and the association between them. As a result of this failure, many United States Nationalist groups and organizations make many accusations against groups that are merely used by the conspiracies rather than being part of the conspiracies.

Much of this confusion seems to have originated through the unwitting action of a man named *Dan Smoot*, an ex-FBI agent whose sincerity cannot be doubted. Many years ago, Mr. Smoot wrote a book called, *"The Invisible Government"* in which he identified the *Council on Foreign Relations* as the dominant controlling influence within the communist conspiracy of the United States. Apparently, Smoot was led to this conclusion through his failure to identify individual members of the Fabian Society as they worked within the Council on Foreign Relations to influence other members and manipulate their influence upon the business and political communities. As a result of this misunderstanding, many important persons have been wrongly stigmatized by accusations of CFR membership. Naturally, these false claims made repeatedly, tend to alienate otherwise patriotic persons, causing them in this way to become hostile toward Nationalist organizations and making them susceptible to friendly overtures from the Fabians who work subtly among their ranks. *The Bilderbergers* is another favorite target of United States Nationalist groups and propaganda. *Prince Philip of Netherlands* is a Fabian Socialist as are a few other prominent participants in the Bilderberger meetings. But here again, Nationalists of the United States fail to understand that the Bilderberger's meetings are simply held by the Fabian Socialists as a means of influencing other important people who are not Fabians. This propaganda by United States Nationalist organizations simply confuses their own people as to the true nature of the enemy and the true identity of the most important Fabian manipulators within their own country. The real and actual infiltrators into United States Nationalist organizations are always helped by an even greater number of profiteers and charlatans who will do anything to make money or boost their own ego, even at the expense of their nation's freedom.

Some of these profiteers act in very effective and seemingly honorable ways to collect and waste large amounts of money that might otherwise be put to good use. Some of these charlatans give reasonable stories and others tell tales so ridiculous as to be pathetic. It is a poor testimonial regarding the gullibility of United States Nationalists that they fall so easily for these things.

One such charlatan is a phoney *"Polish General"* who pretends to have been responsible for identifying several communist spy networks. As part of his ever continuing campaign to establish his own false identity, this charlatan has made claims to the effect that *Henry Kissinger* was an agent for the KGB. Since Henry Kissinger acts in ways continually favorable to the communists, this claim did not seem as being absurd. Even such a usually accurate reporter as *Frank* (Jew) *Capell* used this false story in writing a book claiming Henry Kissinger to be a KGB agent.

Although this claim may seem reasonable to supposedly knowledgeable United States Nationalists, it sounds completely ridiculous to the average citizen of the United States. Thus, this false information often serves to convince ordinary citizens that the American Nationalists are fools.

The truth is of course that Henry Kissinger is a prominent leader in the Fabian Society. As such he works diligently in behalf of the socialist conspiracy but without any connection to the bolshevik controlled KGB. If United States Nationalists understood the extent and nature of the Fabian Socialist movement and if they could clearly identify Henry Kissinger's actual role in this conspiracy both they and their fellow citizens would find this much more believable and good would be done rather than harm.

One of the Fabians early political efforts in the United States was the organization of the *Socialist Party* long identified with Norman Thomas but always controlled by the Fabian Society. A splinter group of the Socialist Party was reorganized as the *Americans for Democratic Action* (*ADA*) which is also under Fabian control.

The Fabian Society's first front group in the United States was the *Intercollegiate Socialists Society* which later became the *League for Industrial Democracy*. The ADA and the LID have interlocking directors and membership which comprises the control of both groups by the Fabian society.

Robert Welch, founder of the *John Birch Society* was for many years a member of the League for Industrial Democracy and is, to this day, a member of the Fabian Society. The John Birch Society receives much money from the sale of books and publications to United States Nationalists and some money as contributions from sincere members. Much of their considerable financial strength comes through secret transfer of money from Jewish individuals and/or organizations in the amount of $300,000. to $800,000. yearly. In this way the John Birch Society has become a major instrument for the confusion of American Nationalists. This is done by hiding the true nature of the Jewish, homosexual and socialist phases of the anti-nationalists conspiracy while reporting exaggerated claims regarding the almost mythical *"order of the Illuminati"*. [1]

Going back to the bolsheviks in Russia. As noted previously most of the original bolsheviks were Jews. One however was not a Jew and he was *Joseph Stalin*. Stalin had a great lust for personal power and to obtain this power it was necessary for him to eliminate most competitors within the original bolshevik movement. He did this through a long series of purges and public trials culminating with the Moscow Treason trials of 1938. With these trials Stalin rid himself of all the old bolsheviks and in doing so largely destroyed Jewish control over the communist party of the Soviet Union.

With Stalin's death, a new battle for control developed between Jewish and non-Jewish elements in the communist party of the Soviet Union. *Nikita Krushchev* who was half Jewish helped establish partial Jewish control through his denunciations of Stalin.

---

[1] The enmity for the staunchly anti-communist John Birch Society may be traced back to 1963 when Robert Welch responded to a number of voices within the organization who were demanding that the organization adopt an anti-Semitic posture under the theory that communism was and is a facet of a wider Jewish conspiracy. Welch demurred, responding with *The Neutralizers*, a book that explicitly decried anti-Semitism as both divisive and a distraction from the larger goal of battling the communist conspiracy. Many radical right wing figures, men such as Revillo P. Oliver, Jack Mohr, and Tom Metzger to name a few, passed through Birch Society ranks only to leave or be expelled for their expressions of blatant anti-Semitism. See Robert Welch, *The Neutralizers* (Belmont, MA: The John Birch Society, 1963).

Still, to this day, the Jews do not have control of the communist party in the Soviet Union.

Within the Soviet Union today many Jews are accepted and influential within government positions. Many others have been expelled or executed. During the past five years an enormous number of Jews have immigrated from the Soviet Union to the United States, Israel or other nations. Some of these Jewish immigrants were actually dedicated communist spies. Most of them have simply been Jewish dissidents of which the Soviet government was glad to be rid of. You may say, why do they not simply shoot these Jews if they wish to be rid of them? The reason lies in a new policy by the Soviet Government of demanding ransom from those persons wishing to immigrate who have relatives in foreign countries. The average ransom paid for permission to immigrate from the communist bloc to the Western World is $15,000 per family. In some cases of Jews having wealthy relatives in the United States, as much as $250,000 has been asked and has been paid. Another reason is that by not shooting dissident Jews they retain the loyalty of other communist Jews.

In addition to the Fabian Socialist movement within the United States, the Bolsheviks have also set up numerous organizations, usually under the control of the Communist party of the Soviet Union. The conflict that has been discussed between Jewish and non-Jew segments of the Communist Party of the Soviet Union has led to considerable splintering among the Bolshevik organizations within the United States.

An early leader of the Bolshevik movement was Leon Trotsky who would have been heir to Lenin's power except for the seizure of this power by Joseph Stalin. Trotsky escaped from the Soviet Union and lived in Mexico until he was finally assassinated. Under Trotsky's direction a Fourth International was organized. From this *Fourth International* a number of different organizations have grown including the *Socialist Workers Party*, *Young Socialists Alliance*, *National Peace Action Coalition*, *National Student Conference against Racism*, *International Socialists*, *International Workers Party* and the *Spartacist League*. For the most part, the leaders of all these organizations have been Jewish followers of Leon Trotsky who was also a Jew.

The Communist Party USA was led for a long time by William Z. Foster who was not a Jew but is now led by *John Hall* who is a Jew. From the Communist Party USA has developed the *Young Workers Liberation League*, *Peoples Coalition for Peace and Justice*, *National*

Alliance against Racism and Political Repression, the *National Lawyers Guild*, the *Puerto Rican Socialist Party* and many other Communist fronts. At the time of the split between Stalin and *Mao Tse Tung*, a portion of the Communist Party USA broke away and accepted leadership from Red China. Thus was formed the *Progressive Labor Party* which attempted in 1969 to take over the *Students for Democratic Society*. The SDS was destroyed during these inter-organizational battles and from their membership evolved the *United States Labor Party, National Caucus of Labor Committees, The New Solidarity Group* and the *Weather Underground*.

A publication called *"The Guardian"* has long promoted the Socialists propaganda line and has accepted financing from the *Communist Party USA* as well as solicited financial support from the wealthy Fabian Socialists. At the time of the split between Stalin and *Mao Tse Tung* The Guardian became largely subservient to the Red Chinese. From this activity has developed the *Revolutionary Communist Party* as well as the *Revolutionary Student Brigade, Unemployed Workers Organizing Committee*, and the *Vietnam Veterans Against the War*.

The *Venceremos Brigade* evolved as a cooperative action between the Communist Party USA and the Revolutionary Communist Party.

In many cases we see Jewish and non-Jewish cooperation between the *Socialist Workers Party* and the Communist Party USA. Examples of these cooperative efforts include the *November Mobilization Committee*, the *National Mobilization Committee, Coalition to Stop Funding the War*, and the *Fifth Estate* with its publication, *"Counter spy"*.

As the original "weathermen" faction of the *SDS* took in many radical feminists, the name changed to *Weather Underground*. A major project of the weather underground is the front group called *Prairie Fire Organizing Committee* (PPOC) which in turn organized a *"Hard Times Conference"* to help unify youth groups among the *Maoist, Trotskyite* and *Workers World* parties.

The *October League* (OL) is a Maoist controlled communist group now organizing secret cells of "professional revolutionaries". Their stated purpose is to form a party of insurrection which will go underground to ferment violent revolution within the United States. Another front group of the October League is called the *National Fight Back Organization* to take advantage of the fact that many large cities are forced to cut down on their expenditures for welfare, and unnecessarily large number of city employees. The

"Fight Back" mean to fight back against city cuts in welfare checks and similar expenditures.

The National Fight Back Organization works in close coopera- tion with the *Communist Youth Organization* and the *Southern conference Educational Fund*.

To defend their nation against communism, the Nationalists of the United States must have a clear understanding of these various factions within the socialist conspiracy. Also essential is a clear understanding of the interaction between the socialist conspiracy as described in this section and the Jewish conspiracy and the homosexual conspiracy as described in the next two sections of this communication.

THE JEWISH CONSPIRACY

No other subject has caused so much debate and division among United States Nationalists as have questions regarding the nature of the Jewish Conspiracy or in fact, if such a conspiracy even exists.

The answers to these questions are not difficult and would be obvious except for the fact that the Jews themselves disseminate a great deal of misinformation regarding these matters. This is a fact which seems to have escaped most Nationalists within the United States. Another important fact, equally obscured to United States Nationalists is the fact that many anti-Jewish organizations are actually organized and supported financially by the Jews them- selves. The reasons for the Jews actions in doing these things, is also obvious to those who are not misled by the Jewish propaganda.

Although the Jewish people vary greatly from one geographical area to another, all Jews have certain things in common. Nearly all Jews tend to be clannish among themselves. They are, almost with- out exception, suspicious of non-Jews. Those Jews who have never once in their lives experienced prejudice or discrimination from non-Jews, nevertheless always seem to be expecting that they will run into such prejudice. At any time they feel some other Jew has been subjected to prejudice, they will immediately come to his defense. Almost always, in any difference of opinion between a Jew and a non-Jew, all Jews will assume that their fellow Jew is in the right, regardless of what the facts may show. These tendencies work to the advantage of all Jews and of special advantage to those that are active within the actual Jewish conspiracy. It is for this reason that Jews themselves help organize and finance anti-Jewish organizations and it is for these same reasons that they dissemi- nate both false and true information about themselves so long as the combination tends to obscure the facts regarding the Jewish conspiracy.

The first and foremost objective of all Jewish propaganda is to convince their own people that non-Jews are always against them and thus insure cohesiveness within their own community. To help do this they have set up anti-Jewish organizations and printed much anti-Jewish propaganda. Although the exact origin of the *"Protocols of the Learned Elders of Zion"* is in doubt, there is proof that Jewish conspirators have revived the popularity of this book and have financed the distribution of hundreds of thousands of copies because it serves these purposes for them.

A classic example of anti-Jewish propaganda which was financed by the Jews is a newspaper now out of print but long popular with American Nationalists and called, *"Common Sense"*. This paper was edited by a sincere Nationalist of strong anti-Jew convictions named *Conde NcGinley*. He put out a paper that was well done and was usually factual in most of the articles printed.

McGinley was however, completely duped by a Jew named *Benjamin Freedman* who pretended to have turned against his own people and who pretended a desire to help finance truthful information regarding the Jewish Conspiracy.

Conde McGinley had a number of very sincere assistants who assumed that the publication was financed by subscription rates and donations from non-Jews. When Conde McGinley died they made a great effort to continue the publication but were unable to do so without the secret financial help of Benjamin Freedman so their operation soon went bankrupt and the "Common Sense" ceased publication.

To understand the Jewish conspiracy as it really is we must look deeply into the nature of the Jewish people and the organization of Judaism itself.

Although, through most of the last two thousand years, the Jews have not had any territory to call their own, it is still proper to speak of the Jews as a "nation". Here we use the word in the sense of a people having many common ties of culture, religion, language, with relatives and friends living in close association and everything else (except in this case territory) that makes up a nation. Thus, Judaism is a nation that for its most part exists in the geographical territory of other nations.

To prevent their nation from being intermingled and absorbed by the peoples of other geographical nations in which they exist, has long been the first and most important objective of Jewish leaders. Thus, it is that vast numbers of Jews immigrate from one country to another not with any intent of becoming true citizens of the country in which they reside but as the would-be secret conquerors and masters of such countries.

In the past many Jews, to avoid exposure and exile, have pretended to convert to other religions while actually maintaining their own religious beliefs and practice in secret. In some cases these secret Jews have existed in this manner for generations and comprise a secret subversive force within the countries where they reside. This process continues even in the present days, especially in countries such as the United States where Jews find it advantageous to hide their racial and religious origins or where they need to strengthen their fifth column within the Christian community.

The Jewish religion is an aggressive and imperialist religion, filled with hatred for other religions and with a burning desire to enslave all mankind. This religion is unique to the Jewish people and this is the reason they are not interested in converting others to Judaism. The Jews believe that their religion resulted from Abraham's agreement with God and that as such, it is the obligation of the Lord's chosen people to dominate the world. They look upon other human beings as mere animals, lacking any right to be considered a part of mankind except to act as either real or economic slaves to the future aristocracy on supposed command of God.

The only time that Jews sincerely seek to convert a Christian or Moslem to Judaism is when that person is actually a person of the Jewish race whose parents or grandparents lost interest in Judaism for some reason. The conversion of such a Christian or Moslem is intended to recover the lost blood. The Jewish religion is one to which Gentiles will never be admitted. They may be enrolled in a special religion made for them which will have the outward appearance of Judaism but which is actually different from the ancient organization of spiritual Jews and is designed to make the supposed converts into more willing tools of the true Jewish conspiracy. Since the time of the Inquisition, it has been considered the utmost duty, both of public and secret Jews to recover the lost blood and they cannot rest until they have secretly initiated the renegade's children and brought them back to Judaism once again.

Judaism, in addition to being a people and nation spread out through the world with its own religion, is also a sect or a secret society because most Jews consider the country in which they live to be a colony of Israel. This applies Even to the political state of Israel as it now exists. They are organized into secret ceremonies of initiation at age of 13, holding political-religious meetings and rendering oaths of secrecy and absolute obedience to the leaders. All this is done as in secret societies and participating in ceremonies in which the rituals of free masonry are a weak imitation. It is this complex society, conspiring as a people, religion, and sect of the Israelite nation that has been called Judaism.

The family is the basic unit of Judaism and is patriarchal in most countries. The father is a kind of high priest in the family where he leads the family's religious activities which are practiced by means of daily prayers and very secret ceremonies. These are solemn rituals whose purpose is to impress on Jews from childhood the idea that they are God's chosen people. They are taught through all their family activities that it is their right and goal to take over the world's riches, forging an imperialist ideology that converts them into fanatical instruments of Jewish imperialism.

Among the family ceremonies of secret Jews can be mentioned the Passover with its solemn ceremonial and secret banquets and the Saturday family celebration which starts on Friday at sunset when the parents join with those children over 13 years old and also their grandchildren over the age of 13 and the wives of those children who are already married. The house is locked and no one is allowed to enter the room where ceremonies are held. This secret ceremony is followed by a ritual banquet in which prayers and speeches are delivered and it lasts until midnight unless the adults have to attend some public function to keep up their pretext of Christianity. Children younger than 13 are excluded from this and other ceremonies in order to keep secret the fact that the family is Jewish and to hide from the younger children all activities of secret Judaism.

At the age of 13 and after extensive preparation, only those children who have proven their ability to keep secrets are very cautiously initiated into the family's clandestine Judaism. Those who fail to pass the tests of discretion will only be initiated into secret Judaism when they prove their ability to keep such secrets. Those who cannot pass the test of secrecy and loyalty or who are mentally unreliable are left outside of this underground Judaism but both the family and the clandestine Jewish community will do the best they can to win back the children of such racial Jews if they are later considered capable and worthy of membership into the secret Jewish order.

Most Jewish parents are exemplary in their conduct of family affairs and are extraordinarily good parents. Unfortunately, all these good virtues are directed to the perverted goals of political and religious order imposed by their hatred of other peoples which hatred is also taught to Jewish children from infancy in the very heart of their family affairs. Such a situation seems incomprehensible to those who are unaware of the dimensions of this problem and who do not realize that both secret and open Jews will use all means available to destroy the unity of Gentile families.

To maintain the Jewish conspiracy, it is precisely their purpose to weaken the families of other people and to degrade their morality and loyalty to each other. They know that a nation with strong family ties will be better able to resist their advances than a nation whose families have been unhinged by immorality and disunity. For these reasons, many Jews deliberately spread ideas which are aimed at dissolving the Gentile's faith in marriage and the loyalty of children to their parents and to each other.

In every state and large city, Jews compose a secret organization called a community which includes the Israelite families of that area whose patriarchs are represented in the Kelilah or Supreme Council of that Jewish community. Jews are also organized in fraternities and similar organizations where their goal is to take control of those associations and institutions important to all political and economic affairs.

These fraternities were previously called synagogues because "synagogue" means assembly. It is necessary to distinguish between the assembly-synagogue as different from the building in which that assembly meets which is also called a synagogue. Judaism as a whole is sometimes referred to as the world synagogue.

World-wide Judaism is divided into different rites which have generally a common cultural background. The Sephardite rite includes all Jews dispersed from Spain in the 15th Century and from Portugal during the times of King Manual as well as the crypto-Jewish Christians that were expelled from Spain and Portugal in the times of Philip IV in the 17th Century. The Askhenazi rite includes the Jews of German descent who are also dispersed throughout the world. The Bene-lsrael rite includes the Jews that about 18 centuries ago arrived in India and infiltrated into many Indian castes and have since immigrated to various countries in Africa, Asia and even to England. In India many people believe them to be Hindus but in fact they are clandestine Jews. The present control of the congress and the Indian government is firmly held by such secret Jews.

Since the time of the Jewish prime minister of Britain, *Benjamin Disraeli*, in the last century, the British government has been largely an instrument of Jewish imperialism. Through the combined efforts of Jewish leaders in the British Islands and secret Jews in the *Church of England* was formed the *British Israelite movement* which teaches that the English are descendants of the lost tribes of Israel and are thus the true "chosen people" but in actuality are constantly promoting the desired policies of Judaism.

A Jew named *Herbert W. Armstrong* made a modest start in promoting the British Israelite movement in the United States, promptly received generous financing from wealthy Jews and has become fantastically wealthy himself. He and his son, *Garner Ted Armstrong*, now have churches throughout the United States which prohibit their members from taking any part in political activities which thus neutralizes hundreds of thousands of citizens who would be otherwise more than generally inclined to take part in Nationalist activities. Their various publications including *THE PLAIN TRUTH* and *THE WORLD TOMORROW* are circulated by millions with a very clever one world, anti-Nationalist theme woven into their varied and often interesting articles.

A competitive group, comprised of California attorney *Bertrand Comparet* and his followers, preach a modified version which they call the *"Identity"* message but these people strongly advocate pro-Nationalist activities, even going so far as to store arms and military supplies for future violent resistance to the forces of anti-Nationalism. Unfortunately, this group has been deeply infiltrated as will be dealt with in a future section.

Jewish imperialism even in the Soviet Union is still partially maintained through the secret cells or Jewish committees of control that operate very secretly behind the Central Committee of the Communist Party.

When we see disputes among Jews, it may be that they have different opinions as to how to achieve the same end or they may differ in their religious beliefs or in the degree of loyalty to the Jewish religion. Even Jews who have lost all belief in God and fallen into atheism, are kept as members of the Jewish nation while other Jews respect their atheistic beliefs so long as they submit to the political and economic resolution of the highest authorities of the Jewish nation. Nevertheless, it is a fact that the more religious Jews are most fanatical in the imperialistic activities of the Jewish nation.

During the past three decades, especially in the United States, there has been a falling away of Jews from the Jewish nation. In the United States, the Jews have disseminated great amounts of propaganda advocating racial equality, world brotherhood, etc. Many young and idealistic Jews have come to believe their own propaganda. Large numbers have left the Jewish community and have married Christians. Not a few have married negroes. This trend has been greatly resisted by the leaders of the Jewish conspiracy and that is one reason they have made such an effort during this time to give an appearance of anti-Jewish prejudice through the support of false anti-Jew organizations and dissemination of planted anti-Jew propaganda.

If some who are racially Jews become sincerely identified with the territorial nation in which they live and loyal to that government, such as *Admiral Hyman Rickover* and *General Curtis Lemay* have done, the Jewish conspiracy uses even these events to its own purpose. The existence of United States Nationalists of Jewish racial extraction, is used to further confuse the issue and hide the basic nature of the Jewish conspiracy.

THE HOMOSEXUAL CONSPIRACY

It may safely be presumed that being a homosexual does not directly determine a person's political beliefs. On the other hand homosexuals do have strong feelings of comradship toward others of their own kind. Their lives are frequently shrouded in secrecy and often take on a somewhat conspiratorial aspect. Many homosexuals feel themselves to be ostracized by normal society and are therefore easily recruited into anti-social organizations.

Within the United States especially, most patriotic, Nationalist and conservative organizations have strong religious overtones and are made up of people naturally repelled by homosexual behavior, such organizations have never openly recruited homosexuals into their ranks. The communists and their various left-wing front groups, recognizing the value of homosexuals and their conspiratorial associations with one another, have made a special effort to recruit such people.

It is frequently observed that one homosexual will have greater loyalty to another homosexual than to any divergent political feelings they may hold separately. This has enabled left-wing homosexuals to use other homosexuals almost as they please, either as tools of various anti-Nationalist organizations or as infiltrators and agents provocateur within various anti-communist organizations .

Like the socialist and Jewish parts of the anti-Nationalist conspiracy, the homosexual conspiracy is as old as history. The priests of ancient Egypt lived in homosexual relationships, never perpetuating their own blood but constantly recruiting the nations most attractive young men into their ranks. In addition, they made a practice to castrate very young boys who were then raised and trained to be homosexual concubines to the priests.

The homosexual cult religions of Egypt penetrated deeply into the social life of ancient Greece and contributed significantly to the decline of both Greek democracy and Greek culture. Some of [the] young boys who were then raised and trained [by] the more satanic-acting Emperors of Rome were known homosexuals. The extent of homosexuality within the royal families of Europe and England is too well documented to bother repeating here. But it was among these homosexuals of royal blood that the International Brotherhood as we know it today first originated. The founding fathers of the United States were not entirely free from this influence. *Benjamin Franklin*, well known for his wit and his wisdom, was both a homosexual and a member of the International Brotherhood which is often confused with the *Illuminati*.

Incidentally, contrary to popular belief among United States Nationalists, the Illuminati of Adam Weishaupt no longer exists as a significant part of the International Communist Conspiracy. Only three small remnants have deteriorated into pseudo-science societies that milk the gullible out of their money in return for supposed secrets of the ancients that are in truth, little more than mythology and superstition.

George Bernard Shaw was a member of the International Brotherhood as well as an early member of the *Fabian* socialist society. He used his many contacts among wealthy and influential homosexuals throughout Europe and the United States to advance the cause of socialism and extend the influence of the Fabian Socialist Society. This is typical of the manner of interlock between the socialists and homosexuals. Of all homosexuals who actively aid the anti-Nationalist apparatus, it is probable that less than one in four does so knowingly and for political reasons. For the most part these willing tools are influenced on a person-to-person basis by politicized homosexuals who are either active communists or are of Jewish extraction.

In spite of the Jewish emphasis on strong family units within their own race, Jews have always had a high propensity toward homosexuality. This in fact accounts for the low birth rate among Jewish intellectuals who may be married for the sake of appearances and perhaps to obtain heirs for their family businesses, but nevertheless depend on homosexual activities for a major part of their sexual gratification.

These intellectual Jewish homosexual socialists are the extreme center core of the world-wide communist conspiracy. Locked as they are into all three major conspiratorial networks: the international socialist apparatus, the nation of Judaism and the International Brotherhood, they envision themselves as the super elite, the direct descendants of an all-powerful ancient priesthood and as the rightful supreme rulers of a one world socialist oligarchy.

Although there exists an organized International Brotherhood, it would be a mistake to believe that any sizable percentage of the world's homosexuals are actually members of this central conspiracy. For the most part they act as continually floating pieces of driftwood on a restless sea, moving this way and that in response to their own emotions and the emotions of other homosexuals that they may encounter by chance or by design. Thus, the homosexual influence is both extremely important and at the same time extremely *difficult to define*.

Within the United States, the *"Lavender and Red Union"* which publishes its paper, *"Come out Fighting"* from *Hollywood, California* is an unwelcome tip of the socialist-homosexual iceberg so far as the International Brotherhood is concerned as they prefer not to have their secrecy scratched in such a manner.

Individual homosexuals may be communists or Jews or they may be neither or both. Without doubt, a very high percentage of all homosexuals are loyal citizens of the nation in which they live. In their general, overall effect however, homosexuals exert a continuous subtle influence that is destructive to that foundation upon which each new generation must build in their attempts to improve both their society and their species.

SOCIALIST INFILTRATION

The membership of *Robert Welch* in the *Fabian Society* has already been mentioned. The fact that this organization was set up under the auspices of the *League for Industrial Democracy* and heavily subsidized by Jewish money, along with the fact that it has been constantly publicized by the Fabian-Jewish controlled news media within the United States, has caused this organization to rapidly become the dominant anti-communist and supposedly Nationalist organization in that country. At the same time many truly Nationalist organizations have been killed off by the constant drain on their membership and the draining away of contributions from sincere Nationalists who have been duped into joining and supporting the John Birch Society.

Perhaps it is because of their great success with this one organization that the socialists have not found it necessary to infiltrate most other nationalist organizations within the United States directly. Or possibly, it was their consistent failure to penetrate into other organizations that caused them to take the course of setting up the John Birch Society as an alternative. In any event, it is safe to say that the direct socialist infiltration into other major Nationalist organizations such as *The Foundation for Economic Education, Liberty Lobby, The Citizens Councils, American Security Council, The United Klans of America*, the various *tax strike* organizations, the *Minutemen, Posse Comitatus*, etc. has been very limited. In competition with the heavily financed John Birch Society all of these organizations however, have declined proportionately.

An unusual example of socialist-homosexual coordination may be seen in the person of *Hans J. Schneider*. This individual lives in Oregon but travels extensively throughout the United States by private plane, always in the company of one or two teenage boys that he sometimes introduces as his son or step-sons. He uses these young boys to establish homosexual relationships with various right-wing persons that he suspects of having such tendencies. He then uses this to blackmail them and control their further activities within the Nationalist movement. Schneider is an immigrant from East Germany.

JEWISH INFILTRATION INTO THE NATIONALIST MOVEMENT OF THE UNITED STATES

As previously noted, the *John Birch Society* in the United States has been deeply and systematically infiltrated by Jews. This tactic was hardly necessary inasmuch as the Belmont Headquarters is largely financed with Jewish money and its founder, Robert Welch (although not a Jew) is a member of the Fabian Society. The JBS not only accepts Jewish members but solicits them and furthermore, gives preference to Jews in the hiring of their paid coordinators.

For the most part, Jewish infiltrators into the United States Nationalist movement have preferred to set themselves up as leaders their own organizations or as publishers of some supposedly anti-communist periodical. By these maneuvers they damage the Nationalist movement in two ways (1) by drawing off money needed by other truly Nationalistic organizations and (2) spreading subtle confusion within apparently bonafide anti-communist material.

One of the first prominent Jewish infiltrators into the American Nationalist movement was X-FBI agent and former Salt Lake City police chief, *W. Cleon Skousen*. This Jew (also a member of the Mormon church) established himself as an "authority" on communism by writing a book called *"The Naked Communist"*. This book reads fairly well to the average American conservative but when passed on to a novice, the inexperienced reader receives a picture of communism so awesome and powerful as to cause him to think "what is the use in resisting this?"

A similar but far more successful tactic has been used by *Dr. Fred Schwartz*, an Australian Jew who came to the United States to organize the *Christian Anti-communist Crusade*. During the late 1950's and early 1960's, Schwartz held large and frequent rallies and training seminars in "anti-communism". He still conducts such activity but to a lesser extent. Schwartz is best known for his *"You can trust the Communists"*. This book, like the one written by Skousen pictures the communists as extremely clever, totally dedicated, well-financed and overwhelmingly powerful. Although it seems authoritative when read by most American conservatives, the average citizen finds the picture so terrifying that he tends to say, "why waste my time fighting this. I had better spend the few years we have left with the enjoyment of life." Thus, another prospective worker for the Nationalist movement is turned away.

Although *Fabian Society* member, *Carrol Quigley* is not a Jew this might be an appropriate place to mention his 1400 page book, *"Tragedy and Hope"*. This book really convinces the American citizen that all of their most prominent business leaders, educators, politicians, military officers, etc, are already working hand in hand with the communists and therefore there is nothing the poor average citizen can do to combat such an all-powerful conspiracy. The *NAKED CAPITALIST* by *Leon Skousen* is a popularized and shortened version of Quigley's book.

A more recent entry into the fold is the Java-born, Dutch Jew *Jack Greenways*, who puts out a small magazine titled *"Last Call"*. Greenway's specialty is to build up peripheral issues so as to cause United States Nationalists to devote large amounts of time to projects that are of secondary importance. Greenways is a strong supporter of *Col Arch Roberts* and of *Dr. Peter Deter*, a fellow Jew that specializes in the invention of plausible but purely imaginary stories that are fed out as fact to gullible American conservatives. The Last Call editor's daughter, *Joyce Greenways*, was one of the first volunteers to go cut cane (and study urban guerrilla warfare) in Communist Cuba with the *Venceremos Brigade*.

J. B. Stoner, leader of the *National States Rights Party*, has been an especially destructive Jew infiltrator into the US Nationalists movement. His specialty is running for political office so as to gain public exposure where he spews forth a stream of such venomous hatred toward the negro race as to convince most fair minded citizens that the typical leader of an American Nationalist organization must be totally insane. Stoner, is also a homosexual and more will be said of him in a separate section.

There is no better example than that of *Marvin Liebman* with which to illustrate the interlock between the socialist and Jewish infiltration into the United States Nationalist movement.

While still a high school junior in Brooklyn, New York, Marvin Liebman was recruited by his civics teacher into the *American Students Union*. His hard work and enthusiasm soon resulted in an invitation to join the *Young Communist League* and after a short probationary period, Liebman was accepted into full membership and came under the direct discipline of the *Communist Party USA*.

After high school and part of a semester at New York University, Marvin Leibman rented an apartment in Greenwich Village and began writing short stories for various left-wins magazines. This activity was soon cut short when Liebman found himself to be one of those very few unlucky Jews to be drafted into the Army as a buck private. While in the service, Liebman was a typical Jewish gold brick. Whenever assigned to an unpleasant work detail, he promptly broke his glasses. As soon as he was assigned KP, he sliced his fingers open with a knife. On the drill field he continually stumbled over his own feet and every time the sun came out from behind a cloud he keeled over in a pretended sunstroke. Marvin Liebman must rank as truly unique. He is without doubt the only soldier ever given a medical discharge for sunstroke.

Back in his Greenwich Village apartment once again, Liehman became editor of the *Spotlight*, a publication of *American Youth for Democracy*, one of the most active communist fronts of that time. The Spotlight was a slick publication, strong on ideology but with a distinctly artistic flavor.

In 1946 the *Communist Party USA* switched its line (from the WWII line that anyone fighting the fascists was good) to accommodate the new cold war atmosphere. Liebman left the Communist Party USA to work with the *Trotskyites* for a period of time again exercising his literary political skills.

It seems that in 1947 Marvin Liebman began to yearn for the military action he had so carefully avoided while in the U.S. Army. He signed up with an Israeli terrorist outfit known as the *Irgun* which was dedicated to breaking the British blockade of Palestine. Liebman had his fun, racing back and forth between Marseilles, Haifa, Cyprus and other ports of the Mediterranean. During this time Leibman obviously saw himself as a dashing soldier of leftist fortune. In time he found that Irgun was too right wing for him and he joined the communist "forces of liberation" in Northern Greece. When the bullets started coming too close however, Liebman played it true to form. He quickly returned to the U.S.A. to become a fund raiser for the *United Jewish Appeal*. While with the *UJA*, he attended one of their organizational fund raising schools.

Moving on to a fund raising job for pre-communist *Henry Wallace* in his 1948 campaign he picked up further expertise from Hollywood leftists and then moved back to New York and joined a public relations firm headed by pro-communist *Harold Oram*.

Together, Liebman and Oram sent out mailings, formed committees, raised funds and lobbied energetically for causes of the far left.

In time Leibman decided that it was easier and more profitable raising money from conservatives. Since most of the money raised was wasted in the process of getting it, he could actually help the left more by working for the right.

After the communists had taken over mainland China, they began agitating for membership in the *United Nations*. This seemed like a good cause so Liebman joined up with several other pseudo-patriots (including Representative *Walter Judd*, former New Jersey governor *Charles Edison* and former Ambassador *Joseph Grew* and his old boss Oram) to form the *Committee of One Million* (against the admission of Red China to the United Nations). Using conservative mailing lists purchased from naïve United States Nationalist organizations and many conservative political candidates, they began soliciting funds for their new committee. It was a spectacular financial success.

In 1955, Marvin Liebman teamed up with two energetic young anti-communists, one a recently graduated attorney named *Brent Bozel* and the other a promising young writer named *William Buckley*.

Marvin Liebman Associates became keeper of the mailing lists for a long series of organizations founded by Bozel, Buckley and other supposed conservatives. These included: *The Committee Against The Treaty of Moscow, Young Americans for Freedom, American*

Afro-Asian Educational Exchange, Public Action, Conservative Party of New York, Draft Goldwater, Miller for Vice-President, Buckley for Mayor, American Conservative Union, African-American Affairs Assoc., and the *International Youth Crusade.*

On five different occasions he filled Madison Square Garden with huge YAF rallies. He has sponsored *National Review* testimonial dinners for *Alfred Kohlberg, George Sokolsky,* and *Charles Edison.*

One of Liebman's current major projects is the *"American Chilean Council".* The supposed purpose of this organization is to give public relations support for the new anti-communist government of Chile. The real purpose is to raise funds for Marvin Liebman from companies having property there and to draw off additional funds from the legitimate Nationalist movement in the United States.

At least five officers in the *American-Chilean Council (Dr. Lev. E. Dobriansky, Prof. Joseph Dunner,* Ex-Congressman *Walter H. Judd, David A. Keene* and *Prof. Stefan T. Possony)* are all false Nationalists and are also all directors or officers in the *American Council for World Freedom.*

Although the *A.C.W.F.* published strongly worded anti-communist literature it was organized almost specifically to provide a legitimate seeming background from which its members could infiltrate into genuine Nationalist organizations. In this they were able to trick *Fred Schlafly,* husband of *Phyllis Schlafly,* by obtaining him to serve as president of this pseudo anti-communist organization.

One of Marvin Liebman's most enthusiastic pupils is an interesting young Fabian Society member named *Richard Viguerie. Viguerie* got his start in Harris County, Texas with a list of Republican party contributors. This list landed him a job with Liebman whose techniques and politics Viguerie found completely to his liking.

Following in Marvin Liebman's footsteps, Viguerie has built himself a tremendous mailing list of conservative Republicans as well as conservative Democrats and is now launching his own conservative "third party" movement. Along the way he has used his mailing lists to milk unsuspecting patriots out of their money in support of a series of seemingly good but actually hollow shell organizations.

The *National Association to keep and Bear Arms* was formed in Oregon as one of many fronts for the *Minutemen* but while the Minutemen organization's national leader was in prison NAKBA was taken over by a light haired, blue eyed secret Jew, *Charles Adams* and a suspected Jew, *Rod Rose*. In 1975 the headquarters was moved to Missouri and both Adams and Rose expelled from membership.

Adams is now working with the *Council to Restore the Constitution* of *Col Arch Roberts* as is *Robert Preston*, a confidence man who previously swindled United States Nationalists of $3,000,000.00 on silver they paid for but he never delivered.

Among other secret Jews that have drained money from the United States Nationalist movement for decades can be named *Harry Everingham* of "*We The people*" (first in Chicago, now in Phoenix) and also *Willis Stone* who has recently turned the leadership of the *Liberty Amendment Committee* over to another secret Jew, *Cleon Skousen*.

Willis Stone was one of the speakers at a July 4, 1976 meeting of *Liberty Lobby* as was also *Dan Pills*, another obnoxious Jew silver peddler.

Another socialist Jew who has falsely pretended to change sides is *Phillip Abbot Luce*. After many years of dedicated service to the left, Luce now publishes a newsletter called the *Pink Sheet of the Left*. In this he pretends to expose secrets of the various communist organizations for the information and as assistance to United States Nationalists. The truth is that he prints nothing except what the socialists print in their own publications or what they want him to print in his which serves their own purposes.

HOMOSEXUAL INFILTRATION INTO THE U.S. NATIONALIST MOVEMENT

Within the United States, the Nationalist movement has been infiltrated by homosexuals to an extent that is almost incredible. The following account will trace only the broad and general outlines of this infiltration.

We can begin with the now aging homosexual James Madole who has, for about thirty years, led a small neo-Nazi organization called the *National Renaissance Party*". Located in New York City, Madole has been always financed by wealthy Jews. What Madole's true political beliefs may be is hard to ascertain. He may sincerely subscribe to the Nationalist Socialist policies that he advocates. Be this as it may, his primary purpose in maintaining the National Renaissance Party has been to keep himself surrounded by a never-ending supply of young homosexual converts.

The purpose which Madole serves for his financial angels is to help keep alive the threat of "Nazism" in the public mind. He also helps the communists and Jewish leaders maintain the pretext that the Jews are continually threatened by new waves of persecution and a thus helps maintain solidarity within their ranks.

An early member of the NRP was *George Lincoln Rockwell* who had been a Commander in the United States Navy during World War II. While stationed in Iceland he met the daughter of the head of the Iceland Communist Party and later she became his wife. When Rockwell was discharged from the Navy his wife returned to the United States with him and they lived together for several years. It was during the time that George Lincoln Rockwell was openly friendly with James Madole that his wife finally divorced him and returned to Iceland. Rockwell broke with Madole to form his own organization, the *American Nazi Party* with headquarters in *Arlington, Virginia.*

In his national headquarters, George Lincoln Rockwell was constantly surrounded by a group of "storm troopers" that included a few good men but consisted mostly of social misfits, a surprising number of Jews, and a high percentage of homosexuals. Among the homosexuals that served in the Nazi Party headquarters, at one time or another, were *John Patler* (who was later convicted of having murdered Rockwell) *Roy Frankhouser, Dan Burros, James K. Warner, William Pierce* and many others.

Roy Frankhouser left the *American Nazi Party* to serve as Grand Dragon for the *Ku Klux Klan* in Pennsylvania and later became a Band Leader in the *Minutemen* Organization before finally being exposed as a paid informant for the FBI and the Alcohol, Tobacco and Firearms Tax Division of the Treasury Department who received his reward money through the Jewish Community Center in Reading, Pennsylvania.

Dan Burros, who had an intermittent homosexual affair with *Roy Frankhouser* was later murdered in Frankhouser's apartment (probably by Frankhouser himself) after it was proven that Burros was really a Jew whose true name was *Daniel Sonnstein.* Burros also carried on an intermittent homosexual affair at the Nazi Headquarters with *James Warner* who at the time considered himself an *Odinist* and therefore anti-Christian. Apparently, *Warner* knew that *Burros* was a Jew long before the other members of the American Nazi Party learned this fact. It is said that *Warner* and *Burros* spent their time discussing hideous ways to torture and kill Christians and some day setting up a phoney organization to blackmail Christians and get their money before exterminating them.

Among *Roy Frankhouser's* other queer friends are *the two Gerhardt brothers* who operate a post office tripe organization out of Columbus, Ohio, which they call the *American White Nationalist Party*. These two perverts limit their homosexual activities mostly between themselves although they enjoy occasional visits with their so-called Iowa organizer, another half demented pervert named Mike Papich.

Among those who know them well, *the Gerhardt boys* are referred to as the "dingaling brothers". Without meaning to do so, they carry on a continuos Bud Abbott and Lou Costello routine, continually bumping into each other and falling over each other's feet and doing all that they can (quite unintentionally) to convince any chance observer that United States Nationalists must all be insane.

Another of the Gerhardt brothers' pals is paid government informant *Lou Card* (better known by his *alias Joe Chance*) who is part Jewish and in spite of being married to a very attractive wife, is homosexual also. Both the *Gerhardts* and *Lou Card* are friendly with paid ADL informant *William Sickles* who has been instrumental in organizing a group known as the *White Confederacy*. This confederacy includes a weird mixture of different organizations, both good and bad. Among these are:

> *Adamic Knights of the Ku Klux Klan*, (mostly good people).

> *American Revolutionary Army*. This is the address of the Federal Penitentiary in Atlanta. The American Revolutionary Army consisted of exactly one man named *A. H. Williams* who was convicted of kidnapping newspaper editor *Reg Murphy*. Williams has been diagnosed by prison psychiatrists as schizophrenic. Even Williams own defense attorney called him "crazy as a bedbug".

> *American White Nationalist Party*, organized and operated by the *Gerhardt brothers* referred to above.

> *Christian Vikings of America*, (strictly a front group).

> *Marion County Sheriffs Posse Comitatus*.

> *Minutemen of Indiana*. This organization is operated by the paid agent of the ATFD, *Lou Card* which has been referred to above. This group is not to be confused with

the National Minutemen Organization operating from Norborne, Missouri, a bonafide anti-communist group.

Western Guard Party. This is a small group composed of real Canadian nationalists.

National Socialist Liberation Front. A splinter group of the old Nazi Party commanded by 50 per cent Jew *David Rust* who is at least friendly with some of the homosexual Nazis, friendly to homosexual *William Morrison*, publisher of the "Gay Nazi" publication *National Socialist Mobilizer*.

National Socialist Party of America. Although somewhat confused ideologically, members of this group are generally high caliber individuals.

National Socialist White People's Party of Ohio.

NSDAP. Generally a group of weird characters.

Social Credit Association of Ontario, Inc. Higher type economic-political

United White Peoples Party. Very few members, but generally good.

A separate organization calling themselves *"Alpha Circle"* operates out of ... Portland, OR. They recommend the following organizations: *American White Nationalist Party* of Columbus, OH; *Knights of the Ku Klux Klan* of Metairie, LA; *National Alliance* of Washington, D. C.; *National Socialist White People's Party of Arlington*, VA; *National States Rights Party* of Marietta, GA; and *Western Guard Party* of Canada. Of all these organizations, Western Guard is the only one not having a homosexual among their top leadership.

Another Jew that served briefly with *George Lincoln Rockwell* and the *American Nazi Party* was a chiropractor known as *Dr. Edward R. Fields*. Fields left the ANP to join the *National States Rights Party* in Alabama which was headed by a sincere but slightly senile old man named *Ned Dupes*. It did not take long for Fields to acquire operating leadership of the NSRP and complete control of its publication, *The Thunderbolt*.

In 1960 *James Warner* decided to leave the American Nazi Party. He told Rockwell that his mother was dying in Wilkes-Barre, Pennsylvania, and needed to visit her immediately. Rockwell gave Warner some money, loaned him his car and even helped him pack the car. Among the things that Warner took with him was a copy of Rockwell's mailing list.[2] Rockwell first learned that Warner had stolen a copy of his mailing list when everyone on that list received an expose regarding the communist affiliations of Rockwell's wife as well as the fact that Rockwell was receiving funds from the same people that were still financing *James Madole*.

In the spring of 1961 *The Thunderbolt* denounced Warner as a profiteer but strangely enough, *James K. Warner* soon showed up as an employee in the *NSRP* headquarters.

Dan Burros had confided to his "girlfriend" *James Warner* that like himself, *Ed Fields* was a Jew. Actually, Fields is the "poor relative" of two very wealthy Chicago Jewish families. On his father's side he is related to the Jewish Fields dry goods family and on his mother's side to the Jewish Morrell meat packing family. Warner was able to use this information to blackmail Fields into dropping his expose and into actually taking him into his own headquarters.

It was only a few months later that Warner talked one of Field's secretaries into thinking that he planned to marry her. The two disappeared from the *NSRP* headquarters (along with a copy of Field's mailing list) and the next thing Fields heard about it was a phone call from his secretary saying that Warner had left her stranded and asking for bus fare home.

After Warner left the NSRP, leadership of the Party was taken over by *J.B. Stoner*, a homosexual Jew who formerly worked as an ADL investigator out of the Miami, Florida office of the B'nai B'rith.

Warner formed an organization called "*Sons of Liberty*" using the various mailing lists he had stolen from the *American Nazi Party*, the *National States Rights Party*, etc. Warner's organization called *Sons of Liberty* should not be confused with at least two other

---

[2] Leaders of the racialist right wing hold tightly to their mailing lists. For most of these men, the mailing list is their sole economic lifeline, and without it most simply could not operate. For these leaders, the option of a "nine to five" job is both unappealing and unlikely. Unappealing because of the time and energy a real-world job would require that could otherwise be spent on the movement. Unlikely because, for well-known leaders, the possibility that an employer would offer a job is remote. Moreover, even in the case of lesser lights, should local watchdog organizations get wind of the situation, it is safe to assume that pressure would soon be brought to bear to fire the racialist leader. This state of affairs has in some cases inhibited defections from the movement, but at the same time, has made the mailing list "a pearl beyond price." The suspicion that an activist might have once absconded with such a list is thus, in movement circles, far more serious than involvement in the putative communist, Jewish and/or homosexual conspiracies.

organizations of the same name, directed by sincere Nationalists of good reputation. This was only marginally profitable so he then [went] into partnership with *Willis Carto* and *Roger Pearson* in the publication of *"Western Destiny"*. For unknown reasons, this combination soon broke up. Carto continued to find considerable success with his publication *"Washington Observer"*, his organization *"Liberty Lobby"* and many other organizational activities. Pearson began printing the *"New Patriot"* but after this folded, Pearson claimed that *Warner* had stolen his mailing list also.

Going back to 1961, in the state of Missouri a genuinely anti-communist organization called the Minutemen had been formed and was now getting considerable national publicity. A photographer for *"Life"* magazine, assigned to do a story on the Minutemen, happened be a homosexual and he devised his own rather cute scheme to personally discredit the Minutemen organization. Returning to his home base in California, the Life photographer gathered together a number his homosexual associates in San Diego, took a number of photos of them. He then turned in a story to his magazine about the California section of the Minutemen organization. Apparently, the original idea was to have the California "Minutemen" identify themselves as homosexuals thus helping to smear the national Minutemen organization but it didn't work out that way. Among the San Diego group of homosexuals, one was a rather power hungry individual who saw in the Minutemen concept an easy way to boost his ego, get a little adventure and perhaps earn himself an easy living in the process. This man, *Troy Haughton*, telephoned to *Robert DePugh* the leader of the National Minutemen Organization and offered to merge his organization with the national group. DePugh, anxious to see his own organization expand, unsuspectingly welcomed the San Diego homosexuals into his organization.

Haughton was later publicly identified as a homosexual but apparently convinced *DePugh* that this was part of some "communist frame-up" and DePugh continued to let *Haughton* serve as his West Coast Coordinator for several years. Eventually Haughton disappeared and it has been rumored that he was assassinated by the Minutemen Organization to avoid further embarrassment from his ever more flagrant sexual deviations.

In 1963 or 1964, one of Haughton's homosexual partners was a young man named *Dennis Mower* who had formally been a chauffeur for *"Identity"* preacher *Dr. Wesley Swift*.

After Haughton's disappearance, *Dennis Mower*, along with another homosexual ex-Minuteman named *Don Sisco (who uses the pen name of Kurt Saxon*) joined the *Satanic church of San Francisco* whose high priest was a Jew named *Anton LaVey*. *Warner* began attending the Satanic church about this time and became acquainted with Dennis Mower. They formed a brief homosexual association during which Mower gave Warner a considerable amount of information about *Wesley Swift's* church and the very profitable manner in which he preached the "Identity" message. Warner began reading Swift's material and listening to his tape recorded lectures. Having decided that this was the money making racket he had been looking for, *Warner* proclaimed himself Director of the *New Christian Crusade Church*. From a number of wealthy homosexuals within the Identity movement, Warner obtained an expensive house where he lived with a series of other perverts. Well meaning followers of the Identity Church pitched in to buy Warner an expensive printing press upon which he turned out literature for the New Christian Crusade Church and on which he also printed a militantly "gay" publication called *Pride*.

About this time James Warner became closely associated with a man named *William Morrison* (now owner of *Angriff Press*) who had a long police record as a child molester and homosexual. On and off for most of two years, Warner and Morrison lived together in a homosexual arrangement often attending "gay" parties together where they were seen dressed in women's clothing on frequent occasions.

Between 1970 and 1975 both *Warner* and *Morrison* received considerable sources of income unexplained by the sale of their literature, contributions, etc. Morrison has specialized in publishing and selling books that would be of particular interest to militant Nationalists in the United States. This has now become a very profitable business for him as well as an excellent means of obtaining additional names and addresses of United States Nationalists.

Going back to *Roy Frankhouser*. After being expelled from membership in both the *United Klans of America, Inc.* and the *Minutemen*, Frankhouser teamed up with another homosexual named *Frank Draeger*. They purchased a printing press in partnership and for a time attempted to earn their living at reprinting plagiarized Minutemen training manuals and similar materials. This association broke up when Draeger found himself a new boyfriend, stole the printing press which he subsequently sold to buy a pickup truck and camper. For about eighteen months after that, Draeger and his new homosexual partner traveled around the country until he was finally arrested in Springfield, Illinois on charges of homosexual conduct, possession of marijuana and possession of illegal firearms. The ATFD, for whom Draeger had long been an informant, quickly came to his rescue and he was soon released on minimum bond. He was never called back to Springfield to face these charges.

Moving back to New Jersey, Draeger then put out a "call to revolution" and soon succeeded in trapping a number of sincere patriots in that area into a situation where they were arrested for possession of illegal weapons by ATFD agents. For the sake of appearances, Draeger was arrested along with the others but whereas they were all held on high bonds, Draeger was again released quickly and on his own recognizance.

Turning now to another part of the country we can pick up still another line of homosexual infiltration into the United States Nationalist movement. In New Orleans, *Ned Touchstone* has been known for many years as one of the most dedicated and capable publishers in the right wing movement. His newspaper, *The Councilor*, was long admired for its original material and expose of the communist apparatus. As the right wing movement changed and The Councilor met increasingly stiff competition from other publications, Ned Touchstone began to neglect his paper and turn his attention to other business affairs. It would not be fair to say that these other "business affairs" were confidence games but to a large degree they did entail the sale of essentially valueless gimmicks to the subscribers of his newspaper and to other American Nationalists of his acquaintance.

Yet, we have no reason to believe that Ned Touchstone was not sincere in his patriotic beliefs or that he failed to promote the cause of Nationalism within the limits of his financial and personal capabilities.

Touchstone, like many other patriotic Americans of his generation had the unhappy experience of sending his son away to college as a good young American patriot but watching him become brainwashed by the ultra-liberal college environment. Whether or not the young Touchstone was a sexual deviate before entering college or not is unknown. At any rate, within a year he was keeping company with a group of homosexual students and had become active in the *Students for Democratic Society*. Needless to say, this was a source of considerable anguish to his father and probably contributed at least in part to the elder Touchstone's loss of efficiency.

One of the SDS members that made young Touchstone's acquaintance was a man named *David Duke*. Duke was a liberal that overflowed with sympathy for the negro people. He hated the way that his fellow whites had treated the negroes so badly that he began his own business which he called "Black Products" and which operated out of P.O. Box 1234 Denham Springs, Louisiana. "Black Products" advertised in Sepia magazine to sell a book on African methods of self-defense which gave instructions in how the blacks could rid themselves of their hostile feelings by disabling whites with their bare hands.

This apparently did not prove too profitable so David Duke was more than interested in the stories told to him by young Touchstone as to how easy it was to sucker gullible Nationalists out of their money.

Since the *Ku Klux Klan* was handy, Duke began hanging around their meetings, picking up literature and learning the routine. Once he felt he had his technique perfected, Duke proclaimed himself Director of the *Knights of the Ku Klux Klan* and began soliciting speaking engagements and television interviews.

Since Duke likes girls as well as boys, he began a convenient affair with a young secretary, capable of running his mail order business while he was away. Ultimately, Duke showed good faith by getting married to this girl but only after her pregnancy was becoming conspicuous.

Meanwhile, in Hollywood, California, *James K. Warner* had built up a very prosperous business. Using the mailing lists he had stolen from the *American Nazi Party*, *NSRP*, *Willis Carto* and *Dr. Wesley Swift* he was able to build up a large subscription to his own publication, *The National Vanguard*. With working capital obtained from unknown sources he was able to maintain a large inventory of books which he sold through his mail order bookshop. With the help of well meaning volunteer workers such as Ruth van Slyke and Barbara Updegraff, Warner was able to operate with a minimum overhead and maximum profit. He did little work himself, leafing through the day and attending gay parties most nights. Occasionally he would take time away from Hollywood to attend Nationalist meetings held by other organizations in hopes of making still more contacts.

It was at such a meeting in 1974 that James Warner first met David Duke. Apparently it was love at first sight because Warner immediately invited Duke to come to California as a speaker before his own group and helped Duke arrange a number of radio and television interviews in the Los Angeles area. James Warner was soon following David Duke around, holding hands with him in public bars and casting long loving glances his way, such as only a new bride would be expected to cast upon her husband. Within a matter of weeks, *Warner* announced that he was leaving Hollywood. He sold his property there, abandoned most of his faithful workers and moved his entire operation to Louisiana, literally turning everything he owned over to *David Duke*.

Having milked Warner for most of his money and property, David Duke then began to personally orchestrate a smear campaign against Warner. No doubt he will ultimately ask Warner to leave Louisiana "for the good of the movement".

After Jim Warner left California, his old boy friend, *William Morrison* teamed up with a few local queers and a homosexual ex-Nazi from Ohio to form a new organization known as the "Gay Nazis". They publish a magazine called *National Socialist Mobilizer*, which has included photographs of pretty young men, stark naked except for their swastika arm bands. Most issues contain large advertisements for William Morrison's *Angriff Press* and for Jim Warner's mail order book shop, as well as an occasional ad promoting *David Duke*.

The most common type of advertising however, which is carried by this publication is classified ads placed by Nazi queers wanting to make contact with other Nazi queers. A typical ad reads as follows: "Subservient young man, dedicated to national Socialism, desires to provide complete oral service for dynamic male holding leadership position within the American Nazi movement".

Now going back to *Dennis Mower*, *Don Sisco* and the Satanic Church of *Anton LaVey*. Warner maintained his homosexual alliance with Dennis Mower only long enough to enlist Mower's help in stealing the mailing list from *Wesley Swift*.

Don Sisco found it less profitable to publish books and pamphlets on Satanism than to publish such material on survival, demolitions and guerilla warfare. Using the pen-name *Kurt Saxon*, Sisco began his own company which is called *Atlan Formularies*. Among the books he has published are *"The Poor Mans James Bond" "Explosives Like Grandfather Used to Make"*, and *"Wheels of Rage"*. The latter book is a somewhat fictionalized account of Sisco's experiences with a Nazi motorcycle gang giving peripheral insights into the more far-out elements of the Minutemen organization and other right wing groups. He devotes a couple of pages to snide remarks regarding his old friend and fellow homosexual *James Warner* as well as Warner's boyfriend, *Bill Morrison*.

About 1970, Don Sisco was called before a congressional investigating committee on internal violence. He took along all of the names and addresses of those people that had bought books from him and devoted most of his testimony to statements of ridicule about the various patriotic leaders and organizations of his acquaintance. Still using the name Kurt Saxon, Sisco's latest enterprise is the publication of a monthly tabloid newspaper called *"The Survivor"*.

During the 1950's and early 1960's a newsletter called *Tocsin* was published in Berkeley, California by a man named *Charles Fox*. Although Fox was a flagrant homosexual, we have no other reason to doubt his patriotism or the effectiveness of his work against the communist movement.

Using homosexual contacts in the *Berkeley Socialist Society*, Fox was able to keep himself informed as to almost all important activities of the various communist organizations and communist fronts throughout the state of California. Their activities, including the names, addresses and phone numbers of individuals involved, were dutifully reported in his newsletter, Tocsin.

Over a period of two decades, Fox was able to compile an uncomparably complete set of intelligence files regarding individuals on the West Coast that were active in all types of communist organizations. When Fox died in the early 1960's the publication of Tocsin was discontinued and all of his intelligence files were inherited by another supposed "right wing" homosexual named *George Bundy*. Bundy operates the *"The Church League of America"* located in Wheaten, Illinois.

The Church League of America published a considerable amount of worthwhile anti-communist literature and they allow other anti-communist organizations and individuals to have limited access to their intelligence files. All of this is to be expected from an organization that wants to keep the contributions rolling in. At the same time, much of the material published by the Church League of America is deceptive, evades the real issues and probably does more harm than good. Other workers at the Church League of America office report that the really hard core intelligence files kept there are never made available to other Nationalist groups.

Over the past ten years we have received numerous reports from persons who begin work in George Bundy's offices only to move on after he had made homosexual advances toward them or after they had observed him in homosexual activities with others. Bundy does not limit his homosexual affairs to other American nationalists. One of his most feverish romances involved a male Russian ballet dancer that was touring the United States. There may be some who wonder how Church League Director George Bundy would happen to know a homosexual Russian male ballet dancer. The answer lies in their mutual membership within the International Brotherhood. The International Brotherhood is not comprised of ordinary homosexuals. It includes only homosexuals who are rich, famous or counted among the intellectual elite. Within nationalist circles of the United States perhaps the most influential member of the International Brotherhood was a young (at that time) attorney and author named Francis Parker Yockey of which we will have more to say later on.

Returning again to Berkeley, California. Among those who learned their first lessons in anti-communism from Charles Fox, were two young men, *Willis Carto* and his roommate, *Kent Steffgen*.

Kent Steffgen refers to himself as an author. His three books include one called *"Bondage of the Free"* and two books devoted to successive smears of Governor Ronald Reagan and later Presidential candidate Ronald Reagan. Later in their careers both *Carto* and *Steffgen* served further apprenticeship as paid workers for the *John Birch Society*. During most of his life however, Kent Steffgen has earned his money acting as an escort for plump old ladies and has spent most of his money to buy the services of plump young men.

Self-proclaimed genius, Francis Parker Yockey was a Harvard Law School graduate and assistant prosecutor at the Nuremberg trials of WW II Nazi leaders. Yockey left this job before the trials were over but not before he developed a strong feeling of sympathy for the Nazi ideology and for his fellow homosexual Hermann Goering. Having made contact with Goering through a friendly guard, Yockey provided him with the cyanide capsule which Goering used to avoid his date with the hangman. For the next few years Yockey traveled around the world as an unofficial organizer and messenger of the International Brotherhood. As a welcome guest into the homes of many of the world's most famous and wealthy homosexuals, Yockey had time to pursue his further knowledge of Nazism and political philosophy. Drawing heavily on Spengler's book *"Decline of the West"* Yockey wrote his own book which he called *"Imperium"*.

Eventually Yockey was arrested in San Francisco on a passport violation and held under $50,000 bond. While in jail there, he had only one visitor, Willis Carto. Carto helped repay Yockey's kindness to Goering by slipping him the cyanide capsule with which Yockey himself committed suicide. After his visit to Yockey, Carto's fortunes began to improve rapidly. He quickly left the ranks of poverty stricken right-wing followers to become an eminently successful conservative leader. Naturally, one of his first projects was to publish the book *"Imperium"* and form an organization to help promote its ideology, the *Francis Parker Yockey Society*. During the next few years, Carto launched one of the most expensive and spectacular mailing campaigns ever seen among United States Nationalist organizations. He quickly built up the circulation of his newsletter *"Washington Observer"* to about 150,000 subscribers. At $1.00 per year subscription rate it is obvious that neither the mailing campaign or the publication could pay for themselves. Admittedly, Carto lives frugally and works hard. Frugal living and hard work are not enough however to account for the sums of money which this man has spent in promoting his publications and building his *"Liberty Lobby"* organization. It seems probable that at least part of this money comes from wealthy friends of the late Francis Parker Yockey among the International Brotherhood.

Our investigations do not reveal whether or not *Willis Carto* is himself a homosexual but during his early years of political indoctrination he was a close companion of such known homosexuals as Charles Fox, Kent Steffgen and James Warner. Carto married rather late in life and it is said by some that his obtaining a bride was more of a purchase than a marriage. His wife is a blue-eyed blonde German girl that he brought back from a business trip to Germany.

According to one of Carto's very few close friends, his wife was "purchased" not so much as a bed partner but to improve Carto's personal image within the National Socialist Movement.

In more recent years also Carto has been a close associate of other known homosexuals such as *Kurt Saxon*, *C. B. Baker*, *Pat Tifer*, and *William Pierce*, *Oren F. Potito*.

Another sometimes associate of Willis Carto was devil-worshipper *Ken Duggan*, who hanged himself in his jail cell after having been convicted of shooting another homosexual named *George Wilke* in a gay bar. The homosexual *Wilke* is by chance, a grand dragon in homosexual David Duke's Knights of the Ku Klux Klan.

An especially revolting example of homosexual activity among American National movements is the case of *Billy James Hargis*. This vulgar and obscene beast, using the disguise of Christianity, induced Christian Nationalist parents into sending their children to his various church camps and university. Using his prestige and honored position to best advantage for himself, the so-called Rev. Hargis committed homosexual acts upon a long series of young boys and a few young girls. Some of his activities were finally disclosed in a 1976 issue of Time magazine.

Several months before the publication of this article, four boys and one girl, all students at *Billy James Hargis's Christian Crusade College* in Tulsa, Oklahoma, had gone before a group of University officials and had all accused Hargis of committing sodomy on them. Called before these University officials, Hargis admitted that he was guilty of performing these acts.

Because they wished to save their children from public disgrace, the parents of these students have refused to bring criminal charges against Rev. Hargis. Since Hargis was the principal means of raising funds for the Christian Crusade university and since these officials' salaries depended on such funds, it took them about a year to admit that they had been present and had witnessed the full confession by Hargis of these homosexual activities.

For about one year, Hargis removed himself from Tulsa and hid out on a farm in Southern Missouri. However after the publication in Time magazine, Hargis brazenly returned to Tulsa and demanded his position as leader of the *Christian Crusade Church*. It is a sad commentary on the hypocrisy of most of the workers and other associates of this supposed Christian organization that they accepted Hargis back rather than to see a reduction in their own financial income.

The Church College did break away from Hargis' domination and the officers of that church published a full account of the accusation by four boys and one girl that Hargis committed sodomy on them and his open confession to the truth of these accusations.

The number of young persons who have accused Hargis openly is small compared with the actual number involved. Our investigators have located not less than nine boys with whom Hargis had homosexual relations and two additional girls upon which he committed sodomy between the years of 1960 and 1974.

That persons who call themselves Christians continue to send this beast money is almost unbelievable but strange to say, the Rev. Billy James Hargis is still taking in millions of dollars per year and living in complete luxury at the expense of the other United States Nationalists.

Almost apologetically, we mention the pathetic case of General Edwin Walker and the not so pathetic case of his former associate, *Col. Arch Roberts.* Papers available to us relating to the Board of inquiry which resulted in General Walker's resignation prove the facts of this case.

General Edwin Walker was without doubt a fine military commander and expert military tactician. In addition, he was without doubt a sincere American nationalist and strong anti-communist. While serving in the European theater, General Walker prepared and disseminated among his troops an excellent indoctrination against communism which was referred to as the "pro-blue" program. This program was very beneficial and much needed. It should have been made available to all troops of the United States everywhere.

Unfortunately this excellent work was done by a man who was known to his enemies as being a secret homosexual. To destroy the effectiveness of Walker's pro-blue program, evidence was given to higher military authorities regarding his homosexual relationships with other men in and out of military service. Arch Roberts, then a Major serving under General Walker, was one of several persons named as being active in these homosexual contacts.

In the face of undeniable evidence, General Walker was forced to resign. After his return to the United States he began giving lectures in which he stated that he had been removed solely because of the pro-blue program and that he had voluntarily refused to accept any retirement benefits. These papers, referred to previously, prove that Walker was forced to resign and waive all retirement benefits in return for an agreement by military authorities not to bring criminal charges against him which would have resulted in public disclosure of his homosexual behavior and that of others.

After his return to Dallas, Texas, General Walker [decided] to run for Governor of that state and became temporarily active in the Nationalist movement in that area. Gradually he became shunned by other Nationalists who observed his living in obvious homosexual relationship with a young man that he referred to as his "adjutant". For several weeks, *General Walker* traveled with *Billy James Hargis* sharing the speaker's platform and often times sharing his bed as well. During this period and in subsequent years, Walker's mental abilities began to deteriorate and he began wandering aimlessly through the streets and parks of Dallas. On several occasions he was arrested as a public nuisance or for soliciting homosexual contacts but released by police officers that did not want to discredit his previously fine reputation. Finally, in 1976, Walker was arrested and stood public trial for making homosexual solicitations to a Dallas park plain clothes security officer.

The "tax-strike movement" is a unique phenomenon found only in the United States involving persons of a generally different type

from most Nationalist organizations but having definite Nationalist strengths. Perhaps it is due to the unique nature of these organizations that they have remained relatively free from all types of
infiltration. Two notable exceptions can be mentioned; disbarred
attorneys *Jerome Daley* and *William Drexler* who are not only
homosexuals but alcoholics and outright thieves as well.

SUMMARY

In this communication, we have discussed the nature of the anti-
Nationalist Conspiracies with special attention to the United
States and also a discussion of socialist, Jewish and homosexual
infiltration into Nationalist organizations.

It has not been our intention to give a full assessment of Nationalist organizations within the United States or to discuss their relative merits. Neither has it been our intention to dwell unduly on the
bad side of the picture. There are several active Nationalist organizations that have succeeded fairly well in keeping their ranks free
of socialist, Jewish and homosexual infiltrators.

There are many good Nationalist Organizations within the
United States and numerous smaller organizations that show
promise. Only time will tell which, if any of then, can survive the
struggle and ultimately provide the leadership which will be so
badly needed in the years ahead.

A Brief History of White Nationalism
Rick Cooper, National Socialist Vanguard

"A Brief History of White Nationalism" is an important document in that it is one of the first truly internal histories to emerge from the movement. Rick Cooper is to be commended for the research and thought that went into its production. As he hoped, this history is a valuable scholarly resource, and it is as a primary historical source that it is reproduced here. At the same time, the discourse, which is typical of the internal discussions within the White Nationalist movement, may be unfamiliar to or uncomfortable for some readers of this encyclopedia. In particular, internal movement documents tend to characterize some widely recognized movement figures as secret Jews, secret homosexuals, secret government agents, and, during the Cold War years, secret communists. Perhaps the best extant example of this style of discourse may be found in the "Deguello Report." It goes without saying that the editor of this encyclopedia has no evidence of, nor indeed interest in, the accuracy of these charges. Rather, it was felt that the historical value of "A Brief History of White Nationalism" merits its inclusion in these pages and that the reader should be allowed to draw his or her own conclusions as to the merits of Cooper's arguments. It should be noted in this context as well that, virtually alone in the highly divisive world of the American racial right, Cooper has made some considerable effort to investigate and verify the welter of charges and countercharges that are the "meat and potatoes" of internal movement discourse. Moreover, he writes candidly of his unsuccessful efforts to obtain documentary evidence of particular charges—even when there is widespread agreement as to the veracity of this or that charge. This has been true in the historical cases noted in this document, as well as in more contemporary controversies such as the recent (1997) movement dispute that saw Tom Metzger accused of allowing a representative of the Southern Poverty Law Center to intercept his mail as a condition of settling a judgment the Center won against Metzger in the wrongful death of an Ethiopian immigrant who was beaten by skinheads.

———————————————

INTRODUCTION: This brief history of the White Nationalist Movement is being published for two reasons—(1) to provide an insider's view since almost all of the history of the Movement available to scholars, researchers, book authors, historians and sociologists is the history given by the establishment educational system and any combination of government agencies such as the Justice Department, the Federal Bureau of Investigation (FBI) and various law enforcement agencies, most of which get their information directly or indirectly from the Anti-Defamation League (ADL) of the B'nai B'rith and other anti-White groups; and (2) to educate the novices within the Movement about Movement history and a little about some of the people involved in the Movement.

This article will upset some people, anger others and bring humor to yet more. For those of you who disagree with this historical overview, you are free to write your own version and publish it, hoping that the historians and researchers of today will consider your views worthy of publishing tomorrow. Perhaps these historians and researchers will find this article to be a good chronological outline for their works, and they are encouraged to contact the National Socialist Vanguard for details.

THE BEGINNING: By the term "White Nationalist Movement", we refer to that movement by White people who want a nation for White people only and advocate total geographic separation of the world's races. After World War II, the first White Nationalist group to emerge was the National Renaissance Party (NRP) in 1949 under the leadership of James H. Madole in the New York City area. We say the NRP was the first White Nationalist group because the American Bund was disbanded during World War II by the United States government and no Klan group existing at that time ever had a program for a White territorial imperative. Rather, these Klan groups advocated separate but equal policies regarding race. Not one Klan group advocated total geographic separation of the races as far as we know. The NRP, which consisted of a small number of sincere patriots, was backed, at least in part, by Jewish money and infiltrated by a group of homosexuals, some of whom are still around today, posing as White Nationalist leaders. In case some of you are unaware, historically Jewish organizations have helped finance and even lead anti-Jewish groups for the purpose of scaring and intimidating other Jews to donate money to these Jewish organizations so the organizations can "fight" the anti-Jewish groups. For this reason, Jewish money helped finance the

NRP. There have been many stories, many of them consistent, over the years regarding the homosexuals in the NRP.[1] At least three names are prominent and worth mentioning -all others are insignificant.

Closely associated with the NRP was a group called the Free Ezra Pound Committee (FEPC) which was headed by three homosexuals - Eustace Mullins was chairman of the FEPC and an NRP member, Attorney Edward Fleckenstein was legal counsel of the FEPC whose NRP membership status is unknown, and Matthias Koehl, Jr., who was secretary of the FEPC and not an NRP member. The homosexuality of these three was no secret. The Free Ezra Pound Committee was formed to work for the release of incarcerated poet Ezra Pound (now deceased) who was locked up in St. Elizabeth's mental hospital in Washington, D.C., for political reasons. Ezra Pound was an American citizen who made pro-Axis and anti-Allied radio broadcasts in Italy during World War II. During the middle 1950s, Eustace Mullins and Matt Koehl went on tours down South, the East Coast and Mid-West area to speak out on behalf of the imprisoned Ezra Pound.

In about 1955, Mullins, Koehl and Fleckenstein were arrested in New York State regarding the sodomizing of a teenage boy in the back seat of a car on a county road. As the story goes, the three queers picked up a hitch hiker, Fleckenstein was the aggressor, Mullins the observer and Koehl the driver. After Fleckenstein was finished with the boy, the boy was dumped off the side of the road where the boy noted the car license number and reported the incident to his parents. The parents filed a police report, supposedly with the Middletown police, and the three queers were arrested. Eventually, the parents decided not to press charges. When James Madole learned about the incident, he expelled Eustace Mullins from the NRP as this was apparently the "last straw" of embarrassment that Mullins and his queer associates had caused to the image of the NRP. On July 15, 1985, NSV Director Cooper, posing as an independent writer, paid a visit to the Middletown police to inquire about the arrest which, by this time, had occurred about 30 years previously. Lieutenant Dino seemed very interested in the story about the homosexual involvement in the "American Nazi Movement's" beginning. Lieutenant Dino thumbed through a file of 3x5-inch cards which went back to the early 1950s but found nothing under the names of "Edward Fleckenstein", "Eustace Mullins"

---

[1] *National Socialist Vanguard*, P.O. Box 328, The Dalles, OR 97058.

and "Matthias Koehl, Jr." It is noted, however, that anybody could have just plucked any card he wanted out of the file and destroyed it. On July 16, 1985, Director Cooper went to the county court house in Goshen and found nothing; however, if no charges were pressed, then there would be no court record.

During 1959 and 1960, both Mullins and Koehl volunteered to assist Retired Rear Admiral John G. Crommelin on Crommelin's bid for Vice President of the United States. Crommelin allowed Mullins and Koehl to stay in the basement of his Wetumpka, Alabama, farmhouse as they helped work on his campaign until the day when Crommelin found the two playing around and ordered them off his property. Because Crommelin never did like homosexuals, he never kept it a secret why he booted Mullins and Koehl off his property. Years later, Crommelin told former deputy commander of the American Nazi Party (ANP), Karl Allen, that Mullins and Koehl were queers. Karl Allen later told former ANP member Christopher Bailey, and Chris then told Director Cooper in the early 1980s. It should be noted that neither Crommelin nor Allen have answered Director Cooper's registered letters to them, asking specific questions about the Mullins-Koehl relationship on Crommelin's farm or anywhere else. On July 22, 1985, NSV Director Cooper checked the court records in Wetumpka for a restraining order which Crommelin supposedly filed against Mullins and Koehl to keep them legally off his property. Although the date of this occurrence is not known, court records were checked back as far as the available records there. Records previous to that were in the archives which were kept in the old jail and those were not checked.

THE NATIONAL STATES RIGHTS PARTY

During the 1950s, the National States Right Party (NSRP) was formed. This party advocated total geographic separation of the races and an all-White America, which means that it was a White Nationalist group by the definition previously given. Under the chairmanship of J. B. Stoner and with Dr. Edward R. Fields as national secretary, who also edited *The Thunderbolt*, which was the NSRP's official publication, the NSRP quickly became the largest White Nationalist organization in the country. J. B. Stoner and other NSRP members were running for political offices, mainly in the South, *The Thunderbolt* had the largest circulation of any White Nationalist paper in the country and probably the world, and the NSRP had more dues-paying members than any other White Nationalist group in the country. Although the NSRP advocated the same basic beliefs and principles as National Socialism, there was still no Nazi Party that the Jewish groups wanted. Apparently the NSRP's watered down version of National Socialism was not good enough for the money-hungry leaders of Jewish scam groups.

THE AMERICAN NAZI PARTY

In the late 1950s, a White racialist named DeWest Hooker, then leader of the Nationalist Party, was approached by a Jewish representative or two and asked if he would be willing to start an American Nazi Party. Hooker was not interested. Once in a letter and once over the telephone, Director Cooper mentioned this to Hooker to verify whether or not this was true. Hooker never responded to the issue either time, neither admitting nor denying the allegation. In a subsequent telephone conversation after Hooker read this report, Hooker denied that he was approached by any Jews to start an overt National Socialist or Nazi group. In 1959, the late George Lincoln Rockwell founded the American Nazi Party (ANP) -not as a front group for Jewish scammers but out of dedication and sincere belief. Again, some Jews tried to control Rockwell where they failed with Hooker. Rockwell accepted Jewish money but he had no desire to form a phony group. Instead, Rockwell built the ANP and attracted some of the most dedicated White Nationalists in the country and perhaps some of the kookiest too.

Other White Nationalists, some of whom are still around today, joined Rockwell's ANP from 1959 through August 25, 1967, the day when Rockwell was assassinated, and many of these new ANP people were former NSRP people, and many of the new ANP financial supporters were former NSRP financial supporters. In 1961, Matthias Koehl, Jr., joined the ANP, resigning from the NSRP of which he was a member at the time. The NSRP was losing members and financial contributors because of the ANP. The resentment of the NSRP leaders built up until finally Dr. Ed Fields, with the backing of J. B. Stoner, attacked Rockwell in *The Thunderbolt* of August 1962 as being some sort of FBI collaborator, being on the Jewish payroll, being a phony patriot and being a communist. As stated, Rockwell took all the money that the Jews wanted to give him and he reportedly did submit names of prospective ANP members to the FBI so the FBI could screen out the kind of people that would cause Rockwell legal problems, however, a phony patriot and a communist Rockwell was not. Rockwell demanded a retraction from Fields but Fields refused. Consequently, Rockwell filed a law suit against Dr. Edward R. Fields for slander in late 1964 or early 1965, CIVIL

ACTION NO. 64-570. Letters went back and forth between Rockwell and Matt H. Murphy, Ed Fields' attorney in the case. Before the trial date, Murphy realized that Field's case was weak and so told Fields that if the case went to court, it would cost Fields $2,500 minimum, even if he lost the case. Rockwell, however, offered to settle the case out of court by asking that Fields print a retraction of his (Fields') attack on Rockwell in a future issue of *The Thunderbolt* and pay Rockwell $1,000 which was even a bargain in those days. Fields capitulated, gave Rockwell the $1,000 and printed a retraction in *The Thunderbolt* of October 1965. During the entirety of these legal proceedings, J. B. Stoner backed Dr. Fields against Rockwell.

On January 1, 1967, George Lincoln Rockwell changed the name of the American Nazi Party (ANP) to the National Socialist White People's Party (NSWPP) because the old name pertained to American workers whereas the new name pertained to all White people. Rockwell and the NSWPP had reached their highest peak to date at this time. There was a lot of NSWPP activity to report in the NSWPP's publications - *White Power* and *NS Bulletin* - donations were good and Rockwell was booked well in advance for speaking engagements at colleges and universities throughout the country.

On August 25, 1967, George Lincoln Rockwell, Commander of the NSWPP, was assassinated in a laundromat parking lot in Arlington, Virginia, by John Patler [Patsalos]. The NSWPP members went through the protocol of selecting a new leader. The majority of the members present selected Major Matthias Koehl, Jr., to succeed as the new NSWPP leader. When Matthias Koehl was selected, the NSWPP lost a good percentage of its members, stormtroopers, activists and financial supporters. Rockwell's assassination was the greatest setback the NSWPP could have because Rockwell was at his peak and climbing, and he kept the party together although there were the usual defections which any group experiences. In fact, one former ANP member told us that there were very few people who wouldn't do whatever Rockwell asked of them. Koehl was primarily a bureaucrat who was good at following orders but could not talk to people. If Koehl's personality was not enough to cause massive discontent, if not resignations, Koehl's homosexual background was, and Koehl's background was no secret within the NSWPP membership, especially among the old timers. Many of the loyal NSWPP members resigned and dropped out totally from the White Nationalist Movement, preferring not to align themselves with any phony White Nationalist group or any "sneaky Nazi" group such as the NSRP. However, some dedicated NSWPP members resigned to form their own National Socialist groups or similar groups with different names.

Some of you people may wonder why anybody supported Matt Koehl at all but you must consider that many of these dedicated people were faced with the choice of NSWPP under Koehl or no NSWPP at all so, since there was no "proof" of Koehl's homosexuality or background, they backed Koehl. Considering the other high ranking NSWPP members at the time, Dr. William Pierce, the NSWPP National Secretary, told Director Cooper personally that he often viewed Koehl as an "island of sanity amid a sea of insanity." While Koehl was leader of the NSWPP, he expelled any member who spoke of his homosexual background on the grounds of "character assassination" and "rumor mongering", however, there still remained a few members, supporters and other associates of the NSWPP who kept silent about Koehl's homosexual background so as to not damage the NSWPP any more than the NSWPP had been already.

When word got out that Matthias Koehl, Jr., was to be the new national Nazi leader, a group of concerned sympathizers in the New Jersey area feared that the subsequent exposure of Koehl's homosexual background would be embarrassing to the NSWPP and the Movement. After all, these sympathizers did not want to see everything that Rockwell built go down the drain. During the summer of 1970, a man named Wilfried Kernbach approached Dr. Pierce and gave Dr. Pierce incriminating evidence against Matt Koehl, evidence that was stolen from the home of an Anti-Defamation League (ADL) associate or member who had infiltrated the National Renaissance Party over 10 years previously. It was suggested to Dr. Pierce that he present this evidence to Koehl and then ask Koehl to resign due to health or some other reason so as to not cause suspicion about the NSWPP in the public eye. Koehl said he would sleep on the matter. Dr. Pierce went to his house that evening but, when he returned to the NSWPP headquarters building the next morning. Koehl had instructed the duty officer to ban Dr. Pierce from the building permanently. A short time after that, two of Koehl's blindly loyal backers approached Dr. Pierce at his house and demanded that Dr. Pierce return the things that he had "taken" from the NSWPP headquarters.

It is not clear whether Dr. Pierce took the anti-Koehl evidence to his house or left it at the NSWPP headquarters because Dr. Pierce is yet another one of these guys who refuses to answer letters or state the truth orally. What Wilfried Kernbach told Director Cooper

in 1981 was that Dr. Pierce was given a man's job to do and he han-
dled the situation like a boy scout. What Dr. Pierce told Director
Cooper, when Cooper visited Pierce in his National Alliance office
in 1980, was that he (Pierce) did not want to feud with Koehl. Also,
Dr. Pierce told Director Cooper that at first, he was bitter when
Koehl double-crossed him (about 13 years previously) but that his
bitterness has waned away over the years. Well, it has been 14
years now since Koehl double-crossed Director Cooper but Cooper's
righteous indignation prevents him from forgetting or forgiving
Koehl's treason to the Movement and theft from his own backers,
all to cover up his homosexual background and to live out his fantasies at the expense of others. After Director Cooper's visit with Dr.
Pierce in 1980, Dr. Pierce called Matt Koehl to report on Cooper's
visit and what Cooper wanted.

A PERIOD OF STAGNANCY

From the fall of 1979 to the fall of 1984, the mainstream White
Nationalist Movement was in a state of relative stagnancy. During
this 5-year period, most of the White Nationalist Movement activity
was done by five groups and most of the Movement activists were
active with one of these five groups - the National Socialist White
People's Party (NSWPP) under Matt Koehl, the National States
Rights Party (NSRP) under J. B. Stoner and Dr. Edward R. Fields,
the National Alliance under Dr. William Pierce, the New Christian
Crusade Church (NCCC) under James K. Warner, and the Knights
of the Ku Klux Klan (KKKK) under David E. Duke. None of the
above individuals were gainfully employed. All of the above individuals lived off their mailing lists. Any challenger to the group leader
or any member who showed better leadership ability either
resigned to form his own group, resigned totally from the Movement in disgust, or was expelled by the leader. All of the above
group leaders know each other, and each of these, except for Dr.
Pierce, has something to hide in his personal life and/or background
about which he is very sensitive and fears exposure to his supporters and general public as he knows such would cause him to lose his
current relative position of prestige within the Movement - not to
mention a significant decrease in financial support. Consequently,
none of the above individuals attempted to expose the rot and corruption within the Movement or another one of the specified individuals above because he himself could be exposed in turn. Thus,
this clique of individuals just maintained the status quo, selling

memberships, asking for donations and selling subscriptions to publications, and made little progress.

Of course, some progress had been made previously by these groups but most of the financial supporters, necessary for any organization, could not see any considerable progress made during this 5-year period, started to become demoralized, began to lose faith and cut back on their financial donations. The supporters essentially sent in money for subscriptions, books and various items offered for sale. In late 1979, the donations for the above groups and individuals began to dwindle as a result of their lack of accomplishment and achievement.

As of December 31, 1983, the clique of Movement phonies began to show more visible symptoms of their being phased out of the overall Movement view. Since most of the financial support of the various Movement figures and organizations comes from their same respective supporters, it is no wonder that the Movement beggars were beginning to fall along the wayside. The supporters like to see success and progress made by the groups they support. In fact, the more successful and victorious an organization is, the more support it will earn. The Movement had reached a point where many of the long-time supporters were not able to see anything of significance being accomplished by the "paper tiger" organizations and the phony, begging leaders. Consequently and understandably, the supporters cut back their support while the operating costs for the organizations constantly increased. The five major White Nationalist groups faced problems as follows.

Dr. William Pierce, leader of the National Alliance and publisher of *The National Vanguard*, decreased the frequency of his publication to about two issues per year because his supporters did not send enough money. Since subscriptions paid for the publication, one can only conclude that there was financial mismanagement involved. Although Dr. Pierce has no record of financial scamming, kinky sex or fraud in his Movement dealings, we can only surmise that his unwillingness to expose wrongdoing among other Movement people and groups, or even cooperate with somebody who is willing to expose such wrongdoing, is based on cowardice alone.

David Duke, in 1980, after assuring everybody at his Knights of the Ku Klux Klan (KKKK) leadership conference in Metairie, Louisiana, the previous Labor Day weekend (September 1979) that he would not disband the KKKK and subsequently pressing his Klan members to get their dues up to date, did dump the KKKK. Duke then founded the National Association for the Advancement of

White People and published the *NAAWP News*. After a couple years, he threatened to decrease the frequency of his publication unless his supporters sent more money. Since subscriptions or dues paid for the publication, we must again conclude that there was financial mismanagement involved. David Duke is very immoral sexually, is a con-artist, a cheat, an egoist and is highly self-serving. Duke was once an associate - not a member, but maybe an official supporter - of the NSWPP for a brief period of time. During one of his trips to Arlington, Virginia, in about 1971, Duke stopped by to visit Dr. Pierce of the National Alliance across Interstate 95 from the NSWPP headquarters. Dr. Pierce offered to give David Duke the information regarding Matt Koehl's homosexual background if Duke would publish this information in his Klan publication at the time, *The Crusader*. Duke refused for reasons which should be obvious by now. After visiting Dr. Pierce, Duke visited Matt Koehl at the NSWPP headquarters. Subsequently, Duke spoke with an NSWPP duty officer, James N. Mason, and told Mason of Dr. Pierce's offer. Jim Mason, years later told this to Director Cooper who then wrote to Duke, asking for an account, confirmation or denial that Dr. Pierce made such an offer. Duke refused to answer Director Cooper's letter. Instead, Duke's right-hand man, Tom Wilson, replied in a form letter without even addressing the issue. Director Cooper wrote Wilson back, asking him to ask Duke to respond to his question regarding the offer that Dr. Pierce had made to Duke what must have been about 10 years previously. Wilson finally wrote back and said that Mr. Duke did not remember the offer and does not think discussing the matter, let alone publishing this, would help the Movement. Since that time, Tom Wilson ended up in a mental institution as a result of abusing PCP, a dangerous drug primarily used to tranquilize wild animals in Africa and other places so they can be captured alive.

James K. Warner, another former member of Rockwell's ANP, was, during this time period, leader of the New Christian Crusade Church, and publisher of both the *CDL Report* and the *Christian Vanguard*. Warner discontinued publishing the *CDL Report* because of financial problems. Despite Warner's history of transvestitism and widely discussed bisexuality, Warner was married to a woman who was part of his financial problems. On February 28, 1982, Director Cooper wrote to Warner, asking specific information about the homosexuality of his close friend, Eustace Mullins, and also about Matt Koehl. The letter was never answered. Warner has next to no friends, but a person named Jerry Dutton seemed to be close to him, so Director Cooper asked Dutton to ask Warner if Warner got Director Cooper's letter and when Cooper could expect a reply. Dutton told Cooper subsequently that Warner did get the letter and that Warner told Dutton that he didn't know what he was going to do. Here is another example of one pervert covering up for another pervert.

J. B. Stoner, chairman of the NSRP, was convicted in 1980 and was imprisoned for 3.5 years for supposedly attempting to bomb a Black church back in 1958. Just prior to his imprisonment, Stoner had been keeping peace at the NSRP headquarters building in Marietta, Georgia, between those who were supportive of Dr. Edward R. Fields and those who were against Fields. After Stoner went to prison, warfare erupted among the NSRP staff. This internal dissension was not as a result of any Anti-Defamation League plot or government COINTELPRO operation, but was something that was destined to happen sooner or later. Fields is a money-grubber and there were those on the NSRP staff who did not like Fields personally because he had at least two wives, patronized prostitutes, frequented discos and misused NSRP funds. Mind you, Fields had no job but all his income came from the NSRP. Director Cooper wrote to Ed Fields on February 28, 1982, asking specific questions about what happened to cause Admiral Crommelin to boot Eustace Mullins and Matt Koehl off his Wetumpka farm in late 1959 and 1960, as well as what he knew about Koehl's homosexual background. At least Fields answered the letter but his statement that he had heard nothing bad about Koehl is not believable -these guys all know each other going back at least 2 decades! Director Cooper sent J. B. Stoner a letter on June 5, 1982, asking for the same information sought from Fields but Stoner never answered. As a result of the NSRP infighting, the NSRP fell apart with Fields and Stoner blaming everyone but themselves.

Matthias Koehl, Jr., leader of the NSWPP and publisher of *White Power* and the *NS Bulletin*, ran out of scams to save the dying NSWPP, a death that could only be attributed to Koehl himself and his Jewish masters who threaten to expose his homosexual background publicly unless Koehl does their bidding. NSV Director Cooper was the NSWPP Business Manager from August 12, 1978, to February 5, 1980, and he saw how Koehl's decisions and the manner of doing things directly led to a morale problem among the staff. Koehl's personality and lack of idealism that he expects from others caused continued internal dissension. He relates poorly to individuals; in fact, he avoids people and ignores problems, apparently

thinking that problems resolve themselves. Cooper eventually realized that Koehl is incompetent as a leader and, considering Koehl's
very high intelligence, logically concluded that Koehl's continued
destruction of Commander Rockwell's party was deliberate.
Indeed, when Director Cooper first arrived on the NSWPP staff as
business manager, Koehl informed him that it was vital financially
for the Party to keep active in the streets, to report on the activities
in the publications which must reach the supporters fairly regular
(once monthly for *White Power* and twice monthly for the *NS Bulletin*) and to thank all people who submit donations - dues, pledges or
otherwise. On Labor Day of 1979, Koehl disbanded the NSWPP
stormtroops, a decision which Koehl knew would cost the Party
activists and supporters. The *White Power* newspaper was published more and more infrequently until its last issue of #109 in
1984. The *NS Bulletin*, a special newsletter for members and supporters, was expanded to include propaganda for the masses and
was published infrequently. Koehl's loyal right-hand man, publications editor and go-between, David Martin Kerr, gave Koehl a
year's notice in December 1982, after the suicide of Kerr's ex-wife,
Perry Kerr. Although the NSWPP's last day was December 31,
1982, Kerr continued to work with Matt Koehl in the New Order for
another full year.

A PERIOD OF TRANSITION

Concurrent with the period of relative stagnancy, from the fall of
1979 to the fall of 1984, was a period of transition from the old
Movement to the new Movement. The old White Nationalist Movement was mainly characterized by leaders who sold memberships,
books and paraphernalia, asked for donations and gave fancy
speeches for a living; and the new White Nationalist Movement was
mainly characterized by Viking-type youth who have no leaders
and are their own kings and queens. The Skinheads first began to
receive national attention around 1980. They were not linked up
with any older established groups and some Skins were still relatively isolated from the older more established groups. Today, there
are no Skinhead groups that are isolated from the older more established groups and the Skinheads are currently the largest segment
of the White Nationalist Movement.

In 1976, Pastor Richard G. Butler, head of the Church of Jesus
Christ Christian and leader of Aryan Nations, began holding
annual Aryan Nations Congresses in Hayden, Idaho, which are
now called Aryan National Congresses. The Church of Jesus Christ

Christian welcomed all activists with no regard to group affiliations. "The Lake", as it came to be called, provided a meeting ground for White Nationalists of all types. Leaders of the old Movement were often featured speakers, but most people in attendance were local people along with various leaders and activists of many smaller groups. The yearly gatherings in Hayden Lake were noted only by the local press until a group of militants decided that something must be done to save our race other than listening to sermons and speeches at the Church. Thus, a group that later became known worldwide as "The Order" was formed apart from the Church and formed the vanguard for our country's second revolution and our race's first revolution against the beast system. The Order's activities spanned from the early 1980s to the death of its leader and founder, Robert J. Mathews, on Whidbey Island, Washington, on December 8, 1984. Although Pastor Butler had no involvement with the militants and their activities, he has nevertheless been nicknamed "Godfather of The Order".

In 1976 when the clique and their respective groups started facing survival problems, the late Pastor Robert E. Miles was released from prison. He understood the state of the White Nationalist Movement and he dedicated the remainder of his life to assist the Movement in its transition from the old Movement to the new Movement by forming The Mountain Church in Cohoctah, Michigan. Gatherings at "The Mountain" were held three times a year and everybody was welcome regardless of group affiliation. Because of these gatherings at The Mountain, Pastor Miles received the reputation for being the Movement's "hate broker" -he will connect you with whatever group fits your needs. These free association gatherings were essential for salvaging the many activists who were not accepted or were expelled by the old Movement leaders and for providing a place of welcome for the Skinheads. Pastor Miles did in the Midwest what Pastor Butler did in the Northwest. Their operations not only paralleled each other but they reinforced each other.

Another person arose to facilitate the transition of the Movement from that of relative stagnancy to that of rebirth was Tom Metzger of the White Aryan Resistance. Tom, as with many of us, was both angered and disgusted with The Clique in the way that they were quick to condemn The Order as gangsters and criminals, and equally quick to sell memberships, to beg money from and recruit as activists the Skinheads who were now entering the Movement en masse. In the mid-1980s, Tom made it his special project to steer these young people away from the con-artists and educate them regarding The Order and other bona fide revolutionary leaders of our people.

The timing seemed to many as ominous and even prophetic. A new type of unity was emerging, possibly signaled by the coalition of Klansmen and Nazis as they stood shoulder to shoulder during a shoot-out with communists in Greensboro, North Carolina, on November 4, 1979, resulting in five dead Reds. As the old Movement was dying, Pastor Butler, Pastor Miles and Tom Metzger picked up the pieces and began putting the new Movement together. For the first time in the history of the White Nationalist Movement, a unity was emerging - not a unity of one distinct group headed by one leader but a unity rooted in basic White Nationalism and race survival. It was a unity in spirit more than anything else but that is where any real unity must begin in the first place. Of course there were other gatherings in the country with an uncountable number of activists, but the enemies of our race made it no secret whom they feared the most by whom they attacked the most. Our enemies attacked and still attack the Skinheads as being their largest immediate threat with respect to violence and physical harm, our enemies attacked The Order as being their largest long-term threat with respect to the entire beast system of our enemies, our enemies attacked Pastor Richard G. Butler and Pastor Robert E. Miles for being significant in giving hope to those in despair and providing friendship for the isolated with their free association forums, and our enemies still attack Pastor Butler and Tom Metzger for all of the above. And so it has come to pass, the Movement experienced a transition period from the fall of 1979 to the fall of 1984, a time for "out with the old and in with the new" or, as one associate put it, "from Greensboro [North Carolina] to Whidbey Island [Washington]".

UPDATE ON THE CLIQUE

Most of you in the White Nationalist Movement know the current situation of some of The Clique (Dr. William Pierce, David Duke, James K. Warner, J. B. Stoner, Dr. Edward R. Fields, Matthias Koehl, Jr.) but there are some things that you don't know. For the scholars, book authors, historians and researchers, we are including this update on The Clique.

During the 5-year tribulation period, Dr. William Pierce, leader of the National Alliance (NA), was facing serious financial problems. In the following manner, Pierce kept the NA intact. Pierce informed his supporters that the NA inherited a lot of money which was willed by an elderly woman before she died. What happened was that after the death of Robert Jay Mathews, founder and leader of The Order, Mathews' life insurance company paid a large sum of money to the Cosmotheist Church which was a church corporation established by Dr. Pierce as primarily a tax shelter. Dr. Pierce subsequently moved his operations to rural southeast West Virginia where he is at this time. The *National Vanguard* publication is still only published a couple times per year - not because of lack of money but because Dr. Pierce spends too much time puttering around and doing things of no earthshaking consequence. Additionally, the former Church of the Creator property in Otto North Carolina was supposedly bought by Dr. Pierce for $100,000 on June 15, 1992, was recently sold for $200,000. The National Alliance's current address is P. O. Box 330, Hillsboro, West Virginia 24946.

After David Duke took everything that he wanted out of his Knights of the Ku Klux Klan (office equipment and money), he handed the Klan over to Don Black. David Duke had trouble getting his new National Association for the Advancement of White People (NAAWP) off the ground but he struggled with it and eventually got big money coming into his organization after he began running for public office. Win, lose or draw, David Duke made money just by running for public office. This action on Duke's part saved the NAAWP from financial disaster. Currently, David Duke has some kind of a job to support himself since he is no longer a politician. The NAAWP seems to be standing on its own as well. The address for the NAAWP is P. O. Box 10625, New Orleans, Louisiana 70181.

James K. Warner is still in operation because of his extensive book and literature list that he has built up over the years. Currently, Warner has *CDL Report* as the only publication of his New Christian Crusade Church and runs a mail order book and literature sales business. In spite of a costly divorce from his previous and only wife, both live together at this time at Warner's home in Baton Rouge, Louisiana. James Warner can be reached at NCCC, P. O. Box 462, Metairie, Louisiana 70004.

The National States Rights Party (NSRP) of National Chairman J. B. Stoner and National Secretary Edward R. Fields never survived the 5-year tribulation period. Fields, with the assistance of an old attorney friend, maneuvered to gain control of the old NSRP P. O. Box in Marietta, Georgia. Dr. Fields has managed to stay on his feet financially because of his publishing abilities. Although *The Thunderbolt* no longer exists as the publication of the NSRP, it remains as a private publication published and edited by Dr. Fields and is now called *The Truth At Last*. Dr. Fields and his publication can still be reached at P. O. Box 1211, Marietta, Georgia 30061. After J. B. Stoner was released from prison on the phony bombing charge, he started his Crusade Against Corruption which primarily glorifies AIDS as God's way of destroying homosexuals and non-Whites, and promotes AIDS as being the White man's best ally. J. B. Stoner can be reached at P. O. Box 4063, Marietta, Georgia 30061.

The National Socialist White People's Party of Matthias Koehl, Jr., never survived the 5-year tribulation period for reasons previously explained. To rationalize Koehl's destruction of the NSWPP to Party supporters, Koehl insisted that The Leader never meant for the Movement to be political after World War II which, according to Koehl, is why the NSWPP under his leadership failed. Koehl goes further to say that the only true NS Movement today is a religious one and he has appointed himself guru (who else?). Also, over this same time period, he has embezzled all the NSWPP money, kept the money from property sales and liquidated the gold stocks and certificates of deposit accounts to finance a personal retirement estate in New Berlin, Wisconsin, in Arthur Beneker's name. Matt Koehl does not stop here. It is not bad enough to cheat unknowing supporters out of their money, destroy Rockwell's party and insult The Leader's Movement, but he now condemns those who want to be politically active on behalf of the Movement! Whether Koehl's actions are based on genetic background (His father is Rumanian and his mother's maiden name is Bierbaum) or his fear of having something in his social background exposed (which would hurt his life style and dry up most of his financial support from naive supporters) is an academic issue. However, we should all be aware that Matt Koehl will never lead us, will only waste our time and money, and would best serve White society by selling shoes somewhere.

Currently, Koehl lives on the aforementioned 80-acre (not 88-acre) estate described by *Milwaukee [Wisconsin] Sentinel* staff writer Tim Cuprisin as "quite nice". There are two structures on this property, a smaller house (21288 Barton Road, West) that can be seen from the road and then Koehl's private domain (21200 Barton Road, West) which is the larger house which cannot be seen readily from the road but which is reached by following a gravel road past the smaller house, both of which are reportedly uninsured wooden structures. Ironically, it was one of Koehl's most loyal supporters, former NSWPP Tracy-Stockton Unit leader Paul Raymond, who, almost 15 years ago, stated that he suspected Koehl would one day close down the NSWPP, take all the money and go retire somewhere. Well, that is exactly what happened. Despite the illusion of success that Koehl gives, he is now politically insignificant and has been outside the Movement mainstream for years. His occasional *NS Bulletin* basically discusses the problems which our people face and pie-in-the-sky solutions with activities limited to writing letters and attending small meetings of people who do not know Koehl personally. Koehl has no known income other than what he receives through the mail in donations, dues and book orders. Several years ago, Koehl wrote to the late Ken Stoddard, then of Coquille, Oregon, asking how one could work without a Social Security Number, so finances were a problem for Koehl then. Ken and Ann Stoddard subsequently shared this information with Director Cooper. Koehl's only helper at his estate is "William Wallace", an alias for Barbara Mapp (nee von Goetz) who was once George Lincoln Rockwell's secretary and through whom is the long-suspected control over Koehl, a logical conclusion reached by a person familiar with their relationship. Matthias Koehl, Jr., and his New Order can be reached for comment at P. O. Box 27486, Milwaukee, Wisconsin 53227, or he can be reached personally at his unscrupulously acquired physical residence (addresses above).

On a final note, people should know the current status of Matt Koehl's former lickspittle, David Martin Kerr. Since Kerr's resignation from the New Order (formerly NSWPP) effective January 1, 1984, he has hit rock bottom, starting with a court decision, barring his custody of his daughter, Christina, after the death of Kerr's ex-wife, Perry, down through and including two police searches and arrests in close succession during which Martin Kerr was charged with using and dealing PCP. Kerr's legal adviser during these cases was former attorney Gary Gallo, then leader of the now-defunct National Democratic Front, and for whom Kerr worked as a pizza delivery boy. As far as we know, David Martin Kerr is the proprietor behind White Lightning Enterprises, P. O. Box 6143, McLean Virginia 22106, and Gary Gallo is at P.O. Box 30505, Knoxville, Tennessee 37930, but it is doubtful that anyone will get much information out of either should they care to write.

CONCLUSION

Lest some people get the wrong idea about this *NSV Report* and lose faith in the Movement, we offer the following for consideration. This report is not a continuation of *Deguello* which is an anonymous 54-page report published in the 1970s and which contained a mixture of truth and lies about many prominent people in the White

Nationalist Movement at the time. There is nothing sneaky or anonymous in this report. Since we have nothing to hide, addresses are given without reservation in order that anybody can contact those mentioned in this report to get another viewpoint. Should any of "The Clique" levy an attack on us, we expect our address to be run with the attack so that we may respond in turn. An attack against us should be considered sinister with ulterior motives unless our address is given. It is our expectation that The Clique will continue to remain silent as they have in the past which is something that suits us just fine because future historians, authors and researchers will only have us as their source of information. We ask that any published material about this *NSV Report*, NSV or its directors be brought to our attention.

Indeed, there is a great deal of suppressed anger and resentment on our part as we attempt to find facts and learn truth about our Movement only to encounter silence, stonewalling and sometimes lying. The vast majority of Movement activists today are Skinheads and other young people who know nothing about the con-artists who await them. It is unfortunate that many of our new activists and various supporters will learn about these dinosaurs (because they are outdated) and mossbacks (because they accomplish little) through bitter experiences. We hope to save a lot of people a lot of trouble. To keep things in perspective, we must give credit where due. The Clique all contributed to the earlier stages of the Movement in their own ways. In fact, many of us entered the Movement through The Clique's organizations. Today, some of The Clique still contribute to the Movement and are worthy of support in some ways. We will not tell you whom to support but we advise that you carefully weigh the pros and cons of those whom you plan to support before you make a final decision. If you want truth in the Movement, don't expect it from The Clique, although you are free to consult with any of them. Of course, we are available for our opinion should you ask (and even sometimes if you don't ask).

CURRENT STATE OF THE MOVEMENT

Before George Lincoln Rockwell died, he divided the NSWPP's program into four phases: (1 - establishment of the party in the minds of the public by getting attention in a variety of ways; (2- creation of a leadership cadre to guide the party; (3- adjustment to the mass movement of the people; and (4 - assumption of power. Although Rockwell's NSWPP no longer exists, we can determine from the present state of the Movement that the Movement is now in phase

(2). During phase (1), 25 or so years ago, mass media coverage on any aspect of the contemporary White Nationalist Movement may have occurred once per month. The vast American public now knows of our existence and there is almost daily news regarding some aspect of the Movement. The Movement does have a leadership cadre around the country but they are not all in the same organization. There will be more leaders arising in the future whose overall competence will be greater than ours just as our current overall leadership competence is greater than our leaders of the past. The Movement's entrance into phase (3) will coincide with our race's entrance into a period of oppression and suffering (Tribulation), that period during which time our people will be forced to face the terrible reality of their situation and, much worse, to face the fact that a race war (Armageddon) is inevitable. The race war will climax phase (3) and then our assumption of power will coincide with the commencement of a worldwide era of long-lasting peace (Millennium). THE VICTORY OF OUR RACE WILL NOT OCCUR IN ANY OTHER WAY

The White Nationalist Movement today consists of many varied groups and they all differ in some ways. There is no single organization with a single leader. Today, all Ku Klux Klan groups are White Nationalist groups. All the various National Socialist (Nazi) and Identity Christian groups have always been White Nationalist in conviction. There is neither the time, space nor inclination to list all the heroes and groups in our Movement today but there are four people who are outstanding and should be mentioned: (1) Pastor Richard Butler of the Church of Jesus Christ Christian (P. O. Box 362, Hayden Lake, Idaho 83835) in the field of Identity Christianity; (2) Tom Metzger of the White Aryan Resistance (P. O. Box 65, Fallbrook, California 92088) who is the most effective public spokesman that the Movement has today; (3) Gerhard Lauck of the NSDAP/AO (P. O. Box 6414, Lincoln, Nebraska 68506) in the field of international orthodox National Socialism; and (4) George Dietz of Liberty Bell Publications (P. O. Box 21, Reedy, West Virginia 25270) who is the largest publisher of White Nationalist literature in the country and probably the world.

It has been said by our racial philosophers and theoreticians for hundreds of years that the Jews create "anti-Semitism" where there is none just to get public support for Jews and their causes. Our Movement is a good example in support of this concept. Our Movement has come a long way but we also have along way to go. It was Jewish money that backed the National Renaissance Party

(NRP) in the late 1940s and early 1950s to not only control the NRP but to scare the Jewish community enough that they would support financially such an "anti-Nazi" group to stop the birth of a National Socialist movement in this country. It was a Jewish interest group that offered to set up DeWest Hooker as head of an American Nazi Party in the 1950s but Hooker declined the offer. It was Jewish money that went to George Lincoln Rockwell's newly founded American Nazi Party (ANP) until the Jews learned that Rockwell could no more be controlled than could Adolf Hitler in the 1920s when the Jewish bankers tried to control Hitler in a similar way. Finally, it is believed that Jewish interests were behind Rockwell's assassination in the hopes that Matthias Koehl, Jr., would become the new NSWPP leader because Koehl could be controlled with Koehl's Achilles Heel being his homosexual background.

As we look at the Movement now, we can see that the Jewish con-artists have made some money on their puppet leaders and groups but, in the long run, they always lose control over the movement when our real leaders take control. This is what has now happened. Our militants such as The Order and Skinheads cannot be controlled through phony Jewish front groups nor can the many thousands of sincere patriots in this country today who know the score. As we all see before us our unstoppable Movement, arising as a Phoenix bird, blossoming flower or some other symbol of rebirth, we must not become demoralized or think it odd that our Movement had its beginning with a small group in New York City, infiltrated by a group of homosexuals and financed by Jewish money for such is not a weird phenomenon but a natural metamorphosis; after all, isn't that the way it has been with all great religious and political movements?

Part II Various Movement Documents

In Hoc Signo Vinces
by George Lincoln Rockwell

"In Hoc Signo Vinces"—literally "under this sign you shall win"—refers to the swastika banner and is perhaps George Lincoln Rockwell's most important essay. It was written in pamphlet form in 1960 for the fledgling American Nazi Party, as a way both to announce the existence of the party and to make a forthright statement of his National Socialist faith. In the America of the day, with memories of World War II still fresh for those of Rockwell's generation, the essay was nothing short of revolutionary. "In Hoc Signo Vinces" contains some of the most incendiary prose to emerge from American National Socialism, and the effect of the essay was considerable, both in right-wing circles in the United States and among the scattered band of National Socialist true-believers in Europe as well. The essay remains a National Socialist staple to this day on both sides of the Atlantic.

Long lasting success in any human endeavor is never the result of blind luck. The achievement of a clearly defined goal, whether it be the act of walking from point "X" to point "Y", the building of a house, or the organization of a business, is always the product of three things:

(1) The intellectual ability to perceive the problem involved, the opposition which must be expected, and the best way to overcome that opposition to reach the goal.

(2) The will and determination to do whatever may be necessary to reach the desired goal, regardless of opposition.

(3) The physical means, strength, and courage to enforce and carry out the plan or fight conceived by the mind and determined by the will.

If any of these three elements be lacking on one's purpose, failure is the inevitable, predictable result.

A man who is too stupid to understand the various factors involved in trying to walk from point "X" to point "Y", where the path between us is a jungle infested with snakes, dangerous carnivores and fever, and who fails to arm himself with weapons and maps, medicine and other equipment will never arrive at "Y" no matter how dogged his determination or how mighty his muscles. Another man attempting the same journey, though he clearly perceives the dangers and prepares for them, and though he be mighty of muscle, will yet fail to reach "Y" if he is so irresolute and weak of will that he does not persevere at the struggle and ruthlessly use whatever force might be necessary to crush and destroy the forces opposing him. And a third man who has the intellect to perceive the dangers and to prepare for them, and the will and determination to fight his way through even with the utmost heroism, but who is frail of body and so physically weak that he cannot carry out the commands of his mind and his will cannot but succumb to the stronger adversaries he will meet.

It is with civilizations as it is with the struggles of individual men. Dozens of great civilizations have perished because of failure in one or more of these three elements necessary in the struggle for survival.

Savage societies usually perish, not so much from lack of vigorous will or lack of physical strength, as from lack of ability to perceive the real situation. Drowning in superstition and stumbling in the darkness of ignorance, they are overwhelmed by the physical forces of violent natural occurrences, catastrophes and diseases which more civilized societies have learned to overcome.

On the other hand, civilizations, for all their intellectual achievements and sciences, perish most often because of failure of the will, the diminishing of the savage and ruthless drive for survival and dominance which originally created society. They become "humanitarian", selfish, and soft. They become physically weak and dependent on paid armies and police to do their fighting. The fighting spirit of honor and self-sacrifice and heroism of their ancestors gives way to a growing love of ease and luxury and cowardice masquerading as "humanitarianism".

When a civilization reaches this effete stage in its decay, only a very rare historical occurrence can halt the final collapse of the society as the decadence grows daily more apparent. Only when the dying society still has enough life-energy to produce a spiritual giant, a godlike throwback to the ancient heroism of its people who is able to shock and drive the civilization out of its natural historical night of sleep and death, in spite of the suicidal opposition of the dying peoples who long only for "peace" and the slumber of death, can a society once again rise for a while.

Western, Aryan civilization passed the historical point of no return on its journey into limbo during the nineteenth century, as was duly noted by Spengler, Chamberlain, and others. Were it not for the unbelievable, miraculous arrival of Adolf Hitler at the last possible moment, the only bearable course for an intelligent, perceptive, and sensitive man surrounded by a disgusting and suicide-bent civilization would have been resigned enjoyment of such momentary pleasures as provided escape from the soul-crushing reality of a Judaized, cannibalized and boob-ized civilization rushing headlong back to the jungle in the name of "humanitarianism".

But the appearance in history of Adolf Hitler is evidence that there still remains in White, Western civilization a sufficient spark of self-sacrificing, creative vigor to permit, perhaps, another thousand years or so of survival for the White man. This infinitely precious spark will remain just that, however, and quickly fade into darkness, so long as the tiny elite minority of humanity with the wit to see what Hitler did is too selfish, cowardly, and short-sighted to apply the lessons of history before it is too late forever, and fan the spark Hitler gave us into the roaring flame of creative civilization founded by our courageous ancestors.

So far, the fearful punishment meted out to Adolf Hitler's fighting heroes of civilization by Jewish forces of decay and destruction has so unnerved and terrified the world that even those able to see and understand the peril to humanity, and the way to salvation as shown by Adolf Hitler, are so pitifully attached to their lives and liberties and comforts that they dare not pick up the sacred spark of White survival and fan it with their own life's breath, which it must soon have—or go out forever.

Aryan, White humanity is on the precipice of darkness and oblivion. Strewn on the crags in the eternal blackness below are the bones of other know-it-all, pompous civilizations which were doubtless unable to imagine their own demise at the very time when they were surrounded by the outward power and magnificence of empire. They were unable to realize or face up to the TOTAL threat of a growing weakness and "humanitarianism", unable to muster the TOTAL will necessary to reverse the historical march to death and oblivion. They were too lazy and selfish, greedy and cowardly to heed the tiny few who have been burned, crucified, stoned, fed to the lions or handed the cup of hemlock.

If there is any history a thousand years hence, and any people able to study it, they will marvel in disbelief most of all at the stubborn refusal of the White man to use his overwhelming strength, his knowledge and the providential gift of Adolf Hitler's leadership to save himself from the most incredible and cringing slavery at the hands of a relatively tiny gang of disgusting, pathologically unbalanced, physically weak and cowardly, arrogant, tyrannical Jews.

Our problems today are not "American" problems, "British" problems, "French", "German" or "European" or "African" problems—they are problems of SURVIVAL FOR ALL WHITE MEN.

What, in the name of the most elementary reason, is the difference between whether Bartholomew Buckingham is born near the Thames, Hans Schmidt on the Rhine, Pierre Dubois on the Seine, Per Olafson in Stockholm, Eric Erasmus in Durban, Joe Doaks in Podunk, Ohio or John Smith in Auckland, New Zealand compared to the question of "Shall there BE any more Bartholomews, Hanses, Pierres, Per, Erics, Joes or Johns?"

Our planet swarms with colored creatures who outnumber us by more than FOUR TO ONE—and in all of our nations these inferior beings, we are told, are our "equals", able to vote away our money, our liberties, our lives and our honor. By the old-fashioned notions of nationalism and democracy I, Lincoln Rockwell, am supposed to treasure and care for and be loyal to some of the lowest spawn of the jungle, providing only that their Black dam gave them to the world in some American ditch or filthy crib—because then, of course, they are "Americans", and aren't we all out for "America"?

Or am I to be loyal and die for these miserable and pitiable half-animals, my "fellow Americans", by slaughtering millions upon millions of the finest biological specimens of my own race, because a gang of Hollywood Jews teaches us that Americans must hate Germans?

Or again, is it a certain piece of geography to which I am to be loyal, and for which I must kill my own people and perhaps die myself? Does my loyalty to this hunk of geography stop at the Canadian border?

But perhaps it is "Americanism" to which I am to be loyal and for which I must make war upon German men, women and children. When I examine what they tell me is "Americanism", however, I find that it consists primarily in being willing to submit meekly to Jewish direction of my culture, government, religion, entertainment, and even my sex life.

No, all this is nonsense.

The only thing to which I can be loyal with any deep conviction —the only loyalty which makes any sense —is my RACIAL, and therefore cultural, brotherhood with my own people, no matter where they happen to have been born! When that loyalty is challenged, and my people are in danger, it is monstrous to pretend that we must be suspicious of each other just because we live across imaginary geographical lines, and that, upon proper preparation and agitation by a gang of international Jews, we White men must march forth to kill each other and bomb each other to ashes and everlastingly hate each other because we are "trade rivals" or for "American democracy" or the "British Empire" or for anything else in the world.

I am a WHITE MAN, and a brother to all other White men, and I mean to stand with all of them and, if necessary, lead them in battle to survive against the unspeakable menace of the colored populations of the earth rising to slaughter and rapine against the White men —and led by the scheming Jew!

But like the first man in the analogy of the walk through the snake-infested jungle, too many of our White "leaders" fail to perceive the cosmic proportions of the problem and imagine it is something which can be solved in "their" country, and by half measures.

The tiny few who do see the dreadful and total urgency of the White man's situation have, until our arrival on the scene, attempted to fight with less than the total weapons required in a total fight for survival. Most of the best leaders have imagined that small groups of beleaguered White men, gathered into little geographical huddles behind imaginary lines and waving different colored bits of cloth bravely in the breezes, can survive by themselves, and the hell with the other White men who have different bits of colored cloth.

The Jews have NEVER made the mistake of seriously dividing themselves into these phony geographical "teams". On the contrary, the Jews —with their Bolshevism, Zionism, and mongrelism —are attacking ALL White men, EVERYWHERE and ALL THE TIME. They are sending their black armies into all of our nations in an all-out attack against the White elite of the world, with absolutely no considerations of "national" boundaries or flags or languages or cultures. In the face of this total international threat of annihilation by RACE, millions of those who already see the danger are to be found babbling darkly of "Yankee imperialism", "British Empire", "dirty Catholics", "immoral atheists", "Republicans", "Laborites", "damned Yankees", "Germany first", etc., etc., ad nauseam.

Like little boys besieged by a mob of kidnappers and murderers, they cannot resist squabbling about who has the most marbles in the face of deadly danger they temporarily forget. The battle of our times —if there is to be any battle —is for the SURVIVAL OF THE WHITE RACE!

And to survive, the White man will have to RE-CONQUER the earth once conquered and civilized at the cost of so much blood by his ancestors. Under the banners of international Jewry, the colored masses are threatening to return civilization to savagery. Under the Swastika banner of Adolf Hitler, White men around the world will master the planet to save civilization.

The Jewish war against civilization has actually been a world-wide, gigantic REVOLUTION, in the course of which they got millions of us to murder each other shouting "Democracy!" "Gott mit uns!", "Free the slaves!", "Liberty, equality, fraternity!" And now they are preparing for the final bloodbath during which we will shout "Capitalism!" and "Communism!" respectively, as the two teams of White men slaughter each other with Jew-financed H-bombs.

In the course of these fratricidal and suicidal wars, the Jews have not been afraid to sacrifice thousands of their brethren in their devilish cause, as they did in the last monstrous slaughter in the 1940s. The Jews realize what WE must realize: that they are playing for the highest stakes in the knowledge of mankind— mastery of the whole earth—and they do not shrink from the inescapable conclusions of strategy and tactics dictated by knowledge of such stakes. If we are to survive then we too must have the wit and the strength of mind to face up to the deadly facts of the situation and act RUTHLESSLY, RAPIDLY, and EFFECTIVELY.

The Jews have almost won the final step in their 4,000-year revolution—OPEN world power. They now have total secret power to manipulate and control all world activities, and lack only a little more brainwashing and breaking of the will of the masses to make their world domination an acknowledged and formal power. They have fought and won their way to this incredible power by unsurpassed determination and iron will over forty centuries, and only a miracle can prevent the final victory of such fanatical warriors, tragically and viciously wrong as such a victory would be for humanity.

Even the atheist Jews—which is most of them—have an inexplicable belief in the ancient Jewish prophecies that when "the law comes forth from the hills of Zion" and Jerusalem, it will be the millennium for the Jews and they will own and rule the earth. THEY ARE IN JERUSALEM NOW, and lack only a few blocks of it for total possession! They are experiencing a worldwide frenzy as they can already sense the total victory we are about to give them, and they are even now preparing their sacrificial orgy of victory in Tel Aviv!

In the face of this unspeakable threat, that the whole world and all of us will fall to the tyranny of a gang of criminal paranoiacs, the narrow chauvinism, conservatism, and regionalism of most right-wing leaders is the utmost stupidity! With the masters of mongrels, the Jews, leading MILLIONS of savages in a worldwide attack against the White-elite bearers of civilization, and with the end only moments away in terms of history, only the most short-sighted leaders can continue to keep our children divided and helpless into "teams" of Americans, Dixiecrats, Catholics, Germans, Yankees, atheists, Dutchmen, conservatives, Irishmen, etc. down through the whole pitiful, heartbreaking list. The Jew may be all of these things—but FIRST HE IS A JEW!

It is the first task of him who would save civilization—which requires saving the White man—to make White men supremely and totally conscious of RACE above all other allegiances. Our people can be Democrats or Germans or Catholics or Englishmen if they want to and if it suits their purposes, but FIRST THEY MUST BE WHITE MEN! Otherwise, the Jew will keep us divided and helpless and unconscious of our racial unity and strength, while they fanatically fight as Jews, no matter where they are, until it is all over.

The world of TV, rockets and jet transportation has become too small to permit any group of White men anywhere to enjoy the suicidal luxury of fighting each other on behalf of the Jew ever again, no matter what the reason which may be advanced in the propaganda. We simply cannot afford to fight each other when we are under such overwhelming and deadly attack by such endless hordes led by such a fanatical and devilish enemy as the Marxist, Zionist Jew. The reason that the White man has been losing for so long in the first place is that he has failed or refused to see the enormity and the pressing urgency of his problem. He has permitted himself to be distracted into a million little squabbles over trifles, while his race has been driven almost to extinction.

Like the first man in the analogy, we haven't understood the path, the nature of the obstacles and, worst of all, we haven't even realized the goal we must win—or die. That goal is and must be MASTERY OF THE EARTH BY THE WHITE MAN, since civilization depends solely on such White mastery. Any lesser goal is utterly worthless, just as it would be worthless for a man scheduled to hang to take vitamins and attain perfect health.

And such a fantastically difficult and cosmic goal as world mastery cannot be won by luck, sneaking, half-measures, prayers, hopes, fine speeches, pamphlets, or sporadic violence. What we must aim at and achieve is a WORLD COUNTER REVOLUTION against the Jewish Marxist-Zionist revolution. And revolutions are never, never, NEVER the result of spontaneous and fortuitous uprisings, but ALWAYS the product of ruthless, scientific planning and fighting, based on the immutable laws of great social upheavals. Behind the pitchforks and the barricades there is always the story of the candle-lit conspiracies by the planners—otherwise the revolution would be over in a trice. Not only have our handful of leaders so far failed to realize the unheard-of proportions of the goal at which we must aim, but they have singularly failed to face up to their terrifying responsibilities in planning. Time after time, would-be leaders have arisen and led us in pitiful efforts to nip the end of the tiger's tail, only to waste our substance and blood and heroism in a fruitless struggle which always ends in being crushed by a single, smashing blow from the paw of the beast.

The Jewish world revolution can only be broken and beaten by a counter world revolution.

Any revolution must be planned with care and precision in accordance with the iron laws governing human conduct in the mass. A world revolution, in the face of the international and staggering power of Jewry, must be planned and executed with a brilliance and ruthlessness unmatched in the history of the world.

The most fundamental rule of such a cataclysmic social upheaval as a revolution is: "The blood of the martyrs is the seed of the church!" Perhaps it sounds cruel and brutal, but it is nevertheless true, that the greater the proportion of human upheaval aimed at, the greater quantity of blood and torrents of tears which must be poured out in vast quantities to gain the goal. The kind of unprecedented, colossal movement which can alone reverse the suicidal trend of the Western world, and usher in even another thousand years of survival for the White man, can never be launched—let alone won—in any safe, painless, or easy way. Even ordinary sufferings and martyrdom are too minuscule for the kind of movement we must set aflame to survive. Everything about the current deadly battle for world mastery is and must be Olympian, and we cannot shrink from Olympian AGONIES if we are to hope to win.

Mighty movements always require millions of people to immolate themselves in a passion of self-sacrificing devotion to the cause. And these enormous masses of people can never be moved to fling themselves into the flames of revolution with shouts of "Favorable trade balance!" or "States' rights!" etc. Only the FUNDAMENTAL drives from deep inside the human psyche can lift the slow-moving masses from their ignorant apathy to the wild pitch of emotion which carries them entirely away in the tidal wave of revolution. Nothing so affects these fundamental emotions of the masses as HEROISM, and only the utmost heroism can now save the White man from his lethargy and paralyzing fear of the Jews.

And there is no symbol other than the Swastika and no name other than Adolf Hitler which is so beautifully calculated to produce the persecution and consequent heroism which alone can unite and inflame the White man into an irresistible wave of anti-Jewish Marxist-Zionist revolution. Until the advent of Adolf Hitler, the White men of the world had nothing, absolutely NOTHING in the way of a common cause, common heroes, common martyrs, sacred shrines, names and symbols. But now, after millions of young German White men heroically flung their precious lives away in the first real fight in history for the White elite, we finally have the blood-soaked shrines, symbols, and martyrs which are the most elementary stuff of revolution.

Millions of equally precious young White men on the opposing side, fighting for the devilish Communist-Zionist Jews, will have lost their lives for absolutely nothing unless we accept this stupendous blood-sacrifice, and use it to ensure that never again will precious White blood be spilled fighting for Jews and negroes. Nevertheless, and unbelievably, the lucky heirs of all this self-sacrifice and heroism—the recipients of these precious bloodstained banners and sacred names—reject their heritage as "impractical".

"We can never win with open adherence to National Socialism and the Swastika," these gentlemen explain feebly. "The Jews have taught people to hate them too much," they add. "If we use the Swastika and praise Hitler too openly, they will throw us in prison or kill us!" And did they not throw ALL makers of revolutions, including the Jew makers of the Red revolution, in jail—and even kill some of them? Are we National Socialists to be more fearful and cowardly than a gang of Jews? The very persecution and bloodshed such irresolute characters seek to avoid is the *sine qua non* of our victory!

These are not empty words. I have personally proved their truth here in America, the power center of world Jewry, by being beaten, by going to jail and the insane asylum, losing my dear family, and living like an animal. Twelve days from today, as I write this, I face jail again. These things are unpleasant and even heartbreaking—but they MUST BE!

I have risen in two years to a commanding position in the world-wide fight for the White man, starting as a penniless, unknown and unaided single individual like millions upon millions of others—simply and solely because I have gratefully and lovingly used the precious names and symbols which have been bathed and soaked in such oceans of blood and tears—the Swastika and the name of the Leader, Adolf Hitler.

Temporary and flashy political successes are always easy. It is always simpler and quicker to put pads in one's jacket that to build the human muscles to fill the coat by months or years of work and sweat. For fifty years now, there has been a steady rise and fall of "right-wing" or White movements built entirely of pads.

By endorsing motherhood and virtue and patriotism, etc., and by avoiding brutal statements of the real purpose of such organizations—which must necessarily be the extermination of the Communist-Zionist enemies of humanity—great flocks of skittish "patriots", "conservatives", and even a few "tough" anti-Semites could be corralled. But these people are not attracted to such a movement because they are so inflamed with revolutionary zeal that they can hardly be restrained from attacking their tormentors in the streets. Rather they join the "patriot" society to relieve their guilty consciences by pretending to fight the Jews and their treason and terror by what they call "clever underground methods". They relieve themselves of their pent-up frustration at the tyranny of the Jews and negroes once a week at a "Rally" (private, of course) and then hurry home happily for another week of profits, parties and TV.

Such Mighty Mouses are horrified when it is suggested that perhaps they should hand out pamphlets in the street, or picket some outrageous example of Jewish-Communist arrogance. And if one exposes not only the Jews for what they are, but also exposes these political loafers who siphon off the support and energy for a real battle, these heroes reply by howling that one is an agent provocateur working to get them all crucified as a bunch of Nazis—which, except for their disgusting cowardice, they might otherwise be.

It is not the task of the world anti-Jewish revolution to attract and organize these contemptible sneaks, but to drive them out of the way and out of business, where they will be unable to milk the Movement of the tiny bit of available support for useless "projects", as they have been doing for years. Nothing accomplishes that task like the Swastika. The political drones, profiteers, prostitutes and cowards scoot with their tails between their legs from this hooked cross, as the devil does from holy water.

On the other hand, the Swastika has an irresistible attraction for the kind of daring, bold, devil-may-care fighting YOUNG men we need. In America, most of them are simply nigger-haters because of their pure White man's instinct. When they learn the Jews' part in the disgraceful negro situation they become Nazis in minutes. Then it is the work of only months until they also understand the deeper significance, the idealism, and the true aims of the Movement.

But even more important than these advantages, the blood-soaked Swastika has a supernatural effect on Jews. It is after all only a few black lines—but it drives the Jews out of their usual sly and calculating frame of mind and makes them hysterical and foolish. To them, it is not just the lines, but the awful threat of ruthless exposure, swift justice, and terrible vengeance which their guilty consciences tell them they richly deserve. It is like a picture of the electric chair to a hunted murderer.

A calm, calculating Jew is the most dangerous beast on the face of the earth. By the exercise of his devilish, perverted but brilliant reason, the Jew has almost mastered all the rest of us. But a hysterical, screaming Jew, out of his mind with hate and fear of punishment for his crimes, is helpless putty in the hands of a calculating National Socialist.

We have proved this time and again—when Jewish councils have spent millions of dollars to spread the word among the Jews to ignore us. But the hordes of guilty little sinners can't do it! When they see that Swastika and hear us praising Adolf Hitler and describing the gas chambers for traitors, they become screaming, wild ghetto Jews who have eternally blown up their victories at the last moment by their insane passions of hate and revenge.

The result is the lifeblood of a political movement: PUBLICITY! In spite of the Jewish domination of all the media of public information, the parading of Swastikas and National Socialists in public streets cannot be hidden or ignored without giving the game away. They can suppress the news, to be sure. But then too many people realize their press power and censorship. And when the young Movement is able to force publication of its existence on the giant national TV networks, in magazines, the press, etc.—it serves as a clarion call to the frustrated millions who are looking for such a movement. It is only thus that we have been able to contact thousands of people all over the world who have never before been in any "patriot" outfit but couldn't resist the American Nazi Party and the World Union of National Socialists.

The Swastika and Hitler, far from being millstones, are actually the answer to the eternal problem of the right wing—money! When you don't have money for paper, meeting halls, etc.—as our side never does—you can go into the streets and march and distribute homemade handbills and picket—for nothing. The Jews go wild, attack—and you then have free use of millions of dollars worth of Jewish TV, newspapers, magazines, etc. Of course, you may get bloodied and have to sit in jail a while recuperating. But this is a small price to pay for the astonishing results.

In addition to the free publicity attendant on open operation as a Nazi, you also find that the very audacity of the thing will attract the young fighting men you need, even though they know nothing and care less about the politics of the business. They admire raw courage and daring. Later, when they have come to know the facts a little better, they will fight for ideals and the White man. But until then, these valuable protectors of your free speech will fight just for fun.

Above all, the Swastika will save you from the fundamental error of the right wing—that sweet reason will change the world and save us from the Jewish tyrants.

Reason is still an infant in human affairs, a precious and rare development found in the mutational brains of an infinitesimal minority of Homo sapiens. And even the few geniuses able to exercise genuine, independent reason are almost entirely incapable of acting in accordance with the dictates of that reason—which is one of the reasons so many of them end up as failures in a world which does not appreciate them or their reason.

It is FORCE, POWER, STRENGTH which rules the world, from the ebb and flow of the tides to the decision of your neighbor to join the Rotary. Only a negligible fringe of oddball humans change their mind as a result of being convinced by a superior argument. The overwhelming masses, including the mass of today's "intellectuals", change their minds only in order to CONFORM. In other words, the minds of the vast majority ALWAYS bow to the strongest opinion—the opinion which brings rewards and avoids punishment.

The right wing examines its reasons and arguments and facts and finds them true and good—as they may be. They then become outraged which the slobs next door cannot see and appreciate this rightness and, very probably, throw them out of the house for preaching "hate." But this is only as things are. The slobs will hold whatever opinion seems to show the most strength and WILL TO POWER. They are completely, hopelessly female in their approach to reason and always, ALWAYS prefer strength to "rightness".

When they say "no" to our Swastika and National Socialism, they are only the eternal female saying "no" but meaning, "If you accept my no, then you are a weakling and have no right to my favors. Let us see if you have the manhood and the strength to MAKE me say yes!"

They hate us now because we are weak and powerless. All the reason in the world will never make them love us or our ideas in ANY guise, no matter how we try to sugar-coat them, until we COMMAND THEIR RESPECT AND ADMIRATION FOR OUR WILL, our guts, our force! As stupid as they are, their instincts in smelling force and strength are still pure, and the attempt to SNEAK National Socialist ideas in the guise of "patriot leagues" and other nice, safe groups very properly repulses them as being the actions of cowards and sneaks.

To HELL with the sneaky, safer approaches! They get us persecuted every bit as much as the direct, open approach, and they doom us to miserable, sneaking failure every time. If we are to be the last of the White men who conquered the world; if we are finally to be overwhelmed by a pack of rats, let us at least face the death of our race as our ancestors faced their death—like MEN. Let us not crawl down amongst the rats begging for mercy or trying to out-sneak them and pretend to be rats ourselves!

Let us stand on the scaffold of history—if hang we must—like the martyrs of Nuremberg, tall and proud! Is life so sweet, is comfort so precious and a job in a Jewish counting house so sacred that we are AFRAID to grasp the mighty hand of ADOLF HITLER reaching down to us our of our glorious past? Again, to HELL with sneaking and safety!

It is part of the Jews to be sneaky and sly. The genius of our people has ever been joyous strength, robust forcefulness, directness, manly courage, and flaming heroism. When the Jews, with their economic terrorism, jails, bullies and hangmen, scare the White man into laying down his cudgel and goad him into trying to out-sneak Jewish tyranny, the Jews have completely emasculated the once-strong White man, and doomed him to dishonor and defeat. The White man can NEVER win by sneaking!

In the dawn of Nordic civilization, lesser races used to cringe in their rude huts and pray, "Lord, save us from the fury of the men of the North!" It was THAT kind of man who built Western civilization. If civilization is now to be saved from the swarms of degenerate Jews, their cannibal accomplices and their unspeakably depraved liberal friends, it will be THAT kind of man who saves it, NEVER sneaks!

WHITE MAN! The same iron blood of your mighty ancestors flows in your veins! The towering figure of ADOLF HITLER reaches out a giant hand to lift you up to world-conquering POWER! You have cringed long enough before pygmies! Now RISE! Defy the rats and vermin at your feet! Let them feel the toe and heel of your boot! Stamp them out!

You have been sleeping. When you rise and stand up, and the masses once more see what a man of FORCE looks like, they will love you as they now imagine they hate you. With the spark of National Socialism, struck by Adolf Hitler, burning in your breast, you are unconquerable! IN HOC SIGNO VINCES! In the sign of the Swastika, YOU will conquer!

Join hands with the heroes in America, Britain, Iceland, Denmark and other White countries who have raised the holy Swastika banner and defended it with their blood. It has risen from the ashes of Berlin, and never shall it be hauled down again. Stand with us before the altar of Adolf Hitler and the world-conquering White race, and pledge your life as we have, to bring the order and justice of Western, White civilization once more into the world. Let us teach the traitors and rats and pygmies once more to cringe in terror in their huts and pray, "Lord save us from the FURY OF THE MEN OF THE NORTH!"

—Lincoln Rockwell

The White Party Report

by Max Amman

The "White Party Report," originally published in 1968 by a Texas-based American Nazi Party veteran under the pseudonym Max Amann, is the earliest available document recording the intense disaffection with the leadership of Matt Koehl that soon became the common coin of the American National Socialist world in the wake of the 1967 assassination of George Lincoln Rockwell. The document is included in its entirety here to give readers an insight into the deeply emotive and highly personal ties of loyalty and enmity that characterize the tiny and divisive American NS community. Unlike the "History of White Nationalism" and the "Deguello Report," both given in the "Resources" section and both intended for the disparate audience of the American radical right, "The White Party Report" was written for the National Socialist community alone. As such, it was mimeographed and passed hand to hand for a number of years until Harold Covington scanned it into a text file and disseminated it on the Internet to commemorate the thirtieth anniversary of Rockwell's assassination in 1998. However, as with the "History of White Nationalism," "The White Party Report" should not be read literally as an indictment of Matt Koehl, and the various charges leveled in the document are certainly *not* to be read as literal fact. Rather, it is the highly emotive quality of writing that is important, for it is in the intensity of Max Amman's loyalty to Rockwell and his bitter estrangement from Matt Koehl that the reader is afforded an insider's view into the world of a subculture that is popularly seen to be a pariah in the American body politic.

THE WHITE PARTY REPORT June 1968

TO: Admirers and Supporters of the late George Lincoln Rockwell

FROM: Max Amann, personal friend of George Lincoln Rockwell and former business manager of the American Nazi Party.

The ability to make a clear-cut decision is not a part of most men's make-up. The average man, faced with an unpleasant situation requiring decisive action, prefers to "ride the fence until FORCED in one direction or the other—and the tendency of the fence straddler is to lean in the direction of the status quo; that is, in the direction which requires the least thought and effort on his part.

It is that very lack of decisiveness on the part of the masses of our people which has taken our race and nation to the brink of catastrophe, and it is that same lack of decisiveness on the part of many of the Commander's most ardent supporters which now threatens to destroy the Cause for which he gave his life.

George Lincoln Rockwell's American Nazi Party is DEAD!

In its place is a German Nazi cult that would be violently repudiated by the Commander if he were here to speak. Evidence mounts daily to show us that immediate action is needed if our Cause is to be saved. But while the evidence mounts and our Cause grows dim, many continue to support thestatus quo; that is, the hollow remains of the American Nazi Party—because it's easier than embarking on a new course.

Matt Koehl's American Nazi Party and George Lincoln Rockwell's American Nazi Party are TWO DIFFERENT ORGANIZATIONS ENTIRELY! Only the name is the same.

The time has come to make a decision! History proves beyond any doubt that chaos and defeat is the fate awaiting those who face an either/or situation with a "wait and see" attitude. Victory goes to the man who weighs the facts, makes a decision based on those facts, and ACTS! And we who are the admirers and followers of Lincoln Rockwell's dream are faced with just such an either/or situation. The facts must be weighed, a decision must be made, and we must act. The Cause is at the crossroads and further procrastination will bring us certain defeat.

THE SITUATION

When the Commander was assassinated in August of 1967, there was a great effort made by all of us to keep the Party unified. And for a time, it appeared that all would go smoothly.

But as weeks passed into months, and months into almost a year, it became obvious that we who had trusted Matt Koehl with the leadership of the Commander's party had made a terrible mistake. We had put the Party into the hands of a man who had been repeatedly rejected as leadership material by the Commander himself, and we were faced with the consequences. My recent decisions and actions have been an effort to rectify that mistake and put the Cause once again on a course that does not blaspheme everything for which the Commander lived and died. Lincoln Rockwell's dream deserves better than death at the hands of Matt Koehl.

Because Matt Koehl seized LEGAL control over the name, American Nazi Party, almost before the Commander was cold, we have no alternative but to push the Commander's dream forward under another Party name.

But the Commander himself said, just a few weeks before he was assassinated, at a top level staff conference in June, that the time had come to change our "Nazi" image to one of a White People's movement. As one step in accomplishing that, he (the Commander) changed the name of the Party to the National Socialist White People's Party. So in reality, we are being forced to do what the Commander said should be done anyway. And we have chosen a name to which he would unquestionably give his wholehearted approval—THE WHITE PARTY.

Some feel that to abandon the American Nazi Party name is to abandon the Commander's memory. But it is quite the contrary. The Commander would have called his Party "The Purple People Eater's Party" if he had thought that was the way to victory. He, himself, changed the name of the Party before he died. We have merely simplified the name, and made it more appealing to the masses of the people. The principles, aims and purposes of THE WHITE PARTY are identical to those of the Commander.

ALL—I repeat—ALL of the Commander's closest friends and associates have withdrawn support from Matt Koehl's cult. The reasons will be outlined in this letter, and you are asked to decide, one way or the other, which course of action you shall follow. A divided force will destroy all the Commander worked and sacrificed to build. Weight the facts, make a decision—and ACT!

MATT KOEHL: ILLEGITIMATE HEIR

Matt Koehl demands subservience to his dictates under what he calls the "leadership principle", as though it had some bearing on this particular circumstance. He has used the "leadership principle" to convince young idealists, who tend to be guided more by emotion than by reason, that the current actions of those people whom the Commander trusted most constitute a mutiny. But mutiny is defined as "a rebellion against duly constituted authority", and Matt Koehl can hardly claim to be anything other than a recipient of a peculiar circumstance, for it is circumstance ALONE which catapulted him into the position of leadership in the Commander's Party.

As the LEGITIMATE successor to Lincoln Rockwell, Matt Koehl was REJECTED time after time after time. The position of Deputy Commander carried with it the Commander's stamp of approval for his successor. Karl Allen once held that position, and Alan Welch once held that position, but Matt Koehl never held that position, albeit there was no Deputy Commander of the ANP for more than a year prior to the Commander's death, and Koehl was next in line (in terms of rank) for that entire period.

If the Commander had felt that Matt Koehl had the qualifications and capabilities needed to lead the Party in the event of his death, it would have been a simple matter to have made him Deputy Commander. But he didn't. Alan Welch was promoted OVER Matt Koehl when he assumed the duties of Deputy Commander, and the position was left unfilled when Welch resigned from active duty.

The Commander apparently knew from long association and experience what we were to learn only through trial and error; i.e. that Matt Koehl would destroy everything he had built if he ever gained control. We've learned—but undoing an error is not easy.

MATT KOEHL'S OBSESSION

Matt Koehl is now, and always has been, a cultist who worships the past at the expense of the future. He can quote extensively from almost every German manual, but is completely lost when the time comes to put those words into action. If given an ironclad guarantee tomorrow for worldwide WHITE POWER, with the one stipulation being that the name of Adolf Hitler never be mentioned again, Matt Koehl would reject the offer. In his obsession with THE IDEA of National Socialism, he has lost sight of the goal of National Socialism, and you need only look at the last issue of the White Power newspaper to see the proof of that statement. The newspaper, contrary to everything the Commander said and emphasized at the June conference, smacks the American people in the face with GERMAN heroes, GERMAN history, and terms popular to GERMAN people. The newspaper epitomizes the cultist thinking of Matt Koehl, and blasphemes everything the Commander felt was necessary for our victory.

I, as much as any of you, would like to see the name of Adolf Hitler and other German heroes gain their rightful place in history. However, this is America, 1968—NOT Germany, 1933—and the White race is faced with a crisis such as the world has never seen. This is not the time nor the place for cramming German history and heroes down the throats of Americans. Certainly Rudolf Hess should be freed. But the American people today are a good deal more interested in freeing AMERICAN boys from Communist prisons, and we must appeal to THEIR primary interest if we are to gain their support. Worldwide White Power is dependent on AMERICAN support, and regardless of our personal feelings about Germans in particular, we must use propaganda techniques that have a strong appeal to White AMERICANS!

THE JUNE CONFERENCE

In June of 1967, two months before his death, the Commander called a top-level conference to announce changes in Party policy. In that three day meeting, he made clear that the time had come to change the Party's image from German Nazism to an American White People's movement. He proposed a newspaper for mass circulation and mass appeal, to be called "WHITE POWER"; the Swastika was to be played down, and all propaganda was to be aimed at AMERICAN acceptance; the salutation "Heil Hitler" was to be replaced by "White Power", and the name of the Party was changed. All of his proposals were directed toward denazification of the American Nazi Party.

Karl Allen and several of his men (most of whom are mentioned all through *This Time the World*) were invited to the conference for the express purpose of uniting all National Socialists under one banner. The Commander, concerned over the fact that the position of Deputy Commander had gone unfilled for so long, and recognizing a very real possibility of his assassination, discussed with me prior to the meeting the possibility of getting Karl Allen to return to the Party as Deputy Commander. He discussed the same possibility with Karl Allen at the conference. The proposal was met with interest by Allen, and they both agreed to talk further about it at a later date.

WHY DOES MATT KOEHL LIE?

The June conference was a very real success in the Commander's eyes—the newspaper he had dreamed of so long was launched; plans for a new headquarters were already under way with one third of the money already raised; and differences were resolved between him and Karl Allen, making Allen's return to the Party only a matter of time.

It is a well known fact that Matt Koehl despised Karl Allen. It must surely have infuriated him that the Commander was seriously planning once again to put Allen in the position of Deputy Commander, and thus eliminate his hope of attaining that position of potential power. The prospect of having a man he despised promoted over him, making the second time he had been rejected, must have been a bitter pill to swallow. And along with that, he was going to have to stop eulogizing German Nazism. With his obsession for everything German, Koehl undoubtedly saw his world crumbling beneath him.

In a recent *NS Bulletin*, Koehl had this to say about Karl Allen: "Next to Patler, the most dangerous traitor with whom the Commander had to deal was a sly, ingratiating person named Allen who, after being promoted to the position of National Secretary, (Allen was in fact DEPUTY COMMANDER), deliberately attempted to seize the leadership of the Party, and then failing that, to wreck the Party by organizing a mutiny."

Compare that statement with this one from Barbara, the Commander's secretary of many years: "The Commander was quite serious about getting Karl Allen and his group back with our Party....the national conference was held the first part of June, 1967. On June 27th someone tried to kill the Commander. This was AFTER the Commander and Karl Allen had decided to work together. On Monday, August 28th, the Commander was to meet with Karl Allen again for very serious plans..."

What is Koehl's purpose in telling such lies about Karl Allen? Does he hope to keep Party members from meeting and talking with Allen to learn his true character for themselves? If so, he almost accomplished his purpose with me. Fortunately, I make it a practice to base my opinions only on first-hand knowledge. Karl Allen is the leader of the White Party with my full backing and support.

The Commander was killed on August 25th. If he had lived to have that meeting with Karl Allen on the 28th, Karl Allen would today be the head of the American Nazi Party—NOT Matt Koehl.

WHO KILLED LINCOLN ROCKWELL?

A jury said John Patler did it, but the evidence was entirely circumstantial. The Jews undoubtedly wanted the whole affair over and done with as soon as possible to insure that Commander Rockwell would not become a martyr in the people's eyes—so a thorough investigation was too much to hope for. John Patler was arrested, tried and convicted in probably the speediest trial in the last thirty years.

The dirt from John's clothes was tested to see if it matched that of the assassin's getaway path. It didn't. His tennis shoes had a different pattern on the soles than the prints found on the top of the tar roof. Hairs and other markings from the black jacket that was found failed to match anything that would tie it with Patler. The gun admittedly belonged to Robert Lloyd (one of Koehl's current crew), who said that he had loaned it to Patler, (he later said that Patler stole it), but no evidence was ever produced to prove that Patler was in possession of the gun at the time of the shooting, while considerable evidence is available to prove that Patler did NOT have the gun for months prior to the shooting.

When the Commander was assassinated, there was no doubt in my mind that John Patler was the killer. And the fact that he was arrested within minutes after the shooting merely confirmed what I already believed to be true beyond any reasonable doubt. And I was far from alone in that conviction—almost everyone was convinced of Patler's guilt because of the circumstances surrounding his dismissal from the Party and because of his many volcanic eruptions in the past. But as facts began to emerge at the trial, i.e. facts which proved John's innocence rather than his guilt (facts which Matt Koehl never saw fit to make known to ANP members), many began to waver in their belief of his guilt.

At first the tendency was to believe that John "had something to do with the murder" even if he didn'tpull the trigger. But finally, when evidence piled on evidence, and vital questions remained unanswered by those who had control of the Party as a result of the Commander's death, the people who were the Commander's closest associates and friends became as convinced of John's innocence as they had previously been convinced of his guilt. And the question of WHO, if not Patler, had killed the Commander was once again in everybody's mind.

The ONLY thing which was proven beyond any reasonable doubt at Patler's trial was that Patler and the Commander had violently disagreed several times before they had finally parted company. But that could be proven of many people who have been in and out of the Party ranks. We Nazis are highly emotional people, and violent disagreements are part of our nature—but being highly emotional does not make us murderers. It proves nothing when all is said and done.

The Commander's secretary, convinced of Patler's guilt in the beginning, is today as equally convinced of his innocence. Floyd Fleming, one of the Commander's oldest and closest friends, and the man who gave him the HQ on Randolph Street, is another who first believed John to be guilty and who now believes him to be innocent. Ray York, the man who put up the money for *This Time The World*, and who gave financial support to the Commander throughout the years, is still another.

Karl Allen, the man who would have been Deputy Commander of the Party if the Commander had lived another few days, was among the first to notice the total lack of evidence against Patler, and among the first to rise to his defense. J. V. Morgan, an extremely close friend of the Commander, is of a like opinion. And on and on I could go with names of people whose loyalty to the Commander is above question.

And to that list, I'd like to add my name, for I too have become convinced that John's explosive temper, and the circumstances surrounding his separation from the Party, were recognized by someone as factors needed for a perfect "frame". And his presence in the area at the time of the shooting just added to the good fortune of those who planned to use him as a perfect made-to-order patsy for their crime. So shallow was the evidence against John Patler that even the judge later voiced amazement that the jury found him guilty. The jury said it was a "compromise verdict".

GUILTY OR NOT GUILTY?

Patler lived in the vicinity of the area where he was arrested. He established via receipts and witnesses that he was in the area doing errands, and that at the time of the shooting he was so far from the point where the Commander was killed that he would have had to RUN all the way to arrive there in time to fire the fatal shot. And the point of just how he would have known the Commander would be there at that particular moment has never been established.

Witnesses said the killer was wearing a black jacket. The police covered every inch of the area with a fine tooth comb, looking for the jacket, since John was wearing only a T-shirt when he was picked up, and they used mine sweepers and scuba divers to look for the jacket and the gun. Nothing was found. John was put in jail.

The next day an "informer" (who was never identified) called the police and told them that they could find bullet casings from the murder weapon on the farm of Patler's father-in-law, and told them the EXACT tree out of about 5,000 where these items could be located. The black jacket was found stuffed behind a bush, and the gun was seen by someone in a stream which had already been thoroughly searched, with the barrel sticking up prominently between two rocks.

Can anyone honestly believe that the police are THAT inept?

Bullets could be fired into a tree by anyone, and no evidence whatever was presented to prove that John, and not someone else, shot those bullets into the tree. And it requires a stretch of the imagination that I don't have to believe that the police, with all of the investigative equipment at their command, could overlook a gun and a jacket that were both visible to the naked eye the next day.

Patler says that only two people knew the location of his father-in-law's farm, the Commander and Matt Koehl. He says that he gave the location in a sealed envelope to Koehl. Maybe John is lying, but then again, maybe someone else is lying.

The Scripps-Howard newspaper chain, convinced of Patler's innocence and looking for a big story, has paid $6,000 for the trial transcript and assigned a full time reporter to the case. If someone besides John Patler did kill the Commander, they are undoubtedly getting nervous—and with good cause.

STRANGE FACTS EMERGE

Matt Koehl is either a compulsive liar, or he has something to hide. Having no investigative facilities at my command, I cannot say which. But he has told so many lies that they are now coming back around to meet him. He lied about Karl Allen when he labeled him "the most dangerous traitor with whom Commander Rockwell had to deal". He lied when he said that Allen was National Secretary, when in fact he had been Deputy Commander. He lied and distorted the facts outrageously in the Frank Smith-Chris Vidnjevich affair, just as he lied about Frank Drager and me. In short, he lies with almost every breath he takes.

A case in point: Bill Kirstein, the young boy who was put in charge of the California unit when Ralph Forbes left, called Koehl to find out the reason behind so many of the Commander's supporters rejecting his leadership. Since Bill was in Dallas for a while, and knows the work I have done with the ANP Order Department, he asked Koehl specifically about me. Koehl lightly brushed off the loss of my support and said: "Dallas (meaning me) has made no significant contribution since Commander Rockwell's assassination." Bill wanted to be loyal to Koehl, but feeling that something was seriously wrong, wrote to me after the conversation with Koehl. I have since gotten many such letters.

The Commander was assassinated in August of 1967. Since that date, I personally have (1) raised $7,500 from ANP supporters and contributed $1,500 of my own money to publish the Commander's book, White Power; (2) arranged for and followed through the entire business of printing the book, editing, proof reading, advertising, mailing, etc., etc.; (3) contributed my home as an office and warehouse for the ANP Order Department; (4) spent approximately four hours every day in the business of filling orders, answering correspondence, ordering more material, etc. (until Koehl seized the Dallas post office box and redirected all mail to Arlington); and (5) entertained Matt Koehl twice in my home while he had meetings with a group that was openly antagonistic to my wife and me—the group that was led by a half-literate man who was stripped of his rank and thrown completely out of the Stormtroop Section by Commander Rockwell himself.

Do YOU consider my actions since the Commander's death "no significant contribution" to the ANP?

KOEHL'S LIES AND STRANGE BEHAVIOR

At one of the meetings in Dallas, i.e. the one which was held for no other reason than to vilify my name and undermine the work I had done, Matt Koehl was asked, "What were YOU doing on the day of the assassination?" (I had one lone friend in this group, otherwise I would never have known about this particular lie.) Koehl's answer to that was, "I did not leave HQ all day." The Commander took the car and went somewhere. When he returned, he said he was going to do his laundry, and I tried to get him not to because we needed the car for a distribution of the White Power newspaper that was planned for that afternoon."

According to recorded testimony at Patler's trial, Matt Koehl told a flat lie when he said he did not leave the HQ all day. WHY he lied is something only Matt Koehl can answer—and he seems disinclined to discuss it. An answer, however, might be MOST enlightening.

To again quote the Commander's secretary: "This is what happened on the morning of the assassination. The Commander, having no one dependable to clean the camper, decided to do it himself. It was not his clothes he took to the laundromat, but curtains, towels, etc. from the camper. He put them in the back of the car and was going down the hill to the laundromat when Matt Koehl asked him to wait until he had made an errand, which turned out to be a visit to the Niles' and a stop at the post office on the way back."

For those of you who don't know, Peggy and Doug Niles left the Party under most disagreeable circumstances just a short time before the assassination. Doug Niles, who has a criminal background, has the distinction of being the only man ever to receive a DISHONORABLE discharge from the Party. Not even Patler was reduced to that.

The only truth in Koehl's statement to that group was that there was supposed to be a distribution of the newspaper that afternoon, and the car WAS needed. The Commander was undoubtedly hurrying (knowing him) to get to the laundromat and get back with the car. It was the first issue of the long awaited newspaper, and he was most anxious to see the people's reaction to it.

With the Commander on the way down the hill to the laundromat, Koehl stopped him and asked to run an errand first. The Commander agreed. Koehl got in the car, with the laundry still in the back, and drove to the home of Doug Niles. His reason? According to testimony, to deliver two theater tickets to the movie *Triumph of the Will*. When he arrived at Niles' house, Doug was at work and only Peggy, his wife, was home. Though Matt Koehl is not known for his love of small talk, particularly from women, he stayed so long drinking tea and chatting with Peggy Niles that he got a parking ticket—which is how we happen to know his movements on that fateful morning.

While he was there, he called Doug Niles at his office and talked to him. According to Niles' boss, Niles asked for some time off "to do an errand", which was given to him. When finally Koehl left the house of the man who had been dishonorably discharged from the Party, he went by the post office and then returned to HQ with the car and the laundry. The Commander, who had undoubtedly been pacing the floor during Koehl's extended absence, immediately took the car to the laundromat where he was met by an assassin's bullet.

George Lincoln Rockwell was murdered about 11:30. Niles returned to work about 12:30. And Matt Koehl became top ranking officer in the American Nazi Party.

THE FUNERAL

The strangeness of the events surrounding the Commander's assassination didn't end with his death.

At the funeral, with dozens of loyal Party officers in attendance, the man who assumed the LEAD POSITION in front of the hearse was none other than Doug Niles. When an officer asked who put Niles in charge, he was told, "Matt Koehl". It's a certainty that Koehl knew Niles was occupying that strategic position—he was sitting in the hearse and Niles was standing right in front of him.

It seems exceedingly strange that Matt Koehl, a man who is well-known for his strict disciplinarian manner, would choose a man who had been DISHONORABLY DISCHARGED from the Party to occupy the lead position at the Commander's funeral. And it seems particularly strange when you learn, as we did later. that Koehl visited the same man's home on the morning of the assassination for a purpose so insignificant as the delivery of two theatre tickets. Add to Koehl's strange actions the fact that Niles left his job, after receiving a telephone call from Koehl, and did not return until an hour after the assassination, and you are forced to say that "strange" is hardly sufficient to describe the whole affair.

Since Koehl told the Dallas group that he "did not leave HQ all day" on the day of the assassination, it seems safe to say that our knowledge of his movements on that day would be limited to his less than trustworthy word if he hadn't gotten that parking ticket while visiting the Niles' home that morning.

AN INTERESTING PIECE OF INFORMATION

Shortly after the assassination, Patler's private investigator Bob Hunt found a tennis shoe under a bush in the back of Doug Niles' home which had tar on it. As the case is not in their jurisdiction, the FBI cannot test to see if the print matches the one taken from the roof at the shopping center. So Bob Hunt gave a photograph of the print to the Arlington Police Department for their investigation, but he has not yet received a report. Since Patler's tennis shoes did NOT match the prints on the tar roof, it would be interesting to know whether the shoe found behind Niles' house DID match, but only the Arlington police can tell us—and they don't seem too interested. Does anyone besides me smell a Jew in the woodpile?

MATT KOEHL, NATIONAL LEADER OF THE ANP

Almost from the first moment Matt Koehl assumed command of the Party, there were rumblings across the country that all was not as it should be. No one could get any information about anything, and the people who had been the Commander's staunchest and most loyal supporters were being told, in effect, to drop dead. Those who would not blindly follow Koehl's dictates, regardless of their irrationality, were purged from Party ranks.

Don Zinn, a longtime supporter of the Commander, was one of the first men to feel the sting of Koehl's biting tongue. Frank Drager, the only man I ever knew of who had the initiative and drive to get ANP publications out ON TIME, was driven out of the Party by every underhanded means at Koehl's command. George Ware, a man whom the Commander had labeled "the greatest guy who ever lived", was repaid for his many kindnesses by having the press and the building at Spotsylvania maliciously destroyed prior to Koehl's departure. After giving his word that the property would be left in good order after his men vacated the premises, all the windows were broken out, the roof was torn to shreds, signs were painted all over the building reading "Traitors Live Here", and the press had been run after having sand put in it. THAT for a man who went out on a limb for the Commander and the Party when it was needed most.

Ray York's property in California suffered the same fate as the property in Spotsylvania. Ray York has GIVEN over $15,000 to the Party over the years, besides buying property for their use which they rented when no one else would rent to them, and these are the words he used to describe the aftermath of Koehl's men:

"I have just lived through a horrible experience which has really shook me...after letting the Party have the building for eight years, and with their rent being so spasmodic I could no longer make the payments, I told them that I was going to have to sell the building and they would have to move. When the man in charge here related that to the insane man in Arlington (i.e. Koehl), he sent back word to abandon the building. When I went over after they had moved, no one who did not see it could believe the maniacal destruction of my property that greeted me. Fifteen windows were broken out; the gas stove, the refrigerator, a beautiful wardrobe piece, were all smashed with an axe or something. The bunk beds were busted to pieces. Debris was piled up almost to the ceiling, glass jars of food were broken against the walls, and much other damage. It cost me over $700 and three weeks hard work to get the building in decent condition. Much more could be said.

"All this after I have contributed to the Party approximately $15,000." (Bear in mind that Ray York put up ALL the money for the Commander's book *This Time The World*.)

And I, of course, came in for my share of Koehl's insane determination to purge the Party of anyone and everyone who was even suspected of having enough intelligence to see through his demonic scheme of destruction. Koehl's plan was (and is) entirely dependent on using the emotions of the young and naive; i.e. those whose blind loyalty renders them incapable of rational thought, and using the brawn of the downright stupid to accomplish his ends—and he has apparently gathered about him quite an array of both types.

Everywhere there are people whose greed exceeds their patriotism, and whose ambitions exceed their talents. Dallas is no different. The man who heads the group in Dallas was stripped of his rank and ordered out of the Stormtroop Section by Commander Rockwell, after a Party court had shown him to be an incompetent do-nothing, among other things. The people he attracts are mostly those who made long-term financial commitments when we bought the $9,000 press and who, after a few months, defaulted on those commitments because their patriotism didn't quite measure up to their greed.

But that type of person is too dishonest to admit to sheer greed as their reason for defaulting on a commitment (which YOU are going to have to pay if they don't), so they attack and vilify the people with whom they made their voluntary agreement. In Dallas, my wife and I were the villains—WE took the money from OUR pocket and made good on THEIR commitments; WE used our money for bails and fines for the Stormtroopers; WE contributed our home as an office and warehouse for the Order Department; WE filled the orders, answered the letters of inquiry, and kept things running on a day to day basis; and WE raised better than $20,000 in a three year period for the Party.

It was too black a record for them to stand—they lied, connived, and schemed for more than a year on how to destroy us. The Commander would have nothing to do with them. When they called him, he called us to ask how we would like him to handle the latest request or complaint. But after the Commander was assassinated, things were different—the "good guys", that is to say the malefactors whose sole aim in life was to destroy those whose presence served to remind them of their own shortcomings, found a receptive ear. Matt Koehl needed such people and they needed him. And so a mutual admiration society was formed.

When the ANP Order Department was first moved to Dallas under my supervision, the head of the Stormtroopers, who was later to become the leader of the Dallas malefactors, was sent by me as an errand boy to obtain a post office box. Either through stupidity or deliberate intent, I don't know which, he put his own name in the place on the application form where ANP-Dallas should have been listed as holder of the box. I had the only keys; I paid the rent on the box with ANP checks; and it was I who picked up the mail every day. But because he had put his name as the holder, and because Koehl had the calculated foresight to have himself made the LEGAL heir to the ANP, the post office ruled that the box and all the mail belonged to him and therefore to Matt Koehl. My control over the ANP Order Department ended, and the order which I had createdout of chaos ended with it.

It's said that "where there's a will, there's a way". All the indications are that Matt Koehl has the the will, and with the help of all the destructive forces within and without the ANP ranks, he has thus far found the way to destroy all the Commander worked to build.

BUT HE'S GOT ONE HELL OF A FIGHT ON HIS HANDS!

For Race and Nation,

WHITE POWER!

Max Amann

Aryan Nations Creed

The Aryan Nations Creed sets out the religious beliefs of Richard Butler's Aryan Nations Church. The Creed, as well as the biography of Pastor Richard Butler that follows, has for many years been mailed to all who write a letter of interest to the Church of Jesus Christ Christian—the formal name of the Aryan Nations religious organization. The Creed is included here to offer readers a standard introduction to Christian Identity beliefs, as well as provide a look at the National Socialist political slant that the Aryan Nations under Richard Butler is well known for promoting. The biography that follows, despite its grammatical flaws, is a lionization of Butler and his works that stands as the "official" view of the Aryan Nations' founder as written by true believers. More recently, the texts have been linked and widely disseminated on the Internet.

———————

Aryan Nations is not a new right-wing organization suddenly appearing on the scene. Aryan Nations is the on-going work of Jesus the Christ regathering His people, calling His people to a state for their nation to bring in His Kingdom! We hail His Victory!

WE BELIEVE in the preservation of our Race, individually and collectively, as a people as demanded and directed by Yahweh. We believe our Racial Nation has a right and is under obligation to preserve itself and its members.

WE BELIEVE that Adam, man of Genesis, is the placing of the White Race upon this earth. Not all races descend from Adam. Adam is the father of the White Race only. (Adam in the original Hebrew is translated: "to show blood in the face; turn rosy.") Genesis 5:1

WE BELIEVE that the true, literal children of the Bible are the twelve tribes of Israel, now scattered throughout the world and now known as the Anglo-Saxon, Germanic, Teutonic, Scandinavian, Celtic peoples of the earth. We know that the Bible is written to the family of Abraham, descending from Shem back to Adam. Yahweh blessed Abraham and promised that he would be the "father of nations." This same promise continued through the seedline of Abraham's son Isaac, and again to Isaac's son Jacob, the patriarch of the twelve tribes, whose name Yahweh changed to Israel (Meaning: "he will rule as God"). Genesis 32:28; Exodus 12:31; 16:4; 19:20; Revelations 21:12

WE BELIEVE that there are literal children of Satan in the world today. These children are the descendants of Cain, who was a result of Eve's original sin, her physical seduction by Satan. We know that because of this sin there is a battle and a natural enmity between the children of Satan and the children of The Most High God (Yahweh). Genesis 3:15; 1 John 3:12

WE BELIEVE that the Cananite Jew is the natural enemy of our Aryan (White) Race. This is attested by scripture and all secular history. The Jew is like a destroying virus that attacks our racial body to destroy our Aryan culture and the purity of our Race. Those of our Race who resist these attacks are called "chosen and faithful." John 8:44; 1 Thessalonians 2:15; Revelations 17:14

WE BELIEVE that there is a battle being fought this day between the children of darkness (today known as Jews) and the children of light (Yahweh, The Everliving God), the Aryan Race, the true Israel of the bible. Revelations 12:10-11

WE BELIEVE in the gam-ma'di'on (ga'ma'di-on), n.; pl. -DIA (-a). [MGr., dim. of gamma.] A cross formed of four capital gammas (Γ), esp. in the figure of a swastika. Gamma among early Christians symbolized Christ as a cornerstone of the church. WEBSTERS DICTIONARY.

WE BELIEVE that the present world problems are a result of our disobedience to Divine Law.

WE BELIEVE that there is a day of reckoning. The usurper will be thrown out by the terrible might of Yahweh's people, as they return to their roots and their special destiny. We know there is soon to be a day of judgment and a day when Christ's Kingdom (government) will be established on earth, as it is in heaven. "And in the days of these kings shall the God of heaven set up a kingdom which shall never be destroyed; and the kingdom shall not be left to other people, but it shall break in pieces and consume all these kingdoms and it shall stand forever. The saints of the Most High, whose kingdom is an everlasting kingdom, and all dominions shall serve and obey Him." Daniel 2:44; 7:18; 7:27

WHITE RACISM: Where does it come from?

What is the actual driving force behind the "racist" White Christian Nationalist's fight for the preservation of the Aryan Race? The news media would scream an immense and piercing shriek of "HATE" if they could catch the slightest whisper of such a question coming from ruddy Aryan lips. But those long standing warriors in this Struggle know that the answer has a much greater depth and meaning than the anti-Christ Jews, mongrel hordes and liberal White race-mixers could even begin to fathom. . . that of LOVE.

The depths of Love are rooted and very deep in a real White Nationalist's soul and spirit, no form of "hate" could even begin to compare. At least not a hate motivated by ungrounded reasoning. It is not hate that makes the average White man look upon a mixed racial couple with a scowl on his face and loathing in his hear. It is not hate that makes the White housewife throw down the daily jewspaper in repulsion and anger after reading of yet another child-molester or rapist sentenced by corrupt courts to a couple short years in prison or on parole. It is not hate that makes the White workingman curse over his beer about the latest boatload of mud-creatures dumped upon our shores to be given job preference over the White citizens who build this land. It is not hate that brings rage into the heart of a White Christian farmer when he reads of billions loaned or given away as "aid" to foreigners when he can't get the smallest break from an unmerciful government to save his failing farm. No, it is not hate, IT'S LOVE.

Foundations Biography of Aryan Nations
Richard G. Butler

Who are we, and who is Richard G. Butler? We are the continuing direct-line Church of Jesus Christ Christian as originally founded by Dr. Wesley Swift of Lancaster, California. After Dr. Swift's death, the church has been carried on by Richard G. Butler.

Mr. Butler received his formal education and training in southern California, including Aeronautical Engineering at Los Angeles City College. His early experience in the aircraft industry included management of maintenance assembly and repair of major assemblies for commercial and military aircraft in the United States, Africa and India.

In 1946, and the following 18 years, he organized and operated a machine plant for the production and precision machining of automotive parts and engine assemblies and aircraft parts. Subsequently from 1964 through 1973, Mr. Butler was a marketing analyst for new inventions. In 1968 he became a Senior Manufacturing Engineer for Lockheed Aircraft Co. at their Palmdale, California, plant, where extensive development was under way for the L-1011 aircraft. He resigned from this corporate associateship to devote full energy and time to his greatest and all-consuming desire to serve God and Nation.

Pastor Butler is a co-inventor for rapid repair of tubeless tires and holds both U.S. and Canadian patents thereon. He is a pilot and during World War II was among other duties, a Flight Engineer Instructor in the U.S. Air Force. His background reflects a broad experience in the United States and foreign countries concerning alien races, their work habits, status of "culture" and "religions."

Returning home from wartime activities in 1946, Mr. Butler was deeply troubled concerning the future of his nation from what he had observed first hand overseas and events resulting from governmental edicts that seemed to be always contrary to the best interest of the nation, and of the White Race, in particular. While active in business life, the closest thing to his heart was the future of his nation; therefore, most all available spare time was spent studying and delving into various service and political organizations, trying to arouse attention of friends, acquaintances, members of fraternal organizations, and business associates into action concerning the threat of Jewish communism.

The media publicity received from these efforts, while nearly disastrous to business and professional life, turned out to be the greatest of all blessings, in that he was let to Kingdom Identity with the meeting and forming of the closest, most rewarding of all personal relationships with Dr. Wesley A. Swift, starting in 1961 and continuing until Dr. Swift's passing in 1971.

The years of study were spent under Dr. Swift in his magnificent library with line upon line, precept upon precept, and revelations over the years from Dr. Swift and Rev. Bertrand Comparet. They shared the blows of the enemy from their combined efforts in the Christian Defense League, of which Pastor Butler was the National Director from 1962 to 1965.

Upon the passing of Dr. Swift, Mr. Butler continued holding services for the congregation of the Church of Jesus Christ Christian, until he moved to northern Idaho to expand the Kingdom Identity program and to form the foundation for a "Call to the Nation" or Aryan Nations.

We seek to let every Aryan son and daughter of Yahweh know what their duty is to the Covenant (Constitution) that Yahweh their God has made with them as Nations of His people and His blessings come to, or are withheld from, a Nation—so is it that each citizen of the Nation is either blessed or cursed. The rewards are in direct proportion to the ACTION and WILL of the Nation, for our people have the "Law written on their hearts." We seek to live and establish a government under the Law of God, for Your Race is your Nation.

FIDELITY

That for which we fight is to safeguard the existence and reproduction of our Race, by and of our Nations, the sustenance of our children and the purity of our blood, the freedom and independence of the people of our Race, so that we, kindred people, may mature for fulfillment of the mission allotted to us by the Creator of the universe, our Father and God. Hail His Victory!

Aryan Nations Platform

Postal Address: Church of Jesus Christ Christian,
Aryans Nations—PO Box 362, Hayden Lake, ID 83835

The Sixteen Commandments

by Ben Klassen, Church of the Creator

"The Sixteen Commandments" is the creedal statement of Ben Klassen's Church of the Creator. Adherents of the COTC had to do no more than pledge fealty to the Sixteen Commandments and send in their dues, to be ordained as reverends in the stridently racialist COTC. The Sixteen Commandments are prototypical Ben Klassen. Calls to racial pride and group solidarity are interspersed with Klassen's fascination for eugenics and National Socialist imagery. More intriguing, however, are the ambiguous suggestions of violence contained in commandments 2, 3, 8, and 10. Here, the earth is posited as the exclusive domain of the "White Race" (commandment 2), but no suggestion is offered as to how this felicitous denouement is to take place. In commandment 3, Klassen calls for *lebensraum* by "expand(ing) the White race...shrinking our enemies." Commandment 8 mandates the purging of "Jewish thought and influence" in an effort to cleanse the earth of all but the White race, while commandment 10 urges the faithful to undertake at least one act that will make a lasting difference to the status of the "White Race." Are these calls for a "final solution," or merely an apocalyptic dream? Klassen's writings could easily support either interpretation.

———————

THE SIXTEEN COMMANDMENTS

1. It is the avowed duty and the holy responsibility of each generation to assure and secure for all time the existence of the White Race upon the face of this planet.

2. Be fruitful and multiply. Do your part in helping to populate the world with your own kind. It is our sacred goal to populate the lands of this earth with White people exclusively.

3. Remember that the inferior colored races are our deadly enemies, and the most dangerous of all is the Jewish race. It is our immediate objective to relentlessly expand the White race, and keep shrinking our enemies.

4. The guiding principle of all your actions shall be: What is best for the White Race?

5. You shall keep your race pure. Pollution of the White Race is a heinous crime against Nature and against your own race.

6. Your first loyalty belongs to the White Race.

7. Show your preferential treatment in business dealings to members of your own race. Phase out all dealings with Jews as soon as possible. Do not employ niggers or other coloreds. Have social contact only with members of your own racial family.

8. Destroy and banish all Jewish thought and influence from society. Work hard to bring about a White world as soon as possible.

9. Work and creativity are our genius. We regard work as a noble pursuit and our willingness to work a blessing to our race.

10. Decide in early youth that during your lifetime you will make at least one major lasting contribution to the White Race.

11. Uphold the honor of your race at all times.

12. It is our duty and privilege to further Nature's plan by striving towards the advancement and improvement of our future generations.

13. You shall honor, protect and venerate the sanctity of the family unit, and hold it sacred. It is the present link in the long golden chain of our White Race.

14. Throughout your life you shall faithfully uphold our pivotal creed of Blood, Soil and honor. Practice it diligently, for it is the heart of our faith.

15. Be a proud member of the White Race, think and act positively. Be courageous, confident and aggressive. Utilize constructively your creative ability.

16. We, the Racial Comrades of the White Race, are determined to regain complete and unconditional control of our own destiny.

The Movement's Fatal Fascination

by Harold Covington
June 21, 1998

> *"Stand not upon the order of your going, but go at once."*
> — *Lady MacBeth*

Veteran National Socialist Harold Covington's prose should, and probably one day will, be gathered into a volume that details from an insider's perspective, and in highly amusing terms, the pathology of the racialist movement—especially in its National Socialist guise. Should such a volume appear, this essay would no doubt appear as a concluding chapter. In "The Movement's Fatal Fascination," Covington addresses in tragicomic terms the issue of leaving the movement. The essay is redolent with references to Covington's own travails, all of which are dealt with in epic detail in the "Harold Covington" entry. "The Movement's Fatal Fascination" makes reference to recent movement leave-takers, several of whom are considered in these pages. See for example the entry "Internet Recruiting" by Milton John Kleim, whose departure from the movement is discussed both from his perspective in the entry and from Harold Covington's very different perspective below. "The Movement's Fatal Fascination" was distributed to all subscribers on Harold Covington's "Resistance" e-mail list on June 21, 1998.

All of you need to archive this NSNet, or print it out and keep it handy somewhere for future reference. You may need it. I am going to demonstrate once and for all that my concern for you as people is perfectly genuine. I am going to do what no other figure in the "Movement" will do: I am going to tell you how to get OUT of it. There is some method to my madness here; almost as much damage is done to the racial cause bypeople who try to leave but are unable to do so cleanly and finally than by the weirdos who WON'T leave. A bad exit makes people bitter and angry and wanting to lash out at the Cause itself, because of the foul people who have congregated around that holy and sacred Cause, and I'd like to try and prevent some of this.

The first thing you need to understand is something I suspect most of you have already noticed. The Movement is addictive. It is like heroin. It is like a bag of potato chips; once you start munching you just can't stop until the bag is empty. To some degree this is because it provides a touch of excitement and entertainment to the drab, meaningless lives of so many White people today. The Movement is like a living soap opera; you finally kick the "Days of Our Lives" or "Dallas" habit and then a few months or years later you're flicking the remote, you end up watching a few minutes, and you're hooked again.

Like all addictions, it is a matter of character and will power. You CAN kick your Movement jones if you really want to, but it will require exactly the kind of iron self-discipline and inflexible will that mostof you have proven yourselves incapable of exercising while you were IN the Movement. If the majority of you people had the kind of determination and mature, powerful self control necessary to set an objective and attain it, the White man wouldn't be in the shape he is in today. But possibly you can exercise the kind of inner strength in the service of your own personal interest where you could not exercise it in the service of your Race. That seems to be the White man these days: self-absorption may succeed where idealism and racial pride flopped. We'll see.

The second thing you need to understand is that the Bad Craziness is endemic and it will always be part and parcel of the Movement. Remember Covington's Great Paradox: "The Cause is so right; the people in it are so wrong." This appears to be an immutable condition given the realities of late twentieth century White male character and personality, and I have given up ever expecting to change it. As I said somewhere else, when I am 75 years old, some National Alliance creepoid from this insane period in my life will be toddling over to Carrboro on his aluminum walker or riding in his wheel chair to shit on my doorstep, or commit some comparable piece of idiocy. It is written.

The third thing you need to understand is that YOU CANNOT DABBLE. There are those who have attempted to leave gradually, to "cut back", to "phase out" their involvement. They have the idea "Well, I'll keep my hand in, write a little, post a little to Usenet, just not affiliate myself with any group or personality, just deal with the 'real enemy' (ignoring the fact that WE are the real enemy), etc." It's like a heroin addict or an alcoholic who says, "Hey, I'm more mature now, I can handle it." Or the smoker who won't quit cold turkey but spends years being miserable and cranky trying to restrict himself or herself to ten cigarettes a day. WRRROOOOOOOOONNGG! One thing I have learned: where the Bowel Movement is concerned, you are either in or you're out. You may succeed in toe-dancing along the razor's edge for a while, but eventually you will slip and you will fall right smack dab into the Movement toilet.

Always remember: the Movement has a fatal fascination. It is bigger than you are and you do not use the Movement, it seizes and uses you. Like many addictions it starts out with euphoria, a real rush, a roller coaster ride of the ego as we flatter ourselves that we are part of history and making a difference. But then it starts developing weird mutations and digressions as the Bad Craziness gets a grip on your life.

The Movement leaks into your brain cells and sodomizes your intellect. It corrodes your will power. It putrefies your character and paralyzes every positive trait such as integrity, honesty, altruism, and destroys what minimal, atrophied physical courage remains in White males these days. A kind of moral age regression takes place, an idiot's Fountain of Youth as ordinarily mature family men and businessmen, capable and in control of their lives, return to childhood and begin squabbling in the sandbox. The Internet has accelerated and accentuated all of these tendencies, but they have always been there since 1945.

The symptoms of the Bad Craziness start to manifest themselves. The concept of genuine, honestly held political or ideological difference vanishes. Disagreement becomes treachery and criticism prima facie evidence that the critic is a Federal agent or ADL spy, because surely only a Federal agent would dare to disagree with YOU or dare to criticize YOU? Right? Your skin becomes as thin as tissue paper, your paranoia swells, and every mildly critical remark becomes a personal insult which must be fought to the death in a lifelong vendetta or made the subject of a nuisance lawsuit. Your ethics crumble into dust. You become obsessed to Williams-esque dimensions with your own private Black Beast of the Movement, whoever that Black Beast may be (Ed Fields, Willis Carto, and myself are the top three favorites in the *bete noire* category.) It takes over your life. You lose touch with reality.

Then the "Steve Crisp Syndrome" hits, most especially if you have a computer. Total delusion takes over your mind and you lose every bit of common sense and perspective. The "open letters" and smears and slanders are no longer coming from others; you leap headlong into the madness and start churning out your own brand of crap. You begin to gibber and swagger and boast and threaten, beating your chest and telling us all how big and bad and tough you are, telling us about how you gonna do dis and you gonna do dat and you gonna do de udder 'ting, and ain't you BAAAAAAAAAAAD?.

You have become a terminal Movement headcase. You have met the enemy, and it is you. They're coming to take you away, ha ha, they're coming to take you away, ho ho, hee hee, ha ha, to the funny farm, with trees and flowers and chirping birds and basket weavers who sit and smile and twiddle their thumbs and toes....no, Mother, I won't do it...shut up, Mother, go away, get out of my head, I won't do it, I tell you, I won't hurt that girl....no, Mother, put down that knife....YAAAAAH......

Where was I? Oh, yes. Getting out of the Movement before you become part of the problem.

DON'T BE A KLEIM

If you decide in your own mind that this is it, you have finally had enough of dealing with middle aged men who act like ten year-olds, with con men whose goal in life is to take every penny they can out of your pocket, and with so-called "leaders" who file lawsuits against their critics with your money and who are so obviously Federal assets that it's not even publicly challenged any more, and you decide "This is it, I've had enough, I'm getting out!"—then DO IT. GET OUT. Get ALL THE WAY OUT.

Break CLEAN. Break TOTALLY. Do not be a John Milton Kleim and hang around on the fringe whining once your fifteen minutes is up. Don't be like some operatic character who gets stabbed and takes twenty minutes on stage dying while he sings a last aria. You want to leave, LEAVE, and never try to come back thinking, "Okay, I've had a break, I can handle it now." No, you can't handle it. If you crumpled once, you will crumple again.

CANCEL all your newsletter and publication subscriptions. Don't let them run out, CANCEL them and if they keep coming (a common experience given the inefficiency of most Movement grouplets), do not be tempted to leaf through them. THROW THEM AWAY. Clean out your collection of right wing and racist literature and THROW IT AWAY, do not stave or store it. Years from now you'll be rummaging through the stuff in your attic, you'll find some old copy of something or other and you'll be tempted to write and say hello or ask what's been going on. You are an alcoholic and you cannot have booze in the house; if you do, you will drink it eventually. THROW IT ALL AWAY.

REMOVE all Movement bookmarks from your PC. Change your ISP and e-mail account and user name. Actually, the best thing to do is simply disconnect your computer for a long while and not use it at all, if that is possible, until you have gotten firmly and permanently on top of your Internet jones. Better yet, sell the computer; despite what you may think, you don't REALLY absolutely have to have it. Ten years from now that may be different, but not now. Computers are dangerous, like fast food; it's so easy to be surfing the Net one day, bored and looking for entertainment, and then listen that little demonic voice and bring up that Movement web site just to take a peek. The next step on the slippery slope back to addiction is to subscribe to something reasonably staid and mature like the Z-Grams (rationalizing "just to see what's happening with Ernst [Zundel]"). Then comes the quick sneak peeks into the swirling ultimate madhouse, Usenet, the creeping, slowly overwhelming urge of the addict to just make one little post, just for old time's sake—and all of a sudden there is a splash as you fall back into the toilet. GO COLD TURKEY. It is the only way to break ANY addiction.

NO PARTING SHOTS. No open letters denouncing the Movement or individual people; that kind of thing is part of the Bad Craziness, not an escape from it, and just generates more Bad Craziness. Just a few simple words: "Gentleman, I've had enough. Deal me out." or something to that effect is quite sufficient. Then GO. Don't spend the next ten months TALKING about going. Don't be a Kleim!

BREAK CONTACT completely with all Movement people in your circle of acquaintance, cyber or otherwise, no matter how much you may like them personally. You are an alcoholic and they are your former drinking buddies; if you hang with them eventually they're going to lure you back into the barroom and you won't be able to keep to ginger ale; you will end up with a Swastika martini in your hand and singing The Good Old Songs. Do not try to placate your addiction by imbibing a weakerform of the Movement, some methadone like Constitutionalism or the militias or Buchanan or SPOTLIGHT; these watered-down substitutes will simply keep alive your craving for the Hard Stuff.

The price of escaping the Bad Craziness is that you must become a Solid Citizen and press your lips firmly to the buttocks of the Jews and the liberals on demand, and do not delude yourself that you will escape paying this price; it is what Solid Citizens do in exchange for being (sometimes) left alone by the System. Finding Jesus is a good idea for some; the local Holy Roller church will give you the kind of "meaning-to-life" addiction you sought in the Movement and in a much more socially acceptable manner. You may even win a free trip to the Holy Land where you can jump for Jeeeeeee-zus under the muzzles of the Israeli Uzis! Only please, guys, if you do go the JEEEEEEEE-ZUS route, don't turn on us like treacherous dogs and give the enemy more propaganda mileage with a bunch of crap about being a "repentant racist", okay?

If you want out, LEAVE. Leave CLEAN. Leave COMPLETELY. THROW AWAY all your Movement material. BREAK CONTACT with everything and everyone. Get yourself a large color screen TV and a satellite dish that brings in 520 channels; while I try to get Movement people OFF the electronic drug of television, if you are going to leave us and try to re-program your mind as a Solid Citizen you can use TV to drug yourself into unconsciousness; that's what it's for.

Guys, I am really quite serious about this. God knows I understand how and why people sometimes have enough of this madness. But I don't think I am being entirely unreasonable to ask that when you leave, DON'T LEAVE A MESS BEHIND YOU. Just turn out the lights, leave your keys on the table, close the door, and walk away. There are still those of us who are trying to get something accomplished in this looney bin. God knows why, and we're probably crazy as coots—indeed, one of the reasons you want to leave is most likely so you won't end up like us—but there it is.

Speaking of TV, there's a famous line from M.A.S.H. where Radar is upset about something; he staggers into the Swamp and to Hawkeye and B.J.'s amazement he pours himself a big beaker full of their rotgut homemade moonshine and slugs it down. "Yick!" says Radar. "I thought this stuff was supposed to make you feel better?"

"It's supposed to make you feel NOTHING," replies B. J.

That's your goal, my friend. You are never going to feel BETTER once you leave the Movement. You can't, because YOU KNOW the truth and you cannot erase that knowledge from your mind. But it is possible for you to live a so-called "normal" life, (leaving aside the question of this society's "normality"), by making yourself feel NOTHING. By disciplining your memory to forget as much as you can and creating a state of mind where you simply accept the madness and pain of the "real" world under Political Correctness as something inevitable, simply a part of life like death and disease and the weather and automobile accidents. That's how millions of White people live with it. By schooling themselves to feel NOTHING and when they cannot, by killing the pain in chemical or electronic drugs or mindless material pursuits like trying to catch fish they do not need to eat or building little carpentry knick-knacks which will be smashed by rioting niggers in their childrens' time, or a thousand and one variations.

That is the path you have chosen, and who is to say it is not the right one for you? Love us or hate us, it is only a very, very extraordinary few who have what it takes—be that good or bad—to devote their lives to this Cause. It is clear you are not one of them and by pretending otherwise you pose a danger and a distraction to those of us who still fight on. Just DO it, then. LEAVE it. Walk away from it.

And good luck.

88!

Harold A. Covington

David Duke: The Messenger and His Message
by Chip Berlet and Margaret Quigley

This text is self-explanatory. It recounts a radio confrontation between David Duke and Chip Berlet, a longtime watchdog of the radical right who is associated with the Political Research Associates. It is offered as an illustration of Duke's remarkable ability to tailor his message to any particular audience. Here, Berlet brings Duke's words as addressed to a movement audience into the context of the audience for a radio program on Boston's public radio station WBZ.

Chip Berlet and Margaret Quigley are analysts with Political Research Associates in Cambridge, Mass., an organization that has monitored the political right wing for the past ten years. PRA, 678 Mass. Ave., #205 Cambridge, MA 02139

PARTIAL TRANSCRIPT OF DAVID DUKE'S APPEARANCE ON BOSTON RADIO SHOW, MARCH 28, 1991

WBZ-Radio, David Brudnoy Show, Boston, Mass, March 28, 1991.

Guest: David Duke. Caller: Chip Berlet.

Transcript prepared by PRA.

DAVID BRUDNOY, HOST: Chip Berlet was with my colleague John Keller earlier this evening. Mr. Berlet is an analyst with Political Research Associates. He has called and he joins us now. Chip, good evening. You're on with Mr. Duke.

CHIP BERLET: Good morning.

BRUDNOY: Good morning, I'm sorry, Chip go ahead.

BERLET: Well, I spent the last couple of days looking at your recent speeches, Mr. Duke, including a July 23rd one, 1988 one up in the state of Washington Populist Party nominating convention and I'd just like to run a couple of your quotes there and see if you still agree with them.

DAVID DUKE: OK.

BERLET: I certainly understand that you might change your views but in that speech you said that the single most important issue facing America was the Zionist control of the American media and that Zionists control our media and they try to break down our heritage. I wonder if you could explain that.

DUKE: Well, I think there is a lot of Zionist influence in media and I think it's one of the key issues in our...I wouldn't say it was the key issue in America, but I think it is a key issue in terms of our foreign policy.

BERLET: Yeah, and you followed up that statement by saying that you did know one Jew, Alfred Lilienthal, who you thought was OK, but that Judaism was a vile faith. Your quote—

DUKE: No, I didn't say that. And I—

BERLET: You did. I have the tape right here. I'll play it for you.

DUKE: O.K.

BERLET: You said Judaism is a vile faith, there are many horrible things in the Talmud. I'll play the tape right now. I've got it.

DUKE: Well, I don't know where that was from or what year or what time.

BERLET: It was 1988, July 23rd...

DUKE: Let me hear that where you say I, it was a vile, vile faith.

BERLET: Populist Party. I can say it. You want to hear it? I'll play it right now for you.

DUKE: Well, I don't know, I know, but I need to hear the whole context to see it—

BRUDNOY: Well, let's hear the sentence that applies—

DUKE: Yeah, let's hear that.

BRUDNOY: —Chip if you happen to have it—

DUKE: Let me hear that.

BRUDNOY: —geared up.

DUKE: Let me hear that where you say I, it was a vile, vile faith.

BERLET: Well, I've got a, it will take me a second to find that exact quote, I've got one where you say that God created different races and God separated them and that was a natural law. I can play that right now; it's cued up.

BRUDNOY: Go ahead.

BERLET: OK?

DUKE: OK.

DUKE ON TAPE: There's no question that God created different races on this planet. There's also no question that God created those races and he separated those races. [That's right.] The white races were European, the yellow races were Asian and the Blacks, of course, were African. Now man has a tendency to come along and say, God's law doesn't really make, isn't very important. This natural law that God created isn't very vital. Well, I think that it is. I'm glad that God created different races. I think it offers greater possibilities for mankind and I want my grandkids and greatgrandkids to look something like myself [Yes] and the people that came before me. [Amen] And I'm proud of that fact. [Applause]...

BRUDNOY: Chip, I, we'll have to turn that down because it's so hard to hear—

DUKE: Oh, I could hear it—

BRUDNOY: —OK.

DUKE: —And I don't see anything—God did create different races and he did separate them by continent. I don't see anything that was improper or anything that I'd have to repudiate from that statement because I think it's absolutely correct.

BERLET: Yeah, but in the context of your former views, then it does tend to suggest that, you have in the past suggested that the basic culture of America is European and that if that's lost then we will lose America.

DUKE: Oh, I believe that. And I've never denied that. I think the basic culture of this country is European and Christian and I think if we lose that, we lose America. Yes, I believe that a hundred percent. I stated that in my most recent race for the U.S. Senate in my television programs. I've written about that. I have no argument with that statement. Yes, I believe that. We're predominantly white, we're basically white European in terms of our culture and we're basically Christian and I endorse that. I don't think we should suppress other races, but I think that if we lose that white—ahh what's the word for it—dominance in America, with it we lose America. Yes.

BERLET: Would you like to hear the thing about, that you don't respect Judaism and it's vile.

BRUDNOY: Please. Do that part here now.

DUKE: Yeah, I'd like to hear that.

BRUDNOY: Go ahead, Chip, please.

BRUDNOY: This is right after you mentioned Mr. Lilienthal.

BRUDNOY: Go ahead.

DUKE: OK.

DUKE ON TAPE: But I don't have respect for Zionism, and frankly I don't have respect for Judaism. Because it's a very vile [Yeah], anti-Christian faith, and if you're familiar with it, then you'd realize why I feel that way. It doesn't mean all Jews are that way. But I don't, I don't respect the Talmud, I think it's a very vicious and vile book and it attacks all Christians and non-Jews in the world and I—

BRUDNOY: Mr. Duke, what do you say to those remarks? Was it 1988, Chip?

BERLET: July 1988.

DUKE: I don't think that, I don't remember that at that meeting now.

BERLET: You don't?

DUKE: No.

BERLET: I do have the videotape given to me by the Populist Party.

DUKE: Well, that's, that's fine. Again, there are some certain vile quotes like that against, against Christianity and you can look up those quotes yourself in the Talmud but I wouldn't say, I don't believe that Judaism is a vile faith—

BERLET: But you did then.

DUKE: —but I think there are some, there's some elements in it that I certainly disagree with. [laughs]

BRUDNOY: No, but let's stick to the point that you did then, in July of '88—

DUKE: Yeah.

BERLET: So you're saying that you no longer think Judaism is a vile faith.

DUKE: No, I don't think Judaism is a vile faith.

BERLET: What happened in the intervening year—

DUKE: And if it came off that way, I didn't mean to make it as the entire faith that way but I think there's, I said, I said in the speech there are aspects which are, which are wrong and I think, for instance there are some, some passages in the Talmud which say that Christians should be strangulated [sic] and that Christ was a bastard and Mary was a whore and that kind of thing and to me those, those aspects are very anti-Christian and very vile.

BERLET: Uh huh. And at another point, you said—

DUKE: But obviously I don't think that is the whole tradition of Judaism but certainly some of those, some of those sentiments in the Talmud.

BERLET: That's fascinating. At another point you say that the internationalists want to destroy the American middle class. They want to destroy our heritage. They know they cannot take full control of our lives unless they destroy the vitality, the seed, the spirit, the genetic treasure of this society, of our nation. What, what are you, what is the genetic treasure of our society?

DUKE: I think our heritage. I think when you talk about American—

BERLET: Who are the internationalists who are trying to destroy this seed?

DUKE: Well, I think some of the international financial concerns, for instance, some of the international, powerful corporations and that's what's so odd in this country you have a lot of them who have a lot of power in banking and other areas who are also very liberal and pro-Marxist. That to me is a dichotomy. It doesn't seem, it doesn't seem, it seems like a contradiction in terms, yet communism has flourished often where you've had more money in society than in the poorer areas. Mississippi's probably got the lowest Communists per capita of any state in the United States but there seems to be a lot of Communists in the centers like New York City and some of the major financial markets.

BRUDNOY: Anything else, Chip?

BERLET: No, I'm, I remain skeptical of his change of heart—

BRUDNOY: Thanks.

BERLET: —It's not Saul on the road to Damascus.

Aryan Destiny: Back to the Land
Jost

Jost's "Aryan Destiny: Back to the Land" is one of the best, and most intimate, portraits of the transformation of a disillusioned Vietnam veteran of the early 1970s into a National Socialist true believer. On the way, it details the utopian longings of the movement as Jost sought unsuccessfully to create a communal retreat in the mountains of northern California. The essay offers, as well, a wonderful, first-person account of the disparate subcultures that for a time lived in remarkable harmony in the most rural reaches of the mountains of California, and the changes that occurred to shatter that idyllic life.

In the late 1960's I had just returned from two consecutive tours of combat duty in the rugged mountain highlands of South Vietnam. California had become a very different place from the one I had left, and two years of isolation in the Asian jungles had not prepared me for that to which I had returned.

I was suddenly in an alien world of long hair and beards, drugs and sexual promiscuity, civil disobedience and racial color blindness. It was the day of the "Hippy", "do your own thing", and the encouragement to "drop out" of society.

For a while I was in a state of shock, but as I adjusted, I began listening and observing. I dismissed most of this "new age" philosophy as childish nonsense. However, two years in the jungles had given me a different outlook on life. I could now see the selfishness and materialism into which the White race had sunk, and I had some sympathy for my hairy co-racialists. I especially liked their idea of destroying the system by non-participation, and it has always remained in the back of my mind.

By the early 1970's there was a growing movement among these social drop-outs to go "back to the land", advocating self- sufficiency on the land, free from modern society's support, living simply like our ancestors. Their pioneering in this area has done our Folk an invaluable service.

By the mid 1970's I had given up trying to be part of the urban social and economic system. Already I could see the growing political power of non-whites, and the indifference and growing materialism of the white majority. Seeing no real alternative, I packed up my family and headed back to the land. There, I discovered a whole new world, a much better and more natural way of life, and an Aryan destiny!

In the isolated mountains of Northern California, there were already a number of individuals and families, many college educated, who had fled the cities and begun a new life of homesteading. They were all permeated with an anti establishment idealism which was directly descended from the hey-day of the hippy movement. Their philosophy of life was a combination of left-wing politics, oriental religion, Robin Hood and brotherhood, as well as a tolerance for drugs which ultimately led to an early destruction of the movement.

Nevertheless, these urban refugees had done a staggering amount of research, and a great deal of practical application in the field of self-sufficient homesteading. They learned to build their own simple shelters, everything from log cabins to yurts. They learned the skills of organic gardening, animal husbandry, and home processing of foods. They revived the arts of midwifery, herbal medicine, and such skills of self-sufficiency as spinning, weaving, and leather craft. In the spirit of being anti-establishment, they put great effort into supporting themselves off the system, and made some great progress into the area of cottage industries. They spurned corporations and conducted their business exclusively with thrift shops and small businesses. They made great progress in pioneering alternative education for their children. As their numbers grew, they began manifesting a real spirit of community and Folk.

These modern-day pioneers were happy to help any newcomer, and I spent the next couple of years learning the many skills of homesteading and self-sufficiency. For the first few years our family lived in crude octagon cabins, barns and even tepees. We cut firewood with antique handsaws, used herbal medicines, raised organic gardens, and learned to process our own food. Our lives were simple, yet fuller than ever before. Summer work was hard, but there was always ample recreation at the river swimming hole where numbers of locals from all over the mountain ridges would congregate to relax and cool off. Like our pre-christian ancestors of old, they were not burdened by christian puritanism. They saw nothing evil or dirty about the human body, and they swam and sun-bathed quite naturally unadorned by swimsuits or cutoffs. Winter was the time for enjoying the fruits of summer labor. We joined other modern-day homesteaders in rough-hewn cabins all over the mountains, sitting around the wood stove, repairing tools, watching the rain and snow, and planning the next season's chores.

But these pioneers did not understand the importance of discipline to their own idealism and homesteading success. They generally failed to pass anything on to their children. They opted for Jewish permissiveness. The heirs of the movement can be seen here and there throughout the area - purposeless, undisciplined, drug-using youth.

The end really came with the rise of marijuana cultivation. Ideals began to vanish with the temptation of large amounts of easily acquired cash. Materialism and the greater supply of drugs destroyed both the community spirit and idealism. Today, the mountains are waiting for a new back-to-the-land movement, one imbued with a true idealism, and a sound spiritual philosophy. This time it will not be the pressures of White middle class materialism that will spur a back-to-the-land movement. This time it will be the awesome pressure of mass non-white immigration, and White second-class citizenship.

All of the elements for building an Aryan Folk community are here. The time is now ripe. There is little future for White youth in any city. The cities are becoming more and more non-white. Economically, it is getting more and more difficult to survive in the city. The social welfare system is becoming more and more anti-white. The schools are sorely anti-white. Today, the disenfranchised Aryan youth are beginning to stir. The Skinhead movement is a reaction to the growing non-white terrorism, and White indifference. It pains me to see our youth sitting in government prisons for smashing a few degenerate heads in a futile attempt to fight back against overwhelming oppression. How much more useful it would be to put their energy into hewing themselves a homestead, and ultimately an Aryan community, out of the unsettled rugged mountains. There is still a great deal of open land in this country, and although it is not as easy as it used to be, it is still possible to live there simply, inexpensively, and reasonably independently. It is also quite possible to establish communities which are largely independent of the established system. Why not take up the old hippy slogan to "drop out", and begin destroying this anti-white system by non-participation?

Just as Adolf Hitler advocated the *"Drang nach Osten"* (the acquisition and settlement of the vast, unsettled lands in east Europe), we advocate a new Aryan back to the land movement. We hope that Volksberg, our family homestead in the secluded mountains of Northern California, will serve as an example, a viable alternative for the responsible and self-reliant of our Folk, to begin a new life, a simple, joyful, Aryan life, close to nature, and away from the degeneracy of the urban cesspools. As our Folk grows and grows, we hope to provide a viable destiny for Aryans: Back to the Land!

-Jost

88 Precepts

David Lane

The 88 Precepts of Order member David Lane, like his 14 words—"We must secure the existence of our people and a future for White children"—have been widely distributed and greatly respected throughout the White Power world. The number of precepts on offer is no accident: 88 is a number of considerable importance in the racialist movement. As "h" is the eighth letter of the alphabet, the number 88 has come to stand for "Heil Hitler," and is often used as a salutation in the correspondence of National Socialists and other race activists on both sides of the Atlantic.

———————

This is dedicated to all the brave men and women who have struggled and fought for the benefit of our race. And to those who have made the ultimate sacrifice, this is in their memory.

This edition of 88 PRECEPTS, written by David Lane and laid out by the Aryan Women's League, is a labor of love for The Order Bruder Schweigen, and all other Aryan Martyr's and Political Prisoners.

Until the White race realizes there is only one source from which we can ascertain lasting truths, there will never be peace or stability on this earth. In the immutable Laws of Nature, are the keys to life, order, and understanding.

The words of men, even those which some consider "inspired," are subject to translations, vocabulary, additions, subtractions, and distortions of fallible mortals. Therefore, every writing or influence (ancient or modern) must be strained through the test of conformity to Natural Law.

The White Peoples of the earth must collectively understand that they are equally subject to the iron-hard Laws of Nature with every other creature in the Universe, or they will not secure peace, safety, nor even their existence.

The world is in flames because Races, Sub-races, Nations, Cultures are being forced to violate their own Nature-ordained instincts for self reservation.

Many men of goodwill (but little understanding) are struggling against symptoms which are the result of disobedience to Natural Law. As is the Nature of Man, most take narrow provincial stances predicated on views formed by immediate environment current circumstances, and conditioned dogma.

This is encouraged by that powerful ruthless Tribe which has controlled the affairs of the world for untold centuries by exploiting Man's baser instincts. Conflict among and between the unenlightened serves as their mask and shield. A deeper understanding of the Fundamental laws that govern the affairs of Men is necessary if we are to save civilization from its usurious execution.

These few pages are not intended to provide a detailed system of government, but as PRECEPTS which, when understood, will benefit and preserve a People as individuals and as a Nation.

1. Any religion or teaching which denies the Natural Laws of the Universe is false.

2. Whatever a people's perception of God, or the Gods, or the motive Force of the Universe might be, they can hardly deny that Nature's Laws are the work of (and therefore, the intent of) that Force.

3. God and religion are distinct, separate, and often conflicting concepts. God is the personification of Nature proved perfect by the evidence of Natural Law. Religion is the creation of mortals, therefore predestined to fallibility. Religion may preserve or destroy a People, depending on the structure given by its progenitors, the motives of its agents, and the vagaries of historical circumstances.

4. The truest form of prayer is communion with NATURE. It is not vocal. Go to a lonely spot, if possible a mountain top, on a clear star-lit night, ponder the majesty and order of the infinite macrocosm. Then, consider the intricacies of the equally infinite microcosm. Understand that you are on the one hand inconsequential beyond comprehension in the size of things, and on the other hand, you are potentially valuable beyond comprehension as a link in destiny's chain. There you begin to understand how pride and self can co-exist with respect and reverence. There we find harmony with Nature and with harmony comes strength, peace, and certainty.

5. Secular power systems protect and promote religions which teach of an after-life. Thus People are taught to abandon defenses against the predators of this life.

6. History, both secular and religious, is a fable conceived in self-serving deceit and promulgated by those who perceive benefits.

7. Religion in its most beneficial form is the symbology of a People and their culture. A multi-racial religion destroys the senses of uniqueness, exclusivity, and value necessary to the survival of the race.

8. What men call "supernatural" is actually the natural not yet understood or revealed.

9. A proliferation of laws with the resultant loss of freedom is a sign (and directly proportional to) spiritual sickness in a Nation.

10. If a Nation is devoid of spiritual health and moral character, then government and unprincipled men will fill the vacancy. Therefore, freedom prospers in moral values and tyranny thrives in moral decay.

11. Truth requires little explanation. Therefore, beware of verbose doctrines. The great principles are revealed in brevity.

12. Truth does not fear investigation.

13. Unfounded belief is a pitfall. A people who do not check the validity and effect of their beliefs with reason will suffer and/or perish.

14. No greater motivating force exists than the certain conviction that one is right.

15. In accord with Nature's Laws, nothing is more right than the preservation of one's own race.

16. Discernment is a sign of a healthy people. In a sick or dying nation, civilization, culture, or race, substance is abandoned in favor of appearance.

17. Discernment includes the ability to recognize the difference between belief and demonstrable reality.

18. There exists no such thing as rights or privileges under the Laws of Nature. The deer being stalked by a hungry lion has no right to life. However, he may purchase life by obedience to nature-ordained instincts for vigilance and flight. Similarly, men have no right to life, liberty, or happiness. These circumstances may be purchased by oneself, by one's family, by one's tribe, or by one's ancestors, but they are nonetheless, purchases and are not rights. Furthermore, the value of these purchases can only be maintained through vigilance and obedience to Natural Law.

19. A People who are not convinced of their uniqueness and value will perish.

20. The White Race has suffered invasions and brutality from Africa and Asia for thousands of years, for example, Attila and the Asiatic Huns who invaded Europe in the 5th century raping, plundering, and killing from the Alps to the Baltic and Caspian Seas. This scenario was repeated by the Mongols of Genghis Kahn 800 years later. (Note here that the American Indians are not "Native Americans," but are racial Asians.) In the 8th century, hundreds of years before the Crusades and 8 centuries before Blacks were brought to America, the North African Moors of mixed-racial background invaded and conquered Portugal, Spain, and part of France. So, the attempted guilt trip placed on the White Race by civilization's executioners is invalid under both historical circumstances and the Natural Law which denies inter-specie compassion. The fact is all races have benefited immeasurably from the creative genius of the Aryan people.

21. A People who allow others not of their race to live among them will perish because the inevitable result of racial integration is racial inter-breeding which destroys the characteristics and existence of a race. Forced integration is deliberate and malicious genocide, particularly for a people like the White Race who are now a small minority in the world.

22. In the final analysis, a race or specie is not judged superior or inferior by its accomplishments, but by its will and ability to survive.

23. Political, economic, and religious systems may be destroyed and resurrected by men, but the death of a race is eternal.

24. No race of people can indefinitely continue their existence without territorial imperatives in which to propagate, protect, and promote their own kind.

25. A people without a culture exclusively their own, will perish.

26. Nature has put a certain antipathy between races and species, to preserve the individuality and existence of each. Violation of the territorial imperative necessary to preserve that antipathy leads to either conflict or mongrelization.

27. It is not constructive to hate those of other races, or even those of mixed races. But a separation must be maintained for the survival of one's own race. One must, however, hate with a pure and perfect hatred those of one's own race who commit treason against one's own kind and against the nations' of one's own kind. One must hate with a perfect hatred all those people or practices which destroy one's people, one's culture, or the racial exclusiveness of one's territorial imperative.

28. The concept of a multi-racial society violates every Natural Law for specie preservation.

29. The concept of "equality" is declared a lie by every evidence of Nature. It is a search for the lowest common denominator, and its pursuit will destroy every superior race, nation, or culture. In order for a plow horse to run as fast as a race horse, you would first have to cripple the race horse; and conversely, in order for a race horse to pull as much as a plow horse, you would first have to cripple the plow horse. In either case, the pursuit of equality is the destruction of excellence.

30. The instincts for racial and specie preservation are ordained by Nature.

31. Instincts are Nature's perfect mechanism for the survival of each race and specie. The human weakness of rationalizing situations for self-gratification must not be permitted to interfere with these instincts.

32. Miscegenation, that is race-mixing, is and has always been, the greatest threat to the survival of the Aryan race.

33. Inter-specie compassion is contrary to the Laws of Nature and is, therefore, suicidal. If a wolf were to intercede to save a lamb from a lion, he would be killed. Today, we see the White man taxed so heavily that he cannot afford children. The taxes raised are then used to support the breeding of tens of millions of non-whites, many of whom then demand the last White females for breeding partners.

As you can see, man is subject to all the Laws of Nature. This has nothing to do with morality, hatred, good or evil. Nature does not recognize the concepts of good and evil in inter-specie relationships. If the lion eats the lamb, it is good for the lion and evil for the lamb. If the lamb escapes and the lion starves, it is good for the lamb and evil for the lion. So, we see the same incident is labeled both good and evil. This cannot be, for there are no contradictions within Nature's Laws.

34. The instinct for sexual union is part of Nature's perfect mechanism for specie preservation. It must not be repressed; and its purpose namely reproduction, must not be thwarted either. Understand, that for thousands of years, our females bore children at an early age. Now, in an attempt to conform to, and compete in, an alien culture, they deny their Nature-ordained instincts and duties. Teach responsibility, but, also have understanding. The life of a race springs from the wombs of its women. He who would judge must first understand the difference between what is good and what is right.

35. Homosexuality is a crime against Nature. All Nature declares the purpose of the instinct for sexual union is reproduction and, thus, preservation of the specie. Homosexuality does not reproduce or preserve the specie. It is unnatural and, therefore, a suicidal perversion.

36. Sexual pornography degrades the Nature of all who are involved. The woman is reduced to an object and sex to animal coupling.

37. That race whose males will not fight to the death to keep and mate with its females will perish. Any White man with healthy instincts feels disgust and revulsion when he sees a woman of his race with a man of another race. Those who today control the media and affairs of the Western World, teach that this is wrong and shameful. They label it "racism." As any "ism;" for instance the world "nationalism," means you promote your nation, racism merely means you promote and protect the life of your race. It is, perhaps, the proudest word in existence. Any man who disobeys these instincts is anti-Nature.

38. In a sick and dying nation, culture, race, or civilization, political dissent and traditional values will be labelled and persecuted as heinous crimes by inquisitors clothing themselves in jingoistic patriotism.

39. A people who are ignorant of their past will defile the present and destroy the future.

40. A race must honor above all earthly things, those who have given their lives or freedom for the preservation of the folk.

41. The folk, namely the members of the Race, are the Nation. Racial loyalties must always supersede geographical and national boundaries. If this is taught and understood, it will end fratricidal wars. Wars must not be fought for the benefit of another race.

42. The Nation's leaders are not rulers, they are servants and guardians. They are not to serve for personal gain. Choose only a guardian who has no interest in the accumulation of material things.

43. Choose and judge your leader, also called guardians, thus: those who seek always to limit the power of government are of good heart and conscience. Those who seek to expand the power of government are base tyrants.

44. No government can give anything to anybody without first taking from another. Government is, by its very nature, legalized taking. A limited amount of government is a necessary burden for national defense and internal order. Anything more is counterproductive to freedom and liberty.

45. The organic founding Law, namely the Constitution of a Nation must not be amendable by any method other than unanimous consent of all parties thereto, and with all parties present; otherwise the doors are open for the advent of the most dangerous and deadly form of government, namely, democracy.

46. In a democracy, those who control the media (and thus the minds of the electorate) have power undreamed by kings or dictators.

47. The simplest way to describe a democracy is this: three people form a government, each having one vote. Then two of them vote to steal the wealth of the third.

48. The latter stages of democracy are filled with foreign wars because the bankrupt system attempts to preserve itself by plundering other nations.

49. In a democracy that which is legal is seldom moral, and that which is moral is often illegal.

50. A democracy is always followed by a strongman...some call him a dictator. it is the only way to restore order out of the chaos caused by democracy. Pick your strongman wisely! He must be a guardian in his heart. He must be one who has shown that his only purpose in life is the preservation of the folk. His ultimate aim must be to restore the rule of Law based on the perfect Laws of Nature. Do not choose him by his words. Choose one who has sacrificed all in the face of tyranny; one who has endured and persevered. This is the only reliable evidence of his worthiness and motives.

51. A power system will do anything, no matter how corrupt or brutal, to preserve itself.

52. Tyrannies cannot be ended without the use of force.

53. Those who commit treason disguise their deeds in proclamations of patriotism.

54. Propaganda is a major component in all power systems, both secular and religious; and false propaganda is a major component of unprincipled power systems. All power systems endeavor to convince their subjects that the system is good, just, beneficent, and noble, as well as, worthy of perpetuation and defense. The more jingoistic the propaganda issue, the more suspicious one should be of its truth.

55. Political power, in the final analysis, is created and maintained by force.

56. A power system, secular or religious, which employs extensive calls to patriotism or requires verbosity and rhetoric for its preservation, is masking tyranny.

57. Propaganda is a legitimate and necessary weapon in any struggle. The elements of successful propaganda are: simplicity, emotion, repetition and brevity. Also, since men believe what they want to believe, and since they want to believe that which they perceive as beneficial to themselves, then successful propaganda must appeal to the perceived self-interest of those to whom it is disseminated.

58. Tyrannies teach what to think. Free men learn how to think.

59. Beware of men who increase their wealth by the use of words. Particularly beware of the lawyers or any priest who denies Natural Law.

60. The patriot, being led to the inquisition's dungeons or the executioner's axe, will be condemned the loudest by his former friends and allies; for thus they seek to escape the same fate.

61. The sweet Goddess of Peace lives only under the protective arm of the ready GOD OF WAR.

62. The organic founding Law of the Nation must state with unmistakable and irrevocable specificity the identity of the homogenous, racial, cultural group for whose welfare it was formed, and that the continued existence of the Nation is singularly for all time for the welfare of that specific group only.

63. That race or culture which lets others influence or control any of the following will perish.

    1) organs of information

    2) educational institutions

3) religious institutions
4) political offices
5) creation of their money
6) judicial institutions
7) cultural institutions
8) economic life

64. Just Laws require little explanation. Their meaning is irrevocable in simplicity and specificity.

65. Men's emotions are stirred far more effectively by the spoken word than by the written word. This is why a ruling tyranny will react more violently to gatherings of dissenters than to books or pamphlets.

66. The organic founding Law of the Nation, or any law, is exactly as pertinent as the will and power to enforce it.

67. An unarmed and/or non-militant people will be enslaved.

68. Some say the pen is more powerful than the sword. Perhaps so. Yet, the word without the sword has no authority.

69. Tyrannies are usually built step by step and disguised by noble rhetoric.

70. The difference between a terrorist and a patriot is control of the press.

71. The judgments of the guardians, namely the leaders, must be true to Natural Law and, yet, tempered by reason.

72. Materialism is base and destructive. The guardians of a Nation must constantly warn against and combat a materialistic spirit in the Nation.

73. Materialism leads men to seek artificial status through wealth or property. True social status comes from service to Family, Race, and Nation.

74. Materialism ultimately leads to conspicuous, unnecessary consumption which in turn leads to the rape of Nature and destruction of the environment. It is unnatural. The true guardians of the Nations must be wholly untainted by materialism.

75. The function of a merchant or salesman is to provide a method of exchange. A merchant who promotes unnecessary consumption and materialism must not be tolerated.

76. The only lawful functions of money are as a medium of exchange and a store of value. All other uses including social engineering, speculation, inflation, and especially usury are unlawful. Usury/interest, in particular, at any percent, is a high crime which cannot be tolerated.

77. A Nation with an aristocracy of money, lawyers, or merchants will become a tyranny.

78. The simplest way to describe a usury-based central banking system is this: the bankers demand the property of the Nation as collateral for their loans. At interest, more money is owed them than they created with the loans...so, eventually, the bankers foreclose on the Nation.

79. Interest/usury, inflation and oppressive taxation are theft by deception and destroy the moral fabric of the Nation.

80. Wealth gained without sacrifice or honest labor will usually be misused.

81. Nothing in Nature is static. Either the life-force grows and expands or it decays and dies.

82. Respect must be earned, it cannot be demanded or assumed.

83. Avoid a vexatious man for his venom will poison your own nature.

84. Self discipline is a mark of higher man.

85. One measure of a man is cheerfulness in adversity.

86. A fool judges men by their words. A wise man judges others by their actions and accomplishments.

87. In our relationships or interactions, as in all of Nature's Laws, to each action there is a reaction. That which we plant will be harvested, if not by ourselves then by another or others.

88. These are sure signs of a sick or dying Nation. If you seek any of them, your guardians are committing treason.

1) mixing and destruction of the founding race.

2) destruction of the family units

3) oppressive taxation

4) corruption of the Law

5) terror and suppression against those who warn of the Nation's error.

6) immorality: drugs, drunkenness, etc.

7) infanticide (now called abortion)

8) destruction of the currency (inflation or usury)

9) aliens in the land

10) materialism

11) foreign wars

12) guardians (leaders) who pursue wealth or glory

13) homosexuality

14) alien culture

15) religion not based on Natural Law

ALERTNESS: Be aware of potential hazards; be alert to impending danger. Calculate the odds immediately. Anticipate. Avoid. Prepare.

DECISIVENESS: Select an appropriate course of action: abandoning the field does not constitute cowardice. Overcome your domesticity and civility when necessary. Utilize the hypothesis to train. Do not delay or hesitate. Be confident.

AGGRESSIVENESS: "The best defense is a good offense." Do the unexpected. Develop the morale edge. Be indignant; turn your fear into anger.

SPEED: Retaliate instantly. Calculate the reaction time of your assailant. Remember, there are no Marquis of Queensbury rules in the arena where you will compete. No fair play. No rules of engagement.

COOLNESS: Keep your head; do not panic. Train yourself in a mental attitude for combat.

RUTHLESSNESS: Take no chances when your life is at stake. Make your attacker fear for his life. Be tough. Be harsh. Be merciless until the danger has passed or you are victorious. Counterattack to incapacitation.

TECHNIQUE: Apply the proper techniques but do not press a failed attack. Do not ego tie yourself to pressing a futile counter. Improvise; rearrange. Develop an effective repertoire of techniques. Know the body's weaknesses. Utilize appropriate tactics. Comprehend you own limitations. Gauge your opponent's skill and strength. Sharpen your defensive skills. Practice. Survive.

STRESS: Some observations. Stress. It can eat at your insides, gnaw at your brain. It can disrupt your equilibrium and make you do things that are contrary to your inner goodness. Stress plays the swan song; Just some thoughts before we all move on.

HAIL VICTORY!

Leaderless Resistance

Louis R. Beam
Seditionist *Issue 12, February 1992: Final Edition*

"Leaderless Resistance," by Texas Klansman Louis R. Beam, is one of the most important essays to emerge in recent years from the radical right. Making a virtue of weakness, the leaderless resistance concept recognizes the seeming ease with which government and private watchdog agencies penetrate right-wing organizations, and takes note of the tiny number of activists who will take up arms against the vastly superior forces of the state. Beam's response is the creation of a cadre of lone-wolf fighters or, at best, a number of small, autonomous cells whose activities are undertaken with no central direction by any organization or national leader. Beam's essay, which first appeared in his journal the *Seditionist,* has been widely reprinted and disseminated via the Internet as well.

———————————

The concept of Leaderless Resistance was proposed by Col. Ulius Louis Amoss, who was the founder of International Service of Information Incorporated, located in Baltimore, Maryland. Col. Amoss died more than fifteen years ago, but during his life was a tireless opponent of communism, as well as a skilled Intelligence Officer. Col. Amoss first wrote of Leaderless Resistance on April 17, 1962. His theories of organization were primarily directed against the threat of eventual Communist take-over in the United States. The present writer, with the benefit of having lived many years beyond Col. Amoss, has taken his theories and expounded upon them. Col. Amoss feared the Communists. This author fears the federal government. Communism now represents a threat to no one in the United States, while federal tyranny represents a threat to everyone. The writer has joyfully lived long enough to see the dying breaths of communism, but may, unhappily, remain long enough to see the last grasps of freedom in America.

In the hope that, somehow, America can still produce the brave sons and daughters necessary to fight off ever increasing persecution and oppression, this essay is offered. Frankly, it is too close to call at this point. Those who love liberty, and believe in freedom enough to fight for it are rare today, but within the bosom of every once great nation, there remains secreted, the pearls of former greatness. They are there. I have looked into their sparking eyes; sharing a brief moment in time with them as I passed through this life. Relished their friendship, endured their pain, and they mine. We are a band of brothers, native to the soil gaining strength one from another as we have rushed head long into a battle that all the weaker, timid men, say we can not win. Perhaps...but then again, perhaps we can. It's not over till the last freedom fighter is buried or imprisoned, or the same happens to those who would destroy their liberty.

Barring any cataclysmic events, the struggle will yet go on for years. The passage of time will make it clear to even the more slow among us that the government is the foremost threat to the life, and liberty of the folk. The government will no doubt make today's oppressiveness look like grade school work compared to what they have planned in the future. Meanwhile, there are those of us who continue to hope that somehow the few can do what the many have not. We are cognizant that before things get better they will certainly get worse as government shows a willingness to use ever more severe police state measures against dissidents. This changing situation makes it clear that those who oppose state repression must be prepared to alter, adapt, and modify their behavior, strategy, and tactics as circumstances warrant. Failure to consider new methods and implement them as necessary will make the government's efforts at suppression uncomplicated. It is the duty of every patriot to make the tyrant's life miserable. When one fails to do so he not only fails himself, but his people.

With this in mind, current methods of resistance to tyranny employed by those who love our race, culture, and heritage must pass a litmus test of soundness. Methods must be objectively measured as to their effectiveness, as well as to whether they make the government's intention of repression more possible or more difficult. Those not working to aid our objectives must be discarded or the government benefits from our failure to do so.

As honest men who have banded together into groups or associations of a political or religious nature are falsely labeled "domestic terrorists" or "cultists" and suppressed, it will become necessary to consider other methods of organization—or as the case may very well call for: non-organization. One should keep in mind that it is not in the government's interest to eliminate all groups. Some few must remain in order to perpetuate the smoke and mirrors vision for the masses that America is a "free democratic country" where dissent is allowed. Most organizations, however, that possess the potential for effective resistance will not be allowed to continue. Anyone who is so naive as to believe the most powerful government on earth will not crush any who pose a real threat to that power, should not be active, but rather, at home studying political history.

The question as to who is to be left alone and who is not, will be answered by how groups and individuals deal with several factors such as: avoidance of conspiracy plots, rejection of feeble minded malcontents, insistence upon quality of the participants, avoidance of all contact with the front men for the federals—the news media—and, finally, camouflage (which can be defined as the ability to blend in the public's eye the more committed groups of resistance with mainstream "kosher" associations that are generally seen as harmless.) Primarily though, whether any organization is allowed to continue in the future will be a matter of how big a threat a group represents. Not a threat in terms of armed might or political ability, for there is none of either for the present, but rather, threat in terms of potentiality. It is potential the federals fear most. Whether that potential exists in an individual or group is incidental. The federals measure potential threat in terms of what might happen given a situation conducive to action on the part of a restive organization or individual. Accurate intelligence gathering allows them to assess the potential. Showing one's hand before the bets are made, is a sure way to loose.

The movement for freedom is rapidly approaching the point where for many people, the option of belonging to a group will be nonexistent. For others, group membership will be a viable option for only the immediate future. Eventually, and perhaps much sooner than most believe possible, the price paid for membership will exceed any perceived benefit. But for now, some of the groups that do exist often serve a useful purpose either for the newcomer who can be indoctrinated into the ideology of the struggle, or for generating positive propaganda to reach potential freedom fighters. It is sure that, for the most part, this struggle is rapidly becoming a matter of individual action, each of its participants making a private decision in the quietness of his heart to resist: to resist by any means necessary. It is hard to know what others will do, for no man truly knows another man's heart. It is enough to know what one himself will do. A great teacher once said "know thyself." Few men really do, but let each of us, promise ourselves, not to go quietly to the fate our would-be masters have planned.

The concept of Leaderless Resistance is nothing less than a fundamental departure in theories of organization. The orthodox scheme of organization is diagrammatically represented by the pyramid, with the mass at the bottom and the leader at the top. This fundamental of organization is to be seen not only in armies, which are of course, the best illustration of the pyramid structure, with the mass of soldiery, the privates, at the bottom responsible to corporals who are in turn responsible to sergeants, and so on up the entire chain of command to the generals at the top. But the same structure is seen in corporations, ladies' garden clubs and in our political system itself. This orthodox "pyramid" scheme of organization is to be seen basically in all existing political, social and religious structures in the world today from the Federal government to the Roman Catholic Church. The Constitution of the United States, in the wisdom of the Founders, tried to sublimate the essential dictatorial nature of pyramidal organization by dividing authority into three: executive, legislative and judicial. But the pyramid remains essentially untouched.

This scheme of organization, the pyramid, is however, not only useless, but extremely dangerous for the participants when it is utilized in a resistance movement against state tyranny. Especially is this so in technologically advanced societies where electronic surveillance can often penetrate the structure revealing its chain of command. Experience has revealed over and over again that anti-state, political organizations utilizing this method of command and control are easy prey for government infiltration, entrapment, and destruction of the personnel involved. This has been seen repeatedly in the United States where pro-government infiltrators or agent provocateurs weasel their way into patriotic groups and destroy them from within.

In the pyramid type of organization, an infiltrator can destroy anything which is beneath his level of infiltration and often those above him as well. If the traitor has infiltrated at the top, then the entire organization from the top down is compromised and may be traduced at will.

An alternative to the pyramid type of organization is the cell system. In the past, many political groups (both right and left) have used the cell system to further their objectives. Two examples will suffice. During the American Revolution "committees of correspondence" were formed throughout the Thirteen colonies.

Their purpose was to subvert the government and thereby aid the cause of independence. The "Sons of Liberty", who made a name for themselves dumping government taxed tea into the harbor at Boston, were the action arm of the committees of correspondence. Each committee was a secret cell that operated totally independently of the other cells. Information on the government was passed from committee to committee, from colony to colony, and then acted upon on a local basis. Yet even in these bygone days of poor communication, of weeks to months for a letter to be delivered, the committees without any central direction whatsoever, were remarkable similar in tactics employed to resist government tyranny. It was, as the first American patriots knew, totally unnecessary for anyone to give an order for anything. Information was made available to each committee, and each committee acted as it saw fit. A recent example of the cell system taken from the left wing of politics are the Communists. The Communist, in order to get around the obvious problems involved in pyramidal organization, developed to an art the cell system. They had numerous independent cells which operated completely isolated from one another and particularly with no knowledge of each other, but were orchestrated together by a central headquarters. For instance, during World War II, in Washington, it is known that there were at least six secret Communist cells operating at high levels in the United States government (plus all the open Communists who were protected and promoted by President Roosevelt), however, only one of the cells was rooted out and destroyed. How many more actually were operating no one can say for sure.

The Communist cells which operated in the U.S until late 1991 under Soviet control could have at their command a leader, who held a social position which appeared to be very lowly. He could be, for example, a busboy in a restaurant, but in reality a colonel or a general in the Soviet Secret Service, the KGB. Under him could be a number of cells and a person active in one cell would almost never have knowledge of individuals who are active in another cell. The value of this is that while any one cell can be infiltrated, exposed or destroyed, such action will have no effect on the other cells; in fact, the members of the other cells will be supporting that cell which is under attack and ordinarily would lend very strong support to it in many ways. This is at least part of the reason, no doubt, that whenever in the past Communists were attacked in this country, support for them sprang up in many unexpected places.

The efficient and effective operation of a cell system after the Communist model, is of course, dependent upon central direction, which means impressive organization, funding from the top, and outside support, all of which the Communists had. Obviously, American patriots have none of these things at the top or anywhere else, and so an effective cell organization based upon the Soviet system of operation is impossible.

Two things become clear from the above discussion. First, that the pyramid type of organization can be penetrated quite easily and it thus is not a sound method of organization in situations where the government has the resources and desire to penetrate the structure; which is the situation in this country. Secondly, that the normal qualifications for the cell structure based upon the Red model does not exist in the U.S. for patriots. This understood, the question arises "What method is left for those resisting state tyranny?" The answer comes from Col. Amoss who proposed the "Phantom Cell" mode of organization. Which he described as Leaderless Resistance. A system of organization that is based upon the cell organization, but does not have any central control or direction, that is in fact almost identical to the methods used by the Committees of Correspondence during the American Revolution. Utilizing the Leaderless Resistance concept, all individuals and groups operate independently of each other, and never report to a central headquarters or single leader for direction or instruction, as would those who belong to a typical pyramid organization.

At first glance, such a type of organization seems unrealistic, primarily because there appears to be no organization. The natural question thus arises as to how are the "Phantom cells" and individuals to cooperate with each other when there is no intercommunication or central direction? The answer to this question is that participants in a program of Leaderless Resistance through phantom cell or individual action must know exactly what they are doing, and how to do it. It becomes the responsibility of the individual to acquire the necessary skills and information as to what is to be done. This is by no means as impractical as it appears, because it is certainly true that in any movement, all persons involved have the same general outlook, are acquainted with the same philosophy, and generally react to given situations in similar ways. The pervious history of the committees of correspondence during the American Revolution show this to be true.

Since the entire purpose of Leaderless Resistance is to defeat state tyranny (at least insofar as this essay is concerned), all members of phantom cells or individuals will tend to react to objective events in the same way through usual tactics of resistance. Organs of information distribution such as newspapers, leaflets, computers, etc., which are widely available to all, keep each person informed of events, allowing for a planned response that will take many variations. No one need issue an order to anyone. Those idealist truly committed to the cause of freedom will act when they feel the time is ripe, or will take their cue from others who precede them. While it is true that much could be said against this type of structure as a method of resistance, it must be kept in mind that Leaderless Resistance is a child of necessity. The alternatives to it have been show to be unworkable or impractical. Leaderless Resistance has worked before in the American Revolution, and if the truly committed put it to use for themselves, it will work now.

It goes almost without saying that Leaderless Resistance leads to very small or even one man cells of resistance. Those who join organizations to play "let's pretend" or who are "groupies" will quickly be weeded out. While for those who are serious about their opposition to federal despotism, this is exactly what is desired.

From the point of view of tyrants and would be potentates in the federal bureaucracy and police agencies, nothing is more desirable than that those who oppose them be UNIFIED in their command structure, and that every person who opposes them belong to a pyramid type group. Such groups and organizations are an easy kill. Especially in light of the fact that the Justice (sic) Department promised in 1987 that there would never be another group that opposed them that they did not have at least one informer in. These federal "friends of government" are intelligence agents. They gather information that can be used at the whim of a federal D.A. to prosecute. The line of battle has been drawn. Patriots are required therefore, to make a conscious decision to either aid the government in its illegal spying, by continuing with old methods of organization and resistance, or to make the enemy's job more difficult by implementing effective countermeasures.

Now there will, no doubt, be mentally handicapped people out there who, while standing at a podium with an American flag draped in the background, and a lone eagle soaring in the sky above, will state emphatically in their best sounding red, white, and blue voice, "So what if the government is spying? We are not violating any laws." Such crippled thinking by any serious person is the best example that there is a need for special education classes. The person making such a statement is totally out of contact with political reality in this country, and unfit for leadership of any thing more than a dog sleigh in the Alaskan wilderness. The old "Born on the fourth of July" mentality that has influenced so much of the American patriot's thinking in the past will not save him from the government in the future. "Reeducation" for non-thinkers of this type will take place in the federal prison system where there are no flags or eagles, but abundance of men who were "not violating any law."

Most groups who "unify" their disparate associates into a single structure have short political lives. Therefore, those movement leaders constantly calling for unity of organization rather than the desirable unity of purpose, usually fall into one of three categories. They may not be sound political tacticians, but rather, just committed men who feel unity would help their cause, while not realizing that the government would greatly benefit from such efforts. The Federal objective, to imprison or destroy all who oppose them, is made easier in pyramid organizations. Or perhaps, they do not fully understand the struggle they are involved in and that the government they oppose has declared a state of war against those fighting for faith, folk, freedom and constitutional liberty. Those in power will use any means to rid themselves of opposition. The third class calling for unity and let us hope this is the minority of the three, are men more desirous of the supposed power that a large organization would bestow, than of actually achieving their stated purpose.

Conversely, the last thing Federal snoops would have, if they had any choice in the matter, is a thousand different small phantom cells opposing them. It is easy to see why. Such a situation is an intelligence nightmare for a government intent upon knowing everything they possibly can about those who oppose them. The

Federals, able to amass overwhelming strength of numbers, manpower, resources, intelligence gathering, and capability at any given time, need only a focal point to direct their anger. A single penetration of a pyramid type of organization can lead to the destruction of the whole. Whereas, Leaderless Resistance presents no single opportunity for the Federals to destroy a significant portion of the Resistance.

With the announcement by the Department of Justice (sic) that 300 FBI agents formerly assigned to watching Soviet spies in the US (domestic counter intelligence) are now to be used to "combat crime", the federal government is preparing the way for a major assault upon those persons opposed to their policies. Many anti-government groups dedicated to the preservation of the America of our forefathers can expect shortly to feel the brunt of a new federal assault upon liberty.

It is clear, therefore, that it is time to rethink traditional strategy and tactics when it comes to opposing a modern police state. America is quickly moving into a long dark night of police state tyranny, where the rights now accepted by most as being inalienable will disappear. Let the coming night be filled with a thousand points of resistance. Like the fog which forms when conditions are right and disappears when they are not, so must the resistance to tyranny be.

"If every person has the right to defend—even by force—his person, his liberty, and his property, then it follows that a group of men have the right to organize and support a common force to protect these rights constantly."

—*The Law*. Frederick Bastiat Paris, 1850.

Reichsfolk—Toward a New Elite

David Myatt

David Myatt is a long-time fixture on the British National Socialist scene. He is the founder of the small but influential group Reichsfolk, and his voluminous writings on the occult paths of National Socialism have been widely circulated throughout the National Socialist world. In "Reichsfolk–Toward a New Elite," Myatt introduces the organization's goals. In the text that follows, "Why I Am A National-Socialist," Myatt offers a more personal statement of his beliefs and aspirations.

The fundamental aims of Reichsfolk are: (1) to create a new type of individual - a new Aryan elite; (2) to prepare the way for the creation of a new Golden Age by championing the enlightened and higher religion of National-Socialism, and (3) to fight the Holy War that is necessary to destroy the present profane, tyrannical anti-Aryan System and the sub-human values of the old order on which this System is based.

This new elite will be The Legion of Adolf Hitler, and it is the members of this elite who will create the next National-Socialist Reich, the Golden Age itself. It is this new elite which will stand fast against the rising tide of sub-humans and the rising tide of decadence which is engulfing our societies, as it is the loyal and honourable National-Socialists of this elite who will uphold and champion the noble Aryan ideals of honour, loyalty and duty in a world where these values are little understood and seldom practised. It is this elite which will represent all that is best about the Aryan, as the members of this elite will not only be pure Aryans in race, they will also be pure Aryans in spirit - understanding as they will their glorious Aryan heritage and their glorious Aryan culture. It is this Legion of Adolf Hitler who will think and act and if necessary die like noble Aryans in a world increasingly anti-Aryan and increasingly controlled by the dark, sub-human, uncivilised forces of Zionism.

An individual becomes part of, or joins, this elite when they swear an oath to change themselves - or when they have changed themselves - into real National-Socialists through an act of will. This act of will involves them in striving to live by a Code of Honour; it involves them in mastering the Arts of Civilization (including the art of combat) and it involves them in doing their duty by upholding and championing the noble ideals of individual and racial excellence.

Reichsfolk exists primarily to train and guide this new elite. Thus will Reichsfolk teach *what it means to be Aryan*, as it will instruct its members in the arts of civilization and to uphold the noble ideals of individual and racial excellence. Reichsfolk will preserve, and hand on to future generations, the great legacy of our Aryan culture, as it will strive to add to that culture by its members undertaking deeds of heroism, with others extending our knowledge, our wisdom and making profound, noble and thus beautiful and reasoned contributions to the Arts and Sciences.

Thus the Reichsfolk is and will be a bastion of Aryan, ordered, beautiful, sublime and civilised values in a sub-human, ugly, profane, un-Aryan world, just as it is and will be preparing the way for these glorious and higher values to triumph again in the world and become the basis for a new and higher civilization.

Reichsfolk is not fighting for some sordid "political power" nor to implement some political programme. It is fighting for the holy cause of civilization - *for the development of a higher, more evolved, more civilized humanity*. Reichsfolk seeks the creation of a new race of more evolved beings to whom honour, reason, self-discipline and duty are a way of life. Further, Reichsfolk desires this new race, this higher humanity, to take the light, reason, honour and order of their higher civilization out into the very cosmos itself.

Reichsfolk is thus not just another religious or even National-Socialist organization - it is the future of the Aryan race and thus of civilization itself, just as Adolf Hitler is our future. Reichsfolk is fighting in the name of Adolf Hitler himself and for the holiest cause of all - that of the Cosmic Being itself, manifest to us in Nature, the evolution of Nature that is race and the evolution of race that is individual excellence, civilization and enlightenment. Reichsfolk is thus striving to bring the divine light of the Cosmic Being back into an increasingly dark, uncivilized and sub-human world.

Reichsfolk totally rejects the disgusting, decadent, sub-human world of the present with its dis-honourable values and its dishonourable weak individuals. Reichsfolk seeks to totally destroy the old order, as it is prepared to ruthlessly cast aside anyone who belongs to the old order, who in whatever way upholds the sub-human values of this old order and who, in whatever way, is part of or aids the ignoble System based on this old order. Aryans still cling to this old order and its subhuman values and sub-human ways of living when they cannot, or they refuse, to change themselves for the better by an act of will. Such a change involves them in becoming Aryan again - in striving to live by noble and thus Aryan values.

The goals of the Reichsfolk itself, and the high standards which Reichsfolk has set for its members, will never be changed. Reichsfolk is not interested in gaining large numbers of people unprepared to change themselves through an act of will - it is not interested in those who merely want to pay some subscription, or who merely agree with its goals. Reichsfolk seeks only those prepared to live as Aryans - with honour, loyalty and duty - as it requires them to strive for excellence and develops themselves still further. Belonging to Reichsfolk involves a personal commitment - a personal triumph of the will. Those individuals who are not prepared to totally commit themselves to Aryan values are not wanted, since such a lack of commitment means those individuals are still infected with the Zionist values of the old, dishonourable, order. As such, these individuals cannot join the new Aryan elite which is the Reichsfolk and its Legion of Adolf Hitler.

If you believe you have what it takes to join this new elite - contact us about membership.

Reichsfolk, PO Box 248, York, YO1 2YP, England

Why I Am A National-Socialist
David Myatt

Having traveled widely, having experienced at first-hand many things, and having thought deeply about these things, I believe I have acquired a certain understanding of the world.

I have lived among other peoples and cultures in Africa, the Far East and the Middle East. In the course of my life I have been a monk in a Christian monastery; cared for the sick and the dying; lived in a Buddhist monastery; studied Islam in the Middle East; learnt a Martial Art based on Taoism; taught children; experienced the pain, ecstasy and suffering of combat; wandered homeless and poor across the country of my ancestors; been in Prison - for 'political activities'; studied and translated Greek Tragedy; written poetry; worked in factories, offices, on building sites, farms, in shops..... In the course of all this, I have experienced both the heights and the depths of what has been described as "human nature", and I have come to know and understand myself, and, I believe, the world around me.

My early years were spent in East Africa, and my earliest memories are of Tanganyika: dry dusty tracks through the bush; beautiful sunsets over the plains; swimming in a pool below a small waterfall... My father stayed in Africa, and lies buried in what was, and still is, 'darkest Africa - between the Bangweulu swamp and the Lulua river.

When I was sixteen years of age, I became a National-Socialist and for many years afterwards strove to make real what I understood National-Socialism to be: a noble, honourable, idealism. I had seen through the propaganda lies about Adolf Hitler and National-Socialism to the truth. I understood in a profound but instinctive way the spiritual significance of Adolf Hitler - of what he tried to do, and what really motivated him. I understood why he had become so popular and so loved in Germany. I understood these things because I felt exactly as he did - a great idealistic love for my people and a great desire to act so that a better, a more noble world, could be created. Thus, I became involved in politics and associated with various National-Socialist groups and various racial nationalist' ones.

I can remember many times, in my youth when full of youthful idealism, listening to sublime, beautiful music [such as J. S. Bach] and being often moved to almost tears by a vision of what might be, of what might be possible if goodness, if noble idealism, could be made to live within my people. For me, such music seemed to capture what I felt - a joyous expectation and hope, tinged with sadness. And I knew, in a profound way beyond words, that these noble feelings were what motivated Adolf Hitler all those many years ago. He also had found in music an expression of his noble dreams.

I can remember that sad and ecstatic yearning I felt for a better society, a better way of living. I can remember the anger I felt when I was touched by or came to know of the often brutal, petty reality that existed in the world of my people, created as that petty, brutal reality often was by some stupid, brutal or petty individuals untouched by idealism and honour: their reality was the reality of an elderly War veteran brutally beaten and robbed by a gang of louts; of a school-girl abducted and gang-raped; of a cyclist killed by a callous hit-and-run driver; of a young family - the father in low-paid work - in debt, evicted by their greedy landlord from a decaying house they had striven hard to make presentable and a home ...

I can remember attending a concert of music by Vaughan Williams - it seemed to me, then, that the music captured the real essence of my people and my own land. I knew, hearing it, what civilization was and what it produced - the quietness of a Cathedral town between the Wars, the enthusiasm of an orchestra, the freedom to sit and listen to such beautiful music performed sublimely in such a town and then wander, intoxicated by beauty, by the town's river on a warm Summer's night, as some others had wandered, three decades before me ... I knew, hearing this and similar music, that I should try to make my life a means to make this vision real again: that I should and must strive to show my people there was a better way of living, a more noble purpose to Life. I wanted to try and raise them up - to build a more socially just society where the majority of people worked together for a higher good and where there was a striving for the excellence of exploration. Of course this was idealistic - but I strove hard to try and achieve it. But most people who knew me in those years or heard of my actions did not understand either me or my motives: I appeared simply to be another 'fanatic', another 'extremist'.

I can remember, in those years of struggle, many moments of pure, unalloyed joy - as happens when, travelling in an unknown land, one walks toward the summit of a hill and stands at its top to see spread before one, for the first time, an incredible Vista: a vast panorama of a new and as yet undiscovered country. There is then in such a moment the excitement of a personal discovery, an intensity to life itself and one is so pleased to be alive.

But after some years of striving hard to make my noble vision real, I became disillusioned. There was pettiness and jealousy even from some 'comrades'- often a blindness on the part of some of those who were supposed to be fighting and striving for the same goal as I was. And there was betrayal, a lack of honour, from a few of those given my trust; the spreading of petty lies; the fabrication and spreading of rumours about me, from whatever motive perhaps even they did not understand. In the years of my striving I had become hardened - even prison did not deter me. I had become hardened to my own personal circumstances (a grotty attic flat; often being hungry; few possessions ...) and to facing the enemy and my opponents 'on the streets'. But I had not become hard enough, lacking as I did the qualities of a leader. I wanted things to change - to be able to inspire people, but I knew I lacked the personal qualities necessary to do these things. So I came to find the pettiness, the betrayal, the intrigues of 'comrades', trying and irksome and dishonourable after a while. What were they fighting for? Certainly not - it seemed - what I was fighting for. The desire I felt and had felt since my youth to urgently act, to make politics my whole life and the whole purpose of my life, slowly died.

In those years, my hero had been Adolf Hitler himself, and I had striven to try and do what he did - to rescue my folk from the slavery they were enduring so that a new and better society could be created. But although I felt and understood as he did, I lacked his will, his selfless determination and his spiritual charisma. I was, in the words of Savitri Devi, too much Sun - and not enough Lightning. More of a philosopher than a revolutionary leader.

So I left the overt politics of political parties, and instead in my own covert way saught to keep alive something of what I believed in. I also saught to learn more, to experience more, and to live life in other ways - for I was acutely aware of how much there was still to learn about the world, and myself. Many years went by. Occasionally, I would be moved by some incident, some story and seek in some way to try and express my vision again, mostly by writing articles but occasionally by becoming 'politically active' again. Ten years past, then fifteen, then nearly twenty. Journeys; seeking; a studying of various subjects; the exploration of different ways of life. I liked to believe I had obtained a deeper understanding of "human nature" - and the beginnings of wisdom. For a while, I settled to live in a rural area mostly untouched by the decay and decadence infesting most of modern society. I taught a Martial Art to the few who were interested, won over many people to the noble ideals of National-Socialism, and continued with my slow work of trying by covert means to undermine the tyrannical System imposed upon my people.

Then, quite suddenly and unexpectedly, my personal circumstances changed with the death at a young age of someone whom I loved.

Thus I travelled and wandered again, trying to keep alive beauty and goodness by music and by solitary journeys in isolated, wild, beautiful places suffused with the numinosity of nature. One incident I remember vividly. I was wandering alone in an isolated area when I came across a farmhouse. My presence was announced by the barking of several dogs, and an elderly lady came out to greet me. I only wanted permission to pitch my tent in a field, and some fresh water, but she kindly invited me into her home, made a pot of tea and fetched some cake. Soon, we fell to discussing the countryside, and the state of the country in general. She spoke of the Britain she had known as a girl and a young woman, and of how she lamented the many changes that were occurring and had occurred. She knew what needed to be done to make the country again a decent place for decent people to live in, but she was pessimistic about the future of the country, and about the land around her which she loved and had known all her life, and she said that in some ways she was glad that she was old and would die soon because she could only see things getting worse. Sitting there, I felt again that care and concern for my people and my land that I had felt deeply in the idealistic years of my youth. For days afterwards, her sad words haunted me.

Gradually, my thoughts and feelings formed themselves into an ordered whole and I was able for really the first time in my life to express in meaningful words what I felt and understood about the world, my people and that nobility, that goodness that I had known instinctively, since my youth, was represented by National-Socialism and by the life and work of Adolf Hitler.

Thus, I settled somewhere to write about the practical expression of this inner, noble vision. It seemed to me then, as now, that my whole life had led to these moments of expression - this understanding of what National-Socialism really was, beyond the slogans, beyond the politics, beyond the propaganda lies of others opposed to National-Socialism. Beyond even the many mistakes of my own past.

So it was that I came to publish these writings and so establish for myself, once again, a public role as a National-Socialist. I also gave my support to a political group for I know that to mean anything the noble vision which is the essence of National-Socialism has to be made real. Through my own public role, I will strive to guide others toward the noble idealism, the essential goodness, that National-Socialism expresses.

Of course, my opponents and enemies will not understand this - as they will not understand my noble motives, or the noble motives of other National-Socialists, particularly those courageous ones who place their life and liberty at risk by actively fighting for National- Socialism, as those in the group I now support do.

There is apart of me which would, in all honesty, rather spend my free time fulfilling my ambition to translate Homer's Iliad and the rest of Aeschylus. I would often rather be out walking in the hills or upon the moors, watching clouds, than sitting here writing this or any item others may deem 'political'. But I know that if nobility, if goodness, are not fought for, they will die, and that the ignoble cowards will triumph. Someone has to act; someone has to make a stand and live and if necessary die by their honourable principles. So I have fought, in the past, as I am prepared to fight again in defence of those noble civilized values which I and other National-Socialists know are the essence of National-Socialism itself.

I have a duty to try and reveal the truth to others. It would be easier - more comfortable and less dangerous given the tyrannical nature of the present System which seeks to imprison dissidents like me - if I kept quiet, and busied myself doing the things I personally enjoy doing and would enjoy doing: walking long distances over moors; writing translations; mountain climbing; travelling to and exploring foreign-places .....

Many people will not, despite these words, understand what I am doing and why I am doing it. They will continue with their rather stereotyped view of National-Socialism and National-Socialists as they will believe all the lies the opponents of National-Socialism have created and spread to try and discredit National-Socialism. Some may even try to pry into my life and my background to find 'ammunition' for their cliched prejudices against anyone who avows National-Socialism. So be it. My life, outwardly, seems complex, varied and occasionally contradictory. But outward appearance is not the same as inner essence. Often, rumours or lies about me have obscured and distorted the simple truth - or have been manufactured by the enemies of National-Socialism to discredit me and thus my National-Socialist writings. I have never knowingly done anything I consider to be dis-honourable. I do know what I have done, why have I done things and the mistakes I have made. But I have learnt from these mistakes - and so have grown in understanding. I like to believe I have achieved the beginnings of wisdom, but I am honest enough to know that I might be wrong about this.

In actively upholding National-Socialism, and seeking to convert others to this most noble of Causes, I am acting because I want to see a noble society which aspires to continue the glorious work of evolution. I desire this society to reflect the beauty and harmony which I understand to be the essence of civilization and which I have often experienced in classical music and occasionally in living. I believe that to achieve this, this society has to be based upon reality, and so actively works in harmony with Nature and not against it. My knowledge and understanding - and the wisdom of civilization itself - shows that the reality of Nature is the diversity of race.

To me, National-Socialism is a means to create a better, more wholesome, more civilized future. It really is as simple as that.

(D. Myatt 107 yf)

Declaration of War

Robert J. Mathews

At first glance, the notion that Robert Mathews and his small band of Aryan revolutionaries, the Silent Brotherhood (more popularly known as the Order), could present a credible threat to the power of the American state might remind the reader of the Peter Sellers movie *The Mouse That Roared* in which a microstate barely out of the Middle Ages declares war on the United States with every intention of losing gracefully and collecting much-need foreign aid for its pains. Certainly, this is how most of Mathews's contemporaries felt. At the time of the Order's actions, a considerable body of movement opinion held that Mathews and company were in fact federal agents involved in a scheme to entrap and incarcerate the far-right faithful. In the end, Mathews turned out to be deadly serious, and the Order has today passed into movement legend. Mathews himself today posthumously enjoys a reputation as a movement martyr, and the day of his death is celebrated in many quarters as the "Day of the Martyrs" in an event second only to the celebration of Hitler's birthday on the movement's calendar of holy days. The Order's "Declaration of War" was written at the hopeful inception of the Order, as both a recruiting device and a statement of purpose. The far darker document that follows, Robert Mathews's letter to the editor of a local newspaper, was written in less heady times and is thus far less optimistic. Together, these texts are widely circulated in the world of the radical right.

The Order's "Declaration of War":

It is now a dark and dismal time in the history of our race. All about us lie the green graves of our sires, yet, in a land once ours, we have become a people dispossessed...

By the millions, those not of our blood violate our borders and mock our claim to sovereignty. Yet our people only react with lethargy.

A great sickness has overcome us. Why do our people do nothing? What madness is this? Has the cancer of racial masochism consumed our very will to exist?

While we allow Mexicans by the legions to invade our soil, we murder our babies in equal numbers. Were the men of the Alamo only a myth? Whether by the force of arms or force of the groin, the result of this invasion is the same. Yet our people do not resist.

Our heroes and our culture have been insulted and degraded. The mongrel hordes clamor to sever us from our inheritance. Yet our people do not care.

Throughout this land our children are being coerced into accepting nonwhites for their idols, their companions, and worst of all their mates. A course which is taking us straight to oblivion. Yet our people do not see...

Not by accident but by design these terrible things have come to pass. It is self-evident to all who have eyes to see that an evil shadow has fallen across our once fair land. Evidence abounds that a certain vile, alien people have taken control of our country.

How is it that a parasite has gained dominion over its host? Instead of being vigilant, our fathers have slept. What are we to do? How bleak these aliens have made our children's future.

All about us the land is dying. Our cities swarm with dusky hordes. The water is rancid and the air is rank. Our farms are being seized by usurious leeches and our people are being forced off the land. The Capitalists and the Communists pick gleefully at our bones while the vile hook-nosed masters of usury orchestrate our destruction. What is to become of our children in a land such as this? Yet still our people sleep!

Everyday the rich tighten the chains that lay heavy upon our people. How pitiful the white working class has become. Where is the brave Aryan yeoman so quick to smite the tyrant's hand?

They close the factories, the mills, the mines, and ship our jobs overseas. Yet our people do not awaken. They send an army of agents into our midst to steal from our pockets and enforce their rule. Our forefathers under King George knew freedom more than we. Yet still, still our people sleep!

To those who awaken, the reality is grim. John Singer awoke. Concerned over the rampant drugs, homosexuality, and miscegenation in public schools he tried to teach his children at home. He was a stout Aryan yeoman who loved his family dearly. Government agents shot him in the back.

Gordon Kahl awoke. After four decades of submission to the tyranny of the IRS he tried to resist. He was a stout Aryan yeoman who loved his family dearly. Government agents shot him in the back.

Arthur L. Kirk awoke. For three generations his family farmed the land the usurious banker was trying to steal. Kinsman Kirk tried to resist. He was a stout Aryan yeoman who loved his family dearly. Government agents shot him in the back.

To these three kinsmen, we say: "Rise, rise from you graves, white brothers! Rise and join us! We go to avenge your deaths. The Aryan yeomanry is awakening. A long forgotten wind is starting to blow. Do you hear the approaching thunder? It is that of the awakened Saxon. War is upon the land. The tyrant's blood will flow."

By ones and by twos, by scores and by legions we will drive the enemy into the sea. Through our blood and God's will, the land promised to our fathers of old will become the land of our children to be.

We will resign ourselves no more to be ruled by a government based on mobocracy. We, from this day forward declare that we no longer consider the regime in Washington to be a valid and lawful representative of all Aryans who refuse to submit to the coercion and subtle tyranny placed upon us by Tel Aviv and their lackeys in Washington. We recognize that the mass of our people have been put into a lobotomized, lethargic state of blind obedience and we will not take part anymore in collective racial suicide!

We hereby declare ourselves to be a free and sovereign people. We claim a territorial imperative which will consist of the entire North American continent north of Mexico.

As soldiers of the Aryan Resistance Movement (ARM) we will conduct ourselves in accordance with the Geneva Convention.

We now close this Declaration with an open letter to Congress and our signatures confirming our intent to do battle. Let friend and foe alike be made aware. This is war! —We the following, being of sound mind and under no duress, do hereby sign this document of our own free will, stating forthrightly and without fear that we declare ourselves to be in full and unrelenting state of war with those forces seeking and consciously promoting the destruction of our faith and our race.

Therefore, for Blood, Soil, and Honor, and for the future of our children, we commit ourselves to Battle. Amen.

Letter to the Editor

Robert J. Mathews

TO THE EDITOR:

For the past decade I have been a resident of Northern Pend Oreille County. When I first arrived in Metaline Falls, I had only twenty-five dollars to my name, a desire to work hard and be left alone, and the dream of someday acquiring my own small farm.

During my three years at the mine and seven years at the cement plant, I can safely say that I was known as a hard worker. I stayed out of the bars and pretty much kept to myself. Anyone who is familiar with Boundary Dam Road knows how my late father and I carved a beautiful place out of the woods. All of the goals I had when I arrived were accomplished but one ... I was not left alone.

Within months of my arrival the FBI went to the mine office and tried to have me fired from my job. I was working in the electrical department at the time and my foreman, fortunately, had a deep and lasting dislike for the Feds. He was informed of the situation by the mine secretary. Had it been the mine manager instead of the secretary that the Government goons talked to, I would have lost my job.

This campaign of harassment and intimidation began because of my involvement in the Tax Rebellion Movement from the time I was fifteen to twenty years old. The Government was on me so much in Arizona that during one incident when I was eighteen, IRS agents shot at me for nothing more than a misdemeanor tax violation.

I left Arizona and the Tax Rebellion when I was twenty. I left not out of fear of the IRS or because of submission to their tyranny, but because I was thoroughly disgusted with the American people. I maintained then as I do now, that our people have devolved into some of the most cowardly, sheepish, degenerates that have ever littered the face of this planet.

I had hoped to start a new life in the state of Washington, but the ruling powers had other plans for me. When I learned of their highly illegal attempt to have me fired, I wrote a letter to their Seattle office and told them "I would take no more, to leave me alone, or I would respond in such a way that could be very painful to certain agents."

After the letter they gradually started to let me be.

I soon settled down to marriage, clearing my land, and reading. Reading became an obsession with me. I consumed volume upon

526

volume on subjects dealing with history, politics and economics. I was especially taken with Spengler's "Decline of the West" and "Which Way Western Man?". I also subscribed to numerous periodicals on current American problems, especially those concerned with the ever increasing decline of White America.

My knowledge of ancient European history started to awaken a wrongfully suppressed emotion buried deep within my soul, that of racial pride and consciousness.

The stronger my love for my people grew, the deeper became my hatred for those who would destroy my race, my heritage, and darken the future of my children.

By the time my son had arrived, I realized that White America, indeed my entire race, was headed for oblivion unless White men rose and turned the tide. The more I came to love my son the more I realized that unless things changed radically, by the time he was my age, he would be a stranger in his own land, a blonde-haired, blue-eyed Aryan in a country populated mainly by Mexicans, Mulattoes, Blacks and Asians. His future was growing darker by the day.

I came to learn that this was not by accident, that there is a small, cohesive alien group within this nation working day and night to make this happen. I learned that these culture distorters have an iron grip on both major political parties, on Congress, on the media, on the publishing houses, and on most of the major Christian denominations in this nation, even though these aliens subscribe to a religion which is diametrically opposed to Christianity.

These are the same people who Ex-Senator William J. Fulbright and the late General Brown tried to warn us about. Henry Ford and Charles Lindberg tried vainly to warn us also. Had we been more vigilant, my son's future would not be so dark and dismal.

Thus I have no choice. I must stand up like a White man and do battle.

A secret war has been developing for the last year between the regime in Washington and an ever growing number of White people who are determined to regain what our forefathers discovered, explored, conquered, settled, built and died for.

The FBI has been able to keep this war secret only because up until now we have been doing nothing more than growing and preparing. The government, however, seems determined to force the issue, so we have no choice left but to stand and fight back. Hail Victory!

It is at this point that I wish to address the multitude of lies that the federals have been telling about Gary Lee Yarbrough and myself.

Gary did not "ambush" any agents. For weeks prior to this incident they had been harassing Gary, following him everywhere, even to the hospital to visit his gravely ill daughter. The day of the mythical ambush Gary was out in his yard when he saw a forest service truck driving across his property in obvious disregard to the numerous no trespassing signs scattered about his land. He yelled at the truck to stop but it kept coming towards his house until it crashed into and destroyed a gate. At this point Gary fired warning shots into the air and the truck drove away. That ... was the big ambush.

The newspapers are saying now that Gary not only ambushed three agents but that he hit three of them. Gary did not even realize that they were FBI at the time, which is fortunate for them because Gary is an expert marksman and had he decided to ambush the FBI he easily could have killed every fed within range of his weapon.

It was until 8:00 p.m. that night that Gary realized what was actually taking place. That is when approximately thirty agents drove up to Gary's house. Gary and a young house guest went outside to investigate the commotion. When the Feds started yelling at Gary he dropped to the ground and rolled into a ditch behind the line of government vehicles. The young house guest went running back into Gary's residence. After waiting for three hours the FBI used Gary's wife as a shield and a hostage and went into the house. What brave men they are.

As incredulous as it sounds Gary laid in the ditch behind the agents for five hours with his gun aimed at their backs. Had Gary really wanted to ambush these invaders then that was a wonderful opportunity to do so. Gary chose instead to give them quarter, something he would later come to regret. Gary eventually slipped out of the ditch and into the woods.

The incompetence of these gun toting bureaucrats never ceases to amaze me. Especially after their attempted ambush and murder of myself in a Portland motel. First, let me say that the FBI was not there to arrest Gary but to ambush me. They didn't even know that Gary was in the room. The only reason they were able to find me was because a trusted friend in Room 14 was actually a traitor and an informant. The FBI has vast resources and the latest technology but the quality of their agents is going down hill with every new recruit. That's because most of the best White men in this country are starting to realize that to be an FBI agent is to be nothing more than a mercenary for the ADL and Tel Aviv.

When I stepped out of my motel room that morning, a gang of armed men came running at me. None of the men had uniforms on and the only thing they said was "Stop, you bastard". At this, I yelled at Gary who was still inside and I leaped down the stairwell and took off running into the parking lot. A woman agent shot at my back and the bullet missed and hit the motel manager. I rounded the corner of the motel and took off down the hill into a residential area. After running for two blocks I decided to quit being the hunted and become the hunter. I drew my gun and waited behind a concrete wall for the agents to draw near. When I aimed my gun at the closest agent I saw the handsome face of a young White man and lowered my aim to his knee and his foot. Had I not done so I could have killed both agents and still had the use of my hand which is now mangled beyond repair and which I might very well lose altogether. That is the last time I will ever give quarter.

As for the traitor in Room 14, we will eventually find him. If it takes ten years and we have to travel to the far ends of the earth we will find him. And true to our oath when we do find him, we will remove his head from his body.

I have no regrets or apologies to make for Gary or myself. In fact, I am proud that we had the courage and the determination to stand up and fight for our race and our heritage at a time in history when such a deed is called a crime and not an act of valor.

Approximately nine moths ago the FBI went to my house while I was away and threatened my two year old son. That was a very big mistake on their part. After the Portland shootout they went to my house and threatened my sixty-three year old mother. Such brave men they are.

I am not going into hiding, rather I will press the FBI and let them know what it is like to become the hunted. Doing so it is only logical to assume that my days on this planet are rapidly drawing to a close. Even so, I have no fear. For the reality of my life is death, and the worst the enemy can do to me is shorten my tour of duty in this world. I will leave knowing that I have made the ultimate sacrifice to ensure the future of my children.

As always, for blood, soil, honor, for faith and for race.

Robert Jay Mathews

Alert Update and Advisory

Gary Lee Yarbrough

This text, written by imprisoned Order member Gary Lee
Yarbrough, was written in 1983 as an open letter to the
disparate tribes of the American racialist movement and
intended both as a plea for unity and a call to action.
Strategically, Yarbrough's ideas are similar to those of David
Lane. But where Lane's writings suggest an exclusive embrace
of Odinism, Yarbrough insists that theological and ideological
differences must no longer be allowed to obscure the greater
goal of unity.

———————————

The following advisory is addressed to the diverse elements which comprise the folk who are currently involved in the struggle for the cultivation and advancement of the White Aryan Race.

Whether you are National Socialist, Klan, Odinist, Christian Identity, Skinhead, Creator, or any other cult, creed, faith or persuasion of our cause does not matter. For the essence of our cause, regardless of our diversity is RACE!, our common genetic heritage. Our blood is the tie which binds us together. It is our racial entity which motivates us all, regardless of our diverse philosophies. We would not have a motivating force if we did not have race as our foundation. Anyone currently involved in our struggle who rejects race as the primary compelling factor is absurd, and the advisory is not addressed to the ignorant. OUR FAITH IS OUR RACE, AND OUR RACE IS OUR FAITH!!! It cannot be more simply put... The subject of this advisory is the reformation of our cause. Reformation is a necessity because the forms of resistance and strategies hitherto employed have, by and large, been a failure. Because of this failure, and in light of the recent murders of Samuel and Vickie Weaver, I feel compelled to issue this advisory. In addition, I find this advisory necessary since the so-called "leaders" of our cause neglect to adequately advise the folk and are seemingly oblivious to the vital necessities of our cause. Large scale organized resistance is a failure. It has failed our cause for a number of years now. Why our so-called "leaders" refuse to acknowledge this fact and opt for a more plausible strategy is an inexplicable enigma. Perhaps this is because our cause has no real bona fide leaders. In reality, what we have is "publishing agencies" of which the owner, publisher, and editor has assumed the role of "Leader" and official Spokesman for our cause. These publisher leaders are not elected, they are self-proclaimed and self-appointed by virtue of the fact that they own the publishing agency. They are not true leaders in the proper sense of the term, there is no chain of command, and there is no real organization or membership, only subscribers and supporters. Furthermore, there is no truly organized movement, there exist only a cause. The only "organizing" these leaders do is to set-up rallies, marches, protests, vigils, Aryan Fest, annual conventions and other such events that have proven to be more of a hindrance to our cause than a benefit. These events have reaped very little in the line of progress for our cause. The benefits and advantages derived from organized resistance are a scarcity compared to the impediments and harm it has reaped upon our folk and cause.

If any cause should flourish and prosper it is the cause for which we stand. But our cause simply flounders and stagnates. One faction or sect will flare-up now and then, but soon, like all those that preceded them, they succumb to enemy pressure or strife from within and return to a vegetative state. The cause of this malady is the inadequacy and incompetencies of our so-called leaders. Or more accurately, the lack of competent leaders. The conventional methods and courses our diverse factions have utilized for the past few decades have proven to be a failure. And yet, our leaders continue the same old tired program and follow the same old self-defeating procedures. And our enemies employ the same old counter measures against us. Enough! It is time for the Phoenix to rise from the ashes of the old. And if our leaders will not properly direct us, then we will direct ourselves!

In the past few decades, procedures and tactics employed by our various groups have been of the open and above ground nature, i.e., establish a publication, draw in subscribers and supporters, recruit members from the public and organize meetings, rallies, protests, marches, etcetera. To counter this approach, our enemies establish themselves among us in the guise of undercover agent provocateurs, professional instigators and contentionists, saboteurs, sting operatives, and expert witnesses. And let me not neglect to mention the fact that since these groups recruit from the public, and that any Aryan with the due price can become a member, that our cause attracts its fair share of the mentally unbalanced psychopaths, neurotics and the poseurs whose hearts are really not into the cause. These folks are generally are the weak amongst us who, when pressured arises, become the Judas informants and government paid witnesses against the truly loyal and dedicated folk. The enemy agents, poseurs, and informants amongst us are the major impediments of our cause. Take, for example, the circumstances surrounding the Weaver tragedy. Here we have an enemy agent working through an already established informant to set-up and coerce another individual to likewise became an informant for the purpose of infiltrating an entirely legal above ground organization. As a result, we have an entire Aryan family unit destroyed, the murder of a mother of four, the murder of one of her children, the imprisonment of the father and a foster son, and the displacement of the remaining three children. Is the price worthy of the reason (or excuse) for which it was exacted? Absolutely not! And I dare say that this family unit would most likely still be intact today had it not been exposed to the enemy. To be exposed, it first had to be enticed and drawn-out from the populace via some above ground organization. When a member of our race becomes racially conscious and seeks to become actively involved in the struggle for his or her race, it is natural for the person to search for other like minded people to fellowship and associate with. And, usually, the awakening initiate is not yet fully aware of just what he or she is getting involved in. And by the time this awareness arrives, chances are that person has already been exposed, labeled, and targeted by the enemies of our race. Our "publisher leaders" however are fully aware and not as naive as the newcomers. Our "leaders" know, though experience, the depth and treachery of the beast which seeks to devour our race. They know that their phones and mailings are monitored and recorded by enemy agents. They are aware of the fact that the enemy monitors, both overtly and covertly, every function or event that is "organized" by these "leaders". They know that there will be enemy agents in attendance at every gathering or function to work their wiles amongst the folk. But our "leaders" do not seem to care who mingles amongst us so long as there is a large turn-out for the event with plenty of media coverage for their egos. This approach has been the standard operating procedure of our struggle for decades. Indeed, it is the cause of our struggling!!! Yet still our various groups and their "Directors" continue to implement this same old archaic routine. But then, our leaders are not directing a bona fide resistance struggle, they are managing a publishing and propaganda agency, a front. These publishing agencies main function in the publishing and distribution of propaganda and literature, which is a vital element within our cause, and is the area in which these agencies should exert their energies. But it is when these overt agencies attempt to over extend their capabilities that the problems begin. They are not a well-organized and trained resistance force that is capable of opposing an enemy as well entrenched and sophisticated as the tyranny we are up against. Not in the overt capacity anyway.

Our enemies have rendered it inexpedient and dangerous for us to recruit members from the public or to openly gather at large organized functions and events. The conventional resistance techniques hitherto employed by our causes diverse factions have proven to be a failure to our cause and only aid and abet the enemies more so than our own cause. Therefore we must abandon the old strategies and opt for a more judicious approach to victory. It will only require a few minor changes in our course of operations to correct and eliminate the majority of our causes ills. Primarily, these overt publishing agencies and other above ground institutions of our cause must cease from drawing out and exposing the folk! Recruit subscribers and supporters, but cease from recruiting "members" from the public, or at the least, limit the membership to a small cadre of a loyal and dedicated few. Recruit QUALITY, not QUANTITY. It does not require an army to publish and distribute literature. The publishing and distribution of literature and propaganda should be the main function of any above ground overt organization. This strategy will prevent, or at least limit, the undesirable elements that attach themselves to our operations. The publishing and distribution of our causes literature is a vital component of our struggle. It is imperative that our presses produce quality literature to enlighten, educate, and convert new prospects to our cause and instill a sense of racial unity. Some of our "ink pot commanders" have resorted to using their publications to ridicule, slander and reproach other White racially oriented segments of our cause. As if we do not have a preponderance of enemies already, it would seem that our "leaders" would like to see us all bickering and fighting amongst ourselves over petty differences and ideological rigmarole! The only product of this type of journalistic clap trap is strife and contention between our diverse groups. This sounds suspiciously like the work of any enemy agent provocateur, a professional instigator using the old "divide and conquer" technique. As previously stated: RACE IS THE ESSENCE OF OUR CAUSE. Each faction of our cause has its own characteristics and methods which appeal to individual and diverse folk in all walks of this society. Where one faction or philosophy fails to attract an individual prospect, another faction of our cause may. Each and every faction of our cause benefits our cause and race in its own way. The National Socialist and Klan are not enemies! The Odinist and Christian Identists are not enemies! The Skinheads and Creators are not enemies! And I doubt very seriously if anyone can find me two people, in any one of our diverse factions who agree completely on every aspect and issue of their philosophy or ideology. But there is one aspect that we all agree on, and that is RACE!!! Our causes publications are not the place to argue, ridicule or reproach one another. I say "our" publications because without the subscriptions and support of the rank and file adherents to our cause, these self-styled dictators would be hard passed to publish such journalistic racial treason. This is our cause, we will not tolerate any would-be dictators! You subscribers and financial supporters let your views and opinions be known!

Our enemies, via illegal and subversive tactics have managed to hinder our advance. They have infiltrated and polluted our above ground institution. Conventional tactics such as: recruiting members and associates from the populace, mass gatherings and meetings, rallies, protests, etcetera, are no longer profitable, viable, or judicious to employ. Therefore, we must switch from the conventional approach to irregular tactics and implement strategies that are less of a security risk to ourselves and will augment our success. For if we should fail, it will mean the destruction and death of our RACE!!! We must not take our situation and struggle lightly or squander away the minimal chance we have left for victory. We have inadequately accessed our situation and underestimated our enemies. They are insidiously ruthless and treacherous, as the Weaver incident has shown. They are proficient, sophisticated, and well-equipped, and with unlimited resources, finances and man power. The only way to battle and triumph over such an eminent adversary is via covert, clandestine, irregular and guerrilla tactics. We must utilize the very techniques that the enemy employs against us! They are tyrants and terrorists. The only way to fight terror is with a greater terror!

Fun and games are over folks. It is time to get serious. Our "movement" must be re-vamped from the so-called "top" down. If our leaders will not institute the necessary changes, then we, the rank and file folk will force the changes. Our overt publishing agencies should be the only component of our cause that is revealed to the scrutiny of our enemies, except what "WE CHOOSE" to reveal to them. All other components should be concealed and clandestine. The bulk of our resistance forces should be comprised of individuals, or small nuclear units of teams no larger than five or six members. These individuals or nuclear units will conduct their resistance efforts in whatever capacity they feel capable of instituting. At this time in our conflict, our number one priority is to enlighten, educate and convert new prospects to our cause. This is where our publishing agencies play a vital role. They must supply the individual and nuclear units with quality literature and propaganda for the purpose of distribution. The nuclear units must aid in the financing of the literature. The individual and nuclear units must use caution when contacting any overt agency. Order bulk packages of literature to be received at post office boxes, not street addresses. Never contact an overt agencies message "hot line" direct to the enemy camp. I do not exclude or rule out illegal activity or physical confrontation with the adversaries of our racial cause.

We may not be prepared for this type of warfare, but its time has come nonetheless. As previously stated: it is time to get serious. The enemy must learn that they cannot murder and imprison us with impunity...

We all know what our duties are. We all know our own individual strengths and weaknesses. We know what capacity or level of resistance we as individuals are capable of employing. Place yourself in the service of our cause in whatever capacity you feel is best suited for you. Do not overextend yourself, but do not underestimate your capabilities either. Excel in whatever mode of resistance you choose. Give to your race the best of your abilities! In our leaders resistance capacity, the individual must take the initiative, the individual must motivate himself, he MUST TAKE CHARGE!!! There exists an urgent need for the folk within our struggle to rededicate themselves, and to accentuate their rededication with ACTION!!! We have a monstrous task before us, lets all pitch in and get the job done! Our children have no future. If we are to secure their place in the sun it will require great sacrifice. My brothers and sisters, my folk, our lives are not our own to do with as we please. We are indebted to the sweat, blood and sacrifices of the millions of our causes patriots and heroes who have gone before us, to purchase time for us with their very life's blood! We are obligated to our children and their future, who, without us, have no future. This is the final conflict my comrades, freedom and liberty has its price, we must pay our dues! Let us be off to the fray!!!!

Gary Lee Yarbrough

What We Believe As White Racists

by Tom Metzger

A lthough Tom Metzger is best known for his crude race-baiting and for the inroads that this approach has allowed him to make with skinhead groups across the country, this document, posted online as a position paper for Metzger's White Aryan Resistance, contains a number of ideas that, in the context of the 1980s, were visionary. "What We Believe As White Racists" centers on the idea of White separatism, but in the process of making the case for the separation of the races, Metzger muses upon questions of religion, suggests the convergence of interests between the racialist right and the pro-life movement that occurred a decade later, and argues for the equality of the sexes—a remarkable position for a leader in the milieu of the radical right. This document may be found on WAR's web site.

IMMIGRATION

There are now, by statistics, 14 million Mexicans and Latin Americans in the United States. That is a terrible guess, since the Iron Heel government, in Washington D. C., has no real idea of how many there are. Consider this: the United States border control says that they may stop 10% each day. That, in itself, represents thousands each day. Now simply multiply that amount by ten.

Even beyond immigration, legal or illegal, the very numbers of non-Whites already here, and their high birth rate, are enough to plunge North America into a banana republic status within two decades or less.

On the other hand, imagine a Separatist state or region in the Southwest, that could see the impact each day of thousands of immigrants, climbing on board each day, with no hope of a federal solution. Of course they would do what tribes have done since the dawn of time. They would rally their forces and stop it with a force of arms. How? The same way Syria has no drug problem. Violators are executed. There go the "coyotes", and others that would destroy living space for a quick buck.

For example, if an area like Florida wanted to accept the dregs of the Caribbean, let them, with the understanding that the second this mud flood oozed into the sovereign state of Georgia, it would be "lock and load" time. Now, isn't that simple. It's freedom of choice for all concerned. To the Floridians, they are free to swamp their state and exhaust their natural resources and infrastructure. The Caribbeanites are free to try the border of the sovereign state of Georgia. However, the sovereign citizens of Georgia are free to stop them, using any method necessary, and stop the invasion of their sovereign state.

Those that await a Big Brother Washington D. C. or Los Angeles Cesspool Grande solution, wait in vain, since their solutions are either not forthcoming, or are much worse than those that we propose.

Separatism is a state of mind, whose time has come. The superstate is the enemy of racial and cultural self-determination. It is also the extreme enemy of man's environment. That is enough reason for us.

Good Hunting and Keep Preying!

ABORTION

The White Separatist movement today has no logical or coherent position, on abortion.

A majority, in the Right Wing oriented racialist movement, rightly perceive massive abortion as further impacting the survival of the White race. Unfortunately, this position is more tied to those with a religious position, usually Christians. These same people are usually silent, on how the increased birth rate among non-Whites is just as deadly to our race's survival, especially in North America. Even if they do speak about this issue, they do not address the obvious logic, which is that abortion and birth control among non-Whites, should be a major project.

On the other extreme, many support abortion, as a means of helping to limit an explosion of massive proportions, among non-Whites already living in North America. These people do not address the fact that future leaders and thinkers, of our race, are being destroyed by the millions. What is worse is that it is self induced.

The logic is perfect. Very little abortion should be tolerated, among our White race, while at the same time, abortion and birth control should be promoted as a powerful weapon, in the limitation of non-White birth. Overt support of both non-White population control and non-support of abortion for Whites, has the same desired effect.

Promoting this Third Force position confuses and angers the churches, with their anti-abortion position, and at the same time angers and frustrates the abortion proponent's position, as well. The Third Force position on pro-White life, is played on with demonstrations and well written handouts. This will raise the tempo, in this hot issue.

Imagine a few large signs showing up at anti-abortion demonstrations. For example, a sign which boldly states, "Support White Life" or "Stop White Genocide". That would create an all new debate. At the same time, signs for a pro-abortion demonstration might state, "Free Choice For Non-White Abortion" or "Minorities Have Abortion Rights".

Covertly invest into non-White areas, invest in ghetto abortion clinics. Help to raise money for free abortions, in primarily non-White areas. Perhaps abortion clinic syndicates throughout North America, that primarily operate in non-White areas and receive tax support, should be promoted. At the same time, issue stock. This will help Whites raise their standard of living, in two ways.

A note of caution: both sides in this issue, have a propensity for violence. When you join in a demonstration, on either side, have back-up with you. This is just in case the peace loving Christians or Jews get hysterical.

MILITARY WARFARE

There has been no military war in modern history, that promoted the general welfare of the White race. As the great general, Smedly Butler, lamented, "war is a racket". Only in limited cases, where war has temporarily slowed the birthrate in non-White areas of the world, would war be considered even slightly positive. However, when the destruction of resources and pollution are taken into account, even that method of birth control is like "cutting your nose off to spite your face". Remember, after every such economic adventure, the "spook in the sky" people quickly move in to patch up the non-White populations; to begin anew the cycle of birth, poverty and death.

So, why are so many so-called White racists, military or war oriented? Why do healthy White people salivate, while waving the system's flag, and run off to participate in these slaughter games?

Robert Audrey wrote the great trilogy: *African Genesis, Territorial Imperative,* and *The Evolution of Social Contract.* He put it this way: "Men are motivated by three things: 1) Stimulation, 2) Identity and 3) Security..." It seems that modern warfare appeals to all three.

What then causes a trained killer to go from an unstoppable predator in war (who is prepared to carry out any order), to become a cowardly wimp in the civilian life, in defense of his race or family? Is it the great psychological control by the media, churches, or education which are controlled by occult forces.

White men and women cannot be totally snivelized, when they are capable of rising to primordial brutality, under certain conditions. War is economic for a few, and also a way for many White men to release their natural aggression. Is this the reason that our jails, prisons and mental hospitals are full, due to the White man's straight-jacketed and unnatural society? I think that it is.

The mystics will not admit, and be proud of, man's animal nature. Almost all religious beliefs promote the idea that natural aggression is evil, and that straight-jacket demotions are good. One thing that we know for sure is that the military promotes more race mixing, than any other area of society.

All modern warfare has been at the expense of our White gene pool. All modern institutions are designed to stifle White racial aggression to the betterment and expansion, of lesser races. War breeds phony patriotism of a non-nation nation. The diverse races and religions of North America will ultimately sink into Third World poverty and disease, if internal White aggression is not released, from its men and women.

In short, military warfare benefits a very few, at the expense of the many. This warfare destroys needed natural resources, and diminishes the best breeding stock of our race. It promotes hyper-patriotic race mixing, and racial pollution. Other dangers are that all sophisticated spy satellites and star wars style weapons can and will be used, ultimately against those that were bankrupted paying for them.

Make no mistake. The so-called end of the phony communist struggle, marks the beginning of "Operation Mop-Up", by transnational financial cartels, and the occult forces behind them.

Among our enemies, White racism or Separatism is about to become the new crusade. If need be, the same polyglot forces and weapons tested on the "terrible" Sadam Hussein and Iraq, will be used against you, if it becomes necessary.

Logic: War is a racket. Support at least a 75% cut in defense, not only in this country, but in every country in the world. White Separatists must oppose system controlled warfare!

LAWMAKERS

Otherwise known as legislators, these men and women are held in high esteem, for the most part. The reason is that there is a myth, that is perpetuated by the media. That myth is that your lawmakers are your friends, due to the number of bills that they successfully push through into laws. Those that are unable to create bills, and push them through the hoops into laws, are looked on as ineffective and even called lazy. When it comes election time, woe be it to a lawmaker, that has been unable to enact new laws.

In California, as an example, over 1,000 new laws went into effect in January 1992. White voters ignorantly think that massive creation of new laws may afford them new and better protection. What does it really bring to you? It brings you more control, less liberty and higher taxes.

What an amazing and deceptive machine. The slaves, in the name of law and order, are actually manipulated into believing that more laws means more liberty and more security. The slaves (or zombies, as I like to call them) cannot be excused, for they have a vast history that will plainly show, that legislators are not the friends of liberty or of the peasants (as we are commonly referred to as, by the legislators, in their private circles).

So, you ask, what then is the answer?

It is simple. There are more laws on the books, in the United States, than ever before in history. At the same time, the standard of living has dropped like a rock. Non-White crime has gone through the roof. In fact, in all areas where White working people are impacted, most new laws have not helped at all. In fact, most laws are very expensive and just open up new problems, requiring by system logic, more laws.

The answer is obvious. We need thousands of lawmakers, that will become law eliminators. In other words, a WAR on laws. Repeal should be the word for each new election. Legislators should be judged to be a greater friend of the people, by battling entirely for the elimination of costly and ineffective laws.

The greatest help for the White race today, would be state and national legislators, that run on a platform of no new taxes, coupled with no new laws. For to enact more new laws, guarantees more new taxes. Do you see how simple it would be?

Your enemies control the law making machinery. They also control the unequal application of these laws, that help their friends and destroy their enemies. So, get smart you young White Americans! Run for office, but on the basis of spending your entire effort in repealing laws. Couple your arguments with the obvious. Most laws cause higher taxes and usually don't solve a problem. In fact, they actually appear to call for even more laws, to correct the evils of the law that you just enacted.

Whites who love liberty cannot love the great OZ, the great and deceptive lawmakers.

TAXES

Fact: Virtually all taxes today are directly, or indirectly, used to control and destroy the future of our race.

Logic: Any program or method that circumvents taxes is a White revolutionary act. This even applies to tax avoidance by those that you perceive as your enemies, who are doing it purely for personal financial greed or advancement. In the past, tax avoidance movements were preoccupied with some obvious or special gripe. In the Right Wing, it was many times controlled by arguments such as abortion protest or certain anti-war activity.

Overt methods are not important, when you understand that all tax enforcement today is directly, or indirectly, supporting your destruction as a White Separatist. All tax avoidance, in any way, helps to bleed and weaken the Beast. Your sweat and hard earned wages are the only source of power that is used against you. In short, the old adage applies. " The power to tax is the power to destroy".

There are thousands of ways to play this game. For our more well-off friends, you are probably well aware of many ways to fight this game of financial warfare. To our lower, middle-class and poor Whites, there are also hundreds of easy methods. Try not to buy new, when better quality used merchandise is available, with no taxes involved. Flea markets or shopping through the miscellaneous for-sale columns, or in newspapers and throwaways are great ways to avoid tax. Buy your fruits and vegetables from open air, non-tax style markets, or direct from the farmer whenever possible. The prospects are endless.

The underground economy is a fabulous mechanism, and well-suited to our purpose. There are also a vast number of books on the subject.

Remember that the underground economy is seditious to our enemies, but a great weapon for White racial advancement. Again, bleed the Beast. Spread these ideas among even your non-racial contacts, since all tax avoidance and underground economic activity, directly helps our cause. It is easy and it is fun! Use your imagination, and start your war today.

Good Hunting!

WOMEN

There has always been a strain, in all of the races throughout time, that have over done the male dominance habit. For very early man it must have been such, since much activity was largely compiled of brute strength. However, even then the logic and reasoning of women must have played a part in man's evolution. I cannot picture any advancing tribe or race in which women not only gave birth to the future, but also kept the fires burning and the food coming. Living in a hunter-gatherer society it would be impossible for women not to be thrust, from time to time, into combative positions.

As White settler women in early America, they had to shoot or drive off Indians or wild animals. Thus, it must have been with early man, except for the use of the gun. It is illogical to think that as ancient tribes came under attack by others, that women did not join in the fight for survival.

The role of women seems to have been alternated between goddess and warrior, to outcasts in their own homes, throughout history.

No intelligent White man or woman would deny the physical, biological and chemical differences between the two sexes. No intelligent White man or woman would believe that women in general, are capable in matching men as power lifters, or in areas of brute strength. There are however, always exceptions to almost every rule, that is known to man. Generally, on the other hand, men are not able to replace the special bond of a mother and her child. This again is not to say that there are no exceptions.

In relative modern times, within a few hundred years, what has been man's approach to the women of our race?

The invasion of Rome by occult Judaism, and the late revolution of occult Christianity, perpetuated some of the worst stereotypes of women. The Judaeo basis for Christianity, through the writings of the Old and the New Testaments, are still the worst detractor of women. Jews in particular, operating in western society, brought in the very worst oppression of women. Christianity simply promoted the same negative regard for women. Even worse are the Jew's Talmudic teachings, perpetrated right up to the present day. These ideas, even in the late 20th century, through Hasidic and Orthodox Judaism, are the most ridiculous attitudes ever put to paper about women. To observe the extremes of such activity, simply travel to New York City, or any large American city, and visit a Hasidic Jew or hard-line Orthodox Jew neighborhood, to check it out for yourself. To save time and money, simply read the book entitled Hole in the Sheet, written by a Jewish woman, about the sick and perverted treatment of Hasidic and Orthodox women, by Jewish males.

These attitudes have had a strong influence on White European and American civilization. For example, in many northern areas, blacks received the right to vote before White women. Even today our White women are put at the same level as the non-Whites, in civil "wrongs" legislation. These events in the end of the 20th century, are counterproductive to our race's survival and advancement.

Understand that a majority of the nation's views, on the relationship between men and women, have their origins in Judaeo-Christianity. The same religion that wrongly promotes the myth that all men are created equal, also promotes a negative attitude towards our White women.

The Right Wing or conservative movement and the racial elements thereof, have perpetuated some very negative attitudes also. These positions have caused, in part, the political flight of many capable women, into the arms of the extreme left which includes lesbianism and race mixing. W.A.R. believes that an equal percentage of women are as concerned over our status racially, as the men are. Many women put the men to shame, in their work and in their sacrifice, for the benefit of the White race. When you look around at the weak and wimpy status of a large percentage of White men, it is obvious that millions of hard working, handfighting and hard mothering women are needed, in this great struggle.

Throughout our travels as a race, there have been exceptions to the Judeao-Christian idea of women. Historically, women have been proven to be great leaders, warriors, thinkers, scientists, etc.

Our views must be futuristic and not tied to myths of Asiatic cult religions. Imagine determining today's actions, by adhering to the maniacal ramblings of ancient religious dervishes, who sit in the desert, babbling at the moon. It is simply not productive.

I must add that there is wisdom in the studies of the ancients, along with idiocy. One must carefully screen out the nonsense. You will recognize nonsense, since it is both illogical and irrational.

White women of our race must be rated by several criteria. One criteria is ability, in whatever area that they wish to work in. If they are capable and are able to show that ability, then forget all of the artificial barriers. At the same time, just because a man is White and male, this should carry no special ticket to our struggle. Our most dangerous spies, informants and Iron Heel supporters, at this time, are men. As White motherhood becomes more and more threatened, the number of females entering our ranks. may outnumber the males.

Let's not help our enemies by putting up Middle Eastern and Asiatic based roadblocks to male/female unity.

AMERICA FIRST OR RACE FIRST

W.A.R. and Tom Metzger were probably the first to coin our ideological struggle, as White Separatism. Even though our economic determinist enemies continue to simplistically label us as White Supremacists, our message is slowly getting through. There surely are White Elitist Supremacists, however they operate in the economic determinist camp, while pretending to fight "naughty" racism (belief in one's own race).

From the recent re-emergence of breakaway republics in the Soviet Union, to the Northern Indian colony of Kashmire or even closer, Quebec in Canada, ethnicity and culture are again gaining their proper place on the world stage.

Extremists on the Left rail against the re-emergence of Nationalism, while the Right Wing rail for America first. The Left continues to support the idea of suppression of nationalistic moves, preferring the failed "bigger is better" attitude, of the last several decades. The so-called Right has correctly argued against a world class Big Brother, while at the same time, they have supported an equally dangerous transnational economic program which falsely equates Capitalism with Free Enterprise. When discussing the Right and the Left however, things can become very confusing, in this age. The majority of the Right has followed the lead of the Left, into programs and laws, suppressing discrimination. Discrimination and property ownership are the two issues that separate all mankind from slavery. Without the ability to discriminate, ethnic and racial protection is impossible. Anyone who advocates laws against discrimination, coupled with private ownership of property, becomes your enemy, no matter what racial group they belong to, or which flag they happen to wave.

One must remember that forced integration and the outlawing of discrimination, increased at the same rate as state control of private property. These anti-Separatist ideas were enacted under the various flags of the so-called Democracies. Under Old Glory and the Pledge of Allegiance, our race became enslaved. Remember those anti-Separatist words "...one nation indivisible, with liberty and justice for all..." Separatists are not nationalists. For the most part, a Separatist sees national borders as lines drawn arbitrarily, to the tune of economic guidance, not for racial or cultural best interests.

For today, what is this nation? It is certainly no longer an identifiable, homogenous, racial or cultural group. What, in some cases, may have had its beginnings as race and culture, today are simply an economic outline, that encloses any combination of races and beliefs. This, of course, is not a real nation. This is a bastard nation, with almost no roots, where millions of non-Whites can claim only one generation on the land. That land usually being the asphalted big metropolis. These sad places cannot, without tongue in cheek, be called cities or city-states. They are like overnight mining camps, that rise in population, until they suck out the environmental resources and then collapse, to resemble the early cities of Iraq. The metropolises being the gaping anal cavities of a sick and dying nation. To those unclean places, flock the worst of all races. Only the most degenerate of the White race, struggle to stay on top of the maggot pile in such unnatural settings.

In the face of these twin monstrosities, lie the bastardized metropolis of "Blade Runner" fame and the artificial rainbow nation. Separatist movements, world wide, are truly a renaissance of natural logic.

The drastic differences between a real racist, which is a White Separatist, and a White Nationalist of today, are very important.

To a White Separatist, the overriding importance is race, not what we have known as nation, in this century. The White Separatist, by his or her very nature, must applaud racial and cultural Separatism worldwide. White Separatists are not interested in attempting to build another Tower of Babel. It is discernible in all the cities of North America. Yes, the babble of languages, dialects and people, all of whom are called Americans.

Your masters do not fear you as an economic segregationist, however they do fear you as a true Separatist. For if the Soviet Republics have the ethnic and cultural right of self-determination, why do not the states of the United States? When the economic determinists applaud the various Separatist moves in other areas of the world, why not in North America? Some would say that this is a return to states rights, while in fact it is an advance to state sovereignty. There should follow a competition of the states. The states or regions that are convinced that their future is best protected by the advancement of the black race, should openly advertise that fact. Those states or regions that desire a homogenous Euro-American or White population, should advertise as such. Those states or regions that believe that the Mexican and Central American population would provide the future with the most healthy environment, should advertise as such. In other words, total freedom of choice. We hear a lot about freedom of choice lately, don't we? When was the last time you heard of freedom of choice, on the subject of race or racial separation? The press has, in the last twelve years, for the most part frozen out any portion of an interview, that outlined or even mentioned the idea of Separatism. No matter what you label yourself as, the press always uses the terms, "White Supremacist" or "NEO-Nazi". These terms are then pre-digested, as to what Pavlov's sheep are in turn supposed to say and do, in reaction to those few brave enough to even mention the possibility of Separatism.

Smaller racial and cultural states (if you will), tend to move away from arms races and nuclear war, due to the lack of resources. The only small states that get into the armaments race, are those that are being supplied with weapons from larger states. The environment would certainly benefit, since a people more aware of their smaller amount of resources, could not be "hoodwinked" by political economic shell games which make it seem that there are unlimited resources. Much of what I am saying is found in the writings of well known writers, not only of our race, but also from other races around the world. Smaller states or regions, follow a more Jeffersonian ideal of government, also.

What of population? Today's idea of population control, is no control, at all. North American politicians today look at immigration in a 19th century context. They see unlimited land and unlimited resources, with racial homogeneity being of no or questionable value. This is like running a large 1992 airport, with a 1950 schedule. It will not work and it is not working. The faster we careen to a pluralistic society, the faster the quality of life erodes. The larger the size of government, the greater the mistakes that are made. Population in a smaller state or region, is more easily controlled. It is much easier to see the overall problem, when you are closer to the problem.

RELIGION

Religion is a subject that has existed for thousands of years, and has caused more blood to flow, than almost any other human pastime.

It is my view that the subject must be divided into two parts. One being the strong belief in something (which could be almost anything). Number two is having the faith in something, that is not provable by any present day logical and rational facts or evidence.

It is the opinion of many that religion, in a modern sense, must have had its greatest push forward, at a time when a hunter-gatherer society changed to an organized agricultural way of life. Our best evidence would tend to indicate, that religion of that day, was a method of organizing people, and in short, controlling larger and more complex social structures. It would also seem that this was a "chicken or the egg" proposition. The perceived need for people to control, gave birth to the age old query, "why?". The answer, which was simply given by someone who was perceived to be smarter than the rest, was "that God told me so". Out of fear of death and the unknown, men created abstract gods to help them control men, for good or bad, take your pick. In the early stages, these manufactured gods took the form of symbols of reality such as the sun, the seas, the weather, war, and a host of other realities. Although these beliefs were highly misused by many a witchdoctor or tribal leader, in general the reality behind the symbolic gods, and what they represented, was very real and natural.

As the great power of a religion based on faith and not fact emerged, flocks of would-be Jimmy Swaggarts swarmed over the populations. From then until now, what is broadly recognized as religion, is entirely based on faith in leaders that are speaking to a mono-theistic god, and that god speaks to them, or so they claim. Our studies show that Christianity, Judaism and Islam all spring from a common occult force, which was Egyptian in origin (other material on that subject is available through W.A.R.'s national office).

Faith religionists of today mock the reverence that was held for the sun, by ancient societies. In fact, a religion based on the sun was both factual and provable, while the God of Christianity, Judaism and Islam has no basis in fact, whatsoever. The historical myth of Jesus has been promoted at least sixteen times, by much older civilizations. Jesus is just an updated version of the same myth.

The sun was reality. All could easily see the sun as both a benefactor in the northern and southern hemispheres, and a much more cruel reality at the equator. A man thirsting at the equator at high noon, would cry "why are you punishing me?", while our Nordic ancestors would ask the same question, in the coldest times of winter.

It is plain to see that Judaism could never have gained a large following in Europe. This occult society had its limitations in overt activity, however it did well as a covert occult society.

Since Christianity is in fact a slave religion, it is satirical at least to see the negro adopt a slave religion, after chattel slavery was ended. It simply underlines the fact that consciously or unconsciously, weak humans desire the status of sheep, no matter what they say. For example take the pecking order of the barnyard chickens: very few are able to, or have the desire to, break free. Through fear, men are controlled by occult religious forces. If you would listen to those that are obvious front men for such drivel, they will tell you that "it is for your own good", of course.

The natural control of White tribal society was through natural ways, for the most part. Through the leadership principle, right of combat and natural selection, the weak are weeded out and the fabric of the race is strengthened.

If Aryan White man is unable to confront the enemy within the gates of Christianity and Judaism, then there is no hope. We must prepare our dwindling numbers to move towards a combination of technological and natural barbarianism, if we are to survive and expand, as a race. The medicine men and the witchdoctors, of our race, must be thrown down. You cannot serve two masters; one being the Judeo-Christian myth, and the other being in favor of the White eugenics idea. For yet a little while, we must have patience with those among us that have been unable or unwilling to throw off the subversive middle eastern cult religions. However, time is running out, and the albatross of Christianity will surely destroy our reformation, if not subdued.

Remember the likely evidence that life on this planet, and especially man, may simply be an aberration in the vast universe.

Those of our race, and a few from Judaism, created Christianity to carry forward occult control into pagan Europe. Actually, evidence shows that mythical Jesus was created by the Niciani Council in about 300 A.D.

As White racists, any religion must be based on the real preservation and advancement of our race on the Earth today. No faith promises of heaven or hell need apply. One need not have faith that race exists, it is plain for all to see.

Christianity, so far, is the dominant occult faith religion of western White man. Thus Christianity, even more than Judaism itself, is more destructive to our race. Those that would rise in anger at that suggestion, need to observe our society more closely. Every destructive idea to our race can find its basis in Christianity. Without the occult Judaism, it is very likely that Christianity would never have appeared in Europe. However, once Christianity was entrenched, it drug occult Judaism right along with it. In North America, there would be no Judaism, if there had not been Christianity. Since these are both occult control mechanisms, they tend to, from time to time, heed the other. However, both Judaism and Christianity spring from the same roots, and their "marriage" is one of convenience. Not to realize that the front for these religions is just faith and to refuse to see the reality of this age old control mechanism, is to live in a fog.

Perhaps this is it: "what you see is what you get", nature screams out to us. If that is so (and I see nothing to disprove that), then that makes our adventure even more spectacular. One of those millions of mathematical and chemistry combinations that led to you and I. By the first law of natural selection, we are truly a "bootstrap" race. We may chose the control of this planet and the unlimited possibilities of space, or we may decide to sink into the disgenic failure of culture sand societies that now flourish, mainly because of faith religion and greed that threaten to drag us down and out.

Break out of your death cell White man! Your race and only your race, must be your religion.

GOVERNMENT

Government is the euphemism for the modern state. Since government denotes the perennial lie, "of the people", it is used to mislead those that should know better.

All governments are oligarchies, which are ruled by the few. Some oligarchies have facades, such as the Congress and the Senate. This method of illusion has become quite popular, even in openly straight dictatorial countries. Example: the Peoples Republic of China, or India's late Ismira (sic) Ghandi's oligarchy, which she named "a guided democracy".

Even so-called dictatorships are in reality, oligarchies, and are run by the few. The modern oligarchy, which refers to itself as a democracy, is the most deceptive. That is because democracy is a fraud today, just as it has been throughout history.

Many have said, that the government or the state, is theft. This is true. Even the best of states are a protection racket. These rackets are far more dishonest than unlicensed organized crime (the mafia, etc.). For example, the state takes $1.00 in tax, and you are lucky to receive 20% of that in services. These services are then usually redirected, to people not of your race. The hold-up man, on the street, takes all that you have at the time. The burglar carries off, all that he can, from your house. However, rarely do these men make regular demands upon you, such as the state does, by robbing you and always claiming to be doing it "for your own good" or "for your general welfare". You may rob and kill, without worry of punishment, if you are licensed by the state. The state police kill quite regularly, as do the military, the F.B.I. and the C.I.A. These people are allowed to. Most of us travel through life unlicensed, unless it is perhaps a license to drive or to run a business. Should we attempt to operate anything without the proper license, we are sent to jail or possibly executed.

Much of this con game comes from the historical fraud, known as God-directed government, or the divine right of kings. In the modern time it is referred to as the divine right of the state. Millions believe in this totally baseless conception, and chain their offspring from birth, with this emasculating idea.

The religious zealot promotes the nonsense that a mythical Abraham came down from a mountain, with a code of laws from the great spook in the sky. The politician says that the great emissary of God or the state, such as a Congressman or a Senator, comes down from "the hill" in Washington D.C., with laws for the people.

In general, those Christians, Jews or humanists (Christians without a Christ) etc., superstitiously believe in this myth. Unless they are part of the bureaucracy of small time licensed criminals, who believe out of greed of being part of the mob. In other words, national states are gangs, no less no more. The gangs, by their nature, strive to become larger by gobbling up smaller gangs (smaller states), on their way to becoming syndicates (or as we know them to be now, transnational corporations). Remember that the goal of international Socialism and international Capitalism, was to destroy smaller states, or to absorb them into the "Super Gang". Soviet Russia was a good example, and the term "the West" as opposed to "the East", was another. The result, in that case, was the "Cold War". The "Cold War" gobbled up nations into the specter of the "one big fight". Using this as an excuse, the natural resources of the world were squandered, along with the death of millions. All in the name of peace, brotherhood and national defense. At the same time, unlicensed gangs did the same thing. Instead of small gangs controlling small amounts of turf, the idea was to have one big gang control it all. First in one major city, then in another, until we have national organized crime, complete with Governors and the Board of Directors. Finally, the unlicensed gang power becomes so great, that in many cases it overlaps into, and becomes apart of, licensed gang activity (the Iran Contra Affair, etc.).

Street gangs are the lowest common denominator, and in reality, the most sensible of all gang activity! Most street gangs today are satisfied with control of a few blocks of turf, and a financial cut. These gangs are somewhat beneficial since they, in some ways, erode the confidence in the "Big Gang", which supplies protection. However the "Big Gang" tries to use this as a method of gaining tighter controls of the White non-gang populations. Enters: drunk driving, road blocks, helmet laws and seat belt enforcement, as an example of seemingly "good" plans. These so-called "good" plans guide the sheep(that's you), to a more total control, by the "Big Gang" in Washington D .C.

In summation, international gangs lead us into far more dangerous wars, more dangerous population increases, more dangerous destruction of the environment. All of this is of the greatest threat to the White race.

Not even the wars between the smaller White states (gangs)has had the effect that transnational gangs, with open borders, have had on White nations. In this case, smaller is better. Besides being better, the smaller White state is raised by natural leaders, and those that can be dealt with, should they get out of control.

The international style state is inefficient, to the maximum. Perhaps we are moving towards a time of city states. All-White city states would be desirable and efficient, plus they would be culturally strong. As an example, the greatest time of culture and art, on the Italian Boot, were in the time of the city states. Italy has not since demonstrated anything that comes close. Greece, at its Aryan peak, was comprised of city states.

Perhaps the White idea of the Northwest or Southeast solution is more than can be expected. As smaller becomes more beautiful, why not city states with satellite village states? By effective immigration, this is a reachable goal.

However, a war against the Super State must be fought to the finish. Your ammunition is readily available. Cut economic support for the Beast. In short, starve the bureaucrats out. All of their international gang plans are based on sheep that will finance them. Without your cooperation, they are dead.

Think about it, and then join the hunt, and the underground economy.

White Aryan Resistance
PO Box 65 Fallbrook, CA 92088 (619) 723-8996

Open Letter to Minister Louis Farrakhan
by Thom Robb

T his letter, from the Grand Dragon of the Knights of the
Ku Klux Klan, Thom Robb, to the Nation of Islam leader,
Minister Louis Farrakhan, was published in Robb's newspaper,
the *White Patriot,* in August 1984. It is offered here as a graphic
illustration of the meeting of the minds between Black and
White racial separatists in the 1980s and 1990s. A second
example, a talk show involving Tom and John Metzger and
several black nationalists, is presented in the entry "Tom
Metzger."

Dear Mr. Farrakhan,

I have read with interest the news reports about you in recent weeks and sympathize with much of what you have to say. You and I are from two different worlds and thus view the world from two different racial perspectives. Yet in spite of this perhaps we do share some things in common.

I realize that the Nation of Islam is historically anti-white. I expect you to take what ever stand you feel necessary to reach the hearts of your racial brothers. Yet this doesn't really bother me. Likewise, I must take what ever position I must to reach the hearts of My racial brothers. That's the first law of nature!

It appears that the basic agreement that we share is that neither of us wish to have our people mix with the other. We both realize that to do so brings discord and strife.

The establishment hates you and your doctrine as it hates mine. What you think of me and my people matters little to me, only that we remain apart. I feel that you look upon us the same.

What is important to perhaps both of our people is that there is an element in society that benefits from this discord and in fact actually encourages it. That element sir, as you know, is the eternal Jew.

This is something you and I both realize. The Jew seeks to destroy our society by racial strife. You are so correct in stating that the Jews posses a "gutter religion." In fact your statement of the Jewish "criminal conspiracy" is again quite accurate. There are only a few whites and a few blacks that realize this. But it is true! For this reason, the Jew controlled media does not want your message to reach your people any more than it wants our message to reach my people. In spite of everything you may say about white people or in spite of everything we say about black people - the fact is that we both want the same thing - SEPARATION! I *do not* mean segregation - but separation. Our people need a racial nation unto themselves and your people need a racial nation unto themselves. Separation will thus permit both of our people to reach the destiny plotted out for them by the almighty. This is the only way. Any other path will bring chaos.

It seems ironic, but perhaps it really shouldn't that in face of all those who now stand to condemn you, it is only the Ku Klux Klan that comes to your defense.

We do not view the Black Nationalist as our enemy. OUR enemy is the black integrationist and the white integrationist. I suspect that you feel the same. For that reason I propose that you and I engage in a speaking tour together. For it is the teaching of *racial separation* proclaimed by the Nation of Islam and the Ku Klux Klan that America needs- that your people need- and that my people need. I am sure you must agree. Integration has not been good for your people and integration has not been good for my people. What we think of each other beyond this point is meaningless.

I have a book in my library entitled, "The Plot Against Christianity." I realize that your faith is not Christianity, however, the message of the book should perhaps make the title "Plot Against Civilization." It is a superb book and documented fully. It certainly clearly shows the totally sickness of the Jew "gutter religion." If you do not have this book, I would like to make it a gift to you. Please let me know of I should send it to you.

Again, I appreciate your outspoken testimony against Jewish subversion. At this point I am reminded of the statement by the Apostle Paul, who when speaking of the Jews and how they crucified Christ said, "they please not God and are CONTRARY TO ALL MEN."

Sincerely,

Thom Arthur Robb
Nat'l Chaplain
Knights of the Ku Klux Klan

James K. Warner Open Letter 1968

In 1968, a revolt against state party leader Ralph Forbes took place among the cadre of California members of the National Socialist White People's Party. The ferment gave James K. Warner, a former core member of George Lincoln Rockwell's American Nazi Party who had fallen out with the Commander, the opportunity to attempt to seize control of the group. Warner's putsch failed, but the Open Letter that announced Warner's bid for power to the party faithful is so stereotypically descriptive of the workings of American National Socialism that it is worth reproducing in full. It offers the reader not only an insight into the spirit of the times, but also a timeless vision of the divisive milieu of American National Socialism. The names have changed over the course of the last 30 years, but the vicious infighting so vividly portrayed in this document is timeless.

———————————

Phone: 462-0207

Temporary address:
c/o Major Allen Vincent
227 ½ N. Western Ave.
Los Angeles, Calif. 90004

January 1968

Fellow National Socialist:

The question before us today is this: Is the American Nazi Party going to win power in America, or is it just a game for a gang of over-grown children and petty Napoleons?

For the last few years the leadership of the ANP on the West Coast has been in the hands of incompetent individuals who have found the Party a profitable venture for selfish gain, a means of existing without working, and a way to express their illusions of grandeur. Those who have tried to build the Party have run into insurmountable obstacles thrown up by these who enjoy and profit by this miserable travesty on true National Socialism.

When the Party was launched in 1959, I was one of the five original members, and have been credited by Commander Rockwell with being the one individual who gave the Commander the encouragement to go ahead with organizing the American Nazi Party. In the Commander's words:

> "Just about as I regained 'consciousness', James Warner, the young man who sent the Nazi flag, was discharged from the Airforce for his Nazi sympathies, and appeared at Louis' house ready to do what he could to advance Nazism.
>
> "The fact that this young kid was ready to devote his life to our cause and to *my leadership* was the shock I needed to snap out of depression." (page 342, *This Time the World*).

I worked with Commander Rockwell through bad times and good, sharing his hardships, and fighting along beside him in the street. Later, because of political immaturity and lack of political knowledge, I broke with the Party, thinking that I had better ideas than the Commander. I did a lot or stupid, irresponsible rotten things that hurt the Party. However, the Commander and I came to terms in 1965, and the Commander wrote: "I am in hopes that by showing that Warner and I have been able to come to terms and, although he is not in the Party...we stand together against the enemy, after years of bitter and brutal quarreling." (Rockwell Report, Feb., 1965).

In August, 1967, I was mainly responsible for organizing transportation for the Nazi Motorcycle Corps for the famous street action on August 6th, which made headlines nationwide.

The California "leader" (Ralph Forbes) was so engrossed with "family considerations," or so he claims, that he just couldn't find the time, or the money in his treasury (his wife was his treasurer and wrote and kept all the records) to bring the men from Oakland to Los Angeles. Although not being a Party member, I did work for the interest or the Party and the White Race. The "punch-in" was a gigantic success. However, Forbes got the credit for the operation, when it was Mike Brown who supplied the actual leadership and almost all of the men, while I supplied the funds for their travel.

Complaints against Forbes for misuse of Party funds, inactivity, incompetence and lack of leadership, by the men began to divide the Party. All of the men moved out of Headquarters because of Forbes, and I put them up at my place.

Previously Forbes had become a religious fanatic and constantly talked about "having visions" in order to get the support of religious fanatics...and their money, behind him. However, he could not find a way to make it convincing.

At the same time he used the Party as a recruiting ground for off beat religious cults and for other right wing groups. Dedicated members were put under pressure to join and participate in "KKK rallies" which were under the control of an enemy of the Party.

Over the centuries the Jews have used religious differences to divide the White People into warring factions. That is why the official policy of the Nazi Party has been to guarantee religious freedom to all Whitemen (Jews excluded) and not to take sides. If a man chooses to be a Christian, good and well, but if he chooses to be a Hindu or Atheist, also well and good. The main thing is the loyalty he has for the White Race.

But Forbes has driven many good men away from the Party with his religious intolerance, He openly has stated that any Nazi who doesn't believe in his brand of religion is not worthy to be a member of the Party. Today a fellow friend and cultist of Forbes is openly distributing an anti-Nazi booklet that names Hess, Goebbels, etc. as "Jews."

After the Commander was assassinated all the LOYAL NAZIS here on the West Coast decided to do all that we could to make sure that the Jews would not destroy the Party. The Jews had declared a press blackout on the Party back east, so we decided to break that blackout and let the people know that the Party was still fighting for the White Race as strongly as ever.

Forbes still would not not do anything to build the Party, but members to become religious fanatics first and Nazis second.

Lt. Allen Vincent, myself, and other legal Nazis, organized WHITE POWER rallies in Hollywood. So far three have been held, all successes. Forbes would not help in any way although invited to, and although even those few who had been putting up with him pitched in to help. But Forbes became resentful at our success and his inactivity, so he tried to turn all the members still associating with him into anti-Warner anti-Vincent fanatics. Our activities, however, had shown many of them, members and supporters alike, what COULD BE DONE by fanatic Nazis who wanted to BUILD the Party. ALL continued to work and attend in full Nazi uniform, a heartening sight after heartbreaking years of Forbes' destructive influence.

As expected, we became the object of Forbes' wrath, and he spent all his time denouncing us and promoting his fanatic "faith" on Party time and funds. Party members and supporters decided that something must be done to put an end to his hate campaign and to start building the Party.

When seven Nazis lost a battle to 150 Jews while picketing a movie (but making front page news) Forbes called us cowards, although he hadn't managed to show up, and is famous for assuming a fetal position when attacked in the streets. This was more than we could put up with.

Lt. Vincent's unit raised the money to fly Major Koehl out here to settle matters. He agreed to come to California, so we sent him the money and awaited his arrival.

But when he arrived instead of notifying us, he went straight to Forbes' house, and it was only after he had been here for two days that we accidentally found out that he was here in Los Angeles. Forbes had been busy trying to keep him from us, and had been taking him around to every religious fanatic in the area.

Finally we managed to hold several conferences between Major Koehl and ourselves. We explained the situation and the facts to him, producing witnesses and stating actual instances. All of this was to Forbes' face, as he was in the room, and a tape recording was made of the charges by Major Koehl.

Almost all Party members and supporters, even those from San Francisco, wanted something done about Forbes. However, we could never get a definite statement from Major Koehl on the situation. On the contrary, Major Koehl continued to ignore the fanatic Nazis and continued to see all the religious fanatics.

Captain Forbes then held a meeting intending to impress Major Koehl, by rounding up all the religious fanatics in the area and packing them in the hall (this because he couldn't find enough Nazis to attend). After the meeting he replayed the tape of the charges made against him by us the previous day, and all the openly anti-Nazi fanatics roundly cursed the Nazis, saying that they should *all be booted out of the Party* for denouncing religious fanaticism influence in the Nazi Party. All this in front of Major Koehl and in a Nazi headquarters by non-Party people!

At last, on December 31st, Major Koehl called a meeting to announce his decision. We all arrived at Ralph Forbes' house at 2:00 P.M. the meeting time set by Major Koehl. However, we were kept waiting in the meeting room until 2:30 with a tape recorder running all the time. When Major Koehl finally entered the room he had statements handed out to every man, to be signed, stating that we would unquestionably obey *ANY* decision made by him as final (presumably even if we were told to knuckle under to Forbes). After bringing him out here, showing him every courtesy, and proving our sincerity, expressly for the purpose of settling the issue honorably, this was an insult to every man in the room. Koehl further stated that unless we signed the papers that we may as well all leave. Every Nazi but one or two left en masse, emptying the meeting room.

After leaving Ralph Forbes' place, a meeting was held in the Nazi Los Angeles headquarters. It was decided that Major Koehl was a good National Secretary, but did not have the ability to lead the Party to victory. From our observation, he seemed incapable of making an independent decision based on facts, but was obsessed with the "leadership" principle, even when the "leader" is proven to be incompetent and against the welfare of the Party.

Commander Rockwell always stressed the principle of SURVIVAL OF THE FITTEST. Leadership will always rise above the masses and replace those who do not have the fire and zeal to build mass movements. Leadership cannot be inherited like the titles of worthless royalty who live on the glory of their ancestors. Leadership is something that must be earned, and men follow because of respect and loyalty, not because of inherited worthless titles. If a leader does not have what it takes to build a political movement then he should step aside for the betterment of that movement.

Since the Commander's death I have felt an obligation to carry the National Socialist torch forward, and to complete the work he started. Just as with all movements, zealous fanatics with a divine mission must carry forward the banners of the movement. Nothing will stop me in my MISSION. Of all the Nazis outside of Colin Jordan in England, I believe that I am the best qualified to carry the Commander's work on.

No other Nazi in the United States is as close on political ideology as I am to the way the Commander thought.

On January 1, 1968 a Conference of the American Nazi Party was held at Nazi Headquarters in Los Angeles. In view of the incompetent leadership of the National Socialist White People's Party, I, Dr. James K. Warner, assumed by popular Nazi acclaim, the leadership of the American Nazi Party.

The following officers were appointed:

Allen Vincent *Deputy Leader* and *National Stormtroop Leader*, George Carpenter *Stormtroop Leader for Southern California* and *National Secretary*. Don Musgrove *Stormtroop Leader for Northern California*, Don Anderson *Leader of State Security*, Dick Norris *Deputy Leader of State Security*, Paul Tronvig *Assistant Deputy Leader of State Security*, Bart West *National Organizer*, Bill Cummings *Secretary of Labor*, Don Sisco *Party Spokesman*, and Dave Lea *Party Treasurer*.

In view of the Party's past failure to become a mass movement to win the hearts and minds of our people, the following IMMEDIATE changes were made in Party Policy:

The Blue Dot is to be removed from the Swastika, and the pure Aryan Swastika of our ancestors is to be used unblemished.

The age requirement of 18 for membership is hereby removed.

From this time on no membership information on Party members will be turned over to any investigative agency, national, state, or local. We hold all membership in strict confidence, and if need be will burn membership forms before turning them over to Federal enemies of the White Race.

Party membership forms are limited to one page, giving name, address, age, occupation, education, and telephone. No information on family is required. Membership fee is $5.00 and dues will be $3.00 monthly. Student membership is $2.00.

Official Party publications will be ACTION MAGAZINE and the newsletter ATTACK.

Liaison between the ANP and other anti-Jewish movements will be established, and former members encouraged to rejoin.

All Party funds and mail will be opened and recorded by both the National Secretary and the Party Treasurer.

The no smoking or drinking oaths for officers are abolished.

Three distinct uniforms will be used: Party, SS, and Stormtroop.

National Socialists who want to win victory for the White Race can join with us to defeat Jewish Communism and Race-mixing. We are not going to back down, and we are not going to make the mistakes made in the past by incompetents who have kept us from winning.

We have taken up the banner and now move forward into battle in this final fight for our race and nation. Whiteman, stand up and fight beside us in this hour of decision.

WHITE POWER!

Dr. James K. Warner
National Leader

Index

Contributors

Xavier Cattarinich is a graduate student in the Department of Sociology at the University of Alberta.

Rick Cooper is a National Socialist who heads the National Socialist Vanguard, which is headquartered in The Dalles, Oregon. For a more thorough biography see the entries "Rick Cooper" and "National Socialist Vanguard" in this encyclopedia.

Katrine Fangen is a graduate student in the Department of Sociology at the University of Oslo. Among her English language publications are: "Living out our Ethnic Instincts: Ideological Beliefs Among Right-Wing Activists in Norway," in Jeffrey Kaplan and Tore Bjørgo, eds., *Brotherhoods of Nation and Race: The Emergence of a Euro-American Racist Subculture* (Boston, MA: Northeastern University Press, 1998); and "Separate or Equal? The Emergence of an All Female Group in the Norwegian Rightist Underground," *Terrorism and Political Violence* 9:3 (Fall 1997).

Mattias Gardell is a professor of history at Stockholm University who was awarded a Harry Frank Guggenheim Fellowship in 1998 to study the interactions between black nationalists and white separatists in the United States. He is the author of *Rasrisk* (Stockholm & Uppsala: Federativs & Swedish Science Press, 1998); "Black and White Unite In Fight?: On the Inter-Action Between Black and White Radical Racialists," in Heléne Lööw and Jeffrey Kaplan, *Sekter, sektmotståndare och sekteristiska miljöer, en förnyad granskning* (Swedish National Council of Crime Prevention (BRÅ), forthcoming 1999); and *In the Name of Elijah Mohammad: Louis Farrakhan and the Nation of Islam* (Durham, NC: Duke University Press, 1996).

Milton John Kleim, Jr. was a leading theorist on the use of the Internet as a recruiting tool for the radical right. He is the author of "On Strategy and Tactics for the Usenet." He has since left the movement.

Edvard Lind is a graduate student at Stockholm University.

Heléne Lööw is a professor of history at Stockholm University. She has written two books and published a number of articles on the subject of the Swedish radical right and on National Socialism in Sweden from the 1930s to the present. Among her publications in English are: "White Power—Dark History," *Uppväxtvillkor* 3 (1993); "The Fight Against ZOG—Anti-Semitism Among The Modern Race Ideologists," *Historisk Tidskrift* 1 (1996); "'Wir Sind Wieder Da'—From National Socialism to Militant Racial Ideology—The Swedish Racist Underground In An Historical Context," in *Strommar i tiden*, Mohamed Chaib, ed., (Göteborg: Diadalos Forlag, 1995); "Racist Violence and Criminal Behavior in Sweden: Myths and Reality," in Tore Bjørgo, ed., *Terror From the Extreme Right* (London: Frank Cass & Co., 1995); "White Power Rock 'n' Roll—A Growing Industry," in Jeffrey Kaplan and Tore Bjørgo, eds., *Nation and Race: The Developing Euro-American Racist Subculture* (Boston, MA: Northeastern University Press, 1998).

James Mason is a National Socialist who was associated with the National Socialist White Peoples' Party, the National Socialist Liberation Front, and currently with the Universal Order. He is the author of *Siege* (Denver, CO: Storm Books, 1992). Further biographical information can be found in the entries "James Mason," "National Socialist Liberation Front," and "Universal Order."

Michael Moynihan is a writer, artist, and driving force behind Storm Books, the music group Blood Axis, and the author of *Lords of Chaos* (Venice, CA: Feral House, 1998).

Tommy Rydén is a Swedish race activist, National Socialist, and former head of the Swedish Church of the Creator. Further biographical information can be found in the entries "Tommy Rydén" and "Kreativistens Kyrka."

Frederick J. Simonelli is a professor of history at Mount St. Mary's College. He is the author of *American Fuehrer; George Lincoln Rockwell and the American Nazi Party* (Champaign: University of Illinois Press, 1999); "The World Union of National Socialists and Post-War Transatlantic Nazi Revival," in Jeffrey Kaplan and Tore Bjørgo, eds., *Nation and Race: The Developing Euro-American Racist Subculture* (Boston: Northeastern University Press, 1998); "The American Nazi Party, 1958-1967," *The Historian* 57 (Spring, 1995); and "Preaching Hate with the Voice of God: American Neo-Nazis and Christian Identity," *Patterns Of Prejudice* 30 (no. 2. 1996).

Laird Wilcox is the founder of the editorial research service and a long time observer of the American far right scene. He is the co-author of: John George and Laird Wilcox, *Nazis, Communists, Klansmen and Others on the Fringe* (Buffalo, NY: Prometheus Books, 1992); and John George and Laird Wilcox, *American Extremists, Supremacists, Klansmen, Communists and Others* (Buffalo, NY: Prometheus Books, 1996).